CATHOLICISM

CATHOLICISM

VOLUME TWO

by Richard P. McBrien

WINSTON PRESS

Book design: Maria Mazzara·Schade

Except for citations within citations, all Scripture texts used in this work are taken from the *New American Bible*, copyright © 1970, by the Confraternity of Christian Doctrine, Washington, D.C. Used by permission of the copyright owner. All rights reserved.

Quotations from the documents of Vatican II are reprinted with permission of America Press, Inc., 106 W. 56 Street, New York NY 10019. © 1966. All rights reserved.

The chart entitled "Twentieth-Century Views on the Christology of the New Testament," which originally appeared in *Horizons* (vol. 1, 1974, p. 38), is reprinted with permission.

Copyright © 1980 Richard P. McBrien
All rights reserved. No part of this book may be reproduced or used in any form without written permission from Winston Press, Inc.
Library of Congress Catalog Card Number: 79-55963
ISBN (volume I): 0-03-056668-1
ISBN (volume II): 0-03-056906-0
ISBN (entire work): 0-03-056907-9

Printed in the United States of America

5 4 3

Winston Press, Inc., 430 Oak Grove, Minneapolis, MN 55403

CONTENTS

Volume Two

PART FIVE: CHRISTIAN EXISTENCE—ETHICAL AND SPIRITUAL DIMENSIONS 903

CONCLUSION   1167

CATHOLICISM

PART IV

THE CHURCH

THE CHURCH

INTRODUCTION

We come now to the heart of the distinctively Catholic understanding of Christian faith. Catholics have always more strongly emphasized the place of the Church in mediating salvation than have other Christian traditions. And within the mystery of the Church, Catholics have always stressed the mediating function of certain ministries, structures, and institutional forms. Thus, Catholics have insisted on the importance of the ordained ministries of the bishop, priest, and deacon, and the special role of the bishop of Rome, the pope. Catholics have underlined, too, the essentially sacramental character of Christian existence and have taken care to define precisely the nature, meaning, and number of the sacraments, as well as the conditions under which they are celebrated. Catholics have also accorded a prominent position to Mary, the mother of Jesus Christ, a theological and devotional emphasis that is in keeping with three characteristically Catholic principles: the principle of *mediation*, the principle of *sacramentality*, and the principle of *communion* (see chapter 24).

Consistently with the historical method of this entire book, Part IV begins with an examination of the nature, structure, and mission of the Church and the churches in the New Testament (chapter 17) and traces their development and growth through subsequent centuries (chapter 18). Special emphasis is given the event which, more than any other, has shaped, and continues to shape, contemporary Catholic thought and practice, the Second Vatican Council (chapter 19).

In light of this history, from the New Testament to the present, there is offered a systematic definition of the Church and a description of its mission (chapter 20). An ecumenical spectrum of contemporary ecclesiological views is also outlined. Given the sacraments' significance in expressing the nature of the Church and in fulfilling its mission, the sacraments are accorded separate and relatively extensive treatment: first, the sacraments of initiation, i.e., Baptism, Confirmation, and Eucharist (chapter 21); and then the sacraments of healing, i.e., Penance and the Anointing of the Sick, and the sacraments of vocation and commitment, i.e., Matrimony and Holy Order (chapter 22). Special ecclesiological questions are identified and examined: authority, papacy, ministry, ordination of women, and intercommunion (chapter 23). The chapter on Mary (chapter 24), which illustrates three characteristically Catholic principles—mediation, sacramentality and communion—brings Part IV to a conclusion.

In this book generous attention is given the mystery of the Church, but not because it is the most fundamental of the mysteries of Christian faith. It is not. Nor is our extensive treatment of the Church prompted simply by the view that the mystery of the Church is itself a synthesis of all of the other mysteries of faith. It is that, of course. What is more important, however, is that with the mystery of the Church we come at last to the point at which the distinctively *Catholic* understanding and practice of Christian faith most clearly emerges. So if this book is to be successful in its purpose of identifying, examining, and explaining the reality of Catholicism, sustained study of the mystery of the Church is both imperative and inevitable.

·XVII·

THE CHURCH OF THE NEW TESTAMENT

FROM CHRISTOLOGY TO ECCLESIOLOGY

The interlocking character of Christian doctrine is by now unmistakably clear. Our understanding of Jesus Christ is a function of our understanding of God, and our understanding of God is, in turn, a function of our understanding of human existence. Jesus, after all, has meaning and value for us because he is no ordinary person; he is hypostatically one with the Word of God. And God has meaning and value for us because God is the source, the core, the sustenance, and the destiny of our being as individual human persons and as members of the total human community. God enters into the very definition of our humanity. We are alive by a principle which transcends us.

There is also a connection, therefore, between our understanding of human existence, of God, and of Jesus Christ, on the one hand, and our understanding of the Church, on the other. Or more immediately, our understanding of the nature and mission of the Church depends upon our understanding of the meaning and value of Jesus Christ, who reveals to us at one and the same time who God is and who we are.

This presupposes, of course, that there is some vital link between Jesus Christ and the Church, that the Church somehow issues forth from Christ and is identified with his person and work. It is precisely for the sake of examining and establishing that connection that we turn first to the question of the Church in the New Testament. In keeping with the historical method employed throughout this book, we begin at the beginning and then follow the course of the Church's development down to the present time.

THE PROBLEM

The Church exists. No one questions that fact, even though many would differ when it comes to defining what we mean by *Church*. The initial problem is not with the *existence* of the Church but with its *origins*: (1) *When* did the Church *begin* to exist? (2) Did *Jesus intend* that the Church should exist? (3) Did the Church remain *faithful* to Jesus' intentions even during the so-called foundational period encompassed by the New Testament writings?

These three questions are reducible to one: *What connection, if any, can we establish between the Church's evaluation of itself and Jesus' evaluation of the Church?* This is only a variation of the question which framed the parallel chapter (The Christ of the New Testament) in Part III, namely, the question of the Christ of faith and the Jesus of history.

It requires just as much care and delicacy to answer the question in its ecclesiological form as it did to answer it in its Christological form. The New Testament is the same primary source for both. That source can only be interpreted *developmentally*. The New Testament itself emerged through a three-stage process: (1) the original words and deeds of Jesus; (2) the oral proclamation of the Apostles and disciples (catechesis, narratives, testimonies, hymns, doxologies, and prayers); and (3) the writings themselves. Insofar as the New Testament reports sayings of Jesus on the Church (e.g., Matthew 16:18; 18:17), we have to ask: (1) What did those sayings mean when, and if, spoken by Jesus himself? (2) What did they mean in the earliest stage of the apostolic preaching? (3) What did they mean to the communities which preserved them and to the New Testament author(s) who recorded them?

The writings, in turn, reflect a progressive theological movement as the Gospel is proclaimed and accepted in one setting and then in another: (1) in the *Jewish-Christian* community of Palestine, which was closest to the events of the life, death, and resurrection of Jesus and which was most concerned with establishing the connection between Jesus and the house of David; (2) in the *Jewish-Hellenistic* community, which, in the light of the obvious delay of the Second Coming (*parousia*), stressed the present exalted state of Christ ("Jesus *is* Lord!"); and (3) in the *Hellenistic-Gentile* community, which, under the impact of the missionary activity of the Pauline and Johannine schools of theology, declared that God is even now exercising lordship over the universe in and through Jesus Christ, who is the risen and exalted Lord.

Recognizing such developments in both composition and theological content is one thing; interpreting the finally developed material is another. We should not be surprised, therefore, to discover a diversity of ecclesiological approaches not only *within* the New Testament but also within the present-day body of biblical exegetes and theologians. And since the conclusions of scholars are part of the public domain, a diversity of non-scholarly opinion about the Church is also to be expected.

JESUS AND THE CHURCH: A SPECTRUM OF INTERPRETATIONS
Non-scholarly Conservatism

This view *identifies* the whole of New Testament ecclesiology with Jesus' own evaluation of the Church. Even though the New Testament books were composed over a period of some fifty to eighty years and were addressed to diverse audiences of diverse circumstances, this non-scholarly conservative position maintains that there had been *no significant ecclesiological development* in all of that time. Thus, when Jesus accepted Peter's confession that Jesus was indeed the Messiah and made Peter the rock upon which he would build his Church (Matthew 16:13-20), that acceptance and that designation reflected the self-understanding of Jesus—despite the fact that Peter's confession and Jesus' reaction are very different in the earlier Gospel of Mark (8:27-30). Indeed, the next scene in Mark's Gospel has Jesus reprimanding Peter, "Get out of my sight, you satan!" (8:33).

According to the non-scholarly conservative view, Jesus left the Twelve Apostles a detailed blueprint for a Church: seven sacraments with precise matter and form, the papacy vested with supreme and universal jurisdiction, the monarchical episcopate, doctrines, liturgies, and laws. Indeed, the whole purpose of his "coming down from heaven" was to pay humanity's "debt" to the Father by his death on the cross and then to leave a Church behind in order to communicate the benefits of that saving act to as many people as possible. The view was commonly held by Catholics until the Second Vatican Council and the application of biblical scholarship to ecclesiology in the 1960s. Traces of it continue to be found in the Catholic Church today, sometimes even among its pastoral leaders.

Non-scholarly conservatism cannot withstand biblical criticism. There is no evidence in the New Testament that Jesus indicated in detail the where, the how, or the when of ecclesial development. Not even the Acts of the Apostles presents this type of continuity. On the contrary, the great advances in ecclesiastical life and organization which are reported there are responses to new and unprecedented challenges. One of the first great crises to confront the Church centered on the question of whether Gentiles might also be admitted to membership in the Christian community (Acts of the Apostles 10:1—11:18). When Peter was compelled to justify his eating with, and then baptizing, uncircumcised persons (namely, the Roman centurion Cornelius, his relatives, and close friends), he appealed not to some specific doctrinal or legal directive of Jesus but to the prompting and instruction of the Holy Spirit (11:12). Thus, if we are to speak of *continuity* in New Testament ecclesiology, it must be in terms of the Spirit of Christ who dwells within the Church, in every circumstance, time, and place. There was no institutional master plan.

But continuity does not mean *uniformity*, as if there were some unbroken line of development within the New Testament period. There are strong differences in outlook found among the various New Testament writers. For example, Matthew's attitude toward the Law (5:18; 23:2-3) is clearly not the same as Paul's in Galatians (3) and Romans (2-4; 7; 13). And Luke in the Acts of the Apostles makes no attempt to hide the fact that the Hellenistic Christians vehemently objected to the type of ecclesiastical organization which had begun to prevail among the Jewish Christians (15:1-29).

Non-scholarly Liberalism

The non-scholarly liberal concludes that there is *no continuity* at all between the Church's self-understanding and Jesus' evaluation of the Church. Jesus came to teach us a way of life centered on love and based on freedom from institutional oppression of every kind. He proclaimed the Kingdom of God, but his followers gave us the Church instead.

Although non-scholarly liberalism began as a Protestant movement, it has made a delayed entrance into Catholicism as a reaction against the ecclesiastical authoritarianism and the dogmatic and ethical fundamentalism of the pre-Vatican II period.

Scholarly Liberalism

Scholarly liberalism, unlike its non-scholarly counterpart, does not dismiss the ecclesiology of the New Testament as non-existent or unimportant. On the other hand, scholarly liberalism shares with non-scholarly liberalism the conviction that the ecclesiology of the New Testament is a mistaken evaluation of what Jesus intended. For the liberals, New Testament ecclesiology is entirely a creation of the early church.

The liberals hold that Jesus himself did not intend a Church because he expected the Kingdom of God as imminent: at first within his own lifetime, and then as something that would come about immediately after his death. The disciples, therefore, expected the Second Coming in the very near future. They perceived themselves as the ultimate Messianic Community of the Saints, the elect of the final generation who would soon enter a new form of being in the new aeon. With the further delay of the *parousia*, the post-apostolic Church abandoned this Pauline view and assumed organizational form of a type that suggested some historical permanence.

This view is expressed in Martin Werner's *The Formation of Christian Dogma* (Boston: Beacon Press, 1957) but goes back to earlier figures like Johannes Weiss, Albert Schweitzer, and Adolf Harnack.

Bultmannian Existentialism

Over against the Weiss-Schweitzer-Werner point of view, Rudolf Bultmann argued that Jesus did link entrance into the Kingdom with affiliation with a community, the Jewish people. "Do not live in fear, little flock. It has pleased your Father to give you the kingdom" (Luke 12:32). For Bultmann, the individual will find deliverance "only because he belongs to the eschatological community, not because of his personality" (*Jesus and the Word*, London: Collins, 1958, p. 41). Furthermore, he rejected the scholarly liberal's assertion that Jesus' expectation of the Kingdom of God led to his enunciating only an interim ethic. Jesus was unconcerned with the human future; he was concerned only with God's. Every person *now* stands under the judgment of God's word and will. This is the hour of decision; this is the *final* hour (p. 96).

On the other hand, Bultmann rejects the sacramentalism of the Fourth Gospel and of Hellenistic Christianity in general. For Jesus, it is not sacramental washings or meals that make a person pure, but only a pure heart, i.e., a good will (Mark 7:15). "The teaching of Jesus and that of the oldest group of his followers contained no trace of any such sacramental conception" (p. 111).

Scholarly Conservatism

Most scholars today admit *continuity within development*. They reject the fundamentalistic assumptions of their non-scholarly cousins who deny development and inflate continuity into identity. They also reject the Liberal's stress on discontinuity to the point where there is no discernible connection at all between what Jesus said and did and what eventually emerged as Church.

This so-called scholarly conservative position has its *Protestant* and *Catholic* wings, but their differences have perhaps had less to do with exegesis than with theological and doctrinal commitments. Catholics are more likely than Protestants to underline the Church's role in mediating salvation. Thus, Catholic biblical scholars such as Rudolf Schnackenburg, Anton Vögtle, and Raymond Brown affirm a stronger sacramental and ministerial character to the New Testament Church than Protestant biblical scholars such as Ernst Käsemann, Eduard Schweizer, or Hans Conzelmann. For the Catholics, this structure is constitutive or essential to the Church. For the Protestants, it is at best functional and, therefore, not absolutely necessary to the Church's integrity.

Catholic scholars have tended to emphasize *continuity*; Protestant scholars have tended to emphasize *development*. In recent years, however, the Catholic and Protestant wings of the scholarly conservative school have moved closer to each other. Catholics continue to underline continuity, but without prejudice to development. And Protestants continue to underline development, but without prejudice to continuity. An example of this remarkable ecumenical convergence is provided by the joint exegetical and theological study, *Peter in the New Testament* (New York: Paulist Press, 1973), sponsored by the United States Lutheran-Roman Catholic Dialogue.

(The chart on page 603 summarizes the various approaches to the question of Jesus' relationship with, and attitude toward, the Church.)

DID JESUS INTEND TO FOUND A CHURCH?

The answer is "No" if by "found" we mean some direct, explicit, deliberate act by which Jesus established a new religious organization. The answer is "Yes" if by "found" we mean "lay the foundations for" the Church in various indirect ways. In this second case, it is preferable to speak of the Church as having its *origin* in Jesus rather than as having been founded by Jesus.

Jesus Did Not "Found" the Church

In his preaching Jesus never addressed himself merely to a *select group* of people, even though such groups existed in his day—e.g., the Qumran community which understood itself as God's holy remnant, the chosen of the new Covenant. The Kingdom of God, he insisted, is open in principle to everyone: "Mark what I say! Many will come from the east and the west and will find a place at the banquet in the kingdom of God with Abraham, Isaac, and Jacob, while the natural heirs of the kingdom will be driven out into the dark" (Matthew 8:11-12; see also Luke 13:28-29). He is aware that his mission is not to gather together all of the just and the righteous but to "go instead after the lost sheep of the house of Israel" (Matthew 10:6). It is the whole of Israel, and no group or sect within it, which is called to be God's people in the last days. To the very end, despite the experience of failure, Jesus addressed himself to the whole of the people.

Even the call of *the Twelve* has to be seen in this light. The Twelve were to represent Jesus' call to all of the twelve tribes of Israel, and they were to serve as rulers and judges "when the Son of Man takes his seat upon a throne befitting his glory" (Matthew 19:28; Luke 22:30). So, too, the wider circle of disciples were entrusted with the mission to Israel as a whole (Luke 10:1-20).

Although the missionary mandate makes particular demands upon the disciples, Jesus imposes no specific rule of life, nor is membership in the company of his disciples a condition of salvation. On the contrary, "None of those who cry out, 'Lord, Lord,' will enter the kingdom of God but only the one who does the will of my Father in heaven" (Matthew 7:21). And the will of the Father is often done without explicit awareness: "Lord, when did we see you hungry and feed you...?...I assure you, as often as you did it for one of my least brothers, you did it for me" (Matthew 25:31-46). Neither the disciples nor those Israelites who were disposed to hear his message and repent were ever organized formally into a religious group.

One should not be surprised, therefore, to find no evidence of a specific act of founding a Church or of gathering together a community of the elect. Had Jesus done this, his gesture would have been interpreted as the founding of a separate synagogue and would have minimized and even destroyed the uniqueness of his proclamation. Indeed, the only time in all of the Gospels where Jesus is reported to have made explicit reference to the founding of the Church is given in Matthew 16:18. Apart from the problem of its clashing with Mark 8:27-30, to which we referred above, Jesus speaks here not of the present but of the future. Indeed, not until Jesus is risen from the dead do the first Christians even speak of a "Church."

Jesus Laid the Foundations for the Church

First, Jesus did gather disciples around him. They participated in his healing power, which was a sign for Jesus that the Kingdom of God was breaking through: "He sent them forth to proclaim the reign of God and heal the afflicted" (Luke 9:2). On the other hand, the message of the Kingdom which he preached and which he commissioned them to preach was a divisive one. They would be like "sheep among wolves" (Matthew 10:16). "Brother will hand over brother to death, and the father his child; children will turn against parents and have them put to death. You will be hated by all on account of me" (10:21-22). Consequently, those Israelites who would accept his proclamation of the Kingdom would inevitably be distinguished from those who rejected it.

Secondly, he anticipated an interim period between his death and the *parousia*, even though, as we saw in our discussion of Jesus' knowledge in chapter 15, it is difficult to determine just what his understanding of this time-period was. He foresaw that Jerusalem would reject the call to salvation and that instead the pagans would be invited to the heavenly banquet as a new People of God, without regard for ethnic origins (Matthew 8:11-12).

Thirdly, the community of disciples did in fact stay together after the rejection of Jesus by the majority of the Jewish people. It is from this perspective that one must understand the Last Supper, with the Lord's injunction: "Do this in remembrance of me" (1 Corinthians 11:24). Likewise the word to Simon Peter suggests that the disciples understood Jesus as having intended them to stay together (Luke 22:31-34). In fact, there never was a churchless period in the New Testament following the resurrection.

DID THE EARLY CHRISTIAN COMMUNITY UNDERSTAND ITSELF AS CHURCH?
The Word Church

The Greek word *ekklēsia* originally signified a legislative assembly of citizens. Only those citizens who enjoyed full rights could belong to this assembly, and so the word implies both the dignity of the members and the legality of the assembly. The word, however, had no religious usage. It was adopted by the Septuagint (the Greek version of the Old Testament) to render the Hebrew word *kāhāl*, which, with the Hebrew word *'ēdāh*, signifies the religious assembly of the Israelites. The word appears about one hundred times in the Septuagint, often qualified by the phrase "of the Lord" (*kāhāl yahweh*). Because in its earliest phase the young Christian community did not view itself as distinct from Judaism, the Christians simply took over the term to apply to their own gatherings of prayer. *Not until the admission of Gentiles to the community did the distinction between the Church and Judaism become acute.* Thereafter, the work *ekklēsia* applied to the Christian community alone.

The word appears only twice in the *Synoptic Gospels* (Matthew 16:18; 18:17). Of the first, we have already spoken. The second reference (18:17) may have been to the Jewish synagogue, since the distinction between Jesus' disciples and Judaism had not yet become clear.

The word occurs twenty-three times in the *Acts of the Apostles*. In no passage does it certainly refer to anything except the local church, and usually the Church of Jerusalem, the parent and prototype of the other churches (5:11; 8:1,3). These churches outside of Jerusalem are organized with their own bishops, presbyters, and deacons, and they are founded by the Apostles (e.g., 20:28). Entrance is not by Jewish birth but by rite of Baptism. And it is God who gathers the people together (20:28 again).

The word *ekklēsia* occurs sixty-five times in the *Pauline material*—more frequently, therefore, than anywhere else in the New Testament. In most instances the word signifies a local church. Paul is also the first to use the *plural* form of the word (1 Corinthians 11:16; 14:33; 2 Corinthians 8:18; 12:13; Galatians 1:2,22; Romans 16:4,16; and so forth). In *Ephesians* and *Colossians* the word applies to the whole worldwide assembly of Christians. Christ is the head, and the Church is the fullness of his body (Ephesians 1:22-23; Colossians 1:18-20). It is through the Church that the mystery of salvation is revealed (Ephesians 3:10). The relationship between Christ, who is the great sacrament of salvation, and the Church, which is his body, is a great mystery (Ephesians 5:22-32). The figure of the Church as the body of Christ is the basis of Paul's appeal for Christian unity and fellowship (1 Corinthians 12:12-26; Romans 12:4-5). This unity is symbolized by the one bread of the Eucharist (1 Corinthians 10:17).

On the other hand, sometimes the *ekklēsia* is just a small house community (Romans 16:5; Philemon 2), listed alongside larger communities (1 Corinthians 16:19). It often has a specifically liturgical meaning (1 Corinthians 11:18; 14:23,24), and refers also to particular congregations (1 Corinthians 11:18,20,33-34; 14:23). The churches of the New Testament, whether local or universal, are congregations gathered in the name of Jesus Christ. Indeed, they are churches of Jesus Christ (Romans 16:16; 1 Thessalonians 2:14; Galatians 1:22). The Church is the true Israel and the legitimate heir of the Covenant promises (Romans 9-11).

The word *ekklēsia* appears in the *Johannine writings* in 3 John 6, 9, and 10, and twenty times in Revelation, always referring to particular churches. In the Fourth Gospel the Christian community is described as a flock gathered into a sheepfold (10:1-5), and Jesus, as the Good Shepherd. He is also the true vine; his followers, the branches united to him (15:1-8). He commits the flock to Peter (21:15-17) and prays that all of his followers may be one, as he and the Father are one (17:20-21).

In the *other New Testament writings* the word occurs once in James 5:14, where it probably signifies a particular church. There also appears a clearly defined body of followers of Jesus which is called a synagogue (James 2:2).

The Church of the New Testament is no uniform or monolithic reality. It is at once local and universal, but not in the sense that the local church is simply a subdivision of the Church universal, nor that the Church universal is simply the sum total of local churches. Although the precise relationship between the Church universal and the local church(es) is not made clear in the New Testament, it *is* clear that what is excluded in the preceding sentence is excluded also by the New Testament. There is not a Corinthian division of the Church, for example, but "the church of God which is in Corinth" (1 Corinthians 1:2; see also 2 Corinthians 1:1). On the other hand, the Church universal is a living, integrated organism: "the fullness of him who fills the universe in all its parts" (Ephesians 1:23).

The early Christian community did, in fact, appropriate to itself the title "Church" in both senses. It knew itself to be the community of Jesus the Messiah, whom God raised to his right hand (Acts 2:32-36; 3:13-15,20-26; 5:30-31; 7:55-56; 9:4-5; 10:37-43; 13:27-31). That the original Jerusalem Church traced itself back to Jesus is evident in its maintenance of the circle of the Twelve, listed once again by name (less Judas) in Acts 1:13, and completed at the election of Judas' replacement (1:25-26). The celebration of the Eucharist, in fidelity to the Lord's own command, is yet another crucial link with the company of Jesus' disciples (1 Corinthians 11:23-25).

Thus, a purely individualistic Christianity is unthinkable for the earliest Christians. Belief in Christ and life in Christ are to be found only within the community of believers joined to the Lord. All of the New Testament writers write as members of the one Church of Jesus Christ. There is no fragmentation. All of the particular churches are built on the foundation of the Apostles and prophets, and Christ is always the cornerstone (Ephesians 2:20).

The Coming of the Holy Spirit

The descent of the Holy Spirit upon the Church at *Pentecost* did not inaugurate the Church. It already existed (Acts of the Apostles 1:15). But Pentecost was the moment when the Church was specifically endowed with power from on high (Luke 24:49; Acts of the Apostles 1:18). For the early Church the outpouring of the Spirit upon the Church was an established fact, and the manifestations of the Spirit's gifts were not in doubt (1 Corinthians 12-14). Even in Thessalonica those gifts were perceptible (1 Thessalonians 5:19), and so, too, in the Galatian churches (Galatians 3:2-5) and in Rome (Romans 12:6-8). The Spirit is the gift of God to all who believe and are baptized (Acts of the Apostles 2:38; Galatians 4;6; Romans 5:5). The Spirit is the firstfruits of the final Kingdom (1 Thessalonians 4:8; 1 Peter 1:2; Hebrews 6:4; Jude 19-20; 1 John 3:24; 4:13).

The coming of the Holy Spirit makes Christ's community the temple of God (1 Corinthians 3:16; 2 Corinthians 6:16; Ephesians 2:22), a spiritual building where true spiritual sacrifices are offered (1 Peter 2:5) and where true worship in spirit and in truth occurs (John 4:23-24). Through the Spirit all members of the Church have access to the Father and become fellow citizens of heaven with the saints (Ephesians 2:18-19). It is the Spirit who guides the Church in mission (Acts of the Apostles 5:3,9; 8:29,39; 9:31; 10:19; 13:2; 15:28; 16:6-7; 20:23; 21:11) and who speaks to the churches (Revelation 2:7,11,17,19; 3:6,13,22).

The early Church, therefore, did not understand itself simply as another sect within Judaism or even as another religious organization. The Church of the New Testament proclaimed the Gospel "in the Holy Spirit" (1 Thessalonians 1:5). Its message and preaching were given through "the convincing power of the Spirit" (1 Corinthians 2:4). It was a community transformed by the presence of the Spirit, the firstfruits of redemption (Romans 8:23; 2 Corinthians 1:22), and sealed with the Spirit (Ephesians 1:13). The Church is a community saved "through the baptism of new birth and renewal by the Holy Spirit...that we might be justified by his grace and become heirs, in hope, of eternal life" (Titus 3:5,7).

HOW DID THE EARLY CHRISTIAN COMMUNITIES EXPRESS THEMSELVES AS CHURCH?
The Original Jerusalem Community

The religious life of the original Jerusalem Church is summarized in the Acts of the Apostles 2:43-47; 4:32-35; and 5:12-16. We find apostolic activity, supported by healing and miracles, which, in turn, increased the membership of the community; the sharing of goods among the members; and a rich liturgical and prayer life both in a special meeting place in the Temple and in the houses of members themselves. They gathered for the breaking of the bread (2:46; 20:7,11), clearly the eucharistic meal of 1 Corinthians 11:20 which was the central and common worship of all the Christian churches.

This original Jerusalem community maintained its close links with Judaism: the strong attachment to the Temple (a point clearly opposed by the Hellenists, see Acts of the Apostles 6:13-14; 7), the continuation of Jewish practices, and the voluntary community of goods. The Jerusalem Church was not without inner conflict and tension, however. The dispute between the Jewish and Greek members over the care of widows (6:1-6) and, of course, the great debate over the need for circumcision and the observance of Jewish dietary laws (15:1-31) were major cases in point.

The Church at Antioch in Syria

Antioch was at this time the third-largest city in the Roman Empire. The Christian community here was a mixed group: former Jews and former pagans ("Greeks") alike. The Antiochene Church was a model of harmony between Jews and Gentiles, a fact indirectly confirmed by Paul in Galatians 2:1-14. Here, for the first time, the followers of Jesus Christ were called "Christians." They had regular meetings at which the large congregation was "instructed" (Acts of the Apostles 11:26). Prophets and teachers were active here (13:1-3), and the gifts of the Spirit were evident (11:27; 15:32).

It was from this community that Paul and Barnabas were sent to carry the case against the Judaizers at the Council of Jerusalem (15:1-29). Both attested to the marvelous work of God among the Gentiles (15:12). The Council of Jerusalem resolved the crisis with a principle that has remained normative for the Church ever since (if sometimes more in the breach than in the observance): no burden is to be imposed "beyond that which is strictly necessary"(15:28).

The Church of Corinth

This was a church of predominantly pagan origin whose life is disclosed through the two letters of Paul. What is striking about the church in this busy port city is its charismatic character (1 Corinthians 1:5-7; 12:8-11) and its human weaknesses. The charismatics often created confusion (1 Corinthians 14). Serious disorders arose at the celebration of the Eucharist because of the behavior of the rich (1 Corinthians 11:20-34). Partisan groups attached to particular missionaries emerged (1 Corinthians 1:11;

see also 3:4-5, 22). Many sided with opponents of Paul, as his second letter suggests. Pagan vices, especially of a sexual kind, still prevailed (1 Corinthians 5; 6:12-20).

On the other hand, there was also a flourishing church life at Corinth. The apostolic preaching and instruction were sounded in the assemblies (2 Corinthians 3:4—4:6). Worship occupied a central place (1 Corinthians 11:17-34). Baptism and Eucharist were sources of deep religious experience (1 Corinthians 1:13-16; 6:11; 10:1-11,16-22). They understood themselves as the Church of God (1 Corinthians 1:2; 10:32; 11:22; 2 Corinthians 1:1) which honors the Lord (1 Corinthians 1:2,9; 8:6; 10:21; 12:3; 2 Corinthians 3:17-18; 4:5). It was a church in fellowship with the Church of Jerusalem (for which the great collection was taken up) and with the other churches (1 Corinthians 1:2; 7:17; 11:16; 16:1,19; 2 Corinthians 1:1; 8:24; 12:13; 13:12).

Unity in Diversity

Despite all local differences among the Jewish-Christian, Jewish-Hellenistic, and Hellenistic-Gentile communities, *common elements* stood out clearly: faith in Jesus as Messiah and Lord; the practice of Baptism and the celebration of the Eucharist; the apostolic preaching and instruction; the high regard for communal love; and the expectation of the coming Kingdom of God. Great freedom was allowed in all other matters—a freedom which, when exercised, manifested the limitations as well as the spiritual grandeur of God's Church.

HOW DID THE EARLY CHURCH UNDERSTAND ITS MISSION?
Church and Kingdom of God

Just as Jesus' message and mission are centered on, and framed by, the coming Kingdom of God, so, too, are the Church's. It is indeed what Jesus instructed his disciples to pray for: "your kingdom come" (Luke 11:2; Matthew 6:9). It is the reality signified in the many parables attributed to Jesus. But the Church lives "between the times," i.e., between the decisive inbreaking of the Kingdom of

God in Jesus Christ and the final outpouring of the Holy Spirit at the end. As such, the Church is both a Church of glory and a Church of the cross.

It is a *Church of glory* insofar as it has been sanctified from within: "He gave himself up for her to make her holy, purifying her in the bath of water by the power of the word, to present to himself a glorious church, holy and immaculate, without stain or wrinkle or anything of that sort" (Ephesians 5:25-27). "It was in one Spirit," Paul writes elsewhere, "that all of us, whether Jew or Greek, slave or free, were baptized into one body. All of us have been given to drink of the one Spirit" (1 Corinthians 12:13). Indeed, "There is but one body and one Spirit, just as there is but one hope given all of you by your call" (Ephesians 4:4).

But the Church is also a *Church of the cross*. Although it is to the risen body of Christ that Christians are joined (Romans 7:4), within this age that body continues also to be a *suffering* body. "Continually we carry about in our bodies the dying of Jesus, so that in our bodies the life of Jesus may also be revealed" (2 Corinthians 4:10; see also Galatians 6:17; 1 Corinthians 15:31; Romans 8:36). Being joined to the risen Christ means being baptized "into his death...If we have been united with him through likeness to his death, so shall we be through a like resurrection" (Romans 6:3-5). We share "in the blood of Christ" (1 Corinthians 10:16), and by our own suffering, joined to his, we "fill up what is lacking in the sufferings of Christ, for the sake of his body, the church" (Colossians 1:24).

The glory that, in one sense, is *already* in the Church, is *not yet* revealed. We are "heirs of God, heirs with Christ, if only we suffer with him so as to be glorified with him" (Romans 8:17). The tension between glory and suffering is clearly stated in Philippians: "I wish to know Christ and the power flowing from his resurrection; likewise to know how to share in his sufferings by being formed into the pattern of his death. Thus do I hope that I may arrive at resurrection from the dead" (3:10-11). The process is ongoing: "We do not lose heart, because our inner body is renewed each day even though our body is being destroyed at the same time. The present burden of our trial is light enough, and earns for us an eternal weight of glory beyond all comparison" (2 Corinthians

4:16-17). "This means," Paul continues, "that if anyone is in Christ, he is a new creation. The old order has passed away; now all is new!" (5:17).

As a Church both of glory and of the cross, *the Church is both a sign and an instrument of the Kingdom of God.* Peter receives the keys of the Kingdom (Matthew 16:19). He and the other Apostles are given the power of binding and loosing, of forgiving and of withholding forgiveness (Matthew 18:18), of sharing in Jesus' own power (Mark 2:10; John 20:23), even over the demons (Mark 3:15; 6:7). This is indeed the deepest meaning of Jesus' authority: to break the rule of Satan (Luke 11:20; Matthew 12:28; Mark 11:28, 33) and thereby to establish the Kingdom of God. The Church understands itself as having been sent by Christ to make disciples of all nations and to baptize them in the name of the Father, the Son, and the Holy Spirit (Matthew 28:19). This is the grandeur and the burden of the Church. Not all who are called prove worthy of the call (Matthew 22:11-14). Nonetheless Jesus promises to be with the Church for all ages (Matthew 28:20). In the meantime, healings and other signs of renewal will show that the powers of the future age are already present in the Church (Luke 10:17,19; Mark 16:17).

Nowhere is the orientation of the Church toward the Kingdom more explicitly revealed than in the Eucharist, which anticipates the eating and drinking at the Lord's table in the Kingdom (Luke 22:30). "I solemnly assure you, I will never again drink of the fruit of the vine until the day when I drink it new in the reign of God" (Mark 14:25; see also Matthew 26:29).

Proclamation of the Word

That the Church understood itself as having been commissioned to proclaim the Word of God is beyond any reasonable doubt. To *evangelize*, or to announce the good news of salvation, is a favorite word in Luke, occurring ten times in his Gospel and twenty-five times in the Acts of the Apostles. So, too, does it occur frequently (twenty-one times) in the Pauline material, where he speaks also (sixty times) of "the gospel." The evangelist delivers not his own word but the word of God (1 Thessalonians 2:13). It is a Gospel to be proclaimed throughout the world (Mark 13:10). After Easter it becomes the message of salvation about Jesus crucified and risen (Acts 8:5; 9:20; 1 Corinthians 1:23; 15:12). The preaching itself shows forth "the glory of Christ, the image of God" (2 Corinthians 4:4). It has been announced "to every creature under heaven" (Colossians 1:23). It is "a message about God's reign" (Matthew 13:19).

The proclamation also takes the form of *teaching* (Acts of the Apostles 4:2,18; 5:21, 25, 28, 42; 11:26; 15:35; 18:11; 20:20; 28:31). It takes place publicly in the Temple and in houses (5:42; 20:20). The proclamation applies Sacred Scripture to the daily life of the community as a word of instruction, of encouragement, and of consolation (14:22; 15:30–32; 1 Thessalonians 2:2; 1 Corinthians 14:3,31). It is sometimes *prophetic* (1 Corinthians 14). The prophets are listed even before the teachers (1 Corinthians 12:28; Ephesians 4:11), and the faithful are said to be built on the foundation of the Apostles and the prophets (Ephesians 2:20; 3:5). On the other hand, there were false prophets or pseudo-prophets against whom the Church had to act (1 Thessalonians 5:21; 1 Corinthians 12:3; 1 John 4:1-3).

Worship and Sacraments

Baptism

Even Rudolf Bultmann acknowledged that there never was a time in the life of the Church when there was no Baptism. The testimony of Paul is particularly important. In the spring of 56 or 55 or perhaps even 54, he wrote from Ephesus to the Church of Corinth that "it was in one Spirit that all of us, Jew or Greek, slave or free, were baptized into one body" (1 Corinthians 12:13). This testimony takes us back biographically to about the year 33, just after Jesus' death. Baptism has its roots, therefore, not in the later Hellenistic churches but in the Jewish-Christian Church, and the Gospels themselves point to the prototype, *the baptism of John.*

John's baptism is characterized by eschatological expectation; it involves a call to repentance; it is administered only once; and it does not introduce one into a sect but is demanded for the whole people. Jesus himself was baptized by John (Mark 1:9-11), and because of that the community was convinced that he approved "a baptism of repentance which led to the forgiveness of sins" (Mark 1:4). The Church baptized not only in memory of John's baptism but also in memory of Jesus.

Easter gave Baptism a completely new meaning. Jesus is now perceived as the risen Lord (Acts of the Apostles 2:36). Salvation is through his death and resurrection. Even though Baptism is still a baptism of repentance for the forgiveness of sins, repentance is seen as a turning to Christ, and the forgiveness of sins occurs on the authority of Christ and by his power. Baptism is administered "in the name of Jesus" (Acts of the Apostles 2:38; 8:16; 10:48; 1 Corinthians 1:13-15; Galatians 3:27; Romans 6:3). By being baptized in the "name" of Jesus, a person becomes subject to him and is committed to his rule and care. The word "name" is a legal concept, signifying authority and competence.

That Baptism is closely linked with the proclamation of the Word is evident in the meeting between the deacon Philip and the Ethiopian court official (Acts of the Apostles 8:26-40), where Baptism follows an instruction on the Scriptures. The content of that Word is the death and resurrection of Christ. Baptism is a Baptism into his death and resurrection (Colossians 2:11-13; 3:1-4; Ephesians 2:5). And just as the Holy Spirit is released through the resurrection, so, too, is the Spirit given in a special way at Baptism (Acts of the Apostles 19:2-6; Titus 3:6). But the effect is not automatic. Baptism without faith is empty, and without openness to the Spirit there is no holiness (1 Corinthians 10:1-13; Hebrews 6:4-8; and all of 1 Peter).

Eucharist

Like Baptism, the Eucharist, or Lord's Supper (the term used in the oldest account in 1 Corinthians 11:20), is rooted in the very beginning of the Church. The Last Supper tradition is ancient and is given in four variant versions: 1 Corinthians 11:23-25; Mark 14:22-25; Matthew 26:26-29; and Luke 22:15-20. The Pauline account dates from the years 54-56 and refers to the fact that Paul handed on this tradition to the Corinthians at the beginning of his missionary activity in Corinth (about 49). But Paul also states that this tradition comes directly from the Lord. Peter was still alive and could have repudiated Paul's account if it were inaccurate. Paul himself lived for many years with members of the Jerusalem Church (Barnabas, Mark, Silas) and took part in the Lord's Supper in various communities. His account must have agreed with those of eyewitnesses.

The more strongly Semitic flavor to Mark's account has led some exegetes to conclude that his is even older than Paul's. The differences between the two accounts are too great, in any event, to assume a common Greek source. On the other hand, the agreement between them in content is so great that we must assume a common Aramaic or Hebrew source.

The meal that Jesus shared with his Apostles was the last of a long series of daily meals he had with his disciples. For Orientals, shared meals have always signified peace, trust, and community. But Jesus also shared meals with sinners, outcasts, and tax collectors, as a sign that the reign of God had begun and was open to all and demanded love of all. The Last Supper, however, was a special meal. It was either a Passover meal or perhaps a farewell meal on the night before the Passover feast. Whichever it was, it was celebrated with a view to the coming Kingdom of God. Indeed, the Kingdom was the focus of everything Jesus did and said, not only at this meal but in his whole life and ministry.

The structure was obviously taken over from the Jewish ritual meal: the words over the bread, followed by its breaking and sharing, and the blessing over the wine. But now Jesus identifies himself with the bread and wine. It is his body which is broken and his blood which is poured out in atonement for sin and for the establishment of a new Covenant. All four texts agree on this. The Jews regarded every death, but particularly the death of an innocent one, as having the character of atonement. And so Jesus could have easily seen his own innocent suffering in this way, without necessarily tying it to the more fully developed theology of the post-resurrection Church.

By distributing the bread and wine as his flesh and blood, Jesus gave his disciples a share in the power of his death to make atonement and to establish a new Covenant. This, too, is a familiar Oriental idea: Eating and drinking communicated divine gifts.

After the resurrection the disciples gathered again and again for these shared meals, but now with the conviction that the risen Christ was in their midst as they gathered in his name (Matthew 18:20). There was joy in their new fellowship: joy over the presence of Christ and joy over the approach of the Kingdom of God (Acts of the Apostles 2:46). It is important to note that the celebration of the Lord's Supper after the death and resurrection of Christ was not an arbitrary act on the part of the Church. The Church was convinced it was following the Lord's own injunction, and indeed it referred to the actions of Jesus at the Last Supper as the pattern and authority for what it did.

The Eucharist, therefore, is a meal of remembrance and thanksgiving, of fellowship, and of anticipation. It looks at once to the past, the present, and the future. "Every time, then, you eat this bread and drink this cup, you proclaim the death of the Lord until he comes!" (1 Corinthians 11:26).

Through the Eucharist, therefore, the Church proclaims its faith in the Lordship of Jesus and in the coming of the Kingdom. Through the Eucharist the Church manifests and more fully recognizes and deepens its unity in Christ (1 Corinthians 10:16-17). Through the Eucharist the Church sets a pattern for its own ministry to those in need (1 Corinthians 11:17-34) and exposes itself thereby to judgment (11:34).

(We shall, of course, be returning to the sacraments of the Church in chapters 21 and 22.)

Mission to All and for All

The Church always understood itself as a missionary community. It reached out, first, to the whole people of Israel (Acts of the Apostles 3:11; 4:1; 5:25, 40, 42), even beyond Jerusalem (9:32-43; Galatians 2:8; 1 Corinthians 9:5), and then to the Gentiles (Matthew 8:11 = Luke 13:28). The transition, however, from the mission to the Jews to the mission to the Gentiles as well did not occur without difficulty, as we have already noted. There was hesitation, to say the least, on the part of the Jewish Christians of

Jerusalem, including the Apostles. Luke, on the other hand, gives a theological foundation for broadening the mission (Acts of the Apostles 28:25-28) and points to an intervention from God and the authority of Peter as factors in changing the situation (10:1—11:8). The differences, however, were not irreconcilable. The Jerusalem Church still had very close ties with the Jews and Jewish ways of thought and customs (1:6; 10:14), and yet James, the leader of the Jerusalem community, declared himself in agreement with the Pauline approach, which dispensed with the absolute need of circumcision and with Paul's mission to the Gentiles (Acts of the Apostles 15; Galations 6:10). Previously, Barnabas, the representative of the Jerusalem Church, had approved the conversion of Greeks in Antioch and indeed had accompanied Paul on his first missionary journey (Acts of the Apostles 13-14).

On the other hand, Jerusalem's privileged position is upheld. The mission to "the ends of the earth" begins from Jerusalem (Acts of the Apostles 1:8; Luke 24:47; Romans 9-11). Israel was to be given its last opportunity for repentance through the apostolic preaching (Acts of the Apostles 2:38; 3:19; 5:31; Mark 7:27; Romans 1:16; 2:9). Historically, the Hellenistic Christians, who had a freer and more open attitude toward paganism, were probably the first to proclaim the Gospel to the Gentiles.

Paul sees the conversion of the Gentiles as a mystery of the history of redemption, after which all of Israel will be saved (Romans 11:25). That the Gentiles are co-heirs of Christ and sharers in the promise Paul sees as a matter of recent revelation in the Spirit (Ephesians 3:5-6). Through their incorporation into the Church, "God's manifold wisdom is made known" (3:10).

HOW DID THE EARLY CHURCH ORGANIZE ITSELF FOR MISSION?

First, there is *no uniform order or structure* to the Church of the New Testament. This varied from place to place. It is not clear, for example, how the Twelve function even in the Jerusalem Church, and why they seem to recede into the background after Acts of the Apostles 6:2, or why the elders are mentioned with them at the Council of Jerusalem, or what rank and position "the

Seven" held (6:6). There is no doubt about Peter's special position, but what of the importance of James, the "brother of the Lord," who assumes a position of pastoral leadership in Jerusalem alongside Peter (12:17; 15:13-21; Galatians 1:19; 2:9) and after Peter leaves (Galatians 2:12; Acts of the Apostles 21:18)?

Secondly, however, there is *some* order and structure which shapes the life and mission of the Church. The Church is never without it, nor can it be without it. In this sense, that order is said to be *constitutive* rather than merely functional. This is not to say that all authority and missionary responsibility were given to the hierarchical few to be exercised in the name of, or for the sake of, the many. On the contrary, the whole congregation was involved in important decisions in this earliest of periods (Acts of the Apostles 15; 1 Corinthians 5). But there were also members who served in some leadership capacity. Local churches were guided by presbyters, and others were appointed as overseers (the original meaning of the word for *bishop, episcopos*; see Acts of the Apostles 20:28). And that is not only Lucan theology. A hierarchically structured community is also at the basis of Paul's listing of the various ministers and ministries in 1 Corinthians 12:28, and he derives these various offices from the Lord himself (Ephesians 4:11). Mention of the Apostles first, and then prophets and teachers, cannot be by chance. There is a sacred order of ministers and pastors who are responsible to their heavenly chief shepherd (1 Peter 5:2-4).

Thirdly, there is *no radical opposition between the charismatic and administrative ministries,* as some Protestant scholars had argued in the past. All of the gifts and charisms have the same source, the Holy Spirit (1 Corinthians 12:11). Some of these gifts are clearly "charismatic"—e.g., the gift of tongues. Others are clearly "administrative" or "institutional"—e.g., teaching and presiding (Romans 12:7-8; Ephesians 4:11-12).

Fourthly, *neither is there any radical opposition between the order of the Jerusalem Church and the order of the Pauline communities.* Despite his absence from Corinth, Paul decides the cases of the incestuous man (1 Corinthians 5:3-5), gives directives for the divine service (11: 17, 33), admonishes and gives concrete prescriptions (7:17; 16:1; Titus 1:5), and gives definite moral guidance

(1 Thessalonians 4:11; 2 Thessalonians 3:4,6,10,12). The Church of Corinth must have recognized his apostolic authority. Why else would they have submitted certain questions to him for decision (1 Corinthians 7:1, and following chapters)? Nor is the picture presented by the Pastoral Epistles (1 and 2 Timothy, and Titus) improbable for the period of consolidation of the Pauline communities.

Fifthly, whatever the office or ministry, it is also for the sake of *service*, never for domination. The model is Jesus, who lays down his life for others (Mark 10:45). The one who humbles himself will be exalted, and vice versa (Luke 14:11; Matthew 23:12). Paul consistently refers to his own office as that of a servant (1 Corinthians 4:1, 9-13; 2 Corinthians 4:5,12,15; 6:4-10; Philippians 2:17).

Sixthly, the chief ministry in the Church is the *Petrine ministry*, i.e., a ministry for the universal Church. Indeed, even if one were to conclude that Jesus did not say "You are Peter and upon this rock I will build my church..." in July of the year 29 at Caesarea Philippi, we still have to contend with the clear fact that this tradition, embedded in Matthew 16:18, was maintained somewhere in the first-century Church and represents a Christian evaluation of Peter's position with which every serious Christian must cope.

Peter was one of the first called, and remained prominent thereafter among Jesus' disciples. He is the most frequently mentioned disciple in all four Gospels. Even the distant Gentile converts of Paul in Galatia know of Peter. He functioned as the spokesman of the Apostles and is always placed first on lists of Apostles (Matthew 10:2). Indeed, he was probably the first to whom the Lord appeared after the resurrection (1 Corinthians 15:5; Luke 24:34; Mark 16:7). This fact alone may explain the prominence of Peter in the early Church, not all of which is explicable in the light of his role during the life of Jesus. That Peter served as the spokesman of the Apostles after the resurrection is clear in the Acts of the Apostles, but it was never a unilateral or unaccountable sort of role. He is also portrayed as consulting with the other Apostles and even being sent by them (8:14). He and John act almost as a team (3:1-11; 4:1-23; 8:14). It was Peter who took the decisive step in ordering the Baptism of the Gentile Cornelius (Acts of the Apostles 10). And although Paul spoke of Peter's ministry as being directed to the circumcised (Galatians 2:7), Peter's influence in Gentile areas is obvious (1 Corinthians 1:12; 1 Peter 1:1).

Whatever the minimal facts of Peter's life and ministry, it is also clear that he became a symbol for Christian thought. He is portrayed as having played many different roles in the life of the Church. Modern New Testament scholars speak of a *trajectory* of biblical images of Peter. It begins with Peter as the great Christian *fisherman* (Luke 5; John 21), then as the *shepherd*, or pastor, of the flock (John 21), then as the Christian *martyr* (John 13:36; 1 Peter 5:1), then as the *receiver of special revelation* (Mark 9:2-8, and parallels; 2 Peter 1:16-18; Acts of the Apostles 5:1-11; 10:9-16; 12:7-9), then as the *confessor of the true faith* (Matthew 16:16-17) and as its *guardian* against false teaching (2 Peter 1:20-21; 3:15-16). He is portrayed also as a weak and sinful man, but a *repentant sinner*. He is reproached by Paul (Galatians 2:11-14), misunderstands Jesus (Mark 9:5-6; John 13:6-11; 18:10-11), is rebuked by Jesus (Mark 8:33; Matthew 16:23) and denies Christ (Mark 14:66-72). But he is rehabilitated. The risen Lord appears to him (John 21:15-17), and he becomes again a source of strength to the Church (Luke 22:32).

Other Apostles were also subjects of similar trajectories, but no trajectory outdistanced Peter's, not even the Twelve's or Paul's. This is even implied already in 2 Peter, where the image of Peter is evoked to correct those who are appealing to Paul.

WHAT IS THE CHURCH OF THE NEW TESTAMENT?
People of God

According to Hebrew ways of thinking, the people forms a whole, a *corporate personality*. The individual takes on meaning, importance, and even destiny insofar as the individual is involved with the people. Israel understood itself as the people of God, by God's own call (Exodus 19:5; 23:22; Deuteronomy 7:6; 14:2; 26:18). "I will take you as my own people, and you shall have me as your

God" (Exodus 6:7). The call to peoplehood is linked with the *Covenant:* "I will look with favor upon you...as I carry out my covenant with you...I will set my Dwelling among you, and will not disdain you. Ever present in your midst, I will be your God, and you will be my people..." (Leviticus 26:9-12). The same connection is to be found in the major prophets (e.g., Jeremiah 32:38-41).

The early Church appropriated this image to itself: "You, however, are 'a chosen race, a royal priesthood, a holy nation, a people he claims for his own to proclaim the glorious works' of the One who called you from darkness into his marvelous light. Once you were no people, but now you are God's people..." (1 Peter 2:9-10). The allusions to the Old Testament are evident: in particular Isaiah 43:20-21, and Exodus 19:6. Undoubtedly, the passage intends to show that the Church is the new People of God purchased by the redemptive work of Christ.

That fundamental text from the Old Testament, "I will take you as my own people, and you shall have me as your God," is cited several times throughout the New Testament and applied to the Church itself, as the new eschatological community. Paul quotes it in 2 Corinthians 6:16 from Ezekiel 37:27 in order to distinguish the Church from the unbelievers. In Hebrews 8:10 it occurs in the lengthy quotation from Jeremiah 31:31-34 to show that this great prophecy has been fulfilled in the new Covenant. And the formula appears finally in Revelation 21:3 in the vision of the future Jerusalem. Indeed, the notion of the Church as the new eschatological People of God is the guiding theme of the Epistle to the Hebrews.

This new People of God, formed out of the remnant of Israel and from many Gentiles, arises out of the love and grace of God: "Once you were no people, but now you are God's people; once there was no mercy for you, but now you have found mercy" (1 Peter 2:10). But, again, it is a "purchased" people, "acquired at the price of his own blood" (Acts of the Apostles 20:28). God makes a new beginning for the human community in grace. The Church is itself the new People of God (Titus 2:14, where the reference again is to Ezekiel 37:23).

Nowhere is the Church spoken of explicitly as the "new" People of God, but there *is* explicit mention of the *new* Covenant

(Luke 22:20; 1 Corinthians 11:25; 2 Corinthians 3:6; Hebrews 8:13; 9:15; 12:24), and that Covenant is connected, at least implicitly, to a new community (Hebrews 8:8-12 cites Jeremiah 31:31-34, where such a link is made). But it is no longer a covenant signed by circumcision, but by faith in Jesus Christ and the "circumcision of Christ" (Colossians 2:11), i.e., Baptism.

A tension between the old and new People of God remains, however, and it is most strongly portrayed in Paul, especially in Romans 9-11. Unbelieving Israel is "Israel according to the flesh" (1 Corinthians 10:18), but believing Israel is "the Israel of God" (Galatians 6:16). God calls us, Jew and Gentile alike. "There does not exist among you Jew or Greek, slave or freeman, male or female. All are one in Christ Jesus. Futhermore, if you belong to Christ you are the descendants of Abraham, which means you inherit all that was promised" (Galatians 3:28-29).

But even in the New Testament the new People of God are not identical with the community of the elect. In other words, membership in the Church is no guarantee of participation in the Kingdom of God. There are false prophets in the Church who will be repudiated by the Lord at the end (Matthew 7:22-23). All evil-doers will be cast out (13:41-43). On the other side, many who did not belong to the Church will be acknowledged by the Son of Man as his brothers and sisters (25:31-46). "He will dispatch his angels and assemble his chosen from the four winds, from the farthest bounds of earth and sky" (Mark 13:27). The final test will be a just life. No one will enter the marriage feast without a wedding garment (Matthew 22:11-13).

Body of Christ

If the People-of-God image underlines the Church's intimate connection with Israel and with God's call to a covenant relationship, the Body-of-Christ image underlines the Church's intimate connection with Jesus Christ and with God's call to a communal relationship, one with another in Christ.

The image is, of course, distinctively Pauline, although it bears some affinity with the Johannine allegory of the vine and the branches (John 15:1-8). The Church in the New Testament is the

People of God, but a people newly constituted in Christ and in relation to Christ. The two images, therefore, are not mutually opposed. The Church is the People of God insofar as it is the Body of Christ, and it is the Body of Christ insofar as it is the People of God. In principle, both images are rooted in the Old Testament idea of *corporate personality*.

The conception of the Church as Body of Christ is grounded in the union that exists between the Christian and the *risen* body of Christ. Just as the resurrection is central to New Testament Christology, so is it central to New Testament, and especially Pauline, ecclesiology. When the Christian shares in the bread of the Eucharist, he or she becomes one body with Christ (1 Corinthians 10:16-17). Thus, the one who eats or drinks unworthily profanes the body of the Lord (11:27) and eats and drinks unto his or her own condemnation (11:29). It is in one body that Christ has reconciled us to the Father by his death (Ephesians 2:16-17; Colossians 1:22). The Church has become one body, his own, in which the Holy Spirit dwells (Ephesians 4:4). Christians are called one body (Colossians 3:15).

The physical realism of the union between Christ and the Church lies behind the development from the notion of one body "in" Christ (Romans and 1 Corinthians) to one Body "of" Christ (Ephesians and Colossians). But it *is* a development. In Romans 12:4-21 and in 1 Corinthians 12:4-27, for example, the application of the image refers more to the union of Christians with each other than with Christ. It speaks of a diversity of charisms and offices which, despite their multiplicity, do not compromise the fundamental unity of the Church. The members are one because they are baptized by one spirit into one body (1 Corinthians 12:13). They are called not one body "in" Christ but one body "of" Christ (12:27). The same identity is presupposed in 1 Corinthians 6:15: "Do you not see that your bodies are members of Christ?" Indeed, it is because the Christian is really a member of the body of Christ that he or she can also be called metaphorically a temple of the Holy Spirit (6:19).

The ideas of these earlier letters are presupposed as the Body of Christ image is introduced, with seeming abruptness, in Ephesians 1:23 and Colossians 1:24. Christ is now called the head of his

Body the Church (Ephesians 5:23; Colossians 1:18; 2:19). As head of the Church, Christ is the principle of union and growth (Ephesians 4:16; Colossians 2:19). The Body of Christ is something that is to be built up (Ephesians 4:12,16).

With some measure of urgency, the Pauline author of Ephesians pleads with the community to "live a life worthy of the calling...(to) make every effort to preserve the unity which has the Spirit as its origin and peace as its binding force. There is but one body and one Spirit" (4:1-4; see also Colossians 3:12-15).

Temple of the Holy Spirit

Because the Church is the Body of Christ it can also be called the Temple of the Holy Spirit. Here again the *resurrection* is central. The Spirit proceeds from the "Lord of the Spirit," who through his resurrection has become "a life-giving spirit" (1 Corinthians 15:45). There is, of course, a special outpouring of the Spirit at Pentecost, as the fruit of Christ's saving action (Acts of the Apostles 1:8; 2:3-4,38; 4:8,31; 6:8; 9:17; 11:24; 13:52; 19:2). This thought is particularly clear in John where it is asserted that the Spirit could not be given until the Lord had been glorified (7:39; 6:63). The risen and exalted Lord releases the Spirit and with the Spirit builds his Church. The Body of Christ "takes shape as a holy temple in the Lord...to become a dwelling place for God in the Spirit (Ephesians 2:21-22). Jew and Gentile alike have "access in one Spirit to the Father" (2:18).

Just as Jesus identified himself with the Temple, so the Body of Christ is itself the new Temple (1 Corinthians 3:9, 16-17; 2 Corinthians 6:16; Ephesians 2:19-22). The Church is now the place of God's dwelling. It is, in the theological sense of the word, a *mystery*, i.e., "a reality imbued with the hidden presence of God" (Pope Paul VI, at the opening of the second session of Vatican II, September 1963).

The Spirit is manifested in various ways, witnessing to the presence and activity of God in the Church (Acts of the Apostles 2:3-13; 10:47; 11:17; 15:8). The Spirit teaches the disciples what to say (Luke 12:12), reveals the mysteries of God (Luke 1:41,67; Acts of the Apostles 11:28; 13:9), inspires prophecy (2:18), is the source of wisdom (6:3), faith (6:5; 2 Corinthians 4:13), encouragement (Acts of the Apostles 9:31), joy (13:52), hope (Romans 15:13; 1 Corinthians 14:14-16; 2:4-5; Galatians 3:5), and love (Romans 5:5; Colossians 1:18; Galatians 5:13-36).

The Spirit directs the officers of the Church in important decisions (Acts of the Apostles 13:2; 15:28; 20:28). The Spirit is conferred upon all of the members at Baptism (19:2,6; 2:38-39; 15:8-9; 8:16-18; 9:17; 10:44; 11:16-17) and at the imposition of hands (8:14-17; 19:6). The gifts of the Spirit are for the building up of the Church (1 Corinthians 14:12,26). By his or her union with the Spirit of the risen Christ, the Christian rises in a spiritual body (1 Corinthians 15:35-50). The Christian's and the Church's present possession of the Spirit is a foretaste (Romans 8:23) and a pledge (2 Corinthians 1:22; 5:5) of the salvation, i.e., of the Kingdom of God, that is to come.

SUMMARY

1.   The mystery of the Church flows directly from the mystery of Christ. The Church is the Body of Christ and carries forward his mission.

2.   Did Jesus found the Church? Was his evaluation of the Church identical with the Church's evaluation of itself? There is a spectrum of answers to these questions: *non-scholarly conservatism*, which insists on continuity (between Jesus' intentions and the Church's self-understanding) without development within the New Testament itself; *non-scholarly liberalism*, which denies all continuity and ignores even the ecclesiology of the New Testament; *scholarly liberalism*, which does not ignore the ecclesiology of the New Testament but denies its origin in Jesus because he expected the Kingdom of God as imminent; *Bultmannian existentialism*, which acknowledges some continuity between Jesus' proclamation of the Kingdom and membership in the community of faith here and now, but rejects the development toward sacramentalism in the Fourth Gospel and in Hellenistic Christianity; and *scholarly conservatism*, which admits continuity within development, but which divides Catholic from Protestant on the degree of sacramental and ministerial structure that is necessary or "constitutive" for the life and mission of the Church.

3.   Jesus did *not* intend to found a Church if by *found* we mean some direct, explicit, deliberate act by which he established a new religious organization. He never addresses a select group of people; he

imposes no specific rule of life; he makes no connection between member-ship in his circle with salvation.

4.   Jesus *did* found a Church, at least indirectly; i.e., he laid the foundations for it. First, he gathered disciples around him for the procla-mation of the Kingdom of God. Secondly, he anticipated an interim period between his death and the final coming of the Kingdom. Thirdly, at the Last Supper and in the injunction to Peter, he looked toward the disciples' staying together even after his death.

5.   The word *church* is from the Greek *"ekklēsia,"* which refers in its original political meaning to an assembly of citizens who enjoy full civil rights. It was taken over by the Greek-speaking Jews to translate the Hebrew word *kāhāl*. Not until the admission of Gentiles to the commu-nity did the word *ekklēsia* apply to the Church alone, over against Judaism.

6.   Did the early Christian community understand itself as Church? Yes, in both local and universal senses. *Church* as *local* church is mentioned twenty-three times in the Acts of the Apostles and in most of the sixty-five references to Church in the Pauline literature. In Ephesians and Colossians, however, *Church* is used in its *universal* sense, as the fullness of Christ. At other times, *Church* refers to a small *house* commu-nity (as in Romans 16:5 and Philemon 2) or to *particular congregations* (1 Corinthians 11:18,20,33-34; 14:23). All references in the Johannine literature (at least twenty-three) are to particular churches.

7.   The local Church is not simply a subdivision of the Church universal, nor is the Church universal simply the sum total or composite of local churches. There is not a Corinthian division of the Church, for example, but "the church of God which is in Corinth" (1 Corinthians 1:2).

8.   *There is no individualistic Christianity in the New Testament.* Belief in Christ and life in Christ are to be found only within the community of believers joined to the Lord. All of the New Testament writers write as members of the one Church of Jesus Christ.

9.   The Church did not begin at *Pentecost*. It already existed by that time. But Pentecost was the moment when the Church was endowed in a special way with power from on high, i.e., the power of the Holy Spirit, as the firstfruits of the Kingdom of God.

10.   The early Church did not understand itself as just another Jewish sect or a new religious organization. It was a community trans-formed by the presence of the *Holy Spirit*.

11.   The Jewish-Christian Church of *Jerusalem* maintained many links with Judaism: strong attachment to the Temple, continuation of certain Jewish practices, and a sharing of goods. It was eventually marked by conflict over the need for circumcision and the observance of

the dietary laws. As in all of the churches, the Eucharist was its central act of worship.

12.   The Jewish-Hellenistic Church of *Antioch* was a model of harmony between Jews and Gentiles. Here the followers of Christ were called "Christians" for the first time. Prophets and teachers were active here, and the gifts of the Spirit were evident.

13.   The Hellenistic-Gentile Church of *Corinth* was also marked by the gifts of the Spirit, but they were often sources of division rather than unity. On the other hand, the apostolic preaching and instruction were carried on, as was the worship of God in the Eucharist.

14.   Despite the differences among these three different types of churches, certain *common elements* remain: faith in Jesus as Messiah and Lord, the practice of Baptism and the celebration of the Eucharist, the apostolic preaching and instruction, regard for communal love, and the expectation of the Kingdom of God. Freedom was allowed in most other matters.

15.   The *mission* of the Church, like the mission of Jesus, centered on the *Kingdom of God*. The Church lives between-the-times, between the Kingdom as promised and the Kingdom as realized fully. As such the Church is at once a *Church of glory* (the firstfruits of the Kingdom, i.e., the Holy Spirit, are already present in the Church), and a *Church of the cross* (it continues to be joined to the sufferings and death of Christ).

16.   The Church, therefore, is both *sign* and *instrument* of the Kingdom. It is sent by Christ to proclaim the Kingdom of God, to make disciples of all nations, to baptize them in the name of the Father, the Son, and the Holy Spirit, to forgive sins, and thereby to break the power of Satan. The orientation of the Church to the Kingdom is explicit in the Eucharist.

17.   The mission of the Church, more specifically, includes the *proclamation* of the Word (evangelization): a message about the crucifed and risen Jesus, about the reign of God. It may also take the form of teaching and prophecy.

18.   The mission also includes *worship and sacraments* , especially Baptism and the Eucharist. *Baptism* is always into the death and resurrection of Jesus. As such, it is an act of repentance and forgiveness of sins. The *Eucharist*, or Lord's Supper, whose structure is taken over from the Jewish ritual meal, is an act of remembrance and thanksgiving, of fellowship, and of anticipation of the Kingdom.

19.   The mission is *to all* and *for all*. This did not happen without some reluctance, even sharp conflict. But eventually the Church understood itself as having a mandate to reach out to the Gentiles, who are co-heirs of Christ and sharers in the promise given to Israel in the past.

20.   There is *no uniform order or structure* in the New Testament Church. It varied from place to place. On the other hand, all churches had *some* order and structure. Some members served in leadership roles as presbyters, bishops, elders, etc. All ministers were responsible to the chief shepherd in heaven.

21.   There is no radical opposition between the charismatic and administrative ministries. All have the same source: the Holy Spirit.

22.   Neither is there any radical opposition between the Jerusalem Church and the Pauline churches. Paul's apostolic authority was recognized and exercised even in the freer communities of the Hellenistic world.

23.   All offices and ministries are for the sake of *service*, never for domination. Jesus is always the model.

24.   The chief ministry in the Church is the *Petrine* , a ministry to and for the universal Church. Even if Jesus did not say, "You are Peter...," it is clear that the early Church believed in the primacy of Peter. Among other things, he was probably the first to whom the risen Lord appeared. There is a trajectory of images about Peter (fisherman, shepherd, guardian of the faith, etc.) which tend to support the special status he came to enjoy in the eyes of the New Testament and post-biblical Church.

25.   The Church of the New Testament is also portrayed according to various *images*, the most important of which are three: People of God, Body of Christ, and Temple of the Holy Spirit.

26.   The Church is *People of God*. The image is linked with the Old Testament notions of *corporate personality* and *covenant*. The former reminds us that the destiny of the individual is wrapped up with the fortunes of the whole people, and the latter reminds us that the people are constituted as a people by reason of God's covenant with them: "I will be your God, and you will be my people" (Leviticus 26:12). The Church is founded on a *new Covenant* in Christ. Entrance into the new People of God is not by circumcision but by faith and Baptism. The new People of God are not entirely separate from the old Israel. Many in Israel have come to believe; the rest will enter in God's own good time. All are called as one in Christ.

27.   The Church is the *Body of Christ*. Here, too, the notion of *corporate personality* is significant. Christians are united to the *risen* Christ and therefore to one another "in Christ." We are baptized into his body, and become one with the body by partaking of the body and blood in the Eucharist. Christ is *head* of the body, as principle of unity and growth. All must live according to the calling, to manifest the unity that is the Church.

28.   The Church is the *Temple of the Holy Spirit.* It is "a dwelling place for God in the Spirit" (Ephesians 2:21–22). The risen and exalted Lord releases the Spirit and with the Spirit builds the Church, as a temple. The Spirit is manifested in various ways and is the source of wisdom and strength. The gifts of the Spirit are for the building up of the Church. And the Spirit is itself a foretaste and a pledge of the Kingdom that is to come.

SUGGESTED READINGS

Brown, Raymond E., et al. *Peter in the New Testament: A Collaborative Assessment by Protestant and Roman Catholic Scholars.* New York: Paulist Press, 1973.

Minear, Paul. *Images of the Church in the New Testament.* Philadelphia: Westminster Press, 1960.

Robinson, John A. T. *The Body: A Study in Pauline Theology* . London: S. C. M. Press, 1952.

Schnackenburg, Rudolf. *The Church in the New Testament* . New York: Herder & Herder, 1965.

Schweizer, Eduard. *Church Order in the New Testament.* London: S. C. M. Press, 1961.

Zehnle, Richard. *The Making of the Christian Church.* Notre Dame, Ind.: Fides Press, 1969.

TWENTIETH-CENTURY VIEWS OF THE ECCLESIOLOGY OF THE NEW TESTAMENT

Non-Scholarly Liberalism	Scholarly Liberalism	Bultmannian Existentialism	Scholarly Conservatism	Non-Scholarly Conservatism
There is no continuity at all between the Church's evaluation of itself and Jesus' evaluation of the Church. Jesus came to teach us a way of life centered on love and based on freedom from institutional oppression. Jesus did not intend to found a Church in any sense. He came only to preach the Kingdom of God.	Because of Jesus's own expectation of the Kingdom as imminent, bringing an end to this world order, he did not intend to found a Church. With the delay of the *parousia* until after the death and resurrection of Jesus, the Church perceived itself as the ultimate Messianic Community of the Saints, the elect of the final generation, Jews and Gentiles alike, who would soon enter a new form of being in the new aeon. With the delay of the *parousia* well beyond the death and resurrection, the post-apostolic Church abandoned this Pauline view and assumed some organizational form suggesting some historical permanence.	In reaction to Liberalism, Bultmann insisted that Jesus linked entrance into the Kingdom of God with affiliation with the Jewish people, as the eschatological community. He rejects the Liberal view that Jesus' expectation of the Kingdom as imminent led him to expound only an interim ethic. On the other hand, Jesus never thought of a mission to the Gentiles, nor would he have countenanced the sacramentalism of the Fourth Gospel and of Hellenistic Christianity.	Most scholars today admit a stronger and broader continuity between the Church's self-evaluation and Jesus' evaluation of the Church. Yet they recognize growth and development in New Testament ecclesiology. But there is continuity in development.	Jesus left the Twelve Apostles a detailed blueprint for a Church: seven sacraments with precise matter and form, the papacy as vested with supreme and universal jurisdiction, the monarchical episcopate, doctrines, liturgies, and laws. The Church's evaluation of itself (as given in Counter-Reformation and pre-Vatican II theology) and Jesus' evaluation of the Church are identical.
Liberalism has emerged within Catholicism in recent years as a reaction against ecclesiastical authoritarianism and doctrinal and moral fundamentalism.	Expressed by Johannes Weiss (1892) and especially in Martin Werner's *The Formation of Christian Dogma* (1941).		Differences between Catholic and Protestant scholars are more a reflection of theological and doctrinal commitments than of exegetical differences. Catholics emphasize the Church's role in mediating salvation more than Protestants do, and this accounts for some differences in approach toward questions of sacramental and ministerial order. Recent ecumenical dialogues, however, suggest a growing convergence of views.	A view held by Catholics until the Second Vatican Council and the application of biblical studies to ecclesiology in the 1960s.

· XVIII ·

THE CHURCH IN HISTORY

THE PROBLEM

This chapter is deliberately entitled "The Church in History" rather than "The History of the Church." Even from a practical point of view, the second project would have been impossible, given the limitations of both purpose and space. But the second project would also have been less appropriate on ecclesiological grounds as well. We are not so much interested here in the accumulated past of the Church as in the impact history itself has had upon the Church, and the Church upon history. *The relationship between the Church and history is a theological one.* It has to do with the presence of grace in the world, with the direction and destiny of the world toward the Kingdom of God, and with the role of the Church in proclaiming, celebrating, exemplifying, and serving that reality of grace, as personified in Jesus Christ, by which the world is alive and in movement toward perfection. (The reader is referred again to the discussion of revelation and history in chapter 7.)

But whether one is discussing the history *of* the Church or the Church *in* history, some logical order must be imposed upon the massive amount of data one confronts. To talk at all about the Church from an historical point of view is to talk about *something* historical. What should that be, and in what context(s)? What should be passed over, and why? On what basis can the selected material be systematized (for if not systematized, it is unusable)? Which divisions are to be employed, and why? Who, after all, "consecrated" the usual tripartite structure: ancient, medieval, and modern? What is the "early Church"? If the Church (and the world) is still in existence in the year 20,000, will not the late twentieth century look very much like the "early Church" to our brothers and sisters of that future period? And from the vantage point of the year 20,000, what possible meaning can the term Middle Ages have?

The earliest Christian historians divided history in various ways. Some used the *six world-ages,* analogous to the six days of creation, each world-day the equivalent of one thousand years. "In the Lord's eyes, one day is as a thousand years and a thousand years are as a day" (2 Peter 3:8). The seventh day, the universal Sabbath, would bring the *millennium,* when all those who had died "for their witness to Jesus and the word of God" would come "to life again and (reign) with Christ for a thousand years" (Revelation 20:4-5). *Millenarianism* has always had a sympathetic hearing in the Church, albeit at the fringes rather than at the center of the Christian community: Anabaptists, Adventists, Mormons, Jehovah's Witnesses, and others.

Other historians used the *four world-empires*—Assyrian-Babylonian, Persian, Macedonian, and Roman—by way of interpreting Daniel 2:36-45 and 7:2-27. The fourth of these empires, the Roman, is now Christianized and will last until the end of the world. This explains why so many Christians clung to the Roman "way" well into the Middle Ages.

Still other historians have employed the threefold *Augustinian schema*: before the law (*ante legem*), under the law (*sub lege*), and after the law (*post legem*). There were variations. Some substituted *grace* for *law,* and Joachim of Flora (d. 1202) imposed a trinitarian perspective: the Old Testament as the age of the Father, the New Testament as the age of the Son, and the post-New Testament period as the age of the Holy Spirit. Joachim prophesied that in the year 1260 the Petrine hierarchical Church would be replaced by the new Johannnine Church of the Spirit.

Theologically, the Church has had two major historical moments and is now moving into a third. The *first* was its *Jewish* moment. The Christ-event was proclaimed in the beginning within and to Israel. This is the period of Jewish Christianity, centered in Jerusalem. The *second* is, or was, its *culturally-determined* moment, when the Church became the Church of

Hellenism, of Europe, of North America, and so forth. The *transition* or, perhaps more accurately, the *break* between the first and second moments was signaled by the decision (or series of decisions) to carry the Gospel to the Gentiles without imposing circumcision or other Jewish laws and customs on the new Christians.

As we noted in the previous chapter, Jesus did not explicitly anticipate this widening of the mission. When Peter had to justify his baptizing of Cornelius, the Roman centurion, he appealed not to some specific directive of Jesus but to the prompting and instruction of the Holy Spirit (Acts of the Apostles 11:12). Paul made exactly the same appeal (Acts of the Apostles 16:9; 18:9; 20:22; 22:21; *et passim*; see also Ephesians 3:5-6). But if something as "essential" as circumcision could be set aside, what can and must be retained from the Old Testament? Moreover, the Church would also change the Sabbath, move the center from Jerusalem to Rome, and modify various ethical and disciplinary principles. We simply do not have, at this point, a clear theology of explanation for this substantial, perhaps even radical, break between Jewish Christianity and Gentile Christianity.

The *third* moment, whose inauguration was heralded by the Second Vatican Council, is the movement from a Church of cultural confinement (especially of European and North American confinement) to a genuine *world Church*. There is as much misunderstanding of, and resistance to, this transition to a world Church as there was to the transition to a Church of the Gentiles in the first century. Today's resistance has ample precedent: in the rites controversy of the seventeenth century (to which brief reference will be made later in this chapter), in the insistence on the Latin language in liturgy and in all official communications, in the imposition of canon (Roman) law on the whole Church, in the enforcement of certain culturally conditioned styles of Christian life (e.g., clerical celibacy), and in the rejection of the religious experiences of non-European cultures.

Given this theological schema, which Karl Rahner in particular has proposed, the material in this chapter is not so much an outline of the Church's course throughout all of its history thus far as it is an outline of the Church's course in the *second moment* of its still-very-young history. Even within that second moment, i.e., the period of the Church's cultural confinement especially within European culture, there are transitions and breaks to which attention is given here.

We shall be relying, with some modifications, on the divisions proposed by H. Jedin and August Franzen: (1) the Church within Graeco-Roman civilization (first through the seventh centuries); (2) the Church as the dominant presence in the West (about 700-1300); (3) the disintegration of Christian unity and the transition to a wider mission (1300-1750); and (4) the Church in the period of industrialization and technology (nineteenth and twentieth centuries). The transition from one period to the next has always involved a crisis or series of crises, which we spoke of in chapter 1. Choices had to be made about abandoning older approaches and structures and selecting new ones. We are obviously in another period of crisis today, but one far more profound than any of those which marked the life of the Church within its *second moment* alone.

THE CHURCH AND HISTORY

But the question *"How* shall we organize the data?" is less important than the question *"What* is it that we are organizing?" What do we mean by *Church* and *history?*

If the *Church* is principally a hierarchical society, with the pope at the top of the pyramid and the bishops just below him, then the history of the "Church" is the history of the popes, of ecumenical councils, of heresies and schisms, of contests with the secular government, and the like. And that is precisely what many (indeed, too many) histories of the Church appear to be.

If, on the other hand, the Church is primarily the People of God—laity, religious, and clergy alike—then its history includes more than papal initiatives, conciliar definitions, and struggles for power, whether from the outside or from within. History has to take into account the lives and achievements of the vast majority of the Church's membership: its laity, its religious, and its so-called lower clergy.

If, furthermore, the Church is the Body of Christ, it must be incarnate in history and affected by history, as Jesus was (see especially chapter 15). It is not like some gust of wind that blows through a house, scattering loose items but without any effect upon itself.

And if the Church is, finally, the Temple of the Holy Spirit, it must be infinitely adaptable to the changing circumstances of history, without compromise of its fundamental identity or without loss of the radical unity given by the Spirit.

Here, of course, we raise again the issue of classicism versus historical consciousness. The *classicist* perceives the Church as a static, essentially unchanging reality, by divine decree and guidance immune to process. The Church moves through history, but is affected by it only at the most external levels. Change is always cosmetic, or, as some are fond of saying, "semantic." The *historically conscious* approach understands history as a human as well as a divine phenomenon. What occurs is also the result of human passions, human decisions, and human actions. And just as each person is different from the other, so is each event and each culture. But not only are the "events" of history contingent. So, too, are the *interpretations* of those "events." The historian himself or herself is a particular person, of a particular family and nation, of a particular economic and social status, with particular intellectual strengths and limitations, with particular theological and philosophical commitments, with particular associations and experiences.

We cannot define *history*, therefore, as simply the residue or sum total of "what happened." *Data* have to be translated into *facts,* and facts have to be *interpreted* by reason of their *interrelationship* with other facts. But who, apart from God, has access to all the data? And who, apart from God, knows all the facts? And who, apart from God, sees all the facts in their exact interrelationship with one another?

Consequently, history is always written by those with limited data, fewer facts, and faulty perspective. That is why histories of the same reality can differ so markedly, not only in terms of how facts are interpreted, but even in terms of *which facts* are considered. Thus, we have had histories of the Church which pay no attention at all to the development of spirituality or to the social, political, economic, and cultural impact of Christian faith on the emergence and maintenance of such units as neighborhoods.

The history of the Church is reflection on the *mystery* of the Church, i.e., on the active, continuous, and purposive presence of God in the world through the Christian community. God calls and moves the world to the Kingdom of God. The Church is the sign and instrument of that call and movement. The Church itself is called and is in movement toward the Kingdom. The whole process by which the world, and the Church within the world, is moving toward the Kingdom is what we know as *history*.

Since the call requires a *free response* (see again chapter 5 on the fundamental relationship between nature and grace), history is not only the history of God's interventions in human affairs, as the classicist believes. Furthermore, since both the call and the movement toward the Kingdom are given in *grace*, history is not only the history of contingent human events, as the historicists have contended. (We distinguish here between *historicism* and historical consciousness. Historicism is a form of historical consciousness, but it is not the only form.)

THE CHURCH IN THE GRAECO-ROMAN PERIOD (FIRST THROUGH SEVENTH CENTURIES)
The New Testament Period

This comprises at least the first two generations of Christians, and probably carries forward into the middle of the second century. It is the period already considered in the previous chapter. It is marked, first, by the preaching and ministry of Jesus and his impact on his disciples and those beyond the circle of his followers; secondly, by the preaching and teaching of the disciples and by the prayers and practices of the earliest converts; and, thirdly, by the formation of stable communities, or churches, from which the various New Testament writings emerged.

The principal crisis of this earliest period was the decision to extend the mission to the Gentiles without, at the same time, imposing Jewish law and practice upon them (as the *Judaizers* insisted). This first great controversy was adjudicated at the

Council of Jerusalem (ca. 50), thanks to the "decision of the Holy Spirit" (Acts of the Apostles 15:28), and the leadership of Peter and James (15:1-29).

Second and Third Centuries

As the young Church progressively detached itself from Judaism and entered the mainstream of Graeco-Roman civilization, it confronted the challenge of communicating the message of Jesus across diverse social, intellectual, and cultural lines. This task fell in the beginning upon the *Apostolic Fathers* (so called because they were themselves pupils of the Apostles) and the *Apologists,* or defenders of the faith. By the end of the century a major theological center was established in *Alexandria,* Egypt. Less than a hundred years later, another such center would be founded in *Antioch,* Syria. The two schools, as we pointed out in chapter 13, would become principal competing forces in the great Christological debates of the fourth and fifth centuries.

A correct understanding of the Gospel was a problem not only for those still outside the Church, but for some inside as well. Already the community, summoned to unity by its Lord (John 17:20-23), was wracked by heresy: principally *Gnosticism* (salvation is through "knowledge" available only to an elite few), *Adoptionism* (Jesus was not truly divine), and *Docetism* (Jesus only "seemed" to be human). It was because of the challenge of Gnosticism, with its appeal to private sources of revelation, that the Church was compelled to establish the *canon,* or list, of Sacred Scripture as the sole norm of faith and to underscore the role of the bishops, standing in *apostolic succession* to the Apostles, as official interpreters or guarantors of the apostolic tradition.

From the latter half of the second century, the bishops began meeting in *synods* to present a common defense against these heresies, now including the *purist* (holier than the Church) extremes: *Manichaeism* (material realities, including marriage, are to be renounced), *Montanism* (no sins committed after Baptism can be forgiven) and *Donatism* (a sacrament is not valid if the minister of the sacrament is in the state of mortal sin). The more widespread the heresy, the more broadly based were the synods.

Local synods were replaced by provincial synods. It would not be until the beginning of the fourth century that the Church would hold its first *ecumenical* council (literally, a council representing the "whole wide world") at Nicea.

Once Christianity began making an impact upon society, it came to the notice of those completely uninterested in such internal theological disputes. As one Catholic historian has written, "The established state cult of the emperor could hardly be expected to favor a religion founded by an executed criminal" (John P. Dolan, *Catholicism*, p. 11). But more offensive even than the character of its "founder" was Christianity's absolute claims. It was not proposed as just one new religion among many, but as the *true* religion. "In a culture and civilization toward which they had contributed nothing, the Christians, by rejecting the religious pluralism of the Roman state, made themselves public enemies" (Dolan, p. 11).

Until the middle of the second century, however, the *persecution* of Christians was of a local nature with a relatively small number of victims. It is important to remember that all accounts of the persecutions were written by Christians, whose characterizations of the emperors were not entirely disinterested. On the other hand, there would be many instances of severe repression and cruelty in later years, especially in the reigns of Decius (d. 251) and Diocletian (d. 305), with a forty-year period of peace and missionary success in between, under the emperor Gallienus (d. 268).

Fourth Century

The conversion of Constantine (d. 337) in the year 312 marked another great turning point in the historical progress of the Church. As noted in chapter 1, the new emperor pursued a vigorous campaign against pagan practices and lavished money and monuments upon the Church. Roman law was modified to accommodate Christian values, and the clergy were accorded privileged status. Opinions differ about the long-term effects of this display of imperial favor. For some historians it signaled the beginning of a sort of *Caesaro-papism* (Caesar is pope), with the Church utterly dependent upon the state and forced eventually to subordinate its spiritual interests to political considerations. For others, the conversion of Constantine provided the Church with extraordinary opportunities for proclaiming the Gospel to all nations and for bringing necessary order into its doctrinal and liturgical life. It also allowed the Church to be less defensive about pagan culture, to learn from it and be enriched by it. On the other hand, the end of the age of persecutions and "least favored status" also meant the end of a certain quality of Christian commitment, a development not without parallel today.

The protest against this development gave rise to the *monastic movement*. Although the roots of monasticism reach back into the pre-Constantinian period, the great monastic exodus from society coincided with the era of Constantine. When the multitudes entered the Church, the monks went into the desert, not as an escape but as an encounter with the demons who inhabited those waterless places. Anthony of Egypt (d. 356), generally regarded as the founder of monasticism, had withdrawn into the desert in 285 and remained there for twenty years living a hermit's existence. Only under Anthony's contemporary Pachomius (d. 346) did the movement to the desert (the root meaning of the word *hermit*) become communal, according to organized patterns of life.

Monasticism had an almost-immediate impact on the Church. Bishops began to be recruited from among those with some monastic training. Athanasius, for example, was a disciple of Anthony. According to August Franzen, "The strong missionary impetus, the remarkable development of pastoral care, the effort to Christianize the Roman State, and above all the theological work of the great councils of the 4th to the 7th century are inconceivable without monasticism" ("Church History," *The Concise Sacramentum Mundi*, p. 264). On the other hand, when monks were transferred to episcopal sees, they also tended to bring with them some of their monastic mores, particularly celibacy and a certain disdain for ordinary human experiences. The separation between leaders and the general membership of the Church, therefore, was not only on the basis of office and power but also on the basis of spirituality.

The Doctrinal Controversies
of the Fourth and Fifth Centuries

We have already reviewed in chapters 9, 10, and 13 the history of the doctrinal controversies regarding the Trinity and the mystery of Jesus Christ. All of these occurred in the Greek-speaking East.

Over against pagan polytheism, the Apostolic Fathers and the Apologists had consistently stressed the doctrine of the one God, the Father, the Almighty. In the third century the emphasis shifted to the triune pluralism of God when the Church could no longer avoid the difficult questions posed by the apparent discrepancy between its uncompromising monotheism and the clear testimony of Sacred Scripture and of the Church's liturgical life that Jesus Christ is also Lord, and that upon rising from the dead he gave the Church his Spirit.

One of the earliest attempts at a solution to the problem of the one-and-the-three proved unorthodox, namely, the *Arian* solution, which made Christ something more than man but less than God, the Almighty. The implications were serious: If Christ is a creature like us, he has no special standing before God as savior, and we are still in our sins.

The first general, or ecumenical, council in the history of the Church was called by the emperor Constantine in 325. Over two hundred and fifty bishops assembled at *Nicea,* the imperial summer residence. Representation from the West was negligible: five priests. The pope was not present, nor did he send any special legates. Nonetheless, the council gave what the Church has subsequently accepted as the definitive answer to Arius. The Son does not "emanate" from the Father's will, as a creature. The Son is "begotten, not made." He is "of the same substance" (*homoousios*) as the Father. For the first time, the Church moved officially from biblical to speculative categories to define the faith.

This transition did not occur without opposition. Followers of Eusebius of Caesarea preferred to say no more than what Scripture seemed to be saying, namely, that the Son is "like" (*homoiousios*) the Father. Through the efforts of Athanasius and Hilary of

Poitiers, the two sides were reconciled at the Council of Alexandria in 362, from which emerged a new orthodox formula, "one substance, three persons."

Meanwhile, others pressed the Nicean definition too far in the opposite direction. Apollinaris of Laodicea, a member of the Alexandrian School, placed so much emphasis on the Word as the unique principle of life in Jesus Christ that Jesus was left with no human soul at all. *Apollinarianism* was condemned at the First Council of Constantinople in 381. This was also the council that approved the so-called *Nicaeo-Constantinopolitan Creed,* expressing faith in the fullness of the Blessed Trinity: Father, Son, *and* Holy Spirit. It was the so-called *Cappadocian Fathers* (Basil, Gregory of Nyssa, and Gregory of Nazianzus) who established the coequal divinity of the Spirit with the Father and the Son.

Still another theological approach developed at Antioch. Concerned with the emphasis of the Alexandrians on the divinity of Christ and intent upon preserving the humanity of Jesus, the Antiochenes preferred to regard the relationship between Jesus and the Word more loosely, to the point where Jesus seemed to be divided in two. Thus, Mary was said to be the Mother of Jesus the man but not the Mother of God. This was the position of Nestorius, and of *Nestorianism.* Nestorius was opposed by Cyril of Alexandria and then condemned by the Council of Ephesus in 431.

But Cyril's views were themselves carried to an extreme by Eutyches, a monk in Constantinople, who argued that Christ's human nature was completely absorbed by the divine nature so that we have not only one divine person but also one divine nature (*physis*). Thus, the heresy was known as *Monophysitism.* The Council of Chalcedon in 451 condemned Monophysitism and reaffirmed the earlier condemnation of Nestorianism. The Alexandrians were satisfied with the council's formula, "one and the same Lord Jesus Christ," and the Antiochenes were pleased with the formula, "the same truly God and truly man composed of rational soul and body...like us in all things but sin...."

During this same period theological activity in the Latin West was significantly less pronounced. *Augustine,* of course, was the principal figure and *Pelagianism* the principal heresy. Here the concern was with the doctrines of justification and grace. It was Augustine who led the fight against those who assumed that salvation is the result of human effort alone.

The "Barbarian Invasions"

By the beginning of the fifth century, the West was also caught up in the great Germanic migrations: The Visigoths in southern France (Gaul) and Spain, the Vandals in North Africa, and the Ostrogoths and Lombards in Italy. Augustine died in 430, while the Vandals were besieging Hippo, his episcopal city. Those migrations were to last for six hundred years and were to come in three waves: the continental Germans in the fifth and sixth centuries, the Saracens in the seventh and eighth centuries, and the Scandinavians and Vikings in the ninth and tenth centuries. Although their disruptive effect on the social, political, and religious scenes was serious enough, it has often been exaggerated.

Most of those who turned to Christianity after entering the Roman Empire turned to Arianism. Many of the conversions were tribal rather than individual and deeply personal. Such was the case of the Frankish tribes under Clovis (d. 511). In many cases, therefore, there was only a superficial appreciation of the doctrinal and moral content of the new religion. Hence, superstitious practices and vestiges of pagan worship remained for many centuries.

The position of women among these tribes was extremely low, much lower, in fact, than in Roman society. Divorce was only gradually abolished. Legal matters were settled by ordeal, either by fire or water or combat rather than by the Roman system of proof substantiated by witnesses. Compensation, a practice whereby money was given to make satisfaction for crimes, was encouraged by the Church since at least it avoided bloodshed. It also proved to be the forerunner of the medieval system of indulgences.

The strongly militaristic and feudal elements in Germanic culture influenced Germanic Christian devotion and spirituality: Christ was the *Heiland*, the most powerful of kings; the place of worship was the *Burg-Gottes*, God's fortress; monks were the warriors of Christ; the profession of faith was regarded as an oath of fidelity to a feudal lord.

Since the conversion of the northern lands was largely the work of laymen (Olaf, Erich, Canute), ecclesiastical authority was usually reserved to the warrior chief. The anointing of kings was regarded as a sacramental act. Unlike the ancient Christian-Roman law which had guarded the independence of the Church, German law held to a more political idea of church office and, therefore, was less concerned with the moral qualifications of the officer, whether a bishop or an abbot of a monastery. By the eighth century, politically controlled churches of this kind far outnumbered those under the authority of the local bishops. With the development of feudalism, the system was solidified, preparing the way for the great investiture struggle in the eleventh century between the popes (especially Gregory VII, d. 1085) and the rulers of state, i.e., the struggle about whether ecclesiastical leaders would be appointed by the Church or by the state.

On the other hand, credibly strong ecclesiastical leadership *was* exercised at this time by Pope Gregory the Great (d. 604), who inaugurated the mission to the Anglo-Saxons in the British Isles. He also displayed imaginative and resourceful administrative skills in his distribution of church funds: to ransom captives from the Lombards, to charter vessels to bring grain to Rome from the islands, to ship lumber to churches in Egypt or blankets to the monks at Mount Sinai. The emperor at Constantinople did not like this papal usurpation of imperial power, but the pope was, after all, paying the bills. The rise of the temporal power of the papacy (in response to a vacuum of civil leadership, following the collapse of the Western Empire) is commonly assigned to the middle of the eighth century, but it had its origins here, during the pontificate of Gregory the Great (590-604).

THE CHURCH AS THE DOMINANT FORCE
IN THE WEST (700-1300)
The Germanization of Christianity

When, in the middle of the eighth century, the exarchate of Ravenna fell to the Lombards and the Eastern emperor proved unable to assist the papacy, Pope Stephen II (d. 752) turned to the Franks. In 754 Pepin (d. 768) was consecrated king and given the title of patriarch of the Romans. The process was completed on Christmas day, 800, with the crowning of Charlemagne (d. 814) by Pope Leo III (d. 816) as emperor of the Romans and protector and defender of the papacy. He was to see to it that Roman liturgy and Roman disciplinary practices were introduced and observed throughout his new empire. He appointed all bishops and abbots and presided over all synods. The role of pope receded far into the background. The line between Church and state dissolved.

With the collapse of the Carolingian empire, however, the papacy was plunged into even worse straits. The attacks of the Normans and the Saracens and the absence of any strong personalities among the successors of Leo reduced the papacy to a plaything of the Roman nobility. Throughout the tenth and much of the eleventh centuries the office languished in what historians have called the *saeculum obscurum* (dark age).

Western Monasticism

Eastern monasticism was transferred to the West by St. Martin of Tours (d. 397), who established a monastery near Poitiers in 362. Distinctive shape was given Western monasticism by St. Benedict (d. ca. 550) in the middle of the sixth century. After a period as a hermit, he established a community at Monte Cassino, imposing a sensible rule with vows of poverty, chastity, obedience, and stability. The purpose of the monastery was to honor God by worship and to benefit the community by prayer. Since the monastery was to be self-sustaining, the monks were required also to work in the fields. Thus, the essence of the Rule of St. Benedict: *Ora et labora* (pray and work).

The role of the monastery as a center of scholarship developed only gradually. Benedict thought it desirable that his monks be literate enough to read the Bible and the Fathers of the Church. Later, with the Carolingian renaissance, many of the monks were relieved of manual labor and were able to devote themselves to scholarly pursuits. One of the most practical was the copying of the texts of the classics of Western civilization.

Western monasticism, thus transformed, was to play a crucial part in the Gregorian Reform of the late eleventh century. By the ninth century most monks were drawn almost exclusively from the nobility, and the monasteries had become one of the most important social institutions. Monastic schools were the only effective replacements for the municipal schools of the late Roman Empire. In spite of their personal poverty, the monks had vast landholdings and agricultural enterprises that played an important role in the economy and government. After the eighth century the monks became part of the feudal system. Abbots were made vassals of the king.

The Gregorian Reform

By the middle of the eleventh century, however, sufficient social, economic, and political stability had returned to Europe. There appeared an elite who studied philosophy, theology, and law outside of monasteries. Monks had less and less to do with temporal matters, and the impulse to return to the realm of the spiritual became increasingly strong. Men like Peter Damian (d. 1072) and Cardinal Humbert (d. 1061) were among the leading reformers, carrying their cause even as high as the papal office itself. Not content with purifying the monasteries, they devised a program for the entire Christian world.

Avoiding some extreme proposals, Pope Gregory VII (d. 1085) focused his attack upon three evils: simony (the buying and selling of ecclesiastical offices and/or spiritual goods), the alienation of property (the passing of church property into the private hands of a bishop's or a priest's offspring), and lay investiture. Each reform was designed to free the Church from political control and to restore the authority of the pope over the whole Church. Gregory proclaimed in 1075 that the pope held supreme power over all Christian souls. He was the supreme judge, under God alone. All prelates (bishops and abbots) were subject to him, and his powers of absolution and excommunication were absolute.

This *Dictatus Papae*, alongside the systematic establishment of the Roman Curia as the central organ of Church government, gave one of Gregory's successors, Innocent III (d. 1216), a unique position of authority and leadership among all the Western nations. This was to find expression in the new Western general, or ecumenical, councils (Lateran I-IV; Lyons I-II) and was supported by the Church's canonists, or lawyers. (For an English text of the *Dictatus*, see Dolan, *Catholicism*, pp. 72-73.)

Indeed, this was the beginning of the dominance of canon law in the medieval Church. Because of the systematizing efforts of the monk Gratian (d. ca. 1159), a concordance of ecclesiastical laws appeared about the year 1150, entitled *The Concord of Discordant Canons*. Like the *Sentences* of Peter Lombard (d. 1160) which systematized theology as it existed up to that time, this work was to become the basic text of a new branch of theological studies, canon law. Legal decrees rather than the Gospel became the basis for moral judgments. Even the sacraments assumed a legal cast, and a whole sacramental jurisprudence developed. (Who can administer a sacrament? Who is eligible to receive a sacrament? When? Under what circumstances?) Baptism was portrayed less as a moment of rebirth in Christ than as a juridical act by which a person becomes a member of the Church, with full rights, privileges, and obligations. Matrimony was considered a legal contract whose validity depended upon the absence of any one of a whole list of impediments drawn up by Rome. A knowledge of canon law became the requisite for ecclesiastical advancement, and it remained so until the post-Vatican II period.

By 1234 all former collections of papal decisions were combined and codified by Pope Gregory IX (d. 1241) into *The Five Books of Decretals*. The classical juridical doctrine of the Church was now clearly established. The Church is a visible, hierarchically structured organization with supreme power vested in the pope. The place of the laity and all religious and lower clergy is to obey the directives of the Church's lawfully constituted authority. Indeed, many rights formerly exercised by bishops and synods were now reserved to the pope. Even the election of a new pope was reserved to cardinals who were themselves appointed by the pope. Bishops meanwhile were obliged to take an oath of obedience to the pope that resembled the feudal oaths binding a vassal to his lord.

The pope was no longer only consecrated. He was crowned with a tiara, a helmet-shaped head covering used originally by the deified rulers of Persia. The coronation rite, so redolent of imperial prerogatives, was used in the conferral of the papacy from that time until 1978, when Pope John Paul I (d. 1978) chose simply to be "installed" into his new "supreme pastoral ministry." Pope John Paul II, who succeeded to the papacy the following month, also refused the crown.

The Monastic Renewal

The Gregorian Reform (also known as the *Hildebrandine* Reform, since Gregory VII had been Cardinal Hildebrand before election to the papacy) was not an unqualified success. Emperor Henry IV (d. 1106) sacked the city of Rome, Gregory died a prisoner in Salerno, and the investiture struggle continued for many centuries. On the other hand, simony was effectively prohibited, and celibacy was imposed upon the Latin-rite clergy as a way of dealing with the alienation of property. Concurrently, the same ascetic impulse that worked so powerfully to produce a reform of the central administration of the Church also found a natural outlet in the renewal of monasticism. New orders appeared: Camaldolese (founded by Romuald, d. 1027), Carthusians (Bruno, d. 1101), Cistercians (Robert of Molesme, d. 1111, and Bernard of Clairvaux, d. 1153), and the religious Orders of Chivalry (Knights of Malta, 1099, Templars, 1118, and Teutonic Knights, 1189). The ongoing reform of the clergy was carried forward by the Canons Regular movement: Augustinians, Premonstratensians or Norbertines, the latter founded by Norbert of Xanten (d. 1134). The laity formed Bible groups, and many dedicated themselves to lives of evangelical poverty. The Crusades, for all the negative results they generated (especially the fourth crusade), also released extraordinary religious energy, solidifying the sense of community and widening the horizons of Western Christians through contact with the great Byzantine and Islamic cultures. The development of Western philosophy and theology in the medieval period could not have occurred as it did without this encounter with the East.

Outstanding in all of this movement was St. Bernard of Clairvaux, described as an "admonisher of popes and preacher of Crusades." "If you are to do the work of a prophet," he told the pope, "you will need a hoe rather than a sceptre." Although he believed in the theory of the two swords (namely, that the pope had power not only in the spiritual realm but also in the temporal), he insisted that the temporal power was always to be used for spiritual purposes alone. The pope was a minister, not a lord.

From this point of view, Bernard was a reformer, a progressive by modern standards. But there was another side to him. His approach to spirituality might be summed up in the Latin phrase, *credo ut experiar* (I believe that I might experience), in contrast to Augustine's *credo ut intelligam* (I believe that I might understand) or Anselm's *fides quaerens intellectum* (faith seeking understanding). Bernard, therefore, heralded a turn toward subjective, even individualistic, piety that began to surface throughout Europe. His mysticism was founded on the union of Christ and the soul, and his devotional life was focused on the Blessed Virgin, to whom all Cistercian churches were dedicated. The once-popular Catholic formula, *Ad Jesum per Mariam* (To Jesus through Mary), is ascribed to Bernard. And his opposition to the use of dialectics in the study of revelation is also well known.

Theological Renewal

Bernard's attitude notwithstanding, there was indeed a significant turn in the theological posture of the Church at the outset of the second Christian millennium. The early medieval theology of the monastic schools, so closely wedded to the biblical texts, no longer satisfied the increasingly critical minds of the mid-eleventh century. Independent schools appeared which sought new ways of doing theology. Anselm of Canterbury was himself part of this movement. At the beginning of the thirteenth century several such schools in Paris united to form the first *university*. Other universities followed in Bologna, Padua, Naples, Montpellier, Oxford, Cambridge, Salamanca, and Valencia. Not until a century later did a similar development occur in Germany.

There were also new assaults upon orthodoxy, e.g., the Albigensians, or Cathari, and the Waldensians, to which reference has already been made. The Inquisition was founded at this time, and in 1252 Pope Innocent IV (d. 1254) authorized the use of torture to secure proof of heresy. By all reasonable standards, the Inquisition was one of the shabbiest chapters in the entire history of the Church.

Others found alternate ways of combatting heresy. St. Francis of Assisi (d. 1226) and St. Dominic (d. 1221) founded the Franciscans and Dominicans respectively to express, by way of their example of voluntary poverty and their straightforward preaching of the Gospel, what the true faith required. These new religious movements, in turn, inspired a resurgence of theological scholarship. On the Dominican side: Albert the Great (d. 1280), Thomas Aquinas (d. 1274), and Master Eckhart (d. 1328). On the Franciscan side: Alexander of Hales (d. 1245), Bonaventure (d. 1274), and Duns Scotus (d. 1308). Perhaps equally important, if not more important, was the *pastoral* orientation of these new mendicant (begging) orders. In the older forms of monasticism, people entered religious life for their own spiritual welfare: the glory of God through personal sanctification. But the Franciscans and Dominicans centered their activities in the preaching of the Gospel and the care of souls, i.e., ministry "out in the world."

The East-West Schism

From the time of the Council of Chalcedon (451), when Rome rejected the proposal (canon 28) to grant major jurisdictional powers to Constantinople, relations between the two sees were marked by sporadic tension and conflict. The subsequent controversy over Monothelitism (one divine will in Christ) saw the Roman view triumph over the Constantinopolitan at the Third Council of Constantinople in 680, but even a deceased pope, Honorius, came in for censure (see again chapter 13). The Eastern emperors' attempt to enforce a policy of *iconoclasm* (the abolition of all religious images) in the eighth century widened the gap. The West, which by now no longer understood the Greek language, could not distinguish between *veneration* and *adoration*. Where the Easterners recommended the former, the Westerners thought they meant the latter. And the refusal of the East to send military assistance to the pope in 753 prompted Rome's turning to the Franks, as we have already noted.

The next breach occurred in 858 when the patriarch of Constantinople was deposed by the emperor and replaced by Photius (d. 895), against the wishes of Pope Nicholas I (d. 867). Nicholas sent delegates to Constantinople, who decided in favor of Photius. But then Photius insisted that he did not accept the pope's supremacy, so the pope withdrew his support. After much negotiation, a reconciliation between the patriarchate and the papacy was achieved at a council held in Constantinople in 879. Peace was maintained throughout the tenth century, but it came apart in the middle of the eleventh century and has not been healed even to this day.

Michael Cerularius (d. 1058), patriarch of Constantinople, assumed office in 1043. He brought with him an exceedingly low opinion of the papacy and some measure of ignorance about recent Roman reforms. Because the pope had been insisting that Easterners conform to Latin usage in the West, Michael, in turn, ordered the Latin churches in Constantinople to adopt Greek usages. When they refused, he closed them down and ordered the head of the Bulgarian Church to write to the bishop of Tani in southern Italy, where the Eastern Christians were living, and denounce such Latin customs as the use of unleavened bread in the Eucharist. The letter was to be forwarded thereafter to the pope. It arrived at an inopportune moment. Pope Leo IX (d. 1054) had just been defeated by the Normans and was being held in captivity. His cardinal-secretary, Humbert of Moyenmoutier, also known as Humbert of Silva Candida (d. 1061), with little knowledge of Greek, probably mistranslated some of the letter, thereby exaggerating its offensive tone. Legates were dispatched to Constantinople, Humbert among them.

To compress the story: The legates botched their diplomatic mission, dealing heavy-handedly with the patriarch. On July 16, 1054, they marched into the Church of Santa Sophia just before the afternoon liturgy and laid on the altar a bull excommunicating Michael Cerularius, the emperor, and all their followers, and then departed, ceremoniously shaking the dust from their feet. The general populace, already annoyed at the emperor's concessions to the Latins in their midst, rioted and could be calmed only after a public burning of the bull. A synod condemned the legates, but significantly not the pope. The door was left ajar for still another reconciliation. In the meantime, Pope Leo died, leaving his successor with the option and the opportunity for making peace. Unfortunately, Leo's successors and others in Rome believed Humbert's account of the sorry events, and no peace initiatives were taken.

With the election of Urban II (d. 1099) in 1088, hopes rose. The new pope was a man of good will and calmness. He reopened negotiations with the Byzantine court and lifted an earlier excommunication of the emperor. When the Pope called for a crusade at Clermont in 1095, one of his motives was to bring help to Eastern Christians. But the crusade had the opposite effect. Quarrels between the emperor and the crusaders developed over the status of the reconquered city of Antioch. The conduct of the Western knights disgusted the people, and the situation became inflamed when the crusade leader drove the Greek patriarch out of the city and replaced him with a Latin patriarch. Though no one can give an exact date for the beginning of the East-West Schism, it was this Fourth Crusade (1202-1204) which probably drove the last wedge in. In 1203 the crusaders sacked the city of Constantinople, not even sparing the churches. Two later attempts at bringing the two sides back together—at the Council of Lyons in 1276 and at the Council of Florence in 1439—did not have lasting results. The climate has only just recently begun to change, under the impact of Pope John XXIII and the Second Vatican Council.

THE DISINTEGRATION OF WESTERN CHRISTIAN UNITY AND THE TRANSITION TO A WIDER MISSION (1300-1750)

The unity of the Christian West rested on two universally recognized forces: the papacy and the empire. When the papacy fell from its position of temporal power and the empire was overwhelmed by the growth of national states, the twin supports of "Christendom" buckled and collapsed. The process began in the fourteenth century, continued in the fifteenth, and reached its climax in the Protestant Reformation in the sixteenth century. Not until the middle of the eighteenth century was it arrested.

Church and State in Conflict

With the defeat of the Hohenstaufen emperors after the middle of the thirteenth century, the papacy found itself in mortal conflict with the new dominant powers in France. Philip the Fair (d. 1314) claimed a royal power to tax the Church. Pope Boniface VIII (d. 1303) retaliated with a papal bull, or manifesto, entitled *Clericis Laicos*, threatening excommunication upon anyone interfering with the collection of papal revenues. The situation worsened when Philip demanded the degradation of the bishop of Parmiers, a demand that was calculated as an open affront to ecclesiastical authority. Boniface issued another bull, *Unam Sanctam* (1302), asserting papal authority over the French national state. It has been described as the most absolute theocratic doctrine ever formulated:

> "We are taught by the evangelical works," the document declares, "that there are two swords, the spiritual and the temporal, in the control of the Church.... Certainly he who denies that the temporal sword was under the control of Peter, misunderstands the word of the Lord when he said: 'Put your sword into the sheath.' Therefore, both the spiritual and material sword are under the control of the Church, but the latter is used for the Church and the former by the Church. One is used by the hand of the priest, the other by the hand of the kings and knights at the command and with the permission of the priest.... We therefore declare, say, affirm, and announce that for every human creature to be submissive to the Roman pontiff is absolutely necessary for salvation."

Boniface was arrested by Philip at Anagni in September, 1303, and died soon thereafter. The action sent shock waves throughout Catholic Europe. Boniface's successors Benedict XI

(d. 1304) and Clement V (d. 1314) came increasingly under French influence until the latter moved the papacy in 1309 to Avignon, where it remained until 1378. The period was known variously as the Avignon Exile and as the Babylonian Captivity of the Church. It was not a time of unrelieved disaster for the Church, however. On the contrary, there was much evidence of renewed interest in missionary activity. But this was also a period of intensified financial abuses, and perhaps more than anything else these prepared the way for the eventual breakup of the Church at the Reformation. Those appointed to ecclesiastical office were expected to pay a benefice tax. There seems to have been a price tag on everything. In 1328, for example, Pope John XXII (d. 1334) announced in a public audience that he had excommunicated, suspended, or interdicted one patriarch, five archbishops, thirty bishops, and forty-six abbots for failure to make their appropriate payments. As the financial burden rested more and more heavily on the so-called upper clergy, they, in turn, were forced to seek ways of supplementing their own income to pay these enormous taxes. The money came somehow from the laity. Both groups, the upper clergy and the laity, developed a contempt for the system of taxation. The laity became increasingly anti-clerical, and the clergy increasingly nationalistic.

Conflicts Within the Church

Trouble began brewing as well on the theological front. Two major challenges were pressed against the prevailing ecclesiological and canonical notions of ecclesiastical, and especially papal, authority: one by William of Ockham (d. 1347), an English Franciscan, and the other by Marsilius of Padua (d. 1343), former chancellor of the University of Paris.

Ockham accepted the pope's supreme authority over the Church, but only if exercised in a ministerial, not dominational, way, and for the good of the whole Church, not for the temporal power of the papacy or the ecclesiastical bureaucracy. Placing the pope above all law and placing everyone else under his absolute authority is a direct violation of the principle of Christian liberty. Although the pope was now elected by the College of Cardinals, that system could readily be changed since the responsibility rests on the entire body of the faithful.

Marsilius of Padua was even more radical in his opposition. In his *Defensor Pacis* (1324), which some have characterized as the dividing line between medieval and modern notions of political and religious theory, he argued that the Church is a spiritual and sacramental community, united by a common faith and a common celebration of the sacraments. Relying on Aristotle, Marsilius argued that the clergy-laity distinction had been overdrawn. Each cleric and each lay person is a citizen with inherent rights to participate in the affairs of state. Ordination has nothing at all to do with it. The Church should be governed by those closest to the scene: local bishops and priests, rather than the pope. And sanctions such as excommunication should be ignored since coercive power is foreign to the Gospel. The pope is no more than the executor of the wishes of the whole Christian community. Supreme authority rests with a representative council of all Christians. However, despite his apparently democratic leanings, Marsilius seemed to hold that actual power in the governance of the Church should be exercised by the civil ruler.

The Great Western Schism (1378-1417)

The papacy returned to Rome in 1378. In April of that year the College of Cardinals, long since predominantly French in composition, elected the archbishop of Bari, Bartolomeo Prignano, who took the name Urban VI (d. 1389). Within a few months the same electoral body declared their previous decision null and void and proclaimed a new pope, Clement VII (d. 1394). Now the Church had two claimants to the papacy, and schism resulted. To resolve the terrible ambiguity, key churchmen turned to *conciliarism*, a theory originally developed by canonists in the twelfth century and carried forward by Marsilius of Padua in the fourteenth. According to this theory, the Church is a vast corporation, with some members exercising leadership roles. All power resides ultimately in the whole body of the faithful, but that power is transferred to certain representatives, as in the case of the College of Cardinals in the election of the pope. There are in effect two churches: the Universal Church (the Body of Christ, in the New Testament sense) and the Apostolic Church, the administrative arm of the Universal Church. The latter, however, is always subordinate to the former. The theory was later refined by such theologians as Jean Gerson (d. 1429), who insisted that the pope is subject to the judgment and legislation of a general council, which is the only true representative of the Universal Church.

By 1409 the situation worsened. At a council held in Pisa a third pope was elected, Alexander V (d. 1410). Meanwhile, Benedict XIII (d. 1428) had succeeded Clement VII, and Gregory XII (d. 1415) was in office in the Roman line. By the end of his reign, however, Benedict had no support outside a small Spanish town where he lived, and Gregory had the allegiance only of certain Italian princes. The one who, according to some, had the least claim on the papacy, Alexander V, actually had the widest measure of support. Upon the death of Alexander, the Pisan party elected Baldassare Cossa, who took the name John XXIII. He proved such a poor choice that he alienated most of his original backers. The emperor Sigismund (d. 1437) forced John XXIII to call a new council, which met at Constance in November, 1414. More than one hundred thousand people descended upon the city: one hundred eighty-five bishops, three hundred theologians and canon lawyers, and vast numbers of priests, monks, lay persons, and politicians. Not only the bishops but also the doctors of theology and law were voting members of the assembly. The dominant figure, however, was the emperor.

Realizing that he was about to be condemned and deposed, John XXIII fled Constance but was arrested and placed under guard while the council continued. On May 29, 1415, John XXIII was formally deposed after a trial, and six days later he accepted his sentence. Meanwhile, the Roman Pope, Gregory XII, now eighty-nine years of age, was still holding out at Rimini, where he refused the emperor's invitation to the council. He decided to abdicate, but first sent his representatives to Constance formally convoking the council and then formally announcing his resignation. The third claimant, Benedict XIII, was also condemned, but he refused to accept the judgment and died, as one put it, "excommunicated and excommunicating." On St. Martin's day, November 11, 1417, the conclave, consisting of twenty-three cardinals and five prelates from each of the five nations represented at the council (Italy, France, England, Germany, and Spain), elected a new pope, Martin V (d. 1431). The schism was over.

Conciliarism

Two important pieces of legislation were produced by the Council of Constance, and they have been the subject of much discussion and debate ever since. The one, *Haec Sancta* (1415), espoused the supremacy of a general council and the collegiality of the bishops; the other, *Frequens*, decreed a kind of parliamentary government for the Church, requiring the calling of general councils at specified intervals. Although the new pope generally approved the decrees insofar as they were truly conciliar and did call a council at Pavia five years later, it was obvious that he and his immediate successors were determined to resist the onslaught of conciliarism in the Church. In fact, Eugene IV (d. 1447) suspended the next general council at Basle and transferred it to Florence in 1431. It was at Basle that conciliarism reached its highest development, inspired undoubtedly by the work of a German priest, Nicholas of Cusa (d. 1464). In a work published during the council entitled *De Concordantia Catholica* (On Catholic Concord), Cusa argued for the supremacy of a general council over the pope. The council, in turn, governs the Church only through the consent of the faithful.

In 1460 Pope Pius II (d. 1464) issued a decree condemning the "deadly poison" of conciliarism and forbidding under pain of excommunication any appeal beyond the pope to a general council. The prohibition was repeated by Popes Sixtus IV (d. 1484) and Julius II (d. 1513). Among the strongest opponents of the pope's negative stance toward general councils were members of the reformed monastic groups, especially the Carthusians. The pope's resistance to the conciliar principle, they argued, was rooted in the Roman Curia's fear of being held to account for centuries of evil practices. That was not the first attack upon the Curia, nor would it be the last, as the history of the Second Vatican Council shows.

The Reformation

"The Reformation" is the all-embracing term which describes the disintegration of Western Christianity in the sixteenth century. Like all other major developments in the history of the Church, including even the decision to carry the Gospel to the Gentiles, this one did not occur in a single event and through the efforts of a single person, such as Martin Luther (d. 1546). It was instead an extremely complex process in which religious, intellectual, political, and social forces converged.

Insofar as one can identify specific *causes* of the Reformation, they are as follows: (1) the corruption of the Renaissance papacy; (2) the divorce of piety from theology, and of theology from biblical and patristic tradition; (3) the aftereffects of the Western Schism; (4) the rise of the national state; (5) the close connection between Western Christianity and Western civilization; and (6) the vision, experiences, and personalities of Luther, Ulrich Zwingli (d. 1531), and John Calvin (d. 1564).

1.   The *Renaissance* (literally, "rebirth") of the fifteenth century tried to recapture the literary and artistic achievements of Latin and Greek antiquity. The focus was not upon ideas but upon the aesthetic and the emotional. The movement was, by many accounts, excessive in its celebration of the human. Not only were the works of art of the ancient civilizations brought forward, but so, too, were the mores and morals of those civilizations. Although there were instances of real, substantial advancements in this period (e.g., the establishment of the Vatican Library by Pope Nicholas V, d. 1455), it was also a period marked by nepotism, simony, military expeditions, financial manipulation, political intrigue, and even murder. The year America was "discovered" by Columbus (1492), the notorious Alexander VI (d. 1503) ascended to the papal throne.

2.   At the same time Catholic *piety* grew increasingly away from sound theology, and theology, in turn, from its own best tradition. Religious art and spirituality appealed directly, almost blatantly, to the emotions. Emphasis on the sufferings and wounds of Christ in excruciatingly physical detail became commonplace. Statues of Christ with blood dripping down from his crown of

thorns appeared everywhere. Attention was riveted on the Last Judgment, not as the day of redemption but as the day of reckoning and of terror.

Catholic *theology* also drifted along an anti-intellectual course. In reaction against the excessive abstractions of Scholasticism, a new style of theology known as *nominalism* rejected all forms of mediation between God and humankind: sacraments, Church authority, meritorious deeds, and so forth. Nothing can bridge the gap between God and us except the mercy of God manifested in Christ. Since we are utterly corrupt, justification is exclusively God's work. The rapidity with which this new theological approach spread through Europe—influencing Luther, Calvin, Zwingli, and others—indicates the intensity of dissatisfaction with the status quo of late medieval Catholicism. There was an "alluring simplicity" to the Protestant message, and it caught on almost immediately. And it had its Catholic counterparts—e.g., in the *Imitation of Christ* of Thomas à Kempis (d. 1471), who insisted, among other things, that "it is better to feel compunction than to be able to define it."

3.   The debilitating effects of the *Great Western Schism* are obvious enough. The pope's ability to function as a symbol and instrument of unity was seriously undermined even within the Church of the West. The *East-West Schism* had weakened the office's credibility and effectiveness one to two centuries earlier.

4.   The rise of the *national states* made independence from the influence of the papacy increasingly possible, likely, and then certain. The new slogan was *Rex imperator in regno suo* (The king is emperor in his own kingdom). That political perspective gradually widened to embrace even authority over the Church.

5.   The insistence of the Western Church on tying its identity too intimately to *Western civilization* denied the Church a necessary measure of flexibility and adaptability. The papacy, and ecclesiastical authority in general, had taken on an imperial cast. The Church was less the People of God than a hierarchical, indeed an absolutely monarchical, society. Its rulers tried to impose as a matter of faith what we have since come to recognize all too clearly to be only a matter of culturally-conditioned political theory and churchcraft. (Compare, for example, Boniface

VIII's *Unam Sanctam* with the Second Vatican Council's *Dogmatic Constitution on the Church.*)

6.   In the final accounting, no one can ever ignore the direct *impact of personalities* themselves on the course of events, no matter how much we talk of larger social, political, and economic forces. The Reformation took hold in Europe and in the forms it assumed because of the peculiar strengths and weaknesses of specific men: Luther, Calvin, and Zwingli in particular.

Luther was a monk who, like most medieval Christians, took the "last things" very seriously: death, judgment, heaven, and hell. He was tormented by the thought of God's judgment as he reflected on his creatureliness and unworthiness. Traditional modes of mortification and penance did not work for him. He was still without peace. He concluded that he had to relinquish all forms of self-reliance. God alone would save him if only he would trust in God's power and readiness to save him. All other devices of mediation, including *indulgences* (the remission of a temporal punishment in Purgatory still due to sins which have already been forgiven), are contrary to the simple, unadorned message of the Gospel. The charging of fees for indulgences brought the matter to a head, and on October 31, 1517, Luther posted his now famous Ninety-five Theses on the door of the castle church at Wittenberg. The rest is history.

Zwingli was a Swiss humanist who became vicar of the cathedral at Zurich in 1519, whereupon he announced that he would preach the entire Gospel of Matthew and not only the excerpts available in the liturgy. He would thereby carry the Church back to its simpler, primitive, non-Roman origins. He abolished fast days, removed images, and banned all church music. Zwingli's system of church polity, not surprisingly, was well suited to the city of Zurich, which had a representative government. His ecclesiology was also considerably more democratic, anti-clerical, and anti-institutional than Luther's, who was satisfied to introduce the vernacular into the liturgy and eliminate religious vows and celibacy.

Calvin, a French theologian who left the Catholic Church in 1533, provided Protestantism with its first integrated doctrinal system: *The Institutes of the Christian Religion* (1536). Calvin was especially noted for his theory of *predestination*. We can do nothing at all about our salvation. God has already determined our destiny. Since the fall of Adam, all of us deserve to be damned. And God indeed allows many to be damned to manifest divine justice. But some are saved to manifest divine grace. There are signs in a person's life by which one can tell if he or she is destined for salvation or reprobation: profession of the true faith, an upright life, and attendance upon the sacrament of the Lord's Supper. The Church, therefore, is the company of the elect.

Calvin's ecclesiology was somewhere between the still essentially "Catholic" Luther on the right and the strongly "Protestant" Zwingli on the left. Where Luther still employed the crucifix (with the figure of Christ upon the cross), and where Zwingli abandoned it altogether, Calvin allowed the cross but without the corpus. Calvinism was to become the most international form of Protestantism.

Other Reformation movements included the *Anabaptists* on the far left (to the left even of Zwingli) and the *Anglicans* on the right (to the right even of Luther). The *Anabaptist* movement is often referred to as the "radical Reformation." They were called *ana*baptists (literally, "baptized again") because they held as invalid the Baptism of infants ("dipping in the Romish bath"). For them the Church is a completely voluntary society of convinced believers. Only those who are truly converted and repentant can be baptized.

Anglicanism, on the other hand, is the result of a fusion of nationalism and religious upheaval. The quarrel with Rome was not over doctrine nor even over morality and finances, but over a royal wedding. Pope Clement VII (d. 1534) refused to allow King Henry VIII (d. 1547) to divorce his first wife and take a second. What followed was a moral course of action in search of theological justification. The writings of Marsilius of Padua and others proved useful to this purpose. The state "acquired" the Church, and Henry became in effect his own pope. Even today, the reigning monarch of Great Britain is at the same time the head of the Church of England.

The Counter-Reformation

By the 1530s all of Scandinavia, the British Isles, and much of Germany, Austria, and France had severed the bonds of communion with Rome. In spite of the fact that Luther himself had called for a general council to examine his doctrine, nothing of the sort was done until 1545. The reasons for the delay were for the most part political. The pope as a temporal ruler was caught between the territorial designs of the Hapsburgs, on the one hand, and the king of France, on the other. The threat of conciliarism still hung over Europe. There was a general fear in Rome that should a general council be called, the very office of the papacy might be abolished. Another reason for the delay was the simple failure of the Church's leadership to recognize the seriousness of the Protestant movement, and especially how much opposed it really was to traditional Catholic doctrine. Luther was looked upon at first as a sincere reformer who was merely expressing dissatisfaction with the abuses in contemporary Catholicism.

Not until the election of Paul III (d. 1549) in 1534 did the situation begin to change. Surrounding himself with bona fide reformers, he mandated steps to eliminate the abuses. A call was issued for the reform of the Roman Curia, particularly its financial dealings. When a council finally convened in 1545 in the northern Italian town of Trent, its attendance was skimpy: less than forty bishops, mostly Italian. There was a long debate about the representative character of the assembly, and then about the relative importance of dogmatic over against disciplinary issues. In early 1546 the opposed forces within the council reached a compromise, deciding to deal simultaneously with both matters.

Although its composition was slight in comparison with Chalcedon (about 630 delegates) and Vatican I (about 700), not to mention Vatican II (over 2000), and although its proceedings were twice suspended (from 1548 to 1551, and again from 1552 to 1561), the Council of Trent (1545-1563) is perhaps second only to the Second Vatican Council (1962-1965) in terms of disciplinary decrees and the clarification of Catholic doctrine. Until Vatican II, twentieth-century Catholicism was shaped more by the Council of Trent than by any other historically tangible event or force.

The council definitively articulated Catholic doctrine on the matter of faith and grace against Luther, Zwingli, Calvin, and their followers. Following a middle course between Pelagianism (everything depends on human effort) and Protestantism (everything depends on God), the council insisted that salvation comes from God as a pure gift, but that it requires some measure of human cooperation (see again chapter 5). It has been asserted that "had Trent's decree on justification been decreed at the Lateran Council at the beginning of the sixteenth century, the Reformation would not have occurred and the religious unity of the Middle Ages would have endured" (John P. Dolan, *Catholicism*, p. 149).

The council also clearly and decisively defined the meaning and number of the sacraments, especially the Eucharist, thereby confirming a tradition which first emerged about 1150 and achieved conciliar formulation at Florence in 1439. Its decree on marriage, *Tametsi,* required that a wedding be celebrated before a priest and two witnesses, and held as invalid marriages between Catholics and Protestants. The council also created the Index of Forbidden Books (not abolished until the pontificate of Paul VI, d. 1978) and established seminaries for the training of future priests. Both of these actions, conceived as temporary measures, proved to have lasting effects on the life of the Church: The first kept both the laity and the clergy separated from the major intellectual works of modern times, and the second tended to sharpen the distinction between clergy and laity by encouraging an academic and spiritual formation for priests in isolation from the ordinary workday world of the rest of the People of God. Again, those effects have only recently begun to change under the impact of Vatican II.

At the heart of the Catholic Counter-Reformation was the newly established Society of Jesus, founded by St. Ignatius of Loyola (d. 1556), a former soldier, and approved by Pope Paul III in 1540. Although it was only one of several new communities in the Church, the Jesuits stand out because of their dedication to various forms of the apostolate, especially the education of the young and of future priests, their sense of solidarity as a community and with the pope, their scholarship and learning, and their rapid expansion, growing as they did to more than 13,000 within fifty years of Ignatius' death. To the extent that the Counter-Reformation succeeded, it did so primarily through the worldwide efforts and missionary imagination of the Society of Jesus.

There was a concurrent resurgence of art, piety, and theology in the so-called *Baroque age* (1550-1750). Baroque scholasticism replaced the more obscure pre-Reformation, nominalistic theology. Spanish and Italian theologians like Bellarmine, Soto, Suarez, Cano, and others, distinguished themselves. Suarez (d. 1617) made a particularly strong impact, influencing every branch of theology and philosophy. Theology became exceedingly systematized. The authority of each theological position was precisely identified. Suarezianism had its spiritual effects as well: especially on the Spanish mystics (St. Teresa of Avila, d. 1582, and St. John of the Cross, d. 1591), who, in turn, influenced French spirituality.

But by and large the post-Tridentine Church continued to emphasize those practices which came under particular attack by the Protestants: veneration of the saints, Marian devotions, and eucharistic adoration. The first and second tended, unwittingly or not, to diminish the role of Christ, and the third, the role of the laity in the Church and at the Eucharist. The liturgy was still the affair of the clergy. In 1661 Pope Alexander VII (d. 1667) forbade any translation of the missal into the vernacular under pain of excommunication. The anti-vernacularists wanted instead to preserve the aura of "mystery." Recitation of the rosary at Mass became common, and preaching, when it occurred at all at the Eucharist, was divorced from the biblical readings. The reception of Communion took place after the Mass. The sacrament was primarily to be worshiped rather than taken as spiritual nourishment. Thus, this period saw the spread of eucharistic processions, forty hours devotions, and benediction of the Blessed Sacrament. The baroque character of the age was also manifest in architecture and in sacred music (the works of Mozart, Haydn, and Beethoven, and the growth of polyphonic song). The liturgy became as much a grand spectacle as an act of community worship.

At the same time the seventeenth and eighteenth centuries were marked by religious fervor and holiness. The seventeenth century has been called the century of saints: St. Vincent de Paul (d. 1660), St. Jean Eudes (d. 1680), Jean Jacques Olier (d. 1657),

Jacques Bossuet (d. 1704), and others. Of particular importance was St. Francis de Sales (d. 1622), bishop of Geneva, who was considerably ahead of his time as an ecumenist, a pastoral leader, an encourager of the lay apostolate and of lay spirituality. He gave particular expression to the latter in his *Introduction to the Devout Life* (1590). The section on marriage is the very antithesis of the monastic prejudice which characterized so many earlier treatments of the married state.

Jansenism

By the beginning of the seventeenth century, the papacy was as strong as it had been since the thirteenth. But doctrinal controversy continued to hamper the Church's quest for a unified missionary effort. Michael de Bay of Louvain (d. 1589), also known as Michael Baius, considered grace, immortality, and freedom from concupiscence as due to us and given in creation; they were not gifts freely bestowed by God. Thus, by Original Sin we lost not only goods that were "extra" to begin with, but goods that are constitutive of our human condition. Therefore, the wound of Original Sin is radical.

Baianism was less important in itself than in a movement it influenced, namely, *Jansenism,* generated by one of Michael's pupils at Louvain, Cornelius Jansen (d. 1638). Jansen wrote a defense of Baius entitled *Augustinus,* in which he attacked Thomism and the theology of the Jesuits and argued that Augustine, not Thomas, is the true representative of Christianity. The book appeared two years after Jansen's death and evoked a strong reaction. Protestants were pleased. Jansen had laid bare the Pelagianism of Rome. But Pope Urban VIII (d. 1644) placed the book on the Index. Jansenism spread nonetheless, especially through France, where it influenced the training of large numbers of priests. It promoted the theory of predestination and a morally rigorous style of Christian life.

Since Original Sin has so radically corrupted human nature, everything purely natural is evil. Grace is given only to the few. Reception of Communion, therefore, is to be experienced only rarely, as an occasional reward for virtue. (Since Jansenism was from the outset an anti-Jesuit movement, its stand on reception of Communion was not surprising in view of the Jesuits' promotion of frequent reception.) Jansenism was carried to Ireland from France, and from Ireland to the United States. Much of pre-Vatican II American Catholicism's obsession with sexual morality and its relatively narrow eucharistic piety (e.g., infrequent reception of Communion and then only after "going to Confession") is directly traceable to this Jansenist influence.

Gallicanism

The condemnation of Jansenism by Rome fueled the fires of independence in France. In 1682 the French clergy declared that the pope had only spiritual authority, that he is subject to the decrees of the Council of Constance, and that henceforth all of his pronouncements would have to be approved by the consent of the entire Church. This latter point is especially important because it would be a matter of specific condemnation at the First Vatican Council (1869-1870) when, on the matter of papal infallibility, the Church would officially declare that a pope's authoritative teachings are *not* subject to the consent of the entire Church. Some Catholics in the twentieth century interpreted that to mean that the pope has absolute teaching authority, that can in no way require the consent of the Church. But as we shall see when returning to the question of papal infallibility in chapter 24, Vatican I meant here to rule out the juridical necessity of some subsequent formal vote taken by a general council or other representative agency in the Church. Infallible teachings, on the other hand, do require the consent of the Church in the sense that what the pope teaches must really be consistent with the actual faith of the whole Church.

Gallicanism (so-called because of its French, or Gallic, origins) persisted in France even beyond the Revolution at the end of the eighteenth century. As transplanted to Germany it was called *Febronianism* or *Josephism* (after the emperor Joseph II, d. 1790).

The Enlightenment

Conditions grew substantially worse as the intellectual atmosphere also changed. It was at this time that the West was to undergo the most revolutionary of all movements in Western history. The *Enlightenment* began in the Netherlands and in England in the mid-seventeenth century and reached its highwater mark in French rationalism (Voltaire, d. 1778, *et al.*). Its fullest philosophical expression occurred in Germany (Leibniz, d. 1716, Lessing, d. 1781, and Kant, d. 1804). It had relatively little effect in southern and eastern Europe.

The Enlightenment was characterized by its confidence in reason, its optimistic view of the world and of human nature, and its celebration of freedom of inquiry. It had a decidedly hostile attitude toward the supernatural, the notion of revelation, and extrinsic authority of every kind. It was chiefly in the Protestant countries that a distinctively Enlightenment Christianity took hold in the form of dogmatic reductionism and an anti-sacramentalism. The reconciliation of science and culture, on the one hand, and Christianity, on the other, was facilely achieved.

But there was also a Catholic Enlightenment which brought about a renewal of Church life as early as the eighteenth century, particularly in the Catholic states of Germany. It took the form of advances in historical and exegetical methods, improvements in the education of the clergy, the struggle against superstition, reform of the liturgy and catechesis, and the promotion of popular education. In many ways, its reforms paved the road for the renewal of the nineteenth century.

In the final accounting, the Enlightenment marks the division between an often pre-critical, authority-oriented theology and a critical, historically sophisticated, and philosophically mature theology. The fact that much Catholic theology was written *after* the Enlightenment does not mean that all of it was truly a post-Enlightenment theology. On the contrary, much Catholic theology before Vatican II was still largely unaffected by the Enlightenment.

The Missions

The transition from a culturally confined Church to a genuine world Church might have begun also at this time, but it did not. With the discovery of new territories by the Spanish and Portuguese in the early fifteenth century and with the continuing geographical expansions of the sixteenth and seventeenth centuries, the Church had an opportunity to be enriched not only quantitatively but qualitatively as well. But *colonialism* compromised the missionary efforts on the political side, and *controversies over methods* compromised those efforts on the ecclesiastical side. The debate over the Chinese and Malabar rites (1645-1692, 1704) brought the promising Jesuit missions in China and India to an end. Rome insisted on the Latin way. The movement to a world Church would have to wait.

THE CHURCH IN THE INDUSTRIAL AND TECHNOLOGICAL AGE (NINETEENTH AND TWENTIETH CENTURIES)

The French Revolution (1789)

The crisis that precipitated yet another qualitative leap in the Church's historical course was the *French Revolution,* the Enlightenment's political carrier. It brought about the end of the feudal, hierarchical society that had been so much a part of medieval Catholicism. But it tried to do more than that. It tried to destroy Catholicism itself, and not just its organizational structure. The French Revolution's extremism generated a counter-reaction among some European intellectuals, who once again turned to the basic principles of Catholicism. The Revolution also destroyed Gallicanism by uprooting the clerical system upon which it had been based. The clergy were forced to look to Rome and the papacy for direction. In a few words, the French Revolution gave the Catholic Church the "grace of destitution." It no longer had much to lose. It was free once again to pursue the mission for which it had existed from the beginning.

Nineteenth-Century Renewal

In France and Germany *Romanticism* extolled Catholicism as the mother of art and the guardian of patriotism. Catholic revival groups as well as new theological schools came into existence. Georg Hermes (d. 1831) in Bonn tried to overcome the new rationalism by using the very concepts of Kant and of Fichte, but he was condemned in 1835 as a semi-rationalist. Similar efforts were made by A. Günther (d. 1863) and J. Frohschammer (d. 1893), with similar results. More successful theological ventures were undertaken by the Tübingen school (J. Möhler, d. 1838, *et al.*). The French priest Félicité Lamennais (d. 1854) and the French Dominican preacher Jean Lacordaire (d. 1861) also attempted a reconciliation between Catholic faith and modern freedoms. Thousands who had been alienated from the Church returned to Catholicism. In Italy, Antonio Rosmini's (d. 1855) *The Five Wounds of the Church* called attention to the need for internal ecclesiastical reform and renewal. And in England John Henry Newman (d. 1890) centered his interests on the problems of faith in the modern world, e.g., in his *Grammar of Assent*, and thereby anticipated by many decades the modern theological and philosophical return to the subject, as in the work of Rahner, Lonergan, and Transcendental Thomism. But Newman was not typical of nineteenth-century theology which, for the most part, was *neo-Scholastic*, an essentially *restorative* theology.

Nineteenth-Century Reaction

For every authentic attempt to deal constructively with the new intellectual currents there seemed to be as many, if not more, forces moving in the opposite direction. A rigid traditionalism developed in France (going by the names of *Integralism* and *Fideism*), distrustful of all rational reflection in theology and excessively dependent upon papal direction (*Ultramontanism*, literally those who look *beyond the mountains*, the Alps, to Rome). The papacy, under Gregory XVI (d. 1846) and Pius IX (d. 1878), set its face against the winds of Liberalism, and nowhere more defiantly than in the latter's *Syllabus of Errors* (1864), where he proclaimed that the pope "cannot and should not be reconciled and come to terms with progress, liberalism, and modern civilization."

At the First Vatican Council Pope Pius IX also secured the dogmatic definition of papal primacy and papal infallibility, but at the same time lost the Papal States (September 1870) and with them his remaining political power. Indeed, the pope became "the prisoner of the Vatican." It was not until the Lateran Treaty of 1929 that the pope's temporal rights to the Vatican territory were acknowledged, and then it was not until 1958 that a pope, John XXIII, made pastoral visitations outside that tiny principality. Paul VI was the first pope in modern times to leave Italy while serving as pope. He did so on several occasions: to visit the Holy Land, India, Latin America, the United States, Australia, and the Philippines. Pope John Paul II has continued that practice, traveling to such countries as Mexico, Poland, Ireland, and the United States.

The Social Question

The *second phase of the Enlightenment* occurred at the economic level. Just as the first phase had disclosed how conditioned our thinking is by extrinsic "authorities" (revealed or otherwise), the second phase disclosed how conditioned our very lives are by extrinsic economic and social forces. With the rapid development of industrialism in the nineteenth century, the condition of the workers worsened. Marxism stepped into the gap. The workers were now alienated not only from the fruits of their labor but from their historic faith as well. Religion, Marx had warned them, was but an opiate, designed to make them forget their oppressive situation. By the time the Church responded at the official level in 1891, especially in Pope Leo XIII's (d. 1903) encyclical *Rerum Novarum (On the Condition of the Workingman)*, it was for many already too late.

With the accelerated growth in the population, the move to the industrial cities, the increase of literacy, the dissemination of news, and dramatic improvements in health care, especially in the decline of infant mortality, the Church found itself unable to meet the pastoral needs of its people and to reiterate, without provoking dissent, its traditional moral teaching on birth control and divorce. This new human situation was only the forerunner of what has been described more fully in chapter 3.

Modernism

If Protestantism's initial impulse is to embrace modernity, Catholicism's has always been to repudiate it. Eventually, however, the Catholic Church comes to terms with modernity, sometimes making a few of the same mistakes Protestantism has already made many years before. Accordingly, the Church's first reaction to the continued industrial, social, and intellectual upheavals of the late nineteenth century was to pronounce a condemnation upon them. That was done, for the most part, by Pope Pius X (d. 1914). The enemy this time was not Liberalism but *Modernism*.

Modernism was not a single movement but a complex of movements. It assumed many very different forms: some clearly unorthodox, others clearly orthodox by today's standards. Unfortunately, the distinction was not often recognized or made. The term *Modernism* was applied to all who refused to adopt a strictly conservative standpoint on debatable matters. Indeed, many of the positions eventually taken by the Second Vatican Council would have been characterized as Modernism had they been expressed by individual theologians or church persons in the early twentieth century, and, in fact, that was precisely what sometimes happened.

In its *unorthodox* form, Modernism was so subjectivist and existentialist as to be anti-intellectual. There could be no fixed doctrinal positions. Everything was always in a state of flux. The new methods of interpreting the Bible accentuated this trend. The French biblical exegete Alfred Loisy (d. 1940) insisted that one must study the Bible as any other historical document, without doctrinal or dogmatic presuppositions. The movement found expression in England in the work of the ex-Jesuit George Tyrrell (d. 1909), who insisted that Christ did not present himself as a teacher of orthodoxy and that dogma is just a human effort to put into intellectual terms the divine force working in all of us. Some of his disciples carried the point a step further, coming close to pantheism. In Italy the movement took social and political form, favoring the establishment of society in complete freedom from hierarchical control.

As noted in chapter 7, Modernism was condemned in various documents issued by the authority of Pope Pius X: the Holy Office decree *Lamentabili* (1907), the encyclical *Pascendi* (1907), and the Oath Against Modernism (*Sacrorum Antistitum, 1909*). Although all the clergy were required to take this oath, its imposition produced such a strongly negative reaction in Germany that the German bishops secured an exemption for Catholic university professors.

Much of twentieth-century Catholic theology in the years before Vatican II was written while authors were looking back over their shoulders at the Modernist crisis. Church officials sustained this atmosphere by continuing to equate most deviations from Scholastic or neo-Scholastic theology with Modernist unorthodoxies. But Modernism in its more sophisticated theological forms was *right* about several important matters: (1) The inner religious experience *is* an essential element of the life of the spirit and, in large measure, generates and supports the act of faith; (2) dogmatic formulae are always inadequate to their object, which is God; (3) revelation is first and foremost for the sake of salvation and the quality of human life rather than for the satisfaction of intellectual curiosity; (4) revelation was only gradually unfolded in the life of the Church, and with many fits and starts; and (5) the Bible, and indeed all the sources of Christian tradition, must be studied according to the most scientifically critical methods at hand.

On the other hand, (1) inner religious experience is not the only way to come to a knowledge of God; (2) dogmatic formulae are not completely devoid of objective content; (3) the development of dogma and of our understanding of revelation is not a completely natural process which can just as easily distort the meaning of the Gospel as illuminate it; and (4) the Bible and other authoritative sources are not just historical documents, but are expressions and products of the Church's collective faith and must also be read and interpreted as such.

The Church's official magisterium may have oversimplified the Modernist position and prematurely condemned it, without really understanding its inner substance and its fundamental truth. But the Modernists themselves often exaggerated their partial grasp of that truth, uncritically adopted late nineteenth-century positivist views of history, and individualized theology by tearing it from its broader ecclesial context.

Between the Two World Wars (1918-1939)

Although Catholic theology and its official interpretation remained conservative in the aftermath of the Modernist crisis, the period between the two World Wars was one of unusual progress on several major fronts, each of which would reach a fuller flowering at the Second Vatican Council in the 1960s:

1.   The *liturgical movement* worked to bridge the gap between altar and people by emphasizing the liturgy as an act of communal worship in and through Christ, the head of the Church, and by recovering the Thomistic principle, taught at the Council of Trent, that the sacraments are both signs and causes of grace. As *signs* of grace, they must be intelligible.

2.   The *biblical movement* prudently carried forward the work of critical interpretation without provoking additional papal or curial condemnations. Père Marie-Joseph Lagrange (d. 1938) continued his scriptural studies in Jerusalem and trained a corps of scholars who were available for service to the Church when, in 1943, Pope Pius XII issued the so-called Magna Carta of Catholic biblical scholarship, *Divino Afflante Spiritu*.

3.   The *social action* movement continued to apply the social teachings of the Church, including Pope Pius XI's major encyclical *Quadragesimo Anno* (*Forty Years After [Rerum Novarum]*) in 1931. In the United States, for example, this movement was centered in the drive for the recognition of labor unionism in American industry.

4.   The *lay apostolate* under Pius XI and especially Pius XII sought to involve larger and larger numbers of the laity in the work of the Church ("Catholic Action").

5.   The *ecumenical movement*, in spite of the negative tone of Pius XI's encyclical *Mortalium Animos*, on the occasion of the

Faith and Order Conference of 1927 at Lausanne, began attracting the scholarly attention of such major Catholic theologians as Yves Congar in his pioneering work, *Divided Christendom* (1939).

6. The *missionary movement* was now increasingly carried out with a minimum of colonial and European influence. The first native bishops in the new mission territories were consecrated in 1926, and Pius XII furnished the mission countries with their own hierarchies.

7. A *theological renewal* was signaled by the emergence of a theology inspired by the Catholic Church's renewed respect for Thomas Aquinas but not uncritically wedded to his system. Because of the preceding six items, the new theological approach was more biblically, historically, pastorally, socially, and ecumenically oriented. Prominent among the varieties of developing Catholic theologies was Transcendental Thomism, whose principal and most celebrated exponent has been the Austrian Jesuit Karl Rahner. The new understanding of the mystery of Church as People of God with a mission to the whole world was anticipated in the writings of the century's most important ecclesiologist, the French Dominican Yves Congar.

The Second World War and Its Aftermath (1940-1962)

The change in official Catholicism is evident in the encyclicals that were produced during this period. The *liturgical movement* was given a major push in Pius XII's *Mystici Corporis* (1943) and *Mediator Dei* (1947), and in the restoration of the Easter Vigil (1951) and the rites of Holy Week (1955). The *biblical movement*, as we just noted, received remarkable endorsement in Pius XII's *Divino Afflante Spiritu* (1943)—remarkable certainly in the light of the exceedingly restrictive directives of the Pontifical Biblical Commission at the turn of the century. The *social action movement* and the *lay apostolate* in general were warmly endorsed in John XXIII's *Mater et Magistra* (1961) and *Pacem in Terris* (1963) and in Paul VI's *Populorum Progressio* (1967). The *ecumenical movement* had to await the pontificate of John XXIII before it could surface with official blessing. John XXIII established in 1960 the Secretariat for the Promotion of Christian Unity and invited non-Catholic Christians as official observers at Vatican II. The *missionary movement,* and particularly the need for adaptation and enculturation, was strongly approved in Pius XII's encyclicals *Summi Pontificatus* (1939), *Evangelii Praecones* (1951), and *Fidei Donum* (1957). Finally, the *theological renewal,* after a glaring setback in Pius XII's *Humani Generis* (1950), found itself at the center, not the margin, of the deliberations of the Second Vatican Council.

The next chapter is devoted entirely to that extraordinary event, a moment comparable in historical significance to the early Church's abandonment of circumcision as a condition for membership.

SUMMARY

1.   The relationship between the Church and history is a theological one. It has to do with the movement of the world, and the Church within the world, toward its destiny in the Kingdom of God, and with the presence of God to the world here and now through the Church.

2.   Dividing the history in which the Church has been present and active, however, always reflects certain theological presuppositions. We use here *three major divisions:* the Church of *Jewish Christianity* (a very brief period); the Church of *cultural confinement* (Hellenistic Christianity, European Christianity, etc.); and the Church of the world, or the period of the *world Church.*

3.   The transition, or break, between the first and second periods occurred at the point (or points) at which the Church carried the Gospel to the Gentiles and decided at the same time not to impose circumcision as a condition for membership. The transition, or break, between the second and third periods has only just begun to occur with the Second Vatican Council.

4.   This chapter, therefore, is concerned with the *second period* of the Church's historical pilgrimage, namely, its movement through, and consecutive identification with, various cultures, especially the European.

5.   The historical material of this second period is further divided as follows: (1) the Church within Graeco-Roman civilization (first to seventh centuries); (2) the Church as the dominant presence in the West

(about 700-1300); (3) the disintegration of Christian unity and the transition to a wider mission (1300-1750); and (4) the Church in the period of industrialization and technology (nineteenth and twentieth centuries).

6. By the word *Church* we mean here not just the pope and the bishops, but the whole People of God. By *history* we mean the whole process by which the world, and the Church within the world, is moving toward the Kingdom of God. History is also the *interpretation* of that process. God alone can "interpret" history without error: comprehending all the data, knowing all the facts, and perceiving all the facts in their proper relationships one with another to constitute the whole.

7. *Classicism*, in effect, denies the reality of history as a process as well as the element of human cooperation with the grace of God. *Historicism*, in effect, denies the reality of history as the work of God and as the sign of God's presence in grace. *Historical consciousness* understands history as a process that is grounded in, and sustained and guided by, the grace of God, but which also emerges through human decisions and events according to an often-unpredictable pattern.

8. The Church of the *Graeco-Roman civilization* (first through seventh centuries) began with the transition from Jewish Christianity to Christianity of and for Gentiles, and that, of course, was an occurrence within the New Testament period itself. Overlapping with the latter part of this period was the age of the *Apostolic Fathers* (pupils of the Apostles) and the *Apologists* (defenders of the faith). Early challenges to the faith in this period included *Gnosticism, Adoptionism,* and *Docetism,* and these, in turn, moved the Church to determine its *canon* (list) of Sacred Scripture as the norm of faith and to articulate an understanding of *apostolic succession,* by which the witness of the Apostles as authoritatively interpreted by the bishops is an additional norm and guarantee of faith.

9. By the *latter half of the second century* organizational complexification occurred: local synods, regional synods, and then, in 325, an ecumenical council (Nicea). This development was in response to continuing challenges to the purity of faith from *Montanism* (no sins committed after Baptism can be forgiven) and *Donatism* (a sacrament is invalid if administered by one in mortal sin).

10. *Persecutions* began also at this time as Christianity increasingly set itself at odds with the religious pluralism of contemporary society. Major persecutions occurred under the emperors *Decius* and *Diocletian.*

11.   A major event at the beginning of the *fourth century* was the conversion of the emperor *Constantine* and his edict of 313 granting legal status to Christianity.

12.   The *monastic movement* began at this time at least partially in protest against the lessening of Christian fervor in this new atmosphere of legal status. It originated as a retreat of individuals (hermits) into the desert but soon became a communal movement. Bishops and leading theologians of the period were trained in the monastic way. It shaped their scholarship (and hence influenced the great ecumenical councils of the fourth and fifth centuries) and their spirituality as well.

13.   The *fourth and fifth centuries* were also preoccupied with dogmatic controversies in the East about the relationship between the one God and Jesus Christ, and then about the Holy Spirit in relationship to both. *Arianism* (Christ is a creature, greater than we but less than God) was opposed by the *Council of Nicea* in 325; *Apollinarianism* (Christ had no human soul) was condemned by the *First Council of Constantinople* in 381; *Nestorianism* (the man Jesus is separate from the Word; the two are not united in one person) was condemned by the *Council of Ephesus* in 431; and *Monophysitism* (Christ's human nature was completely absorbed by the one divine person) was rejected by the *Council of Chalcedon* in 451.

14.   In the West, meanwhile, the theological challenge came from *Pelagianism* on the issue of nature and grace (salvation is through human effort alone), and its chief opponent was *Augustine*.

15.   By the beginning of the fifth century also, German tribes began migrating through Europe without discernible control. This movement has been called the *Barbarian Invasions*. These invasions were to last some six hundred years and were to change the character of Christianity from a largely Graeco-Roman religion to a broader European religion. Except for the Franks, most of the tribes converted to Arianism, carrying with them many of their former pagan and superstitious practices. The strongly militaristic and feudal character of Germanic culture was to influence Christian devotion, spirituality, and organizational structure.

16.   The tradition of the warrior chief in these tribes led eventually to the great *investiture struggle* between the rulers of state and the popes, especially *Gregory VII* (d. 1085): Shall ecclesiastical leaders be appointed by the Church, or by the state?

17.   Meanwhile, a mission to the Anglo-Saxons in the British Isles was inaugurated by *Pope Gregory the Great* (d. 604), who also imagina-

tively employed undeniably strong financial resources to draw temporal power to the papacy.

18. The Church entered another major historical period at the beginning of the *eighth century*. Because the Eastern emperor proved incapable of coming to the aid of the papacy when it was under attack from the Lombards in northern Italy, the pope turned to the Franks for help. This was the start of ther Holy Roman Empire, which reached its climactic moment in the year 800 with the crowning of *Charlemagne*. The line between Church and state disappeared, for all practical purposes.

19. When the Carolingian empire collapsed, however, the papacy was left at the mercy of an essentially corrupt Roman nobility. Throughout the *tenth and eleventh centuries* the papacy languished in its "dark age."

20. Meanwhile, *monasticism* was imported into the West from the East, reaching its high point in the middle of the sixth century with the founding of Monte Cassino by *St. Benedict*. In spite of its simple purposes of work and prayer, Western monasticism became the principal carrier of Western civilization during the early Middle Ages. No other institution had comparable social or intellectual influence.

21. Some measure of stability returned to Europe by the *middle of the eleventh century*. Monks, no longer required to bear so many temporal burdens, returned to their monasteries. A spirit of renewal and reform prevailed. *Pope Gregory VII* attacked three evils: simony, the alienation of property, and lay investiture. Each reform was designed to liberate the Church from lay control. The powers of the papacy were enormously strengthened, especially in the pontificate of *Innocent III* (1198-1216).

22. *Canon law* was codified to support the new network of papal authority. Legalism replaced theology in the self-understanding of the Church and in its sacramental life, especially concerning marriage. The classical, juridical, papal-hierarchical concept of the Church was firmly established by the *middle of the thirteenth century*. By now the pope was crowned like an emperor, a practice observed until 1978, when newly elected Pope John Paul I abandoned the coronation rite.

23. Although the Gregorian Reform was not a complete success (the investiture struggle continued, and Gregory himself died a prisoner), there was a renewal of religious life, of the life of the clergy, and even of the Church's central administration. *Bernard of Clairvaux* (d. 1153) was

one of the principal instruments of the renewal, although he also introduced a highly personal, subjectivist, almost anti-intellectual approach to
spirituality and theology.

24. With the consolidation of independent schools at the beginning of the thirteenth century, theology moved from the monasteries to
the emerging *universities* and assumed the speculative character of university disciplines.

25. New assaults upon orthodoxy came from purist groups: The
Albigensians, or *Cathari*, and the *Waldensians*. The *Inquisition* was
founded at this time to deal with these movements. Its excesses are well
known. Others combatted the new heresies through preaching, example,
and pastoral care: *Francis of Assisi* and *Dominic* in particular, and the
mendicant orders they founded. A renewed theological scholarship also
grew out of these communities: *Aquinas, Bonaventure, Duns Scotus, et al.*

26. Concurrently, through a series of unfortunate and complicated
political and diplomatic maneuvers, the historic bond of union between
the Church of Rome and the Church of Constantinople came apart. In
1054 the patriarch of Constantinople, *Michael Cerularius*, was heavy-
handedly excommunicated by papal legates, but the death blow to East-
West unity was dealt by the *Fourth Crusade* (1202-1204) and the sack of
Constantinople by Western knights. Thus began the *East-West Schism.*

27. The Church moved into another major period of its history at
the beginning of the *fourteenth century*, a period of *disintegration* which
reached its climax in the *Protestant Reformation* of the *sixteenth century.*

28. Events which prepared the way for the Reformation included:
the confrontation between *Pope Boniface VIII* and *Philip the Fair*,
leading to the Pope's imprisonment and death; the proliferation of serious financial abuses during the papacy's Babylonian Captivity at Avignon, in France (1309-1378); the rise of nationalism and anti-clericalism
in resentment against papal taxes; the new theological challenges to the
canonical justifications of papal power, especially in *Marsilius of Padua's*
advocacy of a conciliar rather than a monarchical concept of the Church
(1324); the *Great Western Schism* (1378-1417) with, at one point, three
different claimants to the papacy; and the turn to the principle of *conciliarism* to resolve the problem at the *Council of Constance*, which
decreed the supremacy of a general council and the collegiality of the
bishops.

29. Among the *causes of the Reformation* are: (1) the corruption of
the Renaissance papacy of the fifteenth century; (2) the divorce of piety
from theology, and of theology from biblical and patristic tradition;
(3) the debilitating effects of the Great Western Schism; (4) the rise of the

national state; (5) the too-close connection between Western Christianity and Western civilization; and (6) the vision, experiences, and personalities of *Luther, Zwingli,* and *Calvin.*

30.   The *Reformation* itself took *different forms*: On the *right*, it retained essential Catholic doctrine but changed certain canonical and/or ecclesiological forms (Lutheranism and Anglicanism); on the *left*, it repudiated much Catholic doctrine as well as much of Catholicism's sacramental life (*Zwinglianism* and the *Anabaptist* movement); nearer to the *center*, it modified both doctrine and practice but retained much of the old (*Calvinism*).

31.   The Catholic response was belated. When it came, it was vigorous. Known as the *Counter-Reformation*, it began at the *Council of Trent* (1545-1563) and especially under the leadership of *Pope Paul III* (1534-1549). The council, which perhaps did more than any other event or historical factor to shape Catholicism from that time until the Second Vatican Council in the mid-1960s, articulated Catholic doctrine on faith and grace, following a middle course between Pelagianism (it all depends on us) and Protestantism (it all depends on God). The Council also defined the sacraments, created the Index of Forbidden Books, and established seminaries. There were good and bad effects of the council's work.

32.   At the heart of the Catholic Counter-Reformation was the *Society of Jesus* (Jesuits), the strongest single force in helping the Church regain the initiative on several fronts: missionary, educational, and pastoral. Spiritual renewal in the form of Spanish mysticism also occurred at this time in the work of *Teresa of Avila* and *John of the Cross.*

33.   But by and large the post-Tridentine Church continued to emphasize those practices so vehemently attacked by the Protestants: veneration of the saints, Marian devotions, and eucharistic adoration. The centrality of Christ, the communal character of the Eucharist, the responsibility of the laity in the Church—all of these were muted. Exceptions, of course, existed, as in the work and writings of *Francis de Sales* (d. 1622).

34.   Although by the *beginning of the seventeenth century* the papacy was as strong as it had been since the thirteenth, the Church was wracked again by doctrinal and moral controversy, this time provoked by *Jansenism.* The movement drew its inspiration from Augustine, who had always emphasized the priority of grace over nature. Jansenism took Augustine's emphasis many steps further, portraying nature as totally corrupt and promoting a theory of predestination. From these principles there emerged a life-style that was exceedingly rigorous and puritanical.

35. *Gallicanism* developed as a result of Rome's efforts to combat and suppress Jansenism, which was largely a French movement. Gallicanism affirmed that the pope lacks supreme authority in the Church. That belongs only to a general council. Therefore, all papal decrees are subject to the consent of the entire Church, as represented in such a council.

36. These internal problems were complicated by the most fundamental external challenge to traditional Christianity, the *Enlightenment*. It displayed enormous (indeed exaggerated) confidence in reason; it had an optimistic view of human nature and the world (inevitable progress); and it celebrated freedom of inquiry. It made inroads particularly in Protestant countries.

37. A counterpart to the Englightenment occurred within the Catholic Church of the eighteenth century, with advances in scholarship, education of the clergy, reform of the liturgy and catechesis, and so forth.

38. Missionary expansion at this time, especially by the Spanish and Portuguese, was marred by colonialism and Romanism; i.e., the Gospel was tied too closely to certain political, cultural, and legal forms. Flexibility and adaptation were not in order. This was the period of the great controversy over the Chinese rites.

39. The Church was catapulted into the final period of its second great historical moment (i.e., its moment of cultural confinement) by the *French Revolution* (1789), which ended medieval Catholicism once and for all.

40. Catholic reactions to the excesses of the French Revolution included a *romanticist* movement (an attempt at recovering the glories of the Church's past) and a *theological* movement designed to come to terms constructively with the Enlightenment. But the *nineteenth century* does not present a uniform picture. Although *Cardinal Newman's* interest in the problem of faith anticipated the major theological developments of the twentieth century, the Church also witnessed the spread of *Integralism, Fideism,* and *Ultramontanism,* all of which found support in the pontificates of *Gregory XVI* and *Pius IX.* The spirit of the leadership's attitude to this period of pronounced change is captured in the latter Pope's *Syllabus of Errors* (1864), which condemned "progress, liberalism, and modern civilization."

41. The official Church's response to the *social question* was more positive, though belated. *Pope Leo XIII* initiated a series of teachings on behalf of social justice that have remained largely pertinent even to the present day.

42.   The Enlightenment continued to pound at the Church's door, but now in the form of *Modernism* at the turn of the twentieth century. Not a single school of thought so much as a cluster of movements, Modernism emphasized the inner religious experience in the genesis of faith, and correspondingly downplayed the role of revelation, of dogma, and of ecclesiastical authority. The reaction of the Pope, *Pius X*, was unmistakably negative. It was at this time that the *Oath Against Modernism* was imposed upon all priests (1909).

43.   Between the two World Wars, Catholicism lived at once under the impact of the Modernist crisis and under the power of new movements within the Church: liturgical, biblical, social action, lay, ecumenical, missionary, and theological.

44.   These movements were to surface, now with official approval, in the years during or just following the Second World War. They were forerunners of the renewal and reforms of the Second Vatican Council.

SUGGESTED READINGS

Bainton, Roland. *Christendom: A Short History of Christianity and Its Impact on Western Civilization.* 2 vols. New York: Harper & Row, 1966.

Barry, Colman. *Readings in Church History.* 3 vols. Westminster, Md.: Newman Press, 1960-1965.

Bausch, William J. *Pilgrim Church: A Popular History of Catholic Christianity.* Notre Dame, Ind.: Fides Press, 1973.

Bettenson, Henry, ed. *Documents of the Christian Church.* New York: Oxford University Press, 1967.

Dillenberger, John, and Welch, Claude. *Protestant Christianity: Interpreted Through Its Development.* New York: Scribner, 1954.

Dolan, John P. *Catholicism: An Historical Survey.* Woodbury, N.Y.: Barron's Educational Series, 1968.

Franzen, August. *A Concise History of the Church.* New York: Herder & Herder, 1969.

Ruether, Rosemary, and McLaughlin, Eleanor, eds. *Women of Spirit: Female Leadership in the Jewish and Christian Traditions.* New York: Simon & Shuster, 1979.

· XIX ·

THE CHURCH OF THE SECOND VATICAN COUNCIL

THE SIGNIFICANCE OF VATICAN II

The Second Vatican Council was only the twenty-first general or *ecumenical* (literally, "the whole wide world") council of the Church. To a great extent it was convened, organized, and governed by the same laws and processes which shaped its predecessor, Vatican I (1869-1870), and, to a slightly lesser extent, the Council of Trent (1545-1563). This is not to say, however, that all of the councils have followed the same pattern as Trent, Vatican I, and Vatican II. The eight ancient ecumenical councils of the Byzantine East, for example, were convened not by the bishop of Rome but by the emperor. In an official statement released on the eve of Vatican II's opening (September 1962), Pope John XXIII expressed the judgment that "by virtue of the number and variety of those who will participate in its meetings [Vatican II] will be the greatest of the councils held by the Church so far." Why should this have been so?

First, the total number of delegates to this council greatly exceeded the number attending any of the preceding twenty. The largest previous ecumenical council had been Vatican I, with 737 in attendance. Vatican II had more than 2600 bishops from all over the world (2908 would have been eligible to attend the first session). Counting theologians and other experts on hand, the number of participants approached 3000.

Secondly, and more significantly, this council was not only the largest in number but also the most representative in terms of nations and cultures. Even Vatican I, with its 737 delegates, was dominated by Europeans, including European bishops of mission- ary lands. But between Vatican I and Vatican II a major change occurred in the composition of the hierarchies of mission coun- tries. In his encyclical letter *Maximum Illud* (1919), Pope Bene- dict XV insisted on the primary importance of establishing a native clergy and a native hierarchy in mission lands, of the disin- terestedness required from foreign missionaries, and of their full adaptation to their adopted country. The same stress on develop- ing a native clergy and native bishops was carried forward in subsequent encyclicals by Popes Pius XI and Pius XII. Conse- quently, most of the bishops from mission countries in attendance at Vatican II were themselves natives of those lands and products of those cultures. Among eligible bishops, 1089 were from Europe, 489 from South America, 404 from North America, 374 from Asia, 296 from Africa, 84 from Central America, and 75 from Oceania.

Thirdly, the council was also more representative than ear- lier councils in terms of non-Catholic and lay observers. With the arrival of three representatives of the Russian Orthodox Church, sixty-three non-Catholic observers were in attendance by the beginning of the second session (1963), an increase of eighteen over the first session. Almost every major Christian church was represented. In addition, eleven laymen were invited to attend the second session. This number was to increase to fifty-two lay audi- tors by the beginning of the fourth session (1965), twenty-nine of whom were men and twenty-three women, including ten nuns.

Fourthly, this was the first ecumenical council to have availa- ble to it electric lights, telephones, typewriters, and other modern means of communication and transportation. It was also the first to be covered by newspapers and magazines from all over the world, as well as by radio and television.

Finally, the council was also unique in its intended purpose. Unlike so many councils before it, it was not called to confront a serious attack upon the doctrinal or organizational integrity of the Church. It was not called simply to repeat ancient formulas or to condemn dissidents and heretics. On the contrary, Pope John XXIII, in his opening address of October 11, 1962, said that the council's goal was to eradicate the seeds of discord and promote peace and the unity of all humankind. Insofar as it would attend to doctrine, the council was to keep in mind the basic distinction between the substance of doctrine and the way in which it is presented. The Church must employ, to this end, the best methods of research and the literary forms of modern thought. The council would thereby prepare "the path toward that unity of mankind which is required . . . in order that the earthly city may be brought to the resemblance of that heavenly city. . . ."

In a word, Vatican II was a council unique in the history of the Church because it was the first really *ecumenical* council. As such, it signaled the Catholic Church's movement from a Church of cultural confinement, particularly of the European variety, to a genuine world Church.

TWENTIETH-CENTURY CATHOLIC THEOLOGY BEFORE VATICAN II

One must be careful about a purely pejorative understanding of the expression "pre-Vatican II theology." There is no uniform preconciliar theology. In the early and mid-twentieth century we find not only the theology of the textbooks, or manuals, but also the theology of individual theologians whose work was not yet accepted at official levels but who were, in fact, laying the foundation for the documents of Vatican II. Included among these theologians were Karl Rahner, Yves Congar, Henri de Lubac, Edward Schillebeeckx, Hans Küng, and the American Jesuit John Courtney Murray.

Textbook Theology

Nowhere is the traditional pre-Vatican ecclesiology more faithfully or more responsibly set forth than in Joachim Salaverri's "*De Ecclesia Christi*" ("On the Church of Christ") in the first volume of the so-called *Spanish Summa (Sacrae Theologiae Summa,* Madrid: Library of Christian Authors, 1962, 5th ed.). The basic approach is clear in the organization of the material. Salaverri divides his ecclesiology into three main parts, or books. The first is on the "social constitution" of the Church. Here he explains, in chapter 1, Christ's "institution of a hierarchical Church." He suggests that the Church is the visible, earthly, external form of the Kingdom of God and that it is governed by the college of the Apostles, by mandate of the Lord himself. The Apostles were granted the power of teaching, ruling, and sanctifying, with the understanding or proviso that every person would submit himself or herself to this power.

Salaverri argues in his second chapter that the Church is not only a *hierarchical* Church; it is also a *monarchical* Church. This is rooted in Christ's conferral of the primacy on Peter, which the author proves on the basis of the New Testament (employing a form of exegesis not consistent with that accepted and practiced by Catholic scholars today, as already suggested in chapter 17 of this book). According to Salaverri, after the resurrection Christ gave Peter "direct and immediate" authority over the universal Church. Peter is, therefore, the Vicar of Christ and the "superior" of the Apostles. The permanence of this monarchical-hierarchical Church is insured through the act of succession: apostolic in the case of the bishops, Petrine in the case of the pope. The papal primacy, Salaverri argues in his tenth thesis, is "universal, ordinary, immediate, truly episcopal, supreme and full, and is subject to no higher judgment on earth." There is, of course, much here that is reminiscent of the papal claims in the Middle Ages, especially as represented in the *Dictatus Papae* of Gregory VII (1075) and the bull *Unam Sanctam* (1302) of Boniface VIII. Salaverri concludes Book I with the assertion that "the Roman Catholic Church alone is the true Church of Christ" and he "demonstrates" this on the basis of the necessity of a permanent hierarchy and primacy to insure the permanence of the Church as Christ instituted it.

In Book II, Salaverri moves to a thorough discussion of the teaching authority (*magisterium*) of the Church and the sources of that authority. He argues that Christ established in the Apostles a teaching authority that is authentic (i.e., attached to an ecclesiastical office) perpetual, and infallible (immune from error). The pope is infallible when he speaks *ex cathedra* ("from the chair") on matters of faith and morals with the intention of binding the whole Church. The bishops share in this infallibility when they define a dogma of faith in union with the pope either at an ecumenical council or through some other vehicle of common teaching. Doctrinal decrees of the various Vatican administrative offices (the Curia) express the intention of the pope and therefore are to be received with "internal and religious assent of the mind." The source for the Church's official teaching authority is the divine apostolic tradition, including Sacred Scripture, the Fathers of the Church, and theological consensus (especially the opinion of Thomas Aquinas).

In Book III, Salaverri turns finally to the "supernaturality" and "properties" of the Church. But here, too, the discussion is largely in terms of the hierarchical, the organizational, and the juridical. Thus, thesis 23 asserts: "The Church is a perfect and absolutely independent society with full legislative, judicial, and coercive power." When he speaks of the Church as Mystical Body of Christ, the focus is upon conditions for membership. One gains entrance through valid Baptism, and one may be subsequently excluded by heresy, apostasy, schism, or excommunication. The Church, in any case, is necessary for salvation even by "necessity of means." (A distinction was drawn in the older theology between "necessity of means" and "necessity of precept." "Necessity of precept" refers to a condition that "ought" to be fullfilled because the Lord asked us to do so, but it is possible nonetheless to reach a particular end without fulfilling the condition. "Necessity of means" refers to a condition that "ought" to and "must" be fulfilled if the end is to be reached.)

Regarding the properties of the Church, Salaverri proposes that the Roman Catholic Church alone possesses the "notes" of unity, holiness, catholicity, and apostolicity. All other churches, insofar as they lack one or more of these notes, are "false churches." The whole treatise on the Church concludes with the thesis that Christ gave the Apostles and their successors the threefold power of teaching, ruling, and sanctifying, and that this is the primary law for the whole Church.

"Progressive" Theology

Yves Congar

The most important ecclesiologist of this century, Yves Congar perhaps did more than any other single theologian to prepare the way for the Second Vatican Council. The council's major themes are already anticipated in Congar's books. He wrote of the Church as the People of God in his *Mystery of the Temple* (1958). Within the People of God the laity are called to full participation in the mission of the Church (*Lay People in the Church*, 1953). The Church is more than the Roman Catholic Church alone (*Divided Christendom*, 1937). The mission of the Church is not to grow and multiply but to be a minority in the service of the majority. Like the French Underground during the Second World War, the Church is a small community which prepares the way for the salvation of all in the coming of the Kingdom. The Church exists in itself but not for itself (*The Wide World, My Parish*, 1961). This Church, ecumenically conceived, is always in need of reform, even institutional and structural reform, in head as well as in members (*Vraie et fausse reforme dans l'Eglise*, 1950). This book, whose title means *True and False Reform in the Church,* was never translated into English, and in fact was withdrawn from circulation because of its controversial content.

Karl Rahner

Although Rahner's principal theological contributions have not been in the area of ecclesiology as such, he, too, prepared the way for Vatican II with his fundamental notion of the universality of grace (already discussed at length in our earlier chapters on human existence, 4 and 5) and the correlative notion of the *diaspora* Church. In an essay published in 1961 but written earlier than that, "A Theological Interpretation of the Position of Christians in the Modern World" (*Mission and Grace*, London: Sheed & Ward, 1963, pp. 3-55), Rahner notes that some events in the history of salvation "ought not" to be, but are and "must" be so (e.g., the crucifixion, the existence of poverty, etc.) The minority, scattered (*diaspora*) condition of the Church is one of those "musts" of salvation history. This diaspora situation, he argues, is not only permitted by God but positively willed by God. And we must draw our conclusions from this.

It means that the Church is no longer "in possession" and cannot act as if it were. The age of "Christendom" is over. The Church must attract people on the basis of choice, not on the basis of social convention or political pressure. Those who belong to the Church will belong to it as a matter of conviction, not of habit. "Just where is it written that *we* must have the whole 100 per cent? God must have all. . . . Why should we not alter to our use, quite humbly and dispassionately, a saying of St. Augustine's: Many whom God has, the Church does not have; and many whom the Church has, God does not have?" (p. 51).

Edward Schillebeeckx

Another major theological influence before the council was Edward Schillebeeckx's *Christ the Sacrament of Encounter with God*, first published in Dutch in 1960, and translated into English in 1963 (New York: Sheed & Ward). Schillebeeckx's argument is easily summarized: Apart from the sacramental principle, there is no basis for contact (encounter) between God and the human community. God is totally spiritual, and we are bodily creatures. Thus, it is only insofar as God adapts to our material condition that God can reach us and we can reach God. The embodiment of the spiritual in the material and the communication of the spiritual through the material is the sacramental principle. Christ is the great sacrament of God, because God addresses us through the flesh of Christ and we respond through that same fleshly Christ. The Church, in turn, is the sacrament of Christ, who otherwise would be removed from our range of daily, bodily existence. The seven sacraments are, finally, the principal ways by which the Church communicates the reality of Christ and of God, and by which we respond to Christ and to God in worship.

The essence of the Church, therefore, "consists in this, that the final goal of grace achieved by Christ becomes visibly present in the *whole* Church as a visible society" (p. 56). The Church is not only a means of salvation; it is the principal sign, or sacrament, of salvation. It is not only an institution but a community. Indeed, it is an institutionalized community. The important missionary implication is not whether the whole world enters the Church but whether the Church itself gives credible witness to the presence of Christ and of God within the community.

Henri de Lubac

A similarly sacramental perspective was advanced by the French Jesuit Henri de Lubac in his influential work *Catholicism* (New York: Sheed & Ward, 1950). "Humanity is one, organically one by its divine structure; it is the Church's mission to reveal to men that pristine unity that they have lost, to restore and complete it" (p. 19). The Church, de Lubac insisted, is "not merely that strongly hierarchical and disciplined society whose divine origin has to be maintained. . . . If Christ is the sacrament of God, the Church is for us the sacrament of Christ. . ." (p. 29). Indeed, "it is through his union with the community that the Christian is united to Christ" (p. 35).

John Courtney Murray

John Courtney Murray was not formally an ecclesiologist, although his best-known writings touched upon the relationship between Church and state and on the correlative question of religious freedom. Not invited to the first session of the council because of his views on these issues, Murray proved to be the major influence in the composition of the council's *Declaration on Religious Freedom.* His pre-Vatican II contributions were done through scholarly articles in *Theological Studies* in which he subjected certain traditional teachings, especially of Pope Leo XIII, to historical and theological reinterpretation. He argued not that the Leonine doctrine was false but that it was archaic. It was based on a paternalistic rather than a constitutional concept of political authority. Leo's position was also formulated in the context of the Continental laicist state, and Leo confused society with the state just as they were confused in the philosophies of pagan antiquity. But given developments in Catholic social philosophy and in the political character of much of the world, the Leonine teaching can no longer obtain.

Over against this teaching, Murray argued for the four truths which came to be accepted in essence by the council: the dignity of the human person (a principle which pervaded the doctrinal work of Pope Pius XII), our endowment with natural rights and duties (also in Pius XII, but developed by John XXIII in *Pacem in Terris*), the juridical nature of the state, i.e., its primary commitment to the protection of human rights and the facilitation of duties (Pius XII again), and the limitation of the powers of government by a higher order of human and civil rights (Pius XII, as elaborated upon by John XXIII). A brief summary of Murray's position, in light of Vatican II's statement on religious liberty, is available in *Council Daybook, Vatican II, Session 4,* pp. 14-17.

Hans Küng

Hans Küng was only 33 when he published his *The Council and Reunion* (London: Sheed & Ward, 1961). It was undoubtedly the single most influential book in the council's preparatory phase because it alerted so many people in the Catholic world to the possibilities for renewal and reform through the medium of Vatican II. For Küng, reunion of the churches depends upon their prior reform, including the reform of the Roman Catholic Church. This is always necessary because the Church consists not only of human beings but of sinful human beings. Although his book is remarkably comprehensive, its basic ecclesiological point is that "the chief difficulty in the way of reunion lies in the two different concepts of the Church, and especially of the concrete organizational structure of the Church" (p. 188). The difference is most sharply focused in the question of ecclesiastical office: its origin, powers, scope of authority, and forms. And the heart of the matter is the Petrine office: "Do we need a pope?" Pope John XXIII, Küng noted, was giving the papacy a whole new style and perhaps in the process eliminating or diminishing many of the historic objections to the office from the Protestant side.

Almost all of the reforms Küng argued for were eventually adopted—e.g., the establishment of episcopal conferences, the abolition of the Index of Forbidden Books, simplification of the liturgy.

POPE JOHN XXIII

It is difficult to exaggerate the role played by Pope John XXIII in the total event known as the Second Vatican Council, even though he was to die between the first and second sessions (1963). When elected in 1958 Pope John insisted that his was a "very humble office of shepherd" and that he intended to pattern his ministry after that of Joseph in the Old Testament story, who greeted the brothers who had once sold him into slavery with the compassionate and forgiving words, "I am Joseph, your brother" (Genesis 45:4). When the new pope took possession of the Lateran Basilica in Rome, he reminded the congregation that he was not a prince surrounded by the signs of outward power but "a priest, a father, a shepherd." From the beginning he broke the precedent of centuries and visited the sick in the Roman hospitals, the elderly in old-age homes, the convicts at Regina Coeli prison. Every day he celebrated what was then known as the dialogue Mass (i.e., with responses from the people). On Holy Thursday he washed the feet of selected members of the congregation, and on Good Friday he walked in the procession of the cross.

This new-style pope first announced the council on January 25, 1959, and officially convoked it on December 25, 1961, with the hope that it would be a demonstration of the vitality of the Church, a means of rebuilding Christian unity, and a catalyst for world peace. In his address at the council's solemn opening on October 11, 1962, the pope revealed again his fundamental spirit of hope and even optimism about the future. He complained openly about some of his advisers who "though burning with zeal, are not endowed with much sense of discretion or measure. In these modern times they can see nothing but prevarication and ruin." He called them "prophets of gloom, who are always forecasting disaster, as though the end of the world were at hand." On the contrary, "Divine Providence is leading us to a new order of human relations. . . ."

To carry out its purposes, the council would have to remain faithful to the "sacred patrimony of truth received from the Fathers. But at the same time she must ever look to the present, to the new conditions and new forms of life introduced into the modern world which have opened new avenues to the Catholic apostolate." But a council was unnecessary at this time, the pope insisted, if the preservation of doctrine were to be its principal aim. "The substance of the ancient doctrine. . .is one thing, and the way in which it is presented is another." This is not the time for negativism. The Church counteracts errors by "demonstrating the validity of her teaching rather than by condemnations." The council and the Church in council are like Peter who said to the beggar, "Silver and gold I have none; but what I have, that I give you. In the name of Jesus Christ of Nazareth, arise and walk" (Acts of the Apostles 3:6).

Thus, the Church of Vatican II will spread everywhere the fullness of Christian charity, "than which nothing is more effective in eradicating the seeds of discord, nothing more efficacious in promoting concord, just peace and the brotherly unity of all." This means that the council must work for the unity of the whole Christian family and for the unity of the whole human family. "The council now beginning rises in the Church like daybreak, a forerunner of most splendid light. It is now only dawn."

THE COUNCIL DOCUMENTS IN GENERAL

There are sixteen council documents in all. Two were produced in the second session (1963): *The Constitution on the Sacred Liturgy* and the *Decree on the Instruments of Social Communication.* Three were produced in the third session (1964): the *Dogmatic Constitution on the Church (Lumen gentium),* the *Decree on Ecumenism,* and the *Decree on Eastern Catholic Churches.* Eleven were produced in the fourth and final session (1965): the *Decree on the Bishops' Pastoral Office in the Church,* the *Decree on Priestly Formation,* the *Decree on the Appropriate Renewal of the Religious Life,* the *Declaration on the Relationship of the Church to Non-*

Christian Religions, the *Declaration on Christian Education,* the *Dogmatic Constitution on Divine Revelation,* the *Decree on the Apostolate of the Laity,* the *Pastoral Constitution on the Church in the Modern World* (*Gaudium et spes*), the *Decree on the Ministry and Life of Priests,* the *Decree on the Church's Missionary Activity,* and the *Declaration on Religious Freedom.*

Their Authority

These documents are unequal in juridical standing, in content, and in effect. They vary in *juridical standing* in that the dogmatic constitutions are more "authoritative" than decrees and declarations. *Constitutions* touch substantively upon doctrinal matters which pertain to the very essence, or "constitution," of the Church. *Decrees* and *declarations* are directed at practical questions or specific pastoral concerns. As such, they presuppose the doctrine and the theology of the constitutions. Two of the four constitutions (on the Church and on revelation) are called "dogmatic" in that they do indeed touch upon matters which are themselves part of the dogmatic content of Christian faith. One of the constitutions is called "pastoral"—a designation unprecedented in the history of the Church—in that it touches upon the fundamental, "constitutive" relationship of the Church to the world at large. And a fourth constitution, on the sacred liturgy, has no special designation at all. Liturgy is part of the Church's constitutive nature, but it is not part of the dogmatic content of its faith. Rather it is dogma in practice (*Lex orandi, lex credendi* again).

These documents vary also in *content.* Some are substantive—e.g., the *Dogmatic Constitution on the Church,* and others are remarkably thin—e.g., the *Declaration on Christian Education.* Some reflect the progressive theological currents of the preconciliar period—e.g., the *Decree on Ecumenism,* and others reflect the more traditional currents—e.g., the *Decree on the Instruments of Social Communication.*

These documents vary, finally, in their *effect* upon the Church. How a teaching is "received" by the Church is one of the important criteria by which we judge the teaching's authority. It is not enough, in other words, that a document should have issued forth from an ecumenical council. Just as there is a hierarchy of sacraments (Eucharist being the most important, according to the Council of Trent) and a hierarchy even of biblical books (the Epistle to the Romans, for example, is certainly more important than the Epistle to Philemon), so there is a hierarchy of official pronouncements.

Theologians judge the *degree* of any official pronouncement's authority, therefore, by a variety of standards: (1) *What is the nature of the document?* Is it an encyclical? An address to a group of pilgrims to Rome? A disciplinary decree from a Vatican congregation? A declaration of an ecumenical council? A dogmatic constitution of an ecumenical council? (2) *What is the source of the pronouncement?* A pope? An ecumenical council? A synod of bishops? (3) *How representative was the process by which the document was written?* Were all those with competence and a legitimate interest in the question under discussion actually consulted, and did they effectively participate in the formulation of the pronouncement? (4) *Do the concepts and language of the final formulation reflect the current state of the discussion on the topic?* Are the terms of the current debate and the rejected positions clearly understood? (5) *How is the pronouncement received by those with competence on the topic,* either by reason of their academic and scientific qualifications or by reason of their experiential knowledge of the subject? Does the pronouncement, in other words, have any significant impact on the life of the Church?

It is this fifth criterion that is most pertinent to our evaluation here. According to this norm of *reception*, the following seven documents of Vatican II have emerged in this post-conciliar period as the most important: the *Dogmatic Constitution on the Church (Lumen gentium),* the *Pastoral Constitution on the Church in the Modern World (Gaudium et spes),* the *Decree on Ecumenism,* the *Constitution on the Sacred Liturgy,* the *Dogmatic Constitution on Divine Revelation,* the *Declaration on Religious Freedom,* and the *Declaration on the Relationship of the Church to Non-Christian Religions.* In other words, most of the significant changes in thought and practice since Vatican II are traceable to the teachings and orientations of these seven documents rather than to the other nine.

Their Relationship to the Church

All of the documents are concerned, in one way or another, with the mystery of the Church:

The Church in General: Nature and Place in History
Dogmatic Constitution on the Church

The Inner Life of the Church
Proclamation and Teaching
Dogmatic Constitution on Divine Revelation
Declaration on Christian Education
Worship
Constitution on the Sacred Liturgy
Ministries and Forms of Christian Existence
Decree on the Ministry and Life of Priests
Decree on Priestly Formation
Decree on the Bishops' Pastoral Office
Decree on the Appropriate Renewal of Religious Life
Interrelationships among Churches
Decree on Ecumenism
Decree on Eastern Catholic Churches

The Church and the World Beyond the Church
Other Religions
Declaration on Non-Christian Religions
The World at Large
Pastoral Constitution on the Church in the Modern World
Decree on the Church's Missionary Activity
Declaration on Religious Freedom
Decree on the Instruments of Social Communication

THE COUNCIL DOCUMENTS IN PARTICULAR
The Major Documents

Dogmatic Constitution on the Church

The first draft of this document, prepared by the council's Theological Commission in 1962, resembled the standard textbook treatments of the mystery of the Church which were in general use in seminaries, colleges, and universities throughout most of the twentieth century. The successive drafts (there were four in all) disclose the extraordinary development which occurred in the council's self-understanding. Whereas at the beginning the emphasis was on the institutional, hierarchical, and juridical aspects of the Church, with special importance assigned to the papal office, the finally approved and promulgated constitution speaks of the Church as the People of God and of its authority as collegial in nature and exercise.

According to *Lumen gentium*, the Church is a *mystery* before all else, i.e., "a reality imbued with the hidden presence of God" (Pope Paul VI). It is, to use an almost identical theological term, a *sacrament*, "a visible sign of an invisible grace" (Augustine). "By its relationship with Christ, the Church is a kind of sacrament of intimate union with God, and of the unity of all humankind, that is, it is a sign and an instrument of such union and unity" (n. 1). The Church is the visible embodiment of the triune God. It is called by the Father (n. 2) to union with and in Christ (n. 3) through the power of the Holy Spirit (n. 4). It is inaugurated by Jesus' preaching of the Kingdom of God, which he also personified and brought into being by his good works. The Church, too, is called to proclaim, embody, and serve the coming Kingdom of God (n. 5). As such, the Church is the pilgrim People of God in movement through history, sharing in Christ's threefold mission as Prophet, Priest, and King (chapter II).

Not until the council had described the Church as People of God did it direct its attention to the Church's hierarchical structure. An earlier draft of the constitution had the chapter on the hierarchy before the chapter on the People of God. In one of the most crucial arguments waged during the entire council, the point was urged upon the Fathers that the chapters should be reversed.

To speak of the Church's hierarchy before speaking of the Church as People of God would simply carry forward the textbook tradition that the Church is, first and foremost, a hierarchical institution to which people belong for the sake of certain spiritual benefits. The argument prevailed, and the chapters were reversed. The Church is presented in *Lumen gentium* as the whole People of God (chapter II), which happens to have a certain hierarchical structure to help the People of God fulfill its mission in history (chapter III).

The third chapter on the hierarchical structure of the Church, however, is important not only for the position it finally occupies in the dogmatic constitution but also for its content. The governance of the Church is no longer portrayed in purely monarchical terms, as it was in the theology textbooks and in the first draft of *Lumen gentium* itself. Authority is given not just to Peter and his successors but to the whole college of the Apostles and to those who succeed to the apostolic commission: "Together with its head, the Roman Pontiff, and never without its head, the episcopal order is the subject of supreme and full power over the universal Church" (n. 22). This collegial union is especially apparent in an ecumenical council, but it is also manifested "in the mutual relations of the individual bishops with particular churches and with the universal Church. . . . In and from such individual churches there comes into being the one and only Catholic Church. For this reason each individual bishop represents his own church, but all of them together in union with the Pope represent the entire Church joined in the bond of peace, love, and unity" (n. 23). The Church, therefore, exists in each legitimate local congregation, as was the case in the New Testament, and also in the communion of all these local congregations (n. 26). The Church is at once local and universal.

The Church is also at once lay, religious, and clerical. The Church is the whole People of God, not just the hierarchy. "Everything which has been said so far concerning the People of God applies equally to the laity, religious, and clergy" (n. 30). Pastors were not intended by Christ to shoulder the whole mission themselves. On the contrary, their task is one of coordination of the gifts, charisms, and ministries which in fact exist within a given local church, to see to it that "all according to their proper roles may cooperate in this common undertaking with one heart" (n. 30). The laity, therefore, do not simply participate in the mission or the ministry of the hierarchy: "The lay apostolate, however, is a participation in the saving mission of the Church itself. Through their baptism and confirmation, all are commissioned to that apostolate by the Lord himself" (n. 33). And because the laity are as much a part of the Church as religious and clergy, and because the Church is called to holiness in order to be a credible sign of Christ to the world, everyone in the Church—laity, religious, and clergy alike—is called to holiness (chapter V). But this is always an imperfect realization. The Church is still on pilgrimage. "She herself dwells among creatures who groan and travail in pain until now and await the revelation of the sons of God" (n. 48). In the meantime, Mary serves as "a model of the Church in the matter of faith, charity, and perfect union with Christ" (n. 63). She is "a sign of sure hope and solace for the pilgrim People of God" (n. 68).

Pastoral Constitution on the Church in the Modern World

As we pointed out in chapter 3 of this book, the impetus for this unprecedented "pastoral" constitution came from Pope John XXIII and Cardinal Leo-Jozef Suenens of Belgium. With the prior knowledge and approval of the pope, Cardinal Suenens rose at the end of the first session (December 4, 1962) and urged the council to do more than examine the mystery of the Church in itself (*ad intra*). The council must also attend to the Church's relationship with the world at large (*ad extra*). The document (*Gaudium et spes (Joy and Hope)* is the principal result of that important intervention. (It was Pope John Paul II, then a bishop delegate at the council, who suggested the adjective "pastoral" for this unusual constitution.)

The pastoral constitution recapitulates the Church's social teachings as they had developed from Pope Leo XIII's encyclical *Rerum Novarum* (1891), through Pope Pius XI's *Quadragesimo Anno* (1931), and Pope John XXIII's *Mater et Magistra* (1961) and *Pacem in Terris* (1963). But it correlates this teaching with intellectual and scientific developments outside the Church as well: "...the Church has always had the duty of scrutinizing the signs of the times and of interpreting them in the light of the gospel" (n. 4). The ecclesiological theme is sounded at the outset: The Church exists not alongside the world but within the world, and not in domination over the world but as its servant. "Inspired by no earthly ambition, the Church seeks but a solitary goal: to carry forward the work of Christ himself under the lead of the befriending Spirit. And Christ entered this world to give witness to the truth, to rescue and not to sit in judgment, to serve and not to be served" (n. 3). (The reader is referred again to chapters 3 and 6 of this book, where some attention was already devoted to this conciliar document.)

Even though the Church will not fully attain its saving and eschatological purpose except in the age to come, the Church is called even now "to form the family of God's children during the present history of the human race..." (n. 40). The Church is "at once a visible assembly and a spiritual community (and) goes forward together with humanity and experiences the same earthly lot which the world does" (n. 40). In trying to imbue the world and its history with deeper meaning and importance, "...the Church believes it can contribute greatly toward making the family of humankind and its history more human" (n. 40). On the other hand, the Church is not a political party. It has "no proper mission in the political, economic, or social order" (n. 42). Nor is the Church bound to any "particular form of human culture, nor to any political, economic, or social system" (n. 42).

The pastoral constitution nevertheless recognizes and underlines the connection between religious faith and temporal activities. It characterizes the split between the two realms as "among the more serious errors of our age.... Therefore, let there be no false opposition between professional and social activities on the one part, and religious life on the other. The Christian who neglects his temporal duties neglects his duties toward his neighbor and even God, and jeopardizes his eternal salvation" (n. 43). The document acknowledges that this dichotomy between faith and action can occur within the Church as well as outside it, and the council calls upon Christians to close the gap between message and performance wherever it exists. In all, ". . .the Church has a single intention: that God's kingdom may come, and that the salvation of the whole human race may come to pass" (n. 45). The Church is in fact the universal sacrament of salvation. It is the sign of that fellowship "which allows honest dialogue and invigorates it" (n. 92). This means that life inside the Church must be governed always by the principle "Let there be unity in what is necessary, freedom in what is unsettled, and charity in any case" (n. 92). Insofar as the Church offers a credible witness to the truth, it will arouse the world to a "lively hope" in the coming of the Kingdom of God (n. 93).

Decree on Ecumenism

The quest for Christian unity is a missionary responsibility, for the Church is called to be a sacrament of Christ and of the unity of the triune God who is present within the Church (n. 2). The decree is remarkable for a variety of reasons: It describes the ecumenical movement as one of seeking the *restoration* of Christian unity rather than as a *return* of non-Catholics to the already-existing unity of the Catholic Church; it acknowledges the ecclesial reality of other Christian communities, which share the same Sacred Scriptures, the same life of grace, the same faith, hope, and charity, the same gifts of the Holy Spirit, the same Baptism, and many other common elements which constitute the Church; and it admits, finally, that both sides were to blame for the divisions that ruptured the Church at the time of the Reformation (nn. 3,20-23).

The immediate path to unity is through reform and renewal (n. 6). "There can be no ecumenism worthy of the name without a change of heart" (n. 7). This change of heart (which the council calls "spiritual ecumenism") may express itself at times even in joint celebration of the Eucharist. Although it is not simply a means of unity to be employed indiscriminately, eucharistic sharing may at times be necessary for the gaining of the grace of unity (n. 8). In the meantime, ecumenism also requires theological collaboration, dialogue, and joint study, as well as cooperation in social action (nn. 9-12).

Constitution on the Sacred Liturgy

This document is based on the ecclesiological assumption that the liturgy is "the outstanding means by which the faithful can express in their lives, and manifest to others, the mystery of Christ and the real nature of the true Church" (n. 2). It underscores the Church's mission to be a sign, or sacrament, of Christ and of God's presence in and for the world. The Church is called to proclaim the Gospel not only in word but also in ritual: in the sacraments and in the Eucharist particularly (n. 6). Through the liturgy the Church continues Christ's worship of the Father, which Christ achieved principally by the paschal mystery of his passion, resurrection, and exaltation to the right hand of God (n. 5). Through our participation in that same worship, we have a foretaste of the heavenly liturgy that is to come (n. 8). Although the liturgy does not exhaust the entire activity of the Church (n. 9), it can be described as "the summit toward which the activity of the Church is directed; at the same time it is the source from which all her power flows" (n. 10).

Because the Church is the whole People of God, everyone must be encouraged to participate actively in the celebration of the Eucharist and the other sacraments (nn. 26, 28, 29, 31, 47-55). But this is impossible if the liturgy, which is a world of signs and symbols, is not intelligible to those who participate in it (n. 21). And so this principle must govern the reform and renewal of the Church's liturgical life: If the sign is to cause the grace it signifies (as the Council of Trent declared), then the sign must be understandable. Otherwise it is not a sign at all, and, if not a sign, it cannot cause the grace for which it exists. That is why the language of the Eucharist and the other sacraments is once again the language of the people, and that is why the rites or ceremonies have been restructured and simplified since Vatican II. The latter process has been guided by the principles that there should be "legitimate variations and adaptations to different groups" and that there be no "rigid uniformity in matters which do not involve the faith or the good of the whole community" (nn. 37-38).

Dogmatic Constitution on Divine Revelation

The Church is commissioned to preach the Gospel to the whole of creation. What the Church is called upon to proclaim today it draws from Sacred Scripture and from the tradition "which comes from the apostles. . . with the help of the Holy Spirit. For there is a growth in the understanding of the realities and the words which have been handed down. . . . the Church constantly moves forward toward the fullness of divine truth until the words of God reach their complete fulfillment. . ." (n. 8). The teaching office of the Church interprets the word of God as it is communicated in Scripture and in the successive interpretations of the Scriptures (tradition). "This teaching office is not above the word of God, but serves it. . . . It is clear, therefore, that sacred tradition, sacred Scripture, and the teaching authority of the Church. . . are so linked and joined together that one cannot stand without the others, and that all together and each in its own way under the action of the one Holy Spirit contribute effectively to the salvation of souls" (n. 10).

Declaration on Religious Freedom

This document was at first to be a chapter of the *Decree on Ecumenism*, and later an Appendix of that same decree. Finally, it was given independent status as a declaration of the council. Although it is hardly a milestone in the history of the world (the principle of religious liberty had long since been recognized and defended by others inside and outside the Church), the declaration was a major event in the history of the Catholic Church and of the Second Vatican Council. It was by far the most controversial document produced by the council, because it raised in a special way the underlying question of *doctrinal development*. In light of so many seemingly unequivocal condemnations of the principle of religious freedom in earlier papal documents, how could the Church now turn around and endorse the principle? The distance between Pope Pius IX's *Syllabus of Errors* (1864) and Vatican II's *Declaration on Religious Freedom* (1965) is more than chronological. They inhabit two different theological universes.

This declaration ends the so-called double standard by which the Church demands freedom for itself when in a minority position but refuses to grant freedom to other religions when they are in the minority. The council declares as a matter of principle that the dignity of the human person and the freedom of the act of faith demand that everyone should be immune from coercion of every kind, private or public, in matters pertaining to the profession of a particular religious faith (n. 2). No one can be compelled to accept the Christian faith, nor can anyone be penalized in any way for not being a Christian (n. 9). The supreme model is Jesus himself and, after him, the example of the early Church (n. 11).

Declaration on the Relationship of the Church to Non-Christian Religions

This document, too, was originally planned as a chapter in the *Decree on Ecumenism*. It was also to be concerned principally with the Jews. Its vision, however, is considerably broader than that. It acknowledges, first of all, that the whole human community comes from the creative hand of the one God, and that variations in religious faith and expression are a reflection of the diversity that characterizes humankind itself. "The Catholic Church rejects nothing which is true and holy in these religions. . . . [They] often reflect a ray of that Truth which enlightens all persons" (n. 2). And so the Church encourages dialogue and collaboration with the followers of other religions in order to promote common spiritual and moral values.

The declaration recounts the many basic elements the Church has in common with the Jews. Since there is such a close union between Christians and Jews, we must pursue the way of mutual understanding and respect. Specifically, we must eschew the notion that Jews can be blamed as a race for the death of Jesus. Furthermore, the Jews are not repudiated or accursed by God (n. 4). Every form of persecution is to be condemned, and so, too, every kind of discrimination based on race, color, condition of life, or religion (n. 5).

The Minor Documents

Decree on the Church's Missionary Activity

This document presupposes the dogmatic constitution *Lumen gentium* and the pastoral constitution *Gaudium et spes*. It differs from both of them in that they speak of the "mission" of the Church in its total sense of preaching the Gospel in word, sacrament, witness, and service to the whole human community, Christians and non-Christians alike, whereas the *Decree on the Church's Missionary Activity* is concerned with one important aspect of that total mission, namely, "evangelization and the planting of the Church among those peoples and groups where it has not yet taken root" (n. 6). The distinction is between the "mission of the Church" and "the missions."

The decree does not restrict its vision to the de-Christianized West. The Gospel is to penetrate Asia, Africa, and Oceania as well. But wherever missionaries go, they are not to impose an alien cultural reality from outside. They are to recognize and preserve "whatever truth and grace are to be found among the nations, as a sort of secret presence of God. . . . And so, whatever good is found to be sown in the hearts and minds of men and women, or in the rites and cultures peculiar to various peoples, is not lost" (n. 9). This pastoral principle is rooted in the theological principle of the incarnation (n. 10). Finally, "the whole Church is missionary, and the work of evangelization is a basic duty of the People of God. . ." (n. 35).

Decree on the Apostolate of the Laity

This document also presupposes what is contained in *Lumen gentium* and *Gaudium et spes*. Moreover, its subject matter is treated in various other pronouncements of the council—e.g., the aforementioned *Decree on the Church's Missionary Activity*. This decree makes clear, as the *Dogmatic Constitution on the Church (Lumen gentium)* also made clear, that the laity are full members of the People of God and, as such, share directly in the mission of the Church, not simply by leave of the hierarchy but "from their union with Christ their Head. Incorporated into Christ's Mystical

Body through baptism and strengthened by the power of the Holy Spirit through confirmation, they are assigned to the apostolate by the Lord himself" (n. 3). This apostolate is located principally, but not exclusively, in the temporal order: the world of family, culture, economic affairs, the arts and professions, political institutions, and so forth (n. 6).

Decree on Eastern Catholic Churches

This decree is really a complement to the *Decree on Ecumenism*. It relates to the six main Eastern Catholic rites (i.e., to those Eastern churches in union with Rome as distinguished from those Eastern Orthodox churches which are still separate from Rome ever since the East-West Schism at the turn of the thirteenth century): Chaldean, Syrian, Maronite, Coptic, Armenian, and Byzantine. They are also known as "Uniate" churches. They have been sources of much friction between Rome and the Orthodox world because the "Uniate" churches were originally conceived as "substitutes" for, rather than as "bridges" to, the Orthodox East, and as such have always been resented by the latter.

Although the decree proclaims the equality of the Eastern and Western traditions of Christianity (n. 3) as well as the importance of preserving the spiritual heritage of the Eastern churches (n. 5), the decree itself is still very much a Latin text about the Eastern tradition (nn. 7-23). It clearly manifests, however, an ardent desire for reconciliation with the separated churches of the East and opens the door from Rome's side to common eucharistic sharing (nn. 24-29).

Decree on the Bishops' Pastoral Office in the Church

In its earlier stages this document reflected the pre-conciliar ecclesiology which tended to make bishops entirely subordinate to the pope and the Curia and to make the office of bishop more a jurisdictional than a sacramental reality. The finally approved decree, however, reflects the teaching of *Lumen gentium* on collegiality. Thus, bishops exercise their episcopal office "received through episcopal consecration" (n. 3). They exercise that office at three levels: over their own diocese, or "particular church," in collaboration with other bishops on a regional or national level (episcopal conferences), and as a worldwide body in union with the pope (college of bishops). Bishops, therefore, are not simply delegates or vicars of the pope in a diocese, as an exceedingly hierarchical model of the Church once proposed. They are "the proper, ordinary, and immediate pastors" of their own dioceses (n. 11). That pastoral office, which includes preaching the Gospel, presiding at worship, and ministering to those in need, must always be exercised in the mode of a servant (n. 16). The bishop must carry out his episcopal, or supervisory, duties in a manner that encourages communication and integration among the various apostolates (n. 17). Indeed, the decree contains a kind of job description and list of qualifications for the office of bishop (nn. 11-21).

Decree on the Ministry and Life of Priests

This decree emerged as a separate document because many bishops at the council thought there was too little said about priests in the *Dogmatic Constitution on the Church*. The essence of the decree's teaching follows: "Established in the priestly order by ordination, all priests are united among themselves in an intimate sacramental brotherhood. In a special way they form one presbytery in a diocese to whose service they are committed under their own bishop." Whether they are in parish work, teaching, or some other special activity, priests are "united in the single goal of building up Christ's Body" (n. 8). This work includes the proclamation of the Gospel, the celebration of the Eucharist and other sacraments, governance of a community, and ministering to those in need (nn. 4-6).

Decree on Priestly Formation

For four centuries the training of Catholic priests had been shaped by the directives of the Council of Trent, which was itself originally a reform council. Prior to Trent, priests were ordained with little or no theological or spiritual formation. But eventually the reforms of Trent developed into rigid rules, and seminaries tended to become increasingly isolated from the world around them. The essence of the present-day reform, encouraged in such large measure by Vatican II, is the impulse to combine the theological and the spiritual with the pastoral, and thereby to allow seminary training to be adapted to the particular social and cultural circumstances in which priestly service will be rendered. Such a reform required some measure of decentralization of authority, so that national churches could also have a direct hand in determining what is required for effective priestly service. Therefore, the decree proposes the principle of adaptation (n. 1) and insists on a close connection of seminary formation with pastoral realities (n. 4). Meanwhile, theological studies should be biblical, ecumenical, historical, and personally formative (nn. 16-17). Special attention must be given to the relationship between theory and practice (n. 21). Continuing education programs for the clergy are also of great importance (n. 22).

Decree on the Appropriate Renewal of the Religious Life

"Religious life" refers to a corporate form of Christian existence in which members of the Church gather together in common pursuit of the evangelical counsels: poverty, chastity, and obedience (see Matthew 19:10-12, 21). We have already referred to the origins and growth of religious life in the preceding chapter. Renewal of such a life depends on two principles: "(1) a continuous return to the sources of all Christian life and to the original inspiration behind a given community and (2) an adjustment of the community to the changed conditions of the times" (n. 2). Such communities must always see themselves as part of the Church and as participants in its mission, whatever their composition, structure, and apostolate. The generally traditional tone and spirit of the decree have been recognized and embraced by an American-based organization of religious men and women devoted to the preservation of traditional forms of religious life, e.g., traditional religious clothing (habits), traditional places of residence (convents and other religious houses), and traditional modes of exercising authority (more directive than collegial or participative). That organization, *Consortium Perfectae Caritatis*, took for its name the Latin title of this decree.

Declaration on Christian Education

This declaration is different from most of the other council documents in that it deals only with a few fundamental principles and leaves further development to the postconciliar process, particularly in the various conferences of bishops. The focus is on the education of the young as it occurs in the home, the school, and the church. Emphasis is placed most strongly on schooling. Insofar as the declaration does reflect something of the spirit of the council itself, it insists that education must be broadly humane, in keeping with advances in all of the sciences, and with a concern for nurturing personal maturity and social responsibility (nn. 1-2).

Decree on the Instruments of Social Communication

This decree was one of the first two documents approved by Vatican II, on December 4, 1963, at the end of the first session. That may explain why it is so clearly out of touch with the theological and pastoral character of the council as a whole. It is indeed, alongside the aforementioned *Declaration on Christian Education*, one of the two weakest documents produced by Vatican II. The language employed in the opening paragraphs is typical of the spirit which informs the decree: "As a Mother, the Church welcomes and watches such inventions with special concern. . . . Such would be the press, the cinema, radio, television, and similar media, which can be properly classified as instruments of social communication" (n. 1). "Mother Church. . . is also aware that men can employ these gifts against the mind of the divine Benefactor, and abuse them to their own undoing. In fact the Church grieves with a motherly sorrow at the damage far too often inflicted on society by the perverse use of these media" (n. 2).

THE ECCLESIOLOGY OF VATICAN II

The council's distinctive understanding of the nature and mission of the Church is a reflection and embodiment of the following theological and pastoral principles:

1. *The Church is, first and foremost, a mystery or sacrament*, i.e., "a reality imbued with the hidden presence of God" (Pope Paul VI). This principle, articulated in the first chapter of *Lumen gentium*, supplants the pre-Vatican II emphasis on the Church as *means* of salvation.

2 *The Church is the whole People of God.* This principle, expressed in the second chapter of *Lumen gentium*, replaced the pre-Vatican II emphasis on the Church as hierarchical institution, which tended to make the study of the Church more akin to "hierarchology" than to "ecclesiology."

3. *The whole People of God—laity, religious, and clergy alike—is called to participate in the mission of Christ as Prophet, Priest, and King.* This principle, presented in the fourth chapter of *Lumen gentium* (especially nn. 30,33) and reaffirmed in the *Decree on the Apostolate of the Laity*, replaces the pre-Vatican II notion of "Catholic Action," wherein the laity participates only in the mission of the hierarchy.

4. *The mission of the People of God includes service (diakonia) to human needs in the social, political, and economic orders as well as the preaching of the Word and the celebration of the sacraments.* This principle is especially set forth in *Gaudium et spes* and is reiterated in more abbreviated form in such documents as the *Decree on the Apostolate of the Laity*, the *Decree on Ecumenism*, the *Decree on Bishops' Pastoral Office in the Church*, the *Decree on the Ministry and Life of Priests*, and the *Decree on the Church's Missionary Activity*. The principle supplants the pre-Vatican II notion of "pre-evangelization," wherein such service is, or may be, a necessary preparation for the preaching of the Gospel (evangelization) but is not itself essential to the Church's mission in the same way as the preaching or the celebration of the sacraments.

5. *This Church*, so composed and with such a mission, *is realized and expressed at the local as well as the universal level. The Church is indeed a communion of churches* (= collegiality). This principle is articulated especially in *Lumen gentium* (n. 26), and is also expressed in the *Decree on the Bishops' Pastoral Office in the Church*, the *Decree on the Church's Missionary Activity*, the

Decree on Eastern Catholic Churches, and the *Decree on the Ministry and Life of Priests*. The principle supplants the common pre-Vatican II notion that the Church is, for all practical purposes, always understood as the Church universal, centralized in the Vatican under the supreme authority of the pope, with each diocese considered only as an administrative division of the Church universal, and each parish, in turn, an administrative subdivision of the diocese.

6. *This Church*, at once local and universal, *embraces more than the Catholic Church. It is the whole Body of Christ: Catholics, Orthodox, Anglicans, and Protestants alike.* This principle is to be found in the *Decree of Ecumenism* and in the *Dogmatic Constitution on the Church (Lumen gentium).* It sets aside the pre-Vatican II concept that the Roman Catholic Church alone is the one, true Church, and that the other Christian communities (never called "churches" before Vatican II) are somehow "related" to the Church but are not real members of it. This is not to say, however, that all churches are equal.

7. *The mission of the whole Church is* (a) *one of proclamation of the Gospel that is always subordinate to the Word of God*; (b) *one of celebration of the sacraments in a way that always fully engages the intelligent participation of the worshiping community or individuals*; (c) *one of witnessing to the Gospel through a life-style that is marked by humility, compassion, respect for human rights, etc*; *and* (d) *one of service to those in need, both inside and outside the Church.* This multiple principle is grounded (a) in the *Dogmatic Constitution on Divine Revelation*; (b) in the *Constitution on the Sacred Liturgy*; (c) in the *Pastoral Constitution on the Church in the Modern World*, the fifth chapter of the *Dogmatic Constitution on the Church* ("The Call of the Whole Church to Holiness"), the *Decree on the Bishops' Pastoral Office in the Church*, the *Decree on the Ministry and Life of Priests*, the *Decree on the Church's Missionary Activity*, and the *Decree on the Appropriate Renewal of the Religious Life*; and (d) for the service aspect of mission, in the same documents. This multiple principle expands upon a narrower view of mission in pre-Vatican II ecclesiology, namely, one that tended to restrict the mission to the preaching of the Word and the celebration of the sacraments, and one which perhaps paid too

little attention to the missionary responsibility of corporate witnessing to the Gospel. In other words, it is an essential part of the
Church's mission to practice what it preaches.

8. *All authority in the Church is to be exercised as a service
and in a collegial mode.* The principle is particularly proposed in
Lumen gentium (chapter III) and is reaffirmed in such other documents as the decrees on bishops, priests, and religious life. The
principle is intended to transform the exercise of authority from
one of domination and unilateral decision-making, as prevailed in
the pre-Vatican II period.

9. *Religious truth is to be found outside the Body of Christ
and should be respected wherever it is discovered. In no instance is
anyone to be coerced to embrace either the Christian or the Catholic
faith.* This dual principle is set forth in the *Declaration on the
Relationship of the Church to Non-Christian Religions* and in the
Declaration on Religious Freedom. It replaces a too-exclusive
understanding of revelation as "Christian revelation," as well as
the formula "Error has no rights."

10. *The nature and mission of the Church are always to be
understood in relationship and in subordination to the Kingdom of
God.* This principle is expressed in article 5 of *Lumen gentium*
and again in article 45 of *Gaudium et spes.* It replaces what was
perhaps the most serious pre-Vatican II ecclesiological misunderstanding, namely, that the Church is identical with the Kingdom
of God. If it is, then it is beyond all need for institutional reform,
and its mission is to bring everyone inside lest salvation elude
them.

SUMMARY

1. The Second Vatican Council was the largest and most representative council in the Church's history. It was perhaps the Church's first
really *ecumenical* council in that its bishops were drawn from every
major continent and culture. With this council, the Church began its
movement from a Church of cultural confinement to a geniune world
Church.

2. Twentieth-century *ecclesiology before Vatican II* was of two
kinds: *textbook* ecclesiology, which stressed the institutional, juridical,

and hierarchical aspects of the Church (Salaverri), and *progressive* ecclesiology, which understood the Church as the whole People of God,
including laity and other Christians (Congar). Since this Church is not
yet the Kingdom of God, it is always in need of renewal and reform
(Congar, Küng). It does not exist primarily to grow and multiply but to
be a credible and effective sign or sacrament of Christ's and God's
presence in the world (Rahner, Schillebeeckx, de Lubac). The state owes
the Church no special privileges, nor can the Church use the state to
compel Catholic faith (Murray).

3.   The single most influential personality associated with the
event of Vatican II was *Pope John XXIII*. He called and opened the
council and set its tone by the style he himself adopted as pope, namely,
that of a servant-shepherd. The council, he insisted, was not for condemnations but for moving the Church into the future for the sake of its own
vitality, Christian unity, and world peace.

4.   There were *sixteen council documents* of varying authority,
content, and effects. The most authoritative in the *juridical sense* were
the four *constitutions*: on the Church, on the Church in the modern
world, on revelation, and on the sacred liturgy. The most authoritative
in terms of their *reception* in and by the Church have been the four
constitutions, plus the *Decree on Ecumenism*, the *Declaration on Religious Freedom*, and the *Declaration on the Relationship of the Church to
Non-Christian Religions*.

5.   The major documents in summary form are:

a.   *Dogmatic Constitution on the Church*: The Church is a mystery, or sacrament, the whole People of God, in whose service the
hierarchy is placed. The authority of pope and bishops is to be
exercised as a service and in a collegial mode. Bishops are not
simply the vicars of the pope, and the laity participate fully and
directly in the Church's mission.

b.   *Pastoral Constitution on the Church in the Modern World*:
The Church must read the signs of the times and interpret them in
the light of the Gospel. The Church does not exist alongside or
apart from the world; the Church is part of the world, and its
mission is to serve the whole human family in order to make the
human race's history more human.

c.   *Decree on Ecumenism*: Christian unity is a matter of restoration, not of a return to Rome; other Christian communities are
churches within the Body of Christ; and both sides were to blame
for the divisions of the Church.

d. *Constitution on the Sacred Liturgy*: The Church proclaims the Gospel not only in word but also in sacrament, or by sacred signs. Since the whole People of God is involved in this worship, the signs must be intelligible.

e. *Dogmatic Constitution on Divine Revelation*: The Word of God is communicated through Sacred Scripture, sacred tradition, and the teaching authority of the Church, all linked together and directed by the Holy Spirit. The sacred realities are always open in principle to a growth in understanding.

f. *Declaration on Religious Freedom*: No one is to be forced in any way to embrace the Christian or the Catholic faith. This principle is rooted in human dignity and the freedom of the act of faith.

g. *Declaration on the Relationship of the Church to Non-Christian Religions*: God speaks also through other religions, so we should engage in dialogue and other collaborative efforts with them. The Jews have a special relationship to the Church. They cannot be blamed as a people for the death of Jesus.

6. The minor documents in summary form are:

a. *Decree on the Church's Missionary Activity*: The Gospel is to be preached also and always to non-Christians, but not as a culturally alien reality. Evangelization is an obligation for every member of the Church.

b. *Decree on the Apostolate of the Laity*: The laity participates in the mission of the Church, but especially in the temporal order.

c. *Decree on Eastern Catholic Churches*: The Eastern Catholic, or "Uniate," churches can be a bridge to the Orthodox East. The integrity of Eastern traditions of liturgy, spirituality, and discipline is to be restored.

d. *Decree on the Bishops' Pastoral Office in the Church*: Bishops are the pastors of their own local churches, and beyond that collaborate with other bishops through episcopal conferences and with the pope and all other bishops through the episcopal college. Authority is always for service.

e. *Decree on the Ministry and Life of Priests*: Priests are members of a presbytery in union with a bishop, and with him serve the building up of Christ's body.

f. *Decree on Priestly Formation*: There must be a closer connection between seminary training and the pastoral situation.

g.   *Decree on the Appropriate Renewal of the Religious Life*: The renewal of religious life (a life lived according to the evangelical counsels of poverty, chastity, and obedience) must be based on the Gospel, the original purposes of the community, and the changed conditions of the times.

h.   *Declaration on Christian Education*: Education must be broadly humane and up-to-date, with a concern for personal maturity and social responsibility.

i.   *Decree on the Instruments of Social Communication*: The Church must be vigilant toward the media because of the ever-present danger of their abuse, but must also use the media where opportune.

7.   The *distinctive ecclesiology* of Vatican II is based on the following principles:

a.   The Church is a mystery, or sacrament, and not primarily a means of salvation.

b.   The Church is the whole People of God, not just the hierarchy.

c.   The whole People of God participates in the mission of Christ, and not just in the mission of the hierarchy.

d.   The mission of the Church includes service to those in need, and not just the preaching of the Gospel or the celebration of the sacraments.

e.   The Church is truly present at the local level as well as at the universal level. A diocese or parish is not just an administrative division of the Church universal.

f.   The Church includes Orthodox, Anglicans, and Protestants, as well as Catholics.

g.   The mission of the Church includes proclamation of the Word, celebration of the sacraments, witnessing to the Gospel individually and institutionally, and providing service to those in need.

h.   All authority is for service, not domination.

i.   Religious truth is to be found outside the Church as well. No one is to be coerced to embrace the Christian or the Catholic faith.

j.   The Church is always for the sake of the Kingdom of God and is not itself the Kingdom.

SUGGESTED READINGS

Abbott, Walter, and Gallagher, Joseph, eds. *The Documents of Vatican II*. New York: America Press, 1966.

Anderson, Floyd, ed. *Council Daybook: Sessions 1 and 2*. Washington, D. C.: National Catholic Welfare Conference, 1965; *Session 3* (1965); and *Session 4* (1966).

Kloppenburg, Bonaventure. *The Ecclesiology of Vatican II*. Chicago: Franciscan Herald Press, 1974.

Lindbeck, George. *The Future of Roman Catholic Theology: Vatican II—Catalyst for Change*. Philadelphia: Fortress Press, 1970.

Miller, John H., ed. *Vatican II: An Interfaith Appraisal*. Notre Dame, Ind.: University of Notre Dame Press, 1966.

Outler, Albert. *Methodist Observer at Vatican II*. Westminster, Md.: Newman Press, 1967.

Pawley, Bernard C., ed. *The Second Vatican Council: Studies by Eight Anglican Observers*. New York: Oxford University Press, 1967.

Rynne, Xavier. *Vatican Council II*. New York: Farrar, Straus & Giroux, 1968.

Vorgrimler, Herbert, ed. *Commentary on the Documents of Vatican II*. 5 vols. New York: Herder & Herder, 1967-1969.

· XX ·

THE CHURCH TODAY: ITS NATURE AND MISSION

As noted in the preceding chapter, many of the progressive features of the Second Vatican Council were anticipated in the work of theologians writing *before* Vatican II. Some of these theologians continued to exercise leadership in the postconciliar period as well. The spirit of the council has also been reflected in official ecclesiastical statements, in pastoral developments of various kinds, in ecumenical dialogues, and in the work of individual Protestant theologians where a new sense of the sacramentality of the Church has begun to emerge alongside a deepened emphasis on its servanthood toward the world. We have perhaps reached a point in the evolution of twentieth-century ecclesiology where consensus has nearly been achieved, both inside and outside the Catholic Church, on the question of the nature and mission of the Church.

ECCLESIOLOGY SINCE VATICAN II
Catholic Ecclesiology

Karl Rahner

Rahner's understanding of the Church is consistent with his fundamental approach to the theology of *grace*. The Church is the sacrament of God's universal saving activity on our behalf. It is "the historically real and actual presence of the eschatologically victorious mercy of God," or "the sign of the grace of God definitively triumphant in the world in Christ" (*The Church and the*

Sacraments, London: Nelson, 1963, pp. 14,18). The Church is not itself the Kingdom of God. "It is the sacrament of the kingdom of God in the eschatological phase of sacred history which began with Christ, the phase which brings about the kingdom of God" ("Church and World," *The Concise Sacramentum Mundi*, p. 239).

The relationship of Church and world is a function of the relationship of Church and Kingdom. The Kingdom, which is the redemptive presence of God, is not purely otherworldly, spiritual, meta-historical. It is also this-worldly, concrete, and historical. Accordingly, the Church must understand its mission in a way that falls between two extremes: *integrism*, which regards everything in the world as evil or worthless unless and until it is somehow "integrated" with Christianity, and *esotericism*, which regards everything in the world, apart from Christianity, as unrelated to salvation, and therefore to be shunned. Provided that the spirit of detachment from the world, of penance, contemplation, and renunciation remains alive in the Church, there need be no mistrust of the Church's present and recent course in announcing the unity of the love of God and love of neighbor (i.e., we manifest our love of God precisely in and through our love for others), in taking up the cause of the poor and the oppressed, in speaking and acting on behalf of human rights and freedom, and in opening dialogue with the rest of humankind.

Rahner insists that we can never forget that we are sinners, not only we ourselves as individuals but also as a society which creates or tolerates inhuman social conditions and institutions. "The danger of debasing Christianity by confining the struggle with sin to the wholly private sphere is imminent and menacing," because so much sin has been institutionalized and has become part of our taken-for-granted world (*The Shape of the Church to Come*, New York: Seabury Press, 1974, p. 124). If the Church avoids the task of challenging institutionalized sin, it will be regarded as a "merely conservative power, devoted to the defence of things as they are" (p. 125). On the other hand, if the Church is to be outwardly credible, it must allow its commitment to justice and freedom to become more effective in its internal life as well. The Church of the future will be an open Church, ecumenical from its very roots, democratized, and especially declericalized.

Edward Schillebeeckx

Sacramentality is also the key to Edward Schillebeeckx's understanding of the nature and mission of the Church. The key idea which inspired the fundamental change of emphasis at Vatican II, he argues, is that of the Church as the *sacramentum mundi* ("sacrament of the world"). In this context "world" means fellowship, community, or other-oriented existence. It is a way of being human in the world, i.e., of being in dialogue with one's fellow human beings (*God the Future of Man*, New York: 1968, p. 123). The Church is committed to the coming Kingdom of God, but it is not yet in possession of the Kingdom. The Church is still on the way, in history, searching tentatively for solutions to the problems of human existence. Its message is not "This is precisely how the world can be fully humanized" but "Humanity is possible." The task of humanization, in other words, "is not a labor of Sisyphus" (p. 156). The hope of the final Kingdom, where all things will be brought to perfection, stimulates the Church never to rest satisfied with what has already been achieved in this world. The promised future has not yet been given. Therefore, nothing that now exists is beyond prophetic criticism. On the other hand, "The Church's critical function is not that of an outsider, pursuing a parallel path, but rather that of one who is critically involved in the building of the world and the progress of the nations" (p. 161).

Schillebeeckx's post-Vatican II turn in the direction of a more socially and politically critical function for the Church is consistent with his discovery and/or renewed appreciation of sociocritical theory (see his *The Understanding of Faith*, New York: Sheed & Ward, 1974) and with his more recent work in Christology, referred to in chapter 14.

Hans Küng

Hans Küng's major post-conciliar work on the Church is entitled simply *The Church* (New York: Sheed & Ward, 1968). It is a significant book in that it is the first major volume in ecclesiology which attends at some length to the subordinate relationship of Church to the Kingdom of God. Standard Catholic textbooks, as we noted in the previous chapter, usually identified the two. The

Church, for Küng, is first and foremost an historical reality. It is the pilgrim People of God. As such, its essential reality is embodied in changeable forms. Adaptation occurred even within the New Testament period itself. The Church emerged not from the direct mandate of Jesus but as a product of his preaching of the Kingdom of God. The Church's own mission is similarly oriented toward the coming Kingdom.

It is here perhaps that Küng's close contacts with the churches of the Reformation, especially Lutheranism, shape his theology in a manner that is not unequivocally Catholic. Specifically, Küng insists very strongly on the discontinuity between Church and Kingdom. The Church does not bring about the Kingdom but is "its voice, its announcer, its *herald*. God alone can bring his reign; the Church is devoted entirely to its service" (p.96). The emphasis is at least reminiscent of Martin Luther's *Alleinswirksamkeit Gottes* ("God's working-aloneness").

On the other hand, Küng does not want to dissociate completely the Church from the Kingdom. It is the anticipatory sign of the Kingdom. The Church is also the Body of Christ and the Creation of the Holy Spirit, as well as the pilgrim People of God. It is a community constituted by Baptism and the Lord's Supper, and it exists at both local and universal levels. A local church is not merely a section of the universal Church, nor is the universal Church merely an accumulation of local churches. Each local church is a manifestation of the Body of Christ in that place, and the Church universal is a dynamic communion of local churches, something more than the sum total of those churches.

A persistent emphasis in Küng's post-Vatican II books and essays on the Church is the need for ongoing institutional reform. The Church is a credible proclaimer and witness of the Kingdom only if it also follows the way of Jesus as a provisional, serving, guilty, and determined Church. It must be a community marked not only by faith, hope, and charity, but also by truthfulness and freedom (*On Being a Christian*, New York: Doubleday, 1976, pp. 481-484). All authority in the Church must always be ultimately in the service of the Kingdom and immediately in the service of the Church itself. We should speak, as the New Testament did, of service (ministries) rather than of offices. The Petrine ministry (papacy), as important as it is, cannot be the sole criterion of orthodoxy or for identifying what and where the Church is (pp. 494-502). The dividing line between Catholic and Protestant is less sharp than we have traditionally thought. The names represent basic attitudes. *Catholic* expresses a preference for the whole, for continuity, and for universality; *Protestant* embraces a concern for the Gospel (Sacred Scripture) and for constant reform. These two attitudes are not mutually exclusive at all.

Avery Dulles

Avery Dulles, one of the leading Catholic theologians in the United States, has made his principal contributions to post-Vatican II ecclesiology in his *The Dimensions of the Church* (Westminster: Newman Press, 1967) and *Models of the Church* (New York: Doubleday, 1974). The former book, subtitled *A Postconciliar Reflection*, notes that the council moved beyond Robert Bellarmine's (d. 1621) highly institutional notion of church as "a group of men bound together by the profession of the same Christian faith and by the communion of the same sacraments, under the rule of the legitimate pastors, and especially of the one vicar of Christ on earth, the Roman pontiff" (cited, p. 4). Indeed, the great weakness of Bellarmine's view is that it omits "precisely what makes the Church the Church, namely, the communion of minds and hearts through sharing in the same divine life" (p. 5). The council's understanding of the Church as People of God and as sacrament carried our ecclesiology forward, Dulles suggests, and its refusal to identify the Church of Christ exclusively with the Roman Catholic Church broadened that ecclesiology's base (p. 10).

A more mature expression of Dulles' theology of the Church is presented in his widely read and influential *Models of the Church*. Here he insists that the mystery of the Church is too rich and diverse to be confined to any single theological category. It is not just an institution, or a mystical communion, or a sacrament, or a herald, or a servant. It is all these. The *institutional model* makes it clear that the Church must be a structured community, including pastoral officers bearing authority to direct and guide it, to preside over worship, to determine the limits of dissent, and to represent the community in an official way. The *community model* makes it evident that the Church must be united to God by grace, and that its members must be united to one another in Christ. The *sacramental model* reminds us, especially in the community's prayer and worship, that the Church must be a sign of the continuing vitality of Christ's grace and of our hope for the redemption he promises. The *kerygmatic model* underlines the Church's abiding call to herald the Gospel and to summon people to faith in Jesus as Lord and Savior. The *servant model* stresses the importance of the Church's contribution to transforming the world and impregnating human society with the values of the Kingdom of God.

Taken in isolation, however, each model can distort the reality of the Church, Dulles warns. Thus, the institutional model can exaggerate the importance of structures, of official authority, of obedience to rules. The community model can generate an unhealthy spirit of enthusiasm, leading to false expectations and impossible demands. The sacramental model can lead to a sterile aestheticism and to an almost narcissistic self-contemplation. The kerygmatic model can exaggerate the importance of merely verbal faith at the expense of social action. And the servant model can lead to an uncritical acceptance of secular values and a completely this-worldly view of salvation.

Dulles expresses a clear preference for the sacramental model, because it preserves and integrates the values and strengths of the other four models. (1) Official structures give a certain vivid character to the *community*. (2) The Church is an authentic *sacrament* of Christ when it is also a community of *love*. (3) The Church bears witness to Christ through the *preaching of the Word*. (4) And its devotion to worldly *service* testifies to the presence and concern of the servant Christ (pp. 182-188). Although Dulles is least disposed to the institutional model (p. 187), some subsequent writings would suggest that his spirit of caution is more directly focused on the servant model than on the institutional. This is clear in his *The Resilient Church* (New York: Doubleday, 1977, pp. 9-27). Therein, he also reaffirms his preference for the sacramental model, "the universal sacrament of salvation" (*Lumen gentium*, n. 48). He concludes, "After some years of work in ecclesiology, I am inclined to think that there is no better definition" (p. 26). A sacrament is a sign, but not an empty sign. It must always be, or strive to be, what it signifies. Thus, the Church is always summoned to greater perfection and to greater fidelity to its mission, to "bear witness to the wonderful deeds of God and attract others to share in the peace and freedom that Christ alone can give" (p. 27).

Johannes Metz

Metz is best known for introducing the concept of "political theology," i.e., a theology which relates theory and practice. Liberation theology, as already noted in chapter 2, is a form of political theology. Political theology measures all reality in the light of the promised Kingdom of God. And because the Kingdom has not yet come in all its perfection, there is nothing, including the Church, which escapes the critical gaze of political theology (see *Theology of the World*, New York: Herder & Herder, 1969, pp. 107-140).

The Church itself is not exempt from criticism, because the Church is also part of the world. "For it is *that world* which attempts to live from the promised future of God, and to call *that world* in question which understands itself only in terms of itself and its possibilities. . . . The Church is the eschatological community and the exodus community. . . . The Church is not the goal of her own strivings; this goal is the Kingdom of God" (p. 94). The Church has a hope and witnesses to a hope, but its hope is not in itself. The hope is in the Kingdom as the world's future. The Church is the universal sacrament of hope for the salvation of the whole world. It is precisely because of this that the Church must be "the liberating and critical force of this one society" (p. 96). Hope is living for the other.

Gregory Baum

Canadian theologian Gregory Baum recapitulates the central themes already contained in these other theologies, especially Rahner's. The distinctive mission of the Church today is one of dialogue. Proclamation includes listening and learning. It is a way of becoming more aware of the ambiguity of the Church's own situation in the world and of entering more deeply into what is God's will for us. Indeed, it was dialogue with the secular world that taught the Church to cherish religious liberty, pluralism, critical interpretation of texts, etc., as religious values (*Faith and Doctrine*, New York: Newman Press, 1969).

But dialogue is not simply a missionary tactic imposed by circumstances. Dialogue is imperative because God's saving presence is everywhere. Ecclesiology studies the manner in which salvation comes to everyone, and hence it has to do with human life in community. In that sense, ecclesiology may be regarded as "the theological study of human society" (*Man Becoming*, New York: Herder & Herder, 1970, p. 69). The Church is people insofar as they are touched by grace. That grace offers and creates community. Such community is the Church, which comes into being "whenever and wherever people become friends through God's presence to them" (*The Credibility of the Church Today*, New York: Herder & Herder, 1968, p. 47).

This is not to say, however, that the Church has no specific character of its own. "The universality of grace does not obliterate the distinction between Church and humanity. The Christian Church is the community in which Jesus Christ, in whom God reveals himself unconditionally and definitively, is proclaimed and celebrated" (p. 48). The mission of such a Church is a movement of humanization. It serves humankind "to help the redemptive presence of God...triumph in terms of unity, reconciliation, social justice, and peace" (p. 198).

Gustavo Gutierrez

The principal theologian of the Latin American liberation school, Gustavo Gutierrez, of Peru, also embraces the Second Vatican Council's sacramental perspective. The Church's existence is not for itself but for others. On the one hand, the Church rescues the world from anonymity and enables it to know the ultimate meaning of its historical future. On the other hand, the Church must listen to the world and be evangelized by it. As the universal sacrament of salvation, the Church must signify in its own structures the salvation it announces. "As a sign of the liberation of man and history, the Church itself in its concrete existence ought to be a place of liberation.... The break with an unjust social order and the search for new ecclesial structures...have their basis in this ecclesiological perspective" (*A Theology of Liberation*, Maryknoll, N.Y.: Orbis Books, 1972, p. 261).

Although the "primary task of the Church ... is to celebrate with joy the salvific action of the Lord in history" (p. 265), the Church must reflect on and live the Gospel in light of the situation in which it finds itself. Thus, in Latin America the Church must take a clear stand against social injustice and in favor of the revolutionary process which seeks to abolish that injustice and build a more human order. The first step is to recognize how much the Church itself is tied to that unjust system. The Church must truly announce the good news of the Kingdom which "reveals, without any evasions, what is at the root of social injustice: the rupture of the brotherhood which is based on our sonship before the Father..." (p. 269). And the Church must also make its own members aware of their oppressed condition, to affirm their humanity, and to motivate them to take responsibility for the quality of their lives ("The oppressed themselves should be the agents of their own pastoral activity"). "Universal love is that which in solidarity with the oppressed seeks also to liberate the oppressors from their own power, from their ambition, and from their selfishness" (p. 275). In the meantime, the unity of the Church cannot be achieved apart from the unity of the world. "In a radically divided world, the function of the ecclesial community is to struggle against the profound causes of the division among men. It is only this commitment that can make of it an authentic sign of unity" (p. 278).

Protestant Ecclesiology

Jürgen Moltmann

For Moltmann, a Reformed (or Calvinist) Protestant, the Church is "the community of those who on the ground of the resurrection of Christ wait for the kingdom of God and whose life is determined by this expectation" (*Theology of Hope*, New York: Harper

& Row, 1967, p. 326). The Church is the body of the crucified and risen Lord "only where in specific acts of service it is obedient to its mission to the world. . . . it is nothing in itself, but all that it is, it is in existing for others. It is the Church of God where it is a Church for the world" (p. 327). The Church's service of the world and of humanity is not such that it strives to keep everything as it is; its service is rather for the sake of helping the world and humankind transform themselves and become what they are promised to be. "For this reason 'Church for the world' can mean nothing else but 'Church for the kingdom of God' and the renewing of the world" (p. 328). The Church's mission is reconciliation with God, forgiveness of sins, peace. The salvation it proclaims is not merely salvation of the soul but also "the realization of the eschatological *hope of justice*, the *humanizing* of man, the *socializing* of humanity, *peace* for all creation" (p. 329).

Following an approach very close to Metz's, and having also in mind the classic Marxist critique of the Church, Moltmann insists that "mission means not merely propagation of faith and hope, but also historic transformation of life" (p. 330). Christian hope calls everything in question by measuring everything against the future Kingdom. The hope of resurrection, therefore, brings about a new understanding of the world as not yet finished. Our world is a world of unfinished possibilities. "To disclose to it the horizon of the future of the crucified Christ is the task of the Christian Church" (p. 338).

The same themes are carried forward, but with more deliberate attention to the place and role of the Holy Spirit, in Moltmann's more recent *The Church in the Power of the Spirit* (New York: Harper & Row, 1977). The Church is, before all else, the Church of Jesus Christ. "Every statement about the church will be a statement about Christ. Every statement about Christ also implies a statement about the church; yet the statement about Christ is not exhausted by the statement about the church because it also goes further, being directed towards the messianic kingdom which the church serves" (p. 6). The Church's mission "embraces all activities that serve to liberate man from his slavery in the presence of the coming God, slavery which extends from economic necessity to Godforsakenness" (p. 10). It is an ecumenical Church;

the whole Church is present in each church. Therefore, the concerns of one are the concerns of all others, and vice versa. So, too, the Church is a political Church, committed to and ever engaged in the struggle for liberation, in liberation's most comprehensive sense.

Wolfhart Pannenberg

Pannenberg, a German Lutheran, also places the Church in the context of the coming Kingdom of God. It is an eschatological community, "a community of high expectation and hope" (*Theology and the Kingdom of God*, Philadelphia: Westminster Press, 1969, p. 74). It is true to its vocation "only as it anticipates and represents the destiny of all mankind, the goal of history." Protestantism, Pannenberg suggests, has focused too much on the piety and salvation of Church members themselves ("the congregation of saints wherein the gospel is rightly preached and the sacraments rightly celebrated"). The doctrine of the Church begins not with the Church but with the Kingdom of God, "the utterly concrete reality of justice and love" (p. 79).

The mission of the Church is to proclaim the universal significance of Jesus, to be a community through which contemporary men and women can participate in the hope for the ultimate fulfillment of humanity, to witness to the limitations of any given society, to stir the imagination for social action and to inspire the visions of social change (pp. 83-85). But in the end it is the Kingdom of *God*. The Church's function is always and only "preliminary." "Any effort to make man appear to be more than he can be in his historically preliminary moment inevitably makes man less" (p. 82).

Carl Braaten

An American Lutheran, Carl Braaten acknowledges his own indebtedness to Pannenberg's vision of the Church. He defines the Church as "the prolepsis of a new world that is coming into being through the power of God's creative future in Christ" (*The Future of God*, New York: Harper & Row, 1969, p. 109). The Church is not itself the Kingdom of God, but only the "sacramental sign of

the new world that is emerging in, with, and under the manifestations of the present, visible world" (p. 111). He, too, criticizes the
traditional Protestant notion of the Church as the "congregation
of saints." The definition leaves out the Kingdom of God and the
Church's missionary function in world history. That missionary
imperative arises itself from the universal vision of the Church's
eschatological faith (p. 133).

George Lindbeck

Another American Lutheran, George Lindbeck similarly stresses
the sacramental character of the Church. Indeed, the Church's
"essence" is "to be a sacramental sign or witness to God's saving
work in all that it is and does. It exercises this witnessing or
missionary function in its *diakonia* or secular service of the
world . . ., its *leitourgia* or worship of God . . ., and its *koinonia* or
communal unity expressed both interpersonally and in institutional structures. . . and in common faith and dogma" (*The Future
of Roman Catholic Theology*, Philadelphia: Fortress Press, 1970,
p. 5). Apart from this mission to be a sacramental sign and anticipation of the Kingdom of God, there is nothing which differenti-
ates the Church from the rest of humankind (p. 27).

Ecumenical Ecclesiology

In addition to the theological work done by individual theologians, the post-Vatican II period has also witnessed the production
of a new form of theological communication: consensus statements
of bilateral, trilateral, or multilateral groups composed of theologians from various Christian traditions. Reference has already
been made to the work of those groups, and even more detailed
references will be made again, later in this chapter and in the next
three chapters.

In the United States alone remarkable progress has been
recorded since the council on such specific questions as the Eucharist, ministry, even the papacy. A measure of consensus on the
general topic of the Church and its mission has also been achieved

by such bilateral consultations as the Presbyterian-Reformed/Roman Catholic, the Orthodox/Roman Catholic, the United Methodist/Roman Catholic, the Lutheran/Roman Catholic and the Anglican/Roman Catholic. The last may usefully represent the others as an example of the nature and degree of ecclesiological consensus.

It its "Agreed Statement on the Purpose of the Church" (*Documents on Anglican-Roman Catholic Relations III*, Washington, D.C.: United States Catholic Conference, 1976, pp. 1-11), the Anglican/Roman Catholic Consultation in the U.S.A. defines the Church as "that community of persons called by the Holy Spirit to continue Christ's saving work of reconciliation. As Christ proclaimed the Kingdom, so the Church serves the Kingdom..." (p. 2). This mission is carried out in various ways: by the proclamation of the Good News, in the context of the fellowship of believers, in the witness of individual members and in its own structures and agencies, and in its service to those in need. The mission, therefore, is threefold: proclamation, worship, and service.

The proclamation must also be a word of challenge, at times even of confrontation. "The imperative of evangelism...has many dimensions" (p. 6). The Eucharist is the summit and source of the Church's mission, for it "testifies to the dependence of all people upon God and it affirms God's action for humanity in the death and resurrection of Jesus Christ, in the promise of the gift of the Spirit, and in our ultimate destiny of union with the Father" (p. 6). But the witness of worship is "only fully complete when it results in a commitment to service" (p. 7). The contemporary reexamination of mission has emphasized the call of the Church to be an agent and forerunner of God's Kingdom of justice and peace. "Human liberation, we agree, is that aspect of the Church's mission of service which is most challenging for our time" (p. 8).

The statement concludes: "We, as Roman Catholics and Episcopalians charged by our churches to explore the possibility that there is a fundamental unity between us, find that we are in substantial agreement about the purpose or mission of the Church as we have set it forth above. We have uncovered no essential points on which we differ" (p. 9).

The Ecclesiology of Official Church Documents

The Third International Synod of Bishops (Rome, 1971)

An international synod of bishops is second only to an ecumenical council in collegial authority. It is an entirely modern phenomenon, a direct outgrowth of the Second Vatican Council, designed to give structure to the council's desire to draw the bishops of the world into the ongoing governance and direction of the Church. The 1971 synod issued two statements, one on "The Ministerial Priesthood" and the other on "Justice in the World" (Washington, D.C.: United States Catholic Conference, 1972, pp. 33-52).

It is this latter document which contains, in its introduction, the assertion which has been so frequently cited ever since: "Action on behalf of justice and participation in the transformation of the world fully appear to us as a constitutive dimension of the preaching of the Gospel, or, in other words, of the Church's mission for the redemption of the human race and its liberation from every oppressive situation" (p. 34). This document dwells, too, upon the changed circumstances in the world wherein human life is marked by interdependence: "Never before have the forces working for bringing about a unified world society appeared so powerful and dynamic; they are rooted in the awareness of the full basic equality as well as of the human dignity of all" (p. 35). On the other hand, there are now technological forces at work (arms race, nuclear power, e.g.) which also threaten the very survival of the human community. The division between rich and poor only exacerbates that danger. Dialogue among peoples is a matter of urgency today, and not simply a desirable goal. The Church has a special role and obligation.

Its mission is to preach the Gospel, a message of universal brotherhood and sisterhood and a consequent demand for justice in the world. The Church is not alone responsible for justice, but nonetheless "has proper and specific responsibility which is identified with her mission of giving witness before the world of the need for love and justice contained in the Gospel message, a witness to be carried out in the Church institutions themselves and in the lives of Christians" (p. 42). The latter point is highlighted in the document's third chapter: "While the Church is bound to give witness to justice, she recognizes that anyone who ventures to speak to people about justice must first be just in their eyes. Hence we must undertake an examination of the modes of acting and of the possessions and life style found within the Church herself" (p. 44). Everything has to be touched by this overriding concern for justice: the exercise of ministry, education, liturgy, etc. And everything is, in turn, placed in the context of the coming Kingdom of God, a kingdom of justice and love, a kingdom rooted in "the radical transformation of the world in the Paschal Mystery of the Lord ..." (p. 52).

Papal Statements

Ecclesiam Suam (*His Church*, 1964):   Pope Paul VI's inaugural encyclical stressed the fundamental need for *dialogue*. Although the encyclical is not precisely post-conciliar, the council had already established clear ecclesiological lines, and the encyclical itself reflects them. The Church is called to dialogue with humankind at various levels. The pope sketches four concentric circles: The first and widest comprises all men and women, with whom dialogue must be initiated and sustained on each of the great problems of the world; the second circle embraces all religious people; the third, all Christians; and the fourth, all Catholics.

Populorum Progressio (*On the Development of Peoples*, 1967):   This encyclical, so strong in its insistence on the social and political character of the Church's mission, is generally credited with inspiring the growth of Latin American liberation theology and of shaping the remarkable documents of the Second Latin American Bishops' Conference, which met in Medellin, Colombia, in 1968. The pope points immediately to the teachings of the Second Vatican Council on the Church's responsibility to the world at large and especially to those in need, and ultimately to the example of Jesus himself, who preached the Gospel to the poor as a sign of his mission (n. 12). "Sharing the noblest aspirations of men, and suffering when she sees them not satisfied, she wishes to help them attain their full flowering, and that is why she offers men what she possesses as her characteristic attribute: a global vision of man and of the human race" (n. 13).

Octagesima Adveniens (A Call to Action, 1971): This "Apostolic Letter" to Cardinal Maurice Roy, President of the Council of the Laity and of the Pontifical Commission, Justice and Peace, recapitulates the social doctrine of the Catholic Church from *Rerum Novarum* (1891), whose eightieth (*octagesima*) anniversary provided the occasion for the document. What is distinctive about *A Call to Action* is its shift of focus from economics to politics (n. 46). Politics is more comprehensive than economics, the pope declares. It has to do with the common good. Such power, however, is to be exercised in a way that maximizes shared responsibility (n. 47).

And what of the place of the Church in this wider political context? The Church is called "to enlighten minds in order to assist them to discover the truth and to find the right path to follow amid the different teachings that call for their attention; and secondly to take part in action and to spread, with a real care for service and effectiveness, the energies of the Gospel" (n. 48).

Evangelii Nuntiandi (On Evangelization in the Modern World, 1975): This is technically an "Apostolic Exhortation" on the occasion of the Fourth International Synod of Bishops in Rome (1974). The document links the mission of the Church with Jesus' proclamation of the Kingdom of God, as "liberation from everything that oppresses man, but which is above all liberation from sin and the Evil One . . ." (n. 9). Just as Jesus accomplished this proclamation in works as well as in word, so is the Church called to be a servant as well as a herald of the Gospel. "Evangelization would not be complete if it did not take account of the unceasing interplay of the Gospel and of man's concrete life, both personal and social" (n. 29). Thus, ". . . the Church strives always to insert the Christian struggle for liberation into the universal plan of salvation which she herself proclaims" (n. 38).

Redemptor Hominis (Redeemer of Humankind, 1979): This inaugural encyclical of Pope John Paul II focuses more on Christology, anthropology, and the ethical implications of both than it does on the mystery of the Church. The document is primarily concerned with human dignity, rooted in the saving work of Christ. The Church must be a constant champion of human dignity, consistent with the teachings of the Second Vatican Council and especially of its *Declaration on Religious Freedom.* The person with whom the Church is concerned is "man in the full truth of his community and social being" (n. 14). The Church's commitment to humankind is shaped by its participation in the threefold mission of Christ as Prophet, Priest, and King. Every member of the Church, not just the hierarchy, shares in this mission: teaching, worshiping, and serving. "The Church's fundamental function in every age and particularly in ours is to direct humankind's gaze . . . toward the mystery of God, to help every person to be familiar with the profundity of the redemption taking place in Christ Jesus . . ." (n. 10). What is finally "amazing" is the "good news" that we are indeed worth something. "This amazement determines the Church's mission in the world. . . ."

Bishops' Statements

The Church in the Present-Day Transformation of Latin America in the Light of the Council (Second General Conference of Latin American Bishops, Medellin, Colombia, 1968):   Inspired by the Second Vatican Council and by *Populorum Progressio*, the so-called Medellin documents describe the Church as an instrument of liberation, an agent of social justice, a defender of the poor and the oppressed. This understanding of the Church's mission must penetrate every major area of Church life: education, youth ministry, the family, catechesis, and so forth. "No earthly ambition impels the Church, only her wish to be the humble servant of all men" (XIV,18).

Message to the People of God (Third General Conference of Latin American Bishops, Puebla, Mexico, 1979):   The same sense of integration characterizes the work and final message to the people of Latin America in this Third General Conference as in the preceding one: Christ assumed humanity and its real conditions, except for sin. Therefore, the Church must be concerned with the whole person, with the matter of human rights, economic justice, the use of power and force, and so forth. "What interests us as pastors is the integral proclamation of the truth about Christ."

Political Responsibility (Administrative Board, United States Catholic Conference, 1976):   "Christians believe," the statement declares, "that Jesus' commandment to love one's neighbor should extend beyond individual relationships to infuse and transform all human relations from the family to the entire human community." The bishops cite a classic text, Luke 4:18: "He has sent me to bring glad tidings to the poor, to proclaim liberty to captives, recovery of sight to the blind and release to prisoners." The call to feed the hungry, clothe the naked, care for the sick and the afflicted, comfort the victims of injustice (Matthew 25) requires more than individual acts of charity. We must understand and act upon "the broader dimensions of poverty, hunger and injustice which necessarily involve the institutions and structures of economy, society and politics."

Sharing the Light of Faith: National Catechetical Directory for Catholics of the United States (Washington, D.C.: United States Catholic Conference, 1979):   The ecclesiology of this document is essentially that of the Second Vatican Council. The Church is described first as a mystery, and then as People of God, servant, sign of the Kingdom, pilgrim, and hierarchical society. The explanation of each descriptive term is consistent with the council's. Thus, the Kingdom is understood also as a Kingdom of justice, love, and peace, as well as of holiness and grace, and authority is to be exercised collegially and in the spirit of service. Christians are called to be a community of shared beliefs, experiences, ideals, and values. The Church is to be missionary. Every member is called to proclaim the Gospel "to the whole of creation" (Matthew 16:15). The marks of the Church—one holy, catholic, and apostolic—are gifts which the Church must "strive to realize ever more fully in its life" (p. 39). The interpretation of each mark differs in some discernible measure from the pre-Vatican II textbooks. Catholicity, for example, means that "the gospel message is capable of being integrated with all cultures. It corresponds to all that is authentically human" (p. 40). Apostolicity is not portrayed in a purely *chronological* sense—i.e., that the Catholic Church's bishops can trace their episcopal orders all the way back, in an unbroken chain, to the Apostles, but in a *dynamic* sense as well—i.e., as "the continuing fidelity to Christ's loving and saving work and message, to ministry and service inspired by the evangelical vision and teaching of the original apostles" (p. 41).

The Church is also a communion of local churches, of East and West alike. "The Church's unity is not based on a particular language, rite, spiritual tradition, or theological school, but upon the one cornerstone, Jesus Christ" (p. 41). It must always be a Church in dialogue and collaboration with others. First, there must be dialogue and collaboration within the Body of Christ between and among separated Christians. Then there must be dialogue and collaboration with Jews, Moslems, and representatives of other religions. Finally, there must be dialogue and collaboration with those who profess no religion because "the Church is confident that its message is in harmony with the most authentic and profound desires of the human heart" (p. 44).

The Impact of Post-Vatican II Ecclesiology on Pastoral Developments

As a result of the ecclesiological self-understanding of Vatican II and the development of that understanding in post-conciliar theology, the following changes in the life, mission, and structure of the Catholic Church have occurred and continue to occur:

Because the Church is perceived more clearly as the whole People of God, and not just the hierarchy, and because all participate directly in the mission of Christ by Baptism and not simply in the mission of the pope and the bishops ("Catholic Action"), the Catholic Church functions now in a more deliberately *conciliar* mode, emphasizing shared responsibility—e.g., parish councils, diocesan pastoral councils, national advisory boards, priests' senates, leadership conferences of religious.

Because the Church is perceived more clearly as a communion of local churches and not just as a single Church subdivided for organizational purposes, the responsibility of bishops and of the body of bishops, representing as they do the local churches in communion with one another, has increased—e.g., national episcopal conferences, international synods of bishops, the expansion of bishops' authority of dispensation without recourse to Rome.

Because the Church's mission includes as an essential component the call to service (*diakonia*), even in the political realm, the

Church is increasingly attentive to the needs of the wider community in its allocation of resources (e.g., the Campaign for Human Development in the United States) and in its formulation of ecclesiastical priorities (e.g., the "Call to Action" Conference in Detroit, Michigan, October, 1976).

Because the Church's mission also includes as an essential component the call of the whole Church to holiness, the Church is marked today by an extraordinary renewal of interest in Christian *spirituality* (e.g., the Catholic Charismatic movement, directed retreats, Marriage Encounter, cursillos).

Because the Church is perceived to include Orthodox, Anglicans, and Protestants, as well as Catholics, the post-Vatican II period has been one of expanding and deepening ecumenical contacts and cooperation—e.g., theological dialogue at the international and national levels, seminary and divinity school consortia, common prayer.

(For a fuller statement of the relationship between ecclesiology and ecclesiastical structures, see my *The Remaking of the Church: An Agenda for Reform*, New York: Harper & Row, 1973).

THE NATURE OF THE CHURCH: TOWARD A DEFINITION

Models of the Church

The word *model* has, first, an *evaluative* meaning—e.g., "She is a model educator" or "He is a model student," in which the term conveys some notion of excellence. A model is an exemplar of some value. The word may also be used in a more *neutral* sense—e.g., "model home" or a "fashion model." Here it means "This is about how you or your own home might look." A model can also be a *philosophical* category, describing a fundamental perspective or way of understanding some complex reality. It may in that instance be either evaluative or neutral. The word *model* is employed here in the philosophical, or perspectival sense, and in its neutral, rather than evaluative, sense.

There are at least three dominant models of, or ways of perceiving, the Church, and they are presented below not in order of importance but in the chronological sequence in which they have entered the recent history of the Catholic Church.

Institution

This model perceives the Church *primarily* (which is not to say exclusively or exhaustively) as a hierarchically structured, visible society which mediates salvation to its individual members through the preaching and teaching of the Word and the administration of the sacraments. This was, of course, the dominant model in Roman Catholicism before Vatican II, and it inspired the first draft of the council's *Dogmatic Constitution of the Church.* Perhaps the most sophisticated expression of this model is contained in Joachim Salaverri's tract *De Ecclesia Christi* in the socalled *Spanish Summa* (summarized in the preceding chapter).

Strengths: This model was and remains attractive because it affords a strong sense of ecclesiastical *identity* (the Church is a specific, visible, clearly defined reality, rooted in the will of God, the mandate of Jesus Christ, and the power of the Holy Spirit); it gives the members a sense of their *place* and *role* within the Church, even if it be a subordinate one (some have clearly defined authority, others do not); and it is attentive to historical *continuity* (the Church has definite origins and has passed through specific points of development in which its identity was further clarified and determined, and both of these—origins and points of passage—connect the Church of the present with the Church of the past).

Weaknesses: On the other hand, the institutional model tended to exaggerate the hierarchical or societal aspect of the Church at the expense of the communitarian. That indeed was the point of the debate at Vatican II over the placement of chapters two and three in *Lumen gentium.* Is the Church first the People of God with a particular structure, or is is a hierarchical reality which happens to provide spiritual benefits to a particular people? *Secondly*, the institutional model may have also exaggerated the role and importance of the ordained, and especially of bishops, at the expense of the missionary responsibility of the entire community of the baptized. Thus, the mode of decision-making was monarchical and/or oligarchical rather than collegial or democratic. *Thirdly*, the institutional model tended to limit the scope of the Church to the Roman Catholic Church, at the expense of the Christian and ecclesial reality of the other churches (Orthodox, Anglican, and Protestant). *Fourthly*, this model tended to limit the scope of the Church's mission to the preaching of the Word and the celebration of the sacraments, at the expense of the Church's broader social and political responsibilities. *Finally*, this model tended to identify the Church with the Kingdom of God on earth, at the expense of the abiding need for renewal and reform not just of its individual members but of the whole Church, structures and persons, head and members.

Community

This model perceives the Church primarily as a community, or a people, whose principal task is the promotion and sustaining of personal growth through interpersonal relationships. This model was at least partially embraced by Vatican II in its central teaching on the Church as the People of God. It is an understanding of the Church proposed at the beginning of the 1960s by Edward Schillebeeckx in his *Christ the Sacrament of Encounter with God* and at more popular levels by Catholic lecturers with a psychological orientation—e.g., Eugene Kennedy and Henri Nouwen. It is a model that was warmly endorsed by those favoring a theology of festivity and fantasy in the late 1960s and early 1970s—e.g., Harvey Cox in *The Feast of Fools* (New York: Macmillan, 1969). This was also the dominant model in the early years of the Catholic Charismatic movement, and it is consistent with the recent emphasis in contemporary American culture on personal growth and development (the so-called Human Potential movement).

Strengths: The community model emphasizes the reality of the Church as a people and the responsibility of the Church to provide a context for human growth in Christ. Specifically, this model avoids some of the problems associated with the institutional model and conforms better than the institutional model to the bibilical, patristic, and Vatican II stress on the Church as the

People of God. Secondly, this model stresses the responsibility of the Church not only to make certain spiritual benefits available to its members, as in the sacraments, but to contribute positively to the human growth of its members. Thirdly, this model underlines the Church's abiding missionary responsibility to be a sign of Christ's presence by the mutual love shown within the community of his disciples.

Weaknesses: On the other hand, the community model is not always clear in identifying those elements which make such a community distinctive. Is "community" the private preserve of Christianity? Is the Church the only real "community"? If not, what makes the Christian community different from other communities? Secondly, this model tends to concentrate on the value of the individual's growth at the expense of the social and political responsibilities of the whole community and at the expense of the community's abiding commitment to the renewal and institutional reform of the Church itself.

Servant

This model perceives the Church primarily as an agent of social change whose task is the wise and courageous allocation of its own moral and material resources for the sake of the coming of the Kingdom of God among humankind—a Kingdom of justice and peace as well as of holiness and grace. It is a model supported by Vatican II's *Pastoral Constitution on the Church in the Modern World*, the Third International Synod of Bishops' *Justice in the World*, and similar official documents of the Catholic Church. It is also articulated in recent theological writings on the Church—e.g., those of Metz, Moltmann, Schillebeeckx, and Gutierrez.

Strengths: The servant model properly emphasizes the social and political responsibilities of the Church, insisting that the Kingdom of God is indeed a Kingdom of justice, peace, and freedom. Furthermore, this model underscores the principle that *diakonia*, which includes service in the socio-political order, is as essential, or constitutive, to the mission of the Church as are proclamation and sacramental celebration.

Weaknesses: But this model, too, is not always clear in identifying those elements which make such an agent of social change distinctive. Why belong to the Church if one can work more effectively for justice and peace outside of it? *Secondly,* some of those who have emphasized the servant model have also tended to identify the Church with the Kingdom of God, as the institutional model's proponents have sometimes done. Thus, wherever God, or the Spirit of God, is redemptively present as the source of justice and reconciliation, there is the Church. But since, as we shall indicate again below, the redemptive presence of God is the Kingdom of God, such an assertion effectively identifies the Kingdom with the Church.

A balanced theology of the Church would have to incorporate the distinctive strengths of all three models without, however, carrying over their individual weaknesses and especially their common liability, namely, their tendency to absolutize themselves, i.e., to equate the whole mystery of the Church with their own particular perspective. Thus, the Church is an institutionalized servant-community.

Definition of Church

The Church is the whole body, or congregation, of persons who are called by God the Father to acknowledge the Lordship of Jesus, the Son, in word, in sacrament, in witness, and in service, and, through the power of the Holy Spirit, to collaborate with Jesus' historic mission for the sake of the Kingdom of God.

The definition embraces all Christians: Catholics, Orthodox, Anglicans, and Protestants. Thus, although the noun *Church* is singular, it is always to be understood at the same time as having a pluralistic character. There is "the Church" and there are "the churches."

But the distinction between the Church and the churches is not only ecumenical. There is also the distinction between the Church as "Church universal" and the church as "local church."

Church refers at once to the whole Body of Christ and the whole People of God, as well as to the congregation of Christians in a particular place (a parish, a diocese, e.g.). Indeed, the Church universal is itself a *communion of local churches*, as noted earlier.

When does a group of persons at a local level become a church? When the following theological and pastoral conditions are verified: (1) a corporate confession of the Lordship of Jesus; (2) ratification of that confession of faith in Baptism, the Eucharist, and other sacraments; (3) regular nourishment on the biblical word of God as a force that summons the community of faith; (4) a sense of fellowship (*koinonia*) within the group—i.e., a common awareness of the call to become a community; (5) an acceptance of the Gospel of Jesus Christ as the conscious motivation for one's values and ethical commitment; and (6) the existence and exercise of certain formal ministries designed to assist the community in remaining faithful to its mission and providing order, coherence, and stability to its internal life so that it really can be a sacrament of Christ and of the Kingdom. For the Catholic Church this last item also implies union with the pope and the college of bishops, who are themselves related by succession to Peter and the other Apostles.

Each of these ecclesial elements is a matter of degree. On the other hand, the noun *church* is not applicable to a particular group except where all of these elements are present, to one degree or another. Thus, we always have to distinguish between movements and associations within the Church (even *within* a local church), and "the Church" itself (whether universal or local).

The definition and brief explanation presuppose, of course, all that has gone before, in this chapter and in chapters 17-19.

THE MISSION OF THE CHURCH

The mission of the Church is focused, as is Jesus' mission, on the *Kingdom of God*. By *Kingdom of God* is meant *the redemptive presence of God actualized through the power of God's reconciling Spirit*. Literally, the Kingdom of God is the reign, or rule, of God. The Kingdom happens whenever and wherever the will of God is fulfilled, for God rules where God's will is at work. And since God's will is applicable to the cosmos, to nature, to objects, to history, to institutions, to groups as well as to individuals, the Kingdom of God is as broad and as overarching as the claims and scope of the divine will itself.

More precisely, one might argue that the Kingdom of God is indistinguishable from God as such. The Kingdom is not something other than God. The Kingdom *of* God *is* God insofar as God is redemptively present and active in our midst through the power of the Holy Spirit. The Kingdom is the divine redemptive presence, reconciling, renewing, healing, and liberating. (A fuller discussion of the Kingdom of God will be provided in chapter 29.)

The mission of the Church is unintelligible apart from the Kingdom of God. The Church is called, first, to proclaim in word and in sacrament the definitive arrival of the Kingdom in Jesus of Nazareth; secondly, to offer itself as a test-case or sign of its own proclamation—i.e., to be a people transformed by the Spirit into a community of faith, hope, love, freedom, and truthfulness; and thirdly, to enable and facilitate the coming of the reign of God through service within the community of faith and in the world at large.

Each of these three missionary responsibilities generates, or is the foundation of, one of the three models of Church given above. The call of the Church to proclaim the Gospel in word and in sacrament in an organized and authorized manner is consistent with the concerns of the institutional model. The call of the Church to proclaim the Gospel by the quality of its own life is consistent with the concerns of the community model. And the call of the Church to proclaim and apply the Gospel through the struggle for social justice, peace, and human rights is consistent with the concerns of the servant model. Just as no one aspect of the Church's mission is the whole of its mission, so no one model of the Church captures the whole of the mystery of the Church.

Missionary Responsibility	Corresponding Model
Proclamation of the Gospel in *word* and in *sacrament*, in an *organized* and *authorized* manner.	Institution
Proclamation of the Gospel by the *quality* of the *Church's own life*.	Community
Proclamation of the Gospel by *application* of the Gospel to the struggle for *social justice, peace*, and *human rights*.	Servant

Proclamation in Word and Sacrament (*Kerygma and Leitourgia*)

The Church is that segment of humankind which hopes in the future of the world because of its fundamental faith in the unique significance of the life, death, and resurrection of Jesus of Nazareth, and in the abiding power of the Holy Spirit. Its first task is to keep alive the memory of Jesus Christ in word and in sacrament, to call attention to his and the Spirit's continued presence in history, and to profess its hope in his and the Spirit's totally new, creative manifestation in the future Kingdom.

Whatever changes in form and structure this Church assumes in the years ahead, it will always be that community which explicitly and publicly identifies Jesus Christ as the focal point of the whole historical process. The Church will not only announce this in word (preaching, catechesis, teaching), but it will celebrate that faith in sacrament. Through the *Eucharist* in particular the Church gives thanksgiving to God for the confirmation and validation of God's promises of reconciliation and peace in Jesus Christ (2 Corinthians 1:20). Through the Eucharist the Church keeps alive Christ's memory in order to make clear that he is indeed the hinge of history, that he is the final measure of all that is good and human. And finally, through the Eucharist the Church fixes the eyes of the world on the future, where the world's final meaning and destiny reside.

The Church, therefore, is a community of *faith* in the significance of what has already happened in and through Jesus Christ; it is a community of *love* as an expression of the effects of that Christ-event; and it is a community of *hope* in the power of the God of Jesus Christ to re-create all things anew in Christ and the Holy Spirit. The celebration of the Eucharist is the "summit and source" of the Church's mission, to use the terms of Vatican II.

But the Church is not commissioned to proclaim the Kingdom of God in an uncritical or naive manner. The Church can never equate any earthly reality, including itself, with the Kingdom of God. The Pauline appeal to flee the world and not be conformed to it (Romans 12:2) means that we should never forget the relative character of everything this side of the Kingdom. The Church, therefore, proclaims the Gospel with a consciousness of sin in the world and in its own household as well. Its proclamation is always prophetic.

Prophecy means, literally, *speaking on behalf of God*. A prophetic Church is a Church that speaks always on behalf of God, measuring everything against the coming Kingdom of God. The Church's preaching, however, is effective and credible to the extent that the Church itself has been converted by it. And this leads to the second missionary task.

Signification (*Koinonia*, or Fellowship, and *Marturia*, or Witness)

The Church must also be a sign of what God *is* actually doing in history and of what the human community *should* be doing in response to God's saving action. Men and women should be able to look upon this Christian community and thereby take courage with regard to the future course of history. They should be filled with confidence in the core of reality—affirming its intelligibility and its worthwhileness—because the ordinary men and women who belong to this community and maintain close affiliation with that core of reality are constantly being transformed by the Spirit of love, justice, intelligence, compassion, fortitude, and so forth. The Church has the responsibility, therefore, to be so open itself to Jesus, the reconciling Word of God, and to the reconciling power of the Spirit that the Church becomes the unmistakably clear sign of Jesus' and the Spirit's presence in the world. The Church must be a community marked by faith, hope, love, freedom, and truthfulness, not only in its official proclamations but in its life-style as well.

But the Church cannot be a sacrament of God's Kingdom unless the Kingdom exists somehow within the community. A sacrament is both sign and reality. The two are distinct but inseparable. Thus, *the Church is not itself the Kingdom of God*, yet *the Church must be inseparable from the Kingdom.* If indeed the Church were in no way imbued with the hidden presence of God, its preaching would have no force and its service no lasting effect. The Church would not be a mystery, or sacrament, at all.

But insofar as the Kingdom *is* present within the Church, that fact imposes upon the Church the missionary obligation to make the Kingdom's presence visible and instrumental for others. It means that the Church must *be* what it is; it must practice what it preaches. It means, too, that the Church must continually reform itself in fidelity to the Gospel. Accordingly, the question of institutional or structural reform is always an important one. The issues that have been on the Church's agenda in recent years—e.g., the ordination of women, the election of bishops, coresponsibility through diocesan and parish councils, papal and episcopal authority—may not be the issues on tomorrow's agenda. But the underlying problem will always be there: How can the Church best express in form and structure the inner reality which it embodies? The question is a missionary question, because the Church is called to be a sign as well as an instrument of the Gospel and of the Kingdom of God.

It would be illogical, therefore, to argue that the Church should be a vigorous agent of liberation and yet to be indifferent to the processes by which the Church selects its leadership or reaches important decisions regarding the allocation of its limited material and human resources. If the Church is called to be a sacrament of Christ, then how it organizes itself for mission and how it practices the virtue of justice within as well as without the community of faith become matters of some practical consequence.

Service (*Diakonia*)

Because the Kingdom of God is also a Kingdom of justice, peace, and freedom, and because the Church exists for the sake of the Kingdom, the Church's mission must also include responsibility for humanization in its fullest sense. The Church's activities on behalf of social justice or human rights are not merely preparatory to the real mission of the Church, as the notion of "pre-evangelization" had it before Vatican II. Apart from the official church documents already cited (*Gaudium et spes*, the synodal document *Justice in the World*, and various papal statements), the Church's involvement in the social and political orders is justified on the basis of the social and institutional character of sin itself. Since the Church is called to combat sin of every kind, the Church has responsibility in all areas where sin appears. More positively, the Church is called to uphold and practice virtue. Justice is one of the cardinal, or "hinge," virtues (along with prudence, fortitude, and temperance), and social justice is one of the principal kinds of justice (alongside commutative, distributive, and legal justice). Therefore, the Church's commitment to, and involvement in, the struggle for social justice, peace, and human rights is an essential, or "constitutive," part of its mission.

On the other hand, that intervention in the social and political orders must always be responsible, never arbitrary, particularly in the light of the Church's limited resources. Accordingly, such intervention must be governed by the following criteria: (1) The issue must be clearly *justice-related*. (2) The ecclesiastical agency or cluster of churches should have the *competence* to deal with the issue. (3) There should be *sufficient resources* within the particular church(es) to deal with the problem effectively. (4) The issue should have a *prior claim* over other justice-related problems which compete for the Church's attention. (5) the *form* of ecclesiastical action should not unnecessarily or unduly polarize the Church itself, since the Church is always called to be a sign of the Gospel and of the Kingdom of God. A diversity of viewpoints is to be expected and tolerated, so that agreement with the specific form of social or political action selected by the church(es) should not become itself a test of authentic Christian faith and commitment. This is not to say, on the other hand, that the mere risk of *conflict* within the Church should discourage such intervention. Conflict is essential to growth. But *excessive* conflict can be corrosive and finally destructive of the unity of the Church itself.

THE NECESSITY OF THE CHURCH

Do we need the Church? We have already indicated what we mean by *Church*. The question here is, What do we mean by *need?* The need may be *psychological* (the need for meaning), *sociological* (the need for a community of shared meaning), or *theological* (the need for direction in life, and ultimately the need for salvation). The question of the necessity of the Church takes in all three levels of meaning.

Who has the need? *First*, every human being, insofar as he or she needs to find some meaning for life and some sense of community of shared meaning, has at least a fundamental openness to religion of some kind (see chapter 8). *Secondly*, the world at large needs religious communities which testify to values which otherwise might be forgotten and lost, to the detriment of the human community itself. *Thirdly*, insofar as Jesus Christ is the Lord of history and the Savior of all humankind, the world at large also needs a particular religious community which testifies to the significance of Jesus Christ and which somehow carries forward his saving work on behalf of all, members and non-members alike. *Finally*, individuals who are convinced in faith of the Lordship of Jesus need a community where this fundamental conviction can be shared in word, in ritual, and in communal living, and through which it can be applied to the world at large for the sake of the world's salvation.

Accordingly, (1) the Church is necessary *for the world* as a sacrament, an efficacious sign and instrument of God's redemptive activity in Jesus Christ, leading toward the final Kingdom of God. The necessity of the Church *for the world* is an *historically contingent* necessity; i.e., *hypothetically* the Kingdom of God could come about without the Church or even without Jesus, but *in fact* it does not and will not. (2) The Church is necessary *for those individuals* who are in fact called by God to acknowledge the Lordship of Jesus and to collaborate with him in the coming of the

Kingdom of God. The necessity of the Church *for the individual* is similarly *contingent*, but contingent this time on the call of God to belong to *this* community rather than to another. Personal salvation, in other words, is not inextricably linked with one's membership or non-membership in the Church. It is existence within the Kingdom of God, not within the Church, that finally determines our relationship with God and our reception of salvation. It is not the one who says, "Lord, Lord!" who will enter the Kingdom, but "only the one who does the will of [the] Father in heaven" (Matthew 7:21). Where is it said, Rahner asked, that we must have the whole one hundred percent?

THE ROMAN CATHOLIC CHURCH

What is different about the Roman Catholic Church? If the Church is necessary to the world and to individuals within the world, is the Roman Catholic Church also necessary to the Body of Christ as a whole and to individuals inside and outside the Body of Christ?

One must distinguish between what is *characteristic* of Roman Catholicism and what is *distinctive* about it. What is characteristic may also be found in different shape or form in other churches, but what is distinctive will be found in Roman Catholicism alone.

What is *characteristically* Catholic? Its conviction that *grace* is finally triumphant over sin, not only as the declaration of God that we are just but through a real interior transformation by the power of the Holy Spirit. *Secondly,* its sense of *tradition*, of *doctrine*, and of the importance of maintaining *continuity* not only with the Church's origins but with its principal points of passage from its beginnings to the present. *Thirdly*, its sense of *peoplehood*, of *community*, and of *church*. *Fourthly*, and most significantly, its sense of *sacramentality* and its correlative sense of the importance of *mediation*. God is present to us through signs and symbols, and the presence of God is effective for us through these same visible signs and instruments.

What is *distinctively* Catholic? Here the answer given earlier by Hans Küng in his *Council and Reunion* still applies: The ecumenical question is the question of ecclesiastical office, and of the Petrine ministry in particular. It is true that Catholic ecclesiology posits a collegial understanding of the Church—i.e., that it is a communion of churches. But, so, too, does the Orthodox tradition. But Roman Catholicism alone insists on the role of the Petrine minister, the pope, as the "perpetual and visible source and foundation of the unity of the bishops and of the multitude of the faithful" (*Dogmatic Constitution of the Church*, n. 23).

One may become, be, and/or remain a Catholic for any number of reasons which have something to do with what is characteristic about Roman Catholicism but nothing to do with what is distinctive about it. But that fact does not negate Catholicism's distinctive *ecclesiological* feature, namely, the importance it assigns to the place and function of the Petrine ministry exercised by the bishop of Rome.

This is not to say, however, that belief in the Petrine ministry is the *only* distinctive feature of Catholicism. Although the Catholic Church is not alone among Christian churches in affirming the triumph of grace over sin, is not alone in its sense of tradition and doctrine, in its commitment to the principles of sacramentality and mediation, or in its emphasis on the peoplehood of the Church, one can argue that there is within Catholicism a particular configuration of such values as these—a configuration which one does not discover elsewhere in the Body of Christ. (A fuller statement on this central question of Catholic identity is provided in chapter 30.)

It is with this distinction in mind between what is characteristic and what is distinctive about Roman Catholicism that we must confront the question, "Do we need the Roman Catholic Church?"

For one thing, the Catholic Church is a part, and a very large and significant part indeed, of the whole Body of Christ. Therefore, the Roman Catholic Church is necessary *for the world* for the same reason that the Church as a whole is necessary for the world, namely, as a sacrament of Jesus Christ and of the Kingdom of God.

Secondly, The Roman Catholic Church is necessary *for the whole Body of Christ* because the Roman Catholic Church alone has all the institutional elements which are necessary for the integrity of the Body of Christ (e.g., the Petrine ministry, the seven sacraments) as well as the many characteristic values which serve to enrich the rest of the churches (e.g., its regard for community, its confidence in God's grace as transformative, its sacramental perspective, its spiritualities, its systematic approach to the Christian theological and doctrinal tradition).

Finally, the Roman Catholic Church is necessary *for the individual* who is called to the Church as such and who is, beyond that call to confess the Lordship of Jesus, persuaded that the fullness of ecclesial union with Christ requires participation in that church within the Body of Christ, whose unity is expressed not only through faith and its sacraments, but also through the ministry of the Petrine minister, the pope, who stands in the midst of the Church as the "source and foundation" of the unity of the communion of churches.

In light of the teaching of the Second Vatican Council, especially the *Decree on Ecumenism* and the *Declaration on the Relationship of the Church to Non-Christian Religions*, a common pre-Vatican II answer to the question of the Roman Catholic Church's necessity is no longer appropriate, namely, that the Roman Catholic Church alone is the one, true Church of Christ, outside of which authentic religious truth does not exist and salvation can be attained only with the greatest difficulty. This position is challenged by the following theological principles: God is present in grace to every human being; revelation is available apart from the Church; and within the Church itself there are many churches which, to one degree or another, "are brought into a certain, though imperfect, communion with the Catholic Church...are incorporated into Christ...have a right to be honored by the title of Christian, and are properly regarded as brothers in the Lord by the sons of the Catholic Church" (*Decree on Ecumenism*, n. 3).

SUMMARY

1. *Catholic ecclesiology* since Vatican II has carried forward the basic theological insights of the council itself. The greatest emphasis is on the *sacramentality* of the Church ("the universal sacrament of salvation"). This emphasis is seen especially in *Rahner, Schillebeeckx, Dulles,*

and *Gutierrez*. Secondly, there is a stress on the subordination of the Church to the *Kingdom of God* and a wider understanding of the Kingdom to include the coming of peace, justice, and freedom *(Rahner, Schillebeeckx, Küng, Dulles, Metz, Baum,* and *Gutierrez)*. Thirdly, there is renewed attention to the need for ongoing institutional reform as a way of fulfilling the Church's sacramental mission *(Rahner, Küng,* and *Gutierrez)*. Finally, because of the universality of grace, all the foregoing theologians stress the abiding need for dialogue with others and for collaboration in the task of humanizing the world.

2.   A sampling of *Protestant ecclesiology* since Vatican II suggests a new emphasis also on the *sacramentality* of the Church *(Braaten, Lindbeck)* and a movement away from the traditional Protestant notion of the Church as the "congregation of saints wherein the gospel is rightly preached and the sacraments rightly celebrated" *(Pannenberg, Braaten)*. There is an insistence, too, on the subordination of the Church to the *Kingdom of God* and on the Church's correlative responsibility to participate in the struggle for *liberation, social justice,* and *humanization (Moltmann, Pannenberg, Braaten, Lindbeck)*.

3.   Similar convergences have been noted in recent *ecumenical dialogues*—e.g., in the *Agreed Statement on the Purpose of the Church* by the Anglican/Roman Catholic Consultation in the U.S.A.

4.   *Official documents* of the Catholic Church have also reaffirmed the principal teachings of the Second Vatican Council; those documents focus particularly on the Church's responsibility for social justice and liberation, e.g., *Justice in the World* (Third International Synod of Bishops, 1971), *Populorum Progressio* (Pope Paul VI, 1967), *Octagesima Adveniens* (Paul VI, 1971), *Evangelii Nuntiandi* (Paul VI, 1975), *Redemptor Hominis* (John Paul II, 1979), the Medellin and Puebla statements of the Latin American Bishops Conference, and recent statements from the United States Catholic Conference, including the *National Catechetical Directory*.

5.   This post-Vatican II ecclesiology has had a *practical impact* on the life of the Catholic Church: on parish and diocesan councils (reflecting the principle that the Church is the whole People of God), national episcopal conferences and international synods of bishops (the Church is a communion of churches), the development of various social action and social ministry projects (the mission of the Church includes the struggle for justice, peace, and human rights), the emergence of new movements and forms of spirituality (all are called to holiness since the whole Church is to be a sign of the Gospel), and ecumenical dialogues and common prayer (the Church is the whole Body of Christ).

6.   There are at least three basic perspectives (models of the Church) in ecclesiology today: Church as *institution,* as *community,* and as *servant.* The first was the dominant perspective in the pre-Vatican II period (Church as a hierarchically structured, visible society, means of salvation, through word and sacrament); the second was encouraged by the council itself (Church as people, fellowship, community); and the third was impelled by the activist concerns of the 1960s and a renewed appreciation of the Church's social doctrine (Church as agent of social change, instrument of liberation, etc.).

7.   *Institutional model:*

strengths: clear sense of Christian identity, of each member's place and role within the Church, and of the continuity of the Church's present faith with the past.

weaknesses: too hierarchical, too clerical, too Roman, too much focused on word and sacrament, and too disposed to identifying Church and Kingdom.

8.   *Community model:*

strengths: consistently with Bible, Fathers of Church, and Vatican II, stresses responsibility of Church for human growth of members, and underlines call to be a sign to others through mutual love and concern.

weaknesses: not always clear on distinctiveness of Christian community, and may exaggerate growth of the individual at the expense of social and political mission.

9.   *Servant model:*

strengths: recognizes wider meaning of Kingdom of God as a Kingdom of justice and peace, and incorporates *diakonia* into the essence of mission.

weaknesses: not clear on distinctiveness of Church, and can lead to identification of Church and Kingdom also.

10.   A balanced theology of the Church must incorporate all three models.

11.   *Definition:* The Church is the whole body, or congregation, of persons who are called by God the Father to acknowledge the Lordship of Jesus, the Son, in word, in sacrament, in witness, and in service, and, through the power of the Holy Spirit, to collaborate with Jesus' historic mission for the sake of the Kingdom of God.

12.   The definition embraces Catholics, Orthodox, Anglicans, and Protestants alike, and applies at once to the Church universal and to the local church. The Church is, in fact, a communion of churches.

13.   Church comes into being where there is (1) a confession of Jesus as Lord, (2) sacramental ratification of that faith, (3) reverence for the Bible, (4) a sense of fellowship, (5) a readiness to apply the Gospel to life, and (6) some ministerial structure to insure stability and direction to the community.

14.   The *mission* of the Church is directed to the *Kingdom of God,* which is the redemptive presence of God actualized through the power of God's reconciling Spirit. The mission is threefold: *proclamation* in word and sacrament *(kerygma* and *leitourgia),* signification *(koinonia* and *marturia),* and service *(diakonia).*

15.   *Proclamation* focuses on the significance of Jesus Christ and is principally expressed in the *Eucharist,* which looks to the past (when God acted in Christ), the present (where God continues to act in Christ and the Spirit), and the future (when God will bring all things to perfection in Christ, by the power of the Spirit). That proclamation, whether in word or sacrament, is always *prophetic* (prophecy means speaking on behalf of God). Everything is measured against the standard of the coming Kingdom of God.

16.   *Signification* emphasizes the sacramentality of the Church. The Church is called to be a sign of what it proclaims and of what it embodies (mystery). Accordingly, the Church must be holy and must engage in continuing institutional reform.

17.   *Service* even in the socio-political order is required by the social and institutional character of sin, and by the Church's obligation to practice and uphold virtue, including social justice.

18.   *Intervention* in the political arena must meet the following criteria: (1) justice-related issue, (2) competence of the Church to deal with it at all, (3) sufficient resources within the Church to deal with it effectively, (4) priority of this issue over other issues, and (5) form of action that is not unnecessarily or unduly polarizing.

19.   The Church is *necessary* insofar as it helps answer the quest for meaning (the psychological need), for a community of shared meaning (the sociological need), and for guidance and example in the pursuit of salvation (the theological need). This need is incumbent on every human being in principle and on the world at large, but specifically upon those individuals in the world who are persuaded by the proclamation of the Lordship of Jesus.

20.   The Church is a *sacrament for the world,* to disclose what God is doing for all. Its necessity for the world is *historically contingent;* i.e., the Kingdom hypothetically could come about without the Church or even without Jesus, but *in fact* it will not come about without them.

21.   The Church is necessary for those *individuals* who are called by God to confess Jesus as Lord, but that necessity is also *contingent* on the call of God to this community (the Church) rather than to some other community.

22.   Roman Catholicism *characteristically* emphasizes the triumph of grace over sin as a transforming presence; tradition, doctrine, and continuity; peoplehood, community, and church; and especially the principles of sacramentality and mediation. Roman Catholicism is *distinctive* in its conviction regarding the fundamental importance of the Petrine ministry to the life and mission of the Church and in its comprehensive (catholic) grasp of the preceding characteristics.

23.   Roman Catholicism is as *necessary* for the *world* as the whole Church is necessary, namely, as a sign and instrument *(sacrament)* of the world's salvation. It is necessary for the whole *Body of Christ* because Roman Catholicism alone has all the institutional elements necessary for the integrity of the Body of Christ as well as the many characteristically Catholic values which enrich and enhance the life and mission of the whole People of God. Finally, Roman Catholicism is necessary for the *individual* who is called not only to confess the Lordship of Jesus but also to enter into explicit union with that communion of churches whose visible center of unity is the Petrine minister within the college of bishops.

24.   This understanding of the necessity of Roman Catholicism differs from the common pre-Vatican II understanding of the Roman Catholic Church as the "one, true Church of Christ." The deeper theological reasons for the shift in understanding are the renewed appreciation of the universality of grace and revelation, and the recognition that the Church (i.e., the whole Body of Christ) is composed of many churches, some of which are not in communion with the bishop of Rome.

SUGGESTED READINGS

Dulles, Avery. *Models of the Church*. New York: Doubleday, 1974.

Gilkey, Langdon. *Catholicism Confronts Modernity: A Protestant View*. New York: Seabury Press, 1975.

Gutierrez, Gustavo. *A Theology of Liberation*. Maryknoll, New York: Orbis Books, 1972.

Küng, Hans. *On Being a Christian*. New York: Doubleday, 1976.

McBrien, Richard P. *Church: The Continuing Quest*. New York: Newman Press, 1970.

——————. *Do We Need the Church?* New York: Harper & Row, 1969.

——————. *The Remaking of the Church: An Agenda for Reform.* New York: Harper & Row, 1973.

——————. *Who Is a Catholic?* Denville, N.J.: Dimension Books, 1971.

——————. "On Being a Catholic." *Why Catholic?* Ed. John Delaney. New York: Doubleday, 1979, pp. 115-136.

Pannenberg, Wolfhart. *Theology and the Kingdom of God.* Philadelphia: Westminster Press, 1969.

Schineller, Peter, et al. *Why the Church?* New York: Paulist Press, 1977.

THE SACRAMENTS OF INITIATION: BAPTISM, CONFIRMATION, AND EUCHARIST

THE PLACE OF SACRAMENTAL THEOLOGY

As has been noted several times throughout this book, a major theological, pastoral, and even aesthetical characteristic of Catholicism is its commitment to the *sacramental principle*. Catholicism has never hesitated to affirm the "mysterious" dimension of all reality: the cosmos, nature, history, events, persons, objects, rituals, words. Everything is, in principle, capable of embodying and communicating the divine. God is at once everywhere and all-powerful. There is no finite instrument that God cannot put to use. On the other hand, we humans have nothing else apart from finite instruments to express our own response to God's self-communication. Just as the divine reaches us through the finite, so we reach the divine through the finite. The point at which this "divine commerce" occurs is the point of *sacramental encounter*. For Christians, *the* point of a sacramental encounter with God is Jesus Christ.

Catholicism has also historically emphasized the notion of peoplehood and of church as a *mediating* principle. God's relationship to us and our relationship to God is not exclusively, nor even primarily, individual and personal. It is corporate and communal. "In Adam's fall, we sinned all." If indeed our relationship with God were not primarily corporate and communal, rather than individual and personal, the doctrines of Original Sin and of redemption would make no sense. But the principle of human solidarity is not only a theological principle. It is also firmly grounded in modern social science (e.g., Max Scheler, Alfred Schutz, Emile Durkheim, George Herbert Mead, Georges Gurvitch) and, beyond that, in the contemporary human experience of *interdependence* (see chapter 3).

Those points of encounter between God and humankind, therefore, are never simply "transactions" between the divine and *this* person, although they are also clearly that as well. God touches all of humankind, and the human community as a whole responds to its experience of the divine through a sacramental mode. The word *sacramental* is being used here in its *widest sense*, of course. It applies to *any finite reality through which the divine is perceived to be disclosed and communicated, and through which our human response to the divine assumes some measure of shape, form, and structure.* (We cannot go into any detail regarding this wider understanding and manifestation of sacramentality. The interested reader should consult the work of Mircea Eliade—e.g., *Patterns in Comparative Religion*, New York: Sheed & Ward, 1958, and *Myths, Rites, Symbols: A Mircea Eliade Reader*, W. C. Beane and W. G. Doty, eds., New York: Harper & Row, 1976.)

Taken in the more *specific* sense as *those finite realities through which God is communicated to the Church and through which the Church responds to God's self-communication,* sacraments are directly ecclesiological in character. This is not to say that sacraments are not also linked closely with theological anthropology, with Christology, with eschatology, or with Christian moral life. But their immediate context is the Church. The redeemed human person (theological anthropology) is made visible in the Church. Christ is mediated through the Church. The Church is the sign and instrument of the Kingdom of God (eschatology). Christian moral life is Christian existence, i.e., our way of being Church.

The Church is the *fundamental sacrament* of God's promise and deliverance of the Kingdom of God in Jesus Christ. It is the "sacrament of universal salvation" (*Lumen gentium*, n. 48). The sacraments, i.e., those seven specific actions which the Church has defined to be sacraments (Eucharist, Baptism, Confirmation, Penance, Anointing of the Sick, Marriage, and Holy Order), are acts of God, to be sure. They are acts of Christ, to be sure. But they are immediately *acts of the Church*. They are expressions of the nature and mission of the Church. The sacraments are not simply actions which the Church performs, or means by which the Church makes grace available. They are moments when the Church becomes Church, manifesting itself as Church to itself and to others.

Correspondingly, those who receive the sacraments are not only related anew to God or to Christ. The sacraments immediately relate the recipient to the Church. The *lasting effect* of the sacrament (the *res et sacramentum*, to be explained in due course) is one of *relationship with the Church*. Thus, the sacrament of Penance has as its immediate purpose and effect not the restoration of friendship with God but reconciliation with the Church. Why else, for example, is a penitent who has committed a serious sin but who has made an act of perfect contrition (which restores union with God) still required to seek forgiveness in the sacrament? The reason is that serious sin compromises the mission of the Church to be a holy people, a credible and effective sacrament of Christ and of the Kingdom of God. It is not just God who is "offended" by the sin. The Church, too, has been violated. Its sacramentality has been tarnished. The sinner also has to "make up" with the Church.

This is not to say that sacramental theology is not at the same time closely connected with Christology, with which it has usually been placed in the past. It is Christ who is encountered in the sacraments. It is Christ who acts in the sacraments. It is Christ's worship of the Father that is carried forward in the sacraments. On the other hand, a too-close connection between sacramental theology and Christology tends to lead to an exaggeration of such questions as the "institution" of the sacraments by Christ and the power of the sacraments to "infuse" the grace of Christ, earned on Calvary, to the individual recipient, even when that individual is a seven-day-old infant. Doing sacramental theology as part of Christology rather than ecclesiology also tends to ignore the sacramental principle itself. We do not encounter Christ directly, but in the Church, which is his Body. Although it is Christ who is present and active in every sacramental celebration, it is the Church which makes that celebration available and which mediates the presence and action of Christ.

SACRAMENTS IN GENERAL
Signs of Faith

It is not an exaggeration to suggest that Catholic sacramental theology and practice, from the time of the Reformation until the full flowering of the liturgical renewal at the Second Vatican Council, concentrated too much on the *causality* of the sacraments and too little on their role as *signs*. Accordingly, it seemed to make little difference if the congregation failed to grasp the meaning of the words and rituals of the Eucharist and the other sacraments, so long as the sacraments were validly administered by an authorized minister using the prescribed matter and form, to a properly disposed recipient (i.e., someone not placing an obstacle in the way, such as lack of faith or serious sin). But it was the clear teaching of the Council of Trent (*Decree on the Sacraments,* Session VII, 1547), and before that of Thomas Aquinas (*Summa Theologica* III, qq. 60-65), that *sacraments cause grace insofar as they signify it*. Indeed, the twentieth-century renewal of sacramental theology is essentially a rediscovery of that Thomistic perspective.

Before the time of Aquinas, moreover, the emphasis had been on the sign. It was Augustine who gave the first technical definition of a sacrament as a sign of grace ("a visible sign of invisible grace"). The priority of sign over cause continued until the scholastic revival of the twelfth century. Its thinking was climaxed and balanced by Thomas, who added the notion of *efficacious* sign of grace; i.e., the sacraments *cause* what they signify. Thomas' own great contribution lay in his exposition of *how* the sacraments cause grace. Although Thomas himself was exceedingly well balanced in his understanding of the relationship between sign and cause, post-medieval theology was not. The sign aspect of sacraments receded from the center of ecclesial consciousness. The sacraments were perceived as instruments of grace, producing their spiritual effects by the very performance of the ritual according to the prescribed manner (*ex opere operato*, "from the work worked").

Thomas devoted his entire first question in sacramental theology (III, q. 60) to the sign, and it is a motif that runs through his whole treatment of the sacraments. The purpose of a sign, he insisted, is to instruct, to call to mind the reality that it signifies. In using the sign, we, from our side, express our *faith* in the unseen reality hidden underneath the sign. Sacraments, then, are signs which proclaim faith.

Secondly, sacraments are signs which express *worship*. Through the sacraments we participate ritually, i.e., through signs, in Christ's own worship of the Father. The Lord's Supper, or Eucharist, is linked from the beginning with the Passover meal, at which Israel gratefully (eucharistically) relived its deliverance from the bondage of Egypt and prayed for the coming of the Messiah. The early Church spoke of Christ as its Passover who had been sacrificed (1 Corinthians 5:7) and related its own fellowship meals to Christ's sacrificial action (1 Corinthians 10:16-17).

Thirdly, sacraments are signs of the *unity of the Church*. The faith that is expressed in each sacrament is the faith *of* the Church and the faith mediated to the individual *by* the Church. Insofar as the celebrants (recipients, ministers, congregation) of a sacrament have a common faith in what they do and in whom they encounter through what they do, the sacrament is also a sign of the Church's faith and of its unity.

Fourthly, sacraments are signs of *Christ's presence*, and ultimately of God the Father's. Since Christ is neither God alone nor a human being alone, but the God-man, the human actions of Christ which are memorialized and represented in the sacraments, especially in the Eucharist, are not confined to the actual time in which they were first expressed (e.g., at the Last Supper, on a particular occasion, in a particular room, during a particular moment in human history). Because Christ himself is also a sacrament, indeed the *primordial* sacrament (or sacrament of the "first order"), God is present in and through him. And since God transcends time as well as space, the saving presence and action of God in Christ is mediated every time the sacrament is celebrated. The risen Lord lives now, at this moment. His presence is signified in every sacrament.

Causes of Grace

The traditional (i.e., post-Trent, pre-Vatican II) explanation of sacramental causality stressed the teaching of Trent's canon 6: "If anyone says that the sacraments of the New Law do not contain the grace which they signify, or that they do not confer that grace on those who place no obstacles in the way...let him be anathema." Neither the merit (holiness) of the minister nor that of the recipient is causally involved, except in a negative way (i.e., the recipient must not put an obstacle in the way). What the Council of Trent was trying to safeguard was the basic truth that the grace of the sacraments is caused not by human forces but by God acting in and through Christ and the Church. We do not merit saving grace; it is a pure gift of God. The phrase *"non ponentibus obicem"* ("for those not placing an obstacle") was taken from Augustine, who had used it to support the argument that infants receive the grace of Baptism because they are clearly not capable of placing any moral obstacle to it. Trent applied the principle across the sacramental board: *It is not the personal merit of the recipient that causes the grace received.* On the other hand, God does not force the human will.

Its balance and good intentions notwithstanding, the teaching of the council was more often misunderstood than understood. Many Catholics came to believe that the graces of the sacraments were theirs if only they placed no obstacle, i.e., were not in mortal sin. The measure of preparation, the intensity of faith, the awareness of the sign's meaning—none of these counted in the end. So long as there is no moral obstacle, the sacrament "works."

Thomas Aquinas, on the other hand, never used the phrase "not placing an obstacle." He refers always to the sign of the sacrament as serving to dispose one more perfectly for receiving sacramental graces (*ex opere operantis*, "from the work of the worker"). He calls for an interior conversion to God, for a personal encounter between the Christian and Christ. Rarely does he speak of "valid reception" of the sacrament. He emphasizes instead the "right disposition" which is worthy of a Christian: faith and devotion.

In fact, this Thomistic stress on the right disposition is so much a part of authentic Catholic tradition that a present-day theologian, Karl Rahner, argues that there is always an element of uncertainty about the effect of the sacrament. "With the sacrament a person knows just as little as he does with his merely 'subjective' actions performed in faith, whether it has really given him God's grace. Just as little and just as much" (*The Church and the Sacraments*, p. 25). The popular notion has been just the opposite, of course. The belief has prevailed among Catholics that they are always more certain that their sins have been forgiven in the sacrament of Penance than are Protestants and others who have to rely solely on the precarious path of personal contrition. "Falsely, therefore, do some accuse Catholic writers as if they maintained that the sacrament of penance confers grace without any good disposition on the part of those receiving it; this is something which the Church of God never taught or accepted" (Trent, *Doctrine on the Sacrament of Penance*, chapter IV, Session XIV, 1551).

But this is looking at the matter from the point of view of the individual who is free and, therefore, has no certain knowledge that his or her own life will end victoriously in the Kingdom of God. On the other hand, it is the faith and hope of the Church as a whole that the world has been redeemed and that history itself will reach final salvation because of what God has already revealed and achieved in Christ. At least to this extent, the individual is assured that the grace of salvation is present and available in and through this sign (*ex opere operato*). We also know that each one of us remains free to give a "Yes" or a "No" (and this is the *opus operantis*).

The sacraments do not cause grace magically. They are free acts of God, and they are free acts of ours. They "work" only to the extent that we bring faith and devotion to them. "Sacraments are nothing but God's efficacious word to man, the word in which God offers himself to man and thereby liberates man's freedom to accept God's self-communication by his own act" (Karl Rahner, *Foundations of Christian Faith*, p. 415).

Effects of Sacraments

The sacraments do not cause grace in the sense that grace is otherwise unavailable. Grace is already present to the individual, to the Church, and to the human community at large in God's original self-communication, as we noted in chapter 5. The sacraments shape and "channel" that original communication of grace so that the divine presence may be effective for this individual or for this group insofar as they are members of the Church and responsible for its mission.

Thus, we do not "need" Baptism to become children of God and heirs of heaven. Every human person, by reason of birth, is already a child of God and an heir of heaven. Unbaptized infants do not go to Limbo, a state of "natural happiness" without the vision and company of God. We do not "need" the sacrament of Holy Order to minister to others. Every person, by reason of his or her humanity, is called and empowered to minister to others. We do not "need" the sacrament of Matrimony to commit ourselves to another for life. And so on. *The sacraments signify and celebrate what God is in fact doing everywhere and for all.* But the sacraments also mandate and equip specific members of the human community, i.e., disciples of Jesus Christ, to be the corporate sign and instrument of God's presence and saving activity in Christ. Once again, sacraments establish a relationship ultimately with God and with Christ but immediately with the Church.

Thus, in every sacrament there is, in addition to the sign or ritual (*sacramentum tantum*, "the sign alone") and the grace, or immediate effect (*res tantum*, "the reality alone"), the lasting effect (*res et sacramentum*). It is that which is signified by the *sacramentum tantum* (the rite) and, in turn, disposes the recipient to grace (the *res tantum*). Why did this distinction arise in sacramental theology? As a way of dealing with one of the major medieval challenges to the Real Presence of Christ in the Eucharist.

According to Augustine, "A good man receives the sacrament and reality of the sacrament, but a bad man receives only the sacrament and not the reality" (*Commentary on John*, 26,11). What Augustine had in mind by "reality" was the grace of the sacrament. Berengar of Tours (d. 1088) accepted the reality of the sacrament, i.e., the grace of union with Christ, but he denied that Christ's true body was present in the Eucharist. For him there were only two elements in the sacrament: the external sign, or symbol, and the ultimate effect, the grace. Theologians did not agree upon a third eucharistic element for almost a century. Not until Hugh of St. Victor (d. 1142) and Peter Lombard (d. 1160) did the concept of the *res et sacramentum* finally emerge. The bread and wine (*sacramentum tantum*) signify the body and blood of Christ (*res et sacramentum*); the body and blood of Christ, in turn, are the basis for union with Christ (*res tantum*) insofar as the body and blood are received worthily. But whether they are received worthily or not, the body and blood of Christ are really present because they have been signified and made present by the *sacramentum tantum* (the rite of the Eucharist).

Only gradually was the triple distinction applied to all of the sacraments, and only more recently, in the closing decades of the nineteenth century, was the *res et sacramentum* understood in a consistently ecclesiological sense, namely, in Matthias Scheeben's (d. 1888) *The Mysteries of Christianity.* For Scheeben, the *res et sacramentum* of the Eucharist is not just the risen body of the Lord, but the whole Christ, the Church.

By tradition the Church does not repeat three sacraments: Baptism, Confirmation, and Order. They are received only once. The *res et sacramentum* for those three sacraments is also called the *"character."* The term was taken over from pagan antiquity, where it referred to the seal by which a soldier or a slave might be identified as belonging to the service of the emperor or an owner. When used by Christians like Tertullian and Augustine, the term was intended to apply to the sacramental rite alone. It was the rite of sealing by which a person became a Christian for life, even if he or she were to lapse into heresy or schism. Only later, in the medieval period, did the word "character" become identified with the *res et sacramentum*, i.e., the lasting effect which is distinguishable from the rite itself as well as from the grace produced by the sacrament. The term *character* does not refer to an indelible mark on the soul, as some catechisms had it. It is simply the word used to describe the permanent effect of three sacraments: Baptism, Confirmation, and Holy Order. These sacraments are not, in fact, administered more than once to the same person during the course of his lifetime. Therefore, they must produce some effect that is permanent (= "the character").

The *res et sacramentum* of *Baptism* and *Confirmation* is membership in the Church and responsibility for its mission. For *Holy Order* it is the abiding responsibility for pastoral service to the Church. For the non-character sacraments, explanations vary: *Matrimony* (the bond of union between man and woman, symbolizing the union of Christ and the Church), *Penance* (reconciliation with the Church), *Anointing of the Sick* (a healing of the separation between the individual and the Church created not by sin but by sickness), and the *Eucharist* (the real presence of Christ). In each instance, the *res et sacramentum* is signified by the rite itself (*sacramentum tantum*) and disposes the recipient(s) for the grace that is appropriate to the special relationship with the Church which is called for in this particular sacrament.

Intention of Minister and Recipient

The Minister

The sacraments do not achieve their intended effect if certain conditions are not fulfilled on the part of the minister of the sacrament and on the part of the recipient. The sacraments are acts of the Church. *The minister represents the Church and acts in its name.* Since everything the Church does, it does as the Body of Christ, the minister of a sacrament also acts in the name of Christ. On the other hand, the sacramental act is not automatic in its effect. The minister must voluntarily carry out the intention of the Church. He or she must intend what the Church intends. This does not mean, however, that the minister must also be a person of profound faith or even of moral probity, although both of these are eminently desirable. But if those qualities were demanded of each minister in every instance, the Church would never know when and to what extent its sacraments were properly celebrated and administered.

It is precisely because the sacraments are acts of the Church, and not simply acts of personal devotion, that the role of the minister is so important. There has been much controversy in the history of Catholic theology over this question of the minister's intention. Is it possible, for example, for a Jewish nurse to baptize validly a dying person who wishes to be baptized? The standard answer has been "Yes, so long as he or she intends to do what the Church intends." The theological problem with this approach is that it tends to conceive of the sacraments as indispensable means of achieving some spiritual effect. But they are not any more "indispensable" than the Church itself. People can be saved without Baptism (unless they know themselves to be called to the Church and deliberately reject the call), and in extraordinary cases people can even enter the Church without Baptism (as in the case of the dying person who wishes to be associated with the Body of Christ in some explicit way but is physically incapable of passing through the normal rite of initiation). Indeed, a catechumen is already in some real sense a part of the Church even before receiving Baptism itself.

It is the official teaching of the Catholic Church that the minister must have at least "the intention of doing what the Church does" (Council of Florence, *Decree for the Armenians*, 1439; and also Council of Trent, *Decree on the Sacraments*, canon 11). The validity of the sacrament is independent of the worthiness of the minister (condemnation of Wyclif by the Council of Constance, 1415; Council of Trent, *op. cit.*, canon 12). But not every member of the Church is qualified to administer every sacrament (Council of Trent, canon 10: "If anyone says that all Christians have the power (to preach) the word and to administer all the sacraments, *anathema sit*").

The Recipient

The *fruitful reception* of the sacraments (in contradistinction to their valid celebration) depends, as noted earlier, on the *disposition* of the recipient. Again, the sacraments are not magic. Sacraments are acts of the Church. The reception of sacraments draws one more fully into the life and mission of the Church. A sacrament can have no ecclesiological impact if the intended recipient has no faith in it or in the reality it symbolizes, or if he or she is morally unprepared for it.

What of a person who receives Baptism, Confirmation, or Holy Order in a state of mortal sin? The traditional answer would have it that the sacrament is validly received but that the grace is not communicated unless and until perfect contrition occurs. The answer is still correct in principle, but the case presupposes that "mortal sin" is relatively common even among active members of the Church who frequent the sacraments and who would be deemed fit candidates for one of the character sacraments. On the contrary, mortal sin involves a fundamental rejection of God and the reorientation of one's whole life away from all that is good and just. It is not something that one "commits" frequently. Certainly it will be rare, even non-existent, in the life of a sincere and active member of the Church (see also chapter 26). Furthermore, this assumption that mortal sin may often obstruct the grace of a character sacrament also seems to forget the principle reaffirmed by the Second Vatican Council's *Dogmatic Constitution on the Sacred Liturgy*: "(The sacraments) do indeed impart grace, but, in addition, the very act of celebrating them most effectively disposes the faithful to receive this grace in a fruitful manner, to worship God duly, and to practice charity" (n. 59). This does not make conversion inevitable, however.

This raises, finally, the question of the *Baptism of infants*, since we have here the case of persons who are manifestly incapable of being "disposed" for a fruitful reception of a sacrament. Two extremes are to be avoided: one which assumes that the primary purpose of Baptism is the "washing away of Original Sin" so that the Baptism of infants is a matter of highest priority no matter what the circumstances; the other which assumes that sacraments are only for adults and that life in the Church is within reach only of adults or of mature young people. Just as one enters a family by birth and is really a part of that family even though for a long period of time there is no real capacity for giving human love but only for receiving it, so one may be brought into the family of the Church before he or she is capable of understanding its significance or of expressing the love that marks this community out as the Body of Christ and the Temple of the Holy Spirit. In the case of infants, the intention is expressed not by the child but by those who bring the child for Baptism—e.g., parents, sponsors, relatives, and friends (*Summa Theologica*, III, q. 68, art. 9). There is a coresponsibility here that is also not foreign to sacraments even for adults. One thinks, e.g., of the role of sponsors and of one's family and friends at Confirmation, of the witnesses and one's family and friends at Marriage, of one's loved ones and others at the Anointing of the Sick.

Institution of the Sacraments

Were the sacraments "instituted" by Christ? Here again, the question is to be answered in its larger ecclesiological context. Just as the Church was not "founded" by Christ in the sense that he immediately and directly established a new religion, with specific organizational structure, doctrines, moral codes, and so forth (see chapter 17), neither do the sacraments issue from some precise mandate of the Lord. On the other hand, the Church does have its origin in Jesus Christ, especially in his proclamation of the Kingdom of God and the call to discipleship; and the sacraments, in turn, have their origin in the Church.

The question is also to be answered in terms of Christology. If one adopts exclusively a Christology "from above" (as in the Johannine writings), then, of course, every possibility is open. The omniscient *Logos* came down from heaven with his program and mission already marked out. He intended the Church as we know it, with the full sacramental life as exists in it. But if one starts instead with the historical Jesus (Christology "from below"), it becomes historically improbable that Jesus would have explicitly determined more than the Synoptic Gospels indicate. *Jesus willed the sacraments to the same degree and extent as he willed the Church.*

The rapidity with which Catholic theology, under the impact of recent developments in ecclesiology, in Christology, and in biblical studies, is moving away from the standard textbook treatments of the institution and the number of sacraments is very remarkable. In 1960 the Dutch theologian Edward Schillebeeckx argued in his important and influential work, *Christ the Sacrament of Encounter with God*, that "Christ...must himself have established the sevenfold direction of grace..." (p. 116).

Just three years later Karl Rahner was beginning to move beyond that cautious view, arguing that "the institution of a sacrament can...follow simply from the fact that Christ founded the Church with its sacramental nature" (*The Church and the Sacraments*, p. 41). And then in a later book (published originally in German in 1976), Rahner questioned even the possibility of tracing Baptism back to the words of Jesus, leaving the Lord's Supper as the only sacrament directly instituted by Christ ("Do this in remembrance of me," Luke 22:19; 1 Corinthians 11:24). He continues to link the "institution" of the sacraments with the "founding" of the Church, in an analogous way. The Church is in its essence sacramental, i.e., "the irreversible presence of God's salvific offer in Christ. This sacramentality is interpreted by the church in the seven sacraments, just as the church developed its own essence in its constitution. From this perspective, an individual Christian can accept without hesitation and live out this seven-fold sacramental order as it in fact exists" (*Foundations of Christian Faith*, p. 413).

The Number of Sacraments

What is essential is not the number seven, but the affirmation that there are certain ritual actions through which the saving presence and activity of God, on the one hand, and the sacramental nature of the Church, on the other, are visibly and effectively engaged. Even according to the most stringent interpretation of the teaching of the Council of Trent that there are seven sacraments, one could say that there are nine, taking diaconate and the episcopate as separate sacramental stages of the sacrament of Holy Order. Or one could say there are only six, considering Baptism and Confirmation as one sacrament. Or one could say that there are eight, combining Baptism and Confirmation but expanding Holy Order from one sacramental order to three.

It was and always is up to the Church to determine whether certain acts flowing from its nature as a sacrament of universal salvation are fundamentally and unconditionally a realization and expression of that nature. Before the number seven was finally settled upon during the medieval period (at Lyons II in 1274, at Florence in 1439, and at Trent in 1547), the Church lived through its entire first millennium and then some without ever having settled upon even a final definition of *sacrament*, let alone their precise number. On the contrary, there were literally hundreds of sacred rites (what we call today "sacramentals") which were simply referred to as "sacraments." These included Sacred Scripture, the mysteries of faith, cultic rites, and even allegory and typology.

Today *sacramentals* are understood as sacred signs which bear a resemblance to the sacraments. Insofar as the sacramentals cause grace, they do so not *ex opere operato*, primarily through the power of the rite itself, but *ex opere operantis*, primarily through the faith and devotion of those who are using, receiving, or celebrating the sacramental. Examples of sacramentals are baptismal water, holy oils, blessed ashes, candles, palms, crucifixes, statues, and medals.

THE RITE OF INITIATION

Most Christians are baptized shortly after birth, but Confirmation and Eucharist are postponed for several years. What is the usual practice is far from the ideal, however. The norm, as set down in the new *Rite of Christian Initiation*, is that a person should receive all three sacraments during the annual celebration of the Easter Vigil, following a suitable period of formation known as the *catechumenate*. But even when the norm cannot be observed, i.e., when Baptism is not followed immediately by Confirmation, or when the sequence of Confirmation and Eucharist is reversed, the ritual still calls for some post-baptismal anointing to replace Confirmation, and at Confirmation itself, the Baptism is renewed and reaffirmed and the Confirmation rite leads to eucharistic Communion.

The doctrine of Christian initiation is summed up in the "General Introduction" to the rite in the revised Roman Ritual:

1.   Through the sacraments of Christian initiation men and women are freed from the power of darkness. With Christ they die, are buried and rise again. They receive the Spirit of adoption which makes them God's sons and daughters and, with the entire people of God, they celebrate the memorial of the Lord's death and resurrection.

2.   Through baptism men and women are incorporated into Christ. They are formed into God's people, and they obtain forgiveness of all their sins. They are raised from their natural human condition to the dignity of adopted children. They become a new creation through water and the Holy Spirit. Hence they are called, and are indeed, the children of God.

Signed with the gift of the Spirit in confirmation, Christians more perfectly become the image of their Lord and are filled with the Holy Spirit. They bear witness to him before all the world and eagerly work for the building up of the body of Christ.

Finally they come to the table of the eucharist, to eat the flesh and drink the blood of the Son of Man so that they may have eternal life and show forth the unity of God's people. By offering themselves with Christ, they share in his universal sacrifice: the entire community of the redeemed is offered to God by their high priest. They pray for a greater outpouring of the Holy Spirit so that the whole human race may be brought into the unity of God's family.

Thus the three sacraments of Christian initiation closely combine to bring the faithful to the full stature of Christ and to enable them to carry out the mission of the entire people of God in the Church and in the world.

(*The Rites of the Catholic Church*, New York: Pueblo Publishing Co., 1976, pp. 3–4)

It is clear from this "General Introduction" and from the introductions to the other separate rites, including the Baptism of children and Confirmation by bishops, that *the premier rite is that of full initiation of adults*. All the other initiatory rites are to be understood in the context of this *Rite of Christian Initiation of Adults*, and their various details often refer back to the full rite of adult initiation as the governing norm of them all.

This represents a major shift in theological and pastoral understanding from the sacramental theology and liturgical practice of the pre-Vatican II Church and those of the post-Vatican II Church. In the pre-Vatican II period, many theological explanations of the sacraments began with the Baptism of infants, as if to underline the principle that the sacraments really do confer grace *ex opere operato*, by the power of Christ alone and not by the faith of the recipient (as some Protestants had insisted). Adult Baptisms were essentially modifications of the rite of infant Baptism (in much the same way as adult religious education was regarded as the exception, and the religious education of youth the norm).

A second major change suggested by the new rites, especially of adult initiation, is the explicit recognition that *the sacraments are closely related one to another*. Baptism is not simply the "ticket" which gives one entrance into the Church's sacred grounds, nor is Confirmation the first moment when the Holy Spirit is conferred (see *The Rites*, n. 34, p. 30). Baptism, Confirmation, and the Eucharist are all of a piece. One is not simply handed a membership card. One is fully introduced into the Spirit-filled life of the community which is God's people and Christ's body.

Thirdly, the sacraments are seen less as means of personal sanctification and more as *empowerments* "*to carry out the mission of the entire people of God in the Church and in the world*." The broader ecclesial vision is sharpened by the directive that the rite of Christian initiation should normally occur during the Easter Vigil which "speaks" about initiation in terms of the evangelization of the cosmos: fire, wind, wax, bees, light and darkness, water, oil, nakedness, bread, wine, aromas, words, and gestures. The full paschal sweep of God's intentions and accomplishments in Jesus

Christ is sketched out. All of the other sacraments and sacramentals find their meaning and purpose only within this salvation-history context (the work of the "economic Trinity" to which we referred in chapters 9 and 10).

Finally, therefore, with the restoration of the catechumenate (the process of pastoral formation of candidates for entrance into the Church), the point is reinforced that membership in the Church is *not simply for individual salvation but for participation in the saving work of God, in Christ, through the Church.* One does not assume this missionary responsibility lightly. The Church, both universal and local, has to take care that those who present themselves for membership understand that missionary responsibility and are properly equipped to fulfill it. All must share in the candidate's growth in faith: the community at large, relatives, friends, the sponsors, catechists, the bishop or his delegate, priests, and deacons.

It is important to note, however, that the catechumenate does *not* apply to those who are seeking entrance into the Catholic Church from some other Christian community. Eastern Orthodox Christians need only make a simple profession of faith, but only after recourse to Rome may they enter the Latin rite. In other cases the admission to the Catholic Church consists of the profession of faith, ordinarily with the Catholic community as a part of the eucharistic celebration, followed by Confirmation (if the person has not already been confirmed in his or her own church), and climaxed by eucharistic Communion for the first time within the Catholic community. No abjuration of heresy is required, as in the past, nor is the candidate to be absolved from any penalty of excommunication. Conditional Baptism ("If you are not already baptized, I baptize you...") is not permitted "unless there is reasonable doubt about the fact or validity of the baptism already received. If after serious investigation it seems necessary—because of such reasonable doubt—to confer baptism conditionally, the minister should carefully explain beforehand the reasons..., and he should administer it in the private form" (*Directory on Ecumenism*, 1967).

BAPTISM
New Testament Origins

Pre-Christian Ablutions and Baptisms

There were already many different kinds of ritual acts in Judaism, including those practiced by the Qumran sect, or Essenes. There were purification rites associated with food preparation and diet, and there were initiatory rites associated with water. This practice of *proselyte baptism* (by which Gentiles became Jews) seems to have developed with the expansion of Judaism outside Palestine. It had three phases: instruction concerning Judaism's persecuted condition and the commandments of the Law, circumcision for males, and a water bath for all. The central element of this ritual process was circumcision, by which solidarity was established with the holy nation of kings and priests (Exodus 19:6). Gradually, the water bath began to absorb the initiatory aspects of circumcision, and finally displaced it altogether. By the Christian era, therefore, proselyte baptism had assumed an increasingly initiatory rather than purificatory character.

This is not to suggest that Christian Baptism was derived from proselyte baptism. What evidence there is leads us to conclude, on the contrary, that Christian Baptism was patterned after the baptism of Jesus by John the Baptist in the Jordan river. There is no hint of a death-resurrection theme, no initiatory motif, no notion of admission to a new community. The emphasis is instead upon repentance as a preparation for messianic work. John's baptism was also a baptism in water. It would give way to another baptism in water and the Holy Spirit (Matthew 3:11; Luke 3:16). John himself regarded his baptism as a temporary rite. In submitting to it, Jesus established his solidarity with those who were the objects of John's preaching, the faithful remnant of Israel.

Baptism in Transition: From Judaism to Christianity

The Fourth Gospel says at one point that Jesus himself baptized, and at another that he did not but authorized his disciples to do so (John 3:22–23; 4:1–4). In any case, baptism continued to be practiced outside Jesus' circle, and it eventually widened the rift between his disciples and the followers of John. These pre-paschal baptisms were no longer Jewish, but neither were they as yet fully Christian. Not until the gathering at Pentecost is the outpouring of the Holy Spirit associated with baptism (Acts of the Apostles 2:1–39). There can be little doubt that the Pentecost occurrence influenced the ways in which the evangelists later interpreted the baptism of Jesus by John and the subsequent initiatory practice of the Church. Both water baptism and the outpouring of the Spirit are necessary as a follow-up to the proclamation of Jesus' resurrection and exaltation. Thus, the normal sequence: proclamation of the Gospel, conversion in faith, water bath, and post-baptismal teaching, fellowship in the Spirit, breaking of the bread, and prayers (Acts of the Apostles 2:42).

Baptism in the New Testament Churches

The relatively sparse data from the Synoptics, the Acts of the Apostles, and the Fourth Gospel is summarized in the preceding paragraph. More detail is provided by non-canonical writings (i.e., writings which were written at the same time as the New Testament but which were not subsequently included on the list, or canon, of inspired books): in the *Didache* (literally, *The Teaching*, composed about the year 100), in the *Apology* of Justin, and later in Tertullian and the *Apostolic Tradition* (ca. 200) of Hippolytus (d. ca. 236). The *theology* of Baptism is worked out later, in the Pauline corpus, in 1 John, and in 1 Peter.

Baptism incorporates us into the death, burial, and resurrection of Jesus, into "life with him" (Colossians 2:12; Ephesians 2:1, 4–6; Philippians 3:10–11). It is a Baptism of repentance (Acts of the Apostles 2:38) and an expression of belief in the Good News (8:37). Baptism purifies (Ephesians 5:26), cleansing our hearts from an evil conscience (Hebrews 10:22). We become "dead to sin but alive for God in Christ Jesus" (Romans 6:11). And what does it require of us? We must lead a wholly different kind of life, no longer "under the law but under grace" (6:12–23). (See also the discussion of Baptism in the New Testament in chapter 17.)

Baptism in Controversy

Donatism

Named after Donatus (d. 347), a false claimant to the episcopal chair at Carthage, this movement was an early rigoristic movement (much like Jansenism in the post-medieval period) which maintained that church membership was restricted to those who are free from sin. Sacraments administered by priests in sin were regarded as invalid. Those who left the Church and then reentered must be rebaptized. Rome's answer was that Baptism should not be readministered; a solemn laying on of hands would suffice. This difference in practice led to an open conflict between Cyprian (d. 258), bishop of Carthage, and Pope Stephen I (d. 257). The two agreed that Baptism could not be repeated. The question was whether or not heretics could validly baptize to begin with. Eventually Roman law prevailed, and the principle (to which we referred earlier in this chapter) was established that the personal holiness of the minister is not required for the efficacy of the sacrament.

Pelagianism

Since Pelagianism (see chapter 5) affirmed that we can attain salvation by our own efforts because we are naturally good, and since, in effect, Pelagianism denied the reality of Original Sin, it denied at the same time the necessity and even the propriety of infant Baptism. Augustine mounted the principal counter-attack, arguing in his treatise *On Baptism* (I,24,34) that we must be in sacramental communion with Christ's redemptive act if we are to reach the Kingdom of God and salvation. On the other hand, Augustine also inveighed against a purely mechanical concept of the sacrament. Without faith there is no sacrament. Thus, against the Donatists he argued that Christ, and not the sinful priest, is the true minister of Baptism; against the Pelagians, that Baptism is necessary for salvation; he also insisted that the fruitfulness of the sacrament depends on the dispositions of the recipient, i.e., the recipient's faith and love.

Thus, by the late fourth and early fifth centuries the theology of Baptism reached a certain level of maturity, weaving together various strands of New Testament and classic patristic theologies. What once happened to Christ now happens to us in Baptism. We are reborn to a new life, and we are given the Holy Spirit as an empowerment to live in Christ and in his body, the Church. (For a fuller treatment of the history of the rite of initiation, see J. D. C. Fisher, *Christian Initiation: Baptism in the Medieval West*, London: S.P.C.K., 1965, and Leonel Mitchell, *Baptismal Anointing*, London: S.P.C.K., 1966. Some of this material is summarized in *Made, Not Born*, pp. 50-98, cited in the Suggested Readings at the end of this chapter.)

The Doctrine of Baptism

The theological development is summed up in the Council of Trent's canons on the sacrament of Baptism (Session VII, 1547): that Baptism is valid even if administered by heretics, that it is necessary for salvation, that it imposes obligations to live a holy life, that its grace can be lost through serious sin, that it can never be repeated, that it can be administered to infants and children, etc. The Second Vatican Council's *Dogmatic Constitution on the Church* notes that Baptism incorporates us into the Church, orients us to the worship of God, and gives us a rebirth as sons and daughters of God (n. 11).

"Baptism of Desire"

The Church has always taught that Baptism is necessary for salvation. On the other hand, we have seen in the chapters 19 and 20 (and also in chapter 8 on the question of religious pluralism) that grace and revelation are universally available. Accordingly, the doctrine that Baptism is necessary for salvation can mean that for those called explicitly to the Church, Baptism is necessary for their salvation. In other words, if we are convinced in conscience that Jesus is Lord and Savior, we are obliged to seek admission to his Church, for there is no other place that we can go where the Lordship of Jesus is proclaimed and celebrated, and where we can collaborate in his historic mission for the sake of the Kingdom of God.

This understanding of the necessity of Baptism for salvation has also been known as "Baptism of desire." A widely held position, taught by Thomas Aquinas, was that prior to Christ it was sufficient to believe in God and in providence. This was tantamount to implicit faith in Christ. After the coming of Christ, however, explicit faith was necessary. It was generally assumed in the Middle Ages, we must never forget, that the world as a whole had already been evangelized. This is long before the geographical discoveries and before the development of modern means of transportation and communication described in chapter 3. After the discoveries of America and the Far East, the question of human salvation was posed with much greater urgency. Some theologians taught that people across the sea who had not yet been evangelized were like those who were alive before the coming of Christ. They, too, could be saved by implicit faith. These theologians were convinced of two principles: Christ is the one mediator of salvation, and every person is touched somehow by the grace of Christ.

This general understanding of a "Baptism of desire" received its most formal expression in the so-called Boston Letter sent by the Holy Office (now called the Congregation for the Doctrine of Faith) to Cardinal Richard Cushing (d. 1970) in 1949. A controversy had developed in the Archdiocese of Boston, Massachusetts, because of the literal interpretation given the principle "Outside the (Catholic) Church, no salvation" by Father Leonard Feeney, S.J. (d. 1978). According to the letter, it is Catholic doctrine that "it is not always required that a person be incorporated in reality (*reapse*) as a member of the Church, but it is required that he belong to it at least in desire and longing (*voto et desiderio*). It is not always necessary that this desire be explicit.... God also accepts an implicit desire, so called because it is contained in the good disposition of soul by which a man wants his will to be conformed to God's will." This teaching is reaffirmed by Vatican II's *Dogmatic Constitution on the Church*, n. 16 (see also n. 9). (See my *Do We Need the Church?*, New York: Harper & Row, 1969, and Gregory Baum, "Baptism of Desire," *The Concise Sacramentum Mundi*, pp. 75-78.)

The Church and Baptism

The sacraments not only signify and communicate grace for the recipient. They also disclose something fundamental about the Church which celebrates them. Thus, Baptism incorporates one into the Church, associates one with the death and resurrection of Christ unto new life, effects a forgiveness of sins, and orients one to the worship of God and the wider mission of the Church. In baptizing, the Church reveals itself to itself and to the rest of the world primarily as a *community*, the Body of Christ, and only secondarily as an institution; the Church identifies itself with the sufferings and death of Christ and so points the way to a share in his resurrection and glorification; it shows itself a forgiving community and, at the same time, a community in need of forgiveness; and its whole life is directed to the glory of God which is achieved in and through the humanization of the world. The Church which baptizes and is baptized has been given "a new birth by water and the Holy Spirit" and as such is a "holy people . . . (anointed) with the chrism of salvation" just as "Christ was anointed Priest, Prophet, and King" unto "everlasting life" (*Rite of Baptism*).

CONFIRMATION
Historical Considerations

In light of what has been noted already regarding the rite of initiation in general and Baptism in particular, the following historical points are pertinent to an understanding of Confirmation and to its relationship with Baptism:

1.   There is no separate rite of Confirmation in the New Testament. Where the Spirit is given, the Spirit is given in connection with Baptism.

2.   The East has never separated Baptism and Confirmation (chrismation). Theologically, the East has viewed them as essentially a single sacrament and, juridically, the East has always

regarded the presbyter as the legitimate minister of Baptism and the post-baptismal rites (including anointing).

3.   In the West, however, the post-baptismal rites (including the anointing) were reserved to the bishop. Two developments eventually led to the separation of Baptism and Confirmation: (a) the sense of urgency about the now-universal practice of infant Baptism (a development linked with Augustine's elaboration of the doctrine of Original Sin against the Pelagians), and (b) the unavailability of bishops to attend immediately to the post-baptismal rites. The bishop now came to those who had already been baptized sometime earlier. Here, too, we have the starting point for the later episcopal visitations, mainly for Confirmation. The prerogative of the bishops as ministers of the post-baptismal rites in the West did not presuppose, but in fact created, two independent sacraments.

4.   At first, the separation of the two rites was regarded as abnormal and less than ideal. Consequently, efforts were made to administer the post-baptismal rites as soon as possible after Baptism, including the Baptism of infants, as was the practice in the East. It was not until the thirteenth century that opposition to the separation of rites began to relax and official allowance was made for the concrete pastoral situation. A provincial council at Cologne in 1280, for example, postponed Confirmation until at least the age of seven. A minimum instead of a maximum age was now imposed. Adults continued to follow the older tradition and received the post-baptismal rites immediately after Baptism. Originally, these rites were relatively simple, as in the baptismal anointing today. From the ninth century on, however, a second anointing which had been known only in Rome was expanded to a self-contained "rite of confirmation."

5.   It was only in the high Middle Ages that a specific theology of Confirmation was developed in order to justify, *after the fact*, the now-autonomous rite carried out only by the bishop. The notion emerged that Confirmation provides a *gratia ad robur* ("grace for strength"), the armor of the soldier of Christ. The False Decretals of Gratian, which formed the basis of all medieval

law, treated Confirmation as a greater sacrament even than Baptism. Peter Lombard, whose *Sentences* influenced much of medieval theology, including Aquinas, followed the same line and described Confirmation as the gift of the Spirit "for strengthening" (*ad robur*) in contrast with baptismal grace, which is "for forgiveness" (*ad remissionem*). Even though this distinction had no basis in Sacred Scripture, the liturgy, or the Fathers of the Church, it was retained in the theology textbooks until the present time (see, for example, *Sharing the Light of Faith, National Catechetical Directory for Catholics of the United States*, p. 68). The distinction was definitively established by the Council of Florence in its *Decree for the Armenians* in 1439, and was confirmed without further reflection by the Council of Trent against Luther. Always the difference between the two ordinary ministers of the sacrament is emphasized: the presbyter for Baptism, the bishop for Confirmation.

6. Today, of course, the rite of Confirmation is often administered, even in the West, by priests rather than bishops. This is to insure that, in the case of a newly baptized adult or a young person capable of being catechized, the full rite of initiation can be given all at once.

Theological Implications

1. *Baptism and Confirmation are*, in essence and in light of their origins and history, *one sacrament*.

2. Confirmation, which comprises the post-baptismal rites of anointing, the laying on of hands, and the words "Be sealed with the gift of the Holy Spirit," is a *ratification* of Baptism. For those who were baptized as infants, Confirmation provides an opportunity to ratify freely and deliberately what was done for them at Baptism. It helps to focus their minds and the minds of the whole community on the essentially *missionary* dimensions of the baptismal commitment.

The Church and Confirmation

As a continuation and/or ratification of the Christian's baptismal commitment, Confirmation expresses the essentially missionary character of the Church and its nature as the Temple of the Holy Spirit. It is a community called to manifest "the spirit of wisdom and understanding, the spirit of right judgment and courage, the spirit of knowledge and reverence. . . the spirit of wonder and awe in (God's) presence" (*Rite of Confirmation*). It is not only a sacred, grace-bearing sign for the good of the recipient, therefore, but it is also a principal moment when the Church reveals itself to itself and to the rest of the world as a particular kind of community, filled with the Holy Spirit and committed to the Spirit's release for the transformation of the whole of creation.

EUCHARIST
General Introduction

Our reflections on the Eucharist are framed by two basic doctrinal principles: the one enunciated by the Council of Trent and the other by the Second Vatican Council. Trent taught that the Eucharist is not simply one of the sacraments but is pre-eminent among them because Christ is present in the Eucharist even before the sacrament is used (*Decree on the Most Holy Eucharist*, chapter III, Session XIII, 1551); Vatican II declared that "the Liturgy. . ., most of all in the divine sacrifice of the Eucharist, is the outstanding means whereby the faithful can express in their lives, and manifest to others, the mystery of Christ and the real nature of the true Church" (*Constitution on the Sacred Liturgy*, n. 2). The Eucharist is indeed the "the source and summit of the entire Christian life" (n. 11).

Biblical Origins

The term *eucharist* is derived from the Greek word which means "thanksgiving." Jesus himself "gave thanks" at the Last Supper (Luke 22:19; 1 Corinthians 11:24; Mark 14:23; Matthew 26:27). The more strongly Semitic flavor of Mark's account has led some biblical interpreters to conclude that its wording is even closer to the original than Paul's. The differences between the Marcan and Pauline accounts are too great for us to assume a common Greek source. On the other hand, there is sufficient measure of agreement between them to assume a common Aramaic or Hebrew source. The essential kernel of the various reports, however, is clearly part of a unanimous tradition in the New Testament churches.

The *meal* which is the object of these reports was only the last in a long series of daily meals which Jesus shared with his disciples. In the Oriental world of his day, a shared meal was always a sign of peace, trust, and communality. Jesus, of course, proclaimed the Kingdom by sharing meals with outcasts, tax-collectors, and the like. But this last meal was special. According to the Synoptics it was a ritual Passover meal, a festive farewell meal. Whether it was a Passover meal or not (John says otherwise), it had the same basic structure: the words over the bread, its breaking and sharing; the words over the wine, and its sharing. But Jesus identified the bread and wine with his own body and blood. And sensing his own impending death, he speaks of himself as a sacrifice. Just as the unleavened bread is broken, so will his body be broken. And just as the wine is poured out, so will his blood. All four texts agree that Jesus' death is an atonement and establishes a new Covenant. The Jews, in fact, regarded every death of an innocent person as an atoning death, and Jesus saw his own death in this light.

There are connections here also with the Old Testament: first, with the idea of the sacrifice of the old Covenant in Exodus 24:8,11 and of the new Covenant in Jeremiah 31:31-34; and, secondly, with the idea of the atoning sufferings of the servant of God in Isaiah 53:12. Thus, the New Testament interprets the death of Jesus as an atoning death which establishes a new Covenant in his blood and brings redemption to all. By distributing the bread and wine, his body and blood, Jesus was indicating that his disciples were to share in his sacrifice and in the power of his atoning death. This, too, is a familiar idea in Oriental thinking: that eating and drinking communicate divine gifts.

With the resurrection the disciples now see the Last Supper and their own subsequent meals together in a new light. They eat and drink with the assurance that Christ will make good his promise to be present among those who are gathered in his name (Matthew 18:20). The new fellowship is now characterized by eschatological joy, a fundamental confidence in the coming of the Kingdom (Acts of the Apostles 2:46).

There are, of course, arguments among New Testament scholars and theologians of various Christian churches regarding the precise meaning and implications of Jesus' words at the Last Supper. We are not going into detail here. It is sufficient for our purpose to note that there is an undeniable continuity between what happened at the Last Supper and what the disciples did together at meals after the resurrection. There is no other explanation for the fact that the disciples repeated this meal and that later communities always referred to the actions of Jesus at the Last Supper to explain and justify what they did at the eucharistic table. The post-Easter Church was convinced that it was doing what Jesus intended it to do when he said: "Do this in remembrance of me" (1 Corinthians 11:24-25).

As an act of remembrance (*anamnesis*) the Eucharist not only recalls to mind what Jesus did but also effectively makes it present again. Thus, Paul affirms the bodily presence of Jesus: "Is not the cup of blessing we bless a sharing in the blood of Christ? And is not the bread we break a sharing in the body of Christ?" (1 Corinthians 10:16). Indeed, to eat and drink unworthily is to sin "against the body and blood of the Lord" (11:27). Because we partake of the same bread, "we, many though we are, are one body" (10:17).

The Lord's Supper establishes and celebrates the communion that exists not only between the Church and Christ but also within the Church—i.e., not only "with Christ" but also "in Christ." And it is a communion that looks always not only to the past—i.e., to the Last Supper and to the redemptive events that followed it—but also to the future, "until he comes" (11:26). Jesus himself had said that he would not drink again of the fruit of the vine until that day when he would drink it new in the Kingdom of God (Mark 14:25; Matthew 26:29; Luke 22:18). Christ's presence in the Eucharist, therefore, is the presence not only of the crucified and risen one, but also the presence of one who is yet to come.

On the other hand, that presence comes about not through some magical formula, but through the proclamatory words of faith. John places a clear warning at the end of Jesus' words about the bread of life: "It is the spirit that gives life; the flesh is useless. The words I spoke to you are spirit and life" (John 6:63). The word is ultimately effective, however, only if it is creative of a sense of community. Where there is no fellowship, where there are divisions, where there is insensitivity to those in need, there is no real community and the Lord's Supper brings judgment, not grace   (1 Corinthians 11:17-34). What is proclaimed must be lived (11:26). (See also the discussion of the Eucharist in the New Testament in chapter 17.)

History of the Eucharist

General Structure

As we have just seen, the Eucharist, or Lord's Supper, was celebrated in the beginning as a *meal*. (The term *Mass* is derived from the Latin word *missa*, which meant "dismissal," the closing blessing at any ecclesiastical celebration. The term was eventually applied only to the Eucharist.) During the second and third centuries the meal disappeared. The prayer of thanksgiving (formerly known as the "canon" and now once again called the "Eucharistic Prayer") became the central feature of the rite. It was during this prayer that the bread and wine were consecrated, after which the people responded "Amen" to ratify what had been said and done. Communion followed. The same introductory prayers that are recited today ("The Lord be with you." "And also with you." "Lift up your hearts." "We lift them up to the Lord." "Let us give thanks to the Lord our God." "It is right to give him thanks and praise.") are to be found in the account of Justin about the year 150 and in a text put forward as a model by Hippolytus about 215. Though the details of the service were left to the discretion of the celebrant, especially the phrasing of the prayers (another practice recently restored), the whole Christian world must have celebrated the Eucharist in much this form until well into the fourth century.

In the earliest centuries, too, the Eucharist was celebrated every Sunday, but on few other occasions. Daily Mass was not the rule. The Eucharist was attended by the whole Christian community of the neighborhood, early in the morning (now that it was separated from the supper meal at the end of the day) and before work (since Sunday was still an ordinary workday). Part of the traditional synagogue service survived and was incorporated into these liturgies. The memoirs of the Apostles or the writings of the prophets were read, and these were followed by a sermon from the president of the assembly and a prayer for the general needs of the community. There are also various indications of an Offertory procession (also since restored) as early as the third century. This ceremony in which bread and wine and other gifts were brought forward to the altar may have been a conscious reaction against Gnosticism, which denied the goodness of matter.

As the Church was liberated from persecution and spread more easily through the empire, cultural diversification set into the liturgy. The entrance rite was expanded to include prayers at the foot of the altar (since eliminated and now incorporated into the introductory greetings and penitential rite). Readings from Scripture, however, formed the core of the early part of the Mass in every celebration, and hence this part of the liturgy was simply called, as it is today, the liturgy of the word. Responses were developed for each reading—songs which survive today in the form of psalm verses and the alleluia. Much solemnity attended the reading of the Gospel: e.g., candles and incense. There followed the recitation of the creed, except in non-Roman rites, where the creed occurred just before the Eucharistic Prayer itself. After the creed came the intercessory prayers (as we have them again today), then the preparation of the gifts (the prayers which are still recited silently over the gifts were not introduced until the ninth century). Finally, the Eucharist itself.

Eucharistic Prayer

For many centuries the canon, or Eucharistic Prayer, was recited in the West in an undertone not audible to the congregation. Today it is once again proclaimed aloud. In the East it was always proclaimed in that manner. The admonition "Do this in remembrance of me" was followed, in all liturgies, by the *anamnesis*: "We remember, we do this to commemorate you." The prayer ends, as it did from Hippolytus' day, with the solemn doxology: "Through him, with him, in him, in the unity of the Holy Spirit, all glory and honor is yours, almighty Father, forever and ever." After Communion there was the blessing (*missa*), and the sacred vessels were cleansed after the liturgy itself.

This basic, straightforward structure was progressively interrupted by the insertion of a variety of petitions for the living and dead, and then by the *epiclesis*, or solemn invocation of the Holy Spirit. Even the breaking of bread came to be embroidered with prayers. The canon was rendered inaudible by the Carolingian liturgists, who wished to make it a sort of sanctuary which the priest alone could enter. To compensate for this, the elevation of the host and chalice after the consecration was introduced in the thirteenth century so that the whole congregation could look upon and adore the sacrament. It was only at the close of the canon that the priest resumed contact with the people. (In the pre-Vatican II Latin Mass, the *per omnia saecula saeculorum* just before the *Pater Noster*, or Our Father, was the first generally audible sound made by the celebrant since the recitation of the preface.)

Congregational Participation

By the seventeenth century frequent Communion had fallen into disrepute, partly through the influence of Jansenism. Not until the early years of the twentieth century was frequent Communion encouraged again, by Pope Pius X. As recently as 1960 most people were still not making responses at Mass. What responses there were the "altar boy," or server, made in their name. The "dialogue Mass" was introduced in the late 1950s just before the Second Vatican Council, but the Latin language was still used. During the Romanticist eighteenth century, choirs had begun to supplant the congregation, singing elaborate polyphonic rendi-tions of the various parts of the Mass: *Kyrie* ("Lord have mercy"), *Gloria, Credo, Sanctus* ("Holy, Holy"), and *Agnus Dei* ("Lamb of God"). As a concession, the congregation was encouraged to sing vernacular hymns not taken from the Eucharist itself, but this was stopped in the nineteenth century.

Private Masses

The practice of private Masses, i.e., Masses celebrated by a priest without a congregation, appeared about the sixth century, chiefly in the form of votive Masses, or Masses for the necessities of the faithful. The Mass was perceived increasingly as an act of peti-tion, something to be performed to receive some particular benefit from God, or it was often regarded as a rite, however complicated, to produce hosts for the tabernacle. And since private Masses became so frequent, they were also regarded eventually as the norm rather than the exception. The Second Vatican Council, however, declared the communal celebration preferable to indi-vidual and quasi-private celebrations *(Constitution on the Sacred Liturgy,* n. 27).

Eucharistic Doctrines

Catholic eucharistic doctrine has been focused on two issues: the sacrificial nature of the Mass and the real presence of Christ in the consecrated elements of bread and wine.

It is official Catholic teaching (Council of Trent) that the Mass is a true *sacrifice*, not only of praise and thanksgiving and of commemoration but also of expiation for the living and the dead, without diminishing the value of the sacrifice of Calvary. Christ is the same victim and priest in the Eucharist as he was on the cross, although the mode of offering is different at Mass. The sacrifice of the cross was a bloody sacrifice; the sacrifice of the Mass is unbloody. Nonetheless, the fruits of the latter sacrifice are the same as those of the former. The sacrifice of the Mass, Trent declared, is "properly offered not only for the sins, penalties, satis-factions, and other needs of the faithful who are living but also for the departed in Christ who are not yet fully cleansed" *(Decree on the Mass,* chapter II).

It is also official Catholic teaching that Christ is *really present* in the consecrated elements of bread and wine. By the Middle Ages the real presence of Christ was being reduced by many (especially Berengar of Tours, d. 1088) to a merely spiritual presence, in reaction to a crudely physical notion (represented, for example, in the belief that if one were to scratch the consecrated host, it would bleed). For the first time in the history of Catholic doctrine, the Fourth Lateran Council (1215) spoke of *transubstantiation*, i.e., the belief that the substance of bread and wine is changed into the body and blood of Christ. This teaching was reaffirmed and made more precise by the Council of Constance (1415) and the Council of Trent (1551). Zwingli and Calvin, however, denied the real presence completely, while Luther held to *consubstantiation*, i.e., the belief that the bread and wine become the body and blood of Christ but that they remain also bread and wine.

The traditional medieval teaching on the real presence was repeated in Pope Paul VI's *Mysterium Fidei* (1965), an encyclical written against the views of certain Dutch Catholic theologians who were attempting to explain the real presence without employing the Scholastic concept of transubstantiation. A mere "transignification or transfinalization," he insisted, is not sufficient to explain the real presence. Rather, the consecrated elements bear not only a new meaning (transignification) and a new purpose (transfinalization) but a new substantial, or ontic, reality as well (transubstantiation). The pope also reaffirmed the teaching that the real presence continues after Mass, and he defended eucharistic adoration and private Masses.

The scope of Christ's presence has been subject to controversy as well. According the the same medieval doctrine of transubstantiation, the whole Christ is present under each form, the consecrated bread and the consecrated wine. For that reason, Trent insisted, it is unnecessary to receive the Eucharist under both species as John Hus (d. 1415) and his disciples in Bohemia had argued. (The practice of Communion under both kinds has recently been reintroduced into the Catholic Church of the Latin rite.) But if Christ is present under each form, that is not to say that he is present *only* there. The Second Vatican Council has taught that the presence of Christ in the Eucharist is not confined to the consecrated elements of bread and wine. Christ is present, first, in the community which has assembled for worship. Secondly, he is present in the person of the minister who presides in his name. Thirdly, he is present in the biblical word which is proclaimed. Finally, he is present in the sacred species themselves (*Constitution on the Sacred Liturgy*, n. 7).

The real presence of Christ in the sacred species comes about through the ordained priest, who "confects" the Eucharist (Lateran Council IV). The power of the priest to consecrate the bread and wine is not dependent upon his personal holiness (Council of Constance). Under the impact of the twentieth-century renewal, this traditional Catholic emphasis on the role of the ordained priest was broadened to include the participation of all the faithful who are present at the celebration of the Eucharist. Both Pope Pius XII's *Mediator Dei* (1947) and the Vatican II's *Constitution on the Sacred Liturgy* insisted that the faithful participate not merely through the priest but along with him (*Constitution*, n. 48). This is not to say, however, that their function is the same as the priest's.

Ecumenical Consensus Today

Eucharist as Sacrifice

It was once assumed that Catholics alone (with the usual exception of the Orthodox) believed in the sacrificial nature of the Eucharist. The ecumenical dialogues and consultations at both international and national levels since 1965 have almost completely undermined that common assumption. The sacrificial nature of the Eucharist is affirmed in varying degrees by the Anglican-Roman Catholic Consultation, Orthodox-Catholic, Lutheran-Catholic, Presbyterian-Reformed-Catholic, and in a 1970 consensus statement of a study commission of the National Council of Churches in the United States. The Lutheran-Catholic dialogue provides the fullest treatment of the subject in its "The Eucharist: Joint Statement" (*Lutherans and Catholics in Dialogue*, vol. 4, Washington D.C.: United States Catholic Conference,

1970, pp. 7-33). The Lutherans join with the Catholics in acknowledging that the Eucharist is also the sacrifice of the Church to the Father through the power of the Holy Spirit. The Eucharist is also a propitiatory sacrifice, "efficacious for the forgiveness of sins and the life of the world." A more recent statement from the International Roman Catholic-Lutheran Commission (*Origins* 8/30, January 11, 1979, pp. 465,467-478) also notes "growing convergence" on this matter.

Real Presence

Here the consensus is even wider and stronger. Every consultation in which Roman Catholics have been involved affirms some measure of basic agreement on the real presence of Christ in the Eucharist. In addition to those mentioned in the paragraph above, there is the Disciples of Christ-Catholic consultation. The Lutheran-Catholic consultation again is emphatic: "We affirm that in the sacrament of the Lord's supper, Jesus Christ, true God and true man, is present wholly and entirely, in his body and blood, under the signs of bread and wine." As to the time or duration of the real presence, the statement declares: "The true body and blood of Christ are present not only at the moment of reception but throughout the eucharistic action" (p. 193). The Lutherans do not reject everything implied in the medieval term *transubstantiation*, but they shy away from it because it is "misleading" (pp. 195-196).

From the other side of the Reformation, i.e., the Presbyterian and Reformed, the same affirmation is made: "The real presence of Christ in the Eucharist...does not depend upon the belief of each individual, but on the power of Christ's Word...and upon his promise to bind himself to the sacramental event as the sign of his person given to us" (*The Unity We Seek*, New York: Paulist Press, 1977, p. 39). This is not to say that there is also fundamental agreement on the "how" of the real presence. But there is agreement on the "that" of it (p. 40). Needless to say, agreement between Catholics and Anglicans and Catholics and Orthodox on this point is clear and unequivocal.

Reflection

What emerges from these consensus statements is the principle that the doctrine and celebration of the Eucharist can make sense only when understood in the context of the doctrine and life of the whole Church as People of God, Body of Christ, and Temple of the Holy Spirit. What also emerges is a general readiness (except among the Orthodox) to call for some eucharistic sharing, or intercommunion, on the basis of these remarkable convergences on eucharistic doctrine. On the other hand, the more sophisticated consultations (especially the Anglican-Roman Catholic and the Lutheran-Roman Catholic) admit that they have not yet solved the fundamental ecclesiological question, "What is minimally required before there can be full ecclesiastical communion and sacramental sharing?" The question of intercommunion will be taken up again in chapter 23.

(For a reliable synthesis and interpretation of the various ecumenical statements on the Eucharist, see John F. Hotchkin, "Christian Dialogue and the Eucharist," *Catholic Mind* 75, March 1977, pp. 11-32.)

The Eucharist and the Church

The first effect of the Eucharist is a more profound incorporation into the unity of the Church. St. Thomas himself regarded the Eucharist as the sacrament of the Church's unity (III, q. 82, a. 2). According the Karl Rahner, the Church is "most manifest and in the most intensive form, she attains the highest actuality of her own nature, when she celebrates the eucharist" (*The Church and the Sacraments*, p. 84). The Church at the Eucharist is a structured community, a community listening to the word of God, a community in continuity with the preaching, ministry, death, and resurrection of its Lord, a community looking forward to the coming of the Kingdom, a community conscious of its sinfulness and repentant of its sins, a community convinced of the power of God's grace, a community ready to serve others, i.e., to carry out "the breaking of the bread" beyond the Church, and a community here and now open to the presence of the Lord and his Spirit.

"Only a person who is prepared in principle to entrust himself to the whole activity of the Church that takes place in the eucharist . . . will share even in the blessings and graces of this sacrament for the individual," Rahner suggests. "For ultimately these are nothing but that deeper and deeper union with the Church, her action and her lot" (p. 87).

SUMMARY

1.   A major theological, pastoral, and even aesthetical characteristic of Catholicism is its commitment to the *sacramental principle*, namely, the conviction that everything is capable of embodying and communicating the divine, that all reality has a "mysterious" dimension insofar as it is imbued with the hidden presence of God.

2.   Just as God reaches us through the finite and the visible, so we reach God through the finite and the visible. The point at which this occurs is the point of *sacramental encounter*. For Christians, *the* point of sacramental encounter with God is *Jesus Christ*.

3.   For Catholics especially, the *Church* also plays an important sacramental, or *mediating*, role in salvation history. Just as Christ is the sacrament of encounter with God, so the Church is the sacrament of encounter with Christ, and, ultimately, with God.

4.   In its *widest sense*, the word *sacrament* applies to any finite reality through which the divine is perceived to be disclosed and communicated, and through which our human response to the divine assumes some measure of shape, form, and structure.

5.   In a *more specific sense*, sacraments are those finite realities through which God is communicated to the Church and through which the Church responds to God's self-communication. As such, sacraments are directly *ecclesial* in character. Although they are certainly the acts of God and of Christ, sacraments are immediately *acts of the Church*, expressions of the nature and mission of the Church.

6.   Since the medieval period, the sacraments have been understood primarily as *causes of grace*. Their function as *signs of faith* was subordinated to concerns about causality. A recovery of the sacramental perspective of *St. Thomas Aquinas* in recent decades has restored balance to Catholic sacramental theology. Sacraments cause grace insofar as they signify it. If they are not intelligible and effective *signs*, then they are not effective *causes*.

7.   Sacraments, therefore, are signs of faith, acts of worship, signs of the unity of the Church, and signs of Christ's presence. They are *signs*

of faith insofar as they express and proclaim belief in the unseen reality of God. They are *acts of worship* insofar as they draw us ritually into Christ's paschal worship of the Father. They signify the *unity of the Church* insofar as all who participate in them share a common faith and enjoy a common fellowship. And they signify *Christ's presence* insofar as the incarnate Word is not confined by time and space but is made available here and now, as he is, the risen Lord.

8.   The *Council of Trent* taught, on the other hand, that the sacraments also *cause* grace for those who place no obstacle to it. The point of the council's teaching was that it is not the personal merit of the recipient that causes the grace received. Nevertheless, God does not force the human will.

9.   Trent's teaching, however, was frequently misunderstood. "Not placing an obstacle" was interpreted to mean that the absence of mortal sin was enough to have the sacrament "work." St. Thomas, on the other hand, insisted on the "right disposition" of the recipient—i.e., interior conversion, faith, devotion. The "fruitfulness" (as opposed to the mere "validity") of the sacrament depends on this.

10.   Sacraments do not cause grace in the sense that grace is otherwise unavailable. Grace is already present to the world in God's original self-communication. Sacramental grace shapes and "channels" that original communication of grace for the sake of the Church's mission. The sacraments signify and celebrate what God is in fact doing everywhere and for all.

11.   In every sacrament there is the sign or ritual (*sacramentum tantum*—e.g., the pouring of the water and the recitation of the formula "I baptize you . . ."), the fruit, or immediate effect (*res tantum*—i.e., the grace of the sacrament), and the lasting effect (*res et sacramentum*—e.g., the permanent membership bond with the Church in Baptism).

12.   The distinction arose as a way of dealing with the challenge posed by *Berengar of Tours*, who acknowledged that the Eucharist is a sign of and causes the grace of union with Christ (*res tantum*) but who denied the real presence of Christ in the sacrament. Theologians insisted that there is a third element that comes into being whether the sacrament is worthily received or not: It is still the body and blood of Christ, even if it does not cause grace in this particular recipient.

13.   Those sacraments which, by tradition, the Church does not repeat are known as "character" sacraments. The term *character* conveys the notion of a "sealing" of the Christian, either as a member of the Church (*Baptism-Confirmation*) or in its service (*Holy Order*).

14.   The lasting effects of the non-character sacraments are the bond of union between a man and a woman (*Matrimony*), a healing of the separation between an individual and the Church caused by sin (*Penance*), a healing of the separation of an individual and the Church caused by sickness (*Anointing of the Sick*), and the real presence of Christ (*Eucharist*).

15.   The *minister* of the sacrament acts in the name of the Church and therefore must intend to do what the Church wishes to be done (Councils of Florence and Trent). But the validity of the sacrament does not depend on the holiness of the minister (Councils of Constance and Trent). Not every member of the Church is qualified to administer every sacrament (Council of Trent).

16.   The *recipient* must be disposed properly (faith, conversion, devotion). If he or she is not, "the very act of celebrating" the sacrament may produce the proper disposition (Vatican II).

17.   *Infant Baptism* is the exception rather than the rule of sacramental reception. Two extremes are to be avoided in explaining it: the one which assumes that Original Sin cannot be "removed" without Baptism, and the other which assumes that sacraments are only for adults or for mature young people. The community's "intention" supplies for the infant's, and it is the community which nurtures the baptized member's faith.

18.   The sacraments were "*instituted*" by Christ in the same way that the Church was "instituted" by Christ. They have their origin in Jesus' proclamation of the Kingdom of God and in his call to discipleship. Jesus willed the sacraments to the same degree and extent as he willed the Church.

19.   There are many sacramental actions celebrated and/or used by the Church to mediate the presence of God. Some few of these so fully engage the nature and mission of the Church that they are placed in a special category. By definition of the Councils of Lyons II, Florence, and Trent, the Catholic Church recognizes *seven* such signs as sacraments in the fullest sense: Baptism, Confirmation, Eucharist, Penance, Anointing of the Sick, Matrimony, and Holy Order. The number seven, however, is not absolute. Thus, one might consider Baptism and Confirmation as one sacrament, or the sacrament of Holy Order as three (diaconate, priesthood, episcopate).

20.   The *rite of Christian initiation* includes three sacraments: Baptism, Confirmation, and Eucharist. It follows a suitable period of formation known as the *catechumenate*. The initiation of *adults* is the pastoral norm, not the exception. All other baptismal rites are referred to

this one. The new rite also underscores the *unity among the sacraments*, their close relationship with the *mission of the Church*, and the *responsibility of the local church* to share in the candidate's growth in faith.

21.   Those entering the Catholic Church from some other Christian church do not become catechumens, nor are they rebaptized, nor do they abjure "heresy." They are already members of the Body of Chirst.

22.   The sacrament of *Baptism* is not without pre-Christian origins—i.e., the purification and initiation rites of Judaism, and the baptism of John the Baptist. Baptism was practiced outside of Jesus' circle during his lifetime, but it was not until Pentecost that the outpouring of the Holy Spirit was associated with it, along with conversion, repentance, the forgiveness of sins, and the call to mission.

23.   The New Testament data on the *practice of Baptism* even in the post-resurrection period is sparse. More detail is provided in the non-canonical writings (*Didache*, Justin's *Apology*, and the *Apostolic Tradition* of Hippolytus). The *theology of Baptism*, however, is worked out in Paul, 1 John, and 1 Peter. Baptism incorporates us into the death, burial, and resurrection of Jesus, into "life with him" (Colossians 2:12, e.g.).

24.   The *post-biblical theology of Baptism* developed under the pressure of the *Donatist* and *Pelagian* controversies: The former insisted on the holiness of the minister for validity, and the latter rejected the necessity of the sacraments for salvation. In each case, the key theological figure was *Augustine*, who insisted, on the one hand, that the sacraments do require faith, but that, on the other hand, Baptism is necessary for salvation. Thus, infants are fit subjects of Baptism, and furthermore they place no obstacle to its effectiveness.

25.   These principles were gathered up and definitively taught by the *Council of Trent*. A wider ecclesiological vision, however, was provided by *Vatican II*, which emphasized our incorporation into the Church and our call to worship.

26.   Many are never baptized during their lifetime, and yet God intends the salvation of all in Christ. With the geographical discoveries of the Middle Ages, theologians were compelled to confront this apparent dilemma. Their solution was the concept of *"Baptism of desire,"* which was tantamount to *implicit faith* in Christ. This approach was adopted by the Holy Office in 1949 in its response to the so-called Feeney case in Boston, Massachusetts, where the principle "Outside the (Catholic) Church, no salvation" had been pushed to extremes.

27.   *Confirmation* is also a sacrament, but it may be regarded as part of the sacrament of Baptism. There is no separate rite of Confirmation in the New Testament. The separation of the rites of Baptism and

Confirmation in the West occurred because the post-baptismal rites
(= Confirmation) were reserved to bishops, and bishops were often
unavailable when Baptism was administered. An elaboration of this
separate rite of Confirmation began in the ninth century, and it was only
in the high Middle Ages that a specific theology of Confirmation developed. The distinction was ratified by the Councils of Florence and
Trent.

28.   Recent reforms of the rite of initiation restore the unity of
Baptism and Confirmation, especially by authorizing priests to be the
ministers of Confirmation.

29.   The separate rite of Confirmation allows one who was baptized as an infant to ratify that Baptism and to embrace freely and
deliberately his or her missionary responsibilities within the Church.

30.   The *Eucharist* is the preeminent sacrament because Christ is
present in it even before it is used. It is also the "source and summit" of
the entire Christian life.

31.   The term *eucharist* means "thanksgiving." It has its origins in
the meal which Jesus celebrated with his disciples, known as the *Last
Supper*, at which he directed them to "do this in remembrance" of him. It
was one of a long series of meals which Jesus shared with his friends as a
sign of fellowship, peace, and trust.

32.   At this meal, however, Jesus identified himself with the bread
and wine ("This is my body..."). He also ate and drank with his disciples with the knowledge that his own death was imminent. Consistently
with Jewish consciousness, he perceived innocent death as *atoning* death.

33.   The disciples and the early Church came to interpret this meal
as establishing a new Covenent in the blood of Christ for the redemption
of all. They continued the practice of shared meals after the death and
resurrection in this light and with fundamental confidence in his
promises and with hope in the coming Kingdom of God.

34.   The Eucharist, or Lord's Supper, became an act of remembrance (*anamnesis*) of what Christ had done, an act of fellowship and
communion not only "with Christ" but also "in Christ," and an act of
eschatological anticipation.

35.   By the second and third centuries the meal aspect of the
Eucharist had disappeared. The prayer of thanksgiving (canon, Eucharistic Prayer), introduced by readings and followed by Holy Communion,
became central. At first the Eucharist was celebrated only on Sundays.

36.   As the persecutions lifted and the Church moved more freely
throughout the empire, the Eucharist assumed many different cultural

forms. The rite became more elaborate. In some cases, there were distortions of its original purpose. E.g., the congregation no longer participated actively, the canon was recited quietly by the celebrant, frequent Communion declined, private Masses for special intentions multiplied. The liturgical reforms mandated by Vatican II restored the Eucharist to its original purpose and structure.

37.   The *real presence* of Christ became a doctrinal preoccupation of the medieval Church because it had been challenged, in particular by Berengar of Tours. Lateran IV, Constance, and Trent all definitively affirmed the doctrine, especially against the Reformers. And Trent also affirmed the doctrine of the *sacrificial* nature of the Eucharist and its *expiatory* value. These traditional themes were sounded again in 1965 by Pope Paul VI's *Mysterium Fidei*. Pope Pius XII's *Mediator Dei* (1947) and Vatican II's *Constitution on the Sacred Liturgy*, however, insisted on the active participation of all the faithful not merely through the priest but along with him. Vatican II also noted that Christ is present at the Eucharist not only in the consecrated elements of bread and wine, but also in the community, the word, and the minister.

38.   There is a remarkable *ecumenical convergence* today on such previously controverted questions as the sacrificial nature of the Eucharist and the real presence of Christ in the Eucharist. The various Christian traditions have come increasingly to perceive the Eucharist in the context of the mystery and mission of the Church.

39.   The first *effect* of the Eucharist is *a more profound incorporation into the Church*. The Church is most manifest and most fully itself in the Eucharist, where the Church is visible as a structured community, listening to the word of God, breaking bread and sharing the cup "until he comes."

SUGGESTED READINGS

Bausch, William J. *A New Look at the Sacraments*. Notre Dame, Ind.: Fides/Claretian, 1977.

Cooke, Bernard. *Christian Sacraments and Christian Personality*. New York: Doubleday, Image Books, 1968.

Davis, Charles. *Sacraments of Initiation: Baptism and Confirmation*. New York: Sheed & Ward, 1964.

Hellwig, Monika K. "New Understanding of the Sacraments." *Commonweal* 105 (16 June 1978), 375-380.

Jungmann, Josef. *The Mass: An Historical, Theological, and Pastoral Survey*. Collegeville, Minn.: Liturgical Press, 1976.

Kavanagh, Aidan. *The Shape of Baptism: The Rite of Christian Initiation.* New York: Pueblo Publishing, 1978.

Murphy Center for Liturgical Research, The. *Made, Not Born: New Perspectives on Christian Initiation and the Catechumenate.* Notre Dame, Ind.: University of Notre Dame Press, 1976.

Rahner, Karl. *The Church and the Sacraments.* New York: Herder & Herder, 1963.

Schanz, John P. *The Sacraments of Life and Worship.* Milwaukee: Bruce, 1966.

Schillebeeckx, Edward. *Christ the Sacrament of Encounter with God.* New York: Sheed & Ward, 1963.

Sullivan, C. Stephen, ed. *Readings in Sacramental Theology.* Englewood Cliffs, N.J.: Prentice-Hall, 1964.

·XXII·

THE SACRAMENTS OF HEALING, VOCATION, AND COMMITMENT

We are initiated into the Christian community by Baptism-Confirmation and the Eucharist, but initiation is only the beginning of a *process*. We are not already fully mature in Christ by the mere fact of having been baptized, anointed, and invited to share the Lord's Supper. We are human. Hence we are prone to sin and vulnerable to illness, physical incapacity, and finally death. And yet the call to Christian existence is a call to perfection: "In a word, you must be perfect as your heavenly Father is perfect" (Matthew 5:48). It is God's will that we be sanctified (1 Thessalonians 4:3; Ephesians 1:4), that we become as saints (Ephesians 5:3). We are to love God with all our mind and all our strength, and our neighbor as ourselves (Mark 12:30). Jesus' proclamation of the Kingdom of God, which shaped his own ministry as well as the mission of the Church, is a call to conversion: "This is the time of fulfillment. The reign of God is at hand! Reform your lives and believe in the gospel" (Mark 1:15).

Two sacraments are celebrated by the Church as a sign and instrument of God's and of Christ's abiding *healing* power. The sacrament of *Penance*, or of *Reconciliation*, is for those whose bond with the Church, and ultimately with God and Christ, has been weakened or even severed by sin. The sacrament of the *Anointing of the Sick* (formerly called *Extreme Unction*) is for those whose bond with the Church has been weakened by illness or physical incapacity. In either case, the purpose of the sacrament is to heal and to restore the morally and/or physically sick member to full communion with the Church so that once again he or she can participate in its life and mission.

Beyond that, the Church itself is disclosed in these sacraments as an essentially healing and forgiving community, as the sacrament of the healing and forgiving Lord. The Church is also the penitent Church, ever bathing the feet of Christ with its tears and hearing his words, "Nor do I condemn you" (John 8:11). And because of its unshakable confidence in the triumph of God's mercy and grace in Christ, when night falls the Church holds high the lamp of hope and reveals itself as the sacrament of *universal* salvation, the community which gives up on no one and no situation, no matter how seemingly hope-less.

All Christians are initiated into the Church through the same essential process, but not all Christians are called to live as Christians in the same mode of existence. Most are called to live in intimate union with another in marriage. Some few others may (also) be called to a life of service of the Christian community itself, specifically through a ministry which attends directly to the order and mission of the Church. So fundamental are both the call to human life itself and the call to the life of the Church that each of these calls and its corresponding commitment is celebrated as a sacrament: the one, the sacrament of *Matrimony*; the other, the sacrament of *Holy Order*.

Like all the sacraments, both these sacraments are directed to the nature and mission of the Church. In Matrimony the Christian community is itself built up and manifested at its most natural and local level. The union of Christ and his Church is symbolized (Ephesians 5:22-32). In Holy Order the Christian community is provided structure and direction for the exercise of its mission. These are the sacraments of *vocation* and of *commitment*. The Church is revealed in them as a community called forth (the root meaning of the word *church* — *ekklesia*) and committed to a life of love and service.

Section One: Sacraments of Healing

PENANCE
History

New Testament Period

The text to which Catholic doctrine has appealed in asserting the sacramentality and divine origin of Penance is John 20:22-23, which records one of Jesus' post-resurrection appearances: "Receive the Holy Spirit. If you forgive men's sins, they are forgiven them; if you hold them bound, they are held bound" (see also Matthew 16:19, 18:18). By itself, the text does not "prove" that Jesus instituted the sacrament of Penance as we know it today or that he conferred the power to forgive sins only on the Apostles, their successors, and their chosen delegates. We have no basis even for concluding that these are the "very words" of Jesus, given the different approach to history in the Fourth Gospel, over against the Synoptics.

On the other hand, the text *is* entirely consistent with Jesus' abiding concern about sin and his readiness to forgive and to heal (Matthew 9:2-8; Mark 2:5-12; Luke 5:20-26). In all three reports of Jesus' cure of the paralytic at Capernaum there is mention of the forgiveness of sins. The forgiveness of sins is also prominent in the preaching of the Apostles (Acts of the Apostles 2:38; 5:31; 10:43; 13:38; 26:18). Accordingly, even though John does not tell us how or by whom this power was exercised in the community for whom he wrote, the very fact that he mentions it shows that it was exercised.

Second and Third Centuries

The material for this period is scant. What evidence there is suggests that Penance was available for the baptized. *The Shepherd of Hermas* (ca. 150), an important para-scriptural document, takes for granted the practice of post-baptismal forgiveness, although it balks at the possibility of a third opportunity for forgiveness. The first to deny the Church's and the bishop's right to forgive those guilty of serious sins were the *Montanists* and the *Novatians*, both arguing that certain sins (e.g., apostasy, murder, adultery) were outside the Church's powers.

Fourth, Fifth, and Sixth Centuries

The purists were condemned by the *Council of Nicea* (325). It explictly directs that the dying are to be reconciled and given *Viaticum* (literally, "on the way with you"; it is the term used for Holy Communion for those at the point of death—i.e., "on the way" to heaven).

During this period Penance was public in character and came to be known as "Canonical Penance" because local councils devoted a number of canons, or juridical decisions, to regulating its practice. Canonical Penance was administered only once in a lifetime, since Baptism was normally received late in life and was seen as calling for a deep conversion, neither easily nor frequently set aside. The Church demanded proof of reconversion before restoring the grace of Baptism through Penance.

Canonical Penance was always reserved for serious sins, e.g., apostasy, murder, heresy, adultery. These were matters of common, public knowledge. The offender would receive a form of liturgical excommunication and was forced to leave the celebration of the Eucharist at the Offertory, along with the catechumens. For less serious offenses there were other forms of penance: almsgiving, fasts, charity to the poor and the sick, and prayers.

Public penance required the sinner's demonstrating a change of heart, presenting himself or herself before the bishop and the local community, and joining the local group of penitents. Then, after a suitable period of probation, he or she would be readmitted to the Christian community by a rite known as the "reconciliation of the penitent." As the needs of the people and the circumstances of the Church changed, private penance became more the rule and so, too, the actual "confession" of sins. By the end of the sixth century Canonical Penance came to be known simply as *Confession*.

Seventh to Eleventh Centuries

This period is marked by a pronounced Celtic influence as the missionary efforts of the Church reached into the British Isles, far removed from the influence of Rome and from all of Europe. (The Irish monks themselves were to bring this Celtic influence to bear upon the Continent in the seventh century.) Since the liturgical life of the Celtic church was monastically oriented, private penance became normative for priests and religious, and under their direction it spread among the laity as well. It was imposed even for trivial offenses and became increasingly divorced from the larger community of faith. In fact, a person could be restored to the Eucharist even before completing the penance. If the penance were deemed too onerous, the penitent could ask for a *commutation* to a lighter penalty. It was also possible to substitute the payment of a sum of money instead of performing the actual penance. This practice was known as *redemption*. Furthermore, Penance was administered by priests as well as the bishop. In order to help the priests in the selection of appropriate penances, a codification of penitential practices was developed, the so-called penitential books (*libri poenitentiales*). These were lists of every kind of sin, with the exact type of penance attached. The minister of the sacrament was no longer the healer and the reconciler. He was now the *judge*. A formula of absolution was also developed at this time.

Eleventh to Fourteenth Centuries

Four principal changes occur in this period. Penance becomes satisfaction, confession, contrition, and absolution. In the ancient Church the emphasis was on the *reconciliation* of the sinner with the Church and ultimately with God. Now the emphasis shifts to the doing of a penance, or the making of *satisfaction*, for sin. When this became too strenuous, the practices of commutation and redemption were introduced. Secondly, *confession* of sins originally served the purpose of insuring that adequate satisfaction was being imposed, but gradually confession came to be considered as having its own efficacy, its own power to reconcile the sinner. Thus, we find at this time the development of arguments urging the necessity of confessing to a priest. Thirdly, in the writings of Abelard (d. 1142) and Peter Lombard there was a shift to *contrition*, i.e., the conversion of heart. The sinner, if truly contrite, was already forgiven even before confession. So pronounced was this new stress on contrition that the purist Albigensians and Waldensians denied any efficacy whatsoever to confession to a priest, a view condemned by the Fourth Lateran Council in 1215. All orthodox theologians and canonists came to the defense of the role of the priest, and this led to a fourth shift: to *absolution* by a priest. Since absolution was *not* part of the practice and teaching of Penance in the early Church, there was some dispute among the medieval authors about its place in the sacrament. By the time of Thomas Aquinas, however, absolution came to be regarded as essential, along with confession and contrition.

From the Middle Ages to Vatican II

Thomas' theology was endorsed in the Council of Florence's *Decree for the Armenians* (1439): (1) Penance is a sacrament; (2) it consists of contrition of the heart (including the resolution not to sin in the future), oral confession to the priest, satisfaction (e.g., prayer, fasting, almsgiving), and absolution by the priest; (3) the effect of the sacrament is the forgiveness of sins.

The Reformers, and Luther in particular, rejected this teaching. Although Luther accepted the sacramentality of Penance, he believed there was an abiding danger of regarding the works of the penitent as more important than faith in God's mercy. He also rejected the reservation of the power of forgiveness to priests. The first official reaction to Luther's views came in a bull of Pope Leo X (d. 1521), *Exsurge Domine* (1520). Calvin also accepted private confession and absolution as a means of arousing faith and confidence in God's mercy, but he denied its sacramentality.

The definitive response to the Reformers came from the Council of Trent (*Doctrine on the Sacrament of Penance*, Session XIV, 1551). It taught that Penance is a sacrament instituted by Christ; that it is distinct from Baptism; that the three acts of the penitent are contrition, confession of all serious sins in number and kind, and satisfaction; that absolution is reserved to priests alone; and that the priest must have jurisdiction, since absolution is a juridical act.

The Tridentine doctrine remained normative in Catholic theology and practice down to the Second Vatican Council. What is to be said of that teaching in light of our present understanding of the historically conditioned character of all doctrinal pronouncements (as acknowledged, for example, by the 1973 declaration *Mysterium Ecclesiae*, from the Sacred Congregation for the Doctrine of the Faith)?

1.   The council taught that the *confession of grave, or serious, sins* is necessary by divine law (*iure divino*). In no way, however, does divine law canonize any concrete form which this confession may have taken in history—e.g., the private confession of sins to a priest. None of those varieties of forms which have been employed in the history of the Church can be said to contradict the intention of Christ. Hence, there are always, in principle, liturgical alternatives to private confession as we have known it from the Middle Ages to the present.

2.   The *detailed* confession of all serious sins was also affirmed by Trent as being *iure divino*. However, this is not to be understood in the strict sense. It was the council's purpose only to defend against the Reformers' teaching that integral confession was manifestly contrary to the venerable tradition of the Church. The council did not intend to make the integral confession of sins the only way in which the sacrament may be received. It is the *normal* form. Other forms are possible according to needs and circumstances.

3.   The council also affirmed that the confessor is a judge and that the sacrament is a tribunal. But this, too, must be seen in light of the council's concerns about the Reformers' new teaching, namely, their utter rejection of the power of the keys and their insistence that the proclamation of the word alone is efficacious in the remission of sins. The council also wished to maintain that absolution is to be given not in an arbitrary fashion but as a result of a working knowledge of the case.

4.   The council's model of judge and tribunal must be understood, finally, in light of the figure employed by the council, namely, that the sacrament resembles more the judgment made by

a physician on a sick person who comes to him for help than by a civil judge who denounces and punishes a guilty person.

Vatican II

The Second Vatican Council called for a revision of the rite and formulae for the sacrament of Penance "so that they more clearly express both the nature and effect of the sacrament" (*Constitution on the Sacred Liturgy,* n. 72). The sacrament's purpose, the council's *Dogmatic Constitution on the Church* declares, is to "obtain pardon from the mercy of God" and to be "reconciled with the Church whom (sinners) have wounded by their sin, and who, by her charity, her example and her prayer, collaborates in their conversion" (n. 11).

The New Rite of Reconciliation

Although not on a par with the new *Rite of Christian Initiation of Adults* (to which we referred in the previous chapter), the new *Rite of Penance* does bring out the ecclesial dimension of the sacrament more fully than does the traditional (i.e., post-Tridentine) practice of private confession. In the new rite, the effect of the sacrament is identified as reconciliation with God and with the Church. The minister functions more as a healer than as a judge. Emphasis is placed on conversion inspired by the Church's proclamation of God's word. And communal celebration of the sacrament is provided for and encouraged.

"The celebration of this sacrament is thus always an act in which the Church proclaims its faith, gives thanks to God for the freedom with which Christ has made us free, and offers its life as a spiritual sacrifice in praise of God's glory, as it hastens to meet the Lord Jesus" (Introduction to the new *Rite,* n. 7).

The Church and Penance

In its celebration of the sacrament of Penance, the Church reveals itself as the sacrament of God's mercy in the world, but also as a sinful community, still "on the way" to the perfection of the Kingdom. Those who sin and who must avail themselves of the sacrament are just as much "the Church" as are those who, in the name of the Church, act to reconcile the sinner with God and the Church. The Church knows what it is both to forgive and to be forgiven, mindful always of the Lord's own prayer, "Forgive us our sins for we too forgive all who do us wrong" (Luke 11:4).

A Church which cannot admit its sin is not the Church of Christ. A Church which cannot forgive the sins of others against itself is not the Church of Christ. *How* the liturgical process of conversion, repentance, and forgiveness is to be structured is always of less importance than *the fact that* it goes on continually within the Church.

ANOINTING OF THE SICK
History

New Testament

Apart from James 5:14 there is no mention of *Anointing* as a sacred rite in the New Testament. The pertinent text is as follows: "Is there anyone sick among you? He should ask for the presbyters of the church. They in turn are to pray over him, anointing him with oil in the Name [of the Lord]." It continues: "This prayer uttered in faith will reclaim the one who is ill, and the Lord will restore him to health. If he has committed any sins, forgiveness will be his. Hence, declare your sins to one another, and pray for one another, that you may find healing" (5:15-16).

The "elders" or "presbyters" are those appointed and ordained by Apostles or disciples of Apostles (Acts of the Apostles 14:23; Titus 1:5). The presbyters are described by James as having extraordinary spiritual gifts which enable them to heal the sick. Sickness, it must be noted, was attributed to sin, as in the Old Testament and contemporary Judaism, and so it posed a problem for the early Church. At the sickbed it is the task of the presbyter to pray for the sick person and to anoint him or her with oil in the name of the Lord. The oil is regarded as a vital substance, a restorative. There is nothing magical implied, however. It is not the oil but the prayers to the Lord which provide the hope of recovery and the forgiveness of sins. (The recommendation that

Christians declare their sins "to one another" is not without relevance to our previous discussion of the sacrament of Penance.)

Although this text by itself does not "prove" the sacramentality of the Anointing of the Sick, it does indicate that there was such a practice in the early Church, that it required the presence of some leader of the community, that it involved prayers, anointing, and the forgiveness of sins, and that its purpose was the restoration of the sick member not only to physical health but also to spiritual health within the community of faith.

Second Century to the Middle Ages

There is, for all practical purposes, no evidence in the early centuries for the actual rite of Anointing. Since it was not a public liturgical act like the rite of initiation, it was passed over in the liturgical books. The first documentary item is provided by a letter of *Pope Innocent I* (d. 417) to Decentius, bishop of Gubbio, in which certain practical points are clarified regarding the administration of the rite of Anointing. It links the Anointing with the text of James and notes that the oil is blessed by the bishop and applied to the sick person by the bishop or a priest. This letter became a basic source for the late Roman and early medieval period inasmuch as it was incorporated into the most important canonical collections and thus became the starting point for theological discussion of the sacrament.

In the first part of the eighth century Bede the Venerable (d. 735), author of the earliest extant commentary on the Epistle of James, states that it has been the custom of the Church from apostolic times for presbyters to anoint the sick with consecrated oil and to pray for their healing. Nowhere in the early tradition does one find mention of the Anointing as a sacrament of *preparation for death*. Where mention *is* made of a "sacrament of the dying," the reference is always to the Eucharist, administered as Viaticum.

The Early Medieval Period

With the Carolingian Reform at the beginning of the ninth century—i.e., the effort guided by the emperor Charlemagne to

impose Roman liturgy and Roman disciplinary practices throughout his new Holy Roman Empire—Anointing becomes established
among the "last rites." By the middle of the twelfth century the
association between Anointing and dying was so taken for granted
that it came to be called *sacramentum exeuntium* ("the sacrament
of the departing") or in the words of Peter Lombard, *extrema
unctio* ("last anointing"). By the close of the twelfth century
Extreme Unction was in fact appropriating to itself the function
and effects previously associated with Viaticum. Thus, Anointing
became more and more a sacrament of the dying, although its
original purpose was to be a remedy against sickness, with the real
hope of recovery. Even in the early medieval period the Church
did not require that a sickness be terminal before the sacrament
could be administered.

Thirteenth and Fourteenth Centuries

In this period the doctrine of the seven sacraments came to its full
development, and Anointing of the Sick was counted among them.
It was understood as the sacrament of spiritual help for the time of
grave illness unto death. Restoration to bodily health was
regarded as a subordinate and conditional effect only. Theologians began to exaggerate the sacrament's spiritual powers: The
Franciscan school argued that all venial (i.e., non-serious) sins
were forgiven as well as serious sins, and the Dominican school
argued that the sacrament removed even the consequences of sin
and anything which lessened a soul's capacity for the life of glory
in heaven. To die immediately after Extreme Unction, in other
words, guaranteed an unimpeded journey to God.

Fifteenth and Sixteenth Centuries

This theological understanding of the sacrament as a sacrament
for the dying was endorsed by the Council of Florence's *Decree for
the Armenians* (1439), which declared that the sacrament could
"not be given except to a sick person whose life is feared for." The
Council of Trent's *Doctrine on the Sacrament of Extreme Unction*
(1551) was formulated as a complement to the council's teaching
on the sacrament of Penance. It defined the Anointing of the Sick

as a true sacrament. The first draft of its doctrinal formulation, however, had directed that the sacrament be given "only to those who are in their final struggle and who have come to grips with death and who are about to go forth to the Lord." The final draft introduced important modifications, declaring that "this anointing is to be used for the sick, particularly for those who are so dangerously ill as to seem at the point of departing this life." It speaks of the sacrament's effects as purification from sin as well as from the effects of sin, comfort and strength of soul, the arousal of confidence in God's mercy, readiness to bear the difficulties and trials of illness, and even health of body, where expedient for the welfare of the soul. Trent's teaching is remarkable not only for what it contains about the spiritual, psychological, and bodily effects of the sacrament but also for what it omits about the sacrament as a last rite. The council thereby struck at the root of a growing abuse which delayed the sacrament until the very last moment of life.

Twentieth Century

The Tridentine doctrine shaped the theological, canonical, and pastoral understanding and practice of this sacrament for centuries thereafter. In the twentieth century some tentative advances were suggested. Theologians and liturgists alike suggested that insofar as this is a sacrament of the dying it is essentially an "anointing for glory." Others, however, pointed out that the prayers of the ritual made no mention of death, and that the sacrament was really a sacrament of the sick. The "last sacrament" is not the Anointing, but Viaticum. Indeed, it was only in the middle of the twelfth century, these theologians argued, that the stress on preparation for death had emerged.

Vatican II

The Second Vatican Council endorsed this second line of thought, recommending that the sacrament be called the Anointing of the Sick rather than Extreme Unction and noting explicitly that it "is not a sacrament reserved for those who are at the point of death"

(*Constitution on the Sacred Liturgy,* n. 73). Indeed, the *last* sacrament to be administered to the dying is Viaticum (n. 68). The *Dogmatic Constitution on the Church* places the sacrament in its larger ecclesial context: "In the holy anointing of the sick with the prayer of the priest, the whole Church recommends the sick to the Lord, who suffered and has been glorified, asking him to give them relief and salvation. She goes further and calls upon them to associate themselves freely with the passion and death of Christ, and in this way to make their contribution to the good of God's people" (n. 11).

The New Rite of Anointing and Pastoral Care of the Sick

The new rite acknowledges that sickness prevents us from fulfilling our role in human society and in the Church. On the other hand, the sick person participates in the redemptive sufferings of Christ and provides the Church with a reminder of higher things and of the limitations of human life. The Church's concern for the sick is in fidelity to Christ's command to visit the sick and is consistent with a wholistic understanding of salvation as reaching the total person (see chapter 5 of this book).

This sacrament is a sacrament of faith: the faith of the Church which looks back to the death and resurrection of Christ and looks ahead to the future kingdom which is pledged in the sacraments. The sacrament provides the grace of the Holy Spirit, heightens trust in God, strengthens us against temptation and anxiety, and may even restore physical health. The sacrament may also provide forgiveness of sins, as a complement to the sacrament of Penance. Anointing is not just for the dying but for anyone who is seriously ill. That judgment is always a prudential one, of course. The last sacrament is Viaticum, received during Mass where possible.

The Church and the Anointing of the Sick

The Church discloses itself in this sacrament as the community of those who are on pilgrimage to the Kingdom of God, with eschatological faith and hope. The Church is a sacrament of Christ the healer, the one who saves us in our human wholeness, body as well as soul. It is at the same time a community always in need of healing, a community subject to physical as well as spiritual reverses.

A Church which is not interested in healing and in the total health of the whole human person and of the human community at large is not the Church of Christ. A Church which abandons those who, by certain of the world's standards, are no longer of practical use is not the Church of Christ. The Church which anoints the sick is the Church of the "Lord Jesus Christ, (who) shared in our human nature to heal the sick and save all mankind" (Prayer After Anointing).

Section Two: Sacraments of Vocation and Commitment

MATRIMONY
History

Old Testament

The Church's understanding of the sacredness of marriage is rooted in the *creation* narrative in Genesis. "The Lord God said: 'It is not good for the man to be alone'.... That is why a man leaves his father and mother and clings to his wife, and the two of them become one body" (2:18,24). The Lord blesses their union and orders them to "be fruitful and multiply" (1:28). Marriage functions primarily in the Old Testament, however, as an institution for the preservation of the husband's clan. That is why children, especially sons, are regarded as a blessing and a gift from God (Genesis 24:60; Psalm 127:3) and why childlessness is a disgrace and a chastisement (Genesis 30:1-6; 1 Samuel 1:6-11). The highest honor paid to marriage in the Old Testament is the application to it of the symbol of the *Covenant* between Yahweh and Israel (Hosea 2; Isaiah 54:4-5; Jeremiah 2:2; 3:20).

New Testament

Jesus deepens the Hebrew concept of marriage, insisting on the oneness that exists between the man and the woman. The woman is not to be cast aside at will. He speaks, therefore, against divorce, so strongly in fact that the one who marries a divorced woman commits adultery (Matthew 5:31-32; 19:3-12). But the early Church adds an "exceptive clause" as a softening of Jesus' demands: " . . . lewd conduct is a separate case" (5:32). On the other hand, Jesus also consistently regards marriage as a state in life proper to this age; in heaven there will be no marrying (Mark 12:25). All of the concerns of marriage must yield to the claims of the Second Coming (Luke 14:20; see also Matthew 24:38-39; Luke 17:27). As always with Jesus, everything is to be seen in light of the Kingdom of God.

This ambivalent view of marriage comes through even more forcefully in the Pauline writings. On the one hand, marriage is a symbol of Christ's union with his Church (Ephesians 5:21-33). The union of man and woman in marriage is not only compared with the union of Christ with the Church; it is actually based on the union of Christ with the Church. When husbands love their wives as their own flesh, they are only doing what Christ does with the Church. On the other hand, Paul in 1 Corinthians wishes that the faithful would renounce marriage in favor of virginity *because he thinks the Lord will soon return* and because he worries about the risk of distraction in the meantime (7:32-35). Paul reduces marriage to something of secondary importance *in view of the Second Coming*. Whereas the creation narrative cautions that it is not good for man to be alone, Paul insists that "a man is better off having no relations with a woman" (7:1). But he does not go so far as to condemn marriage. There are several passages in fact in the New Testament where the messianic period is described as a wedding feast (Matthew 9:15; 25:1-13; Mark 2:19; John 3:29).

Second Century to the Middle Ages

This ambivalence toward marriage continues beyond the apostolic age. Marriage is viewed more and more as the justification of the use of sex which has been infected by sin (a "lawful remedy for concupiscence," the Scholastic textbooks would call it). This trend reached its fullest development in Augustine, who influenced the Church on this subject more profoundly than any other single individual did. Augustine (as we noted in chapter 15 in connection with our discussion of the sexuality of Jesus) linked sexuality with animality. The purpose of marriage is none other than the begetting of children. Indeed, our sexual desires are nothing more than the unfortunate effects of Original Sin. Every child is literally born of his or her parents' "sin" because procreation is possible only with the seductive aid of physical lust. But it is a tolerable "sin" because God wills that we should be fruitful and multiply, and it provides a legitimate way of keeping "perverse desire within its proper bounds."

Why this altered view of marriage developed is not completely clear. It may be because of the influence of Greek philosophy, especially the Stoic insistence on keeping oneself fully under control, and the Gnostic-Manichaean rejection of the goodness of matter. But the Fathers of the Church never went so far as to deny the basic value and sanctity of marriage as upheld, for example, in 1 Timothy 4:1-5 ("Everything God created is good; nothing is to be rejected...").

The Middle Ages to Vatican II

Discussion of marriage continued along a similarly ambivalent course into the medieval period. Abelard acknowledged its sacramentality but insisted that it did not "avail unto salvation .... For to bring home a wife is not meritorious for salvation, but it is allowed for salvation's sake because of incontinence." The goodness of marriage meanwhile was affirmed against the Waldensians and Albigensians, the medieval counterparts of Manichaeism, in the Profession of Faith prescribed by Pope Innocent III in 1208, and marriage itself was accounted a true sacrament in the Council of Florence's *Decree for the Armenians* (1439) and then, most definitely, at the Council of Trent *(Doctrine on the Sacrament of Matrimony,* Session XXIV, 1563).

The Protestant Reformers upheld the sacredness of marriage in the order of creation, but they denied that marriage belonged to the order of grace as a sacrament. They also rejected the Church's authority over marriage, and approved the practice of divorce as a lesser of two evils. Trent affirmed the opposite position in each instance. Among the council's more "historically conditioned" canons is the tenth: "If anyone says that the married state surpasses that of virginity or celibacy, and that it is not better and happier to remain in virginity or celibacy than to be united in matrimony, *anathema sit.*"

The Tridentine perspective remained normative for Catholic theology, canon law, and pastoral practice until the Second Vatican Council. Meanwhile, Trent's teaching was vigorously reaffirmed by Pope Pius XI's *Casti Connubii* in 1930, which set forth as marriage's primary purpose the propagation of life, calling the "mutual faithfulness of husband and wife" the "second blessing" of marriage.

Vatican II

As happened with so many other theological and pastoral questions, the Catholic Church's perspective on marriage was significantly modified by the Second Vatican Council. In contrast with previous official pronouncements and conventional theological and canonical insights, the council adopts a remarkably personalistic standpoint. It no longer uses the traditional term *contract* to describe the marriage bond. Instead, the council speaks of the "marriage covenant" which is sealed by an "irrevocable personal consent" (*Pastoral Constitution on the Church in the Modern World,* n. 48).

Secondly, neither does the council continue to employ the old distinction between primary and secondary ends in which the begetting of children is always more important than the mutual love of husband and wife. "Hence, *while not making the other ends of marriage of less account,* the true practice of conjugal love, and the whole tenor of family life resulting from it, tend to dispose the spouses to cooperate generously with the love of the Creator and Savior who through them day by day expands and enriches His family" (n. 50, italics mine).

Thirdly, the sacrament of marriage is not something added to the marriage union established through mutual human love. "Authentic married love is taken up into divine love and is ruled and enriched by the redemptive power of Christ and the salvific action of the Church ... " (n. 48). This new emphasis in the theology of marriage is consistent with the claims of contemporary sociology that this is the first age in which people marry and remain in marriage because they love each other. And so there is this stress on the mutual exchange of love as constituting the sacrament of marriage, on married love as the source of the institution of marriage, on the need for growth in this love in order to bring the sacrament to its full realization, and on the need for the Church constantly to bring forth the witness value of this sacrament to the whole community of faith. As husband and wife are called to be faithful, generous, and gracious to each other in fulfillment of their marriage covenant, so is the whole Church called to be faithful to its covenant with God in Christ. "When Christian marriage flounders," Father John T. Finnegan, former President of the Canon Law Society of America has written, "the witness of fidelity in all Christian vocations flounders" ("Marriage/Pastoral Care," *Origins* 5/10, August 28, 1975, p. 152).

Fourthly, the council emphasizes the necessity of a faith commitment for the sacrament of marriage (see *Constitution on the Sacred Liturgy,* n. 59). It is no longer sufficient that the two parties be baptized. Marriage is not just a ceremony by which two people are legally bound together. As a sacrament, it is an act of worship, an expression of faith, a sign of the Church's unity, a mode of Christ's presence (as we noted in the previous chapter). Vatican II moves beyond the Code of Canon Law (canon 1012, par. 2, in the present Code; canon 242, par. 2, in the newly proposed revision), which says that there is no valid marriage between the baptized which is not by that very fact a sacrament. The council uses the term *christifideles.* Marriage is not just a union between *baptized* Christians; it is a union between *faithful* Christians.

Fifthly, the full consummation of marriage is more than a biological act. The old theology and the old canon law asserted that a marriage between two baptized Christians, once performed according to the rite of the Church *(ratum)* and once consummated by a single act of physical union *(consummatum)*, can never be dissolved, not even by the pope.

But according to the council, the expression of the mutual love which is at the heart of the sacrament consists of more than biological union. "It involves the good of the whole person. Therefore it can enrich the expressions of body and mind with a unique dignity, ennobling these expressions as special ingredients and signs of friendship distinctive of marriage . . . . Such love pervades the whole of [the spouses'] lives" (n. 49; see also Pope Paul VI's *Humanae Vitae,* 1968, nn. 8-9). Consummation without love is without meaning. It would be difficult to see, in light of the council's teaching, how such purely biological consummation could have a sacramental character. Rather, the council speaks of the "intimate partnership of married life" *(consortium vitae conjugalis,* n. 48).

Finally, the broader ecclesial dimension of the sacrament is maintained. "Christian spouses, in virtue of the sacrament of matrimony, signify and share in the mystery of that union and fruitful love which exists between Christ and the Church (see Ephesians 5:32)" *(Dogmatic Constitution on the Church,* n. 11).

The New Rite of Marriage

The council's theology of matrimony is carried over into the new *Rite of Marriage.* The "Introduction" to the rite speaks of the union of Christ and the Church (n. 1), of the covenantal nature of the marriage bond (n. 2), of the essential element of mutual affection in body and mind (n. 3), of the importance of the procreation and education of children without prejudice to the other purposes of marriage (n. 4), of the virtue of faith required ("for the sacrament of matrimony presupposes and demands faith," n. 7), and of the significance of the eucharistic setting for marriage (n. 6).

Some Canonical Considerations

Indissolubility

The Catholic Church teaches (canon 1013) that marriage is *monogamous* (one husband, one wife at a time) and *indissoluble* (permanent). On the other hand, the Church's own pastoral practice over the years has tolerated certain limited measures of ecclesiastical reconciliation where the rigorous imposition of the full demands of Christian law would require moral heroism. Origen (d. 254) had proposed a formula that was widely quoted throughout the first thousand years of the Church's history: "The matter of divorce and remarriage was contrary to what has been handed down, but not entirely without reason." It was a kind of "lesser-of-two-evils" principle. The Eastern Orthodox churches developed and continue to maintain the principle of *economy* (similar to the Catholic notion of *dispensation)*, by which the unintended harshness of a given law is removed. Thus, the Orthodox churches have permitted remarriage after divorce. "Because the risen Christ has entrusted to the church a stewardship of prudence and freedom to listen to the promptings of the Holy Spirit about today's problems of church unity, a proper understanding of economy involves the exercise of spiritual discernment" (Orthodox-Roman Catholic Consultation, "Unity and Divine Economy," *Origins* 6/9, August 12, 1976, p. 144). The teaching of the Council of Trent (Session XXIV, canon 7, 1563) on indissolubility was formulated against the Reformers, not against the Orthodox. While the official position of the Catholic Church is clear—i.e., that marriage is permanent—it does not absolutely exclude the kind of pastoral flexibility embodied in the principle of economy.

Canonical Form

The Catholic Church requires that all Catholics marry before a priest or deacon, and two witnesses. This is known as the requirement of "canonical form." Before 1966 there were serious penalties incurred by Catholics who married "outside the Church" and before a Protestant minister. Between 1966 and 1970 Pope Paul VI retroactively lifted and abolished all such penalties. Catholics are now permitted to marry in a Protestant church before a Protestant minister with permission from the local bishop. Protestants and Orthodox may also act as official witnesses (bridesmaid or best man) at a Catholic marriage, and Catholics may serve in the same capacity at a marriage which is properly celebrated between separated brethren *(Ecumenical Directory,* May 14, 1967, n. 58).

Mixed Marriage

A "mixed marriage" is one between a Catholic and a non-Catholic. To receive the dispensation to marry a non-Catholic, the Catholic party must make the following affirmation: "I reaffirm my faith in Jesus Christ and, with God's help, intend to continue living that faith in the Catholic Church. I promise to do all in my power to share the faith I have received with our children by having them baptized and reared as Catholics" *(Statement of the United States Catholic Bishops,* January 1, 1971). This promise can be made orally or in writing by the Catholic party. The other party must be informed of the fact and content of this promise.

"Pauline Privilege"

The "Pauline Privilege" is an historical elaboration of 1 Corinthians 7:10-16, where Paul states that, in the case of the marriage of two unbaptized, one of whom later becomes a Christian without the consent of the other, the convert is no longer bound to remain with the non-Christian. "God has called you to live in peace" (v. 15). This principle was used frequently during the missionary expansion of the Church from the sixteenth through the nineteenth centuries and is still employed today.

"Petrine Privilege"

The "Petrine Privilege" is also known as the "Privilege of the Faith." It is not found in the Code of Canon Law but developed as a pastoral practice in the United States after the promulgation of the Code of Canon Law in 1918. The "Petrine Privilege" allows the pope to dissolve a marriage between a Christian and a non-

Christian which, by the very nature of the bond, was not sacramental in the first place (no marriage can be sacramental unless both parties are Christians). There has to be a good reason for such papal action: One of the parties to the first marriage (presumably severed in divorce) wishes to marry a Catholic in a second ceremony, or the non-Christian party wants to become a Catholic and remarry.

Annulment

The Catholic Church does not grant divorces, only annulments. An annulment is an official declaration that a real marriage never existed in the first instance. The traditional grounds for nullity so carefully listed in the 1918 Code of Canon Law have now been broadened to include a whole range of character disorders and deficiencies. Reasons for annulling a marriage now include: lack of discretion (the parties did not really understand what they were committing themselves to), lack of partnership in conjugal life, lack of conjugal love, psychopathic personality, schizophrenia, affective immaturity, psychic incompetence, sociopathic personality, "moral impotence," lack of interpersonal communication.

Internal Forum Solution

The Marriage Tribunal (or court) of a diocese or of the Holy See is referred to as the "external forum." Its proceedings are public. Decisions are rendered in the open. The "internal forum," by contrast, is the realm of conscience. What happens there is private, known only to the parties involved, the priest(s) working on the case, and God. The internal forum solution is used when a public annulment process is impossible by reason of excessive emotional strain or the lack of cooperation from one's former spouse and/or witnesses. In such a case, even though there has been no public, official declaration by the Church, a Catholic, after consultation with a confessor or any competent priest, concludes that he or she is free to marry again, or that he or she can remain in the present second marriage. In either case, the Catholic party makes a judgment of conscience that he or she can return to the Church's sacramental life, assuming that no grave scandal is involved. (For more on conscience, see chapter 25.) This solution goes beyond the traditional "brother-sister" solution, which allowed an invalidly married couple to stay together and receive the sacraments (assuming again there would be no scandal) on condition that they live as "brother and sister."

Ecumenical Reflections

There is agreement between the Catholic Church, on the one hand, and the Orthodox and Anglican churches, on the other, regarding the sacramentality of marriage. The *Orthodox-Roman Catholic* "Agreed Statement on the Sanctity of Marriage" (*Origins* 8/28, December 28, 1978, pp. 446–447) notes that "marriage [is] the fundamental relationship in which a man and woman, by total sharing with each other, seek their own growth in holiness and that of their children, and thus show forth the presence on earth of God's kingdom" (I, par. 2). Although marriage involves a permanent commitment, the statement acknowledges that the Orthodox Church, "out of consideration of the human realities, permits divorce . . . and tolerates remarriages in order to avoid further human tragedies" (II, par. 2).

An *Anglican-Roman Catholic* Commission on the Theology of Marriage and Its Application to Mixed Marriages concluded that there is "no fundamental difference of doctrine between the two Churches, as regards what marriage of its nature is or the ends which it is ordained to serve" (*Final Report*, June 27, 1975, Washington, D.C.: United States Catholic Conference, 1976, p. 20). The report refers favorably to the teaching of Vatican II on the covenantal character of marriage, and to marriage's relationship to the convenantal union of Christ and the Church.

Agreement regarding the sacramental reality of matrimony, however, has not been reached with the churches of the Lutheran and Reformed (Calvinist) traditions. After five years of discussion, Catholic, Lutheran, and Reformed members of an international study commission issued a report in which they insist that they have come "decisively closer" to a common understanding of marriage, but that they could not agree on the sacramentality of marriage or on its indissolubility. (See "An Ecumenical Approach to Marriage," *Origins* 7/31, January 19, 1978, pp. 481, 483–496.)

The Church and Matrimony

When seen as a covenantal rather than contractual bond, Christian marriage is a sacrament of the union between Christ and Church (Ephesians 5:22–32). The sacrament of Matrimony is also a decisive moment when the Church reveals itself as the bride of Christ, as the sign that God is irrevocably committed to the human community in and through Christ. The new community signified and effected by marriage is also a sign of what the Church is, a community of love. The Church comes into being at various levels of Christian fellowship. The family has sometimes been spoken of as "the Church in miniature." Even if that term lacks ecclesiological precision, it does express what the Church discloses in this sacrament, namely, the proclamation that God wills us all to be one in Christ and in his Spirit, and that God is communicated in grace to make that unity possible.

HOLY ORDER
Terminology

This is perhaps the most difficult sacrament of all to treat. It is exceedingly complicated in its origin and in the development of terminology. Tertullian chose the word *ordo* ("order") to apply to the clergy as a whole, probably under the influence of Psalm 109:4 and Hebrews 5–7, which refer to the priesthood "according to the order of Melchisedech." This "order" was composed of various grades of ministers. The bishop, a modern term derived from the Latinization of *episcopos* ("overseer"), was commonly called *sacerdos* ("priest"). The priest was called *presbyter*. The deacon was usually called *minister* ("servant"). In the course of history, the corporate or collegial sense of *ordo* gradually evaporated, only to be rediscovered at Vatican II. Because of these extreme variations in terminology, one must interpret ancient texts with great care, not reading back into them some medieval or modern understanding of the words.

History

Old Testament

As is explained in the Epistle to the Hebrews, Jesus' priesthood must be understood in light of the Old Testament. The patriarchs, as heads of families or tribal groups, performed priestly functions, such as offering sacrifice (Genesis 22:2; 31:54). Eventually, a specific office of priesthood evolved and a priestly professionalism developed, especially in the tribe of Levi (thus, the levitical priesthood). This professionalism involved certain skills and training. It also required sanctity (Leviticus 19:2; 21:8). Deuteronomy 33:8–10 suggests three basic priestly functions: the discernment of God's will through the casting of sacred lots (1 Samuel 14:41–42), teaching (Deuteronomy 33:10), and sacrifice and cultic offering (Deuteronomy 33:10). The priest, therefore, was an intermediary between God and humankind.

New Testament

As noted in chapter 17, the New Testament does not provide an organizational blueprint for the Church. On the contrary, it is practically impossible to say more than that there is some organizational structure in the various New Testament churches, that these are influenced by the political, social, and cultural character of the communities in which these churches existed, and that each organizational or ministerial component was for the sake of the mission of the Church—i.e., for service and not for domination.

Varieties of Ministries and/or Offices: There are *the Twelve* (Matthew 10:2–4; Mark 3:16–19; Luke 6:13–16; Acts of the Aspostles 1:13), called "the Eleven" during the interval between the death of Judas and the election of Matthias (Matthew 28:16; Mark 16:14; Luke 24:9,33; Acts of the Apostles 1:26). The election of Matthias seemed important in order to maintain an apparent symbolic link with the twelve tribes of Israel, which the Twelve will judge (Matthew 19:28; Luke 22:30). All of the Twelve were *apostles* (literally, "those sent forth"), but not all apostles were members of the Twelve—e.g., Paul. (Hereafter, the word apostle is capitalized only when it refers to the Twelve.) And there were other ministries besides those of the Twelve and the other apostles. There were also prophets and teachers, whose authority was very much like that of the Apostles (1 Corinthians 12:28; Acts of the Apostles 13:1; 15:32, Ephesians 2:20; 3:5; 4:11). There were, in addition, wonder-workers, healers, helpers, administrators, speakers in tongues, evangelists, shepherds, elders, deacons, and overseers. The elders (*presbyteroi*), deacons (*diakonoi*), and overseers (*episcopoi*) are of particular interest here because their offices came eventually to be regarded by the Catholic Church as constituting the threefold division of the one sacrament of Holy Order: diaconate, presbyterate, and episcopate—deacon, priest, and bishop. No Christian, however, is ever specifically identified as a priest, probably because early Christians regarded the Jewish priesthood as valid and never thought of a priesthood of their own. They expected, after all, that the Jews would all eventually join the new movement.

Deacons seem to have had their origin in the designation of "the Seven" (Acts of the Apostles 6:1–6) to "wait on tables"—e.g., to distribute food among the widows and to assist the Twelve in other material ways. The *elders* were adult males of a town, city, or tribe, who constituted the community's governing body. In Acts of the Apostles the elders are associated with the Apostles in decisions, especially the council of Jerusalem (15:22). The relationship between elders and *overseers* is more difficult to determine. Sometimes the offices seem interchangeable (Titus 1:5–9); at other times the elders are in charge (1 Timothy 5:17). Some have suggested that the two offices were, in fact, the same; others regard the overseers as the executive board of the elders, a view which is more probable because it is more in harmony with the practices of other social units in which elders appear. In any case, there is no sign that a one single bishop is in charge of a local church.

The elders also became a more select group. They were "established" in each town by election (Titus 1:5), and there was a ritual conferral of office, probably by the imposition of hands (Acts of the Apostles 14:23; 1 Timothy 5:22). Bishops are established by the Holy Spirit (Acts of the Apostles 20:28), whose will is manifested by the assembly of the entire Church. The bishops/elders have care of the Church (1 Timothy 3:4), manage the Church (5:17), are God's stewards (1 Corinthians 4:1), instruct in sound doctrine (Titus 1:7-9), and feed the flock (Acts of the Apostles 20:28; 1 Peter 5:2).

Thus, the bishop/elder, or presbyter/bishop, took up where the Pauline apostles left off. They were responsible for the continued care of churches founded by these apostles. Whereas the apostles, including the Twelve, were ministers "on the move," the presbyter-bishops were ministers in residence. The apostles were charismatic and non-insitutionalized ministers; the presbyter-bishops had to be people who could manage a household well (1 Timothy 3:4-5) and who could organize, stabilize, and combat dangerous innovation (Titus 1:9). They were not to be recent converts, nor married more than once (1 Timothy 3:2,6). They were also to manifest pastoral skills (Acts of the Apostles 20:28-29; 1 Peter 5:2-4).

It is only when we go outside (although not chronologically beyond) the New Testament literature that we find evidence for the so-called *monarchical episcopate*, i.e., a local church presided over by one bishop. The primary source is Ignatius of Antioch (d. 108), and specifically his letters to the *Smyrnaeans* 8:1; 9:1), the *Ephesians* (5:1,3), the *Trallians* (2:1), and the *Magnesians* (4:1; 7:1). Such respect as Ignatius recommended for bishops served as a weapon against disunity and heresy. But we must keep certain qualifications in mind: (1) The local churches over which the bishop presided were not dioceses in the modern sense of the term. They were nothing more than one-parish towns. (2) We have no evidence that the monarchical episcopal structure was universal in the Church at this time. Indeed in Paul's day, some churches had presbyter-bishops (e.g., Philippi) and some did not (e.g., Corinth). (3) On the contrary, in the mid-second century, when *The Shepherd of Hermas* was written, the Roman church still seems to have been ruled by a presbyterate, and Ignatius makes no mention of a bishop in his letter to the *Romans*. (4) Presbyters also served as overseers (bishops) of churches (1 Peter 5:1-3). (5) Neither the presbyter-bishops nor the monarchical bishops can be considered "successors of the Apostles" in the sense that all were duly appointed and ordained by an Apostle, i.e., one of the Twelve.

The Emergence of Christian Priesthood: So long as Christians understood themselves as the renewed, not the new, Israel, they had no idea of replacing the Jewish priesthood with one of their own. The Acts of the Apostles reports that while they broke bread in their homes, the Jerusalem Christians also kept up their daily attendance at the Temple (2:46). Even Paul, who insisted that Gentile Christians were not bound by the Law, still went to the Temple for offerings as late as the year 58 (Acts of the Apostles 21:26).

Not until the early Christians concluded that they were indeed part of a radically new movement distinct from Judaism was there a basis for the development of a separate Christian priesthood. Other events accentuated this process: the increasing numbers of Gentile converts, the shift of leadership away from the Jerusalem church and to the churches of Rome, Antioch, Ephesus, and Alexandria, the destruction of the Temple, and, finally, Judaism's own sectarian tendencies in the post-destruction period. Concomitantly, there was a growing recognition of the sacrificial character of the Eucharist, which called for a priesthood of sacrifice distinct from the Jewish priesthood. This awareness appeared in Christian writings about the end of the first century or the beginning of the second, especially in the *Didache*, in the writings of Clement of Rome (d. 100), and in the *Apostolic Tradition* of Hippolytus of Rome (d. ca. 236).

This historical record requires some modification of the traditional Catholic notion that Jesus directly and explicitly instituted the Catholic priesthood at the Last Supper. As noted in the previous chapter, Jesus' institution of the sacraments is implied and/or included in his proclamation of the Kingdom of God, in his gathering of disciples, and in the special significance he accorded the Last Supper which he ate with his disciples. (The Eucharist, to be sure, was *explicitly* instituted by Jesus at the Last Supper.) The priesthood as we have come to know it represents a fusion of different roles and ministries which are to be found in the New Testament churches. It is not even clear, for example, that anyone in particular was commissioned to preside over the Eucharist in the beginning. Paul never mentions that he presided. In fact, he seems to have been little involved in the administration of sacraments (1 Corinthians 1:14-15). There is no explicit mention that any of the Apostles presided over the Eucharist. Indeed, there is no compelling evidence that they presided when they were present, or that a chain of ordination from Apostle to bishop to priest was required for presiding. Someone must have presided, of course, and those who did so presided with the approval of the community.

We simply do not know how a certain individual came to preside and whether it came to be a permanent or regular function for that person. As we have already seen, there was a remarkable diversity of structure and form in the New Testament churches. The most that can be said is that those who presided did so with the consent of the local church and that this consent was tantamount, but not always equivalent, to ordination.

As the Church grew larger and became more complex in its organizational structure, the element of selection and consent came to be regularized. Presiding eventually became the exclusive privilege of bishops and presbyters. The *Didache* may have been written just at the turning point when the system was placed into effect. There is mention there, for example, of wandering prophets who are not forbidden to hold Eucharist (10:7), and there is an instruction for bishops and deacons to render to the community the ministry (liturgy) of the prophets. By the year 96 Clement's *Epistle to the Corinthians* speaks of the sin of ejecting from office "men who have offered the sacrificial gifts of the episcopate worthily" (44:4). Fifteen years later, Ignatius of Antioch makes it clear that the practice of episcopal and presbyteral presiding is well established (*Smyrnaeans* 8:1). Thus, by the turn of the century or soon thereafter, two roles that were probably once separated are joined together: the role of the presbyter-bishop and the role of the presiding minister of the Eucharist. Significantly, not until the year 1208 is there an official declaration that priestly ordination is necessary to celebrate the Eucharist (Innocent III, *Profession of Faith Prescribed to the Waldensians*), and then, more solemnly, by the Council of Florence (1439) and the Council of Trent (1563).

Third Through Fifth Centuries

The *Apostolic Tradition* of Hippolytus sketches a picture of the third-century Church. The bishop is the *sacerdos*, elected by the people, but he receives the imposition of hands from another bishop. The presbyter, or priest, is ordained by the bishop, with other priests joining in. The deacon is ordained by the bishop alone because the deacon is ordained to the service of the bishop. Significantly, the rite of consecration of a bishop is clearly inspired by the New Testament, while the ordination of the priest is inspired by the Old Testament. This anomaly tends to confirm what was suggested above about the probable origins of the Christian priesthood. At first the Church had no intention of having a priesthood of its own, distinct from the Jewish priesthood. But when the concept of Christian priesthood took hold, the Church understandably drew upon the Old Testament for models, standards, and inspiration.

Early in the fourth century the Church was "blessed" (or "cursed") with the Edict of Constantine, which showered upon the clergy many civil privileges and dispensations. The influence of the Old Testament's notion of priesthood had much to do with this new bestowal of temporal favor.

As the local churches grew, parishes were created outside the major Christian centers, and the presbyters were given pastoral care over them. The Council of Chalcedon (451) would later decree that a priest be ordained for a particular church. The first signs of emphasis on the fundamental equality of bishops and presbyters developed in the fourth century, not only within unorthodox circles, e.g., Arianism, but even within orthodox groups, e.g., John Chrysostom (d. 407) and the *Canons of Hippolytus*. The authors who exercised a decisive influence in this matter on the Middle Ages were Jerome (d. 420) and Ambrosiaster, the unknown author of a series of commentaries on the Pauline epistles. Both stressed the equivalence of the bishop's and the presbyter's power to celebrate the Eucharist and forgive sins.

Sixth Through Twelfth Centuries

With the Germanization of Christianity in the early Middle Ages, the understanding and exercise of priesthood took another turn. Priestly and royal power were fused. Priests themselves were caught up into the feudal system and were ordained not only for the celebration of the Eucharist and the administration of sacraments, but also for certain tax-collecting chores. Their loyalty was to the feudal lords who selected them, not to the bishop. In the Frankish churches new rites of ordination were added. The bishop was anointed with holy chrism, the crozier (staff) and ring were given, and then he was enthroned. The priest was ordained with an anointing of the hands, the giving of bread and wine, and a second laying on of hands in view of the absolution of sins. These developments reflected Germanic customs which attached great importance to the transmission of the emblems of power, a "princely" power for bishops and a cultic power for priests. Toward the end of the tenth century this liturgy was merged with the Roman tradition in the *Romano-Germanic Pontifical* of Mainz. Priesthood became even more of a caste-like existence within the Church with the imposition of *celibacy* in the twelfth century as a universal requirement for priests of the Latin rite.

The Reformation

The increasing alienation of the clergy from the rest of the Church provoked a reaction. The Reformers insisted that there exists in the Church no ministerial power received through the sacrament of Holy Order. There is only a priesthood of all believers. All specialized ministry is delegated by the community. Furthermore, since the Eucharist is not a sacrifice (Calvary cannot, and need not, be repeated), there is no need for a cultic priesthood in the Church. The Council of Trent rejected these views, declaring that priesthood is conferred through one of the seven sacraments, that the Mass is a true sacrifice, and that there is a true hierarchy in the Church consisting of bishops, priests, and deacons and that these ministers do not depend on the call of the community for their authority and powers (*Doctrine on the Sacrament of Order*, Session XXIII, 1563).

The Counter-Reformation to Vatican II

Under the impact of *Trent*, the Catholic Church launched a reform of the clergy. Seminaries for the education and training of future priests were established, and greater emphasis was placed on priestly spirituality. The reform of priestly formation and spirituality was supported by such figures as Charles Borromeo (d. 1584) and Francis de Sales (d. 1622), and by the new religious orders. But the spirituality was still individualistic, and the notion of priesthood on which it was based was still cultic and sacramental. Under the impact of the anticlericalist wave of the *French Revolution* in the eighteenth century, the Church launched yet another spiritual renewal, this time sparked by Vincent de Paul (d. 1660), Jean-Jacques Olier (d. 1657), Pierre de Bérulle (d. 1629), and others. Under the impact of post-Enlightenment *modernity* (see chapter 3), the Catholic priesthood began losing much of its "mystique" as a spiritually elite form of Christian existence. Young Catholic men concluded that there were other ways of living the Gospel and working for the Kingdom of God. A drastic decline in vocations followed, and large numbers of priests resigned from the active ministry. Many of those priests who did resign complained about the misuse of authority by bishops and other Church leaders, and others protested against the continued imposition of obligatory celibacy.

Vatican II

With its stress on the Church as the whole People of God, the Second Vatican Council acknowledged that all the baptized participate in some way in the one priesthood of Christ (*Dogmatic Constitution on the Church*, n. 11). Although the priesthood of ordination and the priesthood of Baptism differ "in essence and not only in degree," they are nonetheless related to this one priesthood of Christ. The ministerial priesthood of ordination consists of three degrees or orders: episcopate, presbyterate, and diaconate (nn. 20-29). Each order is truly sacramental.

Taken as a body (*ordo*), bishops are the successors to the college of the Apostles in teaching authority and pastoral rule (n. 22). United with their head, the bishop of Rome, the bishops constitute a college and are the subjects of "supreme and full power over the universal Church." The union of bishops among themselves and with the bishop of Rome symbolizes the communion of churches which constitutes the whole Body of Christ (n. 23).

The presbyterate is a specific participation in the priesthood of the episcopate (n. 28). Priests are united with their bishop in priestly dignity. They are collaborators with the bishop and constitute a college with him.

The diaconate is also a sacramental degree of Holy Order (n. 29). The council recommends the restoration of the permanent diaconate (as distinguished from reception of the diaconate as the next-to-last step on the way to priesthood).

Since the priesthood of Christ includes prophetic and shepherding as well as "priestly" or cultic functions, the ordained priesthood of the Church embraces more than sacramental and liturgical responsibilities (*Decree on the Ministry and Life of Priests*, nn. 2–6).

The New Rites of Ordination

The rite of episcopal consecration is now modified to include the consecratory prayer from the *Apostolic Tradition* of Hippolytus of Rome, in order to bring out the apostolic succession of bishops and their various duties and functions beyond the purely cultic. The collegial character of the episcopate is also emphasized. In presbyteral ordination the collaborative relationship between the priest and the bishop is more clearly drawn. Significantly, the Old Testament flavor is preserved in the consecratory prayer. Only minor changes have been made in the rite of ordination to the diaconate to take into account recent prescriptions concerning the diaconate as a proper and permanent grade of the hierarchy in the Latin Church and also for the sake of clarifying and simplifying the ceremony.

Ecumenical Developments

Several of the ecumenical consultations have addressed themselves to the question of ordained ministry: Lutheran-Catholic,

Anglican-Roman Catholic, United Methodist-Roman Catholic, Orthodox-Roman Catholic, and Presbyterian-Reformed-Roman Catholic. The *Lutheran-Catholic* consultation issued an important statement, "Eucharist and Ministry," in 1970 (*Lutherans and Catholics in Dialogue*, vol. 4, Washington, D.C.: United States Catholic Conference, 1970, pp. 7-33). It distinguishes between the general ministry (lower case) of the whole People of God and the ordained Ministry (upper case), which is a particular form of service within and for the sake of the Church in its mission to the world. It is a ministry of proclaiming the Gospel, celebrating the sacraments, caring for the faithful, witnessing, and serving. It stands *with* the People of God under Christ, but also speaks in Christ's name *to* his People. The Catholic participants in this dialogue noted a "gratifying degree of agreement" with the Lutherans "as to the essentials of the sacred Ministry." Specifically, they found that the Lutherans hold that the Ministry is of divine institution, that it includes both preaching of the word and administration of the sacraments, and that there is a distinction between it and the general ministry of all believers. The Catholic parties to the Lutheran-Catholic Consultation concluded that they "see no persuasive reason to deny the possibility of the Roman Catholic church recognizing the validity of this (Lutheran) Ministry," and they urged the Catholic authorities to do so.

Similar agreement was recorded by the *Anglican-Roman Catholic* consultation. In its twelve-year report of December, 1977, the dialogue noted only a continuing difference or emphasis on the ministry of *episcope* (literally "oversight"). For Roman Catholics, this ministry is centered in the bishop of Rome; for Anglicans it is less centralized. But certain pastoral developments in the Catholic Church have brought the two churches closer together even on this matter. Collegiality and coresponsibility are now the order of the day: international synods of bishops, national episcopal conferences, national advisory boards, diocesan pastoral councils, parish council, priests' senates. And the ministry of the bishop of Rome is increasingly perceived and exercised as one of service. (*Origins* 7/30, January 12, 1978, pp. 465, 467-473.)

The *Methodist-Roman Catholic* statement, *Holiness and Spirituality of the Ordained Ministry* (Washington, D.C.: United

States Catholic Conference, 1976) is theologically less substantive than the preceding agreements, but it does report consensus on the traditional and contemporary responsibilities of the ordained ministry: preaching the Gospel, presiding at eucharistic worship, exercising pastoral care, e.g., and now the promotion of peace and reconciliation, participation in the struggle for social justice, e.g.

The *Orthodox-Roman Catholic* joint statement of July 1976 on the pastoral office of "Bishops and Presbyters" lists several points of agreement: Ordained ministry is a commissioning by the Holy Spirit to build up the Church; the offices of bishop and presbyter are different realizations of the sacrament of Order; bishops exercise authority over a whole community, and presbyters share in that authority under the bishop; ordination is required for both offices because they are "an essential element of the sacramental reality of the church"; the pastoral officer is distinct but not separated from the rest of the community; on the other hand, he is not dependent on the community for the exercise of his service, since he receives the special bestowal of the Spirit in ordination (*Origins*, 6/9, August 12, 1976, pp. 142-143).

The *Presbyterian-Reformed-Roman Catholic* consultation offers a more congregational approach to the ordained ministry. It stresses, first, the call of all Christians to ministry, for the building up of the Church. Within this general ministry there are ministers who are "called and ordained to represent Christ to the community and the community before Christ. Through the proclamation of the Gospel and the celebration of the sacraments this ministry has endeavored to unite and order the Church for the ministry of the whole people of God." Its function is to see to it that "the Word of God is proclaimed, the sacraments celebrated, individuals led to Christian maturity, and the Christian community built up" (*The Unity We Seek*, New York: Paulist Press, 1977, pp. 11-13).

What emerges from these assorted consensus statements is a measure of convergence at the following points: (1) There is a general ministry to which all baptized Christians are called. (2) Within that general ministry and in its service there are specialized ministries. (3) The ordained ministry at the local level exists to see to it that the Gospel is proclaimed and the sacraments celebrated. Beyond this there is the abiding demand for pastoral care, spiritual direction, and service to other human needs. (4) The ordained minister speaks not only on behalf of or in the name of the community to God, but also on behalf of and in the name of Christ to the community as well. (5) The ordained minister is not called to a different kind of holiness from the rest of the Church but *is* called to "exemplify" the call to servanthood to which all are in fact called. (6) Bishops have a special role in the Church beyond that of the local pastor, in that bishops serve to unify and coordinate the Christian mission and ministries of a community of churches (diocese). This ministry is one of overseeing (*episcope*), and is always exercised as a service, never for domination. Its mode is always collegial, not monarchical. (7) Finally, in the Roman Catholic tradition there is the special place of the bishop of Rome in the service of the unity and mission of the Church universal.

Contemporary Catholic Theology

To the extent that a debate continues on the nature (essence) of the ordained ministry of bishop and presbyter, the discussion centers on two questions: (1) What is the relationship between the two ministries? (2) What makes either or both of these ministries distinctive within the network of ecclesial ministries?

Regarding the first question, a presbyteral tendency is still pressed by some (e.g., Hans Küng and Edward Schillebeeckx), in spite of Vatican II's strongly "episcopal" doctrine. These theologians ask whether the distinction between episcopacy and presbyterate is of divine institution, and whether the episcopacy as it has developed has any real basis at all in the New Testament.

Regarding the second question, answers vary according to one's operative model of the Church. More traditional approaches (e.g., Avery Dulles) continue to insist on the distinctively cultic and sacramental responsibilities of the ordained bishop and priest as that which sets them apart from other ministers in the Church. Others (e.g., Karl Rahner) underline the priest's call to proclaim the Gospel by word and witness. Still other theologians (e.g., Yves Congar, Hans Küng, Walter Kasper, Edward Schillebeeckx) stress the leadership role of the bishop and priest. It is this latter understanding which is perhaps most comprehensive and is most readily integrated with the ecclesiology of Vatican II. Given this perspective, Holy Order is literally a sacrament directed to the *order* of the Church, "that all according to their proper roles may cooperate in this common undertaking with one heart" (*Dogmatic Constitution on the Church*, n. 30).

The Church and Holy Order

The Church is a sacrament. That means it must be and act as a sacrament. Among the principal ways in which the Church manifests itself as a sacrament and acts according to its sacramental nature is the celebration of the sacraments themselves. But the celebration of the sacraments requires those who will see to it that the sacraments are celebrated, that everything is ordered to the benefit of the whole Church and to its upbuilding (2 Corinthians 4:14; 1 Corinthians 14:5). Through the exercise of this sacramental ministry of Holy Order the whole sacramental reality of the Church is expressed: The good news of the Kingdom of God is proclaimed, the Eucharist is celebrated, the death and resurrection of Christ are made real and effective for individuals in Baptism, sins are forgiven, the sick are ministered to and healed, human love is sanctified, the Holy Spirit is poured forth, and the mediating, priestly work of Christ is continued.

SUMMARY

1.   In addition to the sacraments of *initiation* (Baptism-Confirmation and Eucharist) there are the sacraments of *healing* (Penance and Anointing of the Sick) and the sacraments of *vocation* and *commitment* (Matrimony and Holy Order). The former are for the sake of those whose bond with the Church has been weakened or severed by sin and/or by serious illness; the latter are for the sake of the Church itself, so that it will continue to be built up and, at the same time, be faithful to its mission to proclaim the Gospel in word, in sacrament, in witness, and in service.

2.   The *forgiveness of sins*, often linked with the healing of the sick, was an abiding feature of Jesus' own ministry and later of the preaching

and ministry of the Apostles. This is not to say that we can determine a precise moment or event at which Jesus instituted the sacrament of Penance. This sacrament, like the others, issues from the creation of the Church itself which is, in turn, the result of Jesus's proclamation of the Kingdom of God, his gathering of disciples, and his celebration of the Last Supper with his disciples.

3. In the *earliest centuries* of the Church's history, Penance was administered no more than once after Baptism, and then only for the gravest public sins—e.g., apostasy, murder, adultery. There was no private confession of sins to a priest. The bishop was the minister of the sacrament.

4. The character of Penance changed under the influence of the *Irish monks*, who encouraged the practice of private penance for the laity, even for relatively minor offenses. The relationship between sins and penances became very complicated, requiring the publication of special books to help the confessor decide which penance to impose for which sins.

5. By the *Middle Ages* the sacrament of Penance has four separate components: satisfaction (the doing of a penance), confession, contrition, and absolution by a priest. *Trent* made these definitive, over against the opposition to the Reformers. It taught that all grave sins had to be confessed to a priest in kind and number. The priest acted as a judge. The confessional was his tribunal.

6. *Vatican II* mandated a change in the rite of Penance to bring out its *ecclesial* (as opposed to purely private) dimension as an act of *reconciliation*, and to stress the role of the priest as *healer* rather than as judge.

7. Through this sacrament of Penance the Church reveals itself not only as a reconciler of sinners, but also as a community always in need of reconciliation.

8. Apart from James 5:14 there is no mention of Anointing as a sacred rite in the New Testament. Although the text does not "prove" the institution of the sacrament of the *Anointing of the Sick*, it does indicate that such a practice existed in the early Church.

9. The first documentary evidence we have of the administration of this sacrament in the post-biblical period is provided in a letter of Pope Innocent I (d. 417). From the beginning it was not regarded as *the last sacrament*. That function was served by *Viaticum*, one's last Communion. With the Romanization of the Church under Charlemagne, the sacrament of Anointing became "Extreme Unction" and, as such, the sacrament of the dying.

10. Its sacramentality was taught by the Councils of *Florence* and *Trent*. *Vatican II* restored the primitive emphasis on the anointing of the *sick* rather than on the last anointing of the dying. The last sacrament is Viaticum, not the Anointing.

11. The Church discloses itself in this sacrament of Anointing as a *healing community* always on the way to the Kingdom of God and always itself in need of healing. It is a Church which recognizes that salvation is of the whole person, body and soul, and not just of the soul.

12. *Matrimony* is rooted in the Old Testament notions of *creation* and *covenant*. The ambivalence of the New Testament regarding marriage (i.e., that it is at once holy and to be avoided, if possible) may be explained by its sense of the imminence of the Kingdom of God. In later New Testament writings (Ephesians) this sense of the imminence of the Kingdom has waned, and so marriage is linked with the union of Christ and the Church.

13. The ambivalence carries through much of the Church's history. The negative attitude of *Augustine* toward marriage and sexuality is well known, but neither he nor the other Fathers of the Church denied the basic sanctity of marriage. Its sacramentality was affirmed by the Councils of *Florence* and *Trent*.

14. *Vatican II* introduced a whole new perspective on marriage: (1) It is a covenant, not a contract; (2) mutual love is not "secondary" to the begetting of children; (3) mutual love is, in fact, what is sanctified by the sacrament; (4) its sacramentality is not automatic; it requires faith; (5) the consummation of marriage encompasses more than a single biological act; and (6) the sacrament incorporates one more fully into the mystery of the Church. These points are reflected in the new *Rite of Marriage*.

15. The Catholic Church has always taught that marriage is *indissoluble* (permanent) and *monogamous* (one husband, one wife). On the other hand, it has always tolerated certain modifications of this principle through *dispensations* (similar to the Eastern Orthodox application of the principle of *economy*) designed to remove the unintended harshness of the law.

16. Church law requires that Catholics marry before a priest or deacon and two witnesses (*canonical form*). Since Vatican II, however, marriage can, with permission, be performed in a Protestant church before a Protestant minister, and non-Catholic Christians may be permitted to act as witnesses at Catholic marriages, and Catholics at non-Catholic Christian marriages.

17. A *mixed marriage* is one between a Catholic and a non-Catholic; it requires both a dispensation and a promise by the Catholic party to do all in his or her power to share the Catholic faith with any children of the union.

18. The *Pauline Privilege* permits a second marriage to one who converts to Christianity when the first partner does not. The *Petrine Privilege* allows the pope to dissolve a marriage between a Christian and a non-Christain when the Christian wishes to marry another Christian or when the non-Christian wishes to become a Catholic and remarry.

19. An *annulment* is an official declaration that a marriage was invalid form the beginning—e.g., because of the immaturity of the couple. An *internal forum solution* has the same practical effect, but without a public process. The Church does not officially decide anything. The decision is one of conscience alone, after consultation with a confessor or other competent priest.

20. There is fundamental agreement between Catholics and Orthodox, on the one hand, and Catholics and Anglicans, on the other, on the *sacramentality* of marriage. Similar agreement has not yet been reached between Catholics and Protestants of the Lutheran and Reformed traditions.

21. Through the sacrament of Matrimony the Church reveals itself as the bride of Christ and the sign of God's love for us in Christ. The Church is also shown as a community of love.

22. The sacrament of *Holy Order* presents a very complicated history. There are, by present theological and doctrinal standards, three grades of this sacrament: diaconate, presbyterate, and espicopate. The *diaconate* is linked with the call of "the Seven" to assist the Apostles in material chores; the *presbyterate* is rooted in the priesthood of the Old Testament and in the system of elders by which towns and communities were governed; and the *episcopate* emerges from the presbyterate, probably as the executive committee of the council of elders and eventually as the office of pastoral leadership over a particular church.

23. The New Testament does not present an organizational blueprint for the Church. "The Twelve" are not exactly coextensive with "the apostles" (Paul was an apostle, but not one of the Twelve). There were many ministers and officers in the various churches of the New Testament. No clear-cut distinction or job description can be determined. The apostles, however, were missionaries on the move, and the presbyters and presbyter-bishops were ministers in residence, serving the churches established in many instances by the apostles. Evidence for the development of a monarchical espicopate in the early Church is to be

found in the letters of *Ignatius of Antioch*. But this model of governance was not universal.

24.   The notion of a *Christian priesthood* does not emerge early because the Jerusalem Church still regarded the Jewish priesthood as valid. Not until certain events occurred (e.g., destruction of the Temple, large influx of Gentiles into the Church) did the concept of a distinctively Christian priesthood emerge, particularly as the Church's consciousness of the sacrificial nature of the Lord's Supper was heightened.

25.   But there was still no clear principle governing the *celebration of the Eucharist* in churches of the New Testament period. We cannot say that it was restricted to the Apostles or to ordained priests, although eventually it came to that around the turn of the first Christian century.

26.   After the monarchical episcopate was established, the presbyterate was regarded as a *college of priests* in union with the bishop. With the need for parishes outside the Christian centers, the notion of collegiality began to decline. The feudal system, which made the priest more dependent on the nobility than on the bishops, further accentuated this decline. Priests were now ordained principally for the Mass and the sacraments, and with the imposition of obligatory celibacy the priesthood became increasingly a caste within the Church.

27.   The issue of the priesthood of all believers and the priesthood of the ordained was joined at the *Reformation*, with the Council of *Trent* insisting on the latter. *Vatican II* restored the understanding of the Church as the whole People of God and stressed the participation of the laity in the priesthood of Christ, without prejudice to the special priesthood of the ordained. Emphasis was placed on the role of bishops in the Church and on their collegial union, one with another and with the bishop of Rome, as a symbol of the collegial nature of the Church itself. The corporate or collegial nature of the presbyterate was also emphasized once again, and the permanent diaconate was restored.

28.   *Ecumenical consensus* has been reached on the following points, with varying degrees of agreement: (1) There is a general ministry to which all the baptized are called; (2) specialized ministries serve this general ministry; (3) the ordained Ministry exists to see to it that the Gospel is proclaimed, the sacraments celebrated, pastoral care exercised, the needy attended to, etc.; (4) the ordained Minister speaks both *on behalf of* the community and in the name of Christ *to* the community; (5) the ordained Minister is called to "exemplify" the universal call to servanthood; (6) bishops have a special role in the Church, of unifying and coordinating the mission and ministries of a community of churches, or diocese. It is a Ministry of "overseeing" (*episcope*); and (7) in the

Roman Catholic tradition, the bishop of Rome exercises this function for the Church universal.

29.   Contemporary Catholic theology continues to debate the relationship between the episcopate and the presbyterate, and the distinctive purpose of both ministries over against other ministries in the Church. These questions remain open.

30.   Holy Order is a sacrament which attends to the *order* of the Church. It insures that the Church will, in fact, act sacramentally: proclaiming the Gospel in word, in sacrament, in witness, and in service.

SUGGESTED READINGS

Brown, Raymond. *Priest and Bishop: Biblical Reflections*. New York: Paulist Press, 1970.

Cooke, Bernard. *Ministry to Word and Sacraments: History and Theology*. Philadelphia: Fortress Press, 1976.

Dyer, George, ed. "The Pastoral Guide to Canon Law." *Chicago Studies* 15/3 (Fall 1976).

Fransen, Piet. "Orders and Ordination." *Encyclopedia of Theology: The Concise Sacramentum Mundi*. New York: Seabury Press, 1975, pp. 1122-1148.

Neunheuser, Burkhard. *Penance and Anointing of the Sick*. London: Burns Oates, 1964.

Poschmann, Bernard. *Penance and the Anointing of the Sick*. New York: Herder & Herder, 1964.

Rahner, Karl. "Penance." *Encyclopedia of Theology: The Concise Sacramentum Mundi*. New York: Seabury Press, 1975, pp. 1187-1204.

·XXIII·

SPECIAL QUESTIONS IN ECCLESIOLOGY

This chapter addresses five "special questions" in contemporary ecclesiology: *authority, papacy, ministry, women in the Church,* and *intercommunion.* Insofar as authority is rooted in the will of God, authority is the one overarching question; the other four are component parts of the authority issue. How is authority to be exercised, for what purpose, and by whom? How much common consent to authority is necessary before we have a community that can celebrate the sacrament of unity together?

Each of these topics remains a matter of some theological and pastoral controversy today. Accordingly, the presentations and conclusions of this chapter are more tentative than usual. They are principally designed to introduce the reader to the problem, familiarize him or her with the major terms of the discussion, and show the connection of each question with the mystery of the Church.

AUTHORITY

General Philosophical and Theological Considerations

"Authority" is not an easy concept to define. It is perhaps most often identified with legitimate power, and yet philosophers are quick to point out that authority and power are not the same thing. A mugger with knife in hand has power over his victim, but no authority. On the other hand, authority does have something to do with influencing the thinking and behavior of people.

The word is derived from the Latin, *auctor* ("author"). It may be *de iure* or *de facto* authority. Authority is *de iure* (i.e., by right or by law) when it is attached to, or supported by the power of, an office. A policeman has *de iure* authority. Authority is *de facto* (in fact, i.e., the way it really is) when it is actually obeyed and, therefore, achieves its intended effect. A political columnist who influences governmental policy has *de facto* authority. It is not only possible but ideal that those who legitimately hold and exercise *de iure* authority should also possess *de facto* authority. Thus, the policeman who enforces the law should also be perceived as a law-abiding citizen himself and therefore worthy of one's respect as well as one's obedience. Finally, the word *authority* is also applied to inanimate objects—e.g., books (especially the Bible), institutions, codes of law, symbols. But if such authority exists, it resides in the person or persons who stand(s) behind these objects.

Ultimately, all authority is rooted in God, who is the *Author* of all that is. "Let everyone obey the authorities that are over him, for there is no authority except from God, and all authority that exists is established by God" (Romans 13:1).

Biblical Notions

Old Testament

God is the Author, or source, of all creation. Our own authority over nature comes from God (Genesis 1:28), as does the authority of husbands over wives (3:16) and of parents over children (Leviticus 19:3). Even as society becomes more complex, the same principle obtains. It is God who confers on Hazael the government of Damascus (1 Kings 19:15; 2 Kings 8:9-13), and on Nebuchadnezzar the government of the entire Orient (Jeremiah 27:6).

But the authority entrusted by God is never absolute. The law regulates the exercise of authority by listing the rights of slaves (Exodus 21:1-6,26-27; Deuteronomy 15:12-18; Sirach 33:30). Even the father's authority over his children must look to their good education (Proverbs 23:13-14; Sirach 7:23-24; 30:1). Those holding political power must take care not to deify themselves and thereby blaspheme against the God who alone is absolute Author of all life (Daniel 11:36; 7:3-8,19-25). Such pretensions will meet with destruction 7:11-12,26).

This is true also of authority entrusted to religious leaders, such as Moses, the prophets, and the priests (Exodus 19:6), and of the ancients who assist Moses (Exodus 18:21-26; Numbers 11:24-25). All who hold authority exercise it in the name of God. Conflicts are inevitable—e.g., Saul with Samuel (1 Samuel 13:7-15; 15), Ahab with Elijah (1 Kings 21:17-24), and many kings with their prophets. Religious authority can be abused. The power of the Israelite royalty ends in the tragedy of exile. After the exile, Israel is more openly accepting of God's authority. It is from God that Cyrus and his successors have received the empire (Isaiah 45:1-6). But there is also a new attitude toward *de iure* authority—an attitude which appeals to divine vengeance and, in the end, to revolt when the pagan nation turns persecutor (Judith; 1 Maccabees 2:15-28).

New Testament

Authority *(exousia)* is ascribed also to Jesus (John 17:2; 5:27; Revelation 12:10). He preaches with authority (Mark 1:22 and parallels). He has the power to forgive sins (Matthew 9:6-8; Mark 2:5-10). He is lord of the sabbath (Mark 2:23-28 and parallels). He casts out demons and works cures (Mark 1:27; Matthew 12:27-28; Luke 11:19-20). He interprets the law, as the rabbis did, but with definite authority (Matthew 7:28-29). In Matthew he is depicted as speaking in his own name, unlike the teachers of old: "But I say to you . . ." (Matthew 5:21-48). Indeed, so "authoritative" is Jesus' manner that he is specifically confronted with the question "On what authority are you doing these things? Who has given you the power to do them?" (Mark 11:28). The New Testament, therefore, sees the authority of Jesus as something central to his ministry. Here was "something greater than the temple" (Matthew 12:6), greater than Jonah and Solomon (Matthew 12:41-42), and different from the power of "this world" (John 18:36).

After his death and resurrection, the authority of Jesus is perceived anew. He is declared risen and enthroned at the right hand of God (Acts of the Apostles 2:34-36). He is the Lord (Philippians 2:9-11), the son of God "with power" (Romans 1:4). To him "all authority, in heaven and on earth" is given (Matthew 28:18). All creation is subject to him (Philippians 2:10), and he will sit upon God's judgment seat (2 Corinthians 5:10) to judge the living and the dead (Acts of the Apostles 10:42). Past, present, and future are under the authority of Christ, in whom all God's promises are affirmed (2 Corinthians 1:20).

On the other hand, Jesus exercises his authority in the manner of a servant (Mark 10:45; Luke 22:27). It is precisely because he did not cling to divinity that he became Lord of all (Philippians 2:5-11). And so he charges his disciples to follow his example: "Earthly kings lord it over their people. . . . Yet it cannot be that way with you. Let the greater among you be as the junior, the leader as the servant [*diakonos*]" (Luke 22:25-26; John 13:14-15). His kingdom, after all, is not of this world (John 18:36). Therefore, his disciples are not to be engaged in any struggles for power or preferment among themselves (Matthew 20:20-28; Mark 10:35-45).

The absolute power which Jesus claims in Matthew 28:18 is not transferred to his disciples. Not even Peter receives absolute authority. In Acts of the Apostles 1-12, where his leadership is most clearly portrayed, decisions are made by "the Twelve" or "the apostles" or "the church," and not by Peter. His action in Acts of the Apostles 10 is reviewed by "the party of the circumcision" (11:1-18). His devious behavior at Antioch elicits an open rebuke from Paul (Galatians 2:11-14). Nor are the apostles the sole participants in Jesus' authority. There are also prophets, teachers, wonder-workers, evangelists, presbyters, and others (1 Corinthians 12:28; Ephesians 4:11). Paul himself is criticized by some of the Corinthians harshly and unjustly. He responds to the criticisms with warmth, and never suggests that he is above criticism because of his status.

The Spirit is, in fact, given to the whole Church and not exclusively to the leaders of the Church (1 Corinthians 12:1-28; Romans 12:3-8). There is a diversity of gifts and charisms, and all must work together as one for the good of the whole. The power which Christian authority has is grounded in the Holy Spirit, and the Holy Spirit is available to all. Indeed, no one can even profess that Jesus is Lord except in the Holy Spirit (1 Corinthians 12:3). Therefore, authority in the Church is always of a unique kind, not simply another form of standard social or political authority. It is a power existing within the Body of Christ, not just within another human organization. Authority as a function of the Body of Christ is a new concept of authority, just as the Body of Christ is a new concept of society. Authority is an operation of the Holy Spirit, but it is only one operation.

And what specifically of *teaching authority*? "Teacher" was a common category, which applied even to the Scribes. Teaching involved commentary on the Sacred Scriptures (i.e., the Old Testament), but the texts were accommodated to whatever point a teacher wanted to make. Jesus himself was a teacher, and was so regarded. He was preoccupied with proclaiming the reign of God, but his teaching filled out his preaching and explained the nature of the Kingdom and its demands. The people were amazed by Jesus' teaching because, unlike the Scribes, he taught with authority.

On the other hand, the entire New Testament conceives the Gospel as a *way of life*. Only in Matthew are the Apostles *commissioned* to teach, which helps explain why interpreters refer to Matthew as the most Jewish of the Gospels. The Apostles did teach, however. The object of their teaching was Christ (Acts of the Apostles 5:42), the word of the Lord (15:35), the word of God 18:11). In Colossians the object is the person and the mission of Christ; in 2 Thessalonians it is the Second Coming of Christ. When teaching is enumerated among the gifts, it is listed after revelation, knowledge, and prophecy (1 Corinthians 14:6).

At Antioch there were prophets and teachers (Acts of the Apostles 13:1). Teachers are listed with other officers of the Church (Romans 12:7; 1 Corinthians 12:28; and Ephesians 4:11). Their function seemed to have been to explain the person and mission of Jesus Christ and the demands of discipleship in light of the Old Testament. The teachers were not an elite group, like the Scribes, nor was teaching limited to certain persons. As the Church grew and its organizational structure became more complex, concerns were expressed about deviations and unsound teaching (1 Timothy 1:3-7; 6:2-5; 2 Timothy 4:3-4; Titus 1:9-14; 3:9). The sure foundation of sound doctrine is the Old Testament (1 Timothy 4:11-16; 2 Timothy 3:14-17).

But in the New Testament, teaching was simply not one of the primary functions of the Church. That distinction belonged to the proclamation of the Gospel, the announcement of the good news of the Kingdom of God. Teaching was an important subsidiary function. It was the explanation of the Gospel; it was not the Gospel itself. The teaching was not the word which saves. Just as proclamation and teaching are not the same, neither are faith and doctrine. Teaching interprets faith; it is not itself faith. (See our discussion of teaching authority in chapter 2.)

Post-biblical Developments

Second and Third Centuries

The insistence upon authority is strong in Ignatius of Antioch and Cyprian. They, and others at this time, link its religious and spiritual significance with its juridical status, i.e., its status as authority of presiding over a community and regulating its life. Ignatius' assertions, in fact, are so vigorous in this regard that Protestant critics formerly doubted the authenticity of his letters, so outrageously "Catholic" were they. By being subject to their bishop, he wrote, the Magnesians or the Trallians are subject to God or to Jesus Christ (*Magnesians* III,1-2; *Trallians* II,1). For Cyprian, "The bishop is in the Church, and the Church in the bishop."

But the Church is always the whole community, and not just the hierarchy. "I have made it a rule," Cyprian writes elsewhere, "ever since the beginning of my episcopate, to make no decision merely on the strength of my own personal opinion without consulting you (the priests and the deacons) and without the approbation of the people" (*Letters* 14:4). In fact, the whole Church community, laity especially, took part in the election of bishops and the choice of ministers. Even though the early Church already possessed a firm canonical structure, it also wanted to be ready for any movement prompted by the Holy Spirit. And so the intervention of the laity was welcomed as a matter of principle. But the Church also regarded the bishop as possessed of the gifts of the Spirit in a preeminent way. *It was because of the presence of these gifts that one was chosen a bishop in the first place.*

Fourth to Eleventh Centuries

With the *Edict of Constantine* (313) the situation changed markedly. Bishops and presbyters were now invested with civil authority. Monasticism developed, as we pointed out in chapter 18, partly in reaction to this new worldly favor. In monasticism it was possible for a charismatic or spiritual authority to continue to exist, and monastic leaders came to enjoy a kind of independent authority in the Church over against the ordinary hierarchical authority. This was especially true in the East. From the beginning of the eighth century, and as a result of the Monothelite controversy and the iconoclast crisis during which the monks became the defenders of orthodoxy, there was a real transfer of spiritual direction and of the exercise of ecclesiastical authority from the hierarchical priesthood to the monks. It was clear that they were truly men of God. A similar, though less pronounced, development occurred in the West, where saints and abbots developed their own spheres of influence.

This is not to say that there was a fundamental opposition between monastic and hierarchical authority at that time. Many of the bishops were, or had been, monks, or at least men trained in monasteries—e.g., Basil, John Chrysostom, Augustine, Martin, Patrick, Isidore of Seville, Gregory the Great. From St. Augustine of Canterbury's time (d. 604 or 605) until the twelfth century, all archbishops of Canterbury were monks. The connection between the episcopal ministry and the monastic ideal was also evident in the oldest sections of the Latin ritual of ordination, which state the duties, not the powers, of bishops—e.g., assiduous study of Sacred Scripture, prayer, fasting, hospitality, almsgiving, listening, edification of the people by word and through the liturgy. The bishop was to represent the moral ideal of authority, for *genuine authority is moral authority.*

The Church was perceived as more than a juridical organization with rules, regulations, and officials to administer them. It was more fundamentally a body of men and women praying, fasting, doing penance, asking for grace, engaging in spiritual combat to become more like Christ. It was important, therefore, that the bishop and indeed the pope be themselves credible examples of Christian existence. *"Vobis sum episcopus, vobiscum Christianus* ("For you I am a bishop; with you I am a Christian"), St. Augustine of Hippo wrote (*Sermon* 340:1). It is out of this same period (fourth and fifth centuries) that the celebrated formula emerged: *Qui praefuturus est omnibus, ab omnibus eligatur* ("He who would be the head of all should be chosen by all"). The formula is that of Pope Celestine I (d. 432), and it occurs again in the councils of Orleans (549) and Paris (557) and in the *Decretals of Gratian* (d. 1140).

The Middle Ages

The reform of the Church begun by Pope Leo IX (d. 1054) and continued by Gregory VII (d. 1081) represents a turning-point in the history of authority. The reform was aimed not only at the renewal of the Church but also at its liberation from the control of lay princes and other political figures. To do this, Gregory claimed for the Church the completely autonomous and sovereign system of rights proper to a self-contained, spiritual society, and an authority which covered not only the whole Church but kings and their kingdoms as well. To support his argument Gregory ordered the Church's scholars and jurists to comb the archives and uncover every scrap of precedent for his view. Canon law was born, and the foundation was laid for the kind of exaggerated papal claims to be made by Innocent III (d. 1216) and Boniface VIII (d. 1303).

Even the title *Vicar of Christ*, bestowed on the pope, was transformed from an essentially *sacramental* image (Christ and the saints are working through this servant) to a largely *juridical* one (the pope possesses powers given him by Christ). And so a *legalism* was introduced, and it radically changed the originally spiritual notion that obedience to God's representative is obedience to God. The presence of grace in the representative was no longer crucial.

Episcopal authority was no longer *moral* authority but *jurisdiction*, and it was bestowed even before the sacrament was conferred. The bestowal of grace was secondary. And so the idea developed that a priest "governs" his parish, bishops "govern" their dioceses and "judge" in all matters, and the pope rules as a "sovereign"—indeed, is the "Sovereign Pontiff."

A counter-movement developed. Charges were now hurled at the Church's leaders, especially from the spiritual movements of the twelfth century, and later from Franciscanism and from the Hussite movement. Each was saying in effect that the Church, and the pope in particular, had obscured the Gospel with pomp, that it was becoming more the Church of Constantine than of the Apostles. "All this, as well as the claims to prestige and riches, goes back to Constantine, not to Peter," St. Bernard (d. 1153) wrote to Pope Eugenius III (d. 1153).

The new juridicism notwithstanding, Catholic theology preserved many elements of the ancient ecclesiology, at least until the death of the two greatest doctors of the thirteenth century, Thomas and Bonaventure. In Thomas, for example, the idea of the Church as the congregation of the faithful is still very much alive. Authority is not merely juridical. It is linked with spiritual gifts and with the achievement of the perfection of Christian charity. Matthew 16:19 is interpreted as referring principally to Peter's confession of faith. The theology of the new law as formulated in the *Summa Theologica* I-II, q. 106, is completely evangelical. It is a law of love and service, not of fear and slavishness.

But unfortunately this was not the spirit of the Church at large. As Yves Congar has acknowledged, "It is a fact that the authority of prelates of every degree was never insisted on so much as in the fourteenth and fifteenth centuries. The thunderclap of 31 October 1517 [the day Luther posted this ninety-five theses against indulgences on the door of the church at Wittenberg] was only the first of a violent storm" (in *Problems of Authority*, p. 143).

The Council of Trent to the Twentieth Century

The Reformation questioned authority not only in its corrupted forms but in principle. In reaction the Council of Trent (1545-

1547, 1551-1552, 1562-1563) insisted even more strongly on the authority of the hierarchy, so much so that the ecclesiology which developed after Trent was more akin to a *hierarchology* or a treatise on public law. The pope was now regarded as a "universal bishop." Each Catholic was directly under the pope and sub-servient to him, even more than to the individual Catholic's own bishop. The shift of all significant power to Rome occurred at an accelerated pace. Ecclesiastical authority became increasingly centralized. And people were asked to obey because of the status and office of the legislator, not because he and his decrees were obviously prompted by the Spirit. The definition of papal primacy at Vatican I was the culmination of this development.

This understanding of authority prevailed until the Second Vatican Council. Pope Pius XII's *Humani Generis* (1950), for example, insisted that even papal encyclicals, although they do not engage the fullness of the pope's teaching authority, demand both external and internal assent. "And when the Roman Pontiffs care-fully pronounce on some subject which has hitherto been contro-verted, it must be clear to everybody that, in the mind and intention of the Pontiffs concerned, this subject can no longer be regarded as a matter of free debate among theologians."

Vatican II

Although the Second Vatican Council continued to teach that the pope and the bishops exercise supreme authority over the Church, it says that this authority is always to be exercised as a service and in a collegial manner. Furthermore, it is to be used only for the edification ("building up") of their flocks (*Dogmatic Constitution on the Church*, n. 27). Pastors, too, are not intended to shoulder alone the whole saving mission of the Church. They must collabo-rate with their brothers and sisters, including the laity, that all might work together as one for the good of the whole (n. 30). The principle of authority-as-service is reaffirmed in other conciliar documents as well: in the *Decree on the Bishops' Pastoral Office in the Church*, the *Decree on the Ministry and Life of Priests*, and the *Decree on the Appropriate Renewal of the Religious Life*. (See chapter 19.)

Ecumenical Developments

Recent ecumenical statements on the question of authority have come from the Anglican-Roman Catholic International Commission and the Lutheran-Catholic Dialogue in the United States. The Anglican-Roman Catholic document is entitled "An Agreed Statement on Authority in the Church" and is also known as *The Venice Statement* (Washington, D.C.: United States Catholic Conference, 1977). The authority with which it is concerned is the authority of Christ, which is activated by the Holy Spirit to create community with God and with all persons. The model is definitely not political, sociological, or structural, but rather one of *koinonia*, i.e., fellowship of loving service in the truth of Christ. Whatever authority the Church possesses is always and only for the sake of promoting *community*.

There are three types of authority that persons in the Church exercise: of holiness, of the gifts of the Spirit, and of sacramental ordination (the authority of *episcope*, "oversight"). Since there is more to the Church than single local communities, this third type of authority may be exercised at diocesan, regional, and international levels. "Primacy fulfills its purpose by helping the churches to listen to one another, to grow in love and unity, and to strive together towards the fullness of Christian life and witness; it respects and promotes Christian freedom and spontaneity; it does not seek uniformity where diversity is legitimate, or centralize administration to the detriment of local churches" (n. 21, p. 13). Of interest is the response to the *Venice Statement* by the Anglican-Roman Catholic Consultation in the U.S.A., which criticized their international counterparts for concentrating too much on the authority of the pope and bishops and too little on the authority of the whole Church, laity and clergy alike. (See "Authority in the Church: Vital Ecumenical Issue," *Origins* 7/30, January 12, 1978, pp. 474-476.)

The Lutheran-Catholic Dialogue touched upon the question of the teaching authority of the Church in connection with its study of papal infallibility. All Christian authority is rooted in Christ and the Gospel, which is a word of power from God (Romans 1:16). It is proclaimed by various witnesses who share in the authority of Christ. (We shall return to this important consultation in our consideration of the papacy below.)

The Church and Authority

All authority has its origin in God, who alone is the Author of all life. God's authority is at once creative and unitive. Jesus Christ's mission was to re-create and reunite what had been wounded by sin. He proclaimed the good news that the power (authority) of re-creation and reunion was about to be released anew in the Holy Spirit and that it would eventually bring all things together at the end in the Kingdom of God.

The Church shares in the authority of Christ and in the power of the Holy Spirit. Its authority is for the same purpose: to proclaim the Gospel of the Kingdom of God and to manifest and release the power of the Holy Spirit to re-create and reunite the whole human community. The Church is itself the sacrament of community. Whatever authority exists within the Church, as distinct from the general authority to proclaim the Gospel, is for the sake of building and sustaining the reality of community, that Christians themselves might taste the firstfruits of the perfect Kingdom and that others outside the Church might be given reason to hope in it at all.

Because the Church is the whole People of God, authority resides in the community as a whole, although it is exercised in various ways, by various persons, for the good of the whole. Wherever and whenever authority is exercised, it is exercised in the manner of Jesus, who was among us as one who serves (Mark 10:45). Authority that is detached from holiness is not real Christian authority. Authority which seeks to coerce places itself above the grace of the Holy Spirit, and so is not real Christian authority either.

The Church comes into being through the free response of individuals to the call of God in Jesus Christ by the grace of the Holy Spirit. Authority can be exercised only in a way that respects the freedom of the act of faith and the voluntary character of membership in the Church (see again Vatican II's *Declaration on Religious Freedom*, and our discussion of it in chapter 19).

PAPACY

What follows is, in large measure, a summary of the consensus statements of the Lutheran-Catholic Dialogue on the subjects of papal primacy and papal infallibility. It is the author's judgment that these statements are not only a model of ecumenical theology but are fully representative of the best biblical, patristic, historical, and theological scholarship on both subjects today. The reader who wishes to press beyond the schematic presentations of this section of the chapter is advised to consult the more detailed material in the following volumes: *Papal Primacy and The Universal Church, Lutherans and Catholics in Dialogue V*, Paul Empie and T. Austin Murphy, eds. (Minneapolis: Augsburg Publishing House, 1974); *Peter in the New Testament*, Raymond E. Brown, Karl P. Donfried, John Reumann, eds. (Minneapolis: Augsburg Publishing House, 1973); and "Teaching Authority and Infallibility in the Church," *Theological Studies* 40 (March 1979), 113-166.

Papal Primacy

The Issue

The Church is the sacrament of the unity which God wills for all humankind in Christ and through the Holy Spirit. But the fact is that the Church is divided. There are Catholic Christians and Lutheran Christians and Presbyterian Christians and Pentecostal Christians, and so forth. Ironically, a particular ministry within the Catholic Church which exists precisely for the purpose of symbolizing and helping to realize the unity of the whole Church is at the same time one of the greatest obstacles to that unity. Recent ecumenical discussions of the papacy, therefore, are of highest importance.

Separated Christians already embrace and accept realities which serve the unity of the Church as a whole: Baptism, the Sacred Scriptures, liturgies, creeds, confessions of faith, ecumenical councils. The Lutheran-Catholic Dialogue relates these various means of unifying the Church to the "Petrine function," i.e., a particular form of Ministry exercised by a person, officeholder, or local church with reference to the Church as a whole. This Petrine function "serves to promote or preserve the oneness of the church by symbolizing unity, and by facilitating communication, mutual assistance or correction, and collaboration in the church's mission" (*Papal Primacy*, n. 4, p. 12). The function is called Petrine because that is the kind of role the apostle Peter fulfilled among Jesus' original disciples. Among the companions of Jesus, Peter is given the greatest prominence in the New Testament accounts of the Church's origins. He is spoken of in relation to the founding of the Church (Matthew 16:18), strengthening the brethren (Luke 22:32), and feeding the sheep of Christ (John 21:15-17). He is a prominent figure in some of the Pauline letters, in the Acts of the Apostles, and in two of the so-called Catholic Epistles (1 and 2 Peter)—all of which suggests that he was associated with a wide-ranging ministry. The subsequent history of the Church portrayed him as a pastor of the universal Church. Indeed, "...the single most notable representative of this (Petrine) Ministry toward the church universal... has been the bishop of Rome" (n. 5, p. 12).

But at least three areas of controversy have marked the discussion of the ministry of the bishop of Rome: historical, theological, and canonical. Catholics and other Christians have differed about the meaning and implications of Peter's role in the New Testament Church. *Historically*, Catholics have insisted that it was a function of leadership conferred by Jesus himself and that it has been passed down through the centuries, while non-Catholic Christians have tended to minimize the significance of Peter in the New Testament and have clearly rejected the notion of a succession in pastoral authority from Peter to the bishops of Rome. *Theologically*, Catholics have argued that the papacy is of divine law, i.e., that it exists by the will of Christ, while non-Catholic Christians have insisted that it is of human origin only. *Canonically*, Catholics have until recently looked upon the legal power of the pope as supreme, full, ordinary, and immediate (Vatican I), i.e., not subject to any higher human jurisdiction, while other Christians have viewed such claims as leading to intolerable tyranny.

History

New Testament: The New Testament does not call Peter the first pope even though Peter did have, by the will of Christ, a prominent role in the proclamation of the Kingdom of God and in the circle of disciples which formed in response to that proclamation. The terms *primacy* and *jurisdiction* are best avoided when describing Peter's role in the New Testament. They reflect a post-biblical development.

As we noted in chapter 17, the Church of the New Testament is both the church in and of a particular place (e.g., Corinth, Antioch, Jerusalem) and the Church universal (the Body of Christ, as in Ephesians). Although it is not unmistakably clear how Peter relates to the Church universal, it *is* sufficiently clear that he *does* relate to the Church universal in certain significant ways. He is listed first among the Twelve (Mark 3:16-19; Matthew 10:1-4; Luke 6:12-16) and is frequently their spokesman (Mark 8:29; Matthew 18:21; Luke 12:41; John 6:67-69); he is the first apostolic witness of the risen Jesus (1 Corinthians 15:5; Luke 24:34); he is prominent in the original Jerusalem community and is well known to many other churches (Acts of the Apostles 1:15-26; 2:14-40; 3:1-26; 4:8; 5:1-11,29; 8:18-25; 9:32-43; 10:5; 12:17; 1 Peter 2:11; 5:13). His activities after the council of Jerusalem are not reported, but there is increasing agreement that Peter did go to Rome and was martyred there. Whether he actually served the church of Rome as bishop cannot be known through evidence at hand. And from the New Testament record alone, we have no basis for positing a line of succession from Peter through subsequent bishops of Rome.

No single text or series of texts "proves" the primacy of Peter in the New Testament, not even the classic primacy texts: Matthew 16:13-19; Luke 22:31-32; John 21:15-19. The fact that Jesus' naming of Peter as the rock occurs in different contexts in the three Gospels does raise a question about the original setting of the incident. We cannot be sure whether this naming occurred during Jesus' ministry or after the resurrection, with subsequent "retrojection" into the accounts of Jesus' earthly ministry. As for the conferral of the power of the *keys*, this suggests an imposing measure of authority, given the symbolism of the keys. And yet special authority *over others* is not clearly attested. Rather, in the

Acts of the Apostles Peter is presented as consulting with the apostles and even being sent by them (8:14). He and John act almost as a team (3:1-11; 4:1-22; 8:14).

On the other hand, there is a discernible "trajectory" of images relating to Peter and his ministry. He is portrayed as the fisherman (Luke 5:10; John 21:1-14), as the shepherd of the sheep of Christ (John 21:15-17), as an elder who addresses other elders (1 Peter 5:1), as proclaimer of faith in Jesus the Son of God (Matthew 16:16-17), as receiver of a special revelation (Acts of the Apostles 1:9-16), as one who can correct others for doctrinal misunderstanding (2 Peter 3:15-16), and as the rock on which the Church is to be built (Matthew 16:18).

The question, therefore, to be posed on the basis of an investigation of the New Testament is not whether Peter was the first pope, but whether the subsequent, post-biblical development of the Petrine office is, in fact, consistent with the thrust of the New Testament. The Catholic Church says "Yes." Some other Christian churches are beginning to say "Perhaps."

Second Century to Middle Ages: The trajectory of biblical images of Peter did continue in the life of the early Church, and those images were enriched by additional ones: missionary preacher, great visionary, destroyer of heretics, receiver of the new law, gatekeeper of heaven, helmsman of the ship of the Church, co-teacher and co-martyr with Paul. At the same time, the early Church was in the process of accommodating itself to the culture of the Graeco-Roman world, particularly the patterns of organization and administration prevailing in areas of its missionary activity. The Church adopted the organizational grid of the Roman Empire: localities, dioceses, provinces. It also identified its own center with the empire's, Rome. Moreover, there was attached to this city the tradition that Peter had founded the church there and that he and Paul were buried there.

In the controversy with Gnosticism, defenders of orthodoxy appealed to the faith of episcopal sees founded by the Apostles, and especially to the faith of the Roman church which was so closely associated with Peter and Paul alike. During the first five centuries the church of Rome gradually assumed preeminence among the churches. It intervened in the life of distant churches, took sides in theological controversies, was consulted by other bishops on doctrinal and moral questions, and sent delegates to distant councils. The church of Rome came to be regarded as a kind of final or supreme court of appeal as well as focus of unity for the world-wide communion of churches. The correlation between Peter and the bishop of Rome became fully explicit in the term of Pope Leo I (d. 461), who insisted that Peter continues to speak to the whole Church through the bishop of Rome. It was also Leo who decisively intervened in the great Christological controversies and whose letter to Flavian of Constantinople in 449 provided the basis for the definitive formulation of faith two years later at the Council of Chalcedon (see chapter 13).

The Middle Ages: In order to protect the Church at large and the papacy in particular against continuing encroachments by lay powers, Gregory VII and Innocent III, relying on such documents as the *False Decretals* of Pseudo-Isidore (ca. 847-852) claimed monarchical status for their office, in accordance with contemporary secular models of government. Boniface VIII carried the claim even further, insisting on absolute power over the whole world, temporal as well as religious. In the high Middle Ages such prominent theologians as Thomas and Bonaventure stressed the powers of the Roman see, and over against both Conciliarism and Protestantism Scholastic theologians and canonists reaffirmed the monarchical structure of ecclesiastical government. This view received official endorsement in the Council of Florence's *Decree of Union for the Greek and Latin Churches* (1439) in terms very much like those of Vatican I in the nineteenth century.

Post-Tridentine Developments to the Twentieth Century: The inclination of the official theologians and canonists to continue to assert papal prerogatives was accentuated by the rise of nationalism (e.g., Gallicanism), the intellectual challenges of the Enlightenment, and the new liberalism of the nineteenth century. Vatican I (1869-1870) was the culmination of this development. In its *Dogmatic Constitution on the Church of Christ (Pastor Aeternus,* "Eternal Pastor"), the council declared that "the primacy of jurisdiction over the whole Church was immediately and directly promised to and conferred upon the blessed apostle Peter by Christ the Lord." The primacy is passed on to whoever "succeeds

Peter in this Chair, according to the institution of Christ Himself. . . ." This power is full and supreme over the whole Church
not only in matters that pertain to faith and morals but also in
matters that pertain to the discipline and government of the
Church throughout the whole world. This power is ordinary and
immediate over each and every church and over each and every
shepherd and faithful. Vatican I's teaching was reiterated by Pope
Leo XIII in his encyclical *Satis Cognitum* (1896), in the Holy
Office's decree *Lamentabili* under Pius X (1907), in Pius XII's
Mystici Corporis (1943), in the Holy Office's letter to Cardinal
Cushing on the Leonard Feeney case (1949), and in Pius XII's
Humani Generis (1950).

Vatican II: With the Second Vatican Council there begins a
move away from papal absolutism and from a monarchical governmental model of the Church. The pope is not the sole ruler of the
Church, nor the sole possessor of supreme authority. Supreme
authority is vested in the whole college of bishops, with the pope at
its center and head. To be sure, this power cannot be exercised
without the consent of the pope. "This college, insofar as it is
composed of many, expresses the variety and universality of the
People of God, but insofar as it is assembled under one head, it
expresses the unity of the flock of Christ" (*Dogmatic Constitution
on the Church*, n. 22). The pope still has "full, supreme, and
universal power over the Church," but the bishops are no longer
perceived as simply the pope's vicars or delegates. They receive
from the Lord "the mission to teach all nations and to preach the
gospel to every creature" (n. 24). They govern their diocese not as
"vicars of the Roman Pontiff, for they exercise an authority which
is proper to them. . ." (n. 27).

Finally, whatever authority the pope and the bishops enjoy, it
is always to be exercised through the faithful preaching of the
Gospel, the administration of the sacraments, and loving service.
They collaborate thereby in the work of the Holy Spirit, which is
the work of unity: in the confession of faith, in the comon celebration of divine worship, and in the fraternal harmony of the family
of God (*Decree on Ecumenism*, n. 2). Their teaching authority,
too, is subordinate to a higher principle. "This teaching office is

not above the word of God, but serves it . . ." (*Dogmatic Constitution on Divine Revelation*, n. 10).

The Church and Papal Primacy

The Church is at once local and universal. The Body of Christ truly exists in particular locales (*Dogmatic Constitution on the Church*, n. 26) and is also the Church universal. It is indeed a communion of churches. Insofar as the Church is a *communion* of churches, the papal office serves the unity of the Church as "the perpetual and visible source of and foundation of the unity of the bishops and of the multitude of the faithful" (n. 23). The pope's primacy is a primacy of service, in service of unity. Insofar as the Church is a communion of *churches*, the papal office must respect the legitimate diversity of these churches (n. 23), a collegial mode of decision-making (n. 23), and the time-honored Catholic social principle of subsidiarity, which holds that nothing is to be done by a higher group, agency, or level of authority that can be done better or as well by a lower group, agency, or level of authority.

The Church, whether local or universal, is the People of God. The Spirit is given to all. All share in principle in the total mission of the Church: prophetic, priestly, and kingly. The hierarchy, including the pope, exists to serve the rest of the Church in the exercise of that Spirit-rooted mission. The primacy is precisely for that purpose.

Papal Infallibility

The Issue

Infallibility literally means "immunity from error." In theological terms it is a charism of the Holy Spirit which protects the Church from error when it solemnly defines a matter of faith or morals. It is a *negative* gift; i.e., it guarantees that such and such a teaching is *not* wrong. Infallibility does not insure that a particular teaching is an *adequate* expression of a truth of faith or morals or even an *appropriate* formulation of that truth. *Papal* infallibility is a dimension of the *Church's* infallibility, not vice versa. The pope's infallibility is the same infallibility as that "with which the divine

Redeemer willed His Church to be endowed" (*Dogmatic Constitution on the Church*, n. 25).

Papal infallibility is conceptually distinct from papal primacy. There is no reason in principle why the pope would have to possess the charism of infallibility in order to function as the chief shepherd of the Church. Conversely, infallibility could in principle be vested in persons who do not hold the supreme office in the Church. In other words, primacy of itself does not require infallibility, nor does infallibility necessarily presume primacy.

Papal infallibility is related to several larger questions: the authority of the Gospel and of the Church, the indefectibility of the Church, and the certitude of Christian faith. Between the First Vatican Council, which defined papal infallibility, and the Second Vatican Council, which placed it in its wider context, the issue of papal infallibility was often discussed in very narrow terms. In the popular mind and even in some of the theology textbooks it was thought that all papal statements were somehow protected by infallibility. Consequently, the faithful Catholic had to receive all papal pronouncements "as if" they were infallible. Encyclicals were sometimes interpreted as infallibly conveying true doctrine even when they did not meet the specific conditions laid down by Vatican I for infallible definitions. Pope Pius XII's *Humani Generis* (1950) gave some currency to this view by stressing the definitive character of papal teaching even in encyclicals. But this has not been the exclusive tendency of the conservative wing of the Church alone. Hans Küng's *Infallible? An Inquiry* (New York: Doubleday, 1971) argued that the birth control encyclical *Humanae Vitae* (1968) was infallible by traditional standards, but then he attacked the dogma of infallibility because the encyclical's teaching on birth control was, for Küng, obviously wrong (p. 71).

The issue of infallibility is also affected by a new understanding of authority abroad in the world because of a variety of factors, some of which were discussed in chapters 3 and 6. Simply stated, the modern world is a world of pluralism, diversity, and the necessity of choice. Sociologist Peter Berger, for example, describes modern consciousness as living under the impact of this need to make our own choices (the word *heresy* is derived from a Greek word meaning "a choice"). He calls this modern phenomenon *The Heretical Imperative* (New York: Doubleday, 1979). We are no longer governed by fate, he argues, nor do we defer automatically to higher authority.

What possible meaning can the claim of immunity from error have in such a world and in light of modern experience? Does it make sense any longer for the Church to press the point that it and its official representatives (the pope, an ecumenical council, the body of bishops in union with the pope) are, in fact, guaranteed this charism of immunity from error when solemnly teaching about the faith and its moral demands? These are the kind of questions even Catholics are beginning to ask.

History

New Testament: The concept of infallibility, whether of the Church at large, or of the pope, or of the pope and the bishops, does not appear in the New Testament. Related concepts, however, do occur: the authority of Jesus Christ in proclaiming the Kingdom of God, the transmission of that authority in some measure to the apostles, the authority of the Gospel itself, the authority of various witnesses to the Gospel ("He who hears you hears me"—Luke 10:16), the concern for sound doctrine, especially in the Pastoral Espistles, and the conviction that the Spirit has been given to the Church as a guide to all truth (John 16:13).

Post-biblical Developments: A complete history of the development of the notion of infallibility has yet to be written, even though important special studies are now available (e.g., Brian Tierney, *Origins of Papal Infallibility*, Leiden: Brill, 1972). What is clear is that the concern for the faithful transmission of the Gospel did not diminish after the New Testament period. In the late second-century struggle against Gnosticism, the Fathers of the Church linked the reliable handing on of the apostolic teaching with the faith of the episcopal sees founded by the Apostles themselves. By the middle of the third century, special importance was being accorded the faith of the church of Rome, which by tradition was regarded as having been founded by Peter himself. Some Roman emperors included the faith of the bishop of Rome in the official norm of orthodoxy, and the biblical image of the Church "without spot or wrinkle" (Ephesians 5:27) began to be applied to the church of Rome. Rome became *the* apostolic see. According to the *Formula of Pope Hormisdas* (d. 523), written in the year 515, "the catholic religion has always been preserved immaculate" in Rome. This conviction persisted into the Middle Ages and found expression in such influential documents as the Pseudo-Isidorian Decretals, in statements by various popes and theologians, and in assorted collections of canon law.

But this post-biblical development was neither unilateral nor unequivocal. There were challenges to such claims both in the East and the West. Eastern Christians regarded Rome as only one of several apostolic sees to which protection of the faith had been entrusted. But the faithfulness of such Popes as Liberius (d. 366), Vigilius (d. 555), and Honorius (d. 638) was questioned. Certain Western metropolitans (archbishops) even in the early Middle Ages were sometimes wont to contradict papal decisions. Prophetic voices were raised from the eleventh century on—almost five hundred years before the Protestant Reformation—against the style and practice of the papal ministry. Moreover, it was readily admitted by some theologians and canonists that individual popes in the past had been in error on specific points of doctrine, and canon law itself has always reckoned with the possibility that the pope could deviate from the faith (see Brian Tierney, *Foundations of Conciliar Theory*, Cambridge: Cambridge University Press, 1955, pp. 57-67).

Nonetheless, the formula "Rome has never erred" survived, and in the course of time it came to be understood as meaning that Rome "cannot" err. Roman bishops from the fourth century on regarded their confirmation of conciliar actions as an indispensable sign of authoritative teaching, even though their own doctrinal decisions needed to be accepted by secular authorities, councils, and fellow bishops in order to be enforced. But with the growing practice of making appeals to Rome, the bishop of Rome came to be regarded as the court of final appeal, the last word. The legal maxim "The first see is judged by no one" appeared initially in the sixth century and was later interpreted to mean that the pope's teaching authority is supreme. This was restated in the era of the Gregorian Reform, and Thomas Aquinas would describe the pope as one whose judgments in matters of faith must be followed because he represents the universal Church which "cannot err" (*Quodlibet* IX, q. 7, a. 16).

According to Brian Tierney's study (to which reference was made above), the term *infallibility* was first applied to the pope's teaching authority by a fourteenth-century theologian, Guido Terreni (d. 1344). Use of the word was occasioned by a controversy over poverty in the Franciscan order during the late thirteenth and early fourteenth centuries. Advocates of a rigorist position employed "infallibility" to defend the binding authority of statements by earlier popes against the decisions of their successors. Under the impact of the Reformation, the concept of infallibility quickly gained wider theological currency, especially among such Counter Reformation theologians as Robert Bellarmine (d. 1621), Francis Suarez (d. 1617), and Thomas Stapleton (d. 1598). It was appealed to in the condemnations of Jansenism and Gallicanism in the seventeenth and eighteenth centuries and received solemn approbation in the dogma of Vatican I in 1870. The teaching was reaffirmed by Vatican II, but was placed in the larger setting of the infallibility of the whole Church and the collegiality of bishops with the pope.

Ecumenical Convergences

The Lutheran-Catholic Dialogue of 1978 noted, among others, the following points of convergence: (1) The Bible is normative for all of the Church's proclamation and teaching. (2) The apostolic tradition in which the Word of God is transmitted is interpreted with the assistance of creeds, liturgies, confessions, doctrines, structural forms of government, and patterns of devotion and service. (3) The Holy Spirit remains with the Church until the end of time and will not allow it to deviate fundamentally from the truth of the Gospel, from its mission, or from its life of faith (= *indefectibility*). (4) The Church expresses its faith and fulfills its mission especially in the ministry of word and sacrament, supervised and coordinated by specific ministries and structures, including the ministry of bishops and the bishop of Rome.

(5) Their ministries include overseeing the Church's proclamation and, when necessary, the reformulation of doctrine in fidelity to Sacred Scripture. (6) Harmony between the teaching of these ministers and the acceptance of that teaching by the faithful constitutes a sign of the fidelity of that teaching to the Gospel. (7) No doctrinal definition, however, adequately expresses the truth of the Gospel, given the inevitable cultural and historical limitations of language and concepts.

The two sides agreed that the differences which still exist between them are perhaps more verbal than substantive. Catholics are now more attentive to the abuses of papal authority and are committed to the principle that the Church is the whole People of God, subject always to the Word of God in Sacred Scripture. Lutherans are now more conscious of the intent of the dogma of infallibility, namely, to preserve the Church in fidelity to the Gospel. Thus, ". . . in the new context, each side finds itself compelled to recognize that the other seeks to be faithful to the gospel" (n. 42).

Theological Clarifications

1. Vatican I did not state without qualification that the pope is infallible. He is infallible only when he is in the act of defining a doctrine of faith or morals, speaking as head of the Church (*ex cathedra*, "from the chair"), with the clear intention of binding the whole Church.

2. Infallibility is not a personal prerogative of the pope. He is infallible only when he is in the act of defining a dogma of faith. It can be said, without exaggeration, that a pope who never defined a dogma of faith was never infallible. That would apply to such recent popes as John XXIII, Paul VI, and John Paul I.

3. To say that the definitions of the pope are "irreformable by themselves (*ex sese*) and not by reason of the agreement of the Church (*non autem ex consensu ecclesiae*)" does not mean that the pope is above the Church. That phrase was added to the council's definition in order to exclude the tendency of some Gallicans and Conciliarists to regard approval by the bishops as necessary in order to give infallibility to any papal definition. Thus, the term

consensus at Vatican I is to be understood in the juridical sense of official approval and not in the more general sense of agreement or acceptance by the Church as a whole, which, according to Bishop Vincenz Gasser (d. 1879), the definition's author and official interpreter, can never be lacking.

4. A similar difficulty arises with the notion of "irreformability." It does not mean that infallible teachings are immune from change. On the contrary, as formulations written in human language, they are always historically conditioned and therefore subject to revision. According to *Mysterium Ecclesiae* (Congregation for the Doctrine of the Faith, 1973), doctrinal definitions are affected by the limited context of human knowledge in the situation in which they are framed, by the specific concerns that motivated the definitions, by the changeable conceptions (or thought categories) of a given epoch, and by "the expressive power of the language used at a certain point of time."

5. If there is any reasonable doubt about the Church's or the pope's intention to engage the charism of infallibility, then the definition in question is not to be regarded as infallible. "Nothing is to be understood as dogmatically declared or defined unless this is clearly manifested" (*Code of Canon Law*, can. 1323, #3).

6. Infallibility does not apply to non-infallible statements—a truism, to be sure. Although the *Dogmatic Constitution on the Church* (n. 25) restates and carries forward Pope Pius XII's teaching in *Humani Generis*, i.e., that Catholics owe "religious allegiance of the will and intellect" even to non-infallible teachings of the pope, it is significant that the council did not reassert the doctrine of *Humani Generis* forbidding further public discussion of matters settled by the pope, even though this doctrine appeared in the preliminary draft of November 10, 1962.

7. Vatican II also made it clear that the infallibility of the pope and bishops must always be related to the faith of the whole Church, that there must always be close, collegial cooperation between pope and bishops in the process of definition, that the assent of the Church can never be wanting to an authentic definition, that the Church is always a pilgrim Church, subject to sin and weakness, that there is a hierarchy of truths in the Christian

deposit of faith, and that the doctrine of Vatican II on papal infallibility is not itself the last word on the subject.

The Church and Infallibility

The Church is concerned with the truth of the Gospel, not for its speculative but for its *saving* value. The truth is to be put into action, just as Jesus practiced as well as proclaimed the Kingdom of God. Infallibility is of significance to the Church insofar as the Church is called to proclaim the Gospel faithfully and to be a sign of that Gospel through its unity of both life and faith. Insofar as infallibility attends to the fidelity of the proclamation and the unity of the Church which proclaims the Kingdom of God, it is and will always remain a matter of some theological and pastoral importance. Disengaged from exaggerations of papal authority and placed in the wider context of collegiality and the nature of the Church as the People of God, the dogma of infallibility is much less an ecumenical problem than it once was. The Lutheran-Catholic statement on the subject makes that reasonably clear.

MINISTRY
The Problem

From the time of the Council of Trent, and largely in reaction to Protestantism's stress on the "priesthood of all believers," the Catholic Church has tended to restrict the notion of ministry to the ordained (bishops, priests, and deacons) and to those steps taken in preparation for ordination (lector, acolyte, exorcist). Today the opposite extreme has shown itself: Everyone is regarded as called to ministry by Baptism.

The first extreme is outdated by reason of the Church's return to a fuller understanding of the Body of Christ as including the whole People of God, with a variety of ministries necessary for the fulfillment of its mission. The second extreme, not yet fully challenged, tends to confuse mission with ministry and neglects the particularity of ministry in the New Testament itself.

Ecumenical consultations (e.g., Lutheran-Catholic Dialogue) often make a distinction between ministry (lower case), which does apply to the whole Church as a general call to service, and Ministry (upper case), which applies to particular offices and persons in the Church who are specifically charged with the responsibility of seeing to it that the Gospel is proclaimed, the sacraments celebrated, and witness and service carried out.

History

New Testament

The word *ministry* means "service." Jesus himself gave an example of service (Mark 10:45). The apostolate itself is seen as a ministry (Acts of the Apostles 1:17,25). The call of Paul to the apostolate (Romans 1:1) is also a call to a ministry (1 Timothy 1:12; 2 Corinthians 4:1), which Paul tries to fulfill worthily (Acts of the Apostles 20:24). He understands himself as a minister of God (2 Corinthians 6:3-4) and of Christ (11:23), in the service of the Spirit (3:6-9), of reconciliation (5:18) of the Gospel (Colossians 1:23; Ephesians 3:7), and of the Church (Colossians 1:25).

But the word *diakonia* ("service") is applied beyond the apostolate. It refers also to certain material services necessary to the community, such as serving at table (Acts of the Apostles 6:1-4) and the collection for the poor at Jerusalem (11:29; 12:25; Romans 15:31; 1 Corinthians 16:15; 2 Corinthians 8:4; 9:1,12-13). A ministry is entrusted to Archippus (Colossians 4:17) and to Timothy (2 Timothy 4:5), and the title "minister" is given to Apollos as to Paul (1 Corinthians 3:5), to Timothy (1 Thessalonians 3:2; 1 Timothy 4:6), to Tychichus (Colossians 4:7; Ephesians 6:21), and to Epaphras (Colossians 1:7). There was, in fact, a diversity of ministries (1 Corinthians 12:5) and a diversity of charisms in view of the work of ministry (Ephesians 4:12). Every ministry was to be used under the influence of the Holy Spirit (Romans 12:7) as a mandate received from God (1 Peter 4:11). (See the discussion of the sacrament of Holy Order in the preceding chapter, and of the New Testament structure of the Church in chapter 17.)

Post-biblical Developments

No completely satisfactory history of the development of ministry and of ministries yet exists. One may consult Bernard Cooke's *Ministry to Word and Sacraments: History and Theology* (Philadelphia: Fortress Press, 1976) or Yves Congar's *Lay People in the Church* (Westminster, Md.: Newman Press, 1965). The problem with each is that the historical material is not integrally presented. Both divide ministry by reason of function and then provide a good outline of the development of each function in the history of the Church. For Cooke the functions are: formation of community, proclamation of God's word, service to the People of God, ministering to God's judgment, and the celebration of the sacraments. For Congar, the divisions are based on the threefold mission of Jesus and the Church: prophetic, priestly, and kingly.

What emerges from both these studies is the recognition, already noted in the preceding chapters, of (1) a broad diversity of ministries in the history of the Church, as well as of (2) a relatively wide diversity of modes in which various ministries have been exercised. Thus, as Congar has pointed out, lay persons have "heard confessions" (pp. 217-219), and in more recent decades have been mandated explicitly by the hierarchy to participate in various ministries of the Church (Catholic Action).

Vatican II explicitly acknowledged that Christ instituted in the Church "a variety of ministries for the good of the whole body" (*Dogmatic Constitution on the Church*, n. 18; see also *Decree on Ecumenism*, n. 2), among which are liturgical ministries of servers, lectors, commentators, choir (*Constitution on the Sacred Liturgy*, n. 29), and that of catechists (*Decree on the Church's Missionary Activity*, n. 17). Pope Paul VI's apostolic letter *Ministeria Quaedam* (1972) set aside the Council of Trent's notion that all ministries below priesthood are simply steps toward the priesthood, and restored lay ministries to the Latin Church, to be conferred not by ordination but by installation. The apostolic letter established two lay ministries, those of lector and acolyte, and left open the possibility of the creation of others.

Ecumenical Discussions

Although several of the ecumenical consultations have addressed themselves to the question of ordained ministry, especially of bishops and presbyters (priests), none has as yet dealt with the specific question of non-ordained ministries, except in relation to the general ministry of the whole Church. It is not that these consultations have excluded the possibility of formal but non-ordained ministries over and above the general ministry of all baptized. They have just not raised the question of these ministries. The Lutheran-Catholic Dialogue, for example, does acknowledge the existence of such ministries (citing 1 Corinthians 12, Romans 12, and Ephesians 4), but its own study was deliberately limited to valid Ministry in relation to the Eucharist. Even the Presbyterian-Reformed-Roman Catholic Consultation, which has a broadly inclusive understanding of ministry, does not attend directly to the existence of formal, non-ordained ministries.

Theological Clarifications: Ten Theses

1. There is a variety of ministries within the Church, and several possible combinations of each. Thus, one who is called to preside may or may not also be called to teach. There is no set or inflexible pattern established by the New Testament or by theological principle.

2. Each ministry within the Church is a function of the mission of the whole Church.

3. The mission of the whole Church is, in turn, a function of the mission of Jesus Christ: proclamation of the Kingdom in word, in worship, in witness, and in service.

4. Every Christian is called to ministry in the wide sense (Mark 10:45) as an empowerment to serve others, but not every Christian is called to ministry in a strict or formal sense, i.e., as a service designated by the Church to assist in the fulfillment of its mission.

5. The lay apostolate—and all the ministries it encompasses—is not simply a participation in the ministry of the hierarchy, but rather is "a participation in the saving mission of the

Church itself," commissioned by the Lord himself in Baptism and Confirmation (*Dogmatic Constitution on the Church*, n. 33).

6.   The various ministries of social service are true ministries because the services they provide are part of the essential mission of the whole Church (*Pastoral Constitution on the Church in the Modern World*, n. 43; *Justice in the World*, n. 6, Third International Synod of Bishops).

7.   The ordained ministries of presbyter and bishop exist not to suppress the other ministries, but to integrate and coordinate them (*Dogmatic Constitution on the Church*, n. 30; *Decree on the Bishops' Pastoral Office in the Church*, n. 17).

8.   Ordination, therefore, is directed toward the *order* of the Church, indeed the Church's *holy* order. Ordination establishes a new real relationship between the ordained and the community, a relationship that is once-and-for-all, i.e., non-repeatable (which is the meaning of sacramental "character").

9.   Ordination introduces one to a ministry of pastoral leadership within given Christian communities or, in the case of the diaconate, to a ministry of pastoral assistantship. This is not to say that leadership is not exercised by other ministers (e.g., Director of Religious Education), but only that the responsibility for orchestrating all the other ministries falls upon the ordained ministry of presbyter and bishop.

10.   Every ministry is a form of Church life serving the essential function of the Church. Form follows function. The freedom to abolish old forms (e.g., obligatory celibacy), to create new forms, and to modify existing forms of ministry is essential in order to facilitate the function of the community within which the particular ministry exists.

The Necessity of Ordination

There is no evidence in the New Testament that ordination was required even for presiding over the Eucharist. There *is* evidence in the history of the Church that non-ordained Christians heard confessions, and it is the common teaching of the Church today that the ministers of the sacrament of Matrimony are the two parties to the marriage, not the priest. *In principle*, every baptized

Christian is empowered to administer every sacrament. Ordination does not confer a kind of magical power. It is a public act concerned with *order*. It designates someone for particular ministries so that everything will be done properly and the life and mission of the Church will be served.

In fact, therefore, not every baptized Christian is empowered to celebrate any sacrament under any circumstances he or she may choose. For the sake of order, the celebration of certain sacraments is reserved to those who have been set apart by the Church for training and formation, and who have been subsequently approved for ministry.

The sacraments are not simply acts by which grace is conferred, nor are they acts of private devotion. The sacrament of Penance, for example, reconciles a sinner to the Church. To reconcile someone to the Church requires a person who can act truly in the name of the Church and as its representative. That assumes some prior designation and/or authorization. Similarly, the sacrament of the Eucharist is the supreme moment at which the Church manifests and realizes itself as Church. The one who presides over the assembly *at worship* should be the one who presides over the assembly *apart from worship*, or at least one designated to act in the president's stead. The same principle applies to all the other sacraments, with the exception, as stated, of Matrimony. But even there, a representative of the community normally witnesses to the sanctification of the union since that union participates so directly in the mystery of the Church itself.

The sense of disillusionment which prompts some non-ordained Christians to arrogate to themselves the role of an official representative of the community should lead them, and the rest of the Church, to reform the structures which are the source of the disillusionment (e.g., the exclusion of certain qualified Christians from priesthood on the basis of sex or marital status alone). Short-cut strategies often exacerbate rather than improve a defective pastoral situation. The order and unity of the Church can be compromised, and the community is denied its right to test the qualifications of its members for various ministries and to call only those whom it wishes to authorize for ministry.

The Church and Ministry

Ministry is a service publicly or at least explicitly designated by the Church to assist in the fulfillment of its mission. Ministry is not the same as mission; it exists for the sake of mission, as means to end. As such, ministry in this formal sense requires some "call" from the Church, since every ministry is a service to the Church. But "Church" here means more than the Vatican or even the bishop of a diocese. "Church" means any recognizable, integral Christian community (diocese, parish, or other formal grouping) which fulfills the criteria outlined in chapter 20. The public or explicit designation need not be liturgical or ritual (it could be the offering and the signing of a contract after appropriate interviews), although that might be preferable in most cases (e.g., the installation of the Director of Religious Education).

WOMEN IN THE CHURCH
The Issue

"In accordance with the venerable tradition of the Church" (*Ministeria Quaedam*, n. 7), women are excluded from ministries in the Catholic Church today, even from the newly reconstituted lay ministries of acolyte and lector. On the other hand, the recovery of an understanding of the Church as the whole People of God, men and women alike, has led many to question that traditional policy. This ecclesiological development is parallel with an even broader development outside the Church, i.e., a growing recognition of the equality of men and women and of the innumerable ways in which that equality has been denied and thwarted in society. Thus, there is pressure on the Catholic Church from outside, but more intensely from inside, to revise its canon law and pastoral practice, and to admit qualified women to ministry at every level.

History

New Testament

We have evidence of at least two ministries exercised by women in the New Testament: *widows* and *deaconesses*. The prestige and functional roles of the female minister, however, seemed to have varied from area to area. Women ministers who gave service within the community are described as early as the year 58 in reference to Phoebe in Romans 16:1. In the context of a discussion of the qualifications of various ministers, 1 Timothy 3:11 notes that "the women, similarly, should be serious, not slanderous gossips. They should be temperate and entirely trustworthy." The widowhood, on the other hand, seems to have been confined throughout its existence to those who were in fact widows. "To be on the church's roll of widows," 1 Timothy declares, "a widow should be not less than sixty years of age. She must have been married only once. Her good character will be attested to by her good deeds" (5:9–10).

Post-biblical Developments

The earliest description of the duties of deaconesses is given in the *Didascalia Apostolorum* (*The Teachings of the Apostles*), written as a kind of rulebook for a community in Syria in the early third century. Deaconesses are to be sent to minister to other women, to anoint them in Baptism, to instruct them, to visit the sick, and to minister to those in need. A deaconess was ordained by the laying on of hands in the presence of the presbyters, deacons, and other deaconesses. The same Syrian document presents widows as respected intercessors who pray over the sick and lay hands on them. As with all women, including the deaconesses, they were not to teach. The details of the position of widows are not so important as the fact that they eventually developed into a class of senior women within the Church, analogous to the presbyters. They were sometimes linked together with bishops, presbyters, and deacons as "ecclesiastical dignitaries" (Origen, *Homily on Luke 17*), and at other times considered as part of the clergy

(Tertullian, *On Monogamy* 11:1,4; 12:1). The fifth-century *Testament of Our Lord*, written also in Syria, provides an ordination prayer and specifies that there should be thirteen widows who sit in front during the celebration of the Eucharist immediately behind the presbyters, on the left side of the bishop. Widows at this time frequently performed the functions of the deaconess, assisting at the Baptism of women. They led prayer services and generally exercised leadership over women members of a community.

The growth of the Church's membership and its spread from the cities and towns to smaller towns and villages during the latter part of the third and early fourth centuries brought about rapid organizational changes, as we have noted in the previous chapter. Presbyters were now regularly delegated to preside over the Eucharist in place of the bishop and soon were established as permanent pastors in the outlying congregations. The deacon, who was originally an assistant to the bishop, either moved up with the bishop in the larger diocesan structure or stayed behind in a local community as assistant to the presbyter. In both instances the importance of the diaconate was lessened. The deacon's administrative duties were gradually taken over by the presbyters, and deacons in parishes lost prestige.

Meanwhile, the political situation outside the Church exerted additional pressure that led to further organizational change. The loosely knit structure of the first three centuries was not adequate in the face of the manipulation of the Church by the imperial power. Greater centralization seemed required, and the Church simply took over the organizational forms already available in the political realm. Diocesan bishops became like city magistrates. Bishops of provincial capitals were metropolitans, with authority over other bishops in their province. They were the counterparts of the provincial governors. The new ecclesial structure became more and more vertical. Lower offices were now regarded as probationary stepping-stones to higher offices. The line between clergy and laity developed, popular election of bishops disappeared, women were forbidden to go to the altar, and eventually lay men as well were excluded from the sanctuary. The office of deaconess was ordered suppressed by the councils of Epaon (517) and Orleans (533) in the West, but it survived for a longer time in the East, although women were absorbed into the monastic life rather than designated for pastoral ministry.

1960 to the Present

Without prejudice to the fact that women have exercised positions of leadership and influence in the history of the Church (see, for example, *Women of Spirit: Female Leadership in the Jewish and Christian Traditions*, Rosemary Ruether and Eleanor McLaughlin, eds., New York: Simon and Shuster, 1979), it has not been until the thoroughly contemporary phenomenon of the women's liberation movement that a new awareness of the place of women in the Church began to emerge. That movement, we cannot forget, began only in the early 1960s, and in many parts of the world has not yet begun. Its impact was already evident in the remarkable encyclical letter of Pope John XXIII, *Pacem in Terris* (1963), which notes that "women are becoming ever more conscious of their human dignity" and are demanding rights "befitting a human person both in domestic and in public life." He called this development one of three "distinctive characteristics" of the present day.

The Second Vatican Council's *Pastoral Constitution on the Church in the Modern World* recognized the "new social relationships between men and women" (n. 3) and noted that women are demanding equality with men in law and in fact (n. 9). Pope Paul VI's birth-control encyclical *Humanae Vitae* made the same observation (n. 2). In 1971 he issued a "Call to Action" (*Octagesima Adveniens*) in which he referred to the struggle to end discrimination against women in many countries (n. 13). Later that same year *Justice in the World*, of the Third International Synod of Bishops, urged that "women should have their own share of responsibility and participation in the community life of society and likewise of the Church."

In 1972 Pope Paul VI issued an apostolic letter, as we noted above, in which he explicitly excluded women even from the new lay ministries of lector and acolyte (*Ministeria Quaedam*), but in 1976 the Pontifical Biblical Commission reported that it could find no support for the exclusion of women from the ordained priesthood on the basis of the biblical evidence alone. "The Bible does not contain a ready answer to the question of the role of women in the Church or in society" ("Can Women Be Priests?" *Origins* 6/6, July 1, 1976, pp. 92-96). This latter document is of major importance, and merits separate study. The reader should also consult the "Consensus Statement from the Symposium on Women and Church Law," sponsored by the Canon Law Society of America, and published in *Sexism and Church Law*, James Coriden, ed. (New York: Paulist Press, 1977, pp. 150-160).

The Ordination of Women

Arguments in Favor

Positive arguments are advanced by committees of learned societies (e.g., Canon Law Society of America, Catholic Theological Society of America), national associations (e.g., Leadership Conference of Women Religious), various ecumenical consultations (e.g., Presbyterian-Reformed-Roman Catholic Consultation, "Women in the Church," in *Journal of Ecumenical Studies* 9, 1972, pp. 235-241), and the works of individual theologians. Some of these arguments are:

1. The exclusion of women from priesthood violates human dignity and the baptismal mandate to participate in the mission of the Church according to one's qualifications, opportunities, and vocation.

2. Women have in fact served as deaconesses in the early Church.

3. There is nothing in Sacred Scripture which positively excludes the ordination of women.

4. Arguments against the ordination of women are deficient:

    a. To say the tradition of the Church is against it assumes that we are already in the adulthood of the Church. But if the Church is still alive in the year 20,000, the latter part of the twentieth century will look like the "early Church" to those in the two-hundred-first century.

b. Women are equal to men in human dignity and before God. The exclusion of women on the basis of sex assumes a radical inferiority of women and, therefore, a basic incapacity, if not unworthiness, to act on behalf of the Church in the presence of God.

c. Jesus, in fact, called no one to *ordained priesthood* (as distinguished from discipleship and the apostolate).

Arguments Against

Negative arguments are expressed in such Vatican documents as the 1976 *Declaration on the Question of the Admission of Women to the Ministerial Priesthood* from the Sacred Congregation for the Doctrine of the Faith, the statement of the United States bishops, *Theological Reflections on the Ordination of Women* (1972), certain ecumenical consultations (e.g., Catholic-Orthodox, "Bishops and Presbyters," *Origins* 6/9, August 12, 1976, pp. 142-143), and the works of individual theologians.

1. The constant tradition of the Church is opposed to ordination of women to priesthood.

2. Jesus did not call women, not even his mother, to priesthood.

3. The ordained priest must act in the name of Christ, and, therefore, must be able to represent him physically as well as spiritually. The Orthodox refer to this as "iconic" representation.

4. No one has a right to ordination.

5. It is not clear that the women who were called deaconesses in the New Testament were ordained or whether their ordination was sacramental.

(For a fuller discussion of these and similar arguments, both for and against, see the *Research Report: Women in Church and Society*, New York: Catholic Theological Society of America, 1978.)

The Church and Women

Whatever position one takes on the ordination question, recognition of the full Christian and human equality of women with men is essential if the Church is to be perceived, and to function, as the whole People of God. The Church must always be faithful to the example of Jesus Christ, whose sacrament it is. In striking contrast to the contemporary usages of the Jewish world, Jesus surrounded himself with women who followed him and served him (Luke 8:2-3; 10:38-42). It was the women who were charged with announcing the resurrection "to the apostles and to Peter" (Mark 16:7).

The whole purpose of creation and of redemption is the unity of all in God, and the Church is called to be a sign and instrument of the unity of God and humankind, and of the unity of humankind itself (*Dogmatic Constitution on the Church*, n. 1). Therefore, the missionary responsibility of the Church is to attest to the full human and Christian dignity of women not only by word but also by example. The sacramental principle, always central to Catholicism, is here again of utmost importance.

INTERCOMMUNION
The Issue

The mystery of the Church and the mystery of the Eucharist are intimately connected. The Eucharist is the sign as well as the principal instrument of the Church's unity in Christ. Insofar as it is a *sign* of unity, it ought not to be celebrated in common by those who are, in fact, separated from one another. Insofar as the Eucharist is an *instrument* of unity, it can be a means of bringing about the unity which eludes those who find themselves separated.

The term *intercommunion* (also known as *communicatio in sacris*, "communication in sacred realities") refers to this full eucharistic sharing between and among separated Christians. It describes the reception of Holy Communion by a single separated Christian in a church other than his or her own, or it refers to the future possibility of full church-to-church reciprocity in the celebration and reception of the Eucharist. The former is already occurring: Protestants, Anglicans, and Orthodox in fact receive Communion at Catholic Eucharists and vice versa. The latter has not occurred: There has been no public declaration by the Catholic Church, accepted by another church, that full eucharistic sharing between the two churches is now fully operative.

Intercommunion does, of course, occur within the Body of Christ but outside the Catholic Church. Thus, various Protestant churches have the policy that all baptized Christians are welcome to receive Communion at their Lord's Supper service.

The question of intercommunion arises only because there has been some form of *excommunication*, not in the juridical sense of a penalty imposed for some crime (e.g., laying violent hands on the pope), but in the larger ecclesiological sense of declaring another individual or community as unacceptable table companions at the Lord's Supper.

It is not clear what finally determines the possibility of eucharistic sharing. Some churches within the Body of Christ—e.g., Catholic, Anglican, Orthodox, and to a lesser extent Lutheran—already agree in principle on most, if not practically all, major matters of faith, including even the Real Presence of Christ and the sacrificial nature of the Eucharist. What, then, keeps these churches from formal intercommunion?

It would seem that, while common faith is a necessary condition for intercommunion, something is required beyond common faith, namely, a recognition that the other party or community really is a member of one's Christian family and should permanently be welcome to enjoy table fellowship with us. There is a mystery of reconciliation here which has its secular analogue in the reconciliation of friends or of relatives who have fallen out of favor with one another. Only time and some generous and gracious gestures can heal the wounds. A precipitous or prematurely arranged "reconciliation" can do more harm than good. Such an occasion can be painful, or at least awkward and uncomfortable, for both sides. The same situation apparently obtains in the Body of Christ today.

On the other hand, what of the case—frequently attested to—where members of the same church find themselves more sharply at odds with one another in the interpretation and practice of Christian faith than they are with members of other churches? Why is it that they can celebrate the Eucharist together, in spite of their internal divisions, when separated Christians with much closer bonds of faith cannot celebrate together? Once again, the family analogue may be appropriate. Even when there are serious conflicts within a home, people still sit down together at table. They may dislike the company very much indeed, but the other is still "my brother" or "my sister" or "my son" or "my daughter" or "my husband" or "my wife." And the same principle would apply to the extended family of relatives: aunts, uncles, cousins, grandchildren.

If "blood is thicker than water" in these secular examples, then perhaps a "sense of community" is "thicker" than theological and doctrinal agreement in the ecclesiastical realm.

Vatican II

If it were not for the ecumenical movement of the twentieth century, so strongly encouraged by Pope John XXIII and promoted by the Second Vatican Council, the question of intercommunion would be entirely moot. As the Catholic Church's vision of "the Church" expanded beyond the one suggested in Counter-Reformation ecclesiology and in Pope Pius XII's *Humani Generis* (the Body of Christ and the Roman Catholic Church are "one and the same"), there developed a growing awareness that other communities were also part of the Church and could themselves be called churches (*Decree on Ecumenism*, n. 3). The *Dogmatic Constitution on the Church* declared that the Church "subsists in" the Catholic Church (n. 8), not that the Church *is* the Catholic Church.

The possibility of intercommunion was no longer unthinkable: "As for common worship (*communicatio in sacris*), however, it may not be regarded as a means to be used indiscriminately for the restoration of unity among Christians. Such worship depends chiefly on two principles: it should signify the unity of the Church; it should provide a sharing in the means of grace. The fact that it should signify unity generally rules out common worship. Yet the gaining of a needed grace sometimes commends it" (*Decree on Ecumenism*, n. 8).

Post-Vatican II Directives

Implementation of this extraordinary principle was left to the Secretariat for Promoting Christian Unity. This Vatican congregation issued an *Ecumenical Directory* in 1967 and released a special instruction on intercommunion in 1972. The conditions under which intercommunion are allowed by these two documents are these: (1) Admission to the Eucharist is confined to particular cases of those Christians who have a faith in the sacrament in conformity with that of the Catholic Church. (2) Such Christians must experience a serious spiritual need for the eucharistic sustenance. (3) They must be unable for a prolonged period to have recourse to a minister of their own community. (4) They must ask for the sacrament of their own accord. (5) They must have proper dispositions and lead lives worthy of a Christian.

Even if these conditions are fulfilled, "It will be a pastoral responsibility to see that the admission of these other Christians to communion does not endanger or disturb the faith of Catholics." These "rules" do not apply to Orthodox Christians, who, "though separated from us, have true sacraments, above all, because of apostolic succession, the priesthood and the eucharist, which unite them to us by close ties, so that the risk of obscuring the relation between eucharistic communion and ecclesial communion is somewhat reduced."

The Church and Intercommunion

The Church is most fully and most visibly itself at the Eucharist. The fact that there are Christian churches which do not, and feel they cannot, celebrate the Eucharist together reflects the correlative fact that the Body of Christ is divided, in spite of the fundamental unity of faith in the Lordship of Jesus, the common celebration of the sacrament of Baptism, the general commitment to the Gospel of love and reconciliation, and the common hope for the coming of God's Kingdom. To attempt a quick solution to the problem of separate Eucharists is to fail to understand the root causes of ecclesial disunity. Correspondingly, only in discovering the solution to the intercommunion problem can the churches come to the heart of the mystery of unity in Christ. For that reason, this issue remains as important an issue as the Church faces in our time.

SUMMARY

1. This chapter addresses itself to five special questions: authority, papacy, ministry, women in the Church, and intercommunion. Insofar as authority is rooted in the will of God, authority is the one overarching question, and the other four are component parts of it.

2. *Authority,* from the Latin word *auctor* ("author"), has to do with the capacity to influence the thinking and/or behavior of people. It is closely related to *power,* but not identical with it. Authority may be associated with an office (*de iure* authority) or with certain intrinsic qualities which evoke respect and which lead to persuasion (*de facto* authority). God is the ultimate authority, or Author, of all that is.

3. In the *Old Testament* authority is exercised by human agents, but it is never absolute. In the *New Testament,* Jesus provides the model for its exercise. He is one who serves. He uses his power to forgive sins, to heal, and thereby to proclaim the Kingdom of God. He shares his authority with his disciples, but again it is never absolute, nor is its exercise limited to the Apostles. Authority in the New Testament is unique because it is a work of the *Holy Spirit.*

4. *Teaching* authority, while important, is always secondary to the proclamation and practice of the Kingdom. Teaching explains the Gospel; it is not itself the Gospel. Teaching interprets faith; it is not itself the faith.

5. In the *second and third centuries* authority is identified with those who preside over the Christian churches, especially the bishops and presbyters. But the Spirit is perceived to have been given to the whole community, although in a special way to *bishops.* Only those in whom the gifts of the Spirit were discernible were elected bishops in the first place.

6. In subsequent centuries *(fourth to eleventh)* authority becomes confused with *political* authority, especially in the aftermath of the Edict of Constantine. Monasticism grows in reaction to the exercise of worldly authority. The only genuine authority, in the monastic view, is *moral authority.* Most of the great bishops of this era are men trained in monasteries, or are themselves former monks.

7. With the Gregorian Reform (*eleventh century*), in response to lay encroachments against the Church, the papacy claims *monarchical* authority. Papal authority is thoroughly juridicized and exaggerated,

especially under Innocent III and Boniface VIII. This provokes a counter-reaction among certain spiritual groups, e.g., Franciscans.

8. Against the excesses of the Reformation, the Council of Trent *(sixteenth century)* insists even more strongly on the hierarchical authority of the Church. The pope becomes the Church's "universal bishop," the "Sovereign Pontiff." Authority is centralized in Rome. People are asked to obey because of the power of the office, not because of the obvious promptings of the Spirit in the officeholder.

9. This trend culminates in the definition of papal primacy at Vatican I *(nineteenth century)* and is carried forward in the encyclicals of Pope Pius XII *(twentieth century)*.

10. Vatican II *(1962-1965)* stresses the notion of authority as *service* and insists that it must be exercised always in a *collegial* mode. Ecumenical consultations also insist on its rootedness in Christ and on its presence throughout the whole Church, exercised in different ways according to different ministerial responsibilities.

11. *In summary,* authority in the Church exists to serve the mission of the Church, which is to proclaim, celebrate, witness to, and facilitate unity. Ecclesiastical authority is always in the service of a community which is essentially a voluntary society, where the grace of the Spirit, not coercion, is the rule.

12. The *papacy* is an exercise of the *Petrine function,* i.e., a particular form of ministry exercised by a person, officeholder, or local church with reference to the Church as a whole. *Peter* himself seemed to fulfill something of this kind of ministry toward the universal Church, although Protestants have objected to the various forms in which this ministry has been exercised in the subsequent history of the Catholic Church.

13. The *New Testament* does not call Peter the first pope. On the other hand, he exercises a unique role in the early Church. No single text "proves" this. Rather, there is a pattern or *trajectory of images* (e.g., fisherman, shepherd) which suggest that the post-biblical development is indeed consistent with the thrust of the New Testament.

14. The bishop of Rome becomes increasingly important in the *early centuries* of the Church in resolving serious doctrinal controversies. He sends delegates to councils and is appealed to as a court of last resort. The correlation between Peter and the bishop of Rome becomes fully explicit in Leo I (d. 461).

15. *Primacy* becomes an increasingly juridical concept under the impact of the threats posed by the encroachment of lay political power,

Conciliarism, Protestantism, nationalism, the Enlightenment, and nine-teenth-century liberalism. The doctrine of papal primacy, as formulated by Vatican I, reflects the Church's reaction to all these movements.

16.   Vatican II restores a collegial understanding of papal primacy. Supreme authority is vested in the pope and the bishops, forming together a single college. The authority is always fundamentally spiritual, i.e., for the faithful preaching of the Gospel, the administration of the sacraments, and loving service.

17.   The Church is at once local and universal. It is a communion of churches. The papacy exists to serve the *unity* of that communion of churches, but it must always respect the *legitimate diversity* of those churches, *collegiality* in decision-making, and the principle of *subsidiarity,* not appropriating to itself decisions which are better reached at lower levels.

18.   *Papal infallibility* means literally "immunity from error." It is concerned with the faithful transmission of the Gospel, the indefectibility of the Church, and the certitude of faith.

19.   The concept of infallibility does not appear in the *New Testament,* although the concern for sound doctrine does. There was, however, a growing conviction in the *early centuries* of the Church that Rome, and the bishop of Rome in particular, was a reliable touchstone of orthodoxy. And yet popes were conceded to have erred in matters of faith.

20.   The term "infallibility" was first applied to papal teaching authority during the course of a *fourteenth-century* dispute about Franciscan poverty. One side appealed to papal views, defending their binding authority, even against the decisions of later popes. The concept was taken up and accentuated by the Counter-Reformation theologians, in the controversy with Jansenism and Gallicanism, and then made the subject of a dogmatic definition at Vatican I. This definition was reaffirmed at Vatican II but was placed in the larger context of the infallibility of the whole Church and the collegiality of bishops with the pope.

21.   *Vatican I* taught that the pope is infallible only when he is in the act of defining a doctrine of faith and morals, as head of the universal Church, with the clear intention of binding the whole Church. His teachings are not subject to some subsequent vote on the part of the bishops, as the Gallicans had insisted. On the other hand, those teachings are subject to the same process of revision and improvement that all human formulations require.

22. *Vatican II* insisted that papal infallibility must always be related to the faith of the whole Church, whose assent can never be lacking.

23. Infallibility is of significance to the Church insofar as the Church is called to proclaim the Gospel faithfully and to be a sign of that Gospel through its unity of both life and of faith.

24. The question of *ministry* is distorted at two extremes: One side restricts it to the ordained; the other side opens it to everyone, without regard for a call from the Church.

25. In the *New Testament* ministry means service. There is a diversity of ministries, and this diversity continues through the history of the Church. Vatican II acknowledged this, and Pope Paul VI recognized it in reinstating two permanent ministries of lector and acolyte open by "installation" (not ordination) to lay men. Ecumenical discussions have focused on the general ministry of the whole Church, on the one hand, and the ordained ministry of the presbyter and bishop, on the other. They have not attended thus far to the place of formal but non-ordained ministries in the Church.

26. Ministry is always for the sake of mission. In principle, ministry is open to all. By ministry is meant *a service which is publicly or explicitly designated by the Church to assist in the fulfillment of its mission*.

27. *Ordained* ministry is for the sake of the *order* of the Church, that everyone might work together as one for the good of the whole. There is no evidence in the New Testament that ordination was necessary even for the celebration of the Eucharist. In principle, every baptized Christian can celebrate every sacrament. But the Church must retain the right to determine qualifications in order to insure that its mission is effectively and competently carried out.

28. *Women* are presently excluded from all formal ministries in the Catholic Church. In the *New Testament* and in the first five or six centuries of the Church's history, however, women served as *deaconesses* and as *widows* (the latter was also a special office, not simply a civil fact).

29. With the growth of the Church, an increase in its organizational complexity, and its adoption of political and societal models from contemporary Graeco-Roman life, the so-called lower ministries were absorbed upwards, becoming steppingstones to higher ecclesiastical office. Deaconesses were suppressed in the sixth century, and the office of widow disappeared.

30. The women's liberation movement in the 1960s encouraged a new attitude toward the place of women in the Church. This positive

change was reflected in Pope John XXIII's encyclical *Pacem in Terris* and was reinforced by Vatican II's *Gaudium et spes*. Nonetheless, resistance to women in formal ministries continues, and Pope Paul VI's *Ministeria Quaedam* opens the ministries of lector and acolyte to men only.

31.   Those who *favor* ordination of women to the priesthood point to the injustice of the present exclusion based on sex alone, the tradition of deaconesses in the early Church, and the absence of any evidence against it in the New Testament.

32.   Those who *oppose* ordination of women point to the constant tradition of the Church, Jesus' own example, and the necessity of the priest's physical as well as spiritual resemblance to Christ.

33.   Whatever position one takes on this issue, the Church is called to be a sign and instrument of unity. It must attest to the full human and Christian dignity of women, therefore, not only by word but also by example.

34.   *Intercommunion* is an important ecclesiological issue because of the intimate connection between the mystery of the Church and the mystery of the Eucharist. Intercommunion refers to full eucharistic sharing between and/or among separated Christians. It is also known as *communicatio in sacris* ("communication in sacred realities").

35.   If it were not for the ecumenical movement and Vatican II, intercommunion would be a moot question. It is an issue because the Catholic Church now recognizes that "the Church" includes non-Catholic churches also. It has also recovered the Thomistic principle that the Eucharist is not only a sign of unity but also a cause of unity.

36.   Intercommunion since Vatican II is permitted on a restricted basis. The non-Catholic Christian must share Catholic eucharistic faith, have a serious spiritual need, be unable to have recourse to his or her own minister, must ask for the Eucharist, and must display the proper dispositions. These restrictions do not apply to Orthodox Christians.

37.   Since some separated churches already acknowledge profound and extensive theological and doctrinal agreement with the Catholic Church on major matters of faith, why is it that Catholics do not officially celebrate the Eucharist with them? Is something more required, i.e., a sense of community, a readiness to accept the other as part of one's own Christian family? Only in discovering the solution to the intercommunion problem can the churches come to the heart of the mystery of unity in Christ.

SUGGESTED READINGS

Brown, Raymond, *et al. Peter in the New Testament.* Minneapolis: Augsburg Publishing House, 1973.

Butler, Sara, ed. *Research Report: Women in Church and Society.* New York: Catholic Theological Society of America, 1978.

Congar, Yves. *Lay People in the Church.* Rev. ed. Westminster, Md.: Newman Press, 1965.

Cooke, Bernard. *Ministry to Word and Sacraments: History and Theology.* Philadelphia: Fortress Press, 1976.

Coriden, James, ed. *Sexism and Church Law: Equal Rights and Affirmative Action.* New York: Paulist Press, 1977.

Dyer, George, ed. "The Magisterium, the Theologian and the Educator." *Chicago Studies* 17 (1978).

Empie, Paul C., *et al,* eds. *Papal Primacy and the Universal Church: Lutherans and Catholics in Dialogue V.* Minneapolis: Augsburg Publishing House, 1974.

Kirvan, John, ed. *The Infallibility Debate.* New York: Paulist Press, 1971.

McKenzie, John L. *Authority in the Church.* New York: Sheed & Ward, 1966.

Todd, John M., ed. *Problems of Authority.* Baltimore: Helicon Press, 1962.

· XXIV ·

MARY AND THE CHURCH

THE PLACE OF MARIOLOGY

No theological presentation of Catholicism can claim to be at once comprehensive and complete if it leaves out the Blessed Virgin Mary. Mariology is not an exclusively Catholic concern, to be sure, but it is a theological preoccupation that is more characteristic of Catholicism than of any other Christian tradition.

One is faced immediately with the question, "Where do the Marian doctrines and dogmas fit in?" Medieval theology always located Mariology within Christology. For Thomas Aquinas, Mariology became an appendix to Christology. Beginning in the seventeenth century a gap opened between Mariology and the rest of theology. By the end of the nineteenth century the treatise on Mary had acquired its own definite position in systematic theology, situated immediately after the consideration of the incarnation and the redemption. (For a full history of this development, see Hilda Graef, *Mary: A History of Doctrine and Devotion,* 2 vols., 1963.)

One of the more exciting debates at the Second Vatican Council was centered on the placement of the schema on the Blessed Virgin. Would it be an independent document, stressing Mary's unique relationship with Christ, or would it be considered part of the *Dogmatic Constitution on the Church?* By a margin of just four votes the council decided to follow the latter course, but it did so in the spirit of compromise. *Lumen gentium* incorporates Mary into the mystery of the Church, but insists also on her relation with Christ the Redeemer. Although some Mariologists still insist that "the best place for mariology is between the treatise on the redemption and the theological or dogmatic treatise on the Church" (Cyril Vollert, *A Theology of Mary,* p. 47), we are following Vatican II's course here. Mary is seen as a type of the Church, as its mother, as a model of faith, as a sign of the Church's hope in the coming of God's Kingdom, and as the preeminent member of the communion of saints.

HISTORY
New Testament

What follows here is dependent on the most recent ecumenical investigation of the place of Mary in the New Testament *(Mary in the New Testament,* Raymond E. Brown, *et al.,* eds., 1978).

The only reference to Mary in the *Pauline* writings is in Galatians 4:4: "God sent forth his Son born of a woman...." The theological interest of that statement is Christological, pointing to the true humanity of Jesus. The designation "born of a woman" is found in the Old Testament, at Qumran, and in non-Pauline New Testament passages simply as the designation of a human being. There is no other meaning of it in Paul that one can find. Nor is there any other Pauline text referring to Jesus' origin which assigns any unusual part to Mary in Jesus' birth.

The Infancy Narrative of *Matthew* says little about Mary apart from the virginal conception (see our discussion of the virginal conception in chapter 15). In the Gospel of *Luke,* however, the evangelist's estimation of Mary is found principally in his Infancy Narrative. She is hailed by Gabriel as one favored by God (1:28,30); her response shows her to be an obedient handmaid of the Lord (1:38); Elizabeth calls her "the mother of my Lord" (1:43) and declares her blessed because of what God has done for Mary (1:42) and because of Mary's faith "that the Lord's words to her would be fulfilled" (1:45). In her own canticle, the *Magnificat,* Mary acknowledges that "God who is mighty has done great things for me" (1:49). Luke, therefore, depicts Mary as the spokeswoman and representative of the *anawim,* the poor of Israel. She is a faithful hearer of the word, obedient to it and to the God who utters it.

On the other hand, Luke mentions Mary only once in the *Acts of the Apostles* (1:14). It is after the ascension of Jesus into heaven that the disciples return to Jerusalem, go to the upstairs room, and devote themselves to constant prayer. "There were some women in their company, and Mary the mother of Jesus, and his brothers." Although it is not possible to establish the time when Mary's own belief in her Son's messianic significance began, or even the cause of it, it is clear that she shared the faith in Jesus of the earliest Christian community (see chapter 12). She was from the first a member of the post-Easter community.

We find a strikingly negative portrait of Mary in the Gospel of *Mark* (3:20-35). It is just after Jesus' selection of the Twelve (3:13-19). He is in a house with them and a great crowd gathers outside. His own family concludes that "He is out of his mind" (3:21). When his mother and his brothers arrive, they send word for him to come out. Jesus is given the message. "Who are my mother and my brothers?" he asks. Then he looks at his disciples gathered in the circle: "These are my mother and my brothers. Whoever does the will of God is brother and sister and mother to me" (3:33-35). The negative view is strengthened in 6:4, which reports Jesus' return to his home in Nazareth and the skeptical reaction of his neighbors, friends, and relatives. Jesus complains: "No prophet is without honor except in his native place, among his own kindred, and in his own house."

The Matthaen and Lucan parallels to Mark 3:20-35 (Matthew 12:24-50; Luke 8:19-21) present a different picture. Both drop the harsh introduction in Mark 3:20-21. Luke goes further and eliminates Jesus' question, "Who are my mother and my brothers?" Neither Gospel excludes Mary from the "eschatological family" of Jesus. In Luke especially she is the obedient handmaid of the Lord from the beginning. Later in 11:27-28 Jesus responds to a woman who declares his mother blessed by saying that those are blessed who hear the word of God and keep it. In light of Luke's positive description of Mary in 8:19-21, it is likely that Jesus is emphasizing here that Mary's chief blessedness lies in her being one who obediently hears the word of God rather than in being his biological mother. Consistent with this interpretation, Luke's version of the rejection of Jesus at Nazareth speaks only of a prophet's being unacceptable in his own country (4:24). There is no reference to "his own kindred," as in Mark. Matthew, on the other hand, retains the phrase "in his own house."

Thus, in the *Synoptic* depiction of Mary during Jesus' ministry there is a development from the negative estimation of Mark to the positive one of Luke, with Matthew representing the middle ground.

In the Gospel of *John,* Jesus dissociates himself from his mother because she does not realize that the work which the Father has given him takes precedence over the claims and interests of his natural family (2:4). But Mary's misunderstanding does not rank her among the unbelievers, as in the case of Jesus' brothers (7:5). Thus, the Cana story places Mary in a less negative light than in Mark, but because of her still imperfect faith at Cana she is not the equal to the believing and obedient Mary of Luke's Gospel. More important than the Cana story in John is the account of the crucifixion and of Mary's place at the foot of the cross. In giving the "beloved disciple" (John) to Mary as her son, and Mary to the disciple as his mother (19:25-27), Jesus brought into existence a new community of believing disciples, the same "eschatological family" which appears in the Synoptics. The brothers of Jesus have no part in this family. They are unbelievers. But Mary is now associated with that Johannine Christianity which differs in some respects from the Christianity derived from the witness of Peter and the rest of the Twelve. In John's own symbolic treatment of Jesus' mother, an opening is made for the process of further Marian symbolizing within the Church.

The Book of *Revelation,* chapter 12, tells of "a woman clothed with the sun, with the moon under her feet, and on her head a crown of twelve stars" (v. 1) who gives birth to a son who is "destined to shepherd all the nations" (v. 5). A huge dragon appears in hopes of devouring the child. When he fails in that, he pursues the woman. But he fails there, too, and goes off "to make war on the rest of her offspring, on those who kept God's commandments and give witness to Jesus" (v. 17). Pious commentaries notwithstanding, the "woman" here is not Mary. The primary reference is to the People of God, both Israel, which brings forth the Messiah, and the Church, which relives the experience of

Israel and brings forth other children in the image of Christ. A *secondary* reference to Mary remains possible but uncertain. What is more certain is that the author's symbol of the woman who is the mother of the Messiah might well lend itself to Marian interpretation once Marian interest developed in the later Christian community. Eventually, when the Book of Revelation was placed in the same canon of Scripture with the Gospel of Luke and the Gospel of John, the various images of the virgin, the woman at the cross, and the woman who gave birth to the Messiah would reinforce each other.

Before we leave the New Testament, some more explicit mention should be made of Mary's *virginity*. Attention was given this topic in chapter 15, and the reader should review that material in connection with the present discussion. What we noted in that chapter, and repeat here, is that the New Testament provides evidence only of a *belief* in the *ante partum* ("before birth") virginity of Mary, i.e., in the *virginal conception* of Jesus. The New Testament says nothing at all about Mary's virginity *in partu* ("in the act of giving birth"), i.e., that Jesus was born miraculously, without the normal biological disruptions, nor about her virginity *post partum* ("after birth"), i.e., that she had no normal sexual relationships after the birth of Jesus. On the contrary, the New Testament speaks of the brothers and sisters of Jesus. This does not constitute an insuperable barrier to the belief that Mary remained a virgin after the birth of Jesus, but neither is there any convincing argument from the New Testament against the literal meaning of the words *brother* and *sister* when they are used of Jesus' relatives.

Second Century

The literature of the second century is an important link between the emerging canon of the New Testament writings and the broader life-situation of the Church of the Fathers. We do not find here a fully developed interest in Mary. When she appears at all, it is on the margin of more central Christological discussions. The source material, too, is limited. Even in the literature that we do have, Marian references are extremely rare before the year 150 and are difficult to interpret in works written between 150 and 200.

The texts come from two principal groups of writings: the *apocrypha* (non-biblical gospels, epistles, apocalypses) and the *patristic writings*. The former are so called because they were not accorded canonical authority (i.e., they were not included in the canon of Sacred Scripture) and/or were rejected as products of heretical or dissident groups. Among these, the most important source for Marian material is the *Protevangelium of James* (its oldest title was *Birth of Mary: Revelation of James*). It was probably composed around the year 150 or so. The author posed as James, the brother of Jesus. It contains much detail about the early family life of Mary, her birth, her betrothal to Joseph, the annunciation, the birth of Jesus, the coming of the Magi, etc. Despite its condemnation in official documents, it dominated the development of the Marian legend for centuries. Neither in this document nor in any of the other material is there any clear evidence of a reliable historical tradition about Mary unrelated to what was said of her in the canonical Gospels. Some of the literature, in fact, is frankly Docetic. Thus, the Synoptic passage about Jesus' true family (Mark 3:31-35) is taken in this literature as a denial of his humanity.

The picture is the same when we look at the patristic writings. Most do not even mention Mary. The principal exceptions are Ignatius of Antioch, Justin, and Irenaeus. Ignatius gives an early witness to the belief in Jesus' virginal conception (*Smyrnaeans* 1:1; *Ephesians* 7:2; 18:2; 19:1). Justin's interest in Mary serves a Christological and soteriological purpose. Jesus' birth from a virgin is proof of his messiahship and a sign of a new time (see his *Apology*, especially 32:9-35:1). Justin also draws a parallel between the virgin Eve and the virgin Mary. Eve believed and obeyed the serpent; Mary believed and obeyed the angel. Thus, Eve became the mother of sin through her disobedience, and Mary became the mother of the one who destroyed the works of the serpent through her obedience. Irenaeus, finally, spells out the basis of this Eve-Mary typology by showing its parallel to Paul's Adam-Christ typology (*Adversus Haereses* III, 21:10). Mary is the new Eve, the mother of the new humanity in whom God made a new beginning.

These last two witnesses, Justin and Irenaeus, in combination with the *Protevangelium of James*, accelerated the growth of Marian symbolism by the end of the second century. The Mary-Eve parallelism continued in the writings of the Syrian poet Ephrem (d. 373), the Cappodocian Gregory of Nyssa (d. 394), and the Latin Father, Ambrose (d. 397).

The Marian theme with which the second century literature was mainly concerned is the *virginal conception*. The majority of references are affirmative, but there is also a significant amount of dissent. There is, however, no second-century evidence of belief in Mary's remaining a virgin after the birth of Jesus (*post partum*), apart from the implications of the *Protevangelium*. The later development coincided with a newly positive assessment of virginity. The evidence for belief in Mary's virginity during the birth of Jesus (*in partu*), while slight, is more abundant than for belief in her perpetual virginity. Indeed, we do not know the exact origin of the belief in Mary's perpetual virginity. We do know that the idea was actively resisted in the early Church by such writers as Tertullian, lest the Church yield ground to the Docetists and the Gnostics. The tradition of the miraculous birth, on the other hand, clearly originated in the second century. But it created a paradoxical situation for the Church. On the one hand, the Church wanted to uphold the reality of Jesus' birth over against the Docetists and the Gnostics (both of whom denied the humanity of Christ), but the Church fostered at the same time the glorification of the Virgin Mary for ascetical reasons, which allowed an interpretation of the birth in terms of her inviolate virginity and thus introduced a new danger of docetic trends. And that very danger explains again Tertullian's resistance to the *in partu* and *post partum* notions.

Third Century to the Middle Ages

Mary's perpetual virginity, however, came to be almost universally accepted from the third century on. By now consecrated virgins had been established as a special state in the Church, and Mary was presented to them as their model. Both Latin and Greek

Fathers saw in her the model of all virtues, in fact. The outstanding exception was John Chrysostom (d. 407) who, as if in anticipation of modern biblical scholarship, acknowledged the negative flavor of Mark's estimation of Mary, and in his *Homilies on St. John's Gospel*, declared that "she did not cease to think little of (Jesus)...but herself she thought everywhere worthy of the first place, because she was his mother." At Cana, Mary told Jesus there was no more wine only because "she wanted to confer a favor on the others, and render herself more illustrious through her Son." Even at the annunciation she was at fault. The angel had to calm her down lest she kill herself in despair over the news that she was to have a son. Never before had a Christian preacher spoken in such derogatory terms of Mary, and never again for a thousand years would such be heard again.

It was the Nestorian controversy which indirectly promoted Mariology in the fifth century. The Nestorians had so emphasized the distinction of the two natures in Christ, and the integrity of the human nature in particular, that they concluded to two persons as well. The crisis broke out when Nestorius publicly denied to Mary the title "Mother of God" (*theotokos*). According to him, she was only the mother of Christ (*Christotokos*), to whom the Person of the Word of God had united himself. We have already summarized the events surrounding the Council of Ephesus (431) in chapter 13. The council ruled against the Nestorian position and in favor of the term *theotokos*. Mary is indeed the "Mother of God" for there is only one Person in Jesus Christ, not two, and that Person is the very Word of God. The definition, one must remember, was not a Marian definition, but a Christological one. It was intended to safeguard not the motherhood of Mary but the true unity of Christ in one divine Person.

The decision at Ephesus gave a major impetus to Marian devotion. Popular interest in the apocryphal writings increased, especially in the *Protevangelium of James*. It is the source of the belief in her virginity *in partu* (during childbirth), and of the story of her presentation in the Temple (which, in turn, is the source of the liturgical feast of the Presentation). St. Jerome (d. 420), the pioneer Scripture scholar, would have none of this "delirious nonsense." But it caught on nonetheless and was mentioned by the

Council of the Lateran (649) as it formulated its opposition to Monothelitism (one will in Christ).

Before the Council of Ephesus there had been one liturgical feast of Mary, the feast of the Purification, and that was celebrated only in certain parts of the Eastern Church. But after Ephesus the feasts began to multiply. From the beginning of the sixth century various churches celebrated Mary's bodily assumption into heaven. The belief originated not from biblical evidence nor even patristic testimony, but as the conclusion of a so-called argument from convenience or fittingness. It was "fitting" that Jesus should have rescued his mother from the corruption of the flesh, and so he "must have" taken her bodily into heaven. By the middle of the seventh century four separate Marian feasts were observed in Rome: the Annunciation, the Purification, the Assumption, and the Nativity of Mary. At the end of this century the feast of the Conception of Mary began in the East, but it remained unknown in the West until the eleventh century. Andrew of Crete (d. 740) wrote a hymn to Mary, calling her "alone wholly without stain." To Western ears this meant conceived without sin (the Immaculate Conception), but to Eastern ears, which had a different understanding of Original Sin, it meant only freedom from mortality and general human weakness.

Faith in Mary's power of intercession with God received a strong push from the growing belief in her assumption. Germanus (d. 733), patriarch of Constantinople, popularized the view that she had a maternal influence over God, that she could turn away God's anger and vengeance. She is our mediatrix with God. Thus, by the beginning of the eighth century, Mary's intercession and her importance for salvation had become well-established truths, especially in the East, both through popular literature and through preaching. The main contribution of the West at this time, as worked out by Ambrose and Augustine, was the close association of Mary with the Church. But compared with Eastern doctrine and devotion, the West's approach was sober and restrained. It was not yet in touch with the East's Theophilus legend which would so profoundly influence Mariology in the Middle Ages.

The Middle Ages

The idea that Mary appeases the wrath of God, the stern Judge, had been expressed by Germanus in the eighth century. It became one of the most popular themes of medieval Marian piety and devotion. Her power to save us was proclaimed even more dramatically by the story of Theophilus, which was translated into Latin by Paul the Deacon (d. ca. 799), a monk of Monte Cassino who had spent four years at the court of Charlemagne. Paul's version familiarized Western Christians with the story of the man who, like Dr. Faustus, gives his soul to the devil in order to get a desired post. Afterwards he repents and asks Mary to obtain forgiveness for his terrible sin. She does, and the devil is forced to yield control. Mary is seen in the West now, as in the East, as the redemptrix of captives, as refuge of sinners, as mediatrix between God and humankind. The legend was reproduced even by serious theologians and made the subject of a play in which Christ is portrayed as a menacing Judge whose heart is softened only by the pleas of his mother. She also became known as "Star of the Sea" who guides us safely into heaven's port, and as the "Mother of Mercy."

By now theology in the West had become increasingly divorced from the Bible. A rational, deductive kind of argumentation prevailed. One form, to which we referred above, was known as the argument from convenience. Its structure was simple: God (or Christ) *could* do something; it was *fitting* that he should; therefore, he *did* it. *Potuit, decuit, fecit.* This principle would play a large role in the development of medieval Mariology.

One of the most influential of all medieval theologians on the development of Mariology was *Bernard of Clairvaux* (d. 1153). His sermons "In Praise of the Virgin Mary" were as influential as the legend of Theophilus in confirming the medieval Christian in his or her childlike trust in the all-powerful help of Mary. He influenced not only popular devotion but theology as well. It was Bernard's view that Mary had an intimate role in the redemption. She was the aqueduct that leads the waters of divine grace down to earth. God willed us to have "everything through Mary," a saying that became a principle of Mariology, to be repeated again and again by popes, theologians, and spiritual writers down to Pope Pius XII in the middle of the twentieth century.

Bernard did not deny that Christ was the one true Mediator, but felt that men and women might be afraid of him because he is also their God and their Judge. Hence we need "a mediator with that Mediator, and there is no one more efficacious than Mary." If Bernard used the image of the aqueduct, others used the image of the neck. Mary is the neck which joins the Head with the rest of the Body of Christ, which is the Church.

Despite his intense devotion to Mary, Bernard was a strong opponent of the doctrine of the Immaculate Conception, and his whole Order followed his lead. Anselm of Canterbury also opposed the belief as well as the feast. When the feast began making headway in the West, Bernard addressed himself vehemently to the issue. He called the belief a "superstition." It was enough, he insisted, that Mary was sanctified in the womb and remained sinless throughout her life. The doctrine was opposed, because of Bernard and Peter Lombard's *Sentences*, until the beginning of the fourteenth century, at which time two English Franciscans opened a wedge in the opposition: William of Ware (d. early 1300s) and Duns Scotus (d. 1308).

William insisted that he would rather err in giving the Blessed Virgin too much than too little. To that end he employed the medieval formula: *potuit, decuit, fecit.* He also repeated the legend current in England that St. Bernard appeared to a lay brother soon after death in a radiant white garment, on which there was one small stain: his error in the matter of the Immaculate Conception. Scotus' argument was more sophisticated. Christ, he said, was primarily a Redeemer. He came to redeem us not only from actual sin, but from Original Sin. As our most perfect Redeemer, it is to be expected that he would have exercised his power to overcome even Original Sin at least once; and so it was, in the case of his mother. Scotus' approach effectively silenced those who sought to protect the universality of the redemption, and who objected that the Immaculate Conception would leave Mary without any indebtedness to Christ. On the contrary, she owed him more than any other creature because he preserved her alone from sin. The chief opponents were the Dominicans, who followed the lead of their greatest doctor, Thomas Aquinas.

Thomas based his opposition to the Immaculate Conception on the grounds that it would detract from the universality of Christ's redemptive work. Mary was sanctified in the womb and, as such, was the greatest of all the saints of history. Furthermore, her dignity is in some sense infinite because the infinite God took flesh from her. On the other hand, Thomas confined her mediating role to the fact that she gave birth to Christ, the author of grace. He had nothing to say about her connection with the redemptive work on the cross. Bonaventure, contemporary and friend of Thomas, similarly opposed the doctrine, quoting from Bernard. But Bonaventure also ascribed to her some role in the redemptive act of the cross, when she consented to the sacrifice of her Son and paid the price of her compassion. This view led eventually to belief in Mary as Co-Redemptrix of the human race, even though Bonaventure himself insisted on the uniqueness of Christ's redemptive act. One of his sermons, which became widely popular, suggested that Christ reserved to himself the realm of justice while ceding to his mother the realm of mercy.

With this growing reliance on Mary's protection, devotional forms continued to proliferate. "The Little Office of Our Lady" was recommended for use by the laity. The "Hail Mary" became one of the basic prayers to be learned by all the faithful, along with the Lord's Prayer and the Apostles' Creed. Saturday was dedicated to Mary, as Sunday was to Christ. Marian antiphons were composed between the eleventh and twelfth centuries: *Alma Redemptoris Mater* ("Sweet Mother of the Redeemer"), *Ave Regina Caelorum* ("Hail, Queen of Heaven"), *Regina Caeli* ("Queen of Heaven"), and *Salve Regina* ("Hail, [Holy] Queen"). Marian litanies also originated at this time, one of which (the Litany of Loreto) had as many as seventy-three invocations. By the early twelfth century the rosary was in general use. It began as a substitute for the Psalter (a book of one hundred and fifty psalms). The Hail Marys were divided into three groups of fifty and were called *rosarium* after Mary's title *"rosa mystica"* ("mystical rose"). They were eventually counted on beads which had come into use about this time for counting the "Our Fathers" given as a penance. The beginnings of the *Angelus* also appeared: the recitation of Hail Marys and prayers to Mary three times a day, at the ringing of the Angelus bells. The devotion became especially popular when the danger of Turkish invasion in the latter part of the fifteenth century led people to have recourse to the protection of the Blessed Mother.

Marian visions and special revelations, although reported from the earliest centuries, now increased and became more elaborate. St. Brigid of Sweden (d. 1373) claimed that Mary herself confirmed the doctrine of the Immaculate Conception in a private apparition to her. Images of Mary were thought to have miraculous powers, and in the fourteenth century the Holy House of Loreto was believed to have been transported through the air from Nazareth. It became one of the most popular places of pilgrimage. The *Divine Comedy* of Dante Alighieri (d. 1321) sums up the Mariology of the Middle Ages by depicting her as having influence throughout the entire universe: earth, purgatory, heaven, and even hell.

The Reformation to the Mid-Nineteenth Century

All of the great Reformers were brought up as Catholics and shared some measure of contemporary Catholic spirituality—especially Luther, who pointed to Mary as an example of faith and of the goodness of God. But we should ask neither her nor any of the saints for anything. Everything comes from the hand of God alone. The others, Calvin and Zwingli in particular, retained even less of contemporary Catholic spirituality, but they, too, attested to the purity of Mary. They objected, however, to the tendency to ascribe qualities to her which apply only to God—e.g., "our life, our sweetness, and our hope." At first, some of the Marian feasts were retained by the Protestants, but in due course they disappeared from their liturgical calendars.

Defense of Marian devotion and of her important role in our redemption was mounted by the Council of Trent and by various Counter-Reformation theologians: Peter Canisius (d. 1597), Francis Suarez (d. 1617), Robert Bellarmine (d. 1621).

Marian spirituality took another turn with the appearance of the French School: Cardinal de Bérulle (d. 1629), Jean-Jacques Olier (d. 1657), Jean Eudes (d. 1680), and Louis Grignion de Monfort (d. 1716). The last figure had the most enduring influence, having initiated the so-called "true devotion" to the Blessed Virgin, requiring absolute surrender to Mary as mystics had surrendered themselves to Christ. This, he argued, was the only effective way to Christ. If we presented ourselves directly to him, he would see our self-love, but to present ourselves through Mary is to get by his weak side.

With the rise of rationalism in the eighteenth century, Catholic theology assumed a more skeptical posture—e.g., in the works of Cardinal Lambertini, the future Pope Benedict XIV (d. 1758), who laid down rules for the treatment of miracles and mystical phenomena. Benedict protected L.A. Muratori (d. 1750), who had written a treatise on *Moderation in Matters of Religion*, in which he opposed the so-called "bloody vow" to defend the doctrine of the Immaculate Conception even to the shedding of blood. Muratori also attacked other exaggerations of Marian piety—e.g., that Mary could give orders in heaven. In the second half of the eighteenth century, under the impact of the Enlightenment, mild skepticism turned to strong opposition, and the liturgy was stripped of most Marian feasts. Theologians were no longer interested in Mariology, and popular devotions were confined now to Italy, Spain, and a few other places untouched by the general European currents of thought.

In Italy Marian devotion was kept alive through the work of the Redemptorists, and especially of St. Alphonsus Ligouri (d. 1787), whose book *The Glories of Mary* defended two beliefs: the Immaculate Conception and Mary's universal mediation of grace. He repeated the medieval idea that Christ is the king of justice, while Mary is the mother of mercy. She alone knows how to appease an angry God by her prayers. Alphonsus supported his teaching by a large number of quotations from medieval authors, including the revelations of St. Brigid. He also reproduced, without critical comment, a wealth of legends and miracles. His book was warmly received in southern Europe and in France, and it remained popular throughout the nineteenth century.

From the Dogma of the Immaculate Conception (1854) to the Dogma of the Assumption (1950)

The dogma of the Immaculate Conception holds that Mary, the Mother of Jesus, was free from Original Sin from the very moment of her conception. The Immaculate Conception of Mary is often confused with the virginal conception of Jesus. The former was described as a "pious doctrine" by the Council of Basle in its thirty-sixth session (1439), but by that time the council was no longer in communion with the pope and, therefore, its decrees were not regarded as binding. Ten years later, however, all members of the University of Paris were required to take an oath to defend it, and other universities followed suit. In 1476 the feast of the Immaculate Conception was approved by Pope Sixtus IV (d. 1484), and the Council of Trent in the next century explicitly excluded Mary from its decree on the universality of Original Sin (*Decree on Original Sin*, Session V, 1546). In 1661 Pope Alexander VII (d. 1667) forbade any attacks on the doctrine, so that even the Dominicans, who had originally opposed it, began to change sides, taking pains to establish that perhaps St. Thomas had not really been opposed to it in the first place.

Interest in the doctrine waned until early in the nineteenth century when on December 17, 1830, St. Catherine Labouré (d. 1876) claimed to have had a vision of the Immaculate Conception, standing on a globe, rays of light emanating from her hands spread out towards the earth. The vision was surrounded by an oval frame on which appeared the words: "O Mary, conceived without sin, pray for us who have recourse to thee." A voice commanded Catherine to have a medal struck depicting the vision. The medal was named "miraculous" because miracles were attributed to it, and it stimulated renewed interest in the doctrine and in demands for its definition.

Pope Gregory XVI (d. 1846) did not accede to these demands, in deference to objections of liberal Catholics in Europe, especially in Germany, France, and England. The situation changed with the succession of Pope Pius IX (d. 1878) to the chair of Peter. He immediately initiated proceedings leading to a definition.

There was a consultation with some six hundred and three bishops, fifty-six of whom, including the archbishop of Paris, opposed the definition. In a papal bull of December 8, 1854, entitled *Ineffabilis Deus* ("Ineffable God"), Pius IX solemnly decreed that "the most Blessed Virgin Mary was, from the first moment of her conception, by the singular grace and privilege of almighty God and in view of the merits of Christ Jesus the Savior of the human race, preserved immune from all stain of original sin, [that this] is revealed by God and, therefore, firmly and constantly to be believed by all the faithful." Thus, the dogma followed the line taken by Duns Scotus, overcoming the difficulty posed by Thomas Aquinas that the Immaculate Conception would infringe upon the universality of Christ's redemptive work.

The dogma was positively received by most Catholics, but it created a storm of protest from Protestants and Orthodox alike. Protestants rejected the view that Mary was unlike the rest of the human race, and the Orthodox dissented from the dogma's underlying notion of Original Sin. For the Orthodox, sin is human infirmity with which every person is afflicted.

The appearance to Catherine Labouré was only one of many attributed to Mary. In 1846 she was reported to have been seen by a young boy and a young girl at La Salette in the French Alps. She appeared sitting on a stone, her face in her hands, weeping over the sins of desecration of Sunday and of blasphemy. After much controversy the apparition was approved, a shrine was erected in 1852, and a missionary congregation, the Missionaries of La Salette, was founded. In 1858 another well-known series of appearances occurred near Lourdes, in France, to Bernadette Soubirous, a simple girl of fourteen. She was ordered by the Blessed Mother to drink from a previously invisible fountain which sprang up as Bernadette scratched the ground. After much consternation and debate, officials asked Bernadette to seek the lady's name. "I am the Immaculate Conception" was the reply. An increasing number of pilgrims came to the site, which was officially recognized in 1862. By the turn of the century a large church had been built and the place became, and remains, a center of devotional interest, with many physical cures attributed to the spring water.

Still another famous apparition was reported in Fatima, a small Portuguese town, in 1917. Again there were small children involved: a ten-year-old girl and two of her younger cousins, all tending sheep at the time. The apparition revealed herself as "the Lady of the Rosary" and urged everyone to pray for peace. A shrine was built and in 1931 permission was given for devotion to Our Lady of Fatima. Other major Marian shrines are located at Guadalupe in Mexico, Knock in Ireland, Czestochowa in Poland, and Montserrat in Spain.

Although various popes since Pius IX mentioned Mary in their official pronouncements, no pope did more to emphasize the importance of Marian devotion than Pope Pius XII (d. 1958), who was particularly devoted to Our Lady of Fatima. He consecrated the entire world to the Immaculate Heart of Mary in 1942, and on the occasion spoke in Portuguese as if to underline the connection between this act of consecration and the events at Fatima. His major contribution, however, was the definition of yet another Marian dogma, that of the bodily assumption of Mary into heaven. It was her "crowning glory . . . to be preserved from the corruption of the tomb," he wrote in his Apostolic Constitution *Munificentissimus Deus* (1950), "and, like her Son before her, to conquer death and to be raised body and soul to the glory of heaven, to shine refulgent as Queen at the right hand of her Son, the immortal King of ages."

There were, of course, many in the Catholic Church who questioned the opportuneness of such a definition. It seemed to them unnecessarily provocative at a time when ecumenical relations among the churches were just gaining strength. On the other hand, it was argued that the human race had just witnessed two world wars and the horrors of concentration camps, and that this was an appropriate moment to reaffirm the dignity of the human body and to rekindle faith in the resurrection of the body. Many, therefore, welcomed the definition.

The terms of the definition, however, are open to legitimate difference of interpretation. It is not clear whether the pope intended to teach that Mary died at all, and nothing is said about the manner or time of her assumption. Protestant reaction was negative, but this time the Orthodox were more positive, since this was a doctrine they also had held for centuries.

Three years later Pope Pius XII declared a Marian year (December 8, 1953—December 8, 1954) in honor of the centenary of the dogma of the Immaculate Conception. He urged frequent sermons on Mary and encouraged visits to her shrines, especially Lourdes. Marian congresses were held, and many books and articles were published. At the end of the year the pope established yet another Marian feast, her Queenship, on May 31, at which time the consecration of the world to the Immaculate Heart of Mary was to be renewed.

Vatican II

An entire chapter (chapter 8) is devoted to "The Role of the Blessed Virgin Mary, Mother of God, in the Mystery of Christ and the Church" in the Second Vatican Council's *Dogmatic Constitution on the Church*. The Preface notes that Mary, who is "acknowledged and honored as being truly the Mother of God and Mother of the Redeemer" and who "surpasses all other creatures," at the same time "belongs to the offspring of Adam [and] is one with all human beings in their need for salvation" (n. 53). She is also the Mother of the Church since, according to St. Augustine, "she cooperated out of love so that there might be born in the Church the faithful, who are members of Christ their Head." Accordingly, she is "a preeminent and altogether singular member of the Church, and . . . the Church's model and excellent exemplar, in faith and charity. Taught by the Holy Spirit, the Catholic Church honors her with filial affection and piety as a most beloved mother" (n. 53). The council comes very close here to calling Mary "Mother of the Church," but it was left to Pope Paul VI to do so explicitly in his closing speech at the end of the third session, November 21, 1964.

The rest of the eighth chapter is divided into three parts: Mary's role in the economy of salvation, her relationship with the Church, and Marian devotions. Her cooperation in the work of salvation is foreshadowed in the Old Testament (n. 55) and is rooted fundamentally in her assent to become the Mother of God

(n. 56). Throughout this section, however, the council consistently follows the most benign interpretation of her role in Jesus' ministry. Thus, the harshness of Mark 3:31-35 is passed over, and the document simply reads: "He declared blessed (cf. Mark 3:35 and parallels; Luke 11:27-28) those who heard and kept the Word of God, as she was faithfully doing (cf. Luke 2:19,51)" (n. 57).

Mary's role continues in the life of the Church, but without any obscuring or diminution of the "unique mediation of Christ" (n. 60). None of the titles given to her, e.g., Advocate, Auxiliatrix, Adjutrix, Mediatrix, adds to, nor subtracts from, "the dignity and efficacy of Christ the one Mediator" (n. 62). On the other hand, the unique mediation of Christ "does not exclude but rather gives rise among creatures to manifold cooperation which is but a sharing in this unique source. The Church does not hesitate to profess this subordinate role of Mary" (n. 62).

With St. Ambrose the council affirms that Mary is a model of the Church "in the matter of faith, charity, and perfect union with Christ" (n. 63). The Church, too, acts as a mother by accepting God's word in faith and by bringing forth children by Baptism to a new and everlasting life. The Church is also a virgin "who keeps whole and pure the fidelity she has pledged to her Spouse" (n. 64). Although Mary has already reached perfection, the Church continues on pilgrimage (n. 65).

From the most ancient times Mary has been revered as the "God-bearer" (*Deipara*), and this is the foundation of the special devotion, or cult, that is directed toward her. But this cult differs "essentially" from the cult of adoration which is offered to the incarnate Word, as well as to the Father and the Holy Spirit. Thus, although the Church has endorsed many forms of Marian piety, the Church always insisted that they be "within the limits of sound and orthodox doctrine. These forms have varied according to the circumstances of time and place and have reflected the diversity of native characteristics and temperament among the faithful" (n. 66). Furthermore, theologians and preachers should "carefully and equally avoid the falsity of exaggeration on the one hand, and the excess of narrow-mindedness on the other.... Let them painstakingly guard against any word or deed which could lead separated brethren or anyone else into error regarding the true doctrine of the Church. Let the faithful remember moreover that true devotion consists neither in fruitless and passing emotion, nor in a certain vain credulity" (n. 67).

How explain the discrepancy between the Marian maximalism of nineteenth- and twentieth-century devotional life and papal teachings, on the one hand, and the relatively restrained and balanced Mariology of the Second Vatican Council on the other? The answer is the same here as in chapter 19. Before Vatican II there was more than a single theological current, i.e., the "approved theology" of the manuals. While the "approved authors" continued to speak of the Church as a hierarchical society organized according to a papal-monarchical norm, other theologians, such as Congar, de Lubac, and Rahner, spoke of the Church as the People of God and the sacrament of Christ. It was this latter current that entered the conciliar mainstream, not the textbook theology.

The same was the case with Mariology. The "approved authors," assiduously and not a little uncritically, had followed the lead given by Popes Pius IX and Pius XII; other theologians, however, reworked the soil of history, transcended the culturally conditioned devotionalism of the medieval and post-medieval periods, and returned to the sources, i.e., the Bible and especially the Fathers of the Church.

This "return to the sources" began even in the nineteenth century with Cardinal John Henry Newman (d. 1890) and the German theologian Matthias Scheeben (d. 1888), both of whom captured the patristic spirit and made symbolism of the divine motherhood and of Eve the focal points of their reflections. Newman, however, was the more restrained of the two, rejecting suggestions that Mary somehow shares in the redemptive work of the cross or is the sole refuge of sinners. Scheeben, on the other hand, spoke of Mary as being also the bride of Christ, a mediatrix, a co-offerer of the sacrifice of the cross, and the spiritual mother of humankind. By the 1950s and early 1960s, just before the opening of Vatican II, other influential Catholic theologians had turned their attention to Mary, placing the Marian doctrines in the wider context of the mystery of salvation in Christ and the mystery of the

Church, just as the council would do: René Laurentin, Otto Sem-melroth, Karl Rahner, Edward Schillebeeckx, and Yves Congar. This was true also of Cardinal Leo-Jozef Suenens, one of the most important figures at Vatican II (see his *Mary the Mother of God*, 1959).

THE MARIAN DOGMAS
The Immaculate Conception

How one finally understands and explains the dogma of the Immaculate Conception will depend in very large measure on how one understands and explains the doctrine of Original Sin (see chapter 5). If Original Sin means being conceived and born with a "black spot" on the soul, or being conceived and born without grace, then the dogma of the Immaculate Conception means that Mary alone was born in the state of grace. That interpretation assumes, in turn, that "sanctifying grace" is not given for the first time until Baptism or until an unbaptized human being has an opportunity to make a free act of obedience to the will of God (under the impact, or course, of "actual grace").

If, on the other hand, one understands Original Sin as the *sinful condition* in which every human being is born, then we have to propose a different explanation for the Immaculate Conception. It is not that Mary alone was conceived and born in grace, but that, in view of her role in the redemption, God bestowed upon her an unsurpassable degree of grace from the beginning. This is not to be understood in any quantitative sense. Grace is divine life. To be in the "state of grace" is to be in union with God: God in us, and we in God. By reason of Mary's unique call to be the Mother of the incarnate Word, she was from the very beginning of her existence united with God in the most intimate of ways. And this union was, in turn, grounded in the yet-to-be-accomplished redemptive work of the Son she was to bear.

This does not mean that Mary was exempt also from the "consequences" of Original Sin: sickness, suffering, even death. These, too, are part of the human condition, and they are part of the mystery of sin. We do not know why we are subject to physical deterioration; we only know *that* we are. Paul attributed this condition to sin, just as those before him in the Old Testament consistently linked sin and human suffering. But we no longer accept that connection, nor are we required to do so by the doctrine of the Church. Suffering is a part of the human condition, but we do not know why. Sin is also part of the human condition, and we do not know ultimately why either. We *do* know that we freely sin in individual instances, and that this is a reflection of the sinful situation in which we are all born.

The dogma of the Immaculate Conception teaches that Mary was exempt in a unique and exceptional way from the normal and the usual impact of sin, or, more positively, that she was given a greater degree of grace (i.e., God was more intensely present to her than to others) in view of her role as the "God-bearer." So profound is her union with God in grace, in anticipation of her maternal function and in virtue of the redemptive grace of Christ, that she alone remains faithful to God's will throughout her entire life. *She is truly redeemed, but in an exceptional and unique manner.* The Immaculate Conception shows that God can be, and is, utterly gracious toward us, not by reason of our merits but by reason of divine love and mercy.

The Assumption

The dogma of the Assumption complements the dogma of the Immaculate Conception in the same way that the resurrection of Christ complements his crucifixion and life of sacrificial service to others. Just as the Immaculate Conception was not merely a personal privilege conferred upon Mary but a reality bestowed in view of her role in the economy of salvation, so the Assumption is not merely a personal privilege unrelated to the wider mission of her life. Her union with God in Christ was unique from the beginning. Her call to final union with God in Christ, in the totality of her human existence (body and soul), was also unique in the end. The dogma of the Assumption asserts something about human existence in asserting something about Mary: that human existence is bodily existence, and that we are destined for glory not only in the realm of the spiritual but in the realm of the material as well.

In the midst of the anguish and distress of this generation, the Church, so readily accused of being political
and attached to earthly power, of liking to install herself
far too positively in this world, of being insufficiently
eschatological, raises her head and by proclaiming this
doctrine of the faith, gazes towards the only hope in
which she really trusts, the future of God, who is so far
advanced with his Kingdom, that he has already begun
to be wholly present. The Church looks on high and
greets in Mary her own type and model, her own future
in the resurrection of the body.

(Karl Rahner, *Mary Mother of the Lord*, pp. 91-92.)

Binding Force

In defining the dogma of the Immaculate Conception, Pope Pius
IX warned all those who might be tempted to reject his teaching:
"If, therefore, any persons shall dare to think—which God forbid—otherwise than has been defined by us, let them clearly know
that they stand condemned by their own judgment, that they have
made shipwreck of their faith and fallen from the unity of the
Church." Pope Pius XII issued a similarly severe warning in
connection with the definition of the dogma of the Assumption:
"Wherefore, if anyone—which God forbid—should willfully dare
to deny or call in doubt what has been defined by us, let him know
that he certainly has abandoned the divine and catholic faith."

What is to be said, finally, of the binding force of these
dogmas of faith? (1) Is it possible to deny them and at the same time
remain in the Church? (2) Is it possible to deny them and remain in
the *Catholic* Church?

Concerning the first, Catholics do not hold that membership
in Christ's Church is restricted to persons who formally and
explicitly accept these two Marian dogmas. There is "an order or
'hierarchy' of truths, since they vary in their relationship to the
foundation of the Christian faith" (*Decree on Ecumenism*, n. 11).
No one could reasonably hold that the dogmas of the Immaculate
Conception and the Assumption are so central to Christian faith
that the faith itself would disintegrate without either or both.

Such would be the case, on the other hand, if one were to deny the divinity of Jesus Christ or the redemptive value of his life, death, and resurrection.

Furthermore, the Second Vatican Council permitted limited eucharistic sharing between Catholics and Orthodox, even though the Orthodox do not accept both of these dogmas (*Decree on Eastern Catholic Churches*, nn. 26-29). The presumption must be that, in spite of differences on these two dogmas, the unity of Christian faith that *is* present between Catholics and Orthodox is sufficient for eucharistic sharing. The same kind of reasoning could conceivably be extended to the cases of other Christian communities, such as the Anglicans and the Lutherans.

Concerning the second question (Is membership in the *Catholic* Church contingent upon acceptance of these dogmas?), the problem arises because each of these two dogmatic definitions is accompanied by an anathema or its equivalent. According to canon law, an anathema involves an excommunication (Code of Canon Law, c. 2257, #2), but that consequence follows only when the rejection of the dogma is culpable, obstinate, and externally manifested.

What of those Catholics who wish to belong to the Catholic Church, who confess the Lordship of Jesus, who assemble for the Eucharist in faith, who accept the Word of God, and who bear witness to the Gospel in their love of and service to their neighbor? The questioning or even denial of these dogmas should not be regarded today as presumptive evidence of a lapse from Christian faith, nor even from Catholic faith. It could be that in their questioning or denial of these dogmas, some Catholics are reacting not against the Word of God to which these dogmas propose to bear witness, but against the inadequacy, incompleteness, limited expressive power, and historically-conditioned character of these definitions. If such Catholics are otherwise faithful to their Catholic heritage and to the practice of their Catholic faith, would it not be more appropriate to presume the opposite—namely, that they are sincere in their questioning and even denial of these dogmas (i.e., not culpable or obstinate) and that their rejection implies no correlative rejection of the major truths of faith with which these dogmas are related, e.g., the redemptive significance of Christ's life, death, and resurrection; our hope in the resurrection of the body; the power of God's grace to overcome completely the impact of sin?

It is possible, of course, that a Catholic's rejection of either or both of these Marian dogmas would be a sign that one has separated himself or herself from the Catholic tradition and faith, and therefore from communion with the Catholic Church, just as Popes Pius IX and Pius XII warned. A person might, for example, reject these definitions precisely because they are papal actions. That person might believe that the Petrine office has no necessary place in the life and mission of the Church for the benefit of the Church universal. Such a view would effectively disengage one from the Catholic tradition and the community which embodies it. This is not to say, on the other hand, that a faithful and committed Catholic could not question the *process* by which these dogmas were formulated.

MARIAN DEVOTIONS: THEOLOGICAL CRITERIA

There are *two extremes* to be avoided in one's attitude toward devotion to Mary. *First*, there is a temptation to so exaggerate the *divine* role in salvation that the value and importance of *human cooperation* is lost (see the discussion of nature and grace in chapter 5). In this view, human cooperation plays no role at all in our salvation. Therefore, no fellow creature, Mary included, is ever worthy of veneration, because such attention inevitably detracts from the glory owed to God alone and to Jesus Christ in whom and through whom God acted on our behalf for the forgiveness of sins. The consequence of this first extreme is Marian *minimalism*, or "mariophobia."

The *second* temptation is to exaggerate the *human* role in salvation at the expense of the divine and correspondingly to deemphasize the effectiveness of the *mediating work of Christ*, who is perceived as more divine than human. And if he is more divine than human, he is not so much our bridge to God as he is the God from whom we have been alienated by sin. We need access, therefore, not only to the Father but the Son as well. According to this view, we need other ways of reaching God, and these ways must be adapted to our own limited human condition. Consequently, we turn to our fellow human beings who have already won the crown of glory and who have obviously "done something right" in the sight of God. But Mary alone, among the entire "class" assembled by God, achieved a "straight-A record" and earned the enthusiastic favor of her divine Master. It is through the saints, but especially through Mary, the greatest of saints, that we can hope to reach Christ and ultimately reach the Father of our salvation. There is no limit to the help she can give us, nor is there any limit to the veneration we can show her in virtue of her standing before God. The consequence of this second extreme is Marian *maximalism*, or "mariocentricism."

Marian minimalism in effect denies (or at least narrowly applies) the principle of secondary or *instrumental causality*, i.e., that God works through finite agents to achieve infinite ends. It also denies (or narrowly applies) the principle of *sacramentality*, i.e., that God is present to us, is disclosed, and works on our behalf in and through visible, material realities: persons, events, nature, objects, the cosmos. (It is not always clear if the Marian minimalist understands that the humanity of Jesus Christ is also an instrumental cause and sacrament of salvation.) And it denies, finally, that the Church is a *communion of saints*, i.e., that our relationship with God and with Christ is both vertical and horizontal, and that our relationship is always *mediated*. "God vividly manifests to humankind his presence and his face. He speaks to us in them, and gives us a sign of his Kingdom, to which we are powerfully drawn, surrounded as we are by so many witnesses (cf. Hebrews 12:1), and having such an argument for the truth of the gospel" (*Dogmatic Constitution on the Church*, n. 50). Nor is it only by reason of the example the saints give us that we cherish their memory and render them our devotion. "We do so still more in order that the union of the whole Church may be strengthened. . . . For just as Christian communion among wayfarers brings us closer to Christ, so our companionship with the saints joins us to Christ. . . . For by its very nature every genuine testimony of love which we show to those in heaven tends toward and terminates in Christ, who is the 'crown of all saints' " (n. 50). According to the council, that union of all faithful Christians, living and dead, is expressed and celebrated in a particularly effective manner in the sacred liturgy and especially in the Eucharist.

Marian maximalism in effect exaggerates the secondary or *instrumental causality* of Mary and the other saints and demeans the instrumental causality of the humanity of Christ. It also misunderstands the *sacramental principle*. Sacramentality means that God works *in* and *through* some visible, material reality. It is always the inner transforming presence of God that ultimately counts, and not the sign and instrument of that presence. Therefore, it is not because Mary and the saints have the power of influence with God that they are objects of veneration and devotion. Rather it is because the grace of God has triumphed *in them*. They have been transformed by, and have become effective images of, Christ (*Dogmatic Constitution on the Church*, n. 50). It is Christ's, not Mary's, achievement that we celebrate. Finally, Marian maximalism misunderstands the nature of the *communion of saints*. The Church is not just an institution of salvation, with Mary and the saints as "successful graduates" who have some measure of influence with "the administration." It is not comparable to a filling station, where automobiles replenish their supply of fuel. The Church is the People of God, the Body of Christ, and the Temple of the Holy Spirit. It is, first and foremost, a *community (communio, koinonia)*, but not just any community. It is a community of those who have been transformed by Christ and the Holy Spirit and who have explicitly and thankfully acknowledged the source of that transformation. Since transformation is a process, to be completed when the Kingdom of God is fully realized at the end of history, our bond in Christ and the Spirit is not broken by death. Mary is the preeminent member of this communion of saints. Our link with her is an expression of our link with the whole Church. It is a bond, however, not just of advocates and supplicants, but of brothers and sisters in the Lord, the very Body of Christ on the way to achieving "the fullness of God" (Ephesians 3:19).

Between these two extremes of Marian minimalism and Marian maximalism there is wide spectrum of legitimate devotional options. One should be careful not to categorize pejoratively those forms of spirituality with which one is not personally comfortable or from which one feels culturally alienated. The following *theological criteria* might be helpful in evaluating various expressions of Marian devotion:

1.   Devotion to Mary, and to all of the saints, is ultimately devotion to Christ, whose grace has triumphed in Mary and the saints.

2.   Jesus Christ in his humanity and divinity alike is the one Mediator between God and humankind. In him we are forgiven our sins, for he is full of mercy and compassion toward us.

3.   On the other hand, just as God worked through the instrumentality of Jesus' humanity for our salvation, so divine grace is symbolized and mediated through other visible, material, bodily realities, including those fellow creatures who have shown themselves striking examples of the transforming power of this grace.

4.   Since God saves us not just as individuals but as members of a people, we are joined one with another in a community of saints, i.e., of "holy ones" sharing in the holiness (the life) of God. "Be holy, for I, the Lord, your God, am holy" (Leviticus 19:2).

5.   Mary is, by reason of her faith and obedience to the Word of God, a model of the Church and is its preeminent member. She is a disciple *par excellence.*

6.   Insofar as Mary is truly the mother of Jesus Christ, she can be called the "God-bearer." Again, she is a model for the Church in that the Church, too, is a "reality imbued with the hidden presence of God" (Pope Paul VI). Just as the hidden presence of God is the basis of all that we believe about the Church in faith, so it is also the basis of all that we believe about Mary in faith.

7.   And yet just as the Church is not itself the Kingdom of God, even though the Church can be called "the initial budding forth" of the Kingdom (*Dogmatic Constitution on the Church*, n. 5), so Mary is not herself the mediator or the redeemer, even though she is the mother of Jesus and bears the incarnate Word within her.

8.   On the contrary, Mary is, before all else, one of the redeemed. Exemption from Original Sin does not mean that she

was herself in no need of the redemptive work of Christ. She was full of grace from the beginning precisely because of the redemptive work of Christ on her behalf.

9. It is less important *that* one affirms or denies some Marian belief than *why* one affirms it or denies it. Thus, on a relative scale at least, one is actually more "orthodox" in *denying* the Immaculate Conception because it might detract from the universality of the redemption (as Thomas Aquinas feared) than in affirming the Immaculate Conception on the grounds that Mary's closeness to God made the redemptive work of Christ unnecessary in her own unique case.

10. Apparitions, visions, and other unusual occurrences attributed directly or indirectly to Mary may or may not be believed. None of them can ever be regarded as essential to Christian faith, whether they are approved by the official Church or not. If these phenomena do have any final authority, they are authoritative only for those who directly and immediately experience them. No one but the recipient(s) can be bound in conscience by whatever is communicated.

11. In any case, the "contents" (messages, directives, etc.) of such events can never be placed on par with the Gospel itself, neither in terms of their authority nor in terms of the attention they elicit and/or demand. Those "contents," in turn, must always be measured against the totality of the Christian faith and must not contradict or contravene any essential component of that faith.

THE CHURCH AND MARY

"Neither the Gospel nor past Christian tradition have been able to separate Mary and the Church," the Protestant monk and theologian of Taizé, Max Thurian, has written. "To speak of Mary is to speak of the Church. The two are united in one fundamental vocation—maternity"(*Mary, Mother of the Lord, Figure of the Church*, p. 9).

There is, of course, more to the relationship between Mary and the Church than maternity, although that is certainly foundational. The Church is a mother in several senses. It brings forth new creatures in Christ out of the womb of the baptismal font. It nourishes the Christian family at the table of the Eucharist. It is the source of encouragement, of forgiveness, of order, of healing, of love. Each of these maternal activites is linked with one or another of the Church's seven sacraments.

Mary, too, is the mother of all Christians insofar as she is first of all the mother of Jesus Christ. She gives birth to Jesus and so makes it possible for Jesus to give birth to us anew in the Holy Spirit. As a model, or type, or figure, or image of the Church, Mary is preeminently a person of faith, of hope, of love, of obedience to the Word of God.

She is conceived without sin and in the fullness of grace, as the Church was. She is a faithful and undefiled virgin, as the Church is called to be. She is redeemed by Christ, as the Church is. She is the sign of God's presence among us, as the Church is. She is transformed and renewed by the presence of God within her, as the Church is. She shared fully in the resurrection of Christ, body and soul, as the Church is destined to share in it. And she intercedes for us before the throne of God, as the Church does.

Devotion to Mary is a characteristically Catholic phenomenon in that it expresses three fundamental principles of Catholic theology and practice: the principle of *mediation*, the principle of *sacramentality*, and the principle of *communion*.

Just as we say that the world is "mediated by meaning" (Bernard J. F. Lonergan), so the universe of grace is a mediated reality: mediated principally by Christ, and secondarily by the Church and other signs and instruments of salvation beyond the the Church. The Catholic understands the role of Mary in salvation and accepts it because the Catholic already understands and accepts the principle of mediation as applied in the incarnation and in the life and mission of the Church (a point made so effectively by Yves Congar in his *Christ, Our Lady, and the Church*, 1957).

The Catholic also understands that the invisible, spiritual God is present and available to us through the visible and the material, and that these, in turn, are made holy by reason of that divine presence. The Catholic therefore, readily engages in the veneration of Mary, not because Mary is confused with some ancient goddess or supercreature or rival of the Lord himself, but because Mary is herself a symbol or image of God. It is the God who is present within her and who fills her whole being that the Catholic grasps in the act of venerating yet another "sacrament" of the divine.

Finally, the Catholic perceives the Church as itself a communion of saints in its visible as well as its invisible dimensions. It is an institutionalized, structured reality in which and through which the grace of the Holy Spirit is disclosed, celebrated, and released for the renewal and reconciliation of the whole world. Our relationship with God and with Christ is not only bilateral but multilateral, which is to say communal. The Church *as* Church enters directly into that saving relationship with God and with Christ. It is not simply the place where one hears the Word of God and testifies to his or her faith in the Word. The Church is itself the very Body of Christ. To be *in* the church is to be *in* Christ and one *with* Christ. It is to share his "meaning" of reality and the "meanings" of those others who belong to his Body. So, too, devotion to Mary is consequent upon the fact that we are united with her, as with one another, in and with Christ. She is the preeminent member of the community of saints by reason of her unique relationship with Christ, but she is a member nonetheless, and the most exalted one at that. Our unity with her is an expression of our unity in and with Christ.

"In Mary," Otto Semmelroth writes, "the Church affirms her own holy, co-redemptive and redeemed essence.... Thus, the veneration of Mary is the Church's testimony to herself....(to her) own essence and to her task of imparting salvation" (*Mary, Archetype of the Church*, p. 174).

CONCLUDING REFLECTIONS

It was noted at the beginning of this chapter that some theologians still prefer to locate the theology of Mary between the theology of the redemption and the theology of the Church. Without suggesting that such an arrangement is theologically erroneous, the plan we have followed in this book presents Mary less as a collaborator of Christ *above* the Church than as the preeminent member of the *redeemed* community itself. As such, she is not so much a source of grace and power as she is an image, a model, a figure, or a type of the Church and of Christian existence. She provides, therefore, an important bridge between ecclesiology, on the one side, and Christian existence (ethics and spirituality), on the other. And that is precisely how and why our discussion of Mariology fits in here.

SUMMARY

1. *Mariology*, the theological study of the person and role of Mary, began in the Middle Ages as an appendix to Christology. By the end of the nineteenth century it had acquired a separate theological position immediately after the Incarnation and the Redemption and before the mystery of the Church. This book, however, follows the lead of the Second Vatican Council and places Mariology within the discussion of the Church. Mary is the type, model, mother, and preeminent member of the Church.

2. There is relatively little about Mary in the *New Testament*, and what does appear is not unequivocally positive. *Mark's* portrait is remarkably negative: Mary does not understand Jesus' ministry and even tries to interfere with it (3:20-35). *Matthew* and *Luke* tone down the harshness of Mark, and Luke in particular presents her as the obedient handmaid of the Lord from the beginning (see the Infancy Narratives) and as the spokeswoman for the poor of Israel. *John* also reports that Mary's faith was still imperfect during Jesus' public ministry (the Cana story), but at the foot of the cross she is clearly included by her Son in the eschatological family.

3. The New Testament says nothing about Mary's virginity *in partu* (i.e., nothing about a miraculous birth), nor does it say she was a virgin *post partum* (after the birth of Jesus). On the contrary, it speaks of brothers and sisters of Jesus. It is an open question, on the basis of the New Testament evidence alone, whether or not these references are to actual brothers and sisters or to cousins.

4. *Second century* literature on Mary is thin. Among the *apocrypha* (non-canonical writings) the most important was the *Protevangelium of James*, for centuries the source of many legends about Mary and the life of the Holy Family. Among the *patristic writings* (most of which do not even mention Mary), the main sources are *Ignatius of Antioch*, *Justin*, and *Irenaeus*, who witness to the virginal conception of Jesus and

who first develop the Eve-Mary parallel which would influence Christian thought thereafter.

5.   Discussions of Mary's *perpetual virginity* were complicated by the fact that, on the one hand, the Gnostics and Docetists denied the humanity of Jesus, and, on the other, by the fact that virginity was being emphasized within the Church at this time for ascetical reasons, and Mary presented a persuasive model for Christian women. Mary's virginity *post partum* came to be almost universally accepted from the third century on. John Chrysostom was an outstanding exception.

6.   *Nestorianism*, with its insistence on the dual personality of Jesus, *indirectly* fostered Mariological interest by provoking the *Council of Ephesus* (431) into defining that Mary is truly the Mother of God (*theotokos*) and not only the mother of Christ. The definition was directly a Christological one, not Mariological.

7.   Following Ephesus, Marian devotion increased. The apocryphal literature became popular again. *Liturgical feasts* were multiplied: the Annunciation, the Purification, the Assumption, and the Nativity of Mary (by the mid-seventh century all four were being observed in Rome). The feast of the Conception of Mary had its origin in the East at the end of the seventh century but was unknown in the West until the eleventh century.

8.   From the eighth century on, faith in Mary's *intercessory power* received a strong push from growing belief in her assumption, especially in the East.

9.   As popular Eastern legends (e.g., the story of Theophilus, who "sells" his soul to the devil only to have it saved by Mary) were translated and circulated in the West, and as theology in the West became increasingly divorced from the Bible and the Fathers, Mariology took a turn toward some measure of exaggeration. The principle of fittingness or convenience became important: If God *could* do something and it seemed *fitting* that it should be done, then God *must have* done it (*potuit, decuit, fecit*).

10.   One of the most influential Mariologists was *Bernard of Clairvaux*, who stressed Mary's role in the channeling of saving grace ("everything through Mary"). He did not deny that Christ was the one Mediator, but pointed out that he is also our God and Judge. Mary provides the component of mercy.

11.   Two centuries later controversy developed on the *Immaculate Conception*. Aquinas and others argued that such a doctrine would contradict the universality of redemption; Scotus replied that Mary, too, was redeemed, but that she was alone preserved from Original Sin in view of

her relationship with Christ and as a sign of Christ's power over Original Sin as well as over actual sins.

12.   As appreciation of Christ's co-humanity with us diminished, Mary's own mediating role was accentuated. Marian prayers, hymns, devotions, feasts, and reports of apparitions proliferated between the eleventh and fourteenth centuries.

13.   The *Reformers* resisted the underlying assumptions of much of this Marian devotion. God alone is "our life, our sweetness, and our hope," they insisted. Over against the Protestants, the *Council of Trent* and various Counter-Reformation theologians defended Marian devotion and Mary's role in our redemption.

14.   *Marian spirituality* continued to develop new forms in the seventeenth and eighteenth centuries, especially the French School ("True Devotion": absolute surrender to Mary in order to get by Christ's "weak" side). But the rise of *rationalism* and the coming of the *Enlightenment* tempered this spirituality, at least in northern Europe. Marian interest was kept alive where these intellectual movements had no impact—e.g., in the eighteenth century works of Alphonsus Ligouri, which incorporated many legends.

15.   Concern for the doctrine of the *Immaculate Conception* was rejuvenated in 1830 with a reported apparition of Mary to Catherine Labouré. In 1854 Pope Pius IX solemnly defined the Immaculate Conception as a *dogma of faith*, endorsing the approach taken by Scotus against Thomas.

16.   Other reported visions and apparitions (e.g., Lourdes, Fatima) along with various expressions of papal support for Marian devotions between 1854 and 1950 led to a second Marian definition, this time of the *Assumption*. A Marian year was declared in 1954.

17.   But there were *other theological currents* in process between the mid-nineteenth and mid-twentieth centuries. *Cardinal Newman* and *Matthias Scheeben* restored the patristic emphases on the symbolism of the divine maternity and of Eve as focal points for Mariology. Modern theologians such as Otto Semmelroth, Yves Congar, Karl Rahner, placed the Marian doctrines in a wider historical and ecclesiological context.

18.   This more restrained and more biblically and patristically grounded approach entered the mainstream of the *Second Vatican Council*, which emphasized Mary's role in the economy of salvation, her relationship with the Church, and the subordination of all Marian devotions to the unique mediation of Christ. The council also acknowledged that devotions are shaped by circumstances of time, place, temperament, and culture, and warned against exaggerations and excesses.

19. Our understanding of the dogma of the *Immaculate Conception* depends on our understanding of *Original Sin*. If grace is *not* given to all from the beginning, then Mary's Immaculate Conception means that she alone possessed grace from the moment of her conception. If grace *is* given to all from the beginning, then her Immaculate Conception means that she received the fullest degree of it, i.e., that her union with God was as intimate as any creature's could be in virtue of her role as the mother of the Lord. It does not mean, on the other hand, that Mary was also exempted from the "consequences" of our sinful condition: sickness, suffering, and even death. *She is truly redeemed, but in an exceptional and unique manner.*

20. The dogma of the *Assumption* complements the Immaculate Conception. The intimate union with God from the beginning of her existence is fulfilled at the end of her earthly life. The dogma attests to the fact our human existence is bodily existence, too, and that we are destined for glory in the totality of that existence.

21. These two dogmas are not so central or essential to the integrity of Christian faith that one cannot be in the Body of Christ without accepting them. Indeed, Vatican II encouraged limited eucharistic sharing with the Orthodox in spite of differences on these two dogmas. The council also acknowledged that there is a hierarchy of truths.

22. *Catholics who question or deny these dogmas* are not necessarily excluded from the Catholic Church. Such denial must be culpable, obstinate, and externally manifested. Those who do reject the dogmas may often be rejecting certain interpretations of them. Also, we must look at the whole orientation and pattern of a Catholic's life and thought. Is he or she also rejecting correlative doctrines (e.g., resurrection of the body, the redemptive significance of the life, death, and resurrection of Christ) or the very idea of the Petrine ministry? On the other hand, is the person faithful to the Eucharist, the sacraments, the Word of God, and the call to love of neighbor?

23. Two extremes are to be avoided in Marian devotion: a *minimalism* which withholds any and all veneration from Mary, and a *maximalism* which assumes there are practically no limits to such veneration.

24. *Marian minimalism* denies (or narrowly applies) the principle of *instrumental causality*, i.e., that God works through finite, secondary causes, including even the humanity of Christ. Marian minimalism also denies (or narrowly applies) the principle of *sacramentality*, i.e., that God is really present in the instrumental cause and does not simply use the instrument without transforming it from within. Finally, Marian

minimalism denies that the Church is a *communion of saints*, i.e., that our relationship with God is always *mediated*, and mediated through the community of faith and holiness of which Mary is the preeminent member.

25. *Marian maximalism* exaggerates the principle of *instrumental causality* in the case of Mary and deemphasizes it in the case of Christ. It also misunderstands the *sacramental* principle, i.e., that what the sign signifies is more important than the sign. Mary is important, therefore, not for herself but for the presence of God working in and through her. Finally, Marian maximalism misunderstands the nature of the *communion of saints*. Our bond with Mary and the saints is not simply one of supplicants to advocates. We are all brothers and sisters in the Lord on the way to the Kingdom of God.

26. *Criteria* for evaluating Marian devotions include the following: (1) Is Christ at the center? (2) Is he always a merciful and compassionate Christ? (3) Is there room for human cooperation with Christ? (4) Is there a sense of the Church as a communion of saints? (5) Is Mary's discipleship highlighted? (6) Is her sacramentality ("God-bearer") properly emphasized, and is it linked with the sacramentality of the Church? (7) Is Mary's role always properly subordinate to Christ's in the work of redemption? (8) Is it clear that she, too, is one of the redeemed? (9) If there are denials *or* affirmations of dogma, are the *reasons* orthodox? (10) The fact of apparitions is always an open question; no one is bound to accept them in faith except those to whom they are originally given. Who has received them? (11) The *content* of apparitions is always to be measured against the totality of Christian faith. Is the content consistent with that faith?

27. The relationship of *Mary and the Church* is *multilateral*. Both have *maternal* roles in the economy of salvation: the Church through the sacraments, and Mary through her giving birth to Christ. Both the Church and Mary are also filled with grace and redeemed by Christ, are signs of God's presence, are transformed and renewed by that presence, share in the resurrection, and intercede for all humankind before God.

28. *Devotion to Mary* is a characteristically Catholic phenomenon in that it expresses *three fundamental principles of Catholic theology and practice*: (1) The principle of *mediation* affirms that grace is a mediated reality, first through Christ and secondarily through the Church and other human instruments, including Mary. (2) The principle of *sacramentality* affirms that the invisible and the spiritual God is present through the visible and the material, and that these are, in turn, made holy by that presence. This includes Mary, in whom God is very specially

present. (3) The principle of *communion* affirms that the saving encounter with God occurs not only personally and individually but corporately and ecclesially. To be in the Church, i.e., to be in communion with other Christians, is to be in and with Christ. Mary is the preeminent member of this communion of saints. Our unity with her is an expression of our unity in and with Christ.

29.   Since Mary is one of the redeemed and a model of the Church and of Christian discipleship, Mariology provides a *bridge* between our understanding of the redeemed community, the Church, and the nature and dimensions of the redeemed life, i.e., Christian existence.

SUGGESTED READINGS

Brown, Raymond E., et al, eds. *Mary in the New Testament: A Collaborative Assessment by Protestant and Roman Catholic Scholars.* Philadelphia: Fortress Press, and New York: Paulist Press, 1978.

Congar, Yves. *Christ, Our Lady, and the Church.* Westminster, Md.: Newman Press, 1957.

Graef, Hilda. *Mary: A History of Doctrine and Devotion.* 2 vols. New York: Sheed & Ward, 1963.

Greeley, Andrew. *The Mary Myth: On the Femininity of God.* New York: Seabury Press, 1977.

Laurentin, René. *The Question of Mary.* New York: Holt, Rinehart & Winston, 1965.

Rahner, Karl. *Mary, Mother of the Lord: Theological Meditations.* New York: Herder & Herder, 1963.

Ruether, Rosemary, *Mary—The Feminine Face of the Church.* Philadelphia: Westminster Press, 1977.

Schillebeeckx, Edward. *Mary, Mother of the Redemption.* New York: Sheed & Ward, 1964.

Semmelroth, Otto. *Mary, Archetype of the Church.* New York: Sheed & Ward, 1963.

Suenens, Léon Joseph. *Mary the Mother of God.* New York: Hawthorn Books, 1959.

Thurian, Max. *Mary, Mother of the Lord, Figure of the Church.* London: Faith Press, 1963.

Vollert, Cyril. *A Theology of Mary.* New York: Herder & Herder, 1965.

PART FIVE

CHRISTIAN EXISTENCE: ETHICAL AND SPIRITUAL DIMENSIONS

CHRISTIAN EXISTENCE: ETHICAL AND SPIRITUAL DIMENSIONS

INTRODUCTION

Christian faith expresses itself through love (Galatians 5:6). Indeed, such faith does not really exist unless there is a commitment to the Gospel of Jesus Christ. This commitment is initially made, shaped and sustained within a community of faith, which is the Church.

We come in this last section of the book to the question of *Christian existence* in its ethical and spiritual dimensions. What does it mean to be a Christian: a disciple of Jesus Christ and a member of his Body, the Church? What kinds of decisions are consistent with the preaching of Jesus and the faith of the Church? What kinds of behavior advance the Kingdom of God? What styles of life distinguish the Christian from other human beings? What sort of hope does the Christian have that makes the Christian's vision of history different from the vision of others?

We began this book with the *question of ourselves* (Part I). Who are we? What does it mean to be human? How are we shaped by the world in which we live, and how do we, in turn, shape and direct its history?

The question of human existence led us next to the *question of God* (Part II). God is the answer we give to the question of meaning and purpose. The triune God—the God who calls us into being, who identifies with our human condition, who sustains us in our lives—is the God of Christian faith.

The God of Christian faith, more specifically still, is the God of Jesus Christ. Christ is both the Word of God addressed to us, and the way through which we gain access to God in return. And so we raised the *question of Jesus Christ* as the concrete, personal, and historical embodiment of what it really means to be human (Part III).

If Christ mediates the presence of God, so the Church mediates for us the presence of Christ. It is the communal and institutional expression, or sacrament, of Christ and of the Kingdom of God which he proclaimed and practiced. And so we moved from the question of Christ to the *question of the Church* (Part IV).

We raise here in Part V the *question of Christian existence* because we look for some experiential verification of the meaning we embrace in Christ and celebrate in the Church. Do his message and ministry, his life and death, really make sense? Is the way of Christ also the way to resurrection and new life? What does it mean to be converted to the Gospel, individually and as part of the total Christian movement known as the Church?

In chapter 25, therefore, we ask how Jesus understood the shape and substance of Christian discipleship? To what extent was his message in continuity with the faith of Israel, and to what extent was it a departure? How was the call to discipleship understood after the resurrection: within the New Testament churches, in the earliest centuries of the Church through the Middle Ages, and into the twentieth century?

In the light of this long and complex historical development, can we identify any distinguishing marks which set apart the moral vision of Christians in general and of Catholics in particular? Who is the Christian, according to this moral tradition? What kind of person is the Christian called to become? How does one become a Christian? What virtues and what sort of character does the authentic Christian display (chapter 26)?

How are the principles of Christian and Catholic moral theology applicable to specific dilemmas and conflict situations? For example, what is the Christian, and particularly the Catholic, to think of contraception, homosexuality, the use of military power, and the intervention of the state in social and economic matters (chapter 27)?

Beyond the requirements, obligations, and just demands of Christian existence, what sort of style or spirit should characterize the Christian's life, and the Church's? How does one establish a relationship with God, with Christ, with the Holy Spirit; and, once established, how is that relationship cultivated and sustained? Indeed, how does one even know that the relationship exists and/or that it is sound (chapter 28)?

If we are convinced in faith that human existence has meaning, that God is the ground of all reality, that Jesus Christ is the embodiment of God's love for the world, that the Church is the Body of Christ and the Temple of his reconciling Spirit, and that we are empowered by that same Holy Spirit to live according to the vocation to which we have been called (Ephesians 4:1), what do we hope for in the end? Is it a hope for ourselves alone? For the whole of humankind? For the whole of the world? For the whole of the created order? Is it a fragile hope, or a firm hope? Is the way to the Kingdom of God smooth and unimpeded, or is it marked by risk and sacrifice and even death? Can we even now enjoy the firstfruits of the final banquet (chapter 29)?

The Kingdom of God, on which not only Part V but the entire book is focused, is both the beginning and the end of Christian theology. The initial experience of God's renewing and reconciling presence, which *is* the Kingdom of God, evokes our theological quest for understanding and excites the hope that one day our union with God and with one another will be realized to its fullest, when God will be "all in all" (1 Corinthians 15:28).

· XXV ·

CHRISTIAN EXISTENCE: AN HISTORICAL PERSPECTIVE

MORAL THEOLOGY/CHRISTIAN ETHICS

Moral Theology

The standard distinction between "dogmatic" and "moral" theology has been drawn on the basis of a perceived difference between *theory* and *practice*. In dogmatic theology we specify what we must believe; in moral theology we determine what we are required to *do* (or *not* do) because of those beliefs. And the traditional catechisms would thereafter introduce the sacraments as those God-given "aids" to correct belief and moral action.

These distinctions, however, are based on a faulty understanding of the theory-practice relationship. The two are in reality not separate but are united in the one notion of *praxis*. *Praxis* means more than "practice" alone. It is practice-plus-reflection, and it is reflection-in-practice. Truth is not only to be thought but also done, and the doing of truth is a condition of grasping it. "But he who acts in truth comes into the light, to make clear that his deeds are done in God" (John 3:21). Similarly, Paul insists that "faith...expresses itself through love" (Galatians 5:6). Indeed, faith cannot exist, and does not exist, without commitment to the implementation of the Gospel. Systematic theology, therefore, must embrace both dogmatic (or doctrinal) *and* moral theology. This is how Thomas Aquinas understood their relationship in his *Summa Theologica*. The two disciplines were not formally separated until after the Council of Trent, as we shall see below.

On the other hand, reflection and practice do not collapse completely into one another. Although an *integral* understanding

of the Gospel is not possible without a commitment to, and practice of, the Gospel, most people will always find themselves far
short of the ideal. The relationship between theory and practice in
the integrating notion of *praxis* is a *dialectical* relationship, not
one of *identity*. It is possible, in other words, for a person to be a
sincere believer in the Gospel of Jesus Christ and yet not fully
practice what he or she believes and preaches. There is a psychological complexity to faith which is not touched by sociology or
economics alone. Some of the Latin American liberation theologians might not do complete justice to the reality of faith when
they suggest that faith is impossible and non-existent without
works. Indeed, the Council of Trent took pains to assert the
opposite: "If anyone says that with the loss of grace through sin
faith is also always lost, or that the faith which remains is not true
faith, granted that it is not a living faith; or that the man who has
faith without charity is not a Christian, *anathema sit*" (*Decree on
Justification*, canon 28, Session VI, 1547). For a *living* faith, there
must be an expression of love. But faith itself can exist, at least for
a time, without love. Thus, although systematic theology
embraces both dogmatic (or doctrinal) and moral theology, the
two are not the same, no more than faith and action are the same.

Christian Ethics

The other common term to describe and encompass the theological reflections contained in these next three chapters is *Christian
ethics*. Just as the term *moral theology* raises the question of the
relationship between faith and action *within* the field of Christian
reflection and discourse, so the term *Christian ethics* raises the
question of the relationship between *Christian* reflection on
human action and *philosophical* reflections on human action, without reference to the Christian tradition. This is another way of
putting the question: "Is there a distinctively Christian ethics?"

The question moves us back once again to the discussion of
human existence in Part I of the book (especially chapter 5). *How
one understands the relationship between Christian ethics and philosophical ethics will reflect how one understands the relationship
between grace and nature.* If one accepts the premise, as we have,

that all reality is radically graced, that from the very beginning God is present to all that is, then the concept of "pure nature" is only a logical construct, an abstraction. It is possible that God could have created a world without grace, but in fact God did not do so. Thus, although one can make a distinction *in the mind* between grace and nature, the two are *in fact* inseparable. The order of nature (creation) is defined by its relationship to the order of grace (redemption). There is no reality which exists, has ever existed, or ever will exist except in view of the incarnation of the Word.

The Catholic tradition has always insisted that the grace of God is given to us, not to make up for something lacking to us as human persons, but as a free gift that elevates us to a new and unmerited level of existence. Hypothetically, we could have had a purely natural end, but historically we have only a supernatural end. Thus, if grace supposes nature, nature in its own way supposes grace, insofar as the grace of Christ orients our actual human existence to the only end it really has, i.e., the Kingdom of God. Indeed, we should always remember that the very concept of "nature" arises not from the Bible but from subsequent theological reflection on the New Testament's proclamation of "the grace of God through Christ." We infer that we are creatures of God by reflecting on who we have become through Christ.

Human existence is always graced existence. This means, too, that the whole created order is oriented to the glory of God (Romans 8:19-23). The history of the world is, at the same time, the history of salvation. It means also that authentic human progress in the struggle for justice, peace, freedom, etc., is part of the movement of, and toward, the Kingdom of God. It means, too, that human freedom and human action are never to be conceived totally apart from grace, because grace is always modifying and qualifying human freedom and action.

Given this Catholic understanding of the relationship between grace and nature, the question is not so much "Is there a distinctively Christian ethics?" as "Is there a purely philosophical ethics?" "The basic and ultimate thrust of Christian life," Karl Rahner writes, "consists not so much in the fact that a Christian is a special instance of mankind in general, but rather in the fact that a Christian is simply man as he is . . . . From this perspective we could characterize Christian life precisely as a life of freedom," i.e., a life of openness to everything without exception, to absolute truth, to absolute love, to God. "But a Christian believes that there is a path to freedom which lies in going through [the] imprisonment" of ordinary human existence, namely, through the *facticity* of our existence: that we were born without being asked, will die without being asked, and are particular persons without being asked. We do not seize this freedom by force, "but rather it is given to us by God insofar as he gives himself to us throughout all of the imprisonments of our existence" (*Foundations of Christian Faith*, New York: Seabury Press, 1978, pp. 402-403).

It is not adequate, therefore, to suggest that Christian ethics differs from philosophical ethics only insofar as Christian ethics proceeds from reason and revelation, while philosophical ethics proceeds from reason alone. Revelation does not happen where reason gives out, nor is reason completely unaffected by revelation, i.e., by the active presence of God in human experience, in human history, and, therefore, in human consciousness. A similar, although not identical, position is sketched out by Protestant theologian James Gustafson in his *Can Ethics Be Christian?* (see especially pp. 169-179).

It would be preferable to say, in the end, that Christian ethics proceeds from a *conscious* sense of responsibility to the Gospel of Jesus Christ and to the community of faith (Church) which has arisen in response to this Gospel. Thus understood, "Christian ethics is the intellectual discipline that renders an account of this experience [of God in Jesus Christ] and that draws the normative inferences from it for the conduct of the Christian community and its members. The practical import is to aid the community and its members in discerning what God is enabling and requiring them to be and to do" (Gustafson, *Can Ethics Be Christian?*, p. 179).

THE MORAL MESSAGE OF THE OLD TESTAMENT

Faithful *praxis* (practice-plus-reflection, and reflection-in-practice) is linked in ancient Israel with the *Law, (Tôrāh* = "instruction"), and that, in turn, with the *Covenant*. Although scholars do not completely agree, most seem to hold that the Israelites learned and developed their legal traditions from their more sophisticated Canaanite neighbors, after entering the Promised Land. It is also widely assumed that the *Covenant Code* (Exodus 20:22–23:33) belongs to the oldest part of Israelite history because it contains the greatest number of parallels to the pagan laws. Whether this is true, we cannot finally determine here. It is sufficient to note that the Code was inserted into the book of Exodus as part of the terms of the covenant of Sinai (where the Ten Commandments were promulgated). Consequently, the Covenant Code (or Code of the Covenant) is attributed to Moses and given the supreme authority which Israel attributed to all its laws.

Most of the Old Testament laws which have parallels in the ancient Near Eastern law collections are formulated in case form (the common way of teaching law even today); e.g., "If a man strikes his father they shall cut off his hand" (Hammurabi Laws, 195), and "When a man gives money or any article to another for safekeeping and it is stolen from the latter's house, the thief, if caught, must make twofold restitution. If the thief is not caught, the owner of the house shall be brought to God, to swear that he himself did not lay hands on his neighbor's property" (Exodus 22:6-7). In the beginning, of course, such laws were unwritten. When a judge was puzzled about the law, he did not consult the law books but sought the help of a higher official in the capital (Deuteronomy 17:8-11).

Other codes of Israelite law were the "Yahwist ritual decalogue" dealing with the prohibition of images, festivals, and offerings (Exodus 34:17-27), the Deuteronomic Code (Deuteronomy 12-26), which prohibits the worship of gods other than Yahweh, the Holiness Code (Leviticus 17-26), which regulates such matters as diet, worship, hygiene, marriage, and sexual morality, the Priestly Code (scattered throughout the Pentateuch, the first five books of the Old Testament), whose cultic-ritual prescriptions often refer only to priests, and, finally, the Decalogue, or Ten Commandments (Exodus 20:2-17; Deuteronomy 5:6-21).

That ten words (*Dābār* = "word") or commandments were given by God to Moses on Mount Sinai is an accepted part of ancient Hebrew tradition (Exodus 34:28; Deuteronomy 4:13;

10:4). But the enumeration of these ten commandments has taken at least three different forms in subsequent centuries. The best seems to be the one proposed by Philo (d. ca. 50), Josephus (d.ca. 100), the Greek Fathers, and the modern Greek church: (1) Prohibition of false or foreign gods. (2) Prohibition of images. (3) Prohibition of the vain use of the divine name. (4) Keeping holy the Sabbath. (5) Honoring one's father and mother. (6) Prohibition of murder. (7) Prohibition of adultery. (8) Prohibition of theft. (9) Prohibition of false witness against one's neighbor. (10) Prohibition against coveting a neighbor's house, wife, slaves, or possessions.

The first four commandments state one's duties toward God (parents, the source of life, are representative of God), and the last six refer to duties toward other human beings.

The enumeration followed in the modern Latin church, with roots in Origen (d. ca. 254), Clement of Alexandria (d. ca. 215), and Augustine (d. 430), is as follows: (1) Prohibition of false gods *and* images. (2) Vain use of divine name. (3) Sabbath. (4) Parents. (5) Murder. (6) Adultery. (7) Theft. (8) False witness. (9) Coveting of neighbor's wife. (10) Coveting of neighbor's goods. Modern Jews put the introduction, "I am the Lord your God . . .," as (1) and then collapse (9) and (10) into (10). Everything else follows the same order as the Latin form.

One must keep in mind, however, that not even in Jesus' time had the Decalogue acquired the set form and importance as a charter of morality that it would acquire in later Christianity. The separate commandments are mentioned in the New Testament, but never as ten. When Jesus himself was asked by the young man how he could become perfect, Jesus cited some of the ten, but not in the usual order nor completely (Matthew 9:18-19; Mark 10:19; Luke 18:20).

Although the Ten Commandments bear some resemblance to other sources—e.g., the Code of Hammurabi—, they are unique in the sense that they are regarded as the revealed will of God. Other Near Eastern collections were based on the conviction that the gods had authorized their formulation, but the laws themselves were the work of human hands alone. The conception of law as a

sacred *covenant* obligation is indeed peculiar to Israel. It is important also to note that *the Decalogue was not intended as the
ultimate norm of all morality.* On the contrary, it barely touches
upon individual moral obligations. Its consistent focus is *the needs
of the whole community*, and it prohibits those actions which might
injure the community. What was important was the survival of the
People of God. *Thus, the Ten Commandments were not so much an
ethical document as a religious document, i.e., a testimony to the
unbreakable bond between God and Israel.*

The Covenant, of course, is a basic and constant motif in the
whole of the Old Testament. It is the motive for observing the
Law (Deuteronomy 4:23), for Yahweh's punishments (Leviticus
26:15, 25), for Yahweh's coming to Israel's aid in times of distress
(Leviticus 26:9), for Yahweh's mercy and forgiveness (Leviticus
26:42), and for the permanence both of Yahweh's mercy and of
Israel's status as Yahweh's own people (Leviticus 26:45; Psalm
111:9; Isaiah 54:10; 59:21; 61:8; Jeremiah 32:40; Ezekiel 34:25;
37:26). It is never a bilateral contract between equals, but an
agreement between a greater and a lesser party. The greater
imposes its will upon the lesser, but the contract is also an act of
grace and magnanimity. But it is more than a mere contract. It
establishes an artificial blood kinship between the parties that is
second only to the bond of blood. The word used to signify covenant affection and loyalty (*hesed*) is also used to signify the affection and loyalty of kinsmen. The Covenant has its initial historical
grounding in the covenant with *Abraham* (Genesis 15-17), but it
was the covenant with *Moses* on Sinai that established Israel
definitively as God's people (Exodus 19:1-8). The latter is summed
up in the formula: "I will be your God and you shall be my people"
(Jeremiah 7:23; see also 11:4; 24:7; Ezekiel 11:20; 14:11; Hosea
2:25).

The ancient Israelites had come to believe that a God who
asked for righteousness and justice would also supply the means of
instructing the people in the divine ways. Who in ancient Israel
was competent to *interpret* the Covenant? Jeremiah 18:18 refers to
three groups of leaders: the *priests*, who are the source of "instruction" (the root meaning of the word for Law, *Torāh*); the *prophets*,
who convey the word of God; and *wise persons*, who offer counsel.

These three classes of leaders were not mutually opposed to one another, nor indeed to the Law itself. On the contrary, Ezekiel was himself both prophet and priest, and the prophets were within the tradition of the Law. Nor was the teaching authority (*magisterium*) vested in any one group, not even in the priests.

THE MORAL MESSAGE OF JESUS
The Kingdom (Reign) of God

Although the idea of the Covenant is the axis around which the history of ancient Israel revolves, and although there was some expectation of a new covenant among the prophets (Jeremiah 31:31-34; Ezekiel 36:26-28), it was not central to the preaching of Jesus. As we have already noted in chapter 12, the *Kingdom* (or *reign*) *of God* was at the core of Jesus' proclamation and ministry, as it was, and must remain, at the heart of the Church's total mission (chapters 17 and 20). All else flows from that, including our understanding of Christian existence.

The whole of Jesus' preaching is summed up by Mark: "This is the time of fulfillment. The reign of God is at hand. Reform your lives and believe in the gospel " (1:15). Thus, his preaching is at once a proclamation and a warning, i.e., an announcement of a divine act and a demand for a response from men and women. Moral existence is always a response to a divine call. Nowhere in Jesus' preaching, nor in the New Testament at large, do we find an ethical system as such. On the other hand, neither do we find an existence devoid of obligation nor a faith divorced from action.

What Jesus announced was not only a renewal of the Covenant with the people of Israel. His message was even more comprehensive than that. It would embrace the whole world. Jesus returned to his home town of Nazareth to begin his preaching in the synagogue with these words from Isaiah (61:1-2): "The spirit of the Lord is upon me; therefore he has anointed me. He has sent me to bring glad tidings to the poor, to proclaim liberty to the captives, recovery of sight to the blind and release to prisoners, to announce a year of favor from the Lord" (Luke 4:18-19). Then he said, "Today this Scripture passage is fulfilled in your hearing." So obvious was his meaning that his fellow townspeople were filled with indignation and expelled him from Nazareth, attempting even to hurl him over the edge of a hill.

As we noted in chapter 12, Jesus' preaching of the reign of God was often couched in parables in which he often inverted his listeners' whole world view. Thus, the parable of the Good Samaritan (Luke 10:30-37) is not simply an example of neighborliness. If that is all Jesus wanted to communicate, he would have made the Samaritan the injured party and the Israelite the one who comes along to aid him. As it is, no Jew would ever have expected hospitality from a Samaritan (see Luke 9:52-56). Thus, the parable challenges the listener to conceive the inconceivable: The Samaritan is "good." The listener is thereby required to reexamine his or her most basic attitudes and values. The parable is no longer merely instruction; it is proclamation itself.

For Jesus nothing is more precious than the Kingdom of God (see chapter 20), i.e., the healing and renewing power and presence of God on our behalf. "Seek out his kingship over you, and the rest will follow in turn" (Luke 12:31). Like a person who finds a hidden treasure in a field, or a merchant who discovers a precious pearl, everyone must be prepared to give up everything else in order to possess the Kingdom (Matthew 13:44-46). But it is promised only to those with a certain outlook and way of life (see the Beatitudes in Matthew 5:3-12). One can inherit the Kingdom through love of one's neighbor (Matthew 5:38-48), and yet one must also accept it as a child (Mark 10:15). Jesus assured the Scribe who grasped the meaning of the chief of the commandments (love of God and love of neighbor), "You are not far from the reign of God" (12:34). He also insisted to his disciples that their commitment to the Kingdom would make strong demands upon them (Mark 10:1; Luke 9:57-62; Matthew 19:12).

The Call to Conversion and Repentance

Jesus' fundamental though not ultimate demand was that they should *repent*. The Greek word *metanoia* suggests a "change of mind." To the Semite it suggested someone's turning away from his or her former consciousness, now recognized as wrong, and striking out in a completely new direction. Therefore, *metanoia*, or conversion and repentance, is not just sorrow for sin but a fundamental reorientation of one's whole life. Jesus demanded that his listeners not only repent but also believe the Gospel of forgiveness that he preached (Mark 2:10,17). He drove home his point with various parables, especially those in Luke 15 and the parable of the Prodigal Son in particular. Jesus was so committed to the forgiveness of sins in the name of God that he made himself the friend of outcasts—e.g., publicans and sinners (Matthew 11:19)—and did not avoid their company (Mark 2:16). He rejoiced over their conversion (Luke 15:7-10; Matthew 18:13).

The antithesis of a repentant attitude is an attitude of self-righteousness and presumption. Jesus repudiates the proud Pharisee (Luke 18:10-14), the elder brother who resents his father's benevolent reaction to the prodigal son's return (Luke 15:25-30), and the discontented laborers in the vineyard (Matthew 20:1-15). To those who set themselves proudly above others, Jesus declared that publicans and harlots would enter the Kingdom before they would (Matthew 21:31-32). He condemned them for trying to shut the doors of the Kingdom (Matthew 23:13). All of us, he warned, are unprofitable servants (Luke 17:10), ever in God's debt (Matthew 6:12). God will exalt the humble and bring down the proud (Luke 14:11; 18:14). Each must pray that God forgives his or her trespasses. And whoever is without sin should cast the first stone (John 8:7). Repentance, therefore, remains a major requirement of Christian existence. The early Church would continue this message: "You must reform and be baptized ..." (Acts of the Apostles 2:38).

The Demand for Faith

Jesus also demanded *faith*, which is the positive side of conversion (Mark 1:15). He says to the woman afflicted with a hemorrhage for a dozen years and who is cured by touching his clothing, "Daughter, it is your faith that has cured you" (Mark 5:34). From there he went to the official's house where the man's daughter was reported as being already dead. Jesus disregarded the report and said to the official, "Fear is useless. What is needed is trust" (5:36). It was the faith of the lame man's friends which called forth from Jesus the forgiveness of his sins and physical healing (2:5). Faith is central to the narrative of the cured boy (9:14-29). Jesus sighed over this unbelieving generation (9:19) and reminded the boy's father that all things are possible to him who believes (9:23). The great faith of the Syro-Phoenician woman moved Jesus to heal her daughter (7:30), and he drew attention to the faith of the pagan centurion who believed that a mere word from Jesus would heal his sick servant (Matthew 8:10; Luke 7:9). On the other hand, where Jesus encountered an obstinate lack of faith, he was not able to manifest the signs of salvation (Mark 6:5). (See chapter 2 for our fuller discussion of faith.)

The Call to Discipleship

Jesus also gathered disciples around him, a point that is not unrelated to the question of Jesus' intentions regarding the "founding" of the Church (see chapter 17). He encouraged people to leave home, take up their cross, and become his disciples (Luke 14:26-27). He advised the rich young man to sell all that he had, give the money to the poor, and then come follow him (Mark 10:21). To become his disciples meant leaving everything else behind (Luke 5:11; 9:58; 14:26; Mark 2:14). But this was consistent with the traditional Jewish notion of discipleship. *What was not traditional was his sending of disciples to act in his name* (Matthew 10). "Let the dead bury their dead," he chastized the man who wanted to bury his father first. "Come away and proclaim the kingdom of God" (Luke 9:59-60). To do so was to share in Jesus' own destiny. "Where I am, there will my servant be" (John 12:26). There would be an identification of the disciple with the suffering of the master (Mark 8:34-35), but also a participation in his triumph (Luke 22:28-30). *The call to discipleship is a call to the imitation of Christ* (John 13:15).

The Law

It was not Jesus' purpose simply to set aside the Law of the Old Testament. He was in the synagogue on the Sabbath (Mark 1:21; 6:2), went on pilgrimage during the festivals (Luke 2:41-52; John

2:13; 5:1; 7:14; 10:22; 12:12; Mark 11:1-11), taught in the synagogues and in the Temple (e.g., Mark 1:39; 14:49; John 6:59; 7:14; 8:20). He celebrated the paschal feast in the traditional way with his disciples (Mark 14:12-16; Luke 22:14-23), wore the prescribed tassels on his cloak (Mark 6:56; Luke 8:44), sent lepers to show themselves to the priests in accordance with the Law (Mark 1:44; Luke 17:14). He insisted that he had come not to destroy the Law but to fulfill it (Matthew 5:17).

On the other hand, Jesus also found himself at odds with Jewish teachers of the Law. He insisted that the Sabbath was made for men and women, not men and women for the Sabbath (Mark 2:27). He defended his disciples when they had neglected to perform the ritual hand-washing (Mark 7:1-23; Matthew 15:1-20). He argued that the tradition to which the teachers appealed was a merely human institution (Mark 7:8), and he gave a concrete example of what he meant (7:9-13): They neglected the duty of supporting parents (the fourth commandment of the Decalogue) because they permitted so-called *korban* oaths, even to the detriment of their parents' rights. These oaths expressed a son's intention to give money to the Temple, and the money, in turn, was no longer part of the support given to one's parents, even if later on the son decided not to give it to the Temple. *More fundamentally, Jesus attacked the traditional notion that every part of the Law was of equal importance and that the external observance is what finally counted.* For Jesus it is the inner disposition that determines an act's moral value (7:14-23).

But he did not ignore the external action itself (Luke 6:43-45). The final parable of the Sermon on the Mount, the house built on a rock (Matthew 7:24-27), is a call not only to listen to Jesus' words but to put them into action. "Treat others the way you would have them treat you: this sums up the law and the prophets" (7:12). And this must really be done, in deed and not only in word. "None of those who cry out, 'Lord, Lord,' will enter the kingdom of God but the only the one who does the will of my Father in heaven" (7:21). The same insistence on the connection between word and action is given in his indictment of the Scribes and Pharisees (23:1-36). He attacks them for straining at gnats and swallowing camels and for neglecting the weightier matters of the law: justice, mercy, and good faith (23:23). He is especially intoler-ant of their hypocrisy (23:4,28). To return to the notion of *praxis* to which we referred at the beginning of this chapter: Jesus not only proclaimed the Kingdom of God; he practiced it, and he expected the same of others. God's will must be *done*.

The austere demands of Jesus are not to be explained away simply on the basis of his expectation of the coming of the King-dom, but they are to be interpreted always in light of the coming Kingdom. Thus, it is clearly hyperbolic to say, as Jesus did, that it is easier for a camel to pass through the eye of a needle than for a rich man to enter into the Kingdom (Mark 10:25). The disciples expressed alarm: "Then who can be saved?" Jesus answered, "For man it is impossible but not for God. With God all things are possible" (10:27). But as severe as his ethical teaching may have been, his readiness to forgive was even stronger. Thus, a repentant Peter is singled out as the shepherd of the sheep despite his denial of Christ (Luke 22:32; John 21:15-17). Admonition and mercy are found together.

The Commandment of Love

All of Jesus' moral teaching is concentrated in the one command-ment of love: the love of God and the love of neighbor (Mark 12:28-34; Matthew 22:34-40; Luke 10:25-28). On them all the Law and the prophets depend (Matthew 22:40). Apart from the great com-mandment, Jesus did not speak explicitly about loving God. He did say that we should not offer sacrifice to God unless and until we have been reconciled with our brother (Matthew 5:23-24) and that we cannot ask forgiveness for our sins unless we are also ready to forgive those who sin against us (6:12). But it would be wrong to equate love for God entirely with love for neighbor. Religious acts, such as prayer, also belong to the love of God (Matthew 6:1-15; 7:7-11; Mark 14:38). On the other hand, "religious" access to God through prayer cannot finally be divorced from the principal sacramental encounter with God in one's neighbor. The great picture of the Last Judgment in the parable of the Sheep and the Goats (Matthew 25:31-46) offers one of the classic illustrations of this principle.

According to John, Jesus gave himself as an example of unselfish love for others. He humbled himself to wash the feet of the disciples (13:4-15). He insisted that he was in their midst as one who serves (Luke 22:27), who gives his life as a ransom for many (Mark 10:45), and who thereby leaves a new commandment: "Love one another. Such as my love has been for you, so must your love be for each other. This is how all will know you for my disciples: your love for one another" (John 13:34-35). But such love is not to be reserved for one's friends. The disciple of Jesus is also commanded to love the enemy (Luke 6:27-28), to renounce revenge (6:29). We are to avoid judging and condemning others (6:37) and to be careful not to dwell on the speck in our brother's eye while missing the plank in our own (6:41-42). All of this is summed up in Paul's classic hymn to love: "There are in the end three things that last: faith, hope, and love, and the greatest of these is love" (1 Corinthians 13).

Discipleship in the World

Jesus did not come to change the political order, but neither was he indifferent to it. What he preached was bound to affect the consciousness and behavior of those who heard and assimilated his words. The values he proclaimed would surely transform the world of those who shared them. But to make of him primarily a political figure is to put more into the New Testament than is there.

Jesus declared that he was sent to call sinners (Mark 2:17), to save the lost (Luke 19:10), to give his life for many (Mark 10:45). His kingdom was not of this world, he assured Pilate (John 18:36-37). He fled from the desire of his Galilean supporters to make him a political messianic king and national liberator (John 6:14-15). He rejected Peter's plea that he relinquish the path of suffering and death, just as he repelled the temptations of Satan to worldly power (Matthew 16:22-23). He maintained no contacts with the Zealot party. But all of this does not mean that Jesus' moral teaching had no bearing on political life.

He sent his disciples into the world (Matthew 10:16) and prayed, not that the Father would take his disciples out of the world, but that he would keep them safe in the world (John 17:15). He criticized contemporary institutions (Matthew 10). He saw what is dangerous and corrupting in political power as well as in riches: "You know how among the Gentiles those who seem to exercise authority lord it over them; their great ones make their importance felt. It cannot be like that with you" (Mark 10:42-43). When asked if he thought his fellow Jews should pay the tax to Caesar (Mark 12:13-37), he said they should, but he gave this answer only after asking about the image on the coin and pointing out to his interrogators that they already recognized Caesar's political authority over them by using his coinage. And then he added: "Give to Caesar what is Caesar's, but give to God what is God's" (12:17). Always it is the Kingdom which is supreme.

Jesus, of course, was a carpenter's son, and he himself labored for a time as a carpenter (Mark 6:3). His parables reflect his sense of identification with the poor and the workers: on the farm (Mark 4:3-8), in the vineyard (Matthew 20:1-15), on the sea (Matthew 13:47-50), in the home (Matthew 13:33; Luke 12:37-39; 17:7-10). But others also appear in his parables, without his passing judgment on their occupations or professions: e.g., merchants, traders, builders, soldiers, kings, judges, physicians, stewards. He did not attack the notion of private property, nor did he demand a redistribution of worldly goods. "The poor you will always have with you," he declared (Mark 14:7). Although he directed his severest warnings against the rich (Luke 6:24), he accepted hospitality from them (Luke 7:36; 10:38-42; 14:1, John 11:1-3; 12:1-3) and support from women of property (Luke 8:3). He certainly did not intend to exclude from the Kingdom such wealthy men as Nicodemus, Joseph of Arimathea, Zacchaeus the rich publican, and others like them (Luke 19:1-10).

The theme of wealth and property has an important place in the Gospel of Luke, so much so that some scholars have suggested that Luke deliberately intensified Jesus' sayings against the rich and riches. This may have been the case here and there (e.g., 5:11,28; 9:3; 10:4), but not as a general rule. As early as the Infancy Narrative Jesus' earthly origin is characterized as poverty-stricken (1:52-53; 2:7,24). The motif is sounded again in various discourses and parables (12:15-21; 14:12-14,33; 16). In Luke's version of the

Beatitudes, Jesus first blesses the poor, for the reign of God is theirs (6:20)—not just the "poor" in the sense of the "poor in spirit" or the "just," but the economically poor. In the parable of the Rich Man and Lazarus (16:19-31), Lazarus, too, is literally poor. On the other hand, it is not poverty that entitles one to entrance into the Kingdom, but fidelity to the will of God (Matthew 7:21). In comparing the presentation of the Beatitudes in Matthew (5:3-12) and Luke (6:20-26), however, it is clear that Matthew emphasizes the religious and moral attitude of those who are called blessed and to whom the Kingdom of God is promised, whereas Luke stresses their social and economic position. Luke makes the same kind of modification in the parables of the Unfaithful Steward (16:1-7) and of the Rich Fool (12:16-20) and also in Jesus' attack on the Pharisees because of their greed (20:47).

Why do we find such a spirit in Luke? The evangelist had close contacts with certain circles in the original Jerusalem community who were literally poor and may have called themselves "the poor" in the religious sense (see Romans 15:26; Galatians 2:10). He praises the practice of sharing goods within the community of the first Christians (Acts of the Apostles 2:44-45; 4:32; 5:1-11). This contact undoubtedly shaped his own personal theology and piety.

What is of major, if not of revolutionary, significance in all of this is the assertion that *the poor have any place at all in the divine scheme of things.* Not only Luke but Matthew, too, removes the curse on poverty. Poverty is not by any means an obstacle to the Kingdom, as some apparently thought. Although other New Testament writings pay little attention to the poor and to poverty (it must have been discussed intensely in the Hellenistic communities for which Luke wrote), *the Christian movement itself was unique in the Roman world as one springing from the poor and lower classes.*

Marriage and the Family

The linchpin of Jesus' attitude toward marriage and the family was his concern for the *dignity of women*, which went far beyond contemporary Jewish attitudes and customs. He spoke with a Samaritan woman at Jacob's Well, though it was frowned upon for a man and a rabbi to do so (John 4:27). He allowed himself to be touched by the woman with the hemorrhage, even though this made him ritually unclean (Mark 5:27-34). He broke the Sabbath to cure a "daughter of Abraham" (Luke 13:10-17). He healed an unusually large number of women—e.g., Peter's mother-in-law (Mark 1:29-31), Jairus' daughter (Mark 5:21-43), the daughter of the Syro-Phoenician woman (Mark 7:24-30), and Mary Magdalene (Luke 8:2). He praised the widow for contributing her mite to the Temple treasury (Mark 12:41-44) and defended Mary of Bethany for anointing his head and feet (Mark 14:3-8; John 12:1-8). He accepted women among his followers and received help from them (Luke 8:2-3). When he visited the family at Bethany, he wished both sisters to hear what he had to say (Luke 10:38). The risen Lord appeared to Mary Magdalene, who brought the good news of the resurrection to the other disciples (John 20:11-18).

Of special importance was Jesus' insistence that marriage is permanent. Women are not to be cast aside at will, as was the custom. He spoke strongly against adultery and divorce (Mark 10:2-12; Matthew 19:3-9). His injunction "Let no man separate what God has joined" is a clear allusion to Genesis, where women and men are assigned equal dignity, coming as they do from the same creative hand of God. (For a fuller consideration of the so-called "exceptive clause," see Rudolf Schnackenburg, *The Moral Teaching of the New Testament*, pp. 136-141. This has to do with Jesus' apparent willingness to allow divorce in the case of "lewd conduct.")

Jesus' high regard for family life is confirmed by the scene which immediately followed the discussion with the Pharisees on divorce. People brought their children to him to have him touch them, and his disciples began to scold them for it. Jesus became indignant and said, "Let the children come to me. . . . It is to just such as these that the kingdom of God belongs" (Mark 10:13-16). He also emphasized the fourth commandment, "Honor your father and your mother," in his reply to the rich young man (10:19). On the other hand, he spoke almost disdainfully of his family when they came to take him home (3:31-35), and he corrected a woman who blessed his mother (Luke 11:27). His mother, too, must have felt rejected at the marriage feast at Cana when she suggested he might produce more wine (John 2:4). So, too, he seemed to belittle blood ties in his command to his disciples regarding their own families (Luke 9:60; 14:26), and he predicted dissensions within homes on his account (Matthew 10:34-36; Luke 12:51-53; Mark 13:12). What emerges from these assorted sayings is the principle that when Jesus gathers his eschatological family around him, blood ties are of less importance than fidelity to the will of God and readiness for the Kingdom.

Reward and Punishment

The principal motive for living according to the Gospel is, of course, the Kingdom of God and its blessings (Matthew 5:3-11). But Jesus also speaks of both rewards and punishments, and they serve perhaps as secondary motives for Christian fidelity. The standard of measurement is often our attitude to the neighbor (25:31-46). On the other hand, Jesus explicitly warns against those who perform certain actions simply to gain a reward (6:2,5,16). The reward he promises is always the future Kingdom or one of its blessings, such as eternal life (Mark 10:30). The parable of the Laborers in the Vineyard (Matthew 20:1-16) is especially important because it shows that God's criteria and ours are not the same. What finally governs the divine judgment is God's own mercy. Thus, those who come to work in the vineyard at a late hour are rewarded on the same basis as those who come at the first hour. So, too, those who bury their talents are singled out for particular condemnation (25:30). The principle is: "When much has been given a man, much will be required of him. More will be asked of a man to whom more has been entrusted" (Luke 12:48).

In the end, we are called to imitate Jesus (Mark 10:45), to follow his example (John 13:15), to love one another as he has loved us (13:14). This is his first and greatest commandment.

THE MORAL MESSAGE OF THE
CHURCH OF THE NEW TESTAMENT

The reader is referred again to chapter 17 for an outline of the Church in the New Testament. It is a community radically shaped by its expectation of the coming of God's Kingdom and by the conviction that the firstfruits of the Kingdom had already been given in the Holy Spirit (2 Corinthians 1:22; 5:5; Ephesians 1:14). It is the Spirit who is the driving force of Christian existence (Romans 8:12-17; Galatians 5:16-26), which begins at Baptism (Romans 6:4; 1 Corinthians 6:11). The Christian no longer lives according to the flesh but according to the Spirit. The Christian is a "new creature" in Christ (2 Corinthians 5:17).

There is an awareness, too, of being a new community in the Spirit, the new People of God. Christian existence, therefore, is corporate existence. We are called to a life of brotherly and sisterly love. We are all one in Christ, whether Jew or Greek, slave or free, male or female (Galatians 3:28). We are one body, the Body of Christ (1 Corinthians 12:13,27). The ethical significance of this is drawn out in Romans 12:4-8 and Colossians 3:11-17. We are to be clothed with mercy, kindness, humility, meekness, patience. We are to bear with one another and to forgive as the Lord has forgiven us. We are to put on love, which binds the rest and makes them perfect. Christ's peace must reign in our hearts. We are to be grateful people and to do everything in the name of the Lord Jesus. In short, we are "to live a life worthy of the calling [we] have received" (Ephesians 4:1).

As for the Law, it is summed up and fulfilled in this one saying: "You shall love your neighbor as yourself" (Galatians 5:14). The Gospel is a new Law, a perfect law of freedom (James 1:25), the law of love (2:8). Jesus himself is the new Law (John 1:17). "His commandment is this: we are to believe in the name of his Son, Jesus Christ, and are to love one another as he has commanded us" (1 John 3:23). If we do love one another, "God dwells in us, and his love is brought to perfection in us" (4:12). On the other hand, "If anyone says, 'My love is fixed on God,' yet hates his brother, he is a liar. One who has no love for the brother he has seen cannot love the God he has not seen" (4:20). In any case, "perfect love casts out all fear" (4:18).

(For a more complete discussion of the moral teaching of the New Testament Church, see Schnackenburg, pp. 168-388.)

SECOND THROUGH SIXTH CENTURIES

The Church has no moral systems as such until the sixteenth century. Of major concern to the early Church was the threat posed by pagan society and culture. There were prohibitions against pagan worship and the fashioning of idols by Christian craftsmen. Also discussed were the proper Christian attitude toward the theatre, military service, martyrdom, flight from persecution, virginity, prayer. Ignatius of Antioch (d. ca.107) italicized the Pauline and Johannine teaching that Christian existence is life in and with Christ. The Christian is a temple of God and a bearer of Christ (Ephesians 9:1). The Eucharist is the source and center of the Christian life.

Clement of Alexandria (d. ca. 215) made perhaps the first attempt at some modest systematization of moral theology. He strove to point out the connection between the positive values in pagan philosophy and those of the Gospel. Genuine Christian life is imitation of God in Christ. Christ is always our teacher. He is the *Logos*-made-flesh. Against the Gnostic hostility toward marriage, Clement defended the married state as a way of salvation. But he also refused to disparage virginity. What counts in the end is the good of the community of love and the things of the Lord (*Stromata*, III, 12).

Clement's successor in the catechetical school at Alexandria was Origen (d. ca. 254), who was less open to the world than his predecessor but perhaps more realistic. He focused on the imitation of God in the contemplative as well as the active life, and reflected on free will, sin, virtues, and the restoration of all things in God. Ambrose (d. 397) provides the first case-approach to moral theology, laying down the various duties of his priests. He insists on the superiority of the Christian moral ideal over pagan philosophies.

One of the earliest to set Christian moral discourse in the context of sacramental initiation was Cyril of Jerusalem (d. 386). His moral instruction, in keeping with Eastern practice, was drawn principally from the liturgical texts. Christian existence is sacramental existence.

The first great figure in Christian moral theology, however, is Ambrose's disciple, Augustine (d. 430), who attended to such fundamental problems as the relationship of grace and freedom, faith and works, faith and love, original sin and the restoration of grace, grace and the law, natural law and revealed law, and divine love and the natural appetites. Christian morality is the way and means to eternal union with God. Morality, in turn, requires obedience to the divine law of love, but not merely through external observance. The moral disposition of the heart is decisive. And so we find a strongly psychological orientation in Augustine's writings (e.g., his own *Confessions*) which makes him a kind of forerunner of modern thought. But in spite of his obvious genius and the major contributions he has made to Christian theology, all the "returns" are not yet in on the quality of his impact upon the Church. Was he "one of the greatest, if not the very greatest, moral theologian of all time," as Bernard Häring suggested, or was he too much the rigorist, too much the Manichaean, too much the nay-sayer about such fundamental human questions as sexuality?

SEVENTH THROUGH TWELFTH CENTURIES

This is a significant period in the history of moral theology because, as we noted in chapters 18 and 22, it was the period of the Germanization and legalization of Christianity. In particular, moral theology became attached to the specific needs of confessors. The sacrament of Penance, once reserved for public sins, had become more widely used by the sixth century under the influence of the Celtic monks. Appropriate penances had to be determined for particular sins. A new genre of theological literature developed, the so-called penitential books (*libri poenitentiales*), to assist the generally uneducated clergy.

These works did not focus on the ideals of Christian existence but only on varieties of sins. They led to the belief that Christian life is essentially one of avoiding sin; the mere avoidance of sin, in turn, led some to conclude to their own moral righteousness. Absolution was not perceived as an act of forgiveness and mercy, but of judgment. And emphasis was placed increasingly on the nature of the individual moral act, apart from the larger context of one's whole existence. Thus, for example, a basically good person could "go to Hell" if he deliberately missed Mass on a given Sunday and then died before having a chance to recite a "perfect act of contrition" or "get to confession."

THIRTEENTH CENTURY

By now a new institution had come upon the scene in the West: the university. It was to change the character and course of moral theology. Systematization became the rule rather than the exception. There was a push to organize and to integrate, to produce *summae*, or syntheses, of theology. The two great figures were Bonaventure (d. 1274) and Thomas Aquinas (d. 1274).

For Bonaventure, and the Franciscan school generally (e.g., Alexander of Hales, d. 1245), the will, not the intellect, was the primary faculty. The intellect was but the tool of the will, which was the instrument of decision. The purpose of theology is to "make us holy." Thomas Aquinas, on the other hand, stressed the intellectual side of human existence. What Bonaventure played down, i.e., contemplation of the true, Thomas emphasized. Theology is for the sake of understanding. Therefore, there could be no separation of doctrinal from moral theology, because there is no separation of truth from behavior. Thomas' entire moral outlook is based on our relation to creation and the last end, on the fact that we are made in the image and likeness of God, and on the humanity of Christ as our way to God (see the prologues to the second and third parts of the *Summa Theologica*). The foundation for his whole theology is God, the Creator, and Christ, the Redeemer. We shall achieve beatitude or union with God through participation in God's own knowledge and love through the grace of Christ. Indeed, this grace is the heart of the new Law, i.e., "the grace of the Holy Spirit, which is given to those who believe in Christ" (I-II, q. 106, a. 1). The virtues, or God-given "powers" to do what is right and to avoid what is evil, are also explicitly treated: the theological virtues of faith, hope, and love, and the cardinal virtues of prudence, fortitude, temperance, and justice. Aquinas' moral teaching, therefore, centered not upon us and the rewards we seek, but upon God as the source of both created and eternal life. (The reader should not neglect to scan the table of contents of I-II and II-II of the *Summa Theologica* in order to appreciate the comprehensiveness and detailed character of Thomas' reflections on the Christian moral life. Much of the material in the next chapter of this book is rooted precisely in Thomas' vision.)

FOURTEENTH AND FIFTEENTH CENTURIES

Where Thomas had emphasized *habits*, i.e., basic attitudes, the Nominalists who followed him, e.g., William of Ockham (d. 1359), emphasized *individual acts*. Secondly, they defined "the good" as that which conforms with the will of the individual. And so a thoroughly individualistic ethic emerges, one which underlines the unique situation of every person in the face of a moral decision. If society feels threatened by this individualism, it has one recourse: the exercise of power. Individual moral agents can be "collected together" and given some shape and direction by the imposition of law, which demands conformity. Thus, the Nominalist approach generates first an ethical individualism and then an ethical legalism.

This was also a time of extraordinary economic expansion and complexification. Medieval feudalism was yielding to the new middle-class commerce. Such activities as the buying and selling of goods and the making of contracts were commonplace. One could no longer rely on relatively simple principles of charity. It became necessary to state precisely the demands of justice, which has to do with rights and duties. The other virtues, such as faith and love, became secondary to justice. A moral minimalism developed ("What am I absolutely required to do, as a bare moral minimum?").

It was against this state of affairs that Martin Luther (d. 1546) would react so vehemently. "The situation emphasized justice, and Luther was convinced that no one is just. The situation focused on minimums, and Luther felt driven to perfection. The situation cherished good works, and Luther placed his trust in faith" (Timothy O'Connell, *Principles for a Catholic Morality*, p. 16).

This was also the period of the great medieval penitential books, in the tradition of the Irish penitential books of the early Middle Ages. They were not textbooks. They were more akin to reference books, such as a dictionary, presenting basic information on a wide range of topics arranged alphabetically. The most important was that of St. Antonine (d. 1459), which presents a sweeping picture of the moral life of the fifteenth century. It exercised profound influence on subsequent works.

SIXTEENTH CENTURY

Although the first commentary on the *Summa* of Thomas Aquinas had been produced by Henry of Gorkum (d. 1431) in the fifteenth century, it was not until the beginning of the sixteenth century that the *Summa* was used as a textbook in the schools, thereby replacing Peter Lombard's *Book of Sentences*. This Thomistic revival had a pronounced impact on moral theology because Thomas, unlike Peter Lombard, had a relatively complete and well-integrated treatment of moral questions, especially of the virtues (*Summa* I-II and II-II). Conrad Koellin (d. 1536), a German Dominican, published the first complete commentary on the first part of the second part of the *Summa* (I-II), and there followed another major commentary by Thomas de Vio, Cardinal Cajetan (d. 1534), in Italy. The Thomistic revival also took hold in Spain at the school of Salamanca through the teachings and writings of Francis of Vitoria (d. 1546), Melchior Cano (d. 1560), Dominic Soto (d. 1560), Dominic Banez (d. 1604)—all Dominicans, like Thomas Aquinas himself.

Concurrent with this Thomistic revival was the Catholic Church's broader struggle with Protestantism. This effort was focused in the work of the Council of Trent. Its *Decree on Justification* (Session VI, 1547) stressed the freedom of the person to assent to, and cooperate with, grace and thus to dispose himself or herself for justification. Free will was not destroyed by Original Sin. Furthermore, the council also took care to specify the nature and number of the seven sacraments and placed special emphasis on the necessary elements in the sacrament of Penance: contrition, confession, absolution, and satisfaction. Trent also established the Catholic seminary system for the education and training of priests. For the first time in its history, the Church decided that the preparation of its clergy for their ministry should occur apart from the normal world, that future priests should be given precise instruction on what they are to preach and teach, and that they should be impressed with the need for institutional loyalty and obedience. Since priests are also ministers of sacraments, they must know exactly the conditions under which those sacraments can validly and licitly be received.

The Society of Jesus (the Jesuits) was the center of this educational enterprise throughout the sixteenth and seventeenth centuries. Their *ratio studiorum* (order of studies) dictated that those professors who were charged with lecturing on the *Summa* of St. Thomas should limit their courses to the more basic principles of moral teaching. Some professors of moral doctrine, however, were assigned to deal with "cases of conscience" in order to determine the correct solution of problems. As a result, an independent and self-contained field of moral theology emerged. Always the concern was to discover if, in fact, a penitent had sinned. All the necessary sources, including canon law, were incorporated into these moral texts to aid in the solution of each problem. Indeed, some topics such as Matrimony and Penance were treated exclusively from a canonical point of view. The first comprehensive manual of moral theology, whose basic form was followed until the Second Vatican Council, was the *Institutiones Morales*, by John Azor (d. 1603). General principles are followed in order by the commandments of God and the Church, the sacraments, censures, indulgences, and the particular obligations of the various states of life.

SEVENTEENTH AND EIGHTEENTH CENTURIES

Moral theology (or theological reflection on Christian existence) was by now a separate division of theology, no longer flowing from doctrinal theology nor from the classic sources of doctrinal theology, i.e., Scripture and the Fathers. Moralists were expected primarily to answer the question "What morally may I do?" Two extremes developed. On the far right, the *Jansenists* rejected every kind of casuisty (i.e., deciding morality on a case-by-case basis), insisting instead that the strictest standards must always be followed. We are radically corrupted by Original Sin, they argued. Only grace can overcome that corruption, and that grace is given to few. When it *is* given, however, it is irresistible. Jansenism was condemned in 1653 by Pope Innocent X's (d. 1655) Constitution *Cum Occasione*. There was also *Quietism*, which excluded all moral effort from the spiritual life. This was condemned by Pope Innocent XI (d. 1689) in his Constitution *Caelestis Pastor* in 1687. At the far left were the *laxists*, who were devoted exclusively to casuisty and who solved literally thousands of cases, usually in favor of liberty.

These debates led to the growth of a variety of moral systems, one of which was known as "probabilism." This was a method of solving difficult moral cases by allowing the Christian to follow the more lenient opinion, even if it was held by only one reputable theologian. Variations on "probabilism" developed: *Equiprobabilism* required that the two conflicting opinions should have equal support among the experts; *probabiliorism* required that the more lenient opinion should also be the majority opinion.

The principal moderating force at this time was Alphonsus Ligouri (d. 1787). He was regarded as a prudent and balanced theologian, one whose opinions could be relied upon. In an age when extreme views were the order of the day, Alphonsus injected a measure of reason and restraint into moral discourse. His methodological approach to moral theology also had a strong impact on subsequent theologies. He always identified and summarized all the opinions on a particular question, then tried to fashion a position somewhere in between the extremes. He counseled against rigorism, i.e., against imposing more on the penitent than was required by the law or by the Gospel, and against laxism, i.e., against disregarding the clear requirements of either law or Gospel, or both.

NINETEENTH TO MID-TWENTIETH CENTURY
General Developments in Moral Theology

A reaction set in at the German University of Tübingen with the work of Johann Michael Sailer (d. 1832), bishop of Ratisbon, and Johann Baptist von Hirscher (d. 1865). Both attempted a reformulation of moral theology disengaged from its customary casuistry and legalism and reconnected with doctrinal theology. Both were also influenced by the renewal of biblical studies, and hence understandably called for a return to the central New Testament notions of conversion and discipleship. In his *Christian Moral Teaching as Realization of the Kingdom of God* (1834), Von Hirscher focused especially on the Kingdom of God as the basis of Christian morality. But neither theologian was without weaknesses. Their understanding of Scripture was often uncritical, and they displayed too little appreciation of the work of the Scholastics.

Contemporaneous and subsequent events impeded a smooth shift in theological gears, however. Pope Pius IX's *Syllabus of Errors* (1864), the First Vatican Council (1869-1870), and a general atmosphere of suspicion and hostility between German and Italian scholars slowed the process. But the Tübingen theologians kept at it: Magnus Jocham (d. 1893), who focused on the theology of grace and the sacraments; Bernard Fuchs (d. 1854), who emphasized the Mystical Body as the context for rebirth in God and growth in grace; Martin Deutinger (d. 1864), who developed a personalism of love based on the idea of human freedom and the capacity to love God; Karl Werner (d. 1888), who put Christ at the center and held up sacrifice as the moral ideal; and Francis Xavier Linsenmann (d. 1898), who also emphasized the Pauline theme of the freedom of the children of God over against the law. There were at the same time, however, other theologians in Germany who continued the more casuistic approach: Francis Friedhoff

(d. 1865), John the Evangelist Pruner (d. 1907), and Francis Schindler (d. 1922).

But the more integrated, biblically and patristically grounded theology carried the greater authority into the twentieth century, particularly in the works of Joseph Mausbach (d. 1931), Otto Schilling (d. 1956), Fritz Tillmann (d. 1953), and Theodore Steinbuechel (d. 1949). For them the law of love, the ethos of the Sermon on the Mount, is the heart and soul of moral theology. When two other German theologians, Joseph Fuchs and Bernard Häring, assumed teaching positions at the Gregorian University and the Alphonsianum in Rome respectively, a wider dissemination of this evolving German theology was assured. Its effects can be seen outside of Europe in the writings of Charles Curran, one of Häring's first American students. Another major influence on recent Catholic moral thought was Gerard Gilleman, whose *The Primacy of Charity in Moral Theology* (Westminster, Md.: Newman Press, 1959) along with Häring's *The Law of Christ*, 3 vols. (Westminster, Md.: Newman Press, 1961-1966), were among the most widely read books in Catholic seminaries in the years just before and during Vatican II.

But even into the 1950s, this broadly based development on the Continent notwithstanding, moral theology in the United States, for example, remained oriented toward the preparation of confessors. The emphasis was on the individual act to determine whether or not it fell into the category of sin, and, if so, whether it was mortal, or venial. Stress was still placed on obedience to law: divine law, natural law, human law. The "good" is what is commanded by law. Therefore, conformity with law is the fulfillment of the good. Analysis of moral action still tended to abstract from the concrete circumstances and situation of the moral actor. The manuals in use in the United States and other countries were based on an understanding of an essentially unchanging human nature. This was the so-called *classicist* approach. Classicist moral theology was largely unbiblical, unsacramental, and unintegrated with the great doctrinal themes of Christ, grace, the Holy Spirit, and the Church understood as the Body of Christ and the People of God. It should be noted, however, that the classicist approach always enjoyed the favor of official teaching before the council, particularly in the various moral pronouncements issued during the pontificate of Pope Pius XII—e.g., the Instruction of the Holy Office on "Situation Ethics" (1956).

That official situation changed with Vatican II. In its *Decree on Priestly Formation* the council urged the renewal of moral theology: "Its scientific exposition should be more thoroughly nourished by scriptural teaching. It should show the nobility of the Christian vocation of the faithful, and their obligation to bring forth fruit in charity for the life of the world" (n. 16). In general, moral theology should be "renewed by livelier contact with the mystery of Christ and the history of salvation." Elsewhere in its two major constitutions, one on the Church and the other on the Church in the modern world, the council proposes an ideal of Christian existence which goes well beyond the observance of law and of juridical norms. Every member of the Church is part of the People of God, and insofar as the whole Church is called to be the sacrament of Christ, the whole Church is also called to holiness (*Dogmatic Constitution on the Church*, n. 40). This consists in the following of Christ (n. 41), which leads to the perfection of love (n. 42). This is at once a love of God and a love of neighbor. These two kinds of love cannot be separated (*Pastoral Constitution on the Church in the Modern World*, n. 24). But the most significant aspect of the council's moral teaching is its advancement of the Church's social doctrine, to which we now turn our attention.

Development of Catholic Social Doctrine

Catholic social doctrine is to be distinguished from the social implications of the Gospel. Catholic social doctrine is a clearly discernible body of official teachings on the social order, in its economic and political dimensions. It is concerned with the dignity of the human person as created in the image of God, with human rights and duties which protect and enhance this dignity, with the radically social nature of human existence, with the nature of society and of the state, with the relationship between society and state (balancing the principle of subsidiarity and the principle of socialization), and with voluntary associations, e.g., labor unions, which serve as a buffer and a bridge between state and society.

Catholic social doctrine as such did not exist before the end of the nineteenth century, which is not to say that the Catholic Church expressed no official interest in, or concern for, the world outside the sanctuary until Pope Leo XIII's encyclical, *Rerum Novarum*, "On the Condition of the Working Man," in 1891. But not until Leo XIII did the Catholic Church begin to articulate in a consciously *systematic* manner a theology of *social justice* and all that this implies. (A fuller discussion of social justice will be presented in the next chapter.) This is not to say that this theology of social justice was well *integrated* with the rest of theology, and particularly with ecclesiology. It was not. Little attention, in fact, was paid in the social teachings of Leo XIII, Pius XI, and Pius XII to forging a clear link between the social ministry of the Church and the nature and mission of the Church. This link was not forged until Vatican II.

Catholic social doctrine is not a blueprint for the reform of the world. It is rather a broad theological and philosophical framework of social analysis. Thus far it has been developed in three stages:

Stage one consists of the Church's response to the problems posed by the *Industrial Revolution*. The key texts are Leo XIII's *Rerum Novarum* (1891) and Pius XI's *Quadragesimo Anno*, "Reconstructing the Social Order" (1931). The principal issues are the role of government in society and in the economy, the right of laborers to organize, the principle of a just wage, and a Christian critique of both capitalism and socialism.

Stage two emerges during the Second World War and continues to the present (overlapping with a third stage). It is the *internationalization* of Catholic social doctrine, confronting the growing material interdependence of the world and seeking to provide a moral framework for the political, economic, and strategic issues facing the human community. The key texts are those of Pope Pius XII (his Pentecost Message of 1941 and his Christmas Addresses of 1939-1957), John XXIII (*Mater et Magistra*, "Christianity and Social Progress," 1961, and *Pacem in Terris*, "Peace on Earth," 1963), Paul VI (*Populorum Progressio*, "The Progress of

Peoples," 1967), the Second Vatican Council's *Pastoral Constitution on the Church in the Modern World* (*Gaudium et spes*, 1965), and the Third International Synod of Bishops' *Justice in the World* (*Iustitia in mundo*, 1971). The principal issues are the political and juridical organization of the international community, the demands of international social justice in determining the rules and relationships of international economic policy, and the moral issues regarding warfare in a nuclear age.

Stage three is represented by Pope Paul VI's apostolic letter *Octagesima Adveniens* ("The Eightieth Year," 1971), reaffirmed to some extent in his apostolic exhortation *Evangelii Nuntiandi* ("On Evangelization in the Modern World," 1975), and Pope John Paul II's *Redemptor Hominis* ("Redeemer of Humankind," 1979). The keynote is sounded in *Octagesima Adveniens* as it addresses "new social questions." It examines the issues faced in an acute way by post-industrial societies, which have been so transformed by *technology* and its effects, especially in the area of communications and mobility (see our discussion in chapter 3). On the other hand, the papal letter returns to the theme of how post-industrial and developing societies are related internationally. The document focuses on the forms of organization which compete for primacy in society and on the intellectual currents which seek to legitimate other kinds of social and political orders. This broader political approach is carried forward in Pope John Paul II's encyclical, which speaks of our alienation from the products and byproducts of technology—e.g., environmental pollution and destruction, the arms race, the widening gap between rich and poor, increasingly sophisticated methods of torture and oppression, wasteful attitudes and practices, inflation, and modern methods of warfare. What is essential today is the right of citizens to share in the "political life of the community" in service of the common good, whether national or international, and in service of the human person, whose dignity in Christ is the foundation and linchpin of the whole social and political order. "Thus the principle of human rights is of profound concern to the area of social justice and is the measure by which it can be tested in the life of political bodies" (section 17, par. 7).

The Second Vatican Council, although still very much a part of stage two, prepared the way for the expansion of Catholic social doctrine to include the political dimension as well. Among the fundamental principles the council stresses, especially in its *Pastoral Constitution on the Church in the Modern World*, are the dignity of the human person created in the image of God (n. 12), the dignity of the moral conscience (n. 16), the excellence of freedom (n. 17), the social nature of human existence and of our destiny (n. 24), the interdependence of person and society (n. 26), the need to promote the common good for the sake of human dignity (n. 26), respect for persons (n. 27), their fundamental equality as the basis of social justice (n. 29), the value of all human activities because of the redemption (n. 34), the rightful autonomy of temporal realities (n. 36), and the missionary responsibility of the Church to attend to this constellation of values and principles (the document as a whole, especially nn. 40-45). The same insistence on human freedom is sounded in the council's *Declaration on Religious Freedom*, a freedom that belongs not only to individuals but to groups (n. 4) and that is always subject to the common good (n. 7).

The social mission of the Church is even more explicitly articulated in the synodal document *Justice in the World*: "Action on behalf of justice and participation in the transformation of the world fully appear to us as a constitutive dimension of the preaching of the Gospel, or, in other words, of the Church's mission for the redemption of the human race and its liberation from every oppressive situation" (Introduction, par. 6). And later the same declaration applies the principle to the Church itself, for "anyone who ventures to speak to people about justice must first be just in their eyes" (III, par. 2). The Church, which is the sacrament of Christ, is called upon by missionary mandate to practice what it preaches about justice and rights.

CATHOLIC MORAL THEOLOGY: FROM CLASSICISM TO HISTORICAL CONSCIOUSNESS

How explain the movement from pre-Vatican II to post-Vatican II moral theology? At the risk of oversimplifying, it is principally the effect of *a fundamental shift in methodology*: from classicism to historical consciousness.

Classicism conceives the moral life of the Christian as that which conforms to certain pre-existing norms: divine law, natural law, ecclesiastical law. Its emphasis, therefore, is always on law, authority, *magisterium*, precedent. Therefore, it is deductive rather than inductive in its approach, and it deals with moral issues in the abstract, i.e., according to universal norms rather than in light of particular or even peculiar circumstances and situations. Classicism is *teleological*; i.e., it emphasizes the end (*telos*), or purpose, of human existence as if one can find in the nature or essence of humanity a blueprint for growth and development. Classicism is also *deontological*; i.e., it emphasizes duty and obligation (*deontos*) in relation to law.

The *advantages* of classicism are its clarity, its simplicity, and its assurance of certitude regarding what is good and evil in relation to the will of God. Its *disadvantages* are its authoritarianism (the Church has most, if not all, of the answers), its dogmatism (and those answers are final and binding), its anti-intellectualism (authoritative norms, not theological or philosophical speculation, are the principal guides to Christian fidelity), and indeed its restriction of teaching authority to the pope and bishops, while making little distinction among the various levels of even *their* authoritative pronouncements (e.g., ecumenical councils, synods of bishops, papal encyclicals, papal letters, decrees of a Vatican congregation).

Historical consciousness, on the other hand, conceives the moral life of the Christian as one of personal responsibility within changing historical conditions. Indeed, the norms themselves reflect the historical situation in which they were first formulated and subsequently interpreted. The emphasis, then, is on "the subject," as historical and social (see chapters 4 and 5). Therefore, an historically conscious methodology is more inductive than deductive, and it deals with moral issues in the concrete and in terms of the particularities of the historical moment. It emphasizes the empirical, the evolutionary, the changeable. According to Vatican II, "...the human race has passed from a rather static concept of reality to a more dynamic, evolutionary one" (*Pastoral Constitution on the Church in the Modern World*, n. 5). A moral theology founded on an historically conscious methodology stresses personal responsibility: to God, to oneself, to the Church, and to the wider human community. It does not completely reject teleology. On the contrary, it understands history as moving toward the Kingdom of God. But it does not assume some inexorable, predetermined process or plan that is readily knowable in light of reason (natural law) and faith (divine law and ecclesiastical law). Neither does it reject the place of norms and obligations, as in the deontological approach. But those norms and obligations never adequately embody or capture the values which they purport to express. The values (e.g., the dignity of human life) may be absolute, but the norms to realize them (e.g., no killing) are relative to the historical situation.

The *advantages* of historical consciousness are its respect for the dignity of the person, for human freedom and responsibility, and its understanding of the moral life as something always unfinished and in process. Its *disadvantages* are its tendencies toward subjectivism ("I am my own law"), relativism ("Nothing is finally binding upon me"), and anti-nomianism ("Laws of every kind are completely irrelevant").

Properly understood, these two methodologies are not necessarily antithetical. A balanced moral theology cannot prescind from principles, precedent, and ultimate purpose, and so it must to that extent be deductive, deontological, and teleological. But it must always attend to the person and the situation, and so it must also be inductive and historical. It is not a question, however, of preserving fifty percent of classicism and adding fifty percent of historical consciousness. The relationship is not so much one of equality as of dialectical tension. That is to say, there are values in the classicist approach which an historical–consciousness approach cannot neglect: the concern for clarity, precision, order, consistency, objectivity, and respect for the classic sources of Christian faith, i.e., Sacred Scripture, the writing of the Fathers and great theologians, and the official teachings of the Church.

On the other hand, there *is* perhaps one irreconcilable difference between the two approaches. The classicist assumes that one can know and express absolute truth in ways that are essentially unaffected by the normal limitations of our human condition. Classicism neglects the basic Thomistic principle that "whatever is received is received according to the mode [situation] of the receiver" (*Summa Theologica*, I, q. 79, a. 6) and is generally indifferent to the major findings of anthropology, psychology, sociology, and especially the sociology of knowledge (see, for example, Peter Berger and Thomas Luckmann, *The Social Construction of Reality*, New York: Doubleday, 1966). Because the classicist rejects in principle the assertion that the perception of all truth is historically conditioned, the classicist takes the sources of Christian faith (Scripture, doctrines, etc.) at "face value," i.e., as if the language and concepts found in the original documents have exactly the same meaning for their authors as they do for those of us reading those documents today. Two recent official pronouncements of the Catholic Church explicitly transcend the classicist approach: the Pontifical Biblical Commission's *Instruction on the Historical Truth of the Gospels* (1964), and the Congregation for the Doctrine of the Faith's *Mysterium Ecclesiae* (1973). Excerpts from both of these documents are provided in the Appendix.

ECUMENICAL SITUATION

The growing theological consensus noted earlier on the mystery of the Church and the celebration of the sacraments is not duplicated here in the area of moral theology or Christian ethics. None of the ecumenical dialogues, for example, has addressed itself to a major moral issue in the sustained way in which they have faced such questions as the place and function of the ordained ministry, papal primacy and infallibility, the nature of the Eucharist, or the mission of the Church. The ecumenical exchange has been wider and more intensive among the doctrinal or dogmatic theologians than it has been among the moral theologians of the various Christian denominations and traditions. Exceptions on the Catholic side include Charles Curran (see his *Politics, Medicine, and Christian Ethics: A Dialogue with Paul Ramsey*, Philadelphia: Fortress Press, 1973), Franz Böckle (see his *Law and Conscience*, New York: Sheed & Ward, 1966), and Joseph Fuchs (see his *Natural Law: A Theological Investigation*, New York: Sheed & Ward, 1965), and on the Protestant side, James Gustafson (see his *Protestant and Roman Catholic Ethics*, Chicago: University of Chicago Press, 1978) and Paul Ramsey (see his *Who Speaks for the Church?*, Nashville: Abingdon Press, 1966). If we are to take Gustafson's view as reliable, the fault in this case may be more on the Protestant than on the Catholic side.

Protestants (e.g., see Roger Mehl, *Catholic Ethics and Protestant Ethics*, Philadelphia: Westminster Press, 1971) often fail to appreciate the origins of Catholic moral theology or the major changes which have occurred in it since Vatican II alone. Catholic moral theology came into being as a distinct discipline in order to assist the confessor in his sacramental functions. Seldom in Protestantism has such a juridical role existed, and so Protestant ethics has usually been more diffuse and ambiguous. Furthermore, Catholics have always stressed the mediating role of the Church and of certain ministers within the Church. Thus, Catholic moral theology has been attentive to norms and principles formulated and authoritatively taught by the hierarchy, whereas Protestant ethics has developed in a much freer atmosphere, without any supreme court of appeal and without required loyalty to specific moral teachings.

A major difference between the two approaches has to do with the place of Sacred Scripture in moral reasoning. The Reformation principle *sola scriptura* ("Scripture alone") became deeply embedded in the Protestant tradition, so much so that a wide variety of Protestant ethicists—from the liberal, social Gospel left to the conservative, fundamentalist right—grounded their ethics entirely in Scripture. According to Gustafson, ". . . when the centrality of the natural moral law in Catholic moral theology is set in contrast to the centrality of Scripture in Protestant ethics, a historic divergence of great proportions is made clear" (*Protestant and Roman Catholic Ethics*, p. 21).

If Catholic and Protestant moral theologies are coming closer together, it is because of revision of traditional assumptions on both sides. Thus, Catholics have a more nuanced understanding of natural law and ecclesiastical authority, whereas Protestants have a more critical perception of Scripture and a greater sense of tradition. Gustafson draws a comparison on the basis of certain polarities in moral theology: being and becoming, structure and process, order and dynamics, continuity and change, determination and freedom, nature and history, nature and grace, law and Gospel. Catholic moral theologians are paying increasing attention to the second set of terms, while Protestants are focusing more intently on the first set. Another way of putting it: Catholics have moved toward an historically conscious methodology without yielding the abiding values of the classicist approach, and Protestants have moved toward embracing some of those enduring values of classicism without abandoning the best in the method of historical consciousness.

SUMMARY

1. Just as faith and action are united in the one notion of *praxis* (practice-plus-reflection, and reflection-in-practice), so dogmatic and moral theology are united in one systematic theology. On the other hand, they are not simply the same. For a living faith, there must be an expression of love, but faith itself is not the same as love and can exist, at least for a time, without love. So, too, it is possible to distinguish between what we believe and what we are called to be and to do.

2. *Christian* ethics does not differ from *philosophical* ethics simply on the basis that the former proceeds from revelation as well as reason while the latter proceeds from reason alone. Insofar as all reality is graced, the question is not so much whether there is a distinctively Christian ethics as whether there is a purely philosophical ethics, completely untouched by the order of grace.

3. *Christian ethics* may be *defined* as the intellectual discipline that renders an account of the experience of God in Jesus Christ and that draws the normative inferences from it for the conduct of the Christian community and its members. It seeks to aid the Church and its members to discern what God is enabling and requiring them to be and to do.

4. Faithful *praxis* is linked in ancient Israel with the *Law* and that, in turn, with the *Covenant*. The most solemn expression of the Law

was the *Decalogue,* or Ten Commandments. The Ten Commandments are unique in the sense that they are regarded as the revealed will of God and as a manifestation of the bond that exists between God and the people of Israel. The Decalogue was not the ultimate norm of all morality but was concerned primarily with the community and its survival. It was not so much an ethical document as a covenantal one.

5.   The *Ten* Commandments are not recognized *as such* in the New Testament, not even by Jesus. And they had not yet become a charter of morality.

6.   The *Covenant* was always the principal motive for obeying the Law in the Old Testament. Its heart and soul is *hesed*, the affection and loyalty which bound the two unequal partners (God and Israel) together. The Covenant is summed up in the formula: "I will be your God and you shall be my people" (Jeremiah 7:23).

7.   *Interpretation* of the Covenant was not left to any one group, but was given by the *priests*, the *prophets*, and the *wise persons* alike.

8.   The moral message of *Jesus* was centered on the Kingdom of God. His preaching of the Kingdom was both a *proclamation* of good news and a warning and call to *repentance*. Moral existence is always a response to a divine call. We find no ethical system as such in the New Testament, and certainly not in Jesus' teaching.

9.   That is not to say that Jesus made no specific *moral demands*. He repudiated self-righteousness and presumption. He demanded faith in himself. He required heavy sacrifices from his disciples: e.g., leaving home, selling their possessions. He set himself at odds with certain aspects of the law, attacking those who equated observance of the law with moral probity. He commanded us to love one another, even our enemies. He gave an example of this love in his own life and death.

10.   Jesus was concerned with *the world*, but he did not come to change the political order directly. What he preached was bound to affect the consciousness and behavior of those who accepted his word, but he explicitly rejected every effort to make of himself a *political* figure.

11.   Jesus had a special regard for *the poor*, with whom he could identify from his own background and experience, and he warned against the temptations of wealth and power. This is especially evident in the Gospel of Luke. What is revolutionary about Jesus' teaching was that the poor should have any place at all in the divine scheme of things. Poverty is not an obstacle to the Kingdom. On the contrary.

12.   Jesus' teaching on *marriage* and the *family* was founded on his concern for the *dignity of women*, far beyond the concern shown in contemporary Jewish attitudes and customs. He was in the company of

women, healed women, and included them among his followers. He insisted on the permanence of marriage, lest women be regarded as mere objects to be set aside at will.

13. Jesus was not silent about *rewards and punishments*, but he criticized those who acted morally only for the sake of rewards, and he also reminded his listeners that God's standards, dictated by divine mercy, are not our standards. Those who come into the vineyard at the eleventh hour can also be saved.

14. The *early Church's* moral teaching was shaped by the same focal concern for the coming Kingdom of God. Our movement toward the Kingdom is initiated in Baptism and with the outpouring of the Holy Spirit. We have become a new creation, the Body of Christ. Christian existence is existence in *community*. The Law is summed up in the call to love one another.

15. Formal *post-biblical reflection* on the nature and demands of Christian existence was influenced by the threat of paganism. Thus, moral questions were concerned with false worship and the use of pagan images. The imitation of God in Christ was an early theme of Christian moral theology—e.g., Clement of Alexandria and Origen.

16. The first great figure in moral theology was *Augustine*, who attended to such questions as the relationship between grace and freedom, grace and law. He emphasized always the disposition of the heart. On the other hand, there is a negative tone to much of Augustine's work, especially on matters of sexuality, that has had a less happy influence on subsequent moral theology.

17. Moral theology took a significant turn in the *sixth century*, when, under the influence of the Celtic monks, the sacrament of Penance was administered more widely. The fact that a generally uneducated clergy needed to determine appropriate penances for a broad variety of sins brought about the *penitential books*, which were the forerunners of the post-medieval manuals of moral theology.

18. Christian moral life was now perceived primarily as a matter of *avoiding sin*. Absolution was less an act of mercy and forgiveness than an act of *judgment*.

19. With the emergence of *universities* in the high Middle Ages (thirteenth century), attention to moral questions became more systematic: in Bonaventure and especially in *Thomas Aquinas*. However, moral theology was still not separate from theology as a whole. Thomas argued that we must be concerned with the way we act because we are made in the image and likeness of God, we are destined for eternal union with

God, and we have been redeemed by Christ. Thomas' moral teaching, therefore, was framed by the doctrines of creation and redemption.

20. *Nominalism* reintroduced an *individualistic* ethic and an ethical *legalism*. Since each moral act is utterly isolated from all others, the only force that can bring some measure of harmony into human behavior is law.

21. This was also the period of extraordinary *economic* expansion and complexification. Moral theology became preoccupied with such problems as contracts and the buying and selling of goods. A moral *minimalism* resulted, as people asked simply what they were absolutely required to do to avoid sin. It was against this situation that *Martin Luther* reacted.

22. In counter-reaction to Luther and the Protestant Reformation, the *Council of Trent* established a *Catholic seminary system*. This created for the first time in the Church's history a formal need for *textbooks* or manuals to prepare priests for the sacramental ministry, especially the ministry of Penance. The moral theology textbooks were born out of this period (sixteenth century), and moral questions were now treated entirely separately from the broader dogmatic and biblical ones.

23. Extreme approaches to moral theology quickly developed: *Jansenism* followed a rigorist path (the strictest course was always the preferred course), and *laxists* followed a permissive path (when in doubt, follow the easier course). *Probabilism* agreed with the laxist approach if the easier course were approved by at least one reputable theologian. *Equiprobabilism* demanded that the strength of the two positions (the one strict, the other liberal) should be roughly equivalent. *Probabiliorism* demanded that the lenient view be in fact the stronger (i.e., more probable) view as well.

24. The principal moderating force at this time was *Alphonsus Ligouri*, who initiated the practice of identifying and summarizing all opinions and then offering his own prudent view, somewhere near the center.

25. A reaction to the legalism and isolated character of moral theology developed in the *nineteenth century* in Germany, and especially at the University of Tübingen. Moral theology was gradually reconnected with the Bible and with such New Testament themes as conversion, discipleship, and the love commandment. The more traditional (i.e., classicist) approach continued in many countries, including the United States, and in Rome's official teachings, until the work being done in Germany began making a wider impact on the Catholic world.

26. The *Second Vatican Council* called for a renewal of moral theology, stressing its biblical roots, the idea of Christian vocation, the primacy of charity, the mystery of Christ, and the history of salvation.

27. Meanwhile, *Catholic social doctrine*, i.e., the body of official teachings on the social order, began to take shape during the pontificate of *Leo XII*. The Church's social teachings have been formulated in *three stages*: (1) the response to the *Industrial Revolution* (emphasis on labor unions, just wage, e.g.); (2) the response to the growing *internationalization* of life (emphasis on peace and international social justice); and (3) the response to *new social questions* posed by *technology* (arms race, development and liberation of Third World, environmental pollution, e.g.).

28. Catholic social doctrine is focused on the following themes: (1) the *dignity of the human person* as created in the image of God; (2) human *rights* and *duties* which protect and enhance that dignity; (3) the radically *social* nature of human existence; (4) the responsibility of the individual to *society* and vice versa; (5) the responsibility of the *state* to society, and vice versa; and (6) the place of *voluntary associations* as bridges and buffers between society and the state.

29. The broader *social dimensions* of Christian moral existence are especially emphasized in Vatican II's *Pastoral Constitution on the Church in the Modern World* and are reaffirmed strongly in the Third International Synod of Bishops' *Justice in the World*. The latter document teaches that the struggle for justice and liberation is part of the essential *mission of the Church* and that this struggle must occur within as well as outside the Church.

30. *Catholic moral theology today* is incorporating some of the insights of an historically conscious methodology while preserving many of classicism's abiding values. *Classicism* stresses conformity with extrinsic norms based on unchanging truth; *historical consciousness* stresses the subjective responsibility of the person, with attention to the wider community and to the process of history. Properly conceived, the two approaches are somewhat complementary. A balanced moral theology cannot prescind from principles, precedent, and ultimate purpose, and so it must, to that extent, be deductive, deontological, and teleological. But it must also attend to the person and the situation, and so it must also be inductive and historical.

31. In the end, however, classicism rejects the principle that every perception and formulation of truth is historically conditioned. Therein lies the fundamental *opposition* between classicism and historical consciousness.

32.   There is less *ecumenical* progress in the realm of Christian ethics or moral theology than on some of the large ecclesiological questions to which we referred in Part IV of the book. Although there are continued differences about natural law and about specific answers given to specific moral problems (e.g., abortion, birth control), a major difference between Catholic and Protestant ethics has been in their respective *uses of Sacred Scripture* as a norm of moral reflection.

33.   Ecumenical convergence is in process as Protestants appropriate some of the enduring values in the classicist approach and as Catholics move more confidently into historical consciousness.

SUGGESTED READINGS

Gustafson, James M. *Can Ethics Be Christian?* Chicago: University of Chicago Press, 1975.

———————. *Protestant and Roman Catholic Ethics : Prospects for Rapprochement.* Chicago: University of Chicago Press, 1978.

Häring, Bernard. "Historical Survey of Moral Theology." *The Law of Christ.* Vol. 1, Westminster, Md.: Newman Press, 1965, pp. 3-33.

O'Connell, Timothy E. *Principles for a Catholic Morality.* New York: Seabury Press, 1978.

Regan, George M. *New Trends in Moral Theology: A Survey of Fundamental Moral Themes.* New York: Newman Press, 1971.

Schnackenburg, Rudolf. *The Moral Teaching of the New Testament.* New York: Herder & Herder, 1971.

·XXVI·

CHRISTIAN EXISTENCE: PRINCIPLES AND PROCESS

This is an exceedingly ambitious chapter, since it attempts a comprehensive statement of Catholic moral theology. The material is organized around three fundamental questions: (1) *Who is the Christian?* (2) *What kind of person is the Christian called to become?* (3) *How does one become a Christian?* The focus is the theological principles which permeate and shape the Catholic tradition's answers to each of these questions.

The formulation, interpretation, and application of those principles, however, are always historically conditioned. Christian existence itself is always historical existence. One not only *is* a Christian; one is constantly *becoming* a Christian. Conversion to the Gospel is both an act and a process. Accordingly, Christian existence moves between the polarities of principle and process, of being and becoming, of essence and existence, of the universal and the particular, of conviction and risk, of substance and form. But these are not mutually opposed; the one requires and includes the other. Thus, the universal is that which particulars have in common and which gives them meaning. The universal, in turn, is nothing apart from particulars.

So, too, with the polarity of principle and process. Principles do not appear full-blown apart from experience. They are attempts at coming to terms with the multiplicity and ambiguity of experience. Principles are formulations which try to bring a measure of consistency and coherence to human experience, to find common threads which hold that experience together. But their formulation always presupposes experience itself. Once formulated, those principles also have a critical impact on our subsequent evaluation of experience. We reconsider our estimation of past and present experiences, and we revise our anticipation of future experiences in light of these principles. In other words, principles are at once *products* of experience and *shapers* of experience. For that reason, moral theology cannot follow the method of classicism alone (which may underestimate the impact of process on principles) nor the method of historical consciousness alone (which may attend too little to the impact of principles on process). Catholic moral theology is concerned with principles and process alike.

WHO IS THE CHRISTIAN?

The answer to this question can be formulated in only a cumulative fashion. Thus, the Christian is *a radically social human person in whom God is present in grace but who is, at the same time, prone to act against the divine presence.* Thus far we have described any and every human being. The Christian is, first, a human being. But the Christian is a particular kind of human being, not in the sense that a Christian has a different biological or psychic structure, but in the sense that a Christian has moved to *a different level of human consciousness.* The Christian is one who *believes in Jesus Christ, and whose whole life is shaped by that belief.* The process by which the Christian moves to that new level of consciousness is *conversion.*

Since we have already addressed ourselves at some length to the question of human existence in chapters 4 and 5, we shall not repeat that discussion here. We shall focus instead on those elements of our cumulative definition of the Christian to which specific attention has not yet been given in this book, namely, the questions of *sin* and *conversion.*

Sin

Biblical Notions

A first understanding of the word *sin* in the Bible is "to miss the mark." To sin is to fail to achieve one's goal or to fail to measure up to one's highest standards. In the *Old Testament,* with its emphasis on the Covenant, sin is *infidelity to the covenantal relationship* between God and ourselves. It is our failure to live up to the terms of the agreement. It is a missing of the mark. Sin is also a form of idolatry. It is a substituting of human concerns and interests for God's sovereign will (Exodus 32:1-6; Deuteronomy 9:7-21). We sin against the God whom we do not see by violating the rights of our neighbor whom we do see (Leviticus 19:9-18; Isaiah 1:23-25). Rejection of the neighbor is rejection of God (Ezekiel 18:3-32).

The same relationships are present in the *New Testament.* Love of God and love of neighbor are inextricably linked (Matthew 22:34-40; Mark 12:28-31; Luke 10:25-37). It is striking that where the word for sin appears in the *Synoptics,* it almost always is used in connection with the *forgiveness of sins.* Jesus himself associates with sinners and calls them to repentance (Matthew 9:10,13; 11:19; Luke 7:34; 15:1-2; 19:7). For Jesus sin comes only from the heart, and only insofar as it does is the human person defiled (Matthew 15:18-19; Mark 7:20-22). But the sinner need only ask for forgiveness (Luke 18:13-14). There is joy in heaven over the sinner's return (Luke 15:7,10).

The malice of sin is more explicit in John: It is lawlessness (1 John 3:4), wrongdoing (5:17), lust and pride (2:16), darkness (3:9-11). But Jesus is also the conqueror of sin (John 8:46; 1 John 3:5). He is the lamb who takes away the sin of the world (John 1:29). The fullest theology of sin in the New Testament appears in the writings of Paul, and in the first part of the Epistle to the Romans in particular. It is not observance of the Law which brings us victory over sin, he writes. The Law only makes us aware of our sin. In Christ we die to sin. Our old sinful self is crucified with him "so that the sinful body might be destroyed and we might be slaves to sin no longer" (Romans 6:6). Therefore, we are now all "alive for God in Christ Jesus" (6:11). But if we are indeed new creatures in Christ, freed of sin, we must act in accordance with our status. And yet we do in fact sin. We act against who we are and against the God who is within us: "What happens is that I do, not the good I will to do, but the evil I do not intend" (7:19). Our inner selves want to follow the way of the spirit, but our outer selves are still pulled by the flesh. The Spirit has already been given to us as "first fruits" of the new creation, of the redemption of our bodies (8:23). The Spirit helps us in our weakness and makes intercession for us (8:26). "If God is for us, who can be against us?" (8:31). Therefore, Paul is not conceding here the inevitability of sin, only the permanent state of conflict which characterizes human existence: conflict between the spirit and the flesh. We need not be defeated. We can achieve victory in Christ. His Spirit has taken possession of us.

Freedom and Responsibility

The spirit-flesh conflict raises the larger theological question of freedom and responsibility. It is important to note, first, what freedom is *not*. It is not a faculty alongside other faculties (e.g., intellect, will) by which a person decides to do this or that. Freedom enters into the very definition of what it means to be human. To be free is to be present to oneself, to be in possession of oneself, to be conscious of oneself as a distinct, responsible being. Freedom does not so much allow us to *do something* as to *be someone*.

Such freedom, however, is not absolute. Only God is absolutely free, i.e., fully and perfecting self-possessive and responsible. Human freedom is *limited* from without and from within. *From without* our self-possession is qualified by our situatedness in history. Since the world is "mediated by meaning" (Lonergan), our very self-understanding and, therefore, our very freedom are shaped by the meanings which are mediated through our experience (e.g., what our parents tell us we are, what our friends and relatives and neighbors tell us, what society tells us, how our institutions, including the Church, define us, what our economic and social status discloses to us). Our freedom is also limited from without by various natural and physical realities and events—i.e., by the sheer facticity of worldly existence. *From within* our freedom is qualified by the fact that we can never be fully present to ourselves. There is a psychic universe, a portion of which Freud and others have only recently discovered, which remains hidden from our consciousness and yet influences profoundly our awareness, our vision, and our sense of personal responsibility.

Freedom, therefore, is *the relatively limited capacity to decide who we shall be.* It is not something that is active only from time to time, such as at the moment of a choice or decision. Freedom is permanently operative. It governs our whole being all the time. Such freedom is not an immediate datum of our experience. We cannot see it or readily identify it by testing. Nor is freedom (to use Karl Rahner's analogy) like a knife which always remains the same in its capacity for cutting, and in cutting always remains the same knife. Freedom is not simply an instrument for meeting specific needs of choice. It is that fundamental capacity for making a final and irrevocable choice to *be* someone, to be a particular kind of human being. In that sense, freedom is the capacity for the eternal, for God. It is that which allows us to orient ourselves beyond ourselves, to recognize who we are ultimately and to shape our entire life (not just this or that individual act) according to that new self-consciousness of who we are in the presence of God.

And this is precisely what contemporary Catholic moral theologians such as Joseph Fuchs and others mean by the *"fundamental option."* In being truly converted to the Kingdom of God, everything we do assumes its direction, purpose, and meaning in light of the Kingdom, i.e., in light of God's will. This does not rule out the possibility, indeed the probability, that we shall occasionally act against this fundamental choice for God. But only a fundamental reversal of that choice (what the traditional textbooks called *aversio a Deo*, a "turning away from God") is sufficient to cancel out the original decision to understand oneself in relation to God and to orient one's whole life in view of that new self-understanding. In other words, no single act by itself is sufficient to merit eternal punishment in hell unless that act is of sufficient depth and magnitude to constitute a fundamental repeal of the conversion experience. Only a *mortal sin*, Thomas Aquinas wrote, truly deserves the name "sin" (*Summa Theologica* I-II,

q. 88, a. 1). So rare an occurrence should that be in the case of one who is sincerely oriented to God that for the first several centuries the Church expected its members to have recourse to the sacrament of Reconciliation no more than once in their entire lifetimes, if that often! (See chapter 22 on the sacrament of Penance.)

Freedom, then, is a *transcendental* capacity (see chapters 4 and 5 on Transcendental Thomism's understanding of human existence). It is a capacity which allows a person to go beyond himself or herself, to become something other than he or she is, and not simply to do this or avoid that. But because it *is* a transcendental capacity, we can never be directly conscious of it. We acknowledged earlier (in chapter 5) that it is impossible for us to answer completely the question "Who are we?" because we are at one and the same time the questioner and the one questioned. Only God has a view of human existence which is objective and comprehensive. Indeed, as soon as we begin reflecting on our freedom we are already exercising it. We experience ourselves as free, but there is no scientific way of verifying our freedom as we verify, for example, the existence of the lungs or the kidneys. We argue to freedom not only on the basis of our experience, which in any case can be distorted by external and internal forces, but on the basis of the implications of its denial. *If we are not free, we are not responsible. And if we are not responsible, human existence is reduced to mechanical existence.* Without freedom and responsibility there is no love, no faith, no hope, no trust, no compassion, no friendship, no justice. Everything is calculated, predetermined, subject only to accident and/or *mis*calculation.

In summary, in our original, transcendental experience of ourselves as *subjects*, i.e., as distinct, conscious, interrelating, free persons, we know who we are. But we can never objectify with absolute certainty what we know. We know more of ourselves than we can say. No statement, no formulation can ever capture fully what we experience of ourselves as selves, no more than we can adequately report to another the beauty of a symphony, the powerful impact of a speaker, or the horror of an accident. We are at once present to ourselves and distant from ourselves. We are *present* to ourselves in that we are who we are and that we alone are directly conscious of who we are. But we are also *distant* from ourselves in that even our self-knowledge is impaired by factors and forces outside and inside ourselves.

The Capacity for Sin

Freedom is the capacity to say either "Yes" or "No" to God, i.e., to see ourselves either as having ultimate worth because we are alive by a principle which transcends us, or, on the other hand, to see ourselves as merely a constellation and network of biological responses and of psychological and sociological conditioning. Evidence (not overwhelming proof) of our capacity to say "Yes" to God appears in various acts of heroism and of extraordinary generosity where self-interest is clearly subordinated to the interests of others. One need only reflect on the obscenity of Auschwitz and Buchenwald to find similar evidence of our radical capacity to say "No" to God.

On the other hand, we can never point to a particular moment or act in our lives and say that precisely here and not somewhere else we made a fundamental and irrevocable choice for or against God. Whether our lives are oriented toward God or away from God can be judged only on the basis of the totality of our lives, not on the basis of a totaling up virtuous acts and sinful acts and then figuring the difference. Nor are we saying that the possibility of a "No" to God is about the same as that of a "Yes." *Although the Church has always taught that we have the capacity to reject God fundamentally (mortal sin), it has never taught that there are, in fact, persons in hell.* Insofar as Sacred Scripture describes the miseries of eternal punishment, it presents them as possibilities of human life and as instructions about the absolute seriousness of our moral decisions.

Furthermore, *we can never be certain that we have finally and fully said "No" to God, even in an act which appears on the surface to be of such a kind*. We cannot say with certitude to what extent outside and inside forces manipulated us, because that is never obvious to superficial examination. "We can never know with ultimate certainty whether we are sinners. But although it can be suppressed, we do know with ultimate certainty that we really *can* be sinners, even when our bourgeois everyday life and our own reflexive manipulation of our motives appear to give us very good grades" (Karl Rahner, *Foundations of Christian Faith*, p. 104).

What is to be said, finally, of *God's sovereignty*? If we have the capacity to say a final and definitive "No" to God, does not that limit God's power over us? It is God who created us as free beings and who willed and established our freedom. Subjectivity, therefore, must exist without limiting the sovereignty of God. If that seems too simple, consider the alternatives: (a) we are not free, and, therefore, not really human; or (b) God is essentially limited, and, therefore, not really God.

Mortal, Serious, and Venial Sin

As we reflect on our own lives and on the lives of others (the latter is usually the easier task), we recognize that those lives are marked by ambiguity and inconsistency. No one is perfectly good all the time, nor absolutely evil all the time. There is good and bad in everyone, it would appear. This indicates, first, that our fundamental option does not insure uniformity of behavior. It also indicates, secondly, that there are forces which impede our intended course of action. Why this should be so, we can never say. *That* this is so, we know all too well. We call this condition *Original Sin*.

Venial sin is a human act which is not fully human, i.e., not fully consistent with our fundamental orientation toward God. In venial sin there is a genuine decision to do this or that *action*, but there is no decision to become this or that sort of *person*. In venial sin a person chooses to do a particular deed, but he or she also wants even more deeply to be the kind of person who stands opposed to the deed. In every venial sin, therefore, there is a contradiction between the act and the person doing the act.

Venial sin admits of *degrees* of seriousness. Some actions are objectively more serious violations of the Gospel than others. Some sinful motives are more clearly defined than others. Some circumstances make an attitude or a deed more serious than others. *Serious sin*, therefore, is even more inconsistent with the Gospel than is venial sin. But serious sin is not the same as mortal sin. Missing Mass on Sunday is an example of a serious sin.

Mortal sin is an act which fully engages the person. The person chooses not only the act but also the kind of person he or she wants to be or become in and through the act. An older view in moral theology assumed that the commission of every objectively serious act involved or engaged the fundamental option; in other words, it held that every *serious sin* is a *mortal* sin. That is, if (1) an act was seriously sinful, and (2) a person knew it was seriously sinful, and (3) freely consented to it nonetheless, it was a mortal sin.

The insights of both psychology and sociology compel us to revise that assumption. If these actions were always mortally sinful under these three conditions, and if those who committed them had frequent recourse to the sacrament of Penance throughout their lives, then we are left with the conclusion that many people are constantly changing their very self-definition. Is it conceivable that a person could define himself or herself as someone oriented toward God, then repudiate that definition one Sunday morning by deciding against attending Mass in order to watch a sports event, and then reassert that definition in Confession a few hours or a few days later? To suggest this, some moral theologians are saying, is to undermine our very dignity and to cheapen us as persons.

But is this approach really so much opposed even to traditional (i.e., medieval and post-Tridentine) moral theology? Even that theology insisted that every moral act has to be evaluated in terms of *object, end,* and *circumstances.* First, you have to see if, in fact, it is the kind of act that might engage a person's fundamental relationship with God—e.g., murder. Secondly, you have to attend to the purpose, intention, or motive of the agent; e.g., Did X shoot Y in order to protect the life of Z? Thirdly, you have to consider all of the cirsumtances; e.g., Was the killer acting under hypnosis, or had he or she just suffered a traumatic experience? By bringing together the act, the motive, and the circumstances, the traditional theology also brought together subjective and objective morality.

On the other hand, this *three-source theory* may also have confused the two realms of objective and subjective morality. When asked which of the three sources was the most important, some moralists would answer, "The first, the deed itself." But sin is always in the *will*. The primary determinant of morality must be the *motive*, not the act itself. Indeed, some would say that motive is the *only* determinant insofar as morality is not a matter of deeds but of persons acting as persons. To be moral is to be true to oneself, to be seeking always to *be* the one who responds to the call of God and to *act* in ways consistent with that vocation. To be immoral is to refuse to *be* that kind of person, and therefore to refuse to act in ways consistent with that being.

While it is true that some traditional moralists exaggerated the objective morality of the act, traditional moral theology in general has never divorced the act from the other two subjective factors in the three-source principle. Thus, even though the stealing of a loaf of bread might be a "small matter" (*parvitas materiae*), it could become a grave matter (*gravitas materiae*) if the person one stole it from was at the point of starvation. Accordingly, the three traditional questions we might put to ourselves regarding the morality of particular acts still have value: (1) How serious was the act I performed or failed to perform? (2) What was my motive, as far as I can reasonably determine? (3) What were the circumstances surrounding my decision to do what I did, and how did those circumstances affect my decision?

Capital Sins

Some sins are so deeply rooted in our fallen human nature that they are the source of other, related lapses. These are known as the seven capital sins: pride, covetousness, lust, anger, gluttony, envy, and sloth. They are discussed again below, in connection with the moral virtues. Thus, anger and sloth are sins against the cardinal virtue of fortitude, lust and gluttony against the cardinal virtue of temperance, and so forth. (See Henry Fairlee, *The Seven Deadly Sins Today*, Washington, D.C.: New Republic Books, 1978.)

Conversion

A Christian is not only a radically social human person in whom God is present in grace and who is, at the same time, prone to acting against the divine presence. A Christian is also a person who has moved to a different level of human consciousness. The Christian is one who believes in Jesus Christ and whose whole life is shaped by that belief. The process by which the human person moves to that level of consciousness is called *conversion*. More precisely, it is *Christian* conversion, since conversion to God is an invitation and a possibility for every human being.

In the previous chapter we focused on the element of conversion in the preaching of Jesus (Mark 1:15) and of the early Church (Acts of the Apostles 2:38). It was a call to repentance and belief, to a change of mind, or consciousness, and to a new mode of behavior in keeping with that change of mind. The New Testament, therefore, says that we are to live according to the demands of the Kingdom of God. We are to make God the center and source of our being. We are to allow ourselves to be transformed by the redemptive, healing presence of God and then to allow God to continue to work through us to redeem and heal others and the whole world, enemies as well as friends, the outcasts as well as the respectable, the poor as well as the rich, sinners as well as the righteous.

This, of course, is a broader and more profound understanding of conversion than was traditionally proposed since the Council of Trent, with its necessary emphasis on the intellectual and objective character of faith. To be converted was to accept divine revelation as authoritatively presented by the Church. A "convert" was a non-Catholic who had become a Catholic. The determining feature of conversion, therefore, was ecclesiological, not Christological or anthropological. It had to do, primarily, that is, with one's new relationship to the Catholic Church rather than with one's new self-understanding in relationship to God and/or to Jesus Christ.

To use Bernard Lonergan's terms (*Method in Theology*, New York: Herder & Herder, 1972), conversion means shifting horizons. For Lonergan, an *horizon* is that which circumscribes or sets limits to a person's interests and knowledge. Beyond our horizons are matters which we neither know nor care about. Some horizons are relative, others are basic. *Relative horizons* are those which depend on, or are relative to, our psychological, educational, socio-logical, and cultural development. *Basic horizons* are those which relate to three transcendental conversions: intellectual, moral, and religious. A *conversion* is a radical transformation from which follows on all levels of life an interlocking series of changes and developments. What had once gone unnoticed becomes present and vivid. What had once been of no concern is now of the highest importance. According to Lonergan, there is a change in oneself (intellectual conversion), in one's relations with others (moral conversion), and in one's relation to God (religious conversion). Conversion, then, is the transformation of the individual and his or her world. One's direction is altered, one's eyes are opened, and one perceives the world in a new way. Indeed, one perceives a new world.

In *intellectual conversion* there is a turning away from what seems to be to what is, from one's own limited world as defined by one's own psychologically, sociologically, and culturally condi-tioned desires, fears, and achievements to a world that is consis-tent with the intelligent, the true, the good, and even the holy. Intellectual conversion is more than a change of positions or of style. It is a fundamental alteration of a person's basic stance toward reality.

Moral conversion involves a shift from the level of thought (experience, understanding, judgment) to the level of action (deci-sion). It is the recognition of oneself as a free and responsible subject. The morally converted person is able to make decisions for action that are based not on personal satisfaction but on value, not on what gives pleasure but on what is truly good and worth-while. Falling in love is a prime example of moral conversion. One's emotions, decisions, and actions are all shaped and directed anew. The love literally takes over the person.

Religious conversion is a total being-in-love with God: heart, soul, mind and strength. It occurs through the coming of the Holy Spirit, and it is manifested in the love of one's neighbor, who is the sacrament of God. One should not think, however, that religious conversion comes last, after intellectual and moral conversion. On the contrary, the sequence is usually in reverse. First, there is God's gift of love. The inner grace of God discloses values and prompts action to realize those values. Among the values discerned by love's eye is the value of believing the truths articulated and taught by the community of faith. Full religious transformation should include intellectual and moral conversion, but these two kinds of conversion are neither prerequisites nor inevitable results of religious conversion. Furthermore, every conversion is only a beginning. It is both act and process, once-and-for-all and ongoing.

The *final test* of religious conversion is whether or not it leads to and is continually manifested in *love for the neighbor.* "One who has no love for the brother he has seen cannot love the God he has not seen. The commandment we have from him is this: whoever loves God must also love his brother" (1 John 4:20-21).

WHAT KIND OF PERSON IS THE CHRISTIAN CALLED TO BECOME?
Character

The Christian convert is called to become a person of *character*—i.e., with the capacity for self-determination. A person of character is one who takes responsibility for his or her actions. Those actions are not determined simply by rules or principles but by an intelligent and sometimes courageous response to a concrete situation and challenge. An ethics of character, such as proposed in recent years by Protestant ethicist Stanley Hauerwas, focuses our attention more on the person performing an act than on the acts performed by the person. The person does not set out to acquire and cultivate moral goodness. The actions a person performs not only shape a particular situation; they also *form* the person who does them. In other words, doing the act which the situation calls for will take care of shaping us into morally good persons.

Protestant ethics has accorded too little attention to the moral character of persons, perhaps because of Protestantism's traditional denial that the actual shape of a person's life has any efficacy in the attainment of the person's righteousness. Catholic ethics, on he other hand, has stressed the concept of character, especially in treatises on the theological and moral virtues. And insofar as moral theology is emphasizing today the dimension of freedom and responsibility, the concept of "character ethics" is being even more widely considered and developed in Catholic circles.

Emphasis on character, however, should not tempt us to deny the significance of the passive aspects of human existence. Much that we are is the result of what happens to us, as we noted in the previous section of this chapter. Thus, psychological, physiological, and environmental factors are not to be discounted in character formation. However, we must insist at the same time that these passive aspects of our existence enter into character formation only to the extent that we intentionally permit them to. Thus, it is our character which gives orientation and direction to our lives. Indeed, there is an old principle: "Plant an act, reap a habit; plant a habit, reap a virtue; plant a virtue, reap a character; plant a character, reap a destiny." *Habits* are regular patterns of activity. *Virtues* are good habits (and vices are bad habits). *Character* emerges from the network of virtues (or vices). Our final *destiny* depends upon the character we build in response to grace.

Character can never be finished once and for all. Good or bad habits can be reversed or broken. A pattern of habits can be modified or uprooted. Sometimes this occurs gradually; at other times it may happen through a single decisive act (as in a profound conversion experience, or in mortal sin). By definition, we are open always to change as we respond to new elements in our lives. Our moral future is created cumulatively out of our present and our past. That moral future is fashioned not by a resolution to obey certain moral rules but by a resolution to become a certain kind of person.

Since character is so closely linked with personality, and since personality is always unique, rooted as it is in self-consciousness and self-determination, there is no one type of character which is normative for everyone. There are different styles of life, even within the Christian community. Through our beliefs, intentions, and actions we acquire a particular moral history befitting our nature as self-determining persons. (See Stanley Hauerwas, *Character and the Christian Life: A Study in Theological Ethics*, San Antonio: Trinity University, 1975.)

Virtue

A virtue is a *power (virtus)*, in the literal sense of the word. It is the power (ability, skill, facility) to accomplish moral good, and especially to do it joyfully and perseveringly even against inner and outer obstacles and at the cost of sacrifice. (When that power is turned to evil, it is called a *vice*.) Virtues are powers rooted in the presence of God, in grace. They prompt us to act in such a way as to exclude extreme forms of action. Thus, the saying: *In medio stat virtus* ("In the middle stands virtue"). For example, a person may "hope" so strongly in his eventual salvation that he begins to take it for granted. He sins by *presumption*. On the other hand, someone else may be so despondent about her chances for salvation that she "hopes" too little, and falls into *despair*. The *virtue of hope* stands in the middle of these two extremes: It is confidence in the mercy and love of God, but it also accepts responsibility for cooperating with the saving grace that has been bestowed upon us both at birth and in the sacraments. Christ, of course, is the model of all virtue. Christian moral existence, as we noted in the previous chapter, is based on the *imitation of Christ* (John 13:15).

Theology has traditionally distinguished between *natural* and *supernatural* virtues. But in light of our present understanding of the relationship between nature and grace (see chapter 5), this hard and fast distinction seems no longer appropriate. Supernatural virtues are not something added to natural virtues. On the other hand, the distinction does remind us that virtue is rooted in the human, not divorced from it. Another distinction is between *acquired* and *infused* virtues. Seen from the point of view of its source and rootedness, a virtue is "infused" by God. A final distinction—one that we shall employ in this chapter—is between *theological* and *moral* virtues. The former (faith, hope, and charity) have to do immediately with our relationship with God (thus, they are called *theological; theos* = God). The latter (prudence, justice, temperance, fortitude) have to do immediately with our relationships with one another.

The notion of virtue is not without its parallels in contemporary psychology. Erik Erikson, for example, sees the virtues as representing the strengths of the *ego* over against the animal instincts of the *id* and the imposing claims of the *superego*. "Ego strength" is equivalent to virtue. The *id* and the *superego* can rob the person of his or her freedom. In the one case, the person becomes the slave of passions, and in the other, the slave of "higher authorities." It is at the level of the *ego* that a person takes responsibility for his or her life, keeping the animal drives under some measure of control and maintaining a healthy attitude toward the pressures of an overweening conscience. (See William Meissner, *Foundations for a Psychology of Grace*, New York: Paulist Press, 1966, pp. 153-163.) Similar parallels can be drawn from the writings of Abraham Maslow (d. 1970), especially in his notion of "self-actualization" as an unceasing trend toward unity and toward the integration of energy within the person. For example, the self-actualized person has an increased self-acceptance, acceptance of others, increased autonomy, less hostility, less need for honors and prestige. A person who has achieved these characteristics in the course of personal growth has established a life-pattern very similar to that of the traditional "virtuous person, or person of character." (See *Toward a Psychology of Being*, Princeton, N.J.: Van Nostrand, 1968, and *Motivation and Personality*, New York: Harper & Row, 1970, 2nd. ed.)

The Theological Virtues

Faith

We have already addressed ourselves to certain important aspects of the question of faith in chapters 2, 6, and 7. In chapter 2 we described faith as the foundation of theology, belief, and moral action. In chapter 6 we outlined the present crisis of faith and the challenge to belief. In chapter 7 we placed the problem of faith in the larger context of the theology of revelation. Here we shall only touch again upon some of the points in chapter 2 insofar as they directly relate to the shape and character of Christian existence.

Avery Dulles makes a useful schematization of faith as a theological virtue ("The Meaning of Faith Considered in Relationship to Justice," *The Faith That Does Justice*, John C. Haughey, ed., New York: Paulist Press, 1977, pp. 10-46). Faith can be understood as *conviction*, as *trust*, and as *commitment*. The first is an *intellectualist* approach; the second, a *fiducial* approach; the third, a *performative* approach. In the classical tradition, Catholics have tended to emphasize the first, Protestants the second; today both increasingly support the third.

Faith As Conviction: The so-called "intellectualist" approach takes two forms. The *illuminist* school (Augustine, Thomas Aquinas, *et al.*) understands faith as an inner light or as the beginning of wisdom. Its modern exponents—e.g., Bernard Lonergan—regard faith as "the knowledge that is born of religious love," as the "eye of religious love." This is a view of faith, however, which does not regularly foster an intense human concern. Its primary focus is on the relationship between the individual and God in a contemplative union that could unwittingly encourage a spirit of indifference to the needs of others. Pressed too far, the illuminist notion of faith produces a split between faith and daily life.

The "body of doctrine" school, on the other hand, sees faith as a firm assent of the mind to what the Church authoritatively teaches in the name of God. It tends to equate faith with belief, to think of it as an act of intellectual submission and obedience. Although faith is always expressed in some form, its expressions are always historically conditioned. Furthermore, faith is not the acceptance of someone else's point of view on reality but is one's own interpretation of reality. The "body of doctrines" school also focuses the believer's attention so strongly on what there is to believe that he or she tends to ignore the moral (social, political, economic as well as personal and interpersonal) implications of accepting the Gospel in faith.

Faith as Trust: This is usually called the "fiducial" approach. It underlines the elements of personal trust and stresses the personal relationship of the believer with God. God is less the revealer than the savior. This concept of faith is, of course, solidly biblical (as we saw in chapter 2). It was also the emphasis of the Protestant Reformers. The problem with it is the ease with which it can overlook the importance of human initiative and undermine the sense of human responsibility for the future of the world. Everything is left in the hands of God, who will save us in spite of our iniquity. Although the justified person will perform good works and evil works alike, the deeds themselves do not bring about salvation. Faith alone saves.

Ernst Troeltsch (d. 1923), the Protestant Church historian, pointed out how the Lutheran doctrine of justification entails a lack of real interest in social reform (*The Social Teaching of the Christian Churches*, vol. 2, New York: Harper Torchbook, 1960, p. 540). The Protestant ethicist Reinhold Niebuhr (d. 1971) made a similar criticism of Luther's doctrine of the two kingdoms in his *The Nature and Destiny of Man* (New York: Scribner's, 1964, vol. 2, p. 195). If everything depends upon the grace of God and nothing finally depends on human effort, Christian commitment to social justice and peace is of no ultimate interest to the Kingdom of God.

Faith As Commitment: This is the so-called "performative" approach. Faith can never be a matter of disembodied words. It must be incarnate in *praxis* (faith-in-action). Faith is a transforming acceptance of the Word, which challenges us through the cries of the poor and oppressed. Only in liberating *praxis* can we give to the Word the "warm welcome" that constitutes faith. Faith is not a passive waiting upon God's decision to act; rather, it seizes the initiative and reshapes the world by its God-given power. Faith, therefore, is not a passive virture. It does not protect us from the world; it remakes the world. It is active engagement in the service of the Kingdom of God. This is the understanding especially dominant in Latin American liberation theology today, and it has a stronger biblical basis than many have heretofore acknowledged. Thus, "Whoever does what is true comes to the light" (John 3:21). The Gospel is the power of God revealing God's justice and leading to salvation (Romans 1:16-17). Faith works through love (Galatians 5:6). Our faith overcomes the world (1 John 5:4). But neither is this "performative" view a sufficient understanding of faith.

Faith As Synthesis of Conviction, Trust, and Commitment: Each one of these approaches says something that is enduringly true about the virtue of faith. First, faith inevitably seeks understanding, and the understanding achieved is expressed theologically and sometimes doctrinally, as the "intellectualist" approach insists. Faith, therefore, has content; there are truths to be grasped and become convinced of. Faith is also an inner disposition, an illumination of consciousness by which we see and comprehend reality in a wholly new light. Secondly, faith is acceptance of the Word of God. It is trust in God's power to bestow new life, as the "fiducial" approach argues. Finally, faith is an act of self-surrender, demanding total commitment to the Kingdom of God, as the "performative" approach emphasizes. But that Kingdom is not an other-worldly reality alone. It is also a Kingdom of justice and peace here and now. God is present in history, calling us to collaboration in the coming of the Kingdom. To define faith only as conviction or only as trust is to undermine that principle which is so central to Catholicism: the principle of sacramentality. For it is in and through the neighbor whom we see that we respond to the God whom we do not see.

Faith Development: The recognition that faith is not only an act but also a process is not so revolutionary as it may first appear. Faith has always been understood as a virtue, and virtues are in the category of *habits*. Faith, then, can never be merely a once-and-for-all decision; it is an habitual disposition of the mind and heart toward God (in the case of religious faith in general) and toward Jesus Christ (in the case of Christian faith). Recent developments in the cognate disciplines of social and educational psychology have prompted even deeper probings into the processive or ongoing aspect of faith. Specifically the work of Erik Erikson, Jean Piaget, and Lawrence Kohlberg, on the psychological and secular educational side, have been influencing the work of Methodist theologian James Fowler and the many influenced by him, on the theological and religious educational side. What is characteristic of all of these authors is the conviction that human persons grow and develop morally in *stages*.

Thus, Erikson notes a person's advance through early infancy (with its sense of basic trust), later infancy (sense of autonomy), early childhood (sense of initiative), later childhood (sense of industry), adolescence (sense of personal identity), young adulthood (sense of intimacy), older adulthood (sense of concern for guiding the next generation), and twilight of life (sense of ego integrity in the face of possible ultimate despair). Erikson's stages are easily adaptable to the process of Christian faith. The faith commitment can be viewed sequentially or developmentally as: trust in the Church as mother; a sense of personal autonomy in which self-expression and self-control are balanced; a sense of personal initiative, with the aggressive potential of self-growth balanced by the regulating force of authority; entrance into the give-and-take situation of life, and movement from the private society of the family into the larger, more demanding society of other persons; the experience of a certain disintegration catalyzed by doubt and the struggle for reintegration; interpersonal commitment calling for sacrifice; concern for others who are to follow in the next generation(s); and a heightened eschatological sense of reality. (See *Childhood and Society*, New York: W. W. Norton & Company, 1963, 2nd rev. ed., chapter 7, pp. 247-274.)

For Kohlberg, moral maturity does not consist simply in internalizing rules and norms but in developing one's ability to integrate one's conception of social interaction. Moral development is achieved by the stimulation of the natural development of the individual child's own moral judgment and capacities. This occurs either through discussing moral dilemmas which involve a conflict of interests between persons or through establishing "just communities" which offer many opportunities for engaging in social communication and interaction.

According to Kohlberg, an individual moves through the following stages of moral development: (1) Good is done or evil avoided on a reward-or-punishment basis. (2) Good is done or evil avoided as a result of self-centered use of other people. (3) Good is done or evil avoided as a result of a desire for peer approval. (4) Good is done or evil avoided as a result of devotion to a fixed order established by law, authority, and obligation. (5) Good is done or evil avoided as a result of a sense of equity and mutual obligation arising in a democratic view of the social order. (6) Good is done or evil avoided as a result of conscientious decisions made in the light of values which have been internalized. (See his "Stage and Sequence: The Cognitive-Developmental Approach to Socialization," in *Handbook of Socialization Theory and Research*, David Goslin, ed., Chicago: Rand McNally, 1969.)

James Fowler applies the Kohlberg schema of *moral* development to the development of *faith*:

1.   *Intuitive-protective faith.* The imitative, fantasy-filled phase in which the child can be powerfully and permanently influenced by the examples, moods, actions, and language of the visible faith of primal adults.

2.   *Mythic-literal faith.* The person begins to take on for himself or herself the stories and beliefs and observances which symbolize belonging to his or her community. Beliefs are appropriated with literal interpretation, as are moral rules and attitudes.

3.   *Synthetic-conventional faith.* The person's experience of the world goes beyond the family and primary social groups. Coherence and meaning are certified by either the authority of properly designated persons in each group or by the authority of consensus among "those who count."

4.   *Individuating-reflexive faith.* The person begins to take seriously the burden of responsibility for his or her own commitments, life-style, beliefs, and attitudes. This stage develops under the tutelage of ideologically powerful religions or of charismatic leadership. It both brings and requires a qualitatively new and different kind of self-awareness and responsibility for one's choices and rejections.

5.   *Paradoxical-consolidative faith.* The person recognizes the integrity and truth in positions other than his or her own. He or she affirms and lives out his or her own commitments and beliefs in such a way as to honor that which is true in the lives of others without denying the truth of his or her own. This kind of faith requires a regard for those who are different and who oppose one's own position.

6.   *Universalizing faith.* The person dwells in the world as a transforming presence, but is not of the world. He or she discovers that in being-for-others one is being most truly oneself. (See his *Life Maps: Conversations on the Journey of Faith*, with Sam Keen, Waco, Texas: Word Books, 1978.)

The National Catechetical Directory for Catholics of the United States, *Sharing the Light of Faith* (Washington, D.C.: United States Catholic Conference, 1979), basically accepts this developmental approach to faith and moral development. The life of faith is related to human development, and so passes through stages or levels. Furthermore, different people possess aspects of faith to different degrees. It is the task of catechesis to help at each stage of human development and to lead the person ultimately to full identification with Jesus (par. 174, p. 100). The Directory warns, however, against making any one scientific theory normative. There are different schools of psychology and sociology which do not agree in all respects, nor are all developmental theories of equal merit. Catechists should not assume that any one school or theory has all the answers. Furthermore, these scientific disciplines supply nothing of the doctrinal or moral content of catechetical programs (par. 175, pp. 100-101). The Directory seems finally to adopt, or perhaps *adapt*, Erikson's framework: infancy and early childhood (birth to age 5), childhood (ages 6-10), pre-adolescence and puberty (ages 10-13), adolescence (14–17), early adulthood (ages 18-35), middle adulthood, and later adulthood. There are specific recommendations for catechesis at every stage of development (see pp. 102-113).

With regard to the Kohlberg-Fowler approach to moral and faith development, so popular in recent years among Catholic religious educators, criticisms have centered on the following points: (1) Kohlberg's assumption that morality is a matter of *rational* perception; (2) Kohlberg's focus on *justice alone*, which does not touch upon the human quest for intimacy, community, and friendship, nor on the other moral virtues (prudence, temperance, fortitude); (3) Fowler's distinctly and almost exclusively Tillichian notion of faith as a fundamental *attitude*, and his corresponding deemphasis of faith's *content* (*fides quae creditur*, i.e., that which is believed, faith as "conviction") and its broader *social and political dimension* ("transformative" faith); and (4) the tendency of this approach's adherents to "type-cast" their fellow Christians as if these stages were evaluative rather than descriptive and particular rather than general.

Hope

The virtue of hope received little attention from the classical theologians. Even Thomas Aquinas devoted only a few sections to it in his *Summa Theologica* (II-II, qq. 17-22). Where hope was discussed, it was viewed in an individualistic manner, i.e., as *my* hope for *my* salvation. It was understood as the elevation of the will, made possible by grace, by which we expect eternal life and the means to attain it, ever confident of the omnipotent aid of God. We sin against hope by despair (anticipated failure) and by presumption (anticipated success).

Since the mid-1960s, under the impact of such books as Protestant theologian Jürgen Moltmann's *Theology of Hope* (New York: Harper & Row, 1967), the virtue of hope has assumed a different meaning. *It is that virtue by which we take responsibility for the future, not simply our individual future but the future of the world.* Hope is oriented toward the Kingdom of God, not as heaven alone but as the renewal and re-creation of the whole world. God is not above us but ahead of us, summoning us to cocreate the future. The future holds the primacy. Indeed, in one sense all theology is eschatology. It is *hope* seeking understanding (*spes quaerens intellectum*), and not simply *faith* seeking understanding (*fides quaerens intellectum*), as Augustine, Anselm, Aquinas and others insisted. Revelation is not information about another world but promise about this one. Christian existence is life within the horizon of *expectation*: expectation of the Kingdom of God. The *resurrection* of Jesus Christ is the firstfruits of the Kingdom; it is God's "down payment" on the promise. Our future is the future of the risen Christ.

These same themes, also found in such contemporary Protestant theologians as Wolfhart Pannenberg and Carl Braaten (see chapter 20), were taken over into Catholic theology by Johannes Metz in particular. Our understanding of the world, he insisted, is oriented toward the future. We are not so much contemplative as productive. We are called to build a new world (and not only to interpret it), to engage in "political theology," a theology which constantly critiques the "city" (*polis*) according to the standards of the Kingdom of God. Renunciation of the world is not escape from earthly responsibilities. It is simply the refusal to accept anything in the world as absolute, as identical already with the Kingdom. Nothing is as yet the Kingdom. Everything, therefore, is subject to criticism, including even the Church. The Church, after all, is not the "non-world" but that segment of the world which acknowledges the Lordship of Jesus and lives in light of that confession of faith. It is a community of hope, i.e., a community which lives always for the other, in love of neighbor (*Theology of the World*, New York: Herder & Herder, 1969, pp. 107-140). A similar, although not identical, approach has been fashioned by Latin American liberation theology, but its emphasis remains on the virtue of faith as *praxis* rather than on the virtue of hope.

Karl Rahner reminds us that death relativizes all of our grand designs. It italicizes the hardness and the darkness of human existence. Only in God do we have hope. It is hope that makes us free. Yet it is not, to paraphrase Dietrich Bonhoeffer, a "cheap hope." What we hope for we cannot present in advance, and what we enjoy here and now is not what we ultimately hope for. Hence the Christian will always be regarded as a utopian by the absolute pessimists (those who see no life beyond death and see *this* life as absurd) and also by the absolute optimists (those who find this life completely meaningful and worthwhile without any reference at all to a life beyond death). The Christian "is not a person who grasps for something tangible so that he can enjoy it until death comes, nor is he a person who takes the darkness of the world so seriously that he can no longer venture to believe in the eternal light beyond it" (*Foundations of Christian Faith*, p. 405).

Christian existence, of course, is always historical existence. We experience joy at one moment and tears at another. We experience the grandeur and the vitality of human life, and also taste illusions, disappointment, death. "But to be able to open oneself to the reality of life freely and unsystematically, and to do this without absolutizing either earthly life or death, this can be done only by someone who believes and hopes that the totality of the life which we can experience is encompassed by the holy mystery of eternal love" (p. 405).

This new emphasis on the virtue of hope and on the future has had a significant impact on Catholic moral theology. It helps us to see that ethical norms and obligations are always open-ended, imperfect, incomplete, never finished until the Kingdom comes in all its fullness. It helps us see, too, that humankind is itself in process and in development toward a reality beyond itself: ahead and not above. It helps broaden the scope of moral vision because we hope not only in our own salvation but in the salvation of others and of the whole world. And, finally, it underlines the critical function of all moral reflection, analysis, pronouncement, and action within and by the Church, for hope measures everything against the standard of the coming Kingdom.

We have already seen in chapter 19 how and to what extent the Second Vatican Council also embraced this wider understanding of hope. Hope does not diminish the importance of our duties in this life but rather gives them special urgency (*Pastoral Constitution on the Church in the Modern World*, n. 21). Indeed, it is precisely in our recognition of Christ in our brothers and sisters and in our love of Christ in word and deed alike that we give witness to the truth and share with others the mystery of God's love. "As a consequence, men throughout the world will be aroused to a lively hope—the gift of the Holy Spirit—that they will finally be caught up in peace and utter happiness in that fatherland radiant with the splendor of the Lord" (n. 93). Christian existence, therefore, is existence *in* hope, but also existence which seeks to *give* hope to others.

Charity/Love

We saw in the previous chapter that all of Jesus' moral teachings and those of the early Church have been concentrated in the one commandment of love: love of God and love of neighbor (Mark 12:28-34; Matthew 22:34-40; Luke 10:25-37; Galatians 5:14; 1 John 3:23; 1 Corinthians 13). "There are in the end three things that last: faith, hope and love, and the greatest of these is love" (1 Corinthians 13:13). It should be obvious by now that these three virtues are distinct but not separate. Love is a lived faith and a lived hope. The one virtue without the other two is radically incomplete, dead.

First, what does the word *love* mean? In English there is only the one word; in Greek there are four. *Epithemia* is desire, with the connotation of lust. This is sexual love. (All love is, of course, sexual, but not all sexual action is loving.) *Eros* is the drive toward union with others which brings self-fulfillment. *Philia* is affectionate love such as that among brothers, sisters, and friends. *Agape* is total dedication and devotion to the welfare of the other, regardless of sacrifice and personal cost. Many experiences of authentic love by human beings will entail a proportionate blending of these four elements.

Christian love consists in an intimate participation in the life of God who *is* Love (1 John 4:8,16). It is a gift from God that is mediated by Christ and activated by the Spirit. It calls us to share in the paschal mystery by which Christ handed himself over to death and therefore was raised from the dead and exalted by the Father (Philippians 2:5-11). Christian love is rooted in the whole life, death, and resurrection of Christ. He is its model through his life of service (Mark 10:45), through his complete self-giving on the cross, and through his passing over to the Father. Christian love is the same self-giving, even to the point of crucifixion. "There is no greater love than this: to lay down one's life for one's friends" (John 15:13).

Modern psychologists (Erich Fromm, Rollo May, *et al.*) insist that a person's capacity to love depends on his or her *personal maturity*. Love requires self-knowledge, effort, conviction, courage, generosity, respect, a sense of responsibility, sensitivity, patience, and a fundamental acceptance of oneself with all of one's strengths and limitations. Thus, modern psychology often agrees with the basic Christian principle that we are called to love our neighbor as we love ourselves (Mark 12:31). If, however, an individual has not resolved the inevitable crises of human development, he or she may not attain sufficient human maturity for Christian love. The child starts out by being attached to his or her mother as the "ground of being." The child feels helpless and needs the all-enveloping love of a mother. The child then turns to the father as a guiding principle for thought and action. The child is motivated by the need to acquire the father's praise and avoid his displeasure. At full maturity, the child frees himself or herself from the person of both father and mother as protecting and commanding powers. The adult becomes "his or her own father and mother." Love of God passes through similar stages: love of God in helpless attachment; love of God in obedient attachment; and love of God as personal incorporation of the principles of love and justice into oneself.

If we are really to love as Christ intends, we have to overcome our own narcissism. We must strive for objectivity in every situation and become sensitive to the situations where objectivity eludes us. We must see the difference between our picture of another and the other's behavior, on the one hand, and, on the other hand, the way the other really is, apart from our own interests, needs, fears, and hang-ups. Christian loving also means readiness to take risks, to accept pain and disappointment. It means using one's human powers productively. Loving demands a state of intensity and commitment. Christian love cannot coexist with indifference. Indeed, the opposite of love is not hate but *apathy*, a lack of concern, a suspension of commitment (literally, *apathy* means to be "without pain").

Love is also closely related to the *will*. Will without love becomes manipulation; love without will becomes sentimentality. We are afraid, in the latter case, that if we choose one person rather than another, we will lose something, and we are too insecure to take that chance. And so we hold back, remaining cool and aloof. But the same fear of commitment can be expressed in a flurry of seemingly interpersonal activity, especially of a sexual kind. Sensuality then smothers sensitivity. Sex becomes an instrument to express one's anxieties, about death in particular. We try to prove to ourselves that we are still young and can "perform."

If love is the soul of Christian existence, it must be at the heart of every other Christian virtue. Thus, for example, *justice* without love is legalism; *faith* without love is ideology; *hope* without love is self-centeredness; *forgiveness* without love is self-abasement; *fortitude* without love is recklessness; *generosity* without love is extravagance; *care* without love is mere duty; *fidelity* without love is servitude. Every virtue is an expression of love. No virtue is really a virtue unless it is permeated, or informed, by love (1 Corinthians 13).

"Every benefit which the People of God during its earthly pilgrimage can offer to the human family stems from the fact that

the Church is 'the universal sacrament of salvation,' simultaneously manifesting and exercising the mystery of God's love for
man" (Vatican II, *Pastoral Constitution on the Church in the Modern World*, n. 45). It is the cross of Christ which is "the sign of
God's all-embracing love and...the fountain from which every
grace flows" (*Declaration on the Relationship of the Church to
Non-Christian Religions*, n. 4).

The Virtue of Religion

The virtue of religion, or worship, is the ritualization of the
experience of faith, hope, and charity. (See chapters 8, 21, and 22.)
This virtue was traditionally (i.e., in medieval theology) treated as
part of the virtue of justice inasmuch as it entails giving to God
what is due to God. But we already noted in the preceding chapter
how the new economics of the Middle Ages shaped, if not somewhat distorted, Catholic moral theology. Justice was understood
almost entirely in contractual terms, and so, too, was the relationship between God and us.

The virtue of religion is neither exclusively a theological
virtue (oriented toward God) nor exclusively a moral virtue (oriented toward our relationships with others). The religious person
integrates both: Worship demands love of neighbor, and commitment to one's neighbor is directed to the glory of God (1 Corinthians 11:17-22; Matthew 5:23-24). If the human person is merely
economic or political, then worship is a waste of time. If, however,
we are transcendent subjects, open to the Spirit of God, then
worship puts us in touch with, and expresses, that relationship
with the Transcendent.

The virtue of religion is intimately related to the whole
moral life of the Christian. In the words of Vatican II, the exercise
of religion "consists before all else in those internal, voluntary,
and free acts whereby man sets the course of his life directly
toward God" (*Declaration on Religious Freedom*, n. 3).

Religion, of course, is subject to distortion and corruption.
Idolatry is the worship of something less than the Absolute—e.g.,
money, personal gain, political power. We can make an idol even
of the Church or of institutional elements within the Church.

Superstition absolutizes something finite and invests it with saving power in itself—e.g., astrology, wearing amulets to ward off evil spirits. Christians can be superstitious when they assume that the performance of a particular practice in some numbered sequence will of itself insure salvation. *Hypocrisy* in religious matters is an attempt to use religion to advance one's own position in life. It is a manipulative abuse of religion. Hypocrisy is always a temptation for those who exercise religious authority or who derive any material benefits whatever from their status in the Church. *Legalism* is a religious attitude that makes observance the end of religion. Obedience to law is the ultimate sign of religious faith and the principal means to holiness. Legalism is usually based on a false understanding of God as an exacting lawgiver, a stern taskmaster, a vindictive superior. *Self-delusion*, or triumphalism, is a misinterpretation of divine election. We assume that we are God's favored ones, that we have privileged status in the world, that we are better than the rest of humankind. It is a form of deafness and blindness. We do not see the games of power and domination at work, nor do we appreciate how alienating these games are to those outside the Church. (See Gregory Baum, *Religion and Alienation: A Theological Reading of Sociology*, New York: Paulist Press, 1975.)

The Moral, or Cardinal, Virtues

Prudence

This is the first of the *cardinal* virtues, i.e., those virtues which are the "hinges" (the literal meaning of the Latin *cardo*) of other virtues. Prudence is essentially the ability to *discern*. It is *not* simply an attitude of caution, restraint, timidity, or conservatism. Rather, the prudent person is one who can make decisions. *Prudence formulates and imposes the correct dictates of reason upon the human person* (*recta ratio agibilium*, Thomas Aquinas). Prudence does not answer the question: "What is the best way in principle to do the right thing?" Rather: "What is the best way for me, in this situation, to do the right thing?" The prudent person, therefore, must investigate the situation and take counsel from others. A judgment must be formulated in light of this inquiry and advice. And a decision must be made. The prudent person, therefore, is in the moral order what a creative artist is in the intellectual and aesthetic orders. The novelist, for example, is constantly faced with the problem of deciding what to write and how to write it.

Prudence presupposes the following qualities: knowledge of moral principles, experience *and* the ability to profit by it, ability to learn from others, ability to make rational inferences, a certain inventiveness or creativity, vision or foresight, ability to see and weigh circumstances, an ability to anticipate obstacles and plan to surmount them, and finally an ability to decide in light of all the preceding.

The virtue of prudence is closely allied with the *discernment of spirits* and with *spiritual direction*. To be a Christian is to live in communion with the Spirit of God. It is to be open to that Spirit and receptive to the specific promptings of the Spirit. But the promptings of the Spirit are never unequivocally and unmistakably clear. If "no one has ever seen God" (John 1:18), neither has anyone seen the Spirit. One *infers* the Spirit's presence from what we do see and experience. This *discernment* is at once individual and corporate. Community discernment both derives from and leads to individual discernment. Community discernment presupposes prayer, but it also requires community discussion, the free exchange of opinions in a climate of truthfulness and mutual respect.

It is never easy to discern the Spirit. First, the Spirit itself is invisible and transcendent. Secondly, we are prone to rationalize in our own favor—i.e., to highlight those elements which support our predisposition toward one or another course of action and to ignore those elements which work against that predisposition. Thirdly, many issues are complicated and do not admit ready solutions.

Although we can never be absolutely certain that we are indeed responding to the Spirit, there are certain *negative criteria* by which obviously false responses can be exposed: (1) If the discernment process does not issue forth in the classic "fruits" of the Spirit—love, joy, peace, patient endurance, kindness, generosity, faith, mildness, and chastity (Galatians 5:22-23)—it is not "of the

Spirit." (2) If the discernment process leads to doctrinal or moral positions which are clearly inconsistent with the doctrinal tradition of the Church and/or with recognized norms of biblical and theological scholarship, it is not "of the Spirit." (3) If the discernment process intensifies the isolation and even spiritual eccentricities of those involved in it rather than enhancing the life of the whole Body of Christ (Ephesians 4:15-16), it is not "of the Spirit." (4) If the discernment process ignores pertinent information, rejects the counsel of others who have knowledge and experience in the matter at hand, and formulates its judgments by imposition rather than by corporate reflection, it is not "of the Spirit."

Justice

Insofar as the virtue of justice is rooted in Sacred Scripture, it is linked with the idea of *righteousness* (Hebrew, *sedeq,* and Greek, *dikaiosynē*). It is intimately connected with the Covenant, i.e., with the obligations of the Israelite to the community of Israel. A person is righteous insofar as he or she is conformed and faithful to the Covenant. God, too, is righteous insofar as God saves. Yahweh is our righteousness, our salvation (Jeremiah 23:5). Paul developed the Old Testament notion of righteousness in a thoroughly Christian sense. The righteous is "right" with God. He or she is saved and vindicated. A new life has been given because of this vindication. Christian righteousness, therefore, is the state of vindication and deliverance achieved through the death of Christ (2 Corinthians 5:21; Romans 5:16). The Kingdom of God is "justice, peace, and the joy that is given by the Holy Spirit" (Romans 14:17). Accordingly, perfect and complete righteousness is still an object of hope to be achieved beyond history (Galatians 5:5). Christian righteousness requires that the Christian himself or herself live in a way that is consistent with the death and resurrection of Christ and with the new life in the Spirit that flow from Christ's saving work. This righteousness cannot be achieved by the observance of the Law. It is a free gift of God which reaches its fullness in the Kingdom (Romans 3:30; 1 Corinthians 6:11).

Justice is derived from the Latin word *ius*, which means "right." Justice is concerned with *rights* and with *duties* which correspond to those rights. My duty to respect your bodily integrity flows from your right to life in all its fullness. A right, therefore, is a power that we have to do things which are necessary for achieving the end or purpose for which we are destined as rational and free persons. A right is a person's moral claim upon other persons or society in general to the means of reaching an end that is his or hers, and that he or she is responsible for reaching. In that sense, rights flow from duties. This is the so-called *natural right theory*. Others insist that no one has any rights that are not rooted in positive law—that positive law is the source and origin of all human rights. This is the *theory of legal positivism*. Still others propose that all rights are based upon the social good and are subservient to it. One has only those rights which are necessary to advance the common good. This is the *theory of social good*.

Among the principal human rights, as enumerated, for example, in Pope John XXIII's *Pacem in Terris* (1963) are: the right to life and a worthy manner of living; the right to respect for one's person regardless of sex, race, religion, or national origin; the right to freedom in the pursuit of truth and in its expression and communication; the right to be informed truthfully about matters of concern; the right to a basic education; the right to worship God freely; the right to choose one's state in life; the right to gainful employment, to decent working conditions, to a proper compensation, to private property, to organize; the right of meeting and association; the right to freedom of movement (emigration and immigration); the right to participate in public affairs and to contribute to the common good (see pars. 11-45).

There is, however, a *hierarchy* of rights in terms of their relationship to the last end. Rights are also *limited* by the existence of others' rights. When rights are in *conflict*, the virtue of prudence also comes into play. The following criteria apply: (1) Rights to spiritual goods take precedence over rights to purely temporal goods (e.g., the right to live in dignity over another's right to a profit on an investment); and (2) common goods take precedence over individual goods (e.g., the right of the state to exact taxes to pay for social needs over the right to keep what one earns).

It has been said that justice would not be possible unless we were, in fact, separate from one another. Justice regulates relationships between strangers. Where there is perfect love and communion, the question of rights and duties becomes moot. They are completely fulfilled. Justice, therefore, mediates between the otherness which arises from our exteriority and the oneness which arises from our interiority.

But even if unselfish love among all persons were achieved, the virtue of *social justice* would still be required. In the larger community, beyond the small family units or the bonds of love and friendship, there is "a dynamic interpenetration of all those fundamental human rights upon which the aspirations of individuals and nations are based" (*Justice in the World*, Third International Synod of Bishops, 1971). Persons develop fully only in a societal context, since by definition we are fundamentally and radically social. The quality of life in society, the justice of its mode of organization, the orientation of its structures and systems (e.g., political, legal, economic, social, educational, religious) will either enhance or retard the full human development of the person.

Social sin is a situation in which the very organization of some level of society systematically functions to the detriment of groups or individuals in the society. The sinfulness consists in the way social relationships are contrived or allowed to exist. Sometimes people of good will administer those systems. They are caught up in them. Although they may bear no personal guilt, the *situation* is sinful nonetheless. Accordingly, the virtue of justice is engaged even in those situations where there is no discernible culpability on the part of any particular individuals or in the relationships of particular individuals within a given system. The *otherness* from which the demands of justice flow is intrinsic to the human condition itself, apart from the measure of love that exists between or among human beings.

As the Protestant social ethicist Reinhold Niebuhr argued, it is not enough to present Christian ethics as a love ethic. Given the sinful condition of the world, it is impossible to envisage a society of pure love. Christian ethics must come to terms with the reality

of inevitable conflicts and with the demands for their harmoniza-
tion, often on the basis of arrangements that are far from the
Christian idea of disinterested love. Christian realism tells us that
nations, races, classes, and other groups do not love one another.
Nevertheless, their mutual survival demands that they respect
their obligations to others. Interests must be balanced and claims
recognized. To conceive of a world of love without the imperfect
harmonies established by justice is to create an illusion. A simple
Christian moralism, Niebuhr insisted, will counsel men and
women to be simply unselfish. A profound Christian faith must
encourage them to create systems of justice which will save society
from its own selfishness. Indeed, if that portion of society that
benefits from social inequality attempts to counsel only love, forgiveness, and patience to the discontented and disenfranchised
instead of working for justice, it will convict itself of hypocrisy.
(See, for example, *Moral Man and Immoral Society*, New York:
Scribner's, 1932.)

A correct understanding of social justice demands, furthermore, a correct understanding of the distinction beteen society
and the state. *Society* is constituted by the total network of social,
political, economic, cultural, and religious relationships which are
necessary for full human development. The *state* is the center of
coercive power in society. It is the civil authority by which the
purposes of society are procured and preserved. The distinction
between society and the state is presumed in John XXIII's *Pacem
in Terris* and in the Second Vatican Council's *Declaration on
Religious Freedom.*

The extent to which the state should intervene in the life of
its citizens is attended to in the *principle of subsidiarity*, first
enunciated by Pope Pius XI in *Quadragesimo Anno* (1931). This
principle seeks to establish and maintain a balance between individual initiative and governmental assistance and direction. The
principle holds that the presumption is always in favor of individual or small-group action over against governmental intervention.
The state should intervene only when lesser bodies cannot fulfill a
given task required by the common good. In broader terms, the
principle of subsidiarity means that nothing should be done at a
higher level that can be done as well or better at a lower level.

This principle has to be balanced off, however, by the *process of socialization*, first referred to by John XXIII in *Mater et Magistra* (1961) as "the growing interdependence of citizens in society giving rise to various patterns of group life and activity and in many instances to social institutions established on a juridical basis" (par. 59). Thus, given the increased complexity of modern economic and political life, more intervention is required, without prejudice to the principle of subsidiarity. The two—subsidiarity and socialization—must be kept in creative tension.

The virtue of justice, therefore, is divided as follows: *commutative justice*, which relates to contractual obligations between individuals involving a strict right and the obligation of restitution (e.g., one person lends another person a sum of money; the second person is obliged in conscience to return that money according to the agreement); *distributive justice*, which relates to the obligation of a government toward its citizens, by which the government regulates the burdens and benefits of societal life (e.g., a government is to tax its citizens fairly and to distribute those tax monies according to need); *legal justice*, which relates to the citizen's obligation toward the government or toward society in general (e.g., the citizen must pay his or her fair share of the taxes); and *social justice*, which relates to the obligation of all parties to apply the Gospel to the structures, systems, and institutions of society which are the framework in which all human relationships take place (e.g., an individual and/or groups must take an active interest in necessary social reform).

These four kinds of justice are interrelated and mutually limiting. All four are attempts to express the demands of Christian love (*agape*). All four have to do with rights and duties. Such a notion of justice does not provide immediate answers to the complex problems of social existence, but it does provide *principles of discernment and specific guides for judgment*. If the movement of history is toward the Kingdom of God—a Kingdom of "justice, love, and peace" (*Pastoral Constitution on the Church in the Modern World*, n. 39)—the pursuit of justice is itself part of this movement. If we are called in the meantime to participate in the death and resurrection of Christ, justice helps us to specify the terms and demands of that participation. Conversely, efforts toward the fulfillment of human needs, the protection of human rights, and the realization of structures of genuine mutuality are consequences of faith in the saving power of Christ's death and resurrection.

Temperance

One very important dimension of our being human is rooted in what the traditional theology called the "concupiscible appetites," i.e., our desire to achieve the good through food, drink, or sex. The virtue which enables us to achieve some *balance* in these areas while still living in a state of legitimate self-interest is *temperance*. It is a virtue which has attracted the attention of philosophers from the earliest centuries. The ancient Greeks viewed it as a way of insuring "good hygiene." Plato regarded these sensuous cravings as "an ugly brute of a horse" which had to be curbed by the "charioteer" which is the human mind. The Stoics, too, looked upon these appetites as having to be brought under the complete control of reason.

The early Church Fathers saw the virtue as part of the "grace-full" life, as a way of participating in the death and resurrection of Chirst. Death to self leads to greater life in the Spirit. Thomas Aquinas insisted, however, that the virtue is not the *repression* of the desire for sensual pleasure but rather its *tempering* in the service of human growth. Temperance, therefore, is positive, not negative. It is a virtue which humanizes the pleasures of food, drink, and sex. Aquinas referred to three "subjective parts" or divisions of the virtue: *abstinence*, which humanizes our desires for food and other pleasure-producing elements such as tobacco and drugs; *sobriety*, which humanizes our desires for intoxicating drink; and *chastity*, which humanizes our desires for sexual pleasure in accordance with our state in life. Each of these appetites, when properly satisfied, contributes to the preservation of the individual and of the human species. Intemperance makes them ends in themselves.

Moderation of the sensual appetities through the virtue of temperance is closely allied with Christian *asceticism*. The word *askesis* itself means "exercise." Asceticism is concerned with those exercises which help us regulate the conflict between the spirit and the flesh. It involves a painful struggle, self-denial, and renunciation. The medieval and post-medieval notion of asceticism was not unmixed with rationalism, Stoicism, and Pelagianism—all emphasizing the innate power of the human person to live according to a certain pattern *without grace*. This traditional concept of asceticism was also often founded on a dualistic understanding of human existence, as if the bodily aspects of the human person were unholy, even sinful. Indeed, the traditional moral theology textbooks referred to certain organs of the body as *partes inhonestae* ("dishonorable parts").

In light not only of modern psychology but also of contemporary theology, we understand asceticism as the free and faithful acceptance of one's self, of one's painful limitations, weaknesses, inadequacies, of one's sorrows, disappointments, and frustrations, and, finally, of death itself. One is ascetical in not trying to escape the facticity of human existence by immersing oneself in, or distracting oneself by, purely material pleasures. There is nothing wrong with food, drink, or sexual expression. On the contrary. But they can become crutches or escapes from one's human and Christian responsibilities. At the very least, their misuse is symptomatic of a fundamental disorder. Thus, those who are excessively heavy do not simply have healthier appetites than others. Those who are frequently intoxicated to the point where they cannot function are not simply people who like the taste of liquor. Those who move from one sexual liaison to another with commitment to none are not simply people with uncontainable, overflowing love.

The Christian must pattern his or her life on that of Christ, who did not flee suffering and death but who became obedient even unto death (Mark 10:45; Philippians 2:5-11). Christian asceticism is an asceticism of the cross, a readiness to face death in the service of others and ultimately in the service of the Kingdom of God. Asceticism is an affirmation of the cross as the path to resurrection. The ascetic is one who is patient (literally, "suffering"), prepared for the coming of the Lord, ever vigilant, looking toward the Kingdom. It is life on pilgrimage.

How can one tell if his or her asceticism is genuinely Christian or if it is distorted? *First*, is it an expression of self-acceptance, or of self-loathing? Does one deny oneself because self-denial frees one for greater service to others and makes one a more effective sign of Christ to the world, or does one regard the appetites in question as base and unworthy of a Christian? *Secondly*, is the asceticism oriented to dedicated Christian service, or is it finally a way of avoiding commitment, especially the commitment implied in interpersonal intimacy? *Thirdly*, is the ascetic freer to love, more creative, or is the ascetic an isolated figure, closed-minded, difficult to be with?

Fortitude

Whereas temperance balances our concupiscible appetites, *fortitude* moderates our *irascible* appetites. It strengthens them against the passion of *fear*, on the one hand, and on the other restrains their immoderate tendencies toward *audacity* and *rashness*. Fortitude enables a person to face serious challenges, even death, with some measure of calm. It gives the strength to endure suffering for a just cause. It is *the virtue of courage, by which one overcomes an instinctive fear in order to pursue the good*. Fortitude, therefore, has an active and a passive side. Its active side has to do with taking bold action for the sake of the Kingdom of God; its passive side has to do with enduring some pain, suffering, or even death for the sake of the Kingdom. But not even endurance is merely passive. Martin Luther King, Jr. (d. 1968) always insisted that non-violent resistance was still *resistance*, requiring much courage and commitment.

Biblically, courage and strength are linked (2 Samuel 10:12; Deuteronomy 31:7). The prophets were evidently courageous figures. But every form of true courage and every manifestation of real strength is rooted in God (1 Samuel 17:37; Psalms 27:14; 31:25). In the New Testament this *andreia*, or courage, is commended to us by Paul (1 Corinthians 16:13; 2 Corinthians 5:6-7; 10:1-2) and by the Lord himself (Matthew 9:2; 14:27; John 16:33). The early Church looked to Jesus as the model of courage (Hebrews 12:2). Indeed, the whole eleventh chapter of the Epistle to the Hebrews is a tribute to Christian faith and courage. The martyrs followed in Jesus' path—e.g., Stephen (Act of the Apostles 7) and others (Revelation 7:14).

Prudence and justice precede fortitude. Only the prudent person can be truly courageous. Fortitude presupposes a correct evaluation of a situation and must always be in the service of justice. Fortitude marks a path between the extremes of temerity (rashness) and timidity. Without fortitude, growth is impossible. Nietzsche once said that whatever does not destroy us makes us stronger. We can grow in and through adversity. We can be ennobled by suffering—not that we ever seek it or embrace it for its own sake. Fortitude, then, is our affirmative answer to the inevitable shocks of human existence. It is the ability to dare and to endure.

Without fortitude we suffer *frustration*. We become restless and tense, aggressive and destructive against the perceived sources of our frustration, apathetic and sullen, prone to fantasy and escapism, rigid and locked into comfortable routines, or simply regressive, returning to familiar modes of behavior characteristic of an earlier stage of development.

There are various *defense mechanisms* against frustration. Rationalization assigns logical reasons or plausible excuses for the consequences of frustration (e.g., a person insists that his or her excessive weight is a matter of metabolism). Projection assigns one's own undesirable qualities in exaggerated measure to other people (e.g., a conniving person accuses others of always plotting for their own benefit). Reaction-formation conceals a certain emotion from oneself by giving strong expression to its opposite (e.g., an angry, embittered person smiles frequently or goes to great lengths to be courteous to those who are the objects of his or her anger). Dissociation takes the form either of compulsively physical movements (e.g., twitches) or excessive theorizing that prevents action (e.g., an anxious administrator holds frequent committee meetings but comes to no practical decisions). Repression is the total denial of what frustrates us (e.g., the celibate religious never mentions sex). Substitution generates other activities in place of those which lead to frustration (e.g., the classical "cold shower" in the face of sexual temptations). Compensation is one form of substitution. It is an effort to make up for one deficiency by cultivating a different activity that gives some measure of pleasure and satisfaction (e.g., the shy person takes to painting).

Finally, the virtue of fortitude is missing in a person who is always fearful of displeasing others, who remains silent in the face of injustice, who shuns conflict at all costs, who avoids "rocking the boat," and who, therefore, does whatever he or she thinks is "expected."

Works of Mercy

One of the classic problems in theology has been the reconciliation of divine justice and divine mercy. Justice gives to another what the other deserves by right (*suum cuique*, to each his own); mercy gives to another more than the other deserves. Thomas Aquinas argued that when God shows mercy, divine justice is not defeated. By transcending the exact demands of justice and turning a sinner into a just person, God displays the fullness of justice (*Summa Theologica*, I, q. 21, a. 3), and so mercy enables God to be just to the person whom God has made just. All human mercy is founded in, and evoked by, the mercy of God, and all Christian mercy is rooted in the example of Christ himself (Acts of the Apostles 10:38; John 13:15). Human mercy, however, does not give of its own but of what God has bestowed (Romans 11:30-32; Ephesians 2:4). We see the distress of others as our own distress. Mercy is an act which testifies to our solidarity in sin and our common need for redemption and healing.

It is not ritual that the Lord desires, but love, which is the soul of mercy (Hosea 6:6; Hebrews 10:5-8). "This, rather, is the fasting that I wish: releasing those bound unjustly, untying the thongs of the yoke; setting free the oppressed, breaking every yoke; sharing your bread with the hungry, sheltering the oppressed and the homeless; clothing the naked when you see them, and not turning your back on your own. Then your light shall break forth like the dawn, and your wound shall quickly be healed . . ." (Isaiah 58:6-8). In the parable of the Sheep and the Goats (Matthew 25:31-46) the Lord proclaims that we will be judged by our response to the hungry, the thirsty, the stranger, the naked, the prisoner. "I assure you, as often as you did it for one of my least brothers, you did it for me" (25:40).

These works of mercy traditionally have been divided into *corporal* works (concerned with needs of the body) and *spiritual* works (concerned with needs of the soul). Such a dichotomy is no longer appropriate in light of our understanding of the integrity of the human person as at once bodily and spiritual, but the listings provide a useful reminder of the kind of life that the Christian is called to lead. Thus, the *corporal works of mercy* are: feeding the hungry, giving drink to the thirsty, clothing the naked, sheltering the homeless, visiting the sick, ransoming the captive, and burying the dead (the last was added out of respect for the sanctity of the body as a temple of the Holy Spirit; see 1 Corinthians 3:16). The *spiritual works of mercy* are: instructing the ignorant, counseling the doubtful, admonishing the sinner, bearing wrongs patiently, forgiving offenses, comforting the afflicted, and praying for the living and the dead.

Although most of these works have to do with a Christian's obligations to other individuals in need, they also have broader social and political implications today and are to be linked in many cases with the overriding demands of *social justice*. But the dimension of mercy reminds the Christian that his or her obligations go beyond even those required by social justice.

HOW DOES ONE BECOME A CHRISTIAN?

One becomes a Christian, as we have already noted, by being converted to Jesus Christ and his Gospel of the Kingdom of God, and by being initiated into the community through which the encounter with Christ and the Kingdom is mediated (see chapter 21 on the sacraments of initiation). One thereby opens himself or herself to the grace of the Holy Spirit so that God might dwell within oneself as the triune principle of faith, hope, and charity, as well as of prudence, justice, temperance, and fortitude. A Christian is a person whose whole life is ruled by the commandment of love. The Christian's commitment to love is rooted in faith and activated by hope. The Christian, in turn, intelligently, responsibly, and courageously fulfills the Gospel in his or her interpersonal and institutional relationships, and in the manner and style of his or her own life. Everything is oriented to the glory of God.

But it is one thing to sketch this profile of the committed Christian. It is entirely another matter to say precisely *how* the individual Christian determines what the Gospel demands in this particular situation, in these special circumstances, given these conflicting claims. This raises the broad moral question of the interrelationship between *values* and *norms*; and these, in turn, rest on some prior understanding of what it means to be human and how the enduringly human qualifies and shapes our moral vision and decisions. This is the thorny question of *natural law*.

Values and Norms

Values are of two kinds: premoral and moral. *Premoral values* are those concrete good things that ought to be done, to the extent possible. They have to do with the real world of such things as life and death, knowledge and ignorance, health and sickness, friendship and alienation, beauty and ugliness, wealth and poverty. Insofar as anything exists, it has value. It participates in *being*. If it is antithetical to human growth, however, it is a *disvalue*. The attainment of premoral values may or may not contribute to one's moral growth. Thus, one might preserve the value of life in a prison camp by killing a fellow prisoner in one's own place—clearly a disvalue.

Moral values, on the other hand, are those which are essential to proper human living. They are not merely things that we should attend to (as premoral values are), but are things we must possess if we are to be fully human. Thus, one need not be physically attractive to be fully human, but one must be loving. Moral values include such virtues as honesty, justice, chastity, fortitude, temperance. They are not only a matter of *doing* just deeds or courageous acts, but of *being* just and courageous.

Norms are also of two kinds: material and formal. *Material norms* tell us what we should *do*. They point out premoral values which we are to pursue, or premoral evils which we are to avoid.

Some examples of material norms are: Do not kill. Do not take what belongs to another. Tell the truth. Pay your debts.

Material norms are not absolute. There are times when I may have to withhold the truth or even kill. Thus, although material norms are concrete, informational, and instructive, they are also debatable, often tentative, and open to exceptions. These norms do not provide final answers to specific problems. They point to values and illuminate situations. They provide the moral agent with at least some of the factors that must be taken into account in reaching a final judgment.

Formal norms point to moral values which must be pursued. They indicate attitudes which we should acquire. They tell us the "form" our conduct should take. They indicate what is the right thing *to be*. Formal norms do not tell us to "do what is good" but to "do what is right." They are vague and almost totally without specific content. They proclaim goals rather than tactics, strategies, or policies. Examples of formal norms are: Be honest. Respect life. Do not murder. Do not steal.

Formal norms challenge us to be responsible, to be faithful Christians. They remind us of what it means to accept the Gospel of Jesus Christ, particularly in those moments and situations where we may be tempted to act against that Gospel. *Only formal norms are absolute, universal, and exceptionless.* Thus, it is not always wrong to kill (a *material* norm), but it *is* always wrong to commit murder (a *formal* norm). The same contrast could be made between taking what belongs to another (material) and stealing (formal), or between telling the truth (material) and being honest (formal).

As human persons and as Christians, we are called to be moral. We must know what we should *be* (formal norms tell us this) and what we should *do* (material norms tell us this). Formal norms point to moral values, i.e., to those things which the moral person must *be*. Material norms point to premoral values, i.e., to those things which the moral person must *do* in the here and now if he or she is to maximize the good and minimize the evil. To be moral, therefore, it is not enough to be sincere (adhering to material norms); one must also be correct and right (adhering to formal norms as well).

Material norms give us information and direction; formal norms give us motivation and encouragement. Both kinds of norms exist because moral theology goes on at two levels simultaneously. Moral theology not only helps us to determine what we must *do* if we are to live faithfully to Christ, but also the kind of person we should *be* if we are to be perceived by God, by others, and by ourselves as faithful Christians.

In the final accounting, there is no authoritative guidebook by which Christians can determine in almost every conceivable circumstance what is consistent with the Gospel and what is not. The Christian lives in a world of premoral and moral values and of material and formal norms which express those values. But those norms have to be applied in each case, and no case is exactly like another. The challenge of moral education, therefore, is not the teaching of moral rules but the development of Christian character. The rudder of that course toward authentic character is the virtue of *prudence*. It is, as we said above, the ability to *discern*, the capacity to make wise and responsible decisions and to act on them.

Natural Law

Values and norms are rooted ultimately in God and penultimately in *natural law*. The reader should not expect here a substantial historical and philosophical analysis of natural law. On the contrary. It is enough for our limited purposes to note the fundamental difference in outlook between the so-called Greek and Roman versions of natural law, a difference which pervades the history of the question.

In its most general sense, natural law means the whole order of things which, by the will of God, defines us as human persons and contributes to human development. For the *Greeks*, this law is entirely apart from us. Reality is a given. We must simply conform ourselves to it. We find ourselves in a world that is unchanging. If we wish to survive and to prosper, we have to come to terms with reality as it is, and accept it for what it is. The *Romans*, on the other hand, were activists—shakers and movers, so to speak. Where the Greeks emphasized the adjective "natural," the

Romans emphasized the noun "law." Where the Greeks tended to be fatalistic and therefore not inventive, the Romans tended to be innovative. Where the Greeks tended to focus on the essential and the static, the Romans tended to emphasize the empirical and the changeable. Through common sense and intelligence, said the Romans, we are challenged to grapple with life, to solve its riddles and to control its fits and starts.

These so-called alternatives are, of course, only a matter of emphasis. We are, in fact, both time-bound and creative. There is a facticity to our existence, and there is also a wide range of options for human freedom and responsibility. But the emphasis one selects is significant. Thus, we can understand natural law as the obligation, perceived by reason, to conform to nature, or as the obligation, built into nature, to use reason in moral judgment. The first emphasis reflects the *classicist* mentality; the second reflects the *historically conscious* mentality (see chapter 25). Why and how the classicist understanding of natural law lost its hold within the Church has been discussed in different contexts throughout this book (see, for example, chapters 3, 4, 5, and 25). It has to do in large part with the intellectual revolution provoked by the Enlightenment, the work of Darwin, Marx, and Freud, various contemporary developments in psychology, anthropology, history, and the sociology of knowledge, not to mention the extraordinary advances in communications and transportation which have exposed the pluralistic character of human experience and expression.

This is not to say, on the other hand, that the human condition has been completely *relativized* by history, that no dimension of continuity, no abiding elements, remain. Recent works of Piaget, Erikson, Kohlberg, Claude Lévi-Strauss, and others (to whom reference was made earlier in this chapter) suggest that, even apart from the Catholic theological community, there is some scientific readiness to affirm the structured character of human existence. There are patterns of behavior and of growth which suggest intrinsic, enduring qualities in the human constitution. Human persons are not infinitely malleable and programmable. There was, and remains, stiff resistance across the board to the deterministic theories of B. F. Skinner. Although most Catholic moral theologians have moved beyond the rigid, classicist notion of natural law, which is so thoroughly grounded in the Greek over against the Roman concept of the law, Catholic moral theology nonetheless retains and employs some fundamental notion of natural law; but that notion is much closer to the ancient Roman than to the ancient Greek approach. That movement or shift from the Greek to the Roman emphasis is suggested in that oft-cited line from the Second Vatican Council's *Pastoral Constitution on the Church in the Modern World*: "Thus, the human race has passed from a rather static concept of reality to a more dynamic, evolutionary one" (n. 5).

The question is, How much *continuity* is there within the dynamic, evolutionary process? Those who oppose any concept of a natural law deny any underlying continuity. Those who accept at least an historically conditioned notion of natural law affirm some measure of continuity amidst change and development. Those who insist on the classicist idea of natural law regard the process as irrelevant in any case. We shall be returning in the next chapter to a more detailed comparison of the second and third views—namely, the historically conscious and the classicist understandings of natural law as they relate to the discussion of birth control and the encyclical *Humanae Vitae*.

A second question arises: How much continuity is there between the *natural* law and the *supernatural* law of the Gospel? This raises again the discussion in chapters 4 and 5 regarding the interrelationship of nature and grace. Since there is no actual, historically real state of pure nature (all reality is graced, fallen and redeemed), there is no purely natural law, in the sense that some moral obligations are known in the light of reason alone. Human reason or, more broadly, human consciousness, is already elevated by grace. We exist only within a redeemed order. The difference between natural law and the supernatural law of the Gospel, therefore, is not a difference between a law that can be known by reason, on the one hand, and a law that can be known only by revelation, on the other hand. Both "laws" are rooted in the one source and are grasped within the same redeemed order, whether the persons doing the "grasping" are Christians or not.

It is in this context that the official teaching of the Church must be read on the existence and knowability of the natural law. Thus, Pope John XXIII's *Pacem in Terris* declares that "the Creator of the world has imprinted in man's heart an order which his conscience reveals to him and strongly enjoins him to obey...." A citation from Romans 2:15 is included. And Vatican II's *Pastoral Constitution on the Church in the Modern World*, without using the term *natural law*, formulates the basis of a true Christian humanism: "Hence, the norm of human activity is this: that in accord with the divine plan and will, it should harmonize with the genuine good of the human race, and allow men as individuals and as members of society to pursue their total vocation and fulfill it" (n. 35). (See the discussion of faith and theology in chapter 2, of revelation in chapter 7, and of the relationship of Christian and philosophical ethics in chapter 25.)

There are moral theologians, finally, who suggest that the term *natural law* is so ambiguous that it would be better to abandon it altogether. But this need not, and should not, lead also to an abandonment of two principal values which the natural law theory has traditionally upheld—namely, the existence of a source of ethical wisdom and knowledge which the Christian shares with all humankind, and the fact that morality cannot be merely the subjective whim of an individual or group of individuals.

Three alternative approaches have been advanced in recent years: the personalist, the relational and communitarian, and the transcendental. All three work within an historically conscious method.

The *personalist* approach sees the moral act in terms of the person performing the act rather than in terms of the physical structure of the act itself. The *relational and communitarian* approach emphasizes the self as existing within a universal community to which the self is *responsible*. One has to consider the moral act in relationship to that larger community and in terms of the act's impact upon it (see, for example, H. Richard Niebuhr, *The Responsible Self*, New York: Harper & Row, 1963). The *transcendental* approach attends to the structures of the human knowing process itself. Truth, including moral truth, exists not in the mind's grasp of reality itself but in the meaning the mind gives to reality. Our meanings can change in such basic realities as community, family, or the state. This is not to say that there is nothing objective "out there" upon which we impose our meanings. The transcendental approach rejects both naive realism and idealism (see Bernard Lonergan, *Collection*, New York: Herder & Herder, 1967, pp. 221–239).

Karl Rahner speaks of a "moral instinct of faith," i.e., a universal knowledge of right and wrong belief. According to Rahner, on the basis of this instinct we make judgments and moral decisions. It is a synthesizing kind of reasoning, formed by the unity of a prudential judgment and a unique moral situation. It is the kind of knowledge that is engaged in the choice of a career or a marriage partner. One cannot simply list the objective factors and criteria to establish the preference of this occupation or this person over others. The decision takes into account a whole range of elements, but it includes a synthesizing component which transcends any one element or even the sum total of the decision's parts.

There are, according to Rahner, "terrible consequences" to ignoring the universal moral instinct of faith and reason. We can look at a moral problem—e.g., the production of a cheap napalm bomb or other instruments of biochemical warfare—and dissect it to the point where its original and obvious moral horror becomes blurred or submerged in casuistry. "Even the Council was not able unequivocally to overcome this kind of mentality, which paralyzes any action which could be said to be clearly Christian" (see "The Faith Instinct," in *A Rahner Reader*, Gerald A. McCool, ed., New York: The Seabury Press, 1975, pp. 270-277).

Conscience

What Conscience Is Not

Conscience is not a *feeling*, whether good or bad. It is not to be equated, therefore, with the *superego*, our psychic policeman. The fact that we feel that something is right or wrong or that we feel very guilty about some action does not mean that our conscience is telling us something. Someone who is trying to lose ten pounds in time for the summer swimming season may feel terribly "guilty" about having broken his or her diet one day. But that does not make it a matter of conscience. Another person knows that it is not a mortal sin to miss Mass when one is sick but wishes to "confess the sin" anyway because he or she does not "feel right" about it. A third person feels "guilty" about going on his scheduled vacation before finishing a project in the office. In themselves such feelings are morally neutral. They indicate nothing at all about the moral character of the actions in question. They have nothing to do with conscience. Similar examples could be drawn from the other side of the line. For example, the fact that many people do not feel guilty about discrimination based on race or sex does not make such discrimination right. Here again, feelings are not indicative of moral rectitude or deficiency.

Secondly, although conscience involves judgment, conscience itself is not *judgment*. The judgment of an action's moral rightness or wrongness is part of the process of forming one's conscience, but it is not an act of conscience itself. It is an act of judgment, of moral reasoning. Thus, one examines all the facts and all the arguments that one can about a particular moral problem. There are reflection, discussion, and analysis. There is also disagreement. Opinions are in conflict. One still is not sure whether something is right or wrong. But even if one were sure, conscience as such has not yet been engaged.

What Conscience Is

Only when one *decides* to do this or that, or not to do this or that, is one acting out of conscience. Conscience is the *radical experience of ourselves as moral agents. Christian* conscience is the radical experience of ourselves as *new creatures in Christ, enlivened by the Holy Spirit*. But since we never know ourselves completely (self-knowledge is something one works at; it is not ready-made), decisions of conscience are necessarily incomplete and partial. And because our own circumstances are always historically, socially, and culturally defined, decisions of conscience are necessarily fallible and subject to correction and change. (See the section on Faith Development earlier in this chapter, noting its correlation with Moral Development.)

Conscience in Sacred Scripture

There is no Hebrew word for conscience in the Old Testament. The Greek word *syneidesis* occurs only once, in Wisdom 17:11. The closest word to it is *heart*. "Oh, that today you would hear his voice: 'Harden not your hearts . . .' " (Psalm 95:7–8). God is spoken of frequently as probing the heart (Jeremiah 11:20; 17:10; Proverbs 21:2; Psalm 26:2). The "pangs of conscience" are described in Genesis 3. Job insists: ". . . my heart does not reproach me for any of my days" (Job 27:6). Fidelity to conscience is a central theme in the whole book of Job, as it is in the call of the prophets to fidelity to the Covenant and to the Law (Ezekiel 11:14–21; Jeremiah 31:31–34).

Although there are references to the inner disposition of the person in the Gospels (Luke 11:33; 14:28-32; 16:8; Matthew 5:8,28; 6:21–22; Mark 7:21), the word for conscience is absent. The word occurs twenty-five times in the Pauline writings, including Hebrews, three times in 1 Peter, and twice in the Acts of the Apostles, both times uttered by Paul. For him conscience is the fundamental awareness of the difference between moral good and evil. The law is written in our hearts (Romans 2:15). Paul appeals to his own clear conscience (2 Corinthians 1:12; Romans 9:1; Acts of the Apostles 23:1, 24:16). Conscience is a principle of freedom (1 Corinthians 10:29), but such freedom is conditioned by our obligations to our neighbor (10:23). We must commend ourselves to every person's conscience before God (2 Corinthians 4:2; 5:11). Conscience itself can be weak and even erroneous (1 Corinthians 8:10–12), but obedience to such a conscience can still lead to salvation (8:11). Love proceeds from a pure heart and a good conscience and genuine faith (1 Timothy 1:5). The sacrificial ritual of the Law cannot purify the conscience (Hebrews 9:9; 10:2), but Christ purifies the conscience (10:22). Those who finally reject a good conscience can make a shipwreck of their faith (1 Timothy 1:19).

Post-biblical Reflections

In spite of individual references to conscience in the writings of some of the Fathers of the Church—e.g., Tertullian, Origen, Chrysostom, and Augustine—we find no systematic treatment of it until the Middle Ages. The occasion was a dispute over the meaning of a text of St. Jerome, the *Commentary on Ezekiel*, which distinguished between the terms *synderesis* and *syneidesis*. Bonaventure and the Franciscans explained the distinction in one way; Thomas Aquinas and the Dominicans explained it in another way. The Thomistic explanation would influence Catholic moral theology for the next several centuries. Aquinas distinguished between conscience as a permanent natural habit (*synderesis*) and conscience as an act of moral judgment (*syneidesis*). The process of moral judgment is essentially rational. The human will affirms and carries out what is affirmed by right reason. It would seem, however, that the whole distinction was based on an error. In preparing the first Latin text of the Bible, Jerome was working from a Greek manuscript that was not entirely legible. Recent scholarship concludes that Jerome was wrong in finding two different Greek words for conscience. We may still make a distinction, as Bonaventure and Thomas did, between conscience as a habit and as an act of moral judgment but that distinction cannot be attributed to the Bible.

The tradition is summed up at Vatican II in its *Pastoral Constitution on the Church in the Modern World*. Conscience is what summons us to love good and avoid evil, to do this and shun that. "To obey it is the very dignity of man; according to it he will be judged. Conscience is the most secret core and sanctuary of a man. There he is alone with God, whose voice echoes in his depths." But conscience is no infallible guide. It frequently errs from invincible ignorance (i.e., an ignorance for which we are not morally responsible). We Christians search for truth and for the genuine solution of problems in collaboration with others and in fidelity to our consciences (n. 16).

A Contemporary View

Timothy O'Connell suggests that we abandon the language of *synderesis* and *syneidesis* and speak instead of three different levels of meaning of the word *conscience*. At the first and most general level, conscience is a fundamental sense of value and of personal responsibility. The human capacity for self-direction and self-determination implies a human responsibility for right direction and correct determination. Human beings may disagree about what in particular is right or wrong, but there is a general awareness that there *is* a difference between right and wrong. In this meaning of the word, conscience belongs to the whole human community and is part of the definition of what it means to be human. In our experience of ourselves as subjects, as human persons, we have an innate sense of the difference between good and evil.

O'Connell suggests a second level of conscience, which is more exactly an *act* of conscience and not conscience itself. This is the judgment that something is morally good or bad. This judgment is subject to error. There are differences of opinion. Thus, some believe that gambling in itself is evil; others insist that it is morally neutral at worst. When individuals try to make up their minds about what they should do, they have to have as much information about their available options as they can get. Accordingly, they will consult their own experience, their parents, their friends, their colleagues, the findings of various scientific disciplines such as psychology. If they are Christians, they will also consult the opinions of theologians and the testimony of Sacred Scripture. And if they are Catholics, they will also pay attention to the official teachings of the Church. This is known as the process of conscience-formation.

A third level, according to O'Connell, is reached with the decision itself. "I may be wrong, but I am convinced that I should do this." This is the final norm by which a person's act must be guided. It is not that it guarantees correctness of judgment, but only that it allows us to be true to ourselves. And we are judged finally by God on the basis of what is in our hearts, not on what we actually did or did not do. "Everyone, of course, must ultimately follow his conscience; this means he must do right as he sees the right with desire and effort to find and do what is right" (Bernard

Häring, *The Law of Christ*, vol. 1, Westminster, Md.: Newman Press, 1961, p. 151). So strongly rooted is this principle of the primacy of conscience over both external act and external authority that Thomas Aquinas himself argued that "anyone upon whom the ecclesiastical authority, in ignorance of true facts, imposes a demand that offends against his clear conscience, should perish in excommunication rather than violate his conscience" (*IV Sentences*, dist. 38, a. 4). This principle is now taken for granted in Catholic theology, even though the opposite would have been thought to be the case a few decades ago.

The Right and Duty to Follow One's Conscience

The Second Vatican Council's *Declaration on Religious Freedom* declares that we are bound to follow our conscience faithfully in all our activity, and that no one is "to be forced to act in a manner contrary to his conscience. Nor, on the other hand, is he to be restrained from acting in accordance with his conscience, especially in matters religious" (n. 3). This principle applies as well to children (see *Declaration on Christian Education*, n. 1). But what do we do in situations where others oppose our conscientious decision? What do we do if we sincerely believe that another's conscientious act will be harmful to the public good?

There are some traditional guidelines: (1) A person should not be prevented from following even an erroneous conscience, unless the action is seriously injurious to himself/herself or to others. Thus, a person should be prevented from committing suicide, if possible, or from killing his family as an act of "reparation" for his sins. (2) No one may morally coerce or persuade another to act against his or her conscience. Thus, the government cannot force someone to engage in military service if the person is convinced in conscience that all forms of physical combat are gravely sinful (*Pastoral Constitution on the Church in the Modern World*, n. 79). This principle does not prohibit someone, however, from trying to reason with others in order to make them change their judgment about a particular moral action.

Conscience and Church Authority

Having noted the inviolable character of conscience and an individual's right to follow conscience, even when it is erroneous, we move finally to the question of the authority of the Church. Are members of the Church bound to obey all official moral teachings of the Church and to assume, almost as a matter of course, that their consciences are necessarily erroneous and not to be followed if they are in conflict with the Church's moral pronouncements? The following principles must be taken into account:

1.   If, after appropriate study, reflection, and prayer, a person is convinced that his or her conscience is correct, in spite of a conflict with the moral teachings of the Church, the person not only may but *must* follow the dictates of conscience rather than the teachings of the Church.

2.   The Church has never explicitly claimed to speak infallibly on a moral question, so there is probably no question as yet of a conflict between an individual's fallible decision in conscience and a teaching of the Church which is immune from error.

3.   No teaching of the Church can hope to account for every moral situation and circumstance. Every teaching still has to be applied in particular cases. One is not necessarily repudiating the values affirmed in the teaching if one decides that the teaching does not bind or apply in this instance.

4.   The teachings themselves are historically conditioned. What may have been perceived as morally wrong in one set of circumstances—e.g., charging interest on a loan in the Middle Ages—would be regarded as morally justifiable in another situation—e.g., charging interest on a loan today, in the context of modern commercial life.

On the other hand:

5.   No individual or group of individuals can hope to indentify and grasp moral truth by relying entirely on their own resources. We all need assistance. We all rely on the moral vision of others as well as our own. The Church, as the Temple of the Holy Spirit, is a major resource of such moral direction and leadership. It is the product of centuries of experience, crossing cultural, national, and continental lines.

Negatively, one is not a Catholic who deliberately and systematically excludes all reference to official Church teachings in making moral decisions. Positively, a Catholic gives antecedent attention and respect to such teachings, but without prejudice to other sources of moral reflection and counsel—e.g., one's associates, the findings of scientific disciplines, the Bible, the writings of theologians. Thus, the *Declaration on Religious Freedom* of the Second Vatican Council asserts: "In the formation of their consciences, the Christian faithful ought carefully to attend to the sacred and certain doctrine of the Church. The Church is, by the will of Christ, the teacher of truth. It is her duty to give utterance to, and authoritatively to teach, that truth which is Christ himself, and also to declare and confirm by her authority those principles of the moral order which have their origin in human nature itself" (n. 14).

SUMMARY

1.   This chapter raises *three fundamental questions*: (1) Who is the Christian? (2) What kind of person is the Christian called to become? (3) How does one become a Christian? The focus is on the theological principles which permeate and shape the Catholic tradition's answers to each of these questions.

2.   Principles and process are always in a dialectical relationship to one another. *Principles* are formulations which try to come to terms with the process of human experience, and the *process* itself is guided and critiqued by such principles. Principles, therefore, are basic truths which are at once products and shapers of experience. Thus, Catholic moral theology must be concerned with both: principles and process alike.

Who is the Christian?

3.   The Christian is a radically social human person in whom God is present in grace but who is, at the same time, prone to acting against the divine presence. Beyond that, *the Christian is a person who has moved to a different level of human consciousness, i.e., is one who believes in Jesus Christ and whose whole life is shaped by that belief.* The process by which the Christian moves to that new level of consciousness and existence is called *conversion*.

4. The Christian's proneness to act against the divine presence is the tendency to *sin*. There is no single word for "sin" in the *Old Testament*. The closest, *hamartia*, means, in its verb form, "to miss the mark." Sin is infidelity to the *convenantal* relationship with God. In the *New Testament*, and especially in *Paul*, sin is acting against who we are and against the God who is within us. It is at the root of the conflict between the spirit and the flesh. We achieve victory in Christ.

5. Sin presupposes *freedom* and *responsibility*. To be free means to be in possession of oneself, to be conscious of oneself as a responsible being. Freedom is *limited* from without by our historical existence and from within by the fact that we are never fully present to ourselves. Ultimately, freedom is our capacity for God. In freedom we reach beyond ourselves to become something other than we are.

6. This basic orientation toward God is called the *fundamental option*, the state of being converted to the Kingdom of God. Only an equally fundamental reversal of that choice for God is sufficient to cancel out the original act of conversion. Such a reversal is a rare occurrence for one who is sincerely oriented toward God.

7. The Church has always taught that we have the fundamental capacity to reject God (mortal sin), but it has never taught that there are, in fact, human persons in hell. Indeed, because of the forces which limit our freedom, we can never be certain that we have finally and fully said "No" to God, even in an act which appears to involve such a rejection.

8. The situation that makes sin possible is called *Original Sin*. *Venial sin* is a human act which is not fully consistent with our fundamental option for God. There is some contradiction between what we do and the kind of person we are or want to become. *Serious sin* is more inconsistent with our fundamental option than is venial sin, but not so inconsistent as is mortal sin. *Mortal sin* is an act which fully engages the person. The person not only chooses the act but also chooses to be the kind of person who would perform such an act.

9. Although the traditional *three-source theory* is not without criticism today, its threefold norm to judge the morality of a human act is still of some value: (1) How serious was the act I performed or failed to perform (the *object*)? (2) What was my motive, as far as I can reasonably determine (the *end*)? (3) What were the circumstances surrounding my decision to do what I did, and how did those circumstances affect my decision (the *circumstances*)?

10. Some sins are so deeply rooted in our fallen human nature that they are the sources of other lapses. These are the *seven capital sins*: pride, covetousness, lust, anger, gluttony, envy, and sloth.

11.   The process by which we reject sin and turn to God is called *conversion*. It is a determination to live according to the demands of the Kingdom of God. This is a fuller understanding of conversion than was common in the decades before Vatican II, when a "convert" was simply one who became a Catholic.

12.   Conversion means shifting horizons, i.e., shifting those ranges of vision which set limits to our interests and knowledge. We perceive the world in a new way. *Intellectual conversion* is a fundamental change of a person's basic view of reality. *Moral conversion* is a fundamental change of a person's basic motive for making decisions. *Religious conversion* is a fundamental change of a person's basic orientation: away from self and toward God. It is a total being-in-love with God and is manifested in the love of one's neighbor, who is the sacrament of God. Love of the neighbor is the final test of religious conversion (1 John 4:20–21).

What kind of person is the Christian called to become?

13.   The Christian is called to become a person of *character*, i.e., a person who takes responsibility for his or her actions, and not one who simply follows "the rules." It is our character which gives direction and shape to our lives. There is an old adage: "Plant an act, reap a habit; plant a habit, reap a virtue; plant a virtue, reap a character; plant a character, reap a destiny."

14.   *Character is never finished once and for all.* Good or bad habits (virtues and vices) can be reversed or broken. Usually this happens gradually; sometimes it occurs in a decisive experience (e.g., conversion or mortal sin). Since character is so closely linked with personality and since personality is always unique, *there is no single type of character which is normative for everyone.* There are different styles of Christian life and different moral histories.

15.   A *virtue* is a power, rooted in grace, to realize moral good, and especially to do it joyfully and perseveringly even against inner and outer obstacles and at the cost of sacrifice. The opposite of a virtue is a *vice*.

16.   In modern psychology, virtue is equivalent to "ego strength." It is the ability to keep the *id*, or base animal passions, under control, and to make decisions without the interference of the *superego*, or overweening conscience. It is the capacity for self-actualization.

17.   *Theological virtues* are those which have to do immediately with our relationship with God: faith, hope, and charity. *Moral virtues* are those which have to do with our relationship with one another: prudence, justice, temperance, and fortitude.

18.   The first of the theological virtues is *faith*. Faith is *conviction*, *trust*, and *commitment*. It believes something or someone or sees reality in a new way (the *intellectualist* approach). It trusts in the mercy of God (the *fiducial* approach). And it moves a person to action on behalf of others (the *performative* approach).

19.   Such faith is always in process. It develops in *stages*, just as persons develop in stages of self-understanding and moral perception (see Erikson, Kohlberg, *et al.*). According to James Fowler, Christian faith moves through six stages: (1) imitative and fantasy-filled, under the influence of parents and other primal adults; (2) literal understanding of stories and beliefs; (3) acceptance of what is proposed by "those who count"; (4) acceptance of personal responsibility for one's beliefs and attitudes; (5) recognition of, and respect for, legitimate diversity of faith-perspectives; and (6) being-for-others.

20.   *Hope* is that virtue by which we take responsibility for the future, both of ourselves and of the world. It is oriented, therefore, toward the Kingdom of God. Hope measures everything against the future Kingdom, and so it is a virtue which has a prophetic edge. The so-called *theology of hope* movement of the middle and late 1960s brought renewed attention to this virtue and especially to its prophetic dimension.

21.   *Charity* is that virtue by which we participate in the life of God who *is* love (1 John 4:8,16). It is lived faith and lived hope. It is love of God and love of neighbor, i.e., the total dedication and devotion to the welfare of the other, regardless of sacrifice and personal cost. This love is rooted in the crucifixion.

22.   Love is possible only for those who are personally mature, i.e., who can accept themselves and others for who and what they are. Its opposite is not hate but *apathy*, a suspension of commitment, a lack of concern. Love is the soul of all other Christian virtues.

23.   The virtue of *religion*, or worship, directs us to ritualize our experience of faith, hope, and charity. It is a virtue which bridges the gap between the theological and the moral virtues. Worship is oriented at once to the glory of God and the service of one's neighbor. It is opposed by the sins of idolatry, superstition, hypocrisy, legalism, and self-delusion, or triumphalism.

24.   The *cardinal*, or *moral*, virtues are those on which other virtues "hinge." *Prudence* is the ability to discern. It answers the question "What is the best way for me, in this situation, to do the right thing?" It involves inquiry, taking counsel, judgment, and making a decision. It is

closely allied with the discernment of spirits, which also can be a corporate enterprise.

25.   *Discernment* is clearly misguided if it does not issue forth in the fruits of the Spirit: love, joy, peace, etc.; if it leads to doctrinal or moral positions which are clearly at odds with the tradition of the Church and/or with contemporary scholarship; if it intensifies isolation and even eccentricities; and if it ignores information, rejects the counsel of others, and imposes its decisions by force.

26.   The virtue of *justice* is concerned with rights and with the duties which correspond to those rights. It is linked with the biblical notion of *righteousness*, i.e., salvation which is given through fidelity to the Covenant (Old Testament) or through the death of Christ (New Testament).

27.   A *right* is a power to do things necessary for achieving the end or purpose for which we are destined as rational and free persons. In that sense, rights flow from duties. Rights can be in conflict. And there is also a hierarchy of rights.

28.   Since we are radically social and since human growth occurs in a societal context, justice is concerned with our social relationships at various levels: individual(s) to individual(s) (*commutative* justice), government to individual(s) (*distributive* justice), individual(s) to government (*legal* justice), and individual(s) to society at large (*social* justice).

29.   Love of itself is never sufficient for societal life. There are systems and structures, claims and conflicts, which have to be attended to with deliberation and care. Christian moralism must be replaced by *Christian realism* (Reinhold Niebuhr).

30.   A correct understanding of social justice requires a correct understanding of the distinction between society and the state. *Society* is the total network of social, political, economic, cultural, and religious relationships which are necessary for full human development. The *state* is the center of coercive power in society. It is the civil authority by which the purposes of society are procured and preserved.

31.   The *principle of subsidiarity* means that nothing should be done at a higher level that can be done as well or better at a lower level. Thus, the state should intervene only when lesser bodies cannot fulfill a given task required by the common good.

32.   The *process of socialization* refers to the growing interdependence of humankind and of nations. As modern economic and political life becomes more complex, more intervention is required. The principle of subsidiarity, therefore, is balanced off by the process of socialization. The two must be kept in creative tension.

33.   The four kinds of justice—commutative, distributive, legal, and social—are interrelated and mutually limiting. All four are attempts to express the demands of Christian love. They do not provide immediate answers to complex problems of social existence, but rather they are *principles of discernment and specific guides for judgment*. The fulfillment of the virtue of justice is part of the world's movement toward the Kingdom, which is the final realization of justice.

34.   *Temperance* is the virtue which enables us to achieve some balance in the exercise of our concupiscible appetites: desire for food, drink, sex. It humanizes, not represses, these pleasures. The virtue is closely allied with Christian *asceticism,* which is concerned with those "exercises"which help us regulate the conflict between the spirit and the flesh. It involves painful struggle, self-denial, and renunciation. It is the acceptance of one's facticity and the historical limitations of one's existence. Patterned on the cross, asceticism is obedience even to the point of death and leads to the service of others.

35.   *Fortitude* is the virtue of courage by which one overcomes an instinctive fear in order to pursue the good. It brings balance to our irascible appetites: fear and rashness. It has an active and passive side: taking bold action for the Kingdom of God, and enduring pain, suffering, and even death for the sake of the Kingdom.

36.   The Christian is also called to a life of *mercy*. Mercy, unlike justice, gives to another more than the other deserves. All human mercy participates in the mercy of God, by which we are saved. The works of mercy apply to the needs of the body (corporal works) and to the needs of the soul (spiritual works). The *corporal works of mercy* are: feeding the hungry, giving drink to the thirsty, clothing the naked, sheltering the homeless, visiting the sick, ransoming the captive, and burying the dead. The *spiritual works of mercy* are: instructing the ignorant, counseling the doubtful, admonishing the sinner, bearing wrongs patiently, forgiving offenses, comforting the afflicted, and praying for the living and the dead. Mercy reminds us that our obligations go beyond even the demands of social justice.

How does one become a Christian?

37.   One becomes a Christian by being converted to Jesus Christ and his Gospel of the Kingdom of God, and by being initiated into the Church.

38.   How the individual Christian determines what the Gospel demands raises the question of values and norms. *Premoral values* are those concrete good things that ought to be done, to the extent possible

(e.g., the achievement of good health). *Moral values* are those good things which are essential to proper human living (e.g., justice). *Material norms* point out the premoral values we are to pursue (e.g., Do not kill). *Formal norms* point to moral values which must be pursued (e.g., Do not murder). Only formal norms are absolute, universal, and exceptionless. Thus murder is always wrong; killing is not.

39.   Material norms tell us what we should *do*; formal norms tell us who we should *be*. Material norms give us information and direction; formal norms give us motivation and encouragement.

40.   The Christian lives in a world of premoral and moral values and of material and formal norms which express those values. Norms have to be applied in each case, and no case is exactly like another. The challenge of *Christian moral education* is not the teaching of moral rules but the development of Christian character. The rudder of the Christian life is always prudence.

41.   Values and norms are rooted ultimately in God and penultimately in *natural law*, i.e., in the whole order of things which, by the will of God, defines us as human persons and contributes to human development. For the Greeks, natural law was the "given" of reality; for the *Romans*, it was something to be discovered and reshaped through common sense and intelligence. The first emphasis reflects the *classicist* mentality; the second, the *historically conscious* mentality.

42.   The *natural-law theory* has traditionally upheld two principal values: the existence of a source of ethical wisdom and knowledge which the Christian shares with all humankind, and the fact that morality cannot be merely the subjective whim of an individual or group of individuals.

43.   Traditional (classicist) understandings of natural law have been complemented by *three newer approaches*: the personalist, the relational and communitarian, and the transcendental. The first attends to the *person* doing the act; the second attends to the *context* in which the act is done and its *social repercussions*; the third attends to the *knowing process* of the subject who does the act.

44.   With regard to the third approach, Karl Rahner speaks of a *"moral instinct of faith"* by which every person knows the difference between right and wrong and which allows us to synthesize all the factors in a given situation and come to a decision which transcends any one factor or the sum total of these factors.

45.   *Conscience* is not feeling or judgment. It is the radical experience of ourselves as moral agents. We make decisions in terms of our self-understanding. We act insofar as we perceive ourselves to be a

particular kind of person. Decisions of conscience are always fallible because we never know ourselves fully and because, furthermore, we are historically situated.

46.   In *the Bible* conscience is closely identified with "the heart" (Old Testament) and with the fundamental awareness of the difference between moral good and evil (Paul). It is a principle of freedom (1 Corinthians 10:29).

47.   According to *Vatican II*, conscience is what summons us to love good and avoid evil. It is the most secret core and sanctuary of a person. Because conscience can err, all human beings, including Christians, must always search for truth in collaboration with others.

48.   Conscience is the final norm of moral action. It must be properly formed, but once a decision in conscience is made, erroneously or not, it cannot yield even to the directives of the Church. We are judged finally by God on the basis of what is in our hearts, not our fidelity to rules.   A person can be prevented from following a clearly erroneous conscience only when serious injury to oneself or to others will surely follow.

49.   The Church has never explicitly claimed to speak infallibly on a moral question, nor do the non-infallible moral teachings of the Church solve every moral situation and circumstance. The teachings are themselves historically conditioned. On the other hand, the Church does speak from some measure of historical perspective and with collective wisdom and experience. A Catholic will always give antecedent attention and respect to pertinent moral teachings of the Church before reaching a decision.

SUGGESTED READINGS

Böckle, Franz. *Law and Conscience*. New York: Sheed & Ward, 1966.

Curran, Charles E. *A New Look at Christian Morality*. Notre Dame, Ind.: Fides Publishers, 1968.

——————. *Themes in Fundamental Moral Theology*. Notre Dame, Ind.: University of Notre Dame Press, 1977.

Fuchs, Josef. *Human Values and Christian Morality*. Dublin: Gill and Macmillan, 1970.

Gustafson, James. *Christ and the Moral Life*. New York: Harper & Row, 1968.

Hauerwas, Stanley. *Vision and Virtue: Essays in Christian Ethical Reflection*. Notre Dame, Ind.: Fides Publishers, 1974.

McCormick, Richard A. "Notes on Moral Theology," which appear annually in *Theological Studies*.

McDonagh, Enda. *Gift and Call*. St. Meinrad, Ind.: Abbey Press, 1975.

O'Connell, Timothy E. *Principles for a Catholic Morality*. New York: Seabury Press, 1978.

Pieper, Josef. *The Four Cardinal Virtues*. New York: Harcourt, Brace, & World, 1965.

Rahner, Karl. "On the Question of a Formal Existential Ethics." *Theological Investigations*. Vol. 2, Baltimore: Helicon Press, 1963, pp. 217-234.

Regan, George M. *New Trends in Moral Theology: A Survey of Fundamental Moral Themes*. New York: Newman Press, 1971.

· XXVII ·

CHRISTIAN EXISTENCE: SPECIAL QUESTIONS

This chapter seeks to clarify the meaning of the principles described and explained in the preceding chapter by showing how such principles are variously employed and applied to certain contemporary moral questions. There is no attempt here to raise, or even identify, all of the major ethical questions of our day, with the hope of offering the reader guidance toward the solution of such questions. This is clearly beyond the scope of this book. The reader will not find, for example, any explicit discussion of abortion. Catholic theologians do not generally differ among themselves on its morality anyway. On the other hand, some issues must be treated specifically if the material in the two preceding chapters is not to be reduced to moral generalities.

Four questions are addressed in this chapter, two having to do with *interpersonal ethics* and two having to do with *social ethics*. This is not to say that interpersonal ethics have nothing to do with social ethics or vice versa, but only that the immediate focus of such questions is on the one side rather than the other. Indeed, the adjectives themselves are misleading. *Interpersonal* and *social* are not really opposed. One might also call the first *individual* ethics and the second *societal* ethics. But the terms are less important than the issues themselves.

The two issues of an interpersonal character treated here are *birth control* and *homosexuality*. The two issues of a social, and indeed political, character are *warfare* and the *intervention of the state* in the economic order, specifically in the area of health care.

Our emphasis will always be on method, not solutions. This chapter engages in analysis, not advocacy. Comparisons are drawn, but positions are not fixed.

Section One: Interpersonal Ethics

BIRTH CONTROL
An Overview

There are two sides to this question in Catholic moral theology. Neither side, however, rejects birth control totally and absolutely. The traditional, or conservative, position acknowledges, for example, that a married couple may deliberately employ the rhythm method by which sexual union is restricted to those days when the woman is biologically incapable of conceiving a child. That is clearly a form of birth control. What is really at issue here, therefore, is not birth control in this generic sense, but *contraception,* i.e., the intentional placing of a material obstacle to the conception of a child: e.g., a contraceptive pill, an intrauterine device, contraceptive foam, a condom.

One side argues that contraception by such artificial means is always wrong. The other side argues that contraception may be not only legitimate under certain circumstances but even mandatory. This side speaks in terms of "responsible parenthood." The two sides differ on three major counts: (1) their respective understandings of natural law, (2) their respective understandings of the binding force of official Church teachings; and (3) their respective understandings of the development of doctrine.

The argument was joined in 1968 with the publication of Pope Paul VI's encyclical *Humanae Vitae* ("Of Human Life"). The pope had before him the majority and minority reports of a special papal commission established by his predecessor Pope John XXIII and continued in existence by himself. The majority proposed a change in the Catholic Church's traditional teaching by which contraception was condemned; the minority urged the pope to hold fast to that teaching, and raised the question of the impact of a change of view on the credibility of the papal magisterium. Pope Paul VI decided in favor of the minority view, and the rest is history. Theologians and even some episcopal conferences voiced opposition to the encyclical or at least took positions that were less than enthusiastic in their support. Surveys in the United States indicate that the overwhelming majority (more than 80%) of Catholics of child-bearing ages do not, in fact, observe the encyclical's teaching.

Official Teaching Prior to Humanae Vitae

Pope Pius XI (d. 1939), in his encyclical *Casti Connubii* (1930), declared: "Since the conjugal act is destined primarily by nature for the begetting of children, those who in exercising it deliberately frustrate its natural power and purpose sin against nature and commit a deed which is shameful and intrinsically vicious .... any use whatsoever of matrimony exercised in such a way that the act is deliberately frustrated in its natural power to generate life is an offense against the law of God and of nature and those who indulge in such are branded with the guilt of grave sin ...."

Pope Pius XII (d. 1958) in his *Allocution to Midwives* (1951), reaffirmed this teaching: "Our predecessor ... solemnly restated the basic law of the conjugal act and conjugal relations: every attempt on the part of the married couple during the conjugal act ... to deprive it of its inherent power and to hinder the procreation of new life is immoral: no indication or need can change an action that is intrinsically immoral into an action that is moral and lawful. This prescription holds good today just as much as it did yesterday. It will hold tomorrow and always, for it is not a mere precept of human right but the expression of a natural and divine law."

On June 23, 1964, Pope Paul VI (d. 1978), after much discussion at the Second Vatican Council, promised a thorough review of the subject in the light of new knowledge but asked that the traditional teaching be observed in the meantime. He also reserved to himself the final decision on the matter. After much debate within the drafting committee, the council's *Pastoral Constitution on the Church in the Modern World* formulated its view in 1965 in this way: "Therefore, when there is question of harmonizing conjugal love with the responsible transmission of life, the moral aspect of any procedure does not depend solely on sincere intentions or on an evaluation of motives. It must be determined by objective standards. These, based on the nature of the human person and his acts, preserve the full sense of mutual self-giving and human procreation in the context of true love. Such a goal cannot be achieved unless the virtue of conjugal chastity is sincerely practiced. Relying on these principles, sons of the Church may not undertake methods of regulating procreation which are found blameworthy by the teaching authority of the Church in its unfolding of the divine law" (n. 51).

On October 29, 1966, Pope Paul VI stated that the official magisterium was in a state of "reflection" on the issue but not in a state of "doubt." In July of 1968 the matter was officially settled with the publication of the encyclical *Humanae Vitae.*

Arguments in Support of the Traditional Teaching

The *first argument* given in the minority report of the Papal Commission for the Study of Population, the Family, and Birth (1966) is the "constant and perennial" teaching of the Church. The authors (John Ford, S.J., of the United States, Jan Visser, C.SS.R., of the Netherlands, Marcelino Zalba, S.J., of Rome, and Stanley de Lestapis, S.J., of France) cite those sources already referred to in the previous section of this chapter as well as several other assorted addresses of Pope Pius XII, the encyclical *Mater et Magistra* (1961) of Pope John XXIII, statements of various bishops, and the consistent answers given by the Holy See to questions on the subject from around the Catholic world.

"If the Church could err (on this issue), the authority of the ordinary magisterium in moral matters would be thrown into question. The faithful could not put their trust in the magisterium's presentation of moral teaching, especially in sexual matters." The question is not whether this teaching on birth control is "infallible" (i.e., immune from error) according to the traditional criteria of infallibility. "For if this doctrine is not substantially true, the magisterium itself will seem to be empty and useless in any moral matter." The assumption here seems to be that if the Church, or any comparable moral agency, can be found to be in error on *one* important matter, its judgment on *all* matters is automatically suspect.

The *second major argument* in favor of the traditional teaching is based on an analysis of the conjugal act itself. The minority theologians acknowledge, in what is perhaps the most remarkable statement in their entire report, that "if we could bring forward arguments which are clear and cogent based on reason alone, it would not be necessary for our commission to exist, nor would the present state of affairs exist in the Church as it is." What the conservative theologians bring forward, therefore, is suggestions of a line of argument based on natural law, but not of such a character that it can equal the argument from authority in either clarity or force. Thus, " . . . the Fathers, theologians, and the Church herself have always taught that certain acts and the generative processes are in some way specially inviolable precisely because they are generative. This inviolability is always attributed to the act and to the process, which are biological; not inasmuch as they are biological, but inasmuch as they are human, namely inasmuch as they are the object of *human acts* and are destined by their nature to the good of the human species." Contraception is evil, the minority report maintains, because it changes an act which is naturally oriented to procreation into an act which is oriented to the mutual benefit of the spouses.

But the minority report returns immediately to its first argument. The case does not depend finally on the strength of philosophical or even theological points. "It depends on the nature of human life and human sexuality, *as understood theologically by the Church*" (my italics). Indeed, in such a matter we "need the help of the teaching Church, explained and applied under the leadership of the magisterium, so that (we) can with certitude and security embrace the way, the truth, and the life."

Arguments Against the Official Teaching

According to the majority opinion, the argument in favor of the traditional teaching based on authority fails to recognize the *evolutionary* character of that teaching. The early Fathers of the Church held that the use of sex in marriage was justified *only* for procreation. Later it was admitted that a sterile woman might marry and enjoy full conjugal relations. Eventually intercourse during the so-called safe period was approved. The next step would be to admit that the procreative value of the conjugal act is not bound up with every individual act of intercourse. Moreover, the official Church has changed its teachings in other matters—e.g., religious liberty and usury. One need only compare the teachings of Pope Pius IX and even of Leo XIII with Vatican II's *Declaration on Religious Freedom* (see chapters 19 and 25).

Catholic legal and ethical scholar John Noonan has argued that the condemnation of usury, or lending money at interest, was far more authoritative in terms of the biblical, patristic, conciliar, and theological sources adduced in support of the condemnation than was the condemnation of contraception (see his *Contraception: A History of Its Treatment by the Catholic Theologians and Canonists,* Cambridge: Harvard University Press, 1965). And yet the teaching on usury changed because certain theologians in the sixteenth century concluded that economic conditions had changed, making the old condemnations obsolete, and that the experience of lay Christians had to be listened to. Thus, Navarrus (d. 1586), a professor at Salamanca in Spain and author of a *Manual for Confessors,* argued that an "infinite number of decent Christians" were engaged in exchange-banking, and he objected to any analysis which would "damn the whole world." Three papal bulls promulgated over a seventeen-year period (1569-1586) had unequivocally denounced and condemned usury. In a similarly short space of time, thirty years, the bulls were deprived of force to influence anyone's behavior. Theologians refused to support the teachings, and the laity continued about their business as if the teachings did not exist (see John Noonan, "The Amendment of Papal Teaching by Theologians," in *Contraception: Authority and*

Dissent, Charles E. Curran, ed., New York: Herder & Herder, 1969, pp. 41-75).

Furthermore, a change in the traditional teaching would not necessarily undermine the moral teaching authority of the Church. According to the majority theologians on the birth control commission (Josef Fuchs, S.J., of Rome, Philippe Delhaye of Belgium, and Raymond Sigmond of Rome), "such a change is to be seen rather as a step toward a more mature comprehension of the whole doctrine of the Church. For doubt and reconsideration are quite reasonable when proper reasons for doubt and reconsideration occur with regard to some specific question. This is part and parcel of the accepted teaching of fundamental theology."

This majority view also rejects the natural-law theory of those who support the traditional teaching. It is a concept of nature as something so mysterious and sacred, they maintain, that any human intervention tends to destroy rather than perfect this very nature. Because of this mentality many advances in medical science were prohibited for a time, and the same was true of other areas of scientific experimentation. The dignity of the human person consists in this: "that God wished man to share in his dominion .... In the course of his life man must attain his perfection in difficult and adverse conditions, he must accept the consequences of his responsibility, etc. Therefore, the dominion of God is exercised through man, who can use nature for his own perfection according to the dictates of right reason." It follows that we must use our skill to "intervene in the biological processes of nature so that (we) can achieve the ends of the institution of matrimony in the conditions of actual life, (rather) than (to) abandon (ourselves) to chance."

Indeed, the majority report argues, the conjugal act itself must be viewed not as an isolated reality but in the larger context of human love, family life, education, etc. (the *principle of totality).* Sexuality is not ordered only to procreation. Sacred Scripture says not only "Increase and multiply," but also "They shall be two in one flesh," and it shows the partner as another helpful self. "In some cases intercourse can be required as a manifestation of self-giving love, directed to the good of the other person or of the community, while at the same time a new life cannot be received.

This is neither egocentricity nor hedonism but a legitimate communication of persons through gestures proper to beings composed of body and soul with sexual powers."

Vatican II insisted that the decision to have children must take into account the welfare of the spouses and of their children, the material and spiritual conditions of the times, their state in life, the interests of the family group, of society, and of the Church. "The parents themselves should ultimately make this judgment in the sight of God" *(Pastoral Constitution on the Church in the Modern World,* n. 50). And Paul VI, in his encyclical *Populorum Progressio* (1967), acknowledged that "the population explosion adds to the difficulties of development . . . . Parents themselves must decide how many children to have. Parents themselves must consider their responsibilities before God and before each other, before their present children and before the community. Parents themselves must follow their consciences, formed by the law of God" (par. 37).

The final report of the Papal Birth Control Commission (June, 1966) followed this same line of argument, appealing to the *Pastoral Constitution on the Church in the Modern World.* The regulation of conception now appears "necessary for many couples who wish to achieve a responsible, open and reasonable parenthood in today's circumstances." The morality of sexual acts between married people "does not depend upon the direct fecundity of each and every particular act . . . . In a word, the morality of sexual actions is thus to be judged by the true exigencies of the nature of human sexuality, whose meaning is maintained and promoted especially by conjugal chastity . . . ." On the other hand, the final report condemns what it calls a truly "contraceptive" mentality which egotistically and irrationally opposes all fruitfulness in marriage. But the "true opposition is not to be sought between some material conformity to the physiological processes of nature and some artificial intervention. For it is natural to man to use his skill in order to put under human control what is given by physical nature. The opposition is really to be sought between one way of acting which is contraceptive and opposed to a prudent and generous fruitfulness, and another way which is in an ordered relationship to responsible fruitfulness and which has a concern for education and all the essential human and Christian values."

With regard to the contraceptive method to be used, the report of the Papal Birth Control Commission suggested four criteria: (1) it must be consistent with the humanity of the persons and with the love the conjugal act is intended to express; (2) it must be effective; (3) it must exclude as many negative factors as possible—e.g., threats to health or hygiene; and (4) it must inevitably depend on what happens to be available in a certain region at a certain time for a certain couple, and this may depend on the economic situation. In any event, "condemnation of a couple to a long and often heroic abstinence as the means to regulate conception cannot be founded on the truth."

Humanae Vitae

The central teaching of Pope Paul VI's encyclical on the regulation of births is contained in its eleventh paragraph: " . . . the Church calling men back to the observance of the norms of the natural law, as interpreted by constant doctrine, teaches that each and every marriage act must remain open to the transmission of life." The foundation for that teaching is a particular understanding of natural law as it applies to the conjugal act, namely, that there is an "inseparable connection, willed by God and unable to be broken by man on his own initiative, between the two meanings of the conjugal act: the unitive meaning and the procreative meaning" (n. 12). It is "unitive" in that it brings husband and wife together, and it is "procreative" in that it "capacitates them for the generation of new lives." The *principle of totality,* according to which contraception could be considered morally legitimate in the context of the totality of a fruitful married life, is declared erroneous (n. 14).

The encyclical's particular understanding of natural law clearly emerges in its defense of the rhythm method, or the restriction of marital relations to sterile periods of the month. In this case, the couple makes "legitimate use of a natural disposition; in the [other case], they impede the development of natural processes" (n. 16). The encyclical, therefore, rests its argument on the physiological structure of the act, while contemporary theology insists that the basic criterion for the meaning of human actions is the total person and not some isolated aspect of the person.

Indeed, even theologians who accept in principle an inseparable connection between the procreative and unitive elements of sexuality regard the explanation given in the encyclical as too strongly biological. Vatican II allowed for a wider basis for evaluating the morality of such a human act, namely, "the full sense of mutual self-giving and human procreation in the context of true love" *(Pastoral Constitution on the Church in the Modern World,* n. 51).

The encyclical also argues against contraception on the grounds that it leads to certain negative consequences: conjugal infidelity, a general lowering of morality, easy corruption of youth, loss of respect for women (n. 17).

Reaction to Humanae Vitae

The negative reaction of many theologians, ethicists and non-ethicists alike, was vigorous and widespread. These can be sampled in such books as *Contraception: Authority and Dissent* (cited above), *Human Sexuality: New Directions in American Catholic Thought: A Study Commissioned by the Catholic Theological Society of America* (New York: Paulist Press, 1977), pp. 114-128, and Joseph Komonchak's *"Humanae Vitae* and Its Reception: Ecclesiological Reflections," *Theological Studies* 39/2 (June 1978), pp. 221-257. A pro-encyclical view is presented in the same issue of *Theological Studies* by John C. Ford (one of the authors of the Papal Birth Control Commission's minority report) and Germain Grisez, "Contraception and the Infallibility of the Ordinary Magisterium," pp. 258-312.

Many *bishops' conferences* around the world also reacted to the encyclical in a way that fell far short of unqualified support. Each of these focused on the primacy of conscience, the need to be understanding and forgiving, and the judgment that Catholics who sincerely cannot follow the encyclical's teaching are not thereby separated from the love of God through mortal sin. Such themes were sounded by the bishops of Belgium, Germany, the Netherlands, France, Canada, and the Scandinavian countries. Catholics who cannot follow the encyclical's teaching "should not consider that because of this they are separated from God's love" (Belgian bishops). "Pastors must respect the responsible decisions of conscience made by the faithful" (German bishops). Although Catholics must show "respect to the authority and pronouncements of the pope," there are "many factors which determine one's personal conscience regarding marriage rules, for examples mutual love, the relations in a family, and social circumstances" (Dutch bishops). Contraception is always a disorder, "but this disorder is not always culpable." Thus, "when one faces a choice of duties, where one cannot avoid an evil whatever be the decision taken, traditional wisdom requires that one seek before God to find which is the greater duty. The spouses will decide after joint reflection" (French bishops). "No one, including the Church can absolve anyone from the obligation to follow his conscience ... If someone for weighty and well-considered reasons cannot become convinced by the argumentation of the encyclical, it has always been conceded that he is allowed to have a different view from that presented in a non-infallible statement of the Church. No one should be considered a bad Catholic because he is of such a dissenting opinion" (Scandinavian bishops). All of these themes recur in the statement of the Canadian bishops: Such couples "may be safely assured that whoever honestly chooses that course which seems right to him does so in good conscience."

A similar, although more conservative, approach was taken by the Sacred Congregation for the Clergy (April 26, 1971) over the signature of its prefect, Cardinal John Wright (d. 1979), in response to a dispute between certain priests of the archdiocese of Washington, D.C., and their archbishop, Cardinal Patrick O'Boyle. Without equivocating on the clear meaning of *Humanae Vitae,* the Congregation acknowledged that "conscience is inviolable and no man is to be forced to act in a manner contrary to his conscience, as the moral tradition of the Church attests." Thus, in pastoral practice priests must not be too quick to assume either complete innocence or moral guilt in the persons they counsel. One must recognize persons who are "honestly trying to lead a good Christian life." There must be confidence "in the mercy of God and the forgiving power of Christ . . . ."

Declaration on Certain Questions Concerning Sexual Ethics

On December 29, 1975, the Congregation for the Doctrine of the Faith issued a declaration on sexual ethics which reaffirms the teaching of *Humanae Vitae* as well as that encyclical's particular understanding of natural law. But the declaration fixed its attention primarily on three particular issues: premarital sexual intercourse, homosexuality, and masturbation. It is particularly skeptical about the arguments of contemporary Catholic moral theologians regarding the difficulty of committing a real mortal sin, i.e., an act that involves the rejection of one's fundamental option toward God (n. 10). It is true, the Congregation acknowledged, that sins of the sexual order more frequently than other sins may lack full and free consent of the will, but "it in no way follows that one can hold the view that in the sexual field mortal sins are not committed" (n. 10).

Christian Values Underlying This Issue

Whatever decision one makes regarding this disputed question of contraception, there are certain values and principles which Catholics on both sides of the issue have to take into account:

1. The goodness of procreation, as an expression of mutual love and for the welfare of the human community at large.

2. The sanctity of human life.

3. The personal dignity and welfare of the spouses, their children, and their potential children.

4. The inviolability of conscience.

5. The responsibility to act on an informed conscience.

6. The right and responsibility of the Church to teach on matters pertaining to morality ("the Church" here meaning not only pope and bishops, but also other qualified teachers with

varying degrees of ministerial authority and scientific competence).

7. The duty of Catholics to take such teaching seriously into account in the process of forming their consciences.

HOMOSEXUALITY
The Biblical Data

Wherever homosexuality is mentioned in the Bible it is condemned. It is a crime worthy of death (Leviticus 18:22; 20:13), a sin "against nature" (Romans 1:27), which excludes one from the Kingdom of God (1 Corinthians 6:9-10). God is said to have visited a terrible punishment upon Sodom for this sin (Genesis 19:1-29). One must remember, however, that various forms of sexual intercourse, including homosexuality, were considered a necessary part of worship by contemporary pagan groups. The severity of the Old Testament's judgment against homosexuality must be seen in that context. The Israelite would be imitating pagan cultic practices and would thereby defile himself (Leviticus 18:3,20,24,30). The worship of Yahweh was to be unconditionally exclusive. No trace of pagan influence was to be countenanced. Such would be idolatrous and an abomination (e.g., Leviticus 18:26,29-30; Deuteronomy 12:31; 13:14; 17:4; 18:9; 2 Kings 16:3; 21:2,11; 2 Chronicles 33:2; Ezekiel 5:9,11). In a world where worship permeated every aspect of life, anything suggestive of pagan cultic practice—e.g., the fertility rites of the Canaanites—would be for the Israelite tantamount to infidelity to Yahweh.

Even after the danger of ritual intercourse had passed, the prohibition against homosexual activity was retained just as various dietary prescriptions had been maintained. The Talmud extended the prohibition, but not the death penalty, to women as well. The Levitical teaching, of course, had considerable influence on the Church, affecting Paul's estimation of the sexual practices of first-century Greeks. The Genesis story of Sodom and Gomorrah (Genesis 19) was even more influential on Christian thought. The Fathers of the Church would automatically assume that the sin for which Sodom was punished was the homosexual practice of sodomy. A parallel story speaks of the wickedness of the people of Gibeah (Judges 19:22-30) who seize a concubine and abuse her "all night until the following dawn, when they let her go." What is common to the two stories—the one involving the male visitors of Sodom and the other, the female concubine of Gibeah—is rape. If sexuality is involved in the condemnations of both towns, it is less important than the issues of hospitality and justice. Indeed, there is no uniform tradition regarding Sodom's offense: for Isaiah it was injustice (1:10; 3:9); for Jeremiah, adultery, lying, and unrepentance (23:14); for Ezekiel, pride, gluttony, too much comfort, indifference to the poor and needy (16:49); for the Wisdom literature, folly, insolence, and inhospitality (Wisdom 10:8; 19:14; Sirach 16:8). Jesus refers to Sodom but makes no mention of its specific sin (Matthew 10:14-15; 11:23-24; Luke 10:12; 17:29). Not until late in the New Testament is an explicit link made between Sodom and sexuality (Jude 6-7; 2 Peter 2:4,6-10).

Sodom was to become for the early Christians a symbol of the depravity of Greek society. This, in turn, provides some background for the isolated references made to homosexual practices in the New Testament. Jesus says nothing about it. The Epistles mention it three times: in two instances as an item on a list of vices prevalent in first-century Rome (1 Corinthians 6:9-10; 1 Timothy 1:9-10), and in another, extended reference (Romans 1:18,22-28) to those who deliberately choose homosexual over heterosexual relations. There was, of course, no distinction between deliberate perversion and indeliberate homosexual orientation rooted in a particular personality with a particular psychological history and constitution.

Post-Biblical Tradition

The Fathers of the Church were consistent in their denunciation of homosexuality: Augustine, John Chrysostom, *et al.* The sixth-century Code of Justinian added to pre-Christian laws protecting minors from homosexual violation the prohibition of all sodomistic practices under penalty of death by fire. This legal document had influence on both ecclesiastical and civil laws even into the Middle Ages, and perhaps indirectly into our own time in the West.

Thomas Aquinas treated homosexual acts in connection with sins against temperance, specifically lust, and listed sodomy along with masturbation and bestiality as "unnatural vices" *(Summa Theologica* II-II, q. 154). Catholic moral theology, until very recently, made no discernible changes in Aquinas' approach. Although there were exceedingly few references to the sin in the official teachings of the Church, the manuals regularly numbered homosexual acts alongside masturbation and bestiality as against nature and always gravely sinful. The appeal to Scripture is to the Sodom story.

Thus, from the time of Paul, through Thomas Aquinas, down to the Vatican's *Declaration on Sexual Ethics* of 1975, the Catholic tradition has consistently judged all homosexual acts as at once unnatural and gravely sinful. "Underlying this tradition," some theologians have proposed, "are not only a pre-scientific physiology and unhistorical interpretation of Scripture but also the Stoic conviction that procreation alone justifies the enjoyment and use of sexual pleasure" *(Human Sexuality,* p. 199). With the development of scientific research in medicine, psychiatry, and psychology, homosexuality has appeared to some as a much more complex moral problem than the tradition would indicate. (It must also be noted, however, that the Vatican Congregation for the Doctrine of the Faith in 1979 explicitly rejected the theological orientation of the *Human Sexuality* report cited above.)

Three Approaches

There are at least three moral approaches to this issue of homosexuality in recent theological discussion: (1) that homosexual acts are always sinful in themselves; (2) that they are neutral; and (3) that they are essentially imperfect, neither always wrong nor an ideal.

Homosexual Acts Are Always Sinful in Themselves

This position follows the approach of Thomas Aquinas. The order of nature requires that a male should join with a female so that procreation will occur and the human species will continue in existence. Sexual union between persons of the same sex is "unnatural" because procreation is impossible, whereas the act itself is ordered for that purpose alone. A leading defender of this view is Catholic theologian John F. Harvey, O.S.F.S. Harvey argues that, while a homosexual is not responsible for his condition, he or she *is* responsible for controlling actions which spring from that condition. Homosexuals, like all other unmarried people, are called to avoid sexual indulgence (see "Homosexuality," *New Catholic Encyclopedia,* New York: McGraw Hill, 1967, VII, pp. 117-119; and "Contemporary Theological Views," in *Counseling the Homosexual,* John R. Cavanaugh, ed., Huntington, Ind.: Our Sunday Visitor Press, 1977, pp. 235-237).

This remains the position also of the official magisterium. Thus, the *Declaration on Sexual Ethics* from the Sacred Congregation for the Doctrine of the Faith insists that "homosexual acts are intrinsically disordered and can in no case be approved of" (n. 8). And the National Conference of Catholic Bishops of the United States adopted the same approach in its *Principles to Guide Confessors in Questions of Homosexuality* (Washington, D.C.: N.C.C.B., 1973): genital sexual expression may take place only in marriage; each such act must be open in principle to procreation and must as well be an expression of mutual love between a husband and a wife. Because homosexual acts cannot possibly fulfill these principles, they are "a grave transgression of the goals of human sexuality and of human personality, and are consequently contrary to the will of God" (p. 3). Given the factor of compulsion, the confessor must avoid "both harshness and permissiveness . . . . But, generally, [the homosexual] is responsible for his actions, and the worst thing that a confessor can say is that the homosexual is not responsible for his actions" (pp. 8-9). Overt homosexuals are not to be encouraged to receive the Eucharist (pp. 14-15).

Homosexual Acts Are Morally Neutral

This position argues that the morality of the sexual act depends upon the quality of the relationship. The moral determination does not rest on whether the act is heterosexual or homosexual, but rather on the quality of the relationship of the persons. Accordingly, "It is the task of homosexuals to acknowledge themselves as such before God, accept their sexual inclination as their calling, and explore the meaning of this inclination for the Christian life" (Gregory Baum, "Catholic Homosexuals," *Commonweal* 99, February 15, 1974, p. 481). This view in effect denies not only the consistent tradition of Sacred Scripture and the Church but also the majority of all the data from the human sciences which point to the fact that human sexuality has its proper meaning in terms of the love union of male and female. Furthermore, stable homosexual relationships tend to be the exception rather than the rule. "It would seem," some Catholic theologians have argued against this "neutral" view, "that the elements of mutual love, fidelity, and caring need more detailed and specific explanation if this approach is to provide a suitable pastoral norm for counseling homosexuals" *(Human Sexuality,* p. 206). Indeed, freedom is not the only aspect involved in many human relationships—e.g., student-teacher, employer-employee, citizen-government. "Man, human existence, and human relationships can never be merely neutral" (Charles E. Curran, "Dialogue with the Homophile Movement: The Morality of Homosexuality," *Catholic Moral Theology in Dialogue,* Notre Dame, Ind.: Fides Publishers, 1972, p. 209).

Homosexual Acts Are Essentially Imperfect

A third position has been described by one of its principal advocates, Catholic moral theologian Charles E. Curran, of The Catholic University of America, as a mediating one (*op. cit.,* p. 209). It is also called a "theology of compromise." It recognizes that homosexual acts are wrong but also acknowledges that for some people homosexual behavior might not fall under under the total condemnation proposed in the first of these three approaches. The view is somewhat different from that proposed by John J. McNeill, S.J., in his *The Church and the Homosexual* (Kansas City, Mo.: Sheed, Andrews, and McMeel, 1976). McNeill argues that homosexual acts are the lesser of two evils: giving expression to one's sexuality with a person of the same sex, or having no opportunity at all for giving expression to one's sexuality.

Curran's theory of compromise is based on the premise that in the "presence of sin . . . at times one might not be able to do what would be done if there were no sin present . . . . the particular action in one sense is not objectively wrong because in the presence of sin it remains the only viable alternative for the individual. However, in another sense the action is wrong and manifests the power of sin. If possible, man must try to overcome sin, but the Christian knows that the struggle against sin is never totally successful in this world" (*op. cit.*, pp. 216-217; see also his *A New Look at Christian Morality*, Notre Dame, Ind.: Fides Publishers, 1968, pp. 169-173 and 232-233).

Applying this theory of compromise to the issue of homosexuality, Curran asserts two propositions: (1) that "for an irreversible or constitutional homosexual, homosexual acts in the context of a loving relationship striving for permanency can be and are morally good;" and (2) "the ideal meaning of human sexual relationships is in terms of male and female" (see "Moral Theology, Psychiatry, and Homosexuality," *Bulletin of the National Guild of Catholic Psychiatrists*, vol. 24, 1978, pp. 24-25). Thus, the homosexual acts of an irreversible homosexual "in the context of a loving union tending to permanency are objectively good; but at the same time the ideal and normative human meanings of sexuallity are in terms of male and female" (p. 26). On the other hand, Curran does not want to appeal to "the presence of sin in the world" to justify every single action, although some of the Fathers of the Church did make such an appeal to justify slavery. It is necessary rather to "consider all the values involved and on the basis of proportionate reason to decide whether or not something is objectively good" (p. 30; see also *Transition and Tradition in Moral Theology*, Notre Dame, Ind.: University of Notre Dame Press, 1979, pp. 59-80).

Curran's mediating theory of compromise is criticized from both sides: from those who follow the traditional natural law approach and from those who resist the argument that heterosexuality is the ideal (see *Human Sexuality*, p. 204).

Christian Values Underlying This Issue

Whatever decision one makes regarding this moral question of homosexuality, there are certain values and principles which Catholics and other Christians on various sides of the argument have to take into account:

1. The goodness of procreation, as an expression of mutual love and for the welfare of the human community at large.

2. The personal dignity of every human being, regardless of his or her sexual orientation, and the existence of natural and civil rights which flow from that dignity.

3. The need of every person for love, friendship, even intimacy, although not necessarily of a genitally sexual nature.

4. The inviolability of conscience.

5. The responsibility to act on an informed conscience.

6. The existence of many internal and external impediments to full human freedom.

7. The right and responsibility of the Church to teach on matters pertaining to morality ("the Church" here again meaning not only the pope and the bishops, but also other qualified teachers with varying degrees of ministerial authority and scientific competence).

8. The duty of Catholics to take such teaching seriously into account in the process of forming their consciences.

Section Two: Social Ethics

WARFARE
Biblical Data

The wars of Israel were the wars of Yahweh (Exodus 17:16; Numbers 21:14; 1 Samuel 25:28). The war against Amalek was the execution of the anger of Yahweh (1 Samuel 28:18). Yahweh was considered present in the war camp (Deuteronomy 23:15).

Yahweh is called a warrior (Exodus 15:3; Psalm 24:8) who fights on behalf of Israel (Exodus 14:14; Deuteronomy 1:30; 32:41; Joshua 10:14,42; 23:10; 24:12; Judges 5:23), sending panic into the enemy (Exodus 23:27-28). Yahweh delivers the enemy into the hands of Israel (Joshua 2:24; 6:2,16; Judges 3:28; 1 Samuel 23:4; I Kings 20:28). It is Yahweh, not the strength of arms or numbers, who insures the victory (Judges 7:2-22; 1 Samuel 14:6; 17:45,47). It is Yahweh who leads the armies of Israel (Judges 4:14; Deuteronomy 20:4; 2 Samuel 5:24) and who gives the victory (Exodus 15:14-16; 23:27-28). The enemies of Israel are the enemies of Yahweh (Judges 5:23,31). The priestly ideal of a sacred war is set forth in Numbers 31, and the law of war in Deuteronomy 20 is another earlier rationalization of war. In this regard, the Israelites simply reflected the thought patterns and mentality of their times.

On the other hand, there are several instances where the *prophets* explicitly denounced war. War is a judgment of Yahweh upon Israel (Isaiah 5:25-30; Jeremiah 5:15; Amos 5:27; 6:14). It is through faith, not military means, that Israel is destined to survive (Isaiah 2:1-5; 30:15-17; 31:1-3; 22:8-11; Jeremiah 21:3-10; 27; 34:1-5; 38:2-4; Hosea 8:14; 10:13-14; 14:4; Amos 2:14-16).

Jesus and the disciples have no developed theology of warfare. The New Testament community was hardly in a position, as the Israelites had been, of determining policies affecting military expeditions against other nations. Jesus did warn that "those who use the sword are sooner or later destroyed by it" (Matthew 26:52).

Beyond that, however, the idea of warfare only appears in *metaphors* which describe the Christian life or illustrate the proclamation of the Gospel (Matthew 22:7; Luke 11:17; 14:31-32). *Paul* mentions military service to explain the apostolate (1 Corinthians 9:7). The apostle should fight the good fight (1 Timothy 1:18) as a good soldier of Jesus Christ (2 Timothy 2:3-4). The warfare of the Christian is waged against the powers of evil (Ephesians 6:12).

Both Old and New Testaments speak of the final judgment in terms of warfare. The messianic king is a victorious warrior (Psalms 2; 110:5-7). Ezekiel 38-39 describes the attack and defeat of Gog, king of Magog, Meshech, and Tubal. In the New Testament the imagery of an apocalyptic war appears only in Revelation 12:7, the war between the angels led by Michael and the dragon, and in Revelation 20:9, where the dragon's forces are annihilated by God's power.

Post-biblical Developments

Augustine regarded war as both the product of sin and a remedy for it. In a world corrupted by sin, the use of force by public authorities is a legitimate means of avenging evil. Public order must be preserved. On the other hand, Augustine did not approve killing in self-defense. He separated individual morality, which must be dictated by the Gospel mandate of loving one's enemies and turning the other cheek (Matthew 5:39), from social morality, which is for the sake of the common good.

Thomas Aquinas carried forward the Augustinian position but was more specific about the criteria for the just war: (1) The cause must be just; (2) it must be undertaken by legitimate authority; and (3) the intention must be right.

These three basic categories would eventually be expanded into a complex set of criteria and principles. The first set of tests to determine a *just war* are: legitimate authority, just cause, last resort, need for a declaration of war, reasonable hope of success, proportionality between the evil produced by the war and the evil hoped to be avoided or the good hoped to be achieved, and right intention. The second set of principles are: the immunity of non-combatants from direct attack, and proportionality of tactics and of means to end (see James R. Childress, "Just-War Theories," *Theological Studies,* vol. 39, 1978, pp. 427-445).

Since the taking of human life was so obviously opposed to the ideals of the Gospel, warfare remained a serious moral problem for Christians. It could be justified only by an appeal to the common good. *The purpose of the just-war theory, therefore, was not to rationalize violence but to limit its scope and methods.* Thomas' own ambivalence about defending the use of force surfaces in his discussion of the right of self-defense. Whereas Augustine had prohibited it, Aquinas accepted it on the basis of the *principle of the double effect* (two effects follow, one good and one evil, from an essentially good or at least neutral act; if the evil effect is unintended and not a direct result of the act, and if the good effect is proportionate to the evil effect, the act itself is legitimate). Thus, public authorities could directly will the taking of life, but private persons could intend only the deterring of aggression, not the aggressor's death *(Summa Theologica* II-II, q. 64, a. 7; see also F. H. Russell, *The Just War in the Middle Ages,* London: Cambridge University Press, 1977, pp. 16-39, on Augustine, and pp. 60-199, on Aquinas).

The Spanish Scholastics Vitoria (d. 1546) and Suarez (d. 1617) brought the just-war theory to yet another stage of development. By their time the problem of warfare was substantially modified by two changes: the emergence of the nation-state as a new center of secular authority, challenging both the idea of a wider Christian commonwealth and the binding power of any universal moral authority higher than the state, and, secondly, the disintegrative impact of the Reformation on the Christian community. The emphasis in the just-war theory shifted from Aquinas' stress on the just *cause* to the question of *means*. It was acknowledged that both sides might sincerely hold their cause to be just, but they must attend nonetheless to the ways in which they wage war against the other. Indeed, in revising the content of the just-cause category and in enhancing the importance of judgments about the means of warfare, the Spanish Scholastics and also the Protestant theologian Hugo Grotius (d. 1645) provided the foundation for the secular science of international law (see L. B. Walters, *Five Classic Just-War Theories: A Study in the Thought of Thomas Aquinas, Vitoria, Suarez, Gentili and Grotius,* unpublished Ph. D. dissertation, New Haven: Yale University, 1971).

Between the seventeenth and twentieth centuries the only significant change in the just war theory is to be found in the writings of Taparelli d'Azeglio (d. 1862). His efforts to reflect on the international community as a subject of moral law provided the conceptual foundation for some of the major themes in twentieth-century papal teaching, especially that of Pope Pius XII (see, for example, the Christmas Addresses of 1941, 1951, 1952, and

1953 in *Major Addresses of Pius XII,* vol. 2, Vincent Yzermans, ed., St. Paul, Minn.: The North Central Publishing Co., 1961).

Modern Developments

Pope Pius XII (d. 1958) acknowledged that force could be used as an instrument of justice in the international order. However, the destructive capacity of modern warfare had already increased so drastically by his pontificate that he reduced the legitimate causes of war from three (self-defense, avenging an evil, and restoring violated rights) to one, i.e., the defense of one's own nation or that of another against unjust attack. At the same time, the pope rejected pacifism (Christmas Message, 1956).

By the time Pope John XXIII was elected to the papacy in 1958, the just-war doctrine was firmly in place. But development continued, this time in a discernibly pacifist direction. In Pope John XXIII's encyclical *Pacem in Terris* (1963) we find a strong criticism of the arms race and of the balance of terror on which it rests. He called for structural reform of the international political and legal system to deal with this dangerous problem. Significantly, there is no explicit endorsement in this encyclical of the right of self-defense for peoples and for states, although this was the one argument retained by Pius XII. "Therefore, in this age of ours, which prides itself on its atomic power, it is irrational to think that war is a proper way to obtain justice for violated rights" (a text cited by Vatican II's *Pastoral Constitution on the Church in the Modern World,* n. 80).

Is *Pacem in Terris* advocating a pacifist view here? James Douglass thought so *(The Nonviolent Cross: A Theology of Revolution and Peace,* New York: Macmillan, 1966, p. 84). Others, like Protestant ethicist Paul Ramsey contend the opposite *(The Just War: Force and Political Responsibility,* New York: Scribner's, 1968, p. 78). Later official documents of the Catholic Church, however, continue to assert the right of legitimate defense for states and yet make no attempt to reform, correct, or reinterpret *Pacem in Terris.* Nonetheless, it *is* clear that the encyclical heralded a new approach to warfare in Catholic thought.

An explicit endorsement of a pacifist position occurs for the first time in Catholic teaching in Vatican II's *Pastoral Constitution on the Church in the Modern World.* "The horror and perversity of war are immensely magnified by the multiplication of scientific weapons.... (Such) considerations compel us to undertake an evaluation of war with an entirely new attitude" (n. 80). The new attitude generates an acceptance of a philosophy of nonviolence and support for conscientious objection. The council insists that it "cannot fail to praise those who renounce the use of violence in the vindication of their rights and who resort to methods of defense which are otherwise available to weaker parties too, provided that this can be done without injury to the rights and duties of others or of the community itself" (n. 78). *Gaudium et spes* rejects the policy of blind obedience. Conscience must remain supreme. "Moreover, it seems right that laws make humane provisions for the case of those who for reasons of conscience refuse to bear arms, provided however, that they accept some other form of service to the human community" (n. 79).

In the years after the council, Pope Paul VI encouraged this same line of emphasis. He visited the United Nations in 1965 to appeal for the end of all wars and established January 1 as a Day of Peace each year. Protestant theologian John Yoder classified Pope Paul's U. N. speech as an example of "cosmopolitan pacificism" *(Nevertheless: The Varieties of Religious Pacificism,* Scottsdale, Ariz.: Herald Press, 1971). Social ethicists like J. Bryan Hehir, Associate Secretary for International Justice and Peace, United States Catholic Conference, argue that the total content of recent Catholic teaching does not support such a judgment. The Catholic Church has not moved from a just-war ethic to a pacifist position. The reality is more complex. There has been change in the normative doctrine on war, but there is also *continuity.*

The central theme which ties contemporary Catholic teaching to earlier just-war teaching is the repeated assertion of the *right of states to self-defense.* Given the world situation as it is, devoid of any effective international authority, " ... governments cannot be denied the right to legitimate defense once every means of peaceful settlement has been exhausted" *(Gaudium et spes,* n. 79). But this right is not absolute and unrestricted regarding means. Certain forms of force, even in self-defense, may be prohibited. Everything is to be governed by two principles: the *principle of proportionality* (the evil produced by the means of self-defense should not be greater than the evil produced by the aggression) and the *rule of noncombatant immunity.*

Thus, the arms race is condemned in *Pacem in Terris,* in *Gaudium et spes,* and in various statements of the Holy See on disarmament (see *The Holy See and Disarmament,* Vatican City: Tipografia Poliglotta Vaticana, 1976). It is "an utterly treacherous trap for humanity, and one which injures the poor to an intolerable degree" *(Gaudium et spes,* n. 81). The very same theme is sounded in Pope John Paul II's first encyclical, *Redemptor Hominis* (1979) and later the same year in his address to the thirty-fourth General Assembly of the United Nations Organization.

On the other hand, Vatican II does not demand *unilateral* disarmament. Disarmament must proceed "at an equal pace according to agreement, and backed up by authentic and workable safeguards" *(Gaudium et spes,* n. 82). There is a measured political realism in the teaching even in the face of a situation that can only be described as urgent and fraught with the greatest danger. There is a blending here of prophetic vision and political wisdom.

Contemporary Moral Options

In light of these recent developments in official Catholic teaching, it seems correct to suggest that there are two moral options available to Catholics today: the *just-war ethic* and some form of *pacifism.* Within the context of these two broadly stated positions, other specific positions in Catholic moral thought and teaching include: a condemnation of total war *(Gaudium et spes,* n. 80), a condemnation of acts of war aimed indiscriminately against civilians, an indictment of the arms race as a waste of needed funds, and an affirmation that those who do serve in the military may make a genuine contribution to the establishment of peace (n. 79).

There are a number of general moral perceptions and principles which the just-war and pacifist positions have in *common:* the sacredness of life, the seriousness of taking a human life, and the morally restricted nature of any war. The *difference* between the two positions is obvious: The pacifist holds that no conflict of values, even the defense of innocent life, can ever legitimate the use of violent force; the just-war advocate begins with the pacifist presumption but acknowledges the possibility of the presumption's yielding to circumstances which justify a rule-governed use of force shaped by many different moral criteria.

The *difference* is further manifested in their respective approaches to *conscientious objection*. The pacifist option demands *universal* conscientious objection; the just-war option allows also *selective* conscientious objection. For the pacifist, selective conscientious objection is not an option, since it implies that some uses of force are legitimate. During the Vietnam war, the Catholic bishops of the United States voiced their support for both universal conscientious objection and selective conscientious objection *(The Catholic Conscientious Objector,* October 12, 1969; *Declaration on Conscientious Objection and Selective Conscientious Objection,* October 21, 1971). The question is whether or not the two positions are compatible within one and the same community of faith.

But what of the just-war theory itself? Can it still be held in a nuclear age? Jewish political theorist Michael Walzer, of Harvard University, argues that it cannot. "Nuclear weapons explode the theory of just-war. They are the first of mankind's technological innovations that are simply not encompassable within the familiar moral world" *(Just and Unjust Wars: A Moral Argument with Historical Illustrations,* New York: Basic Books, 1977, p. 282). But Catholic theology and official teaching would seem to contradict that assumption. Catholics have, in fact, used the just-war theory to assess the morality of nuclear weapons, and there is a development of Catholic teaching from the time when Pope Pius XII first confronted the question in 1954 to the strongly worded statement of the Second Vatican Council in 1965: "Any act of war aimed indiscriminately at the destruction of entire cities or of extensive areas along with their population is a crime against God and man himself. It merits unequivocal and unhesitating condemnation" *(Gaudium et spes,* n. 80).

The special moral problem, however, is not with the *use* of nuclear weapons but with the *threat* of use in a *policy of deterrence*. Nuclear pacifists are divided on the morality of the deterrence policy. Pius XII did not have to face that problem, and Vatican II gave an imprecise response to it: "Whatever be the case with this method of deterrence, men should be convinced that the arms race in which so many countries are engaged is not a safe way to preserve a steady peace" (n. 81). It is not that the council or moral theologians find the deterrence policy acceptable. Rather, there are no better alternatives to it which are at once morally acceptable and politically viable.

What are the problems in the present deterrence system? First, there is the implicit intention to use the nuclear weapons if necessary. But their use would be immoral. On the other hand, the very threat of their use may in fact be preventing their use (see *Gaudium et spes,* n. 81). "If the intention to retaliate and the actual use of nuclear weapons both violate the ethics of war, is there a lesser evil in a threat which remains unfulfilled?" J. Bryan Hehir asks.

And what effect is there upon the adversary if it seems that the other side does not really intend to act? Would that show of weakness provoke the adversary into action? A radical move like unilateral disarmament may have the opposite intended effect. Rather than cooling off the nuclear atmosphere and making nuclear war less likely, it could conceivably increase the likelihood of a nuclear strike from the other side or put the adversary in the position of a blackmailer.

Three moral positions, not exclusively within the Catholic tradition, have emerged on this difficult issue. The *first,* adopted by the United States Catholic bishops in 1976, condemns not only the use of nuclear weapons but also the policy of deterrence because of the intent to use: "Not only is it wrong to attack civilian populations, but it is also wrong to threaten to attack them as part of a strategy of deterrence" *(To Live in Christ Jesus: A Pastoral Reflection on the Moral Life,* Washington, D.C.: U. S. Catholic Conference, 1976, p. 34). Surprisingly, the statement is more uncompromising about deterrence than it is about use. A *second* position argues that some uses of nuclear weapons are legitimate, and that, therefore, a policy of deterrence is similarly justifiable (Paul Ramsey, *op. cit.*, chapters 13-15). A *third* position prohibits use but tolerates deterrence (J. Bryan Hehir, "The New Nuclear Debate: Political and Ethical Considerations," in *The New Nuclear Debate,* R. A. Gessert and J. B. Hehir, eds., New York: CRIA Special Studies, 1976, pp. 35-76). "We threaten evil," Walzer writes, "in order not to do it, and the doing of it would be so terrible that the threat seems in comparison to be morally defensible" *(op. cit.* p. 274).

If this whole discussion about nuclear strategy illustrates anything about Catholic moral theology and official Catholic moral teaching, it is their conscious effort to mix moral vision with political realism. There is, on the one hand, a clear condemnation of the whole business of nuclear strategy, but there are also concessions to the complexity of the issues. So much so, in fact, that a final judgment on what the Catholic position really is remains an open question. What *is* clear is that two different theological methods are at work: one (the pacifist) which allows for no exceptions on life-and-death issues such as war, capital punishment, abortion, euthanasia; the other (the just-war approach) which emphasizes the principle of proportionality (see Richard A. McCormick and Paul Ramsey, *Doing Evil to Achieve Good,* Chicago: Loyola University Press, 1978, chapter 1, "Ambiguity in Moral Choice," by McCormick).

Christian Values Underlying This Issue

Whatever position one adopts regarding the morality of warfare, there are certain values and principles which Catholics and other Christians, and indeed other persons of good will on various sides of the argument, have to take into account:

1. The sacredness of all human life.
2. The utter gravity of taking another human life.
3. The inherent moral limits on every use of force.
4. The right and responsibility of the Church to articulate a moral vision on matters of social and even international morality ("the Church" here again meaning not only the hierarchy but also

other qualified teachers with varying degrees of ministerial authority and scientific competence).

5. The responsibility of the Church to articulate such a moral vision in a manner that is at the same time politically realistic, or attentive to political realities, such as Pope John Paul II provides in his 1979 United Nations address on peace, human rights, and social justice.

6. The duty of Catholics to take such teaching seriously into account in the process not only of forming their consciences but of expressing their views in the political order (e.g., by voting, communication with political leaders, public statements designed to influence public opinion).

INTERVENTION OF THE STATE IN THE ECONOMIC ORDER
Elements of the Issue

This issue illustrates again the thrust of Catholic teaching on questions of social justice, and indeed shows the nature of the Church as a community of moral discourse. It is "a gathering of people with the explicit intention to survey and critically discuss their personal and social responsibilities in the light of moral convictions about which there is some consensus and to which there is some loyalty" (James Gustafson, *The Church as Moral Decision-Maker*, Philadelphia: Pilgrim Press, 1970, p. 84). The Church does not pretend, and should not be expected, to have precise answers to complex social and political questions. Rather it attempts only to elaborate a framework of values, principles, and responsibilities within which a discussion of such issues can be carried on, the formation of a Christian conscience can be promoted, and decisions fundamentally consistent with the Christian tradition can be made.

The question of the right and duty of the state to intervene in the economic order highlights the relationship between two important elements of Catholic social doctrine: the *principle of subsidiarity* and the *process of socialization*. The *principle of subsidiarity,* according to which nothing is to be done at a higher level which can be done as well or better at a lower level, places the

burden of proof for intervention always on the higher body, principally the state. This is a conservative principle; it leans against
state intervention. The *socialization process* reminds us of our
growing interdependence and the benefits that can be produced
when there is planned interventionist action on the part of the
state. It is not just that a lower group cannot do something as well
or better than the state, but that there are simply too many groups,
institutions, structures, and political factors for any one group or
level apart from the state to meet a problem common to all of these
diverse social elements. To the extent that socialization can also
be considered a principle, it is a liberal principle; it encourages
state intervention.

These two principles are to be understood as dialectically
related, in creative tension. "The thrust of subsidiarity is to preserve a sphere of freedom, while recognizing the need for a certain
degree of centralization and control. The counterthrust of socialization is to highlight the need for coordination and direction of
complex social systems if they are to benefit the citizens for whom
they exist" (J. Bryan Hehir, "Church and State: Basic Concepts for
Analysis," *Origins* 8/24, November 30, 1978, p. 381). In deciding
for or against state intervention, and also regarding the degree and
type of intervention, both values have to be taken into account.

Recent Catholic Teaching

The *principle of subsidiarity* was first formally articulated by Pope
Pius XI in his encyclical *Quadragesimo Anno* (1931): "It is a
fundamental principle of social philosophy, fixed and unchange-
able, that one should not withdraw from individuals and commit
to the community what they can accomplish by their own enterprise and industry. So, too, it is an injustice and at the same time a
grave evil and a disturbance of right order, to transfer to the larger
and higher collectivity functions which can be performed and
provided for by lesser and subordinate bodies" (cited also by Pope
John XXIII's *Mater et Magistra,* 1961, par. 53). Although this is a
conservative principle, it does not justify a laissez-faire approach
by which the state allows the economic order to run by its own
power and according to its own designs. The encyclical

Quadragesimo Anno clearly placed the Church on the side of those arguing that economic activity should be regulated for the sake of the common good.

Pope Pius XII and Pope John XXIII carried this principle of subsidiarity forward to meet the growing complexity of the economic order. Although Pius XII's contributions never took the form of an encyclical letter, they were nevertheless incorporated into the explicit social teachings of John XXIII. Pius XII is cited in thirty-four of the seventy-three footnotes in John XXIII's *Pacem in Terris*. In *Mater et Magistra* John XXIII moved the discussion of state intervention to a new level of clarity and development. First, he reasserted the validity of the principle of subsidiarity as a norm of social policy. Secondly, he called attention to the substantially changed social and political context in which that principle has to function today. And, thirdly, he introduced the notion of socialization as a complement to that of subsidiarity.

John XXIII argued that the role of the state in society had to be understood in light of three contemporary elements: (1) the impact of technological change, (2) the rise of the welfare state, and (3) the growing aspirations of people to participate in the political process (pars. 46-50). From the confluence of these three elements, John XXIII proposed his notion of socialization (par. 59). This process, he argued, is at once the result and cause of increasing state intervention in the socio-economic order. The need to intervene follows from such basic needs as health care, education, housing. Such intervention has both positive and negative effects. On balance, John XXIII finds the benefits outweighing the liabilities.

Also at the heart of Catholic social doctrine and centrally related to the policy judgment the state has to make about intervention is the teaching on *rights and duties*. The clearest statement of which rights are necessary to preserve the human dignity of each person in society is found in John XXIII's *Pacem in Terris* (pars. 8-35). The concept of *right* implies a *moral claim* by a person to some good of the physical or spiritual order which is necessary for proper human development and dignity. When such a right is established, a correlative duty is also established to recognize the right and to see to it that it is fulfilled either through private action or through governmental action. It is one of government's principal responsibilities to balance rights and duties of members and groups within society. The state must recognize and reinforce those rights which protect the individual or groups from undue intrusion by public authority. It must also determine when and in what way the state can be used to promote the socio-economic rights of people, especially those in need and/or the politically weak. *Pacem in Terris* refers specifically to those rights: " . . . the right to life, to bodily integrity, and to the means which are necessary and suitable for proper development of life; these are primarily food, clothing, shelter, rest, medical care, and finally the necessary social services. Therefore a human being also has the right to security in case of sickness, inability to work, widowhood, old age, unemployment or in any other case in which he is deprived of the means of subsistence through no fault of his own" (par. 11).

Pope Paul VI brought Catholic social doctrine yet another step beyond John XXIII when, in *Octagesima Adveniens* (1971), he emphasized the responsibility of the political sector in the task of assuring justice for people in society. The ultimate decision in the social and economic field, both national and international, rests with political power (par. 46). The document does not provide solutions to complex policy questions, but it locates the ultimate arena where such questions are decided, and it thereby calls attention to the role of the state as the final agency of justice if other means fail to provide minimum economic justice for people. Thus, state intervention in some cases may be not only legitimate but even imperative.

Finally, in his address to the Thirty-fourth General Assembly of the United Nations Organization (October 1979), Pope John Paul II argued that "it is a question of the highest importance that in internal social life, as well as in international life, *all human beings* in every nation and country *should be able to enjoy effectively their full rights under any political regime or system"* (n. 19).

Health Care

In a country like the United States of America it is agreed that health care, recognized as a right by *Pacem in Terris,* is not evenly distributed throughout the society. In some parts of the nation there are inadequate facilities and too few trained medical personnel. Many citizens have no insurance policies. Only half the population has any major medical coverage. A prolonged or catastrophic illness can bring immediate financial ruination to a middle-class family. Meanwhile, ordinary health care costs continue to rise dramatically.

Ethically the question of health care is a question of *distributive justice.* How are limited resources to be shared with those with a right to them? How much should the state invest in health care over against, for example, education, food, clothing, defense, transportation, or the environment? Who shall receive the necessary life-giving resources when only a limited number are available and when those who do not receive the resources will probably die? Answers have varied. Significantly, very few Catholic moral theologians have even begun to address themselves to such an issue.

1.   Protestant situation ethicist Joseph Fletcher recommends a *utilitarian* approach. We must strive to bring about the greatest good for the greatest number ("Ethics and Health Care: Computers and Distributive Justice," in *Ethics and Health Policy,* Robert M. Veath and Roy Bransom, eds., Cambridge, Mass.: Ballinger Publishing Co., 1976, pp. 99-109). His approach has been criticized for giving too little importance to the rights of the individual and for neglecting the principle of fairness by concentrating only on the total amount of health care produced.

2.   Others advocate a theory based on the *contribution to society* the sick person is making or is likely to make (Nicholas Rescher, "The Allocation of Exotic Medical Lifesaving Therapy," *Ethics,* vol. 79, 1969, p. 178).

3.   Still others insist on the *equal dignity* of all human beings and resist the tendency to assign more value, dignity, and importance to some lives than to others. To protect this dignity, a third approach proposes a random selection procedure: first come, first

served (James Childress, "Who Shall Live When Not All Can Live?" *Soundings,* vol. 43, 1970, pp. 339-355; Paul Ramsey, *The Patient as Person,* New Haven: Yale University Press, 1970, pp. 239-275).

4.   An extremely *individualistic* position has been taken by Robert Sade, who denies that anyone has a right to health care. It is neither a right nor a privilege, but a service. The doctor has the right to sell his service as he sees fit, and the state has no business interfering ("Medical Care as a Right: A Refutation," *New England Journal of Medicine,* vol. 285, December 2, 1971, pp. 1288-1292).

5.   A fifth approach is rooted in John Rawls' notion of *justice as fairness (A Theory of Justice,* Cambridge: Harvard University Press, 1971). Whatever is done in this particular situation for this particular sick person should be done in all similar situations. Such a theory, according to its proponents, is most compatible with the goal of equal access to health care for all. This is the approach of Protestant ethicists Gene Outka and Robert Veath (Outka, "Social Justice and Equal Access to Health Care," *The Journal of Religious Ethics,* vol. 2, 1974, pp. 11-32; Veath, "What is 'Just' Health Care Delivery?" in Veath and Branson, *Ethics and Health Policy,* pp. 127-153).

6.   A sixth approach is taken by Catholic moral theologian Charles E. Curran, who rejects the fifth as too individualistic. Society does not exist simply as the total aggregate of individuals who live in it, nor does the state exist simply to insure the good of individuals. A correct understanding of society and the state within society is essential if we are to construct a responsible answer to the question of the distribution of health-care resources. Both society and state are concerned with the common good, and since the human person is radically social, the common good can never be simply the sum total of individual goods. It is the complex of spiritual, social, and material conditions needed in society for the person to achieve integral human dignity. What is at issue here is *distributive justice.* How do society in general and the state in particular insure the distribution of those goods which are necessary for the achievement of human dignity?

Curran argues that all individual rights are based on the dignity of human life. Society and the state exist to help the individual achieve true fulfillment. Although health care is not the most fundamental of human needs, it is of great significance for the proper and full functioning of a person's life. The basic formulation is straightforward: "A person has the right to that minimum which is necessary for living a decent human life" (*Transition and Tradition in Moral Theology*, Notre Dame, Ind.: University of Notre Dame Press, 1979, chapter 6, "The Right to Health Care and Distributive Justice," pp. 139-170).

In addition to the dignity and fundamental need of the human person, the right to health care is also rooted in the principle that creation exists primarily to serve the needs of all. We are not the ultimate source of the goods we have, but rather the stewards of what has been given to all of us by a gracious God.

Distributive justice, however, does not even begin to answer all the related questions; it only underlines their relevance and importance. What shall be emphasized: preventive medicine, or crisis medicine? Should the government spend large amounts of money on such exotic lifesaving devices as kidney machines which benefit so few? What role should the state take in regulating the training of doctors and other medical personnel? How should a program of national health insurance be paid for? "Ethics and the ethician are not able to supply answers for all the concrete problems facing our society. Questions such as medical care ultimately must be decided by prudential choices in the political realm. However, the principles of distributive justice can well serve as the basis for making political decisions about the provision of health care which are both just and feasible" (Curran *op. cit.*, p. 167).

Christian Values Underlying the Issue

Whatever position one adopts on the general question of state intervention in the economic order or on the particular question of health care, there are certain values and principles which Catholics and other Christians, and indeed other persons of good will on various sides of the argument, have to take into account:

1.   The dignity of every human person.

2.   The fundamental human right to health care.

3.   The correlation of rights and duties.

4.   The radically social nature of the human person.

5.   The subordination of rights and duties to the common good.

6.   Human stewardship, not absolute ownership, of created goods.

7.   The right and obligation of the state to intervene on behalf of human dignity.

8.   The obligation of the state to respect freedom and local initiative (the principle of subsidiarity).

9.   The importance of both the principle of subsidiarity and the principle of socialization, and of their being held together in creative tension in the formulation of public policy.

10.   The right and responsibility of the Church to articulate a moral vision on matters of social and economic policy ("the Church" meaning again not only the hierarchy but also other qualified teachers with varying degrees of ministerial and scientific competence).

11.   The responsibility of the Church to articulate such a moral vision not as a series of detailed answers to complex questions but as a framework of values and principles within which responsible Christian action can be decided upon and taken.

12.   The duty of Catholics to take such teaching and such a moral framework seriously into account in the process not only of forming their consciences but of expressing their views in the socio-economic and political orders.

SUMMARY

1.   This chapter addresses itself to four separate moral issues: *birth control, homosexuality, warfare,* and *state intervention in the economic order.* The first two issues concern *interpersonal,* or *individual, ethics*; the second two, *social,* or *societal, ethics.*

2.   *Birth control,* or the conscious regulation of births, is not totally and absolutely rejected by Catholic theology and doctrine. The rhythm method, for example, is an accepted way of avoiding pregnancy. What is at issue, therefore, is *contraception* by artificial means—e.g., pill,

IUD, foam, condom. The argument between the two opposing sides in the Catholic Church was joined in 1968 with the publication of *Humanae Vitae*, the papal encyclical which rejected artificial contraception of every kind.

3. The *traditional view*, consistently taught and reaffirmed by such recent encyclicals as *Casti Connubii* (1930) and by various papal statements of Pope Pius XII, rested its case on two principal arguments. The primary argument was drawn from authority and from the consequences a change in the traditional teaching might have on the credibility of the official magisterium; a second argument was based on a structural analysis of the conjugal act itself, i.e., as biologically, and therefore naturally, oriented toward procreation.

4. The argument *against* the traditional teaching emphasized the evolutionary character of the Church's traditional teaching on sexual morality; the fact that the Church had clearly reversed itself on the question of usury; an understanding of natural law requiring the human person to employ reason to shape and control the so-called natural order of things, including the process of procreation; the principle of totality, according to which the conjugal act is to be viewed in relation to such values as human love, family life, education.

5. The Papal Commission for the Study of Population, the Family, and Birth submitted its final report in June 1966 and recommended a change in the traditional teaching, while at the same time condemning what it called a "contraceptive mentality" which egotistically and irrationally opposes all fruitfulness in marriage. The Commission insisted, too, that any method of birth control must be consistent with human dignity, be effective, and be safe.

6. *Humanae Vitae* rejected the Papal Commission's report and reaffirmed the traditional teaching: "Each and every marriage act must remain open to the transmission of life." Unlike the minority report of the Papal Commission, however, the encyclical rested its case more heavily on the purpose of the conjugal act than on the question of authority and its credibility. It also expressed concern for the consequences of contraception—e.g., conjugal infidelity, corruption of youth.

7. The reaction to *Humanae Vitae* was diverse: all the way from unequivocal acceptance to outright rejection. Many other positions fell somewhere in between—e.g., various statements from national bodies of bishops which emphasized the primacy of conscience and the mercy and forgiveness of God. The Vatican carried forward its traditional teaching on sexual ethics in a declaration on the same subject in 1975.

8. There are certain *Christian values* underlying this issue of birth control which must always be taken into account: (1) the goodness of procreation, as an expression of mutual love and for the welfare of the human community at large; (2) the sanctity of human life; (3) the personal dignity and welfare of the spouses, their children, and their potential children; (4) the inviolability of conscience; (5) the responsibility to act on an informed conscience; (6) the right and responsibility of the Church to teach on such matters; (7) the duty of Catholics to take such teaching seriously into account.

9. Wherever *homosexuality* is mentioned in the *Bible* it is condemned. One reason for the severity of judgment against homosexuality was its connection with pagan fertility rites and other cultic practices. The Genesis story of Sodom and Gomorrah was most influential on the Fathers of the Church. Sodom became the symbol of the depravity of Greek society.

10. The *Catholic tradition* has consistently judged all homosexual acts as at once unnatural and gravely sinful. The most recent text is the Vatican's *Declaration on Sexual Ethics* (1975).

11. There are three principal moral approaches to the question today: (1) Homosexual acts are *always sinful* in themselves because they are unnatural, i.e., not open to procreation; (2) homosexual acts are morally *neutral*; i.e., their morality depends on the quality of the relationship; and (3) homosexual acts are *essentially imperfect*; i.e., homosexual behavior is wrong as a general rule, but it is not wrong for those who have no realistic alternative (an irreversible or constitutional homosexual). This last view is also known as a theory of "compromise" in view of the presence of sin in the world.

12. There are certain *Christian values* underlying this issue of homosexuality which must always be taken into account: (1) the goodness of procreation, as an expression of mutual love and for the welfare of the human community at large; (2) the personal dignity of every human being; (3) the need of every person for love, friendship, even intimacy, although not necessarily of a genitally sexual nature; (4) the inviolability of conscience; (5) the responsibility to act on an informed conscience; (6) the existence of many internal and external impediments to full human freedom; (7) the right and responsibility of the Church to teach on matters of this sort; (8) the duty of the Catholic to take such teaching seriously into account.

13. *Warfare* is not automatically condemned in the Bible. In the *Old Testament*, Israel's wars are Yahweh's wars, and Yahweh is himself a warrior. On the other hand, the *prophets* denounced war as a judgment of

Yahweh upon Israel. It is through faith, not war, that Israel is destined to survive. *Jesus and the disciples* had no developed theology of warfare. Jesus spoke only of those who lived by the sword as dying by the sword, and *Paul* spoke in terms of spiritual combat. The final judgment is described in the imagery of warfare.

14.   *Augustine* saw war as both the product of sin and a remedy for it. Public order must be preserved at all costs, even if it means going to war. *Aquinas* listed three criteria for a *just war*: (1) just cause; (2) legitimate authority; and (3) right intention. This was not to rationalize warfare but to limit its scope and methods.

15.   *Later development* of the just-war theory added the following criteria: (1) last resort; (2) formal declaration of war; (3) reasonable hope of success; (4) proportion between the good accomplished or evil avoided and the evil caused by the war itself; (5) immunity of non-combatants from direct attack; and (6) proportionality of tactics and means to end.

16.   In the sixteenth century the *Spanish Scholastics* shifted the focus from just cause to just *means*. Both sides might be sincere about their cause; therefore, both must be attentive to the means employed. A wider *international* dimension was added in the nineteenth century by *Taparelli d'Azeglio*.

17.   *Pope Pius XII* carried d'Azeglio's insight forward in his notion of force as a possible instrument of justice in the international order. Because of the increased destructive capacity of modern weapons, the pope reduced the legitimate causes of war to one: self-defense or the defense of another nation unjustly attacked. He rejected pacifism.

18.   *Pope John XXIII* moved the just war teaching in a pacifist direction. There is strong criticism of the arms race and the balance of terror it creates. War in a nuclear age is "irrational."

19.   *Vatican II* notes that the multiplication of scientific weapons forces us to look at war with "an entirely new attitude." It praises conscientious objectors and condemns a policy of blind obedience. It also denounces the arms race as a "treacherous trap." Granting the right of states to self-defense, everything is to be governed, nevertheless, by the principle of proportionality and by the rule of noncombatant immunity. *Pope Paul VI* and *Pope John Paul II* continued this emphasis, blending prophetic vision and political wisdom.

20.   In light of these recent doctrinal developments, there are two legitimate *moral options* in Catholicism today: the *just-war ethic* and some form of *pacifism*. They hold *in common* the sacredness of human life, the seriousness of taking of human life, and the morally restricted nature of any war. They *differ* in that the pacifist holds that force is never

justified, whereas the just-war advocate acknowledges that circumstances may require the use of force.

21.   The just-war ethic, however, is further challenged by the *threat* of use of nuclear weapons in the *policy of deterrence.* If the *use* of nuclear weapons is immoral, so, too, is their *stockpiling* even for deterrence (U.S. Catholic bishops, 1976). Others argue that the stockpiling is legitimate, even with the intention to use, if it prevents a greater evil, i.e., the use of nuclear weapons by the other side (Paul Ramsey). Still others prohibit the use of nuclear weapons, but tolerate deterrence (Michael Walzer, J. Bryan Hehir).

22.   There are certain *Christian values* underlying this issue of *warfare* which must always be taken into account: (1) the sacredness of all human life; (2) the utter gravity of taking another human life; (3) the inherent moral limits on every use of force; (4) the right and responsibility of the Church to articulate a moral vision of such matters of social and even international morality; (5) the responsibility of the Church to articulate a moral vision in a politically realistic manner; and (6) the duty of Catholics to take such teaching seriously into account in the formation of conscience and in political action.

23.   The question of the right and duty of the *state to intervene in the economic order* for the sake of the common good is answered in terms of the relationship between the principles of *subsidiarity* and of *socialization.* The former discourages intervention; the latter encourages it. The former is attentive to the rights of individuals and groups within society; the latter is attentive to the interdependent character of all individuals and groups in society.

24.   The principle of *subsidiarity* was first formulated by *Pope Pius XI* in *Quadragesimo Anno* (1931); the principle of *socialization* was alluded to in *John XXIII's* encyclical *Mater et Magistra* (1961) and defined more precisely in *Pacem in Terris* (1963).

25.   *Subsidiarity* holds that "one should not withdraw from individuals and commit to the community what they can accomplish by their own enterprise and industry. So, too, it is an injustice and at the same time a grave evil and a disturbance of right order, to transfer to the larger and higher collectivity functions which can be performed and provided for by lesser and subordinate bodies" (Pius XI).

26.   *Socialization* refers to "the growing interdependence of men in society, giving rise to various patterns of group life and activity and in many instances to social institutions established on a juridical basis" (John XXIII).

27.   Besides the principles of subsidiarity and socialization, Catholic teaching on *rights and duties* is also at the heart of the Church's social doctrine. The clearest statement of human rights is found in *Pacem in Terris* (pars. 8-35). *Rights* are *moral claims* to some physical or spiritual good necessary for human development and dignity. A right creates a correlative *duty* on the part of the state to recognize and reinforce it, and to balance it off with other moral claims in conflict with one another. Pope Paul VI in *Octagesima Adveniens* emphasized the *political* character of such responsibility. In his 1979 United Nations address, Pope John Paul II made a similar argument.

28.   *Health care* is one issue of this sort. Should the state intervene to insure health care for all? If so, under what circumstances and according to what conditions? Approaches vary from utilitarian (the greatest good for the greatest number), contributive (health care for the worthier members of society), random selection (first come, first served), individualistic (no right at all; health care is a service), egalitarian (similar cases should be treated similarly), to an argument based on distributive justice: "A person has the right to that minimum which is necessary for living a decent human life. Society has an obligation to provide that which is necessary for a decent human life" (Charles Curran). That minimum includes quality health care.

29.   Ethics and ethicians, however, cannot even begin to answer such questions in any detail. These issues require prudential choices in the political realm. Ethicists can identify the values and principles—e.g., of distributive justice—as a basis for making political decisions.

30.   There are certain *Christian values* underlying this issue of *state intervention in the economic order* which must always be taken into account: (1) the dignity of every human person; (2) health care as a fundamental human right; (3) the correlation of rights and duties; (4) the radically social nature of the human person; (5) the subordination of rights and duties to the common good; (6) the stewardship, not absolute ownership, of created goods; (7) the right and/or obligation of the state to intervene on behalf of human dignity; (8) the principle of subsidiarity; (9) the dialectical relationship between subsidiarity and socialization; (10) the right and responsibility of the Church to articulate a moral vision on such issues; (11) the responsibility of the Church to formulate its vision not as specific answers but as a framework of values and principles for Christian action; (12) the duty of the Catholic to take such teaching and such a moral framework into serious account.

SUGGESTED READINGS

Calvez, Jean Yves. *The Social Thought of John XXIII*. Chicago: H. Regnery, 1965.

Curran, Charles E. *Contemporary Problems in Moral Theology*. Notre Dame, Ind.: Fides Publishers, 1970.

——————. *Transition and Tradition in Moral Theology*. Notre Dame, Ind.: University of Notre Dame Press, 1979.

Dedek, John. *Contemporary Medical Ethics*. New York: Sheed & Ward, 1975.

Gustafson, James. *The Church As Moral Decision-Maker*. Philadelphia: Pilgrim Press, 1970.

Haughey, John C., ed. *The Faith That Does Justice: Examining the Christian Sources for Social Change*, New York: Paulist Press, 1977.

Hollenbach, David. *Claims in Conflict*. New York: Paulist Press, 1979.

Kosnik, Anthony, *et al. Human Sexuality: New Directions in American Catholic Thought*. New York: Paulist Press, 1976.

Macquarrie, John. *Three Issues in Ethics*. New York: Harper & Row, 1970.

McCormick, Richard A. *Ambiguity in Moral Choice*. Milwaukee: Marquette University, 1973.

Murray, John Courtney. "The Issue of Church and State at Vatican II." *Theological Studies* 27 (1966), 580-606.

Reich, Warren T., ed. *Encyclopedia of Bioethics,* 4 vols. New York: Free Press, 1978.

· XXVIII ·

CHRISTIAN SPIRITUALITY

THE MEANING AND PLACE OF "SPIRITUALITY"

The previous three chapters were concerned with principles of
Christian existence and their application to Christian behavior.
They were exercises in moral theology or Christian ethics. This
chapter addresses itself not so much to the substance, or the "just
demands," of Christian existence as to its style, or "spirit." "Those
who live according to the flesh," Paul wrote, "are intent on the
things of the flesh, those who live according to the spirit, on those
of the spirit" (Romans 8:5).

To live according to the spirit is to enjoy "life and peace."
The Spirit of God dwells in such a one as the principle of life
(8:6,8,11). *Spirituality*, therefore, has to do with *our way of being
religious*. We are not only alive by a principle which transcends us
(see chapter 5 on nature and grace); we are consciously aware of,
in touch with, and motivated by, that principle of life.

To be "spiritual" means to know, and to live according to the
knowledge, that there is more to life than meets the eye. To be
"spiritual" means, beyond that, to know, and to live according to
the knowledge, that God is present to us in grace as the principle
of personal, interpersonal, social and even cosmic transformation.
To be "open to the Spirit" is to accept explicitly who we are and
who we are called always to become, and to direct our lives
accordingly.

Since God is not present to Christians alone, spirituality is
not exclusively Christian. What, then, is *Christian* spirituality? It
is *the cultivation of a style of life consistent with the presence of the
Spirit of the Risen Christ within us and with our status as members*

of the Body of Christ. Christian spirituality has to do with *our way of being Christian*, in response to the call of God, issued through Jesus Christ in the power of the Holy Spirit. Christian spirituality, therefore, is *trinitarian, Christological, ecclesiological,* and *pneumatalogical.* It is rooted in the life of the triune God, focused on Jesus Christ, situated in the Church, and ever responsive to the Holy Spirit.

It is also visionary, sacramental, relational, and transformational. Christian spirituality is *visionary* in that it involves a new way of seeing reality and of seeing through things to their spiritual core, of "thus interpreting spiritual things in spiritual terms" (1 Corinthians 2:13). In that sense, Christian spiritual vision is always *sacramental.* Every created reality is imbued, to one degree or another, with the hidden presence of God. Christian spirituality is also *relational.* Neither Christian life nor human life itself is ever isolated existence. We are, by definition, social beings. To be human is to live in community. To be Christian is also to live in community, i.e., the Church. To be spiritually Christian is to live always in relation with others: with our brothers and sisters in the Body of Christ and in the human community at large. Christian spirituality demands sensitivity to the presence, the needs, and the gifts of others. Finally, Christian spirituality is *transformational.* The spiritual Christian is consciously in touch with the presence of the Spirit as the power which heals, reconciles, renews, gives life, bestows peace, sustains hope, brings joy, and creates unity. Christian spirituality requires that the Spirit be allowed to work so that through the instrumentality of the individual and of the Church the transformation of the world into the Kingdom of God might continue to occur.

HISTORY OF CHRISTIAN SPIRITUALITY
Biblical Origins

Although *Christian* spirituality as such did not begin to take shape until Jesus' proclamation of the Kingdom of God and the gathering of the first disciples around him, its foundations were already laid in the *covenantal relationship* between Yahweh and Israel.

The Israelites were convinced of the nearness and even the presence of their God, as the Psalms clearly indicate. Jesus, too, proclaimed that the Father had drawn near to us in a dramatically and definitively new way. The Kingdom of God is "at hand" (Mark 1:15). Jesus suggests that he has a unique relationship with the Father (Matthew 11:25-27). The power of God breaks through in Jesus' words (Mark 4:14; Luke 12:32) and in his healing works (Luke 11:20; Matthew 12:28). To be "in Christ" is to be a "new creation" (2 Corinthians 5:17). It is to be brought to life with Christ "when we were dead in sin" (Ephesians 2:5). It is to have God living in us because God lives in Christ (John 17:23). The love of God for Christ lives in us, because Christ lives in us (17:26).

It is through the death and resurrection of Jesus that we are liberated from sin and for new life (Romans 6:3-11). Jesus was raised from the dead "so that we might bear fruit for God" (7:4). Indeed, the Spirit cannot be given until the resurrection and glorification of Jesus (John 7:39; 16:7), and the first thing the Lord does when he appears to the disciples afterwards is to breathe the Holy Spirit upon them (20:19-23). Our very bodies are given life through the Spirit which now possesses us (Romans 8:11). And the Father will raise us just as Jesus was raised (2 Corinthians 4:14). Christian life and spirituality is knowing that truth, having hope in what we know, and living according to that hope so that our life would not make sense if it were not for such a hope. It is life in possession of "the light of life" (John 8:12).

The Patristic Period:
Second Through Seventh Centuries

If the Kingdom of God was at the center of Jesus' preaching and ministry, it was also necessarily at the center of Christian spirituality from the beginning. But the time of the Kingdom's coming was never clear—not even, it seems, to Jesus himself (see chapter 12). The Thessalonians, for example, thought the Second Coming of the Lord to be so imminent that many of them stopped their normal labors and began waiting in idleness for the end (2 Thessalonians 3:6-15). When it became obvious to all that the *Parousia* was not about to occur and that a considerable span of history would intervene, Christians increasingly perceived their situation as life "between the times": between the initial coming of Christ on earth and the Second Coming at the end. Everything henceforth would be conditioned by this expectation of the Kingdom, but it would no longer divert the Christian community from its earthly mission. On the contrary, the expectation of the Kingdom would add a note of urgency to the Church's call to proclaim the Gospel in word, in sacrament, in witness, and in service.

If spirituality has to do essentially with our union with God in Christ through the Holy Spirit, *martyrdom* provided in the earliest centuries of the Church an ideal, perhaps even infallible, means to such union. Martyrdom's importance was rooted in its close connection with Christ's own death and resurrection. To be martyred (literally, to become a "witness") was to experience ahead of schedule the final eschatological event.

After the persecutions had ended, Christians wondered if the complete union with God in Christ offered by martyrdom was accessible in any other way. Origen (d. ca. 254) suggested that a life of complete self-sacrifice was a kind of unbloody martyrdom, and Clement of Alexandria (d. ca. 215) noted that every death is a true martyrdom provided one approaches it with the proper dispositions.

The first "spiritual" heresy in the Church was Gnosticism, which looked upon matter as evil. Salvation comes only in the rejection of the material world for the world of the spirit. Irenaeus (d. 200) led the counterattack, insisting on the incarnation as a principle of recapitulation of all things, material and spiritual, in Christ. But the Gnostic stress on knowledge, so characteristic of contemporary Greek philosophy, penetrated even orthodox Christian theology and spirituality. The emphasis, however, was much less esoteric and more fully oriented to Christian life. Thus, for Clement of Alexandria, the summit of Christian consciousness is the knowledge of the God of love by loving as God loves. This assimilation to God occurred through *apatheia*, i.e., the domination through grace of everything opposed to Christian love (*agape*). Such a state was itself a kind of anticipation of eternal life. The Gnostic influence was even stronger in Origen, who taught that the soul must struggle to uproot itself from the world in which it is buried by selfish desires. The struggle is won by imitation of Christ and a sharing in his life. The approach carried over into Origen's notion of prayer. For him, the prayer of silence was the ideal since it characterized the state of union with God and liberation from the body.

Monasticism, which developed first as flight from persecution and later as rejection of the Constantinian embrace of the Church in 312, introduced a new expression of spirituality that, for centuries, would mistakenly be regarded as the very norm of Christian life for all. Under the leadership of Anthony of Egypt (d. 356) and others, individual Christians went into the desert to confront the devil and to come to terms with all the dark forces that war against the spirit. Some forms of asceticism were severe. In Syria, for example, various hermits used iron chains to punish themselves; others exposed themselves heedlessly to the elements. Gradually the hermits were joined by others, and a transition was made from the solitary form of monastic existence (anchoritism) to a modified community existence (cenobitism). Almost from the beginning, therefore, monastic life was looked upon as a continuation of apostolic life: perseverance together in prayer, in the community of goods, and in the breaking of the bread (Acts of the Apostles 2:42). The practice of consecrating virgins also developed at this time as yet another way of achieving fuller union with Christ.

Two or three generations passed before a spiritual theology emerged from the new monastic movement. According to Pseudo-Dionysius (d. ca. 500)—probably a Syrian monk who identified himself with Dionysius the Areopagite, mentioned in Acts of the Apostles 17:34—the soul finds union with God only in going beyond itself, by rejecting all particular knowledge and allowing itself to be absorbed totally in the knowledge of God, whose intra-Trinitarian life of love overflows in a stream of self-communicating goodness in creation. Thus, the spiritual life is divided into three stages: purification (*the purgative way*), meditation on the word of God (*the illuminative way*), and union with God (*the unitive way*).

Augustine (d. 430) was himself dependent upon this monastic spirituality as developed and practiced in the East. But he subtly revised it in a more psychological and critical direction. Spiritual discernment does not bring us knowledge of God in Christ so much as *self-knowledge* in the light of Christ, the interior teacher of wisdom. On the other hand, it was also Augustine who wrote in the *City of God* that "no man must be so committed to contemplation as, in his contemplation, to give no thought to his neighbor's needs, nor so absorbed in action as to dispense with the contemplation of God" (Book XIX, chapter 19). It was John Cassian (d. 435), however, who translated the purer form of Eastern monasticism to the West. The monk is not to seek anything beyond the Kingdom of God, and only purity of heart will open the mystery of the Kingdom to him. Christian life is one of constant prayer wholly inspired by the Gospel.

Another key contemporary spiritual leader and writer was Pope Gregory the Great (d. 604), an adept popularizer of doctrine and an influential author on matters of faith and piety. His works are the first major sources of material on the lives of the saints, including Benedict (d. 550), whom he admired and whose rule he observed. One of Gregory's books, *Regula Pastoralis* ("Pastoral Norms"), had almost as much impact on the Church well into the Middle Ages as did Augustine's *City of God*. It was a practical treatise on the spirituality and ministerial skills required of bishops and of all who have the care of souls. The social disruptions created by the so-called barbarian invasions disclosed the fragile character of much of the Christianization that had occurred thus far. Gregory's simple, straightforward style was particularly appealing because reassuring, and the monastic type of life which his work advocated and celebrated proved to be one of the mainstays of the Church and of society generally for the next several centuries.

The Middle Ages:
Eighth Through Fourteenth Centuries

From the time of Gregory the Great until the middle of the eighth century, monks generally maintained a high ascetical ideal and gave an example of Christian life for all: laity, clergy, and bishops alike. Under the new Germanic influence, however, a certain externalism inserted itself into Christian spirituality: devotions to the cross, relics, and tombs of the saints; various forms of penances; the encouragement of confession of sins, etc. But Carolingian piety was also marked by a deep reverence for the Bible and a love of the liturgy—both abiding preoccupations of Christian monks.

By the tenth and eleventh centuries various monasteries began to develop loose federations, which gave rise to congregations of monasteries and eventually to religious orders. The monastic ideal was spread ever more widely throughout the Christian world. Austerity characterized penitential practice even among the laity. Long pilgrimages and self-flagellation were common means of making reparation for sin or for curbing one's unruly appetites. Contemplative prayer, too, was presented as the standard which all Christians should meet. John of Fécamp (d. 1079), one of the most widely read spiritual writers of the time, recommended quiet, meditative reading to induce unimpeded and undistracted thoughts about God.

The new Cistercian Order, founded in 1098, accentuated the *mystical* element in Christian spirituality. Its principal proponents, Bernard of Clairvaux (d. 1153) and William of St. Thierry (d. 1148), regarded the soul as being the image of God because of the gift of free will. But sin marred that image. Only by contemplating the Word of God and conforming oneself to it can the individual soul be restored to its intended perfection, for Christ is the interior Lover who pursues and embraces the soul in a union of intimate love. The stress on contemplation over dialectics (i.e., critical theology) continued into the twelfth century in the Parisian monastery of St. Victor, whose members, known as the *Victorines*, included some of the best-known writers of the period: Hugh of St. Victor (d. 1141), Richard of St. Victor (d. 1173), and others. Richard's work would later be simplified by the English Augustinian Walter Hilton (d. 1396) and Hilton's, in turn, carried forward by Julian of Norwich (d. 1442), a female monk who lived outside the walls of St. Julian's Church in Norwich, England.

But there also appeared at this time another, more idealistic spiritual movement urging radical poverty and an end to all formalism and legalism. Accordingly, by the end of the thirteenth century many lay persons were criticizing the existing social conditions as well as the lives of the clergy and hierarchy. Extreme forms of this new purist tendency were to be found in Waldensianism and Albigensianism. But there were also more mainstream attempts to confront the same abuses and pastoral problems. The rise of the mendicant orders—Franciscans and Dominicans—brought a more realistic, but no less serious, approach to poverty and service. Dominic (d. 1221) provided his new Order of Preachers with an ideal that combined the best of monasticism with the best of the apostolic life. One of his spiritual sons, Thomas Aquinas (d. 1274), would produce an oft-cited formula on the interrelationship between the two: neither contemplation alone nor action alone is the highest form of Christian life, but contemplation in action (a concept not far removed from the modern notion of *praxis*). Francis of Assisi (d. 1226), on the other hand, stressed imitation of the life of Christ in all its simplicity and poverty. God is reflected in the sun, the moon, and stars, and indeed in all of the things of creation. As with the Dominicans, it took another great theologian to systematize, and thereby give wider circulation to, Francis' basic insight. Bonaventure (d. 1274), who saw the whole of creation as a mirror reflecting the power, wisdom, and goodness of God, identified three elements in the Franciscan way of life: (1) following Christ through the evangelical counsels, especially poverty (the other counsels are chastity and obedience); (2) laboring for the salvation of souls by preaching and hearing confessions; and (3) contemplation.

At the beginning of the fourteenth century a new current of spirituality took root in the Rhineland, the Low Countries, and England. A century earlier the works of Pseudo-Dionysius had been translated and made the subject of an extended commentary. Because the author was commonly associated in people's minds with the Areopagite mentioned in Acts of the Apostles 17:34, his newly translated writings were accorded a quasi-apostolic authority throughout the Middle Ages. They had particular influence on Meister Eckhart (d. 1327), John Tauler (d. 1361), and Henry Suso (d. 1366), three German Dominican mystics, and on Jan von Ruysbroeck (d. 1381), a Flemish canon regular of St. Augustine. Their common concern was the soul's union with God, which reached its zenith in contemplation. Such union is impossible, however, apart from complete abandonment of, and detachment from, all creatures and worldly realities. This orientation was most pronounced in *The Cloud of Unknowing*, composed by an anonymous English author. The same stress on the interior life was to be found in Hildegard (d. 1179) and Hedwig (d. 1243), and it is to be found again today in the "centering prayer" approach (see the discussion of *The Cloud of Unknowing* below, under the treatment of post-Vatican II spirituality).

Other spiritual writers, firmly committed to a life of prayer and penance, saw more clearly the pastoral implications and effects of their contemplative life. Catherine of Siena (d. 1380) was exceedingly concerned with the reform of the Church but insisted that her prayers and penances did more for the Church than her public acts did. The same concern for ecclesiastical renewal in the Low Countries stimulated the formation of a lay group, the Brethren of the Common Life, founded by Gerard Groote (d. 1384). The movement's spirituality was known as the *Devotio Moderna*. Its one great product, written probably by Groote or by Thomas à Kempis (d. 1471), was *The Imitation of Christ*, which asserted, among other things, that "it is better to feel compunction than to be able to define it."

This lack of intellectual and theological substance in such popular piety, however, brought with it many serious problems: superstition (e.g., the belief that one could be saved from blindness by gazing on the Communion host), ignorance of the Bible, fascination with reports of visions, exaggeration of the value of relics, emotionalism, inordinate fears of the after-life and of God's judgment, and devotional excesses unrelated to the central mysteries of Christian faith.

The Post-Medieval Period: Renaissance, Reformation, Counter-Reformation

Although Protestantism rejected contemporary medieval spirituality's emotionalism, superstition, and inordinate reverence for such material objects as relics, it did not at the same time reject its *individualism*. Martin Luther (d. 1546) stressed the uniqueness of the Christian believer's relationship with God and the realm of personal conscience (*sola fides*, "faith alone"). His recourse to the Word of God in Sacred Scripture (*sola Scriptura*, "Scripture alone") only underlined his concern for finding a direct approach to Christ, one in which the individual is illumined by the interior witness of the Holy Spirit (*sola gratia*, "grace alone"). Although it was not always obvious in the midst of medieval excesses, it *is* a matter of Catholic principle that the believer's relationship with God is a *mediated* relationship; mediated not only, nor even primarily, through the biblical Word, but in and through the community of faith in which that Word is proclaimed. "Thus Protestantism tends to produce a spirituality which springs entirely from the co-presence and mutual relationship between the Person of God revealed in the Christ of the Gospels and the individual person of the believer. But, for Catholicism, there is no fully authentic Christian spirituality without the realization of an equal co-presence of our fellow-believers with Christ and ourselves, the Church" (Louis Bouyer, *Introduction to Spirituality*, New York: Desclée Co., 1961, p. 11; see also his *Orthodox Spirituality and Protestant and Anglican Spirituality*, London: Burns & Oates, 1969).

Although various Christian humanists were sympathetic toward the contemporary emphasis on mysticism, they were strongly committed to the general restoration of Christian life itself, so much corrupted then by the worst of the Renaissance spirit. Love for classical antiquity and an optimistic view of human nature were characteristic of this so-called devout humanism, and the spiritual writings of Erasmus (d. 1536) are representative of it.

The same emphasis on the unity of prayer and action is found in one of the classics of Christian spirituality, the *Spiritual Exercises* of Ignatius Loyola (d. 1556). Ignatian spirituality was marked by dialectical parallels: between the medieval concepts of *contemplation* and *action*, on the one hand, and between *flight from the world* and *acceptance of the world*, on the other. Contemplation is adherence to the God who transcends this world. Action is the fulfillment of one's duty within the world, consistent with one's own individuality. Hence the Ignatian formula which originated with the first circle of his followers: *"in actione contemplativus"* (contemplative in action). Ignatius' affirmation of the world, therefore, is not a naive optimism. It springs rather from a true grasp of the cross: at once a judgment upon sin and a proclamation of our liberation from it. On the other hand, his profoundly positive evaluation of the contingencies of history puts him at the head of a whole new spiritual tradition—so much so, in fact, that Karl Rahner is convinced that the Holy Spirit raised up in Ignatius an original, creative reinterpretation of the Christian life.

"Work as if everything depended upon you, but pray as if everything depended upon God," another well-known Ignatian formula has it. Although this is not the exact wording, it is close enough to the sense of the original, which says, in effect, that we should trust in God in such a way that we never forget to cooperate with God, and yet at the same time we should cooperate with God in such a way as to remain always aware that it is God alone who is at work. We are always at a *distance*, therefore, from God and even from our own deeds. We are at a distance *from God*, who is never revealed except in works carried out with the cooperation of secondary causes (i.e., free human beings); and we are at a distance *from our deeds*, which must never be taken as something of final value in themselves. The Christian must look to Christ, in whom alone the divine-human interaction is fully realized, and seek to imitate him. This is the core of Ignatian spirituality. (For the original Ignatian text in Latin and a brief commentary on it, see Hugo Rahner, *Ignatius the Theologian,* New York: Herder & Herder, 1968, pp. 25-27; see also Karl Rahner, *The Dynamic Element in the Church*, London: Burns & Oates, 1964, pp. 84-170.)

But the mystical way continued to flourish, especially in *Spain*. For Teresa of Avila (d. 1582) prayer consisted essentially in an exchange of love with God. From our side, proof of our love for God is manifested in the practice of the virtues, leaving to God the communication of grace whenever and however God wishes (see her *Autobiography*, New York: Doubleday-Image, 1960; and *The Way of Perfection*, New York: Doubleday-Image, 1964). John of the Cross (d. 1591), one of Teresa's companions in her work of reform within the Carmelite Order, is regarded by many as the greatest of the mystical writers (see his *Collected Works,* Washington, D.C.: Institute of Carmelite Studies Publications, 1964). His writings were at once poetic and speculative, drawing not only upon personal spiritual experience but upon Sacred Scripture and the classical authors as well. They detail the processes of spiritual purification, through trials and temptations and through deliberate detachment from external things, and they try to explain the life of union with God—a union brought about through the prayer of infused contemplation.

Although Spanish spirituality became increasingly theoretical and scientific after John of the Cross, *Italian* spirituality was more practical. Reform of the Church, renewal of the interior life, and the improvement of priestly ministry were matters of immediate interest. These priorities are reflected in the works of Philip Neri (d. 1595), Charles Borromeo (d. 1584), and Catherine of Genoa (d. 1510).

In *France* developments in spirituality were exceedingly complicated by the theological controversies surrounding the whole issue of nature and grace. Some argued that human nature was so powerless that we can do absolutely nothing to advance our salvation *(Quietism)*. Others insisted on the evil of the flesh and of all human desires and pleasures, urging a life of total abnegation, self-denial, and even repression *(Jansenism)*. Against the Quietists, Jacques Bossuet (d. 1704) taught that abandonment of the soul to God should actually induce the soul to apply itself more deliberately to its religious exercises and to other Christian duties. Against the Jansenists, Francis de Sales (d. 1622) sought to bring Christian piety out of the monasteries and the convents into the world of the average lay person by showing the connection between Christian life and everyday occupations, and by emphasizing the joy of Christian existence (see his *Introduction to the Devout Life*, New York: Doubleday-Image, 1972). A similar orientation appears in Italy in the writings of Alphonsus Ligouri (d. 1787). The spirit of the French school of spirituality, shorn of its heretical excesses, is perhaps best expressed by Jean Jacques Olier (d. 1657), founder of the Sulpicians: "Christianity consists in these three points. . . to look upon Jesus, to unite oneself to Jesus, and to act in Jesus. The first leads us to respect and to religion; the second to union and to identification with Him; the third, to an activity no longer solitary, but joined to the virtue of Jesus Christ, which we have drawn upon ourselves by prayer. The first is called adoration; the second, communion; the third, cooperation" (cited by E. A. Walsh, "Spirituality, French School of, *New Catholic Encyclopedia*, vol. 13, New York: McGraw-Hill, 1967, p. 605).

Nineteenth Century

The nineteenth century provides a bridge between medieval and modern spirituality. Individualism and even regimented piety (e.g., institutionalized devotions to the Sacred Heart, the Blessed Virgin, the Sacred Wounds, the Eucharist) continued, and reactionary theological ideas were still encouraged, and sometimes endorsed, by magisterial interventions of a highly conservative nature (e.g., *Syllabus of Errors*, 1864). But the forces of renewal were also at work: the renewal of theology, of liturgy, of historical studies, and of social ministry. And so, too, were the forces of innovation: e.g., scientific and technological advances, developments in psychology and sociology. Together these forces of renewal and innovation would have a profound impact on Christian spirituality in the twentieth century.

Perhaps nowhere else was this incipient renewal of Christian spirituality more evident than in *England* and particularly in the Oxford Movement, whose driving force was John Henry Newman (d. 1890). His spiritual orientation was primarily interior, a life lived in intimate union with God under the guidance of the Holy Spirit. But it was also a Christocentric spirituality, stressing the incarnation as the basis for an active Christian life in the world. As in Ignatius, therefore, there was a blending of the contemplative and the practical. Newman, however, was not to exert very much influence as a spiritual writer. More influential was Frederick William Faber (d. 1863), who drew his own inspiration from the Italian and French style of spiritual writing, especially that of Alphonsus Ligouri and Cardinal Bérulle (d. 1629). Faber, too, was Christocentric (one of his works was entitled *All for Jesus*), but he was also highly emotional and florid. On the other hand, his emphasis on the psychology of the individual, openness to all people, even non-Catholics and non-Christians, and frequency of reception of the sacraments, all anticipated by a century certain developments that would characterize modern Catholic spirituality.

Twentieth Century

1900-1950

Catholic spiritual writings during the first half of the twentieth century reflected the ambivalent character of Catholic theology itself. On the one hand, traditional scholastic theology was firmly in place in seminaries, in college religion courses, in catechisms, in sermons, and especially in official magisterial pronouncements. The manuals of spiritual or ascetical theology were of the same sort—e.g., Adolfe Tanquerey's *The Spiritual Life* and Reginald Garrigou-Lagrange's *The Three Ages of the Interior Life*. On the other hand, the liturgical movement, spurred by the renewal of historical and biblical studies, guided spirituality in a more Christocentric direction through the writings of such Benedictines as Abbot Columba Marmion (d. 1923) of Belgium, and, in a very different way, in the life and works of Charles de Foucauld (d. 1916).

Tanquerey (d. 1932), by his own account, showed "a certain preference for the spirituality of the French School of the seventeenth century" (*The Spiritual Life*, New York: Desclée, 1930, pp. vii-viii). He was himself a Sulpician priest, a community of priests founded by Olier, one of the leaders of seventeenth-century French spirituality. Certain elements of Tanquerey's system also remarkably anticipate some of the major theological and pastoral developments of the period of Vatican II: (1) the grounding of spirituality in Sacred Scripture and doctrine; (2) an understanding of human existence as spirituality's starting point; (3) the mystery of the Trinity as its primary theological context; (4) the centrality of Jesus Christ and of our union with Christ in the Church, his Mystical Body; and (5) the call of the whole Church, including the laity, to a life of Christian perfection. On the other hand, Tanquerey's use of biblical and doctrinal sources reflects the limitations of scholastic methodology; the human person is conceived as lacking something originally intended by God (which is the more traditional notion of Original Sin and of the relationship between nature and grace); and human existence is portrayed as a process of struggle between higher faculties (especially the intellect) and the lower appetites (including "a lust for freedom and independence"). It is this theological anthropology, or theology of what it means to be human, that appears most inconsistent with the main lines of Catholic theology and of Catholic spirituality today, as we shall see below.

Garrigou-Lagrange (d. 1964), a Dominican professor at the Angelicum University in Rome for many years, presents an even more individualistic approach to the spiritual life than Tanquerey. That life consists of intimate conversation with God, achieved through a threefold process: passing through the purgative, illuminative, and unitive ways successively. Again, the primary emphasis is on the necessity of detaching ourselves from those lower appetites which drag us down and keep us from full union with God. The "one thing necessary" to every human life is the salvation of one's soul. All are called to sanctity, or a life in union with God. Every sin and imperfection will eventually have to be effaced by punishment after death if the soul is to enjoy the eternal vision of God. Having removed the obstacles and purged the senses, the soul moves to a second stage of Christian existence, in which the soul is progressively illumined by the gifts of the Holy Spirit and finds it increasingly easy to contemplate the mystery of God. Finally, there is entrance into a state of perfect mystical union with God in which the theological and moral virtues are practiced to a heroic degree (*The Three Ages of the Interior Life*, 2 vols., St. Louis: B. Herder Book Co. 1947-1948).

The same individualistic emphasis is carried forward in Dietrich von Hildebrand's *Transformation in Christ* (St. Paul, Minn.: Helicon Press, 1948), which describes Christian spirituality in terms of surrender, detachment from self, subordination and abnegation of self, a submerging of oneself in the adoration of God, and always in an I/Thou relationship. Von Hildebrand, formerly a professor of philosophy at Fordham University, rejected various contemporary pastoral developments which underlined the importance of community. He characterized the liturgical movement, for example, as anti-personalist (p. 394). "Our abandonment of self is an indispensable condition of the full unfolding in us of supernatural life" (p. 400). In its highest form, "being possessed" is a state of mystic ecstasy wherein "the mind tends to be aware of nothing besides God" (p. 401). But such an experience of God gives us a clearer perception of all creaturely reality. We see things as they really are in the sight of God (p. 402).

A much less individualistic, more liturgically-oriented, more fully Christocentric and more anthropologically positive approach was taken by Abbot Marmion. It is the last characteristic that is the most significant. Although both Tanquerey and Garrigou-Lagrange assert the importance of the redemptive work of Jesus Christ, they also continue to speak of human existence as if the redemption is, for all practical purposes, a juridical event (i.e., God now "declares" us just) that has not really transformed and renewed the whole human person. The Holy Spirit is given to us in Baptism and Confirmation, filling us with peace and filial confidence in God, Marmion insisted. The Spirit makes us understand that we have everything in Jesus Christ, who is not only holy in himself but has been given to us to be *our* holiness (*Union with God*, Raymond Thibault, ed., St. Louis: B. Herder Book Co., 1934, p. 40).

For Marmion, the Lord is not our distant judge but the source of love, affection, and sympathy, for he is truly human himself. It is above all in the Eucharist that Christ's action in the soul becomes effective and fruitful for us. We are similarly impelled to the love of one another, for we have become one in Christ. This is what *Com-munion* implies and requires, for "to give oneself to Jesus Christ is to give oneself to others for love of Him, or rather to give oneself to Him in the person of our neighbour" (pp. 164-165). "We are neither spirits nor ghosts," he insists, "but human beings" (p. 166). Therefore, we are to love God humanly, that is with all our heart, soul, strength, and mind, and to love our neighbor in the same way. (See also his *Christ the Life of the Soul*, St. Louis: B. Herder Book Co., 1925.)

Another departure from the spirituality of the scholastic manuals of the early twentieth century was taken by Charles de Foucauld (d. 1916), founder of the Little Brothers of the Sacred Heart of Jesus. Foucauld was in the tradition of French rather than Benedictine spirituality, and so his focus on Jesus was less liturgical and less socially oriented than Marmion's. To be a Christian is to follow Jesus in the way of poverty and humility. To take the lowest place among humankind is to be close to Jesus. Foucauld left the Trappist life to establish a small community whose purpose would be to live as nearly as possible the way Jesus lived, following to the letter all the evangelical counsels, possessing nothing, giving to whoever asks (see his *Spiritual Autobiography*, Jean-Francois Six, ed., New York: P. J. Kenedy, 1964). The great Catholic philosopher Jacques Maritain (d. 1973) spent his own last days living in community with the Little Brothers of Charles de Foucauld (see his *The Peasant of the Garonne*, New York: Holt, Rinehart and Winston, 1968).

1950 Through Vatican II (1965)

The turn to a spirituality oriented to the world did not begin in the twentieth century, but the understanding of human existence as *historical* existence *is* a modern development. No Christian spiritual writer contributed more substantially to that new emphasis than Teilhard de Chardin (d. 1955). The more intensely he came to know and experience the world, the closer God was to him. The entire universe is one "divine milieu" (see *The Divine Milieu*, New York: Harper & Brothers, 1960; originally published in French in 1957). We attain an experience of God not, as the traditional ascetical manualists argued, primarily through purgation, contemplation, and mystical union, or a kind of "meditation with closed eyes." Rather we encounter God by turning toward the things of the earth in love and reverence. The natural delight we take in life and in all that exists is the first dawn of divine illumination. The great mystery of Christianity is not that God appears *(epiphany)* but that God shines through the universe *(diaphany)*. Our prayer, therefore, is not that we might see God "as He is in Himself" but that we might see God in all things.

Here again we have an echo of the basic Ignatian vision. It is not merely coincidental that Teilhard himself was a member of Ignatius' company, the Society of Jesus. And yet there is also a trace of Franciscan spirituality in his sense of the presence of God in the physical universe and in his sense of the activating energy of Christ, as the Omega of evolution, across the entire cosmos.

Teilhard's insistence that spirituality is not for the religiously professed alone (priests, nuns, brothers, monks) notwithstanding, monks continued to exercise profound influence on Catholic spirituality in the years immediately preceding the Second Vatican Council. For Dom Hubert Van Zeller spiritual life is a life in search of truth. But the search for truth is not distinct from the quest for love, for the object of both is God, who is at once Truth and Love. Apart from God there is no end to our search, and Christ is the embodiment of God's truth and love.

For the Christian, therefore, the purpose of life is union with Christ, and the Christian's aim is always to live to the fullest possible extent the life outlined in the Gospel. This is no distant ideal proposed only to saints and mystics, but to every baptized person. All are called to a life based on the Christian love ethic, in the individual and the social orders alike. But our search is a prolonged one, involving progressive discovery. We experience frustration and loneliness on the way. "We look for Christ in darkness, and in darkness He reveals Himself. We flounder in unsatisfied longing, and in our floundering we discover love. We think we have lost faith and hope, when in our seeming faithlessness and hopelessness we discover true faith and hope.... We discover that the only thing in life which is worth doing is to search. The man in the Gospel who went digging for his buried treasure had already found it" (*The Inner Search*, New York: Sheed & Ward, 1957, pp. 7,9).

The change from a negative to an increasingly positive attitude toward the world is also apparent within the corpus of writings by the Trappist monk Thomas Merton (d. 1968). There is a discernible shift from his perception of the world as wicked in his *The Seven Storey Mountain* (New York: Harcourt, Brace, 1948) to *Conjectures of a Guilty Bystander* (New York: Doubleday, 1966), where he reports how, on a downtown corner in Louisville, Kentucky, he was suddenly overwhelmed with the realization that he loved all those people and that human beings cannot be alien to one another even though they are total strangers. The whole illusion of a separate holy existence is a dream, he insisted.

In his *Life and Holiness* (New York: Doubleday-Image, 1964) he declares that "a Christianity that despises [the] fundamental needs of man is not truly worthy of the name....There is no genuine holiness without this dimension of human and social concern" (p. 100). Spiritual perfection is available not to those with superhuman powers but to those who, though weak and defective in themselves, trust perfectly in the love of God, who abandon themselves with confident joy to the apparent madness of the cross (p. 119). Perfection means "simple fidelity" to the will of God in every circumstance of our ordinary life. To be a saint means to be oneself, to be what God intended one to be. We are, in fact, called to share with God "the work of *creating* the truth of our identity" (*New Seeds of Contemplation*, New York: New Directions Books, 1961, p. 32; the same point is central to contemporary Catholic moral theology, as we saw in chapter 26).

"Finding God," therefore, "means much more than just abandoning all things that are not God, and emptying oneself of images and desires" (p. 39). Rather, "God discovers Himself in us." To find God, one must find himself or herself. But one cannot find oneself in isolation from the rest of humankind. We must give ourselves to others in the purity of selfless love. "For it is precisely in the recovery of our union with our brothers in Christ that we discover God and know Him, for then His life begins to penetrate our souls and His love possesses our faculties and we are able to find out Who He is from the experience of His mercy, liberating us from the prison of self-concern" (p. 78).

One of the few theologians who attempted a systematic description and definition of Catholic spirituality in the years immediately preceding Vatican II was the French Oratorian Louis Bouyer, perhaps best known for his book *The Spirit and Forms of Protestantism* (Westminster, Md.: Newman Press, 1956). Bouyer acknowledged that spirituality is available to, and practiced by, non-Christians as well as Christians, Protestants as well as

Catholics. Spirituality is engaged wherever there is a personal relationship with God. *Christian* spirituality is engaged where that personal relationship is grounded in God's self-revelation in Jesus Christ. *Catholic* spirituality is more deliberately ecclesial. The Word-made-flesh is proclaimed and encountered in the Church. It is not only the content of the Word that one finds in the Church, but the Word itself.

"It is, therefore, into the Church, the true body of Christ, that we must be incorporated in order to participate in the Spirit of Christ, and, as a consequence, to receive His words, not as a mere dead letter, but as words which remain always living, always uttered by the very Word of God" (*Introduction to Spirituality*, p. 13). Catholic spirituality, for Bouyer, is "Christian spirituality in its fullness" (p. 14). We are called to love as God loves. The Church, which is built up around Christ, is "an extension, an opening out to all mankind of the society of the divine Persons, the Trinity of the *agape*" (p. 17).

Few pre-conciliar formulae provide as clear an introduction to post-Vatican II spirituality, however, as the title of Josef Goldbrunner's essay "Holiness Is Wholeness" (*Holiness Is Wholeness and Other Essays*, Notre Dame, Ind.: University of Notre Dame Press, 1964; originally published in 1955). God, the All-Holy, he argues, is whole. There is "no blemish of disease . . ., no poison of death. . . . The more we seek the perfection that makes man like God, that makes him holy, the more we should become healthy in body and soul, for holiness is health" (p. 1). This is not to say that the way to God is free of suffering and even death. "Only a slow advance in the spiritual life gives the body time to adapt itself, to expel, as it were, the poison of death which it has come to absorb" (p. 2). But there are also many "illegitimate illnesses" which have come to be associated with the spiritual life: sufferings and risks to health that are embraced for their own sake, assaults upon the laws of nature, and the like. The modern Christian should be ready to tread the way of the cross that leads to holiness, but he or she must rebel when "holiness appears in a guise contrary to nature" (p. 3).

Dualism is to be rejected: There is no warring between soul and body as if the two were separate components, the one higher and the other lower and base. The incarnation teaches us that there is a wholeness to human life, which comprehends the bodily as well as the spiritual. But there is more to it even than that. There is as well the universe of the unconscious with which each must get in touch. To live a spiritually healthy life one must find one's own truth; i.e., ". . . one must consciously come to terms with the irrational forces within oneself, incorporating them into the total life of the soul but never allowing them a perfectly free rein" (p. 14). Not every soul is the same. Each has "a certain measure of energy." If the religious life claims a great deal of energy, it must inevitably be subtracted from other spheres of the spirit. It is clear, therefore, that there are limits to our conscious striving for union with God.

Insofar as we *do* manage to continue the lifelong process of conversion, we are empowered by the divine energies known as the three theological virtues: faith, hope, and charity. *Faith* is the ability to think with Christ, to enter into mental communion with him. Fear calls forth the desire for security, but faith demands trust which liberates from fear. *Hope* gives all life a future dimension. All life is waiting, but we are even now "fed with the energies of the coming age" (p. 28). The virtue of hope frees us for the process of maturing, for a growing into the full stature of Christ. It also gives the spirit elasticity and a kind of eternal youthfulness. *Charity*, finally, is a participation in the divine love in which human love can alone find redemption and healing. "In love for man and love for God the yearning heart watches out for the other who can liberate it from the confinement of the single person, break through the wall of isolation, and fill it with the gift of communion" (p. 31).

It was the French philosopher-poet Charles Péguy (d. 1914) who exposed the self-deception of those who believe that the way to God is the way of repression of all desires for intimacy and interpersonal warmth. "Because they love no one," he wrote, "they imagine they love God." This is not to say, of course, that the spiritual life is without paradox. How is one to be wholly worldly and wholly devoted to God? "Through the cross of Christ, holiness and health become one" (Goldbrunner, p. 34).

The Second Vatican Council laid to rest, once and for all, the assumption that spirituality is for priests and religious alone. The fifth chapter of its keynote *Dogmatic Constitution on the Church (Lumen gentium)* is entitled "The Call of the Whole Church to Holiness." The Lord addressed all of his disciples, regardless of their situation, when he said: "You therefore are to be perfect, even as your heavenly Father is perfect" (Matthew 5:48). We are already holy by reason of the Spirit's indwelling within us. Christian spirituality is a matter of living in accordance with who we have become in the Spirit, of manifesting the fruits of the Spirit's presence: mercy, kindness, humility, meekness, patience (Colossians 3:12; Galatians 5:22; Romans 6:22). "Thus it is evident to everyone," the council declares, "that all the faithful of Christ of whatever rank or status are called to the fullness of the Christian life and to the perfection of charity" (n. 40).

The next sentence is almost as significant: "By this holiness a more human way of life is promoted even in this earthly society." Holiness, therefore, is not only for everyone; it also comprehends far more than the individual soul's relationship with God. Furthermore, there is no single mode or style of spirituality for Christians. Each must adapt the call to perfection to his or her own situation. What will always be common to all is love of God and of neighbor. "For charity, as the bond of perfection and the fulfillment of the law (cf. Colossians 3:14; Romans 13:10), rules over all the means of attaining holiness, gives life to them, and makes them work. Hence it is the love of God and of neighbor which points out the true disciple of Christ" (n. 42).

Elsewhere the council reaffirms or elaborates upon these basic principles of Christian spirituality. The call to holiness is a call issued to laity as well as to clergy and religious. The spiritual life of all Christians will be rooted in the mysteries of creation and redemption, in the presence of the Holy Spirit, and in the mission of Christ and the Church (*Decree on the Apostolate of the Laity*, n. 29; see also n. 4). The Christian enters upon the spiritual life in response to the Word of God (*Dogmatic Constitution on Divine Revelation*, n. 21), and the Word of God, in turn, is proclaimed and celebrated in the liturgy of the Church, which is the "summit" and the "fountain" of the whole Christian life. "From the liturgy, therefore, and especially from the Eucharist, as from a fountain, grace is channeled into us; and the sanctification of men in Christ and the glorification of God, to which all other activities of the Church are directed as toward their goal, are most powerfully achieved" (n. 10). And what the council teaches about Catholic spirituality applies to the whole Body of Christ, for there can be "no ecumenism worthy of the name without a change of heart. . . . Let all Christ's faithful remember that the more purely they strive to live according to the gospel, the more they are fostering and even practicing Christian unity. For they can achieve depth and ease in strengthening mutual brotherhood to the degree that they enjoy profound communion with the Father, the Word, and the Spirit" (*Decree on Ecumenism*, n. 7). The council insists that this is "the soul of the whole ecumenical movement, and can rightly be called 'spiritual ecumenism'."

Post-Vatican II (1965-   )

The post-conciliar period has been marked by a full-scale liturgical renewal (vernacular Mass, revised sacramental rites, active participation), by a stronger sense of the ecumenical breadth of the Church, by a more pronounced concern for social justice and the liberating mission of the Church, by a deepening reverence for Sacred Scripture, and by an increased striving for a personal experience of the Holy Spirit. All of these developments—which are outgrowths of movements already at work in the nineteenth century and actively promoted in the pre-Vatican II period—shape contemporary Christian spirituality. Their by-products include the Charismatic Renewal, the Cursillo movement, Marriage Encounter, directed (one-on-one) retreats according to the original Ignatian mode, weekend youth retreats, the resurgence of contemplative prayer, as at the Jesuit Center for Religious Development in Cambridge, Massachusetts, as well as the renewal and reform of religious congregations.

Individual spiritual writers, of course, continue to influence the style of Christian life. Dom Aelred Graham moves beyond the traditional ecumenical boundaries between Catholic and Protestant into the wider dialogue between East and West, in his *Contemplative Christianity: An Approach to the Realities of Religion* (New York: Seabury Press, 1974). What East and West have in common is the conviction that there are three paths to God: the path of self-forgetting adoration, expressed in both private worship and in the Church's liturgy; the path of selfless service of others, which finds expression in compassionate activity for the benefit both of the individual and of society as a whole; and the path of truth-realizing experience, through contemplative meditation (p. 65). Not all three paths have to be traveled. We will be inclined to one or another by temperament. But any one of these paths, selflessly pursued, can lead to union with God. They are not mutually exclusive, and each can be abused. The first can degenerate into mindless piety or an obsessive, even superstitious, preoccupation with rites and ceremonies. The second can be impractical and unrealistic. The third can become an "ego trip" with little regard for the needs of other people. In the end, the spiritual quest is a risk, but a risk that has to be taken in faith. And faith ultimately is "an awareness beyond sense-perception that the power behind the universe is not neutral, but gracious and beneficent, the unshakable confidence that 'all shall be well and all manner of thing shall be well' " (p. 68).

To be spiritual is to have achieved "God-realization," i.e., "to be in a state of awareness such that God is consciously *real*" (p. 74). It means seeing God everywhere and in everything and everyone. Christian spirituality therefore, is incarnational. It welcomes what is fully human, including the physical, the down-to-earth, the concrete. Any yet it is not simply materialistic. There is more to reality than meets the eye. God is present to the world as the power of love which is to be shared with others. The insight is not exclusively Catholic, although one certainly finds it in the Catholic tradition—e.g., in Ignatius, Teilhard de Chardin, Karl Rahner, and many others. It is not even exclusively Christian, although one finds it in such Protestant writers as Dietrich Bonhoeffer. One also finds this insight outside of Christianity—e.g., in Mahayana Buddhism's "man for others" embodied in the Bodhhisattva ideal, succinctly formulated by Shantideva:

"Whoever wishes quickly to rescue himself and another, should practice the supreme mystery: the exchanging of himself and the other" (cited by Graham, p. 94).

Some other post-Vatican II spiritual writings fall to one or another side of Dom Aelred's comprehensive approach. *To the right* are the works of Adrian van Kaam, of Duquesne University in Pittsburgh, Pennsylvania, who carries forward many narrow, pre-conciliar methodological assumptions about the nature of theology, revelation, doctrine, and Sacred Scripture, for example, while at the same time acknowledging, more than Garrigou-Lagrange, Tanquerey, and others, the close relationship between personality development and spirituality (see his *In Search of Spiritual Identity*, Denville, N.J.: Dimension Books, 1975).

And the anonymously produced *Cloud of Unknowing* is a principal guide for the "centering prayer" movement. The term is inspired by Thomas Merton, who stressed in his earlier writings that the only way to come into contact with the living God is to go to one's center and from that point to pass into God. It is a spirituality of *interiority*, of going deeply into oneself in order to get in touch with the divine reality present there. As soon as we become aware of any thoughts, we must disavow them and return to God again. In the spirit of the *Cloud of Unknowing*, everything is to be abandoned except God. Far from removing us from others, this prayer should make us more conscious of our oneness with them. One spiritual writer in this tradition, Jesuit theologian Thomas Clarke, is more insistent upon this than some others appear to be. "The quality and intensity of contemplation is in direct, not in inverse, proportion to the quality and intensity of our action on behalf of justice and peace, and vice versa" ("Finding Grace at the Center," in *Finding Grace at the Center*, Thomas Keating, *et al.*, Still River, Mass.: St. Bede Publications, 1978, p. 59).

Another individually-oriented spirituality, but with a Russian flavoring, is offered by Catherine de Hueck Doherty, foundress of Madonna House in Ontario, Canada. Her approach is developed in a trilogy: *Poustinia* ("Desert"), *Sobornost* ("Unity"), and *Strannik* ("Pilgrimage") (Notre Dame, Ind.: Ave Maria Press, 1975, 1977, and 1978 respectively). We were created to be *one* with

God in paradise. That unity was restored by the incarnation. Christ himself is the total pilgrim, on his way from the bosom of his Father to the hearts of men and women. He invites us to pilgrimage with him, to know God as Adam and Eve once knew God. One goes out to the desert to contemplate the unity God offers us in Christ. Meanwhile, our pilgrimage continues until we meet God again at the Second Coming (see *Strannik: The Call to Pilgrimage for Western Man*, pp. 9-16). Recent biblical, theological, and pastoral developments do not materially enter into the shaping of these works.

To the left are more activist-oriented types, such as Episcopalian Malcolm Boyd's *Are You Running With Me, Jesus?* (New York: Holt, Rinehart and Winston, 1965). Similarly emphatic about the secular and prophetic character of Christian spirituality but perhaps more theologically sober is Johannes Metz, in his *Followers of Christ: Perspectives on the Religious Life* (New York: Paulist Press, 1978). He argues that religious congregations are called in a special way to be a shock force in the Church, giving witness not only to the world but to the Church itself of how the Gospel is to be lived in an uncompromising fashion. Metz's reflections on the evangelical counsels, however, have applicability beyond the concerns of religious orders. *Poverty*, he suggests, is "a protest against the tyranny of having, of possessing and of pure self-assertion. It impels those practising it into practical solidarity with those poor whose poverty is not a matter of virtue but is their condition of life and the situation exacted of them by society" (p. 49). *Celibacy* is "the expression of an uncompromising concentration of longing for the day of the Lord, a concentration that is not afraid of any temptation of loneliness. . . . It impels towards solidarity with those unmarried people whose celibacy (that is to say, loneliness; that is to say, not having anyone) is not a virtue but their social destiny, and towards those who are shut up in lack of expectation and in resignation" (p. 60). *Obedience*, finally, is "the radical and uncalculated surrender of one's life to God the Father who raises up and liberates. It impels one to stand close to those for whom obedience is not a matter of virtue but the sign of oppression and of being placed in tutelage, and to do this in a practical way" (p. 67). For Metz, then, there is a growing proportion between the mystical and the political aspects of Christian discipleship, with the balance apparently tilted in the political direction. It is also a life that is increasingly eschatological, i.e., governed by the expectation of the imminent coming of the Kingdom of God. Since the Lord is close at hand, there is no time for postponement. We must serve the least of the brethren now (p. 79).

Closer again to the middle are the writings of Catholic pastoral theologian Henri Nouwen. Christian spirituality, he suggests, moves through three polarities. The first polarity deals with our relationship to ourselves: the polarity between loneliness and solitude. The second is at the root of our relationship to others: the polarity between hostility and hospitality. And the third, and most important, has to do with our relationship with God: the polarity between illusion and prayer. To live a spiritual life "means first of all to come to the awareness of the inner polarities between which we are held in tension" *(Reaching Out: The Three Movements of the Spiritual Life,* New York: Doubleday, 1975, p. 12). To be Christian we do not have to deny our loneliness, our hostilities, and our illusions. We have to have the courage to allow them to come to our full attention, to understand them, to confess them, and then to convert them into solitude, hospitality, and prayer.

Appealing also to a popular, non-specialist audience is Dominican Matthew Fox, Director of the Institute in Creation-Centered Spirituality at Mundelein College, Chicago, Illinois. The titles of his trilogy of spiritual books tend to veer somewhat from the conventional: *On Becoming a Musical Mystical Bear: Spirituality American Style* (New York: Paulist Press, 1972); *Whee! We, wee All the Way Home: A Guide to the New Sensual Spirituality* (Wilmington, N.C.: Consortium Books, 1976); and *A Spirituality Named Compassion and the Healing of the Global Village, Humpty Dumpty and Us* (Minneapolis: Winston Press, 1979). The first book concentrates on the meaning of the word *prayer* and its relationship to the personal and the psychological (i.e., prayer as "mysticism") as well as to the social (i.e., prayer as "prophecy"). There is a necessary dialectic between the mystical and the prophetic. The second book deals with the recovery of what Fox calls a non-elitist understanding of spiritual experience, especially the experience of ecstasy. Such a spirituality leads, he argues, to a re-examination of the role of body and body politic, of pleasure and the sharing of pleasures that make up the spiritual journey. The third book moves from passion to compassion, which he defines as "a passionate way of living born of an awareness of the interconnectedness of all creatures by reason of their common Creator" (p. 34). Fox draws explicitly from Meister Eckhart, who insisted: "You may call God love; you may call God goodness; but the best name for God is Compassion."

The Humpty Dumpty image reminds us that the egg of our world is cracked. It is the price we have paid for our aggressive, materialistic mode of life. Humpty Dumpty teaches us that the primary issue in spirituality is not redemption of the soul but redemption of the world. We are in the world, and the world is in us. To heal one is to heal the other. The world is only a projection of our inner selves. "It is because we worship upness inside that we build skyscrapers outside. It is because we prefer aggression to gentleness inside that we invest so mightily in armaments and so punily in artists on the outside. Humpty teaches us how the inside is the outside and the outside is the inside. For better or for worse . . . until death do us part" (p. 268).

A quest for balance is evident in the writings of Cardinal Leo Suenens of Belgium, whose *A New Pentecost?* (New York: Seabury Press, 1974) emphasizes both the charismatic and institutional elements of Christian community and the individual and social dimensions of Christian existence. To be spiritual is to be always ready to expect the unexpected from God, for God is even now creating anew. We are not prisoners of determinism or of sociological prognostications. The Holy Spirit is at work in the Church and in the rest of the world, even when unrecognized and unnamed. To those who welcome the Spirit there is liberty, joy, and trust. The Spirit has raised up prophets and saints who, in times of darkness, have discovered "a spring of grace and shed beams of light on our path" (p. xiii). John XXIII and Vatican II were such surprises. Who would dare to say, therefore, that the love and imagination of God are exhausted? "To hope is not to dream, but to turn dreams into reality. Happy are those who dream dreams and are ready to pay the price to make them come true." Pentecost continues.

MYSTICISM

Mysticism is the experiencing of God. It is not confined to the Church. *Christian* mysticism roots the experience of God in Jesus Christ, an experience brought about by the Holy Spirit. All spirituality, and certainly all Christian spirituality, therefore, is oriented toward the experience of God. Individualistic spiritualities assume that we can experience God only to the extent that we *exclude* experiencing everyone else and everything else. Activist liberationist spiritualities assume that we experience God *only* in the other and in the social and political movements of history. Balanced spiritualities insist on a connection between the two: the experience of God as the presence *within,* and the experience of God as the presence *in others* and in the "signs of the times."

Historically, the use of the word *mystical* to describe a special religious experience is peculiar to Christianity. And even at that its use developed only gradually. It was first employed to designate the deepest meaning of Sacred Scripture, a meaning accessible only to faith. For Clement of Alexandria and for Origen, it was equivalent to the Pauline notion of "mystery"—namely, Jesus Christ crucified (1 Corinthians 2:2). The mystery, hidden for ages but now revealed to the saints, is "Christ in you" (Colossians 1:26-27). Christ, in whom are hidden all the treasures of wisdom and knowledge, is the divine mystery (2:2-3).

The term *mystical* next came to be identified with the sacraments—i.e., outward signs of invisible grace. Christ, of course, is the great sacrament, or mystery. With Gregory of Nyssa and Pseudo-Dionysius the word is given another meaning which it retains in Christian spirituality: the fullness of the new life, the divine life communicated in the crucified and risen Christ. Mysticism, therefore, is not something reserved for the few. It is a call to the many. Everyone is invited to intimate union with God, to the experience of God as the principle of one's life and as the meaning and guide of all that is.

To express it another way, mysticism is simply the experience of grace. It occurs within the framework of one's normal, everyday life and within the experience of faith. Therefore, it is correct to say that mystical experience is not specifically different from the ordinary life of grace that is open to everyone. To argue the contrary view would be tantamount to Gnosticism, that earliest of heresies, which supposed that salvation is through knowledge *(gnosis)* and that such saving knowledge is available only to an elite.

Mysticism, furthermore, is not identical with parapsychological phenomena. This is not to suggest, on the other hand, that the experience of God does not have degrees of intensity. Those experiences of the highest intensity available to human consciousness may indeed have an "unnatural" or at least "unusual" character to them. These special, or "peak," experiences do not happen every day, nor frequently within a single lifetime. Many, in fact, would insist that, in spite of their openness to such experiences and the sincerity of their faith, they have never once had such an experience. But to say that one has not ever had a "peak" or exceedingly intense experience of God is not to say that one has not had a *mystical* experience. For a mystical experience is any experience of God, of whatever degree of intensity. Indeed, the adjective *mystical* before the words *experience of God* is perhaps as redundant as the adjective *mystical* before the words *Body of Christ,* when applied to the Church. For the same reason, "mystical theology" is not really distinct from "Christian theology" as such. If the mystic is said to have great difficulty expressing his or her experience of God, so, too, does every theologian. In fact, the process by which we attempt to articulate our experience of God is precisely what we mean by *theology* (see chapter 2).

GLOSSOLALIA: SPEAKING IN TONGUES

The New Testament refers several times to "speaking in tongues" (Mark 16:17; Acts of the Apostles 2:4-11; 10:46; 19:6; 1 Corinthians 14). It is a speech which is unintelligible to the listeners, except in Acts of the Apostles 2:4-11. It is the work of the Holy Spirit, given particularly at Baptism (Acts of the Apostles 10:46;

19:6), and it becomes so routine a part of the life of some churches that the gift has to be regulated (1 Corinthians 14). Furthermore, it is addressed to God, not to "men" (14:2), and it edifies the speaker rather than those who hear the speaker (14:4). Accordingly, what is spoken "in tongues" must be interpreted (14:5-19,27).

It should be noted that one of the effects of religious ecstasy in contemporary Hellenistic and Oriental circles was the utterance of unintelligible speech. The appearance of unintelligible "tongues" in some of the early Christian communities, therefore, may have provided a bridge between the Hellenistic-Oriental world and the emerging world of Christian faith. As the cultural context changed, the gift of tongues gradually disappeared.

Paul, of course, acknowledged that this gift, even in its period of frequent use, was the least important in the hierarchy of gifts (1 Corinthians 12:1-11). It was only occasionally mentioned in subsequent centuries, entering the modern period via small marginal Protestant groups known as Pentecostals. Just after Vatican II, interest in and expression of the gift of tongues surfaced with vigor even in Catholicism. The phenomenon developed in connection with the emergence of the Catholic Charismatic Renewal, whose origin is usually placed at Duquesne University in Pittsburgh, Pennsylvania, in 1967, from where it spread quickly to the University of Michigan at Ann Arbor and the University of Notre Dame in Indiana.

Seen in its most positive light, the gift of tongues is a form of nondiscursive prayer, not unlike the protracted "A" sound at the end of the chanted "Alleluia" or the spontaneous but unstructured communications of a child who has not yet learned to speak. Others have compared it to the gift of tears, i.e., a religious experience by which a person is moved to a profound sense of sorrow for sin, repentance, adoration, or gratitude before God. Such tears are no different from any others, but their religious significance goes far beyond the merely physical. So, too, does that of the gift of tongues.

"In psychological terms, we could say that it is the voice of the subconscious rising to God, finding a manner of praying which is analagous to other expressions of our subconscious in dreams, laughter, tears, painting, or dance," Cardinal Suenens observes. "This prayer within the depths of our being heals at a profound yet often perceptible level hidden psychological wounds that impede the full development of our interior life" (*A New Pentecost?*, p. 103).

On the other hand, the common approach of the great mystics has been to ignore such phenomena, even if they are God-given (John of the Cross, *The Ascent of Mount Carmel,* Part II, chapter 8). One should preserve, in any case, the Pauline principle that in the worship assembly no one should speak in tongues unless an interpreter can explain the meaning to the community, for every gift is, in the final accounting, always for the sake of the Church and ultimately for the sake of the Kingdom of God (1 Corinthians 14:28).

DISCERNMENT AND SPIRITUAL DIRECTION

It is one thing to say, as Ignatius did, that we must see God in all things, but it is quite another matter confidently to affirm that we have, in fact, grasped the reality of God and accurately discerned the divine will for us in these particular circumstances. No one, after all, has ever seen God (John 1:18; 1 Timothy 6:16). One infers the presence and will of God from what one does see and experience.

But our seeing and our experiencing are never isolated acts. We see and experience as part of larger communities: a family, a religious congregation, a parish, an association, a political unit, a business corporation, and so forth. Furthermore, even these larger groups, in which and through which we live our individual lives, are themselves part of a much wider process of social, economic, and political events and of history itself.

Knowledge, in other words, is always conditioned. It is conditioned by who we are (e.g., our age, sex, race, ethnic roots, gifts, native abilities, religious affiliation, economic status), who are our closest relatives, friends, and associates, our occupation, our citizenship, the social, economic, and political events that shape our time, and so forth.

Accordingly, discernment of the presence and will of God is always complex and difficult, especially in a post-Enlightenment age which is at once critical not only of authority (as the first Enlightenment was) but also of the capacity of reason itself (as the second Enlightenment was). There is more to knowing, in other words, than reasoning alone. We are moved not only by external events but also by the dark and utterly mysterious world of the unconscious. To what extent do our emotions, our imagination, and the other affective faculties of human consciousness determine the judgments we make about the will of God for us, for others, for the world, and for history itself? To transcend the limitations of one's own vision and to begin to see reality against a wider horizon ("as God sees reality") is to experience *conversion* (see chapter 26).

As we noted already in connection with the discussion of the virtue of *prudence* (chapter 26), although we can never be absolutely certain that we are indeed responding to the promptings of the Holy Spirit, there are at least certain *negative criteria* by which obviously false responses can be exposed: (1) If the discernment process does not produce the classic "fruits" of the Spirit: love, joy, peace, patience, kindness, generosity, faith, chastity, etc. (Galatians 5:22-23), the discernment process is not "of the Spirit." (2) If the discernment process leads to theological positions which are inconsistent with the Catholic tradition, it is not "of the Spirit" (see the next section of this chapter for a listing of the principal theological criteria). (3) If the discernment process intensifies the isolation and even the spiritual eccentricities of those involved in it rather than enhancing their life and the life of the whole Church (Ephesians 4:15-16), it is not "of the Spirit." (4) If the discernment process ignores pertinent information (even of a social, economic, or political character), if it rejects the counsel of others who have knowledge and experience in the matter at hand (even if they are not members of the Church or even people of religious faith), and if it formulates its judgments by imposition rather than by corporate reflection and with respect for diversity of viewpoints, then it is clearly not "of the Spirit."

The spiritual director is one who assists and guides the discernment process in others. But the "decision" is always made by the individuals themselves, not by the director. The director all the while is guided by the same theological principles which must guide the one who is striving to discern God's will and to enter more deeply into a relationship with God. Indeed, the spiritual director is himself or herself in the same situation, striving to know God's will and to determine the best way to fulfill it now, in these circumstances.

SPIRITUALITY AND SPIRITUALITIES: THEOLOGICAL CRITERIA

We return to the Thomistic philosophical principle: "Whatever is received is received according to the mode of the receiver." Although God is one, the experience of God is individually, socially, historically, even economically conditioned. Thus, there is one God, but there are many religions. There is one Body of Christ but many churches. There is one faith and yet many theologies. And there is one Spirit and yet many spiritualities.

Indeed, as Paul reminded us, "There are different gifts but the same Spirit; there are different ministries but the same Lord; there are different works but the same God who accomplishes all of them in everyone. To each person the manifestation of the Spirit is given for the common good .... But it is one and the same Spirit who produces all these gifts, distributing them to each as he wills" (1 Corinthians 12:4-7,11). According to Thomas Aquinas, the "first cause of this diversity is to be sought on the part of God, who disposes his gifts of grace variously in order that the beauty and perfection of the Church may result from these various degrees" *(Summa Theologica,* I-II, q. 112, a. 4).

But to say that there are inevitably many spiritualities is not to say that all spiritualities are equally good or equally deficient, no more than one could say that all religions, or all theologies, or even all churches are of equal value and are equally faithful expressions of the divine reality. On what basis can one evaluate the worth of spiritualities? What *theological criteria,* consistent with the Catholic tradition, can one apply to the variety of spiritualities?

1. We are neither purely bodily creatures nor purely spiritual; nor are we primarily bodily or primarily spiritual. *We are body-spirits* (for this and the next four principles, see chapter 5). Accordingly, no Christian spirituality can be predicated on a *dualistic* understanding of human existence, as if the flesh (considered separately from the soul) were always at war with the spirit (considered separately from the flesh). The spirit-flesh opposition in Paul is between the *whole person* as oriented toward the Kingdom of God, and the *whole person* as oriented away from God in the pursuit of selfish interests.

2. *We are radically social beings.* Accordingly, no Christian spirituality can attend exclusively nor in an exaggerated fashion to the individual's personal relationship with God, as if other persons and the wider created order did not enter intrinsically into that relationship.

3. *We are individual human persons.* Accordingly, no Christian spirituality can allow the individual to be absorbed into some impersonal collective, as if the experience of God is only corporate or horizontal, never individual or vertical.

4. *We are also subjects,* i.e., distinct centers of consciousness and freedom. Accordingly, there is no single way of experiencing God or of expressing the experience of God. No Christian spirituality can impose itself as the *only* spirituality for *all*.

5. *We are graced.* The presence of God enters into the very definition of what it means to be human. The doctrines of creation and of redemption make it impossible for a Christian to reject the material, the fleshly, the bodily, the natural, the tangible, the visible, the concrete (see also chapter 7). Accordingly, no Christian spirituality can counsel a repression of the human nor dismiss whole components of human existence as if they were somehow dishonorable and bestial (e.g., the passions, or so-called "lower appetites").

6. To be graced is to be alive by a principle that transcends us—namely, the presence of God. For the Christian, *God is always triune* (see chapters 9 and 10). Accordingly, Christian spirituality is trinitarian spirituality. We are created, called, and sustained by the Father; re-created in the Son and given new access to the

Father through the Son; and renewed and empowered to live a fully human life by the Holy Spirit.

7. Since the triune God is present everywhere, *all reality has a sacramental, or mysterious, character.* The invisible is embodied in, and mediated by, the visible (see chapters 7 and 10). Accordingly, the horizon of Christian spirituality will be as wide as the created order itself. It will be as worldly as it is personal; i.e., it will strive always to see God in all things.

8. *Human existence and Christian existence alike are destined for, and therefore oriented toward, the Kingdom of God.* But the Kingdom is a kingdom of justice and peace as well as of holiness and grace (see chapters 20 and 26, and also chapter 29). Accordingly, Christian spirituality will always be sensitive to the demands of justice, of peace, of human rights, and will never be closed off from, or indifferent to, the needs and the cries of the poor and the oppressed.

9. *We are also sinners* (see chapters 5, 12, 22, 25, and 26). Accordingly, there can be no authentic Christian spirituality apart from the cross. It is a spirituality always marked by sacrifice, by denial of selfish interests, even by contradictions. It will be attentive to the impact of Original Sin: to pride, to apathy, to temerity, to lust, to hypocrisy, to sloth, to envy (see chapters 5, 9, and especially 26).

10. *We are ecclesial persons.* Christian faith is given, received, nourished, sustained, and brought to fulfillment in the context of the Church (see chapters 17, 20, and 21). Accordingly, there is no authentic Christian spirituality that is not at the same time ecclesial spirituality, rooted not only in the primitive, foundational proclamation of the Word in and through Sacred Scripture, but also in the Word's constant re-proclamation and celebration in the Church's liturgy and across the whole range of its sacramental and para-sacramental life (see chapters 2, 7, 21, and 22).

11. As ecclesial persons, members of the Body of Christ, *we are called to Christian existence, to the practice of the virtues.* Accordingly, Christian spirituality will be an expression of faith, hope, and charity, and of prudence, justice, temperance, and fortitude (see chapter 26). The center will always be charity.

12.   *The call to Christian holiness is a universal call (Dogmatic Constitution on the Church,* chapter 5). There is no "higher" spirituality for the ordained and the religiously professed than for the laity. Accordingly, Christian spirituality will never be hierarchical or elitist. There will always be different spiritualities, but the differences will not necessarily imply superiority or inferiority in relation to one another, nor on the basis of ecclesiastical "states of life."

SUMMARY

1.   *Spirituality* has to do with one's style of life, with one's way of experiencing God and of shaping one's life on the basis of that experience. It is our way of being religious. Since God is available in principle to everyone, spirituality is not exclusively Christian.

2.   *Christian spirituality* is the cultivation of a style of life consistent with the presence of the Spirit of the Risen Christ within us and with our status as members of the Body of Christ. It is *visionary* (is a way of interpreting reality in "spiritual terms"), *sacramental* (sees God in all things), *relational* (is open to the presence and call of God in other people), and *transformational* (is always in touch with and open to the Spirit of reconciliation, renewal, healing).

3.   The *foundations* of Christian spirituality were already laid in the *covenantal relationship* between Yahweh and Israel in the Old Testament. *Jesus,* however, proclaimed the nearness of God in a dramatically new way in his preaching of the Kingdom of God. Through his death and resurrection, the Spirit of God comes to dwell within us anew, as the source of light, wisdom, hope, peace.

4.   Christian spirituality from the beginning, therefore, is shaped by the Church's *expectation of the coming of the Kingdom of God;* this adds a note of urgency to its mission of proclamation in word, in sacrament, in witness, and in service.

5.   In the time of the persecutions *martyrdom* was regarded as the ideal way of achieving union with God. Thereafter, even "natural death" was perceived as a kind of unbloody martyrdom.

6.   The first division over Christian spirituality occurs with *Gnosticism* and its variants. Matter is evil, according to this heresy. Therefore, the Christian is to disengage from all material reality to seek the true knowledge *(gnosis)* which alone brings salvation. Over against this

view was Irenaeus' doctrine of *recapitulation:* All reality has been redeemed by Christ in the incarnation.

7.   *Monasticism* developed first as a flight from persecution and then as a protest against the newly privileged status of the Church under Constantine. Emphasis was placed on ascetical practices, some of which were severe. It began as a solitary form of existence (anchoritism) and later developed a communal form (cenobitism): common prayers, common goods, and common worship. The *consecration of virgins* was also introduced at this time.

8.   A Christian *spiritual theology* developed only gradually from the new monastic movement: *Pseudo-Dionysius* insisted that the soul finds God only in going beyond itself, being absorbed totally in the knowledge of God, whose goodness is overflowing; *Augustine* focused on the principle of self-knowledge in the light of Christ, the interior teacher of wisdom; for *John Cassian,* Christian life is one of constant prayer. The monastic style of spirituality was given wider currency among the laity through the popular writings of *Pope Gregory the Great.*

9.   Under *Germanic influence,* Christian spirituality became more externalized: devotions, relics, pilgrimages, penances, confession of sins, etc. The influence of the monasteries continued to grow, especially when, in the tenth and eleventh centuries, federations of monasteries were established and the monastic ideal was spread even more widely throughout the Christian world.

10.   Emphasis on *contemplation,* as immediate experience of God without theological reflection, was proposed by the new Cistercian Order, especially by *Bernard of Clairvaux* and *William of St. Thierry,* and by members of the Parisian monastery of St. Victor (the "Victorines": *Hugh, Richard, et al.).*

11.   With the decline of social life and of Christian morals even in the Church, various lay movements developed, urging radical poverty and an end to all formalism and legalism. Waldensianism and Albigensianism were extreme forms. The rise of the *mendicant orders*—Franciscans and Dominicans—had a more sustained effect in these areas. The Dominicans (e.g., Aquinas) emphasized the link between contemplation and the apostolate, while the Franciscans (e.g., Bonaventure) emphasized the link between God and creation and our call to live simply and poorly.

12.   But the stress on contemplation continued with the increasing popularity of Pseudo-Dionysius, whose works were newly translated in the thirteenth century. Christian spirituality was described in terms of the soul's union with God through abandonment of, and detachment

from, all creatures and worldly realities: *Meister Eckhart, John Tauler, Henry Suso, Ruysbroeck, The Cloud of Unknowing* (anonymous). A more extreme form of this anti-intellectual and individualistic spirituality is to be found in the *Imitation of Christ,* edited, perhaps also written, by Thomas à Kempis.

13.   Although *Protestantism* rejected the excesses of medieval spirituality (superstitions and near idolatries), it did not reject its individualism. For Protestantism, access to God is direct and unmediated, guided by the interior illumination of the Holy Spirit.

14.   A reaction to contemplative excesses in Catholic spirituality was mounted by such Christian humanists as *Erasmus* and by such Christian activists as *Ignatius Loyola.* They insisted on the fundamental connection between prayer and the apostolate.

15.   Mysticism continued to flourish, however, especially in *Spain: Teresa of Avila* and *John of the Cross. Italian* spirituality was more practical, oriented toward the renewal of priestly life: *Philip Neri, Charles Borromeo,* and *Catherine of Genoa. French* spirituality was the most complicated of all because of Jansenism and Quietism: the one stressing the corruption of the flesh, the other stressing the powerlessness of the human person to do anything at all toward salvation. On the other side were ranged *Bossuet, Francis de Sales,* and *Jean Jacques Olier*—all emphasizing in different ways the importance of one's worldly duties, the joy of Christian existence, and the goodness of Jesus.

16.   The *nineteenth century* is the bridge between medieval and modern Christian spirituality. Individualism and regimented piety continue (e.g., new devotions) but the forces of renewal are already at work: in theology, liturgy, historical studies, and the social apostolate, as well as in the world of science and technology.

17.   The ambivalence of the nineteenth century carried over into the first half of the twentieth. On the one hand, there were spiritualities based largely on scholastic presuppositions *(Tanquerey, Garrigou-Lagrange)* and underlining the individualistic aspect of Christian existence; on the other hand, a broader, Christocentric piety was being developed by such writers as *Abbot Marmion.*

18.   With an *historical* understanding of human existence increasingly shaping Catholic theology around the middle of the twentieth century, spiritualities begin to emerge which are more world-centered *(Teilhard de Chardin),* neighbor-oriented *(Hubert Van Zeller),* justice-concerned *(Thomas Merton),* and person-integrating *(Josef Goldbrunner),* without prejudice at all to the traditional contemplative elements.

19. The *Second Vatican Council* taught that holiness is for every-one and that it comprehends more than the soul's individual relationship with God. Spirituality is shaped by one's situation in life. It is rooted in the mysteries of creation and redemption, in the presence of the Holy Spirit, and in the mission of Christ and the Church. The liturgy is its summit and fountain.

20. *Post-Vatican II* spirituality has been marked by a full-scale liturgical renewal, ecumenism, a more pronounced commitment to liber-ation and social justice, a deepening reverence for Sacred Scripture, and an increased striving for a personal experience of the Holy Spirit. These developments have, in turn, produced such movements as the Catholic Charismatic Renewal, the Cursillo movement, Marriage Encounter, directed retreats, weekend youth retreats, and the reform and renewal of religious congregations.

21. Individual spiritual writers reflect this new ecumenical out-look, attempting to bridge the gap even between East and West *(Aelred Graham)*. Others continue to see the spiritual challenge as bridging the gaps within the human person, e.g., between loneliness and solitude *(Henri Nouwen)*, between the newly integrated person and the world itself *(Matthew Fox)*, and between the charismatic and institutional dimensions of Christian life *(Cardinal Suenens)*. A continuing emphasis on interiority and individuality continues (the "centering prayer" approach), along with increased stress on the political aspect of spiritual-ity *(Johannes Metz,* and liberation theology).

22. All Christian spirituality is oriented toward experiencing God in Christ and the Holy Spirit, which is to say that all Christian spiritual-ity is also *"mystical."* The term was first applied to the deepest meaning of Sacred Scripture—i.e., to Christ as the source of all wisdom and knowledge. Then it came to be identified with the sacraments, with Christ perceived as the great sacrament, or mystery. Later, in the writ-ings of Gregory of Nyssa and Pseudo-Dionysius, it refers to the fullness of our new life in Christ: union with God in Christ and the Spirit. In other words, *mysticism is the experience of grace*—i.e., of God's presence within us and throughout the whole of creation. Hence mysticism is not for the few but for all. There are, to be sure, degrees of the experience of God.

23. *Speaking in tongues* (usually unintelligible to the listener) is a gift of the Holy Spirit, according to the New Testament. It is a form of ecstatic prayer, not without parallels in then-contemporary Hellenistic and Oriental circles. The gift was subject to abuse and had to be regu-lated. Like all gifts, it must be for the good of the community.

24.   *Discernment* is an exercise of the virtue of prudence. To perceive the presence of God and to discern the divine will are complex and difficult because no one has ever seen God (John 1:18; 1 Timothy 6:16). The process is also complicated by the fact that knowledge itself is historically conditioned and that there is a universe of the unconscious as well as the conscious.

25.   There are some *negative criteria* by which false discernment can be exposed. It is not "of the Spirit": (1) if it does not issue forth in the fruits of the Holy Spirit (love, joy, peace, etc.); (2) if it leads to theological positions inconsistent with the Catholic tradition; (3) if it intensifies the isolation and even the spiritual eccentricities of the discerner and does not enhance the life of the Church; and (4) if it ignores pertinent information, the counsel of others, or if it imposes its judgments without corporate reflection or respect for diversity of viewpoints.

26.   The *spiritual director* assists and guides the discernment process in others, following the same criteria. The discerner, however, must make his or her own decision and take responsibility for it. The spiritual director, too, is always a discerner.

27.   Although there is only one Spirit, there are many gifts of the Spirit. Furthermore, the Spirit is manifested and received in different ways by different people. Accordingly, there are *many different spiritualities,* even within the Church itself. But not all are equally consistent with the Catholic tradition.

28.   Some *theological criteria* for determining such consistency are:

(1)   We are body-spirits. Christian spirituality cannot be dualistic.

(2)   We are social beings. Christianity spirituality cannot be individualistic.

(3)   We are individual human persons. Christian spirituality cannot absorb the individual into an impersonal collective.

(4)   We are subjects, i.e., distinct centers of consciousness and freedom. There is no one Christian spirituality for everyone.

(5)   We are graced. Christian spirituality cannot reject the human nor deny the goodness of the passions.

(6)   God is triune. Christian spirituality must be rooted in the life of the whole Trinity: not the Father alone, not the Son alone, not the Holy Spirit alone.

(7)   The triune God is present to all reality. The horizon of Christian spirituality will therefore be as wide as the created order itself.

(8) Everything is destined for, and oriented toward, the Kingdom of God, a kingdom of justice and peace as well as of holiness and grace. Christian spirituality will be marked by a sense of expectation and readiness and by a commitment to justice, peace, and human rights.

(9) We are sinners. Christian spirituality is a spirituality of the cross: of sacrifice, of denial of selfish interests, of contradiction.

(10) We are ecclesial persons. Christian spirituality will be at once communal, biblical, and liturgical.

(11) We are called to the practice of the virtues. Christian spirituality will be an expression of faith, hope and charity, and of prudence, justice, temperance, and fortitude.

(12) All are called to holiness. Christian spirituality is never hierarchical or elitist, nor of concern only to the ordained and religiously professed.

SUGGESTED READINGS

General Works:

Bouyer, Louis. *Introduction to Spirituality*. New York: Desclée, 1961.
—————— , et al. *A History of Christian Spirituality*. 4 vols. New York: Desclée, 1963.
Dalrymple, John. *Theology and Spirituality*. Cork, Ireland: Mercier Press, 1970.
Rahner, Karl. *The Dynamic Element in the Church*. London: Burns & Oates, 1964.

Ecumenical Spirituality:

Aumann, Jordan, *et. al. Christian Spirituality East and West*, Chicago: Priory Press, 1968. (Catholic, Orthodox, and Evangelical)
Bonhoeffer, Dietrich. *The Cost of Discipleship*. New York: Macmillan, 1959. (Lutheran)
Cox, Harvey. *Turning East: The Promise and Peril of the New Orientalism*. New York: Simon and Schuster, 1977. (Baptist)
Lewis, C. S. *Surprised by Joy: The Shape of My Early Life*. New York: Harcourt, Brace, Janovich, 1973. (Anglican)
Lossky, Vladimir. *The Mystical Theology of the Eastern Church*. London: James Clarke, 1957. (Orthodox)

Thurian, Max. *Modern Man and Spiritual Life*. New York: Association Press, 1963. (Reformed)

Journals and Series:

Chicago Studies 15 (1976). "A Spiritual Life Handbook."
Cross Currents 24 (1974). "Word Out of Silence: A Symposium on World Spiritualities." John-David Robinson, ed.
Spiritual Life
The Way
The Classics of Western Spirituality. New York: Paulist Press, 1978—.

· XXIX ·

CHRISTIAN/HUMAN DESTINY: THE KINGDOM OF GOD

THE MEANING AND PLACE OF ESCHATOLOGY

Catholics share faith in the Lordship of Jesus with all other Christians, faith in the reality of God with all other religious persons and communities, and humanity with all other human beings. All of us inhabit the same earth and are cocreators with God of the same history, even if we "name" God differently or not at all. *Christian destiny* is not distinct from *human destiny*, therefore, nor is either distinct from the *destiny of the world* itself or of its *history*. There is one beginning and one end of all created reality: God.

Eschatology is that area of theology which is directly concerned with the "study of the last thing(s)". The "last thing" is God, or, more precisely, the final manifestation of the reconciling, renewing, and unifying love of God. The "last things" are various moments or stages in the final manifestation process: death, particular judgment, heaven, hell, purgatory, Second Coming of Christ, resurrection of the body, general judgment, consummation of all things in the perfection of the Kingdom of God.

So comprehensive is eschatology's scope that some theologians have argued that all theology begins and ends with eschatology (Jürgen Moltmann, *Theology of Hope*, New York: Harper & Row, 1967, p. 16). At the very least, eschatology provides a wider context for the discussion of every other theological question, for eschatology is about the Kingdom (or "reign") of God, i.e., *the redemptive presence of God actualized through the power of God's reconciling Spirit.* All theology is literally the "study of God." But theology does not reflect on the reality of God as some passive Being or abstract Idea. The God of Christian faith and, therefore, of Christian theology is a God of love (1 John 4:7-21). Love is, by its very nature, active and incarnate. Love is always directed toward the other. Love wishes the other well. Love seeks union with the other. Love heals, renews, reconciles, unites. Love generates peace, joy, kindness, contentment, and all the other fruits of the Holy Spirit, who is the God-of-love in action (Galatians 5:22-23).

But "the other" is not only another individual. "The other" is also *collective*: e.g., family, friends, associates, fellow Christians, the needy. And human existence is always *historical existence*, i.e., existence that is conditioned by social, economic, and political events, by institutions and structures, and by the facticity of life (e.g., we are born at a certain time, of certain parents, of a certain sex, of a certain race, in a certain country). To say, therefore, that God is love and that God loves us means that God loves us as "the other," not only in our individuality but also in our common humanity. Indeed, God loves us in our world and in our history. And because God loves us, God is *active* on our behalf: first in creation, then in redemption, and finally in the consummation of all things in Jesus Christ, by the power of the Holy Spirit. That active love is also an *incarnate* love. God becomes present to us, again not only as individuals but in our total humanity, in our world, and in our history. God is the active, incarnate power of love by which we, our brothers and sisters, our world, and our history are healed, renewed, and brought to the fullness of perfection. And this is precisely what the Kingdom of God is all about.

To reflect on the meaning of the Kingdom of God is to "do eschatology." But to do eschatology is to do what is central to theology: It is to explore the reality of the active, incarnate, redeeming, loving God as that God is known and accepted in faith. Eschatology, however, is not simply coextensive with all of theology, which addresses the total mystery of God. Eschatology centers its attention on that aspect of God by which God is the destiny and consummation of all reality.

This is not to say that eschatology is concerned only with the *future*. On the contrary, the future is being realized even now, in the *present*, and has begun to be realized already in the *past*. We are already redeemed in grace, in faith, in hope, in love (John 5:24; 12:31; 16:8). The Spirit has already been given (Philippians 1:19; Romans 8:23). Our resurrection has already taken place in the Spirit (John 5:25,28). Our *death*, therefore, is, or should be, a participation in the redemptive death of Jesus Christ, which has already taken place. Our *judgment* will be the visible manifestation of the judgment of acquittal already rendered in Jesus Christ (e.g., John 12:31-32; Romans 8:3; Galatians 3:13). The final, *general judgment* will only make clear what is already true— namely, that history is the work of God, that its center is Jesus Christ, and that its moving force is the Holy Spirit. This is, at the same time, the *consummation of all things*, the disclosure of God's acceptance of the world in the incarnation. The Second Coming of Christ (*Parousia*) is simply the final stage of the one coming of Christ (Matthew 12:40). Christ's *return* is really the *arrival* of all things at their final destination in Christ. It is the revelation of God's love for the world (Matthew 24:36; 25:31-46; 1 Thessalonians 5:2; 2 Thessalonians 2:1-8; Revelation 20:11-15; 22:12,20).

The *anticipation* of these final events occurs not only in faith, in hope, and in the active love of one another in charity, but also sacramentally in the *Eucharist*, where we eat and drink of the Lord's body and blood "until he comes" (1 Corinthians 11:26), and in the *Church* itself, which is the eschatological community, the Temple of the Holy Spirit, the carrier even now of the divine glory (Ephesians 5:27).

The movement of history toward its consummation in the Kingdom of God is believed not only because it is *promised* but also because it is *demanded* by graced human nature itself. We are *intentional* beings (see chapters 4 and 5); i.e., we give purpose and direction to our lives. We are constitutionally restless in our quest for truth and in our search for love. Only God, who is the fullness of truth and love itself, can finally satisfy that radical human longing. To say there is no God is to say there is no possibility of ultimate human fulfillment, for the fullness of truth and love obviously transcends our unaided human capacities. There are questions that science can never answer, and problems that science can never solve: What is true justice? How can we create real community? What does it mean to be fully human? Why is there such evil in the world? Why is there such goodness in the world? Why is there being rather than nothing? Where is it all heading? What is the deepest meaning of life?

This "intentionality" is there from the beginning, implanted through God's original self-communication in grace prior even to our free decision to accept or reject it. This is what Rahner has called the "supernatural existential." We are called to accept God's self-communication by responding in faith and love, or we can reject it by sin. The Kingdom of God is the consummation *of* history itself and not just a reward for good deeds *in* history. God completes salvation history by completing history itself. Consequently, there is no such thing as a *purely natural end* for the world or for non-religious people, and a *supernatural end* for the Church and for all who truly believe in God and seek to do the divine will. "For the 'essence' or 'nature' of man is that of a purposeful free being, whose 'nature' it is to be open without limit to the free disposition of God.... And the finality of man is not mechanical, organic, or static, but must be seen from the outset in terms of a dialogal relationship between divine and human freedom.... For the self-communication of God (grace), in spite of being supernatural, is the very 'heart' of man" (Karl Rahner, "Order, IV. End of Man," *The Concise Sacramentum Mundi*, pp. 1119-1120).

Through the mediation of humanity, therefore, the world itself has "intentionality," purpose, direction, conscious freedom. In a word, because of humanity the world itself *has* a history and *is* history. This history has already entered its eschatological phase through the incarnation, the cross and resurrection of Jesus Christ, and the outpouring of the Holy Spirit. The outcome of this history is already decided by Christ, even though that outcome is still hidden and can be grasped only in faith, in hope, and in love. That "outcome" is the finally realized *Kingdom of God*, i.e., *the full and perfect manifestation of the redemptive presence of God through which all things are transformed in the name of Jesus Christ and by the power of the Holy Spirit.*

This is not to say, on the other hand, that history's movement toward the Kingdom of God is smooth and unimpeded. There are powers at work in the world which are hostile to God (e.g., Ezekiel 38-39; Daniel 2:20-45; 7:7-8; Psalm 2) and which are directed immediately against Christ (Revelation 12:1-5) and the Church (12:17), growing in intensity as the end draws near. All of these evil forces are focused in the one known as *Satan* (the Hebrew word *sātān* means "adversary," and it was translated into Greek as *diabolos*, the word which passed into various European languages). He is regarded as the prince of the angels who fell away from God before the creation of the world and who were thrust out of heaven. He becomes in the New Testament the evil one (Matthew 13:19), the enemy (Luke 10:19), the ruler of this world (John 12:31), the father of lies (John 8:44), the evil force behind the passion of Jesus (Luke 22:3,31; John 13:27).

But the passion is also the source of victory over Satan (1 Corinthians 2:8; John 12:31; Acts of the Apostles 12:7-11), who is himself destined to be cast finally into hell (Revelation 20:8,10). (See chapter 9.)

The Church's broadened understanding of the interrelationship between the power of God's love in Christ and the forces of evil personified in Satan is effectively captured in the renewed Rite of Christian Initiation of Adults:

> Father of eternal life,
> you are a God, not of the dead, but of the living:
> you sent your Son to proclaim the good news of life,
> to rescue men from the kingdom of death
> and to lead them to resurrection.
> Free these chosen people
> from the power of the evil spirit who brings death.
> May they receive new life from Christ
> and bear witness to his resurrection.
> We ask this through Christ our Lord. Amen.
>
> (*The Rites of the Catholic Church*, New York: Pueblo Publishing Co., 1976, p. 82.)

THE KINGDOM OF GOD:
THE DESTINY OF CREATION AND HUMANITY
Old Testament

Although Jesus repeatedly referred to the Kingdom of God in his preaching—indeed he began his whole ministry with the announcement that the Kingdom of God was at hand (Mark 1:15)—he never once paused to define it. Nor did any of his hearers ever interrupt him to ask him to define it. Jesus used the term with the apparent assurance that his listeners knew what he meant. And they did. The Kingdom of God was an integral part of contemporary Jewish vocabulary. It was something they all understood and longed for. As we already noted (in chapter 12) and shall note again in the next section (on the preaching of Jesus), the notion of the Kingdom received a radically new interpretation from Jesus, but the interpretation did not break the line of continuity reaching far back into the history of Israel and the pages of the Old Testament.

Although the precise *origins* of the term *Kingdom of God* cannot be determined, it developed sometime during the period of the wandering in the desert. The earliest source we come across is the ancient canticle of the sea, sung by Moses and the children of Israel after their crossing of the Red Sea and the destruction of the Egyptians (Exodus 15:11-13,18). And this was "no idea picked up along the way by cultural borrowing, nor was it the creation of the monarchy and its institutions, nor yet the outgrowth of the frustration of national ambition, however much all these factors may have colored it. On the contrary, it is linked with Israel's whole notion of herself as the chosen people of God, and this in turn was woven into the texture of her faith from the beginning" (John Bright, *The Kingdom of God: The Biblical Concept and Its Meaning for the Church*, New York: Abingdon Press, 1953, p. 19).

Subsequent references to the provident and protecting Lordship of Yahweh show that Israel experienced the kingship of Yahweh in the historical action of God. But that kingship was also beyond history. On the one hand, David becomes aware that his own kingdom was instituted by God and established by God's grace forever (2 Samuel 7:12-16). On the other hand, Gideon, the judge, can declare: "I will not rule over you, nor shall my son rule over you. The Lord must rule over you" (Judges 8:23). Furthermore, the Kingdom is at once localized and universal. Thus, God is said to be in royal residence in the ark of the covenant (Exodus 25:8; 40:34-38; Numbers 14:10), but Yahweh's throne is also in heaven itself, and "All the earth is filled with his glory" (Isaiah 6:3). Yahweh's rule, therefore, is not over Israel alone, but over all people (Amos 9:7; Jeremiah 10:7,10-12; Psalm 22:29-30; Isaiah 44:24-28; 45:1-6). Indeed, the whole of creation, and not merely the Gentiles, is destined to share in the Kingdom of God's peace (Hosea 2:20; Isaiah 35:1-10). Everything will be brought together at the end in a divine banquet (Isaiah 25:6-8).

The *liturgical life* of Israel disclosed yet another dialectical aspect of the Kingdom: It is at once present and future. God even now reigns over and guides the people of Israel, all nations, and the whole created order. But in times of severe affliction Yahweh's rule is perceived to be withdrawn temporarily, and Israel prays in hope that one day Yahweh will powerfully restore the Kingdom and destroy Israel's oppressors. Thus, after the fall of the monarchy the so-called royal Psalms (2, 18, 20, 21, 72, 101, 110, 132, 144:1-11) are "spiritualized," and the king is now identified with the messianic king who is to come.

This hope in a future liberation is particularly emphasized in the *prophetic literature*. All peoples will drink of the cup of God's wrath (Jeremiah 25:15-29). Yahweh will deliver the wicked to the sword (25:30-38). The godless armies will be annihilated (Ezekiel 39:1-7), and all nations will see the glory of God and the divine judgment (39:21). A similarly cosmic vision is sketched by Isaiah (24-27) and in Daniel (2 and 7). Jerusalem is identified as the focal point of God's new reign over Israel (Micah 4:7), and the return of the Israelites shall be like a second Exodus (7:14-15). It is to the mountain of God (Zion) in Jerusalem that all nations will stream (Micah 4:1-4; Isaiah 2:2-4), and the glory of God will be manifested there (Jeremiah 16:19; Isaiah 56:7; 60; 66:19-21; Zechariah 2:14-17; 8:20-22; 14:16).

This universal kingship will bear fruit in a whole new moral order where the will of God is operative. As a result, peace will be achieved among the peoples of the earth (Isaiah 2:4; Zechariah

9:9-10) through the Messiah who is the prince of peace, and God will be revealed again as a shepherd (Isaiah 40:11), but a kingly one (43:15; 44:6). The Lord comes, not to punish and to judge, but to bring peace, goodness, and salvation: "How beautiful upon the mountains are the feet of him who brings glad tidings, announcing peace, bearing good news, announcing salvation, and saying to Zion, 'Your God is King!' " (52:7). Jesus begins his own ministry in the same spirit (Mark 1:14; compare also Isaiah 61:1 with Luke 4:18 and Matthew 11:5). And so it is *Deutero-Isaiah* (or Second Isaiah, chapters 40-55) which most directly anticipates Jesus' own conception of the Kingdom.

In *later Judaism*, however, a more nationalistic orientation develops, and this, too, persists into the New Testament and creates a problem for Jesus. The two sons of Zebedee, for example, vie for the first places in the messianic kingdom of Jesus (Mark 10:37), and Peter himself tries to deter the Lord from the way of suffering (8:32). In direct contrast to this nationalistic eschatology which focused on Palestine and the earthly Jerusalem, *apocalyptic* (from the Hebrew *gālāh* and the Greek *apocalypsis*, meaning "revelation") literature directed its vision rather to the heavenly Jerusalem and to paradise as the abode of the elect and the blessed. The book of Daniel provides the original pattern for this literature. The heavenly origin and character of the Kingdom emerges clearly in the vision of the four beasts and the one who is like the Son of Man, who appears in the clouds of heaven after judgment is rendered on the beasts (7:9-12). The whole scene takes place in heaven. "However we interpret the 'Son of man', he is in no sense an earthly savior who wages war in God's name and exercises justice. He is a heavenly and pre-existent being" (Rudolf Schnackenburg, *God's Rule and Kingdom*, p. 65).

The apocalypses, therefore, place the strongest possible emphasis on God's sovereign action and final intervention without any cooperation at all on our part. They sometimes think they can determine the moment of the divine intervention and recognize the signs that will precede it. Accordingly, they divide the history of the world into periods, on the lines of the four world empires (Daniel 2:37-45), or according to weeks of years and jubilees, seven times seven, or after the seventy shepherds of the people, etc. They inquire how much of the course of world history has already elapsed and then work out the conclusion. And, finally, they look for signs and portents such as earthquakes, plagues, confusion, fighting, the fall of rulers and princes (Daniel 12:1). They dwell upon the fantastic and the fearsome and boast of special apocalyptic knowledge, concealed from the common person. There appear a spirit of revenge and a perverted joy in the annihilation of the wicked. However noble the apocalyptic conception of the Kingdom, much of this literature is marred by pettiness, narowness, and self-righteousness. It is also characterized by an individualism that weakens the community's commitment to the abiding struggle for justice and peace and the transformation of all creation.

The Preaching of Jesus

What caught Jesus' contemporaries by surprise was his proclamation that the Kingdom of God was close at hand (Mark 1:15). Thus, he called for conversion and repentance (Luke 10:13-15; Matthew 11:20-24; Luke 13:1-5; 19:41-44) and underlined the importance of watching and being ready for the Kingdom (Luke 12:35-40; Matthew 25:1-13). In the final accounting, however, the Kingdom comes from divine power and grace (Mark 4:26-29). God gives it (Luke 12:32) or assigns it (22:29-30). It is especially for sinners (Mark 2:16-17; Luke 7:34 = Matthew 11:19; Luke 15:7,10,24,32;18:10-14;19:7; Matthew 21:31). The scandal aroused by Jesus' associating with publicans and prostitutes (Mark 2:15-17; Luke 7:34,36-50;19:7) showed how unexpected his proclamation and interpretation of the Kingdom had been. Jesus emphasizes always the mercy of God (Matthew 18:23-35), and, unlike the prophets, he presupposes in his call for repentance that God's redemptive activity on our behalf has already begun (Mark 1:15). In the beatitudes in the Sermon on the Mount, he insists that God shows special favor toward the poor, the oppressed, the despised, the persecuted (Matthew 5:1-12). In fact, entrance into the Kingdom will be determined in large measure by our response to the neighbor in need (Matthew 25:31-46).

Jesus also excluded a political interpretation of the Kingdom; not that the values of the Kingdom have no political conse- quences, but that its coming is not dependent upon any one politi- cal order. He did not accept the widespread Jewish hope for a political kingdom, nor did he cooperate with the Zealots in their own activities against Roman rule. Why else did he conceal the messianic character of his work, as is evident especially in Mark's Gospel? Indeed, he reminds the Sadducees that after the resurrec- tion from the dead there will be no marrying in heaven (Mark 12:24-25).

But Jesus also excluded an elitist understanding of the King- dom. He carried his ministry to the whole of Israel, just and sinners alike, even the outcasts and the despised. He leaves the separation of the good from the bad to the final judgment (Mat- thew 13:24-30,47-50) and tolerates failures even within his own circle of followers (Mark 14:27,30; Luke 22:31-34). The doors to the Kingdom are open to all, including those from East and West. Some of the children of the Kingdom will be found unworthy and will be cast out into the exterior darkness (Matthew 8:11-23; Luke 13:24-28). What will be decisive is not membership in Israel but the fulfillment of the call to conversion (Matthew 21:43; Mark 12:1-9). To be converted is to seek first the Kingdom of God (Matthew 6:25-33). The Kingdom will come when the will of God is done (6:9-13).

Doing the will of God involves discipleship (Luke 9:57-60 = Matthew 8:19-22; Luke 9:61-62; Mark 10:21; Mark 9:38 = Luke 9:49), which makes absolute demands upon each disciple (Luke 14:33). He calls for a renunciation of earthly goods when these become an obstacle to entry into the Kingdom (Mark 10:24-27). He takes under his influence those who have made themselves eunuchs for the Kingdom (Matthew 19:12) but does not impose celibacy on all.

Jesus' works give substance to his preaching. His healings and exorcisms are signs that the Kingdom has drawn near in him: "But if it is by the finger of God that I cast out devils, then the reign of God is upon you" (Luke 11:20). When the disciples of John the Baptist come out into the desert to inquire whether or not Jesus is the Messiah, he tells them to go back to John and report what they themselves have seen and heard: ". . . the blind recover their sight, cripples walk, lepers are cured, the deaf hear, dead men are raised to life, and the poor have the good news preached to them" (Matthew 11:4-5). Although Jesus had a unique relationship to God (Matthew 11:25-27), it is not his Kingdom but the Father's (Luke 12:32; 22:29-30), who alone knows the hour of its final coming (Matthew 24:36). In the meantime, we can pray for it (Matthew 6:10; Luke 11:2). But because it *is* the Father's work and because the manifestation of the Father's love cannot be understood in this world's terms, Jesus made no attempt to describe the Kingdom, much less define it, except in parables (Mark 4:33-34). (See chapter 12.)

Early Christianity

With the death and resurrection of Jesus there is a remarkable shift from the proclamation of the Kingdom of God to the proclamation of the Lordship of Jesus (Romans 10:9; 1 John 5:1; John 20:31). The historical details of this transition are probably lost to us forever. But this is not to say that the early Church corrupted the original message of Jesus. On the contrary, the Kingdom of God was still at the core of the primitive proclamation (Acts of the Apostles 1:3; 13:16-41; 28:23,31). Furthermore, insofar as Jesus identified himself so closely with his message that he can be regarded as the very incarnation of the Kingdom of God, the early Church's proclamation of Jesus as the Christ represents no fundamental departure from Jesus' own preaching. Jesus' Gospel about the Kingdom of God thereby became the Church's Gospel about Jesus, the Christ of God.

The early Church recognized not only that the Kingdom of God had broken into history in a new and definitive way in Jesus Christ but also that it continued to grow and develop in the course of post-resurrection history. This is particularly characteristic of the *Lucan* writings (the third Gospel and the Acts of the Apostles). We are living now between-the-times: between the decisive inbreaking of the Kingdom in Jesus Christ and the fulfillment of the Kingdom at the Second Coming of Christ when history is brought to perfection.

Paul speaks only rarely of the Kingdom of God (1 Corinthians 6:10; 15:50; Galatians 5:21). It is realized in the Lordship of Christ (1 Corinthians 15:24; Colossians 1:13) and is present to the faithful (Colossians 3:1-4) in the Church (1:18,24). The exalted Christ continues to exercise his sovereignty over the world through the Church (Ephesians 1:21-23; 3:10; 4:8-10), and that Lordship will be brought to completion at the Second Coming, when God will be all in all (1 Corinthians 15:24-28). Christ's rule, therefore, extends beyond the Church.

Except for one text (John 3:5) the term "Kingdom of God" does not occur in the *Johannine* writings. At times there are glimpses into the future: resurrection of the body, judgment, and eternal life (5:28-29; 12:25). History is the battlefield where the powers of Satan war against the reign of God in Christ (Revelation 11:15; 20:4).

The *early Church*, consequently, is always conscious that the Kingdom of God under Christ is still on the way, and that the Church itself is a pilgrim people, strangers and sojourners in this world (1 Peter). Christ's rule is hidden now, but it will be manifested fully in the end, when the Kingdom of God will be realized in all its perfection. And nowhere is the orientation of the Church toward the Kingdom more explicitly revealed than in its Eucharist, which anticipates the eating and drinking at the Lord's table in the Kingdom (Luke 22:30).

Christian Theology: Before the Twentieth Century

Early patristic theology was influenced by the notion of the Lordship of Jesus and the imminence of his Second Coming (e.g., Ignatius of Antioch, *Letter to the Ephesians*, 11). There were also some apocalyptic elements—e.g., the notion of the thousand-year reign in Justin's *Trypho* (80-81) and Tertullian's *Against Marcion* (3, 24). The reign of God in Clement of Alexandria and in Origen tends to be spiritualized. Prayer for the coming of the Kingdom is a petition for wisdom and knowledge (Origen, *On Prayer*, 13). This strongly interiorized concept of the Kingdom prevailed in the East, especially under the philosophical influence of neo-Platonism. Eusebius of Caesarea (d. ca. 340), however, offered a kind of political theology of the Kingdom by referring to the earthly Roman empire, with its enforcement of peace, as the image of the Kingdom.

In the West, the Church became increasingly identified with the Kingdom of God. This is especially evident in *Augustine*: "It follows that the Church even now is the kingdom of Christ and the kingdom of heaven" (*City of God*, book XX, chapter 9). Even more significant is Augustine's notion of the two cities: the city of God and the earthly city. It would seem that the city of God is closely connected, if not simply identified, with the Kingdom of God. The city of God, he says, is "on pilgrimage in this world, and it is by regeneration that it is brought to another world, whose children neither generate nor are generated" (XV, 20). In any case, Augustine introduces a distinction here which probably laid the foundation for Martin Luther's distinctive doctrine of the two kingdoms; and this, in turn, was at the root of so much of the indifference to social and political questions within Christianity between the Reformation and the nineteenth century. The Kingdom of God is God's work alone. We can do absolutely nothing to bring it about. The kingdom of humankind, on the other hand, is destined to pass away without a trace. Therefore, what point is there in striving to alter the face of this earth, since it will not survive? Only God's work will endure.

For Augustine the earthly city is created by self-love and with contempt for God, whereas the city of God, or heavenly city, is created by the love of God and has contempt for self. The earthly city glories in itself; the heavenly city glories in the Lord. The earthly city lusts for domination; the heavenly city seeks to serve others. The earthly city operates according to human standards; the heavenly city fulfills the will of God. The earthly city is destined for eternal punishment; the heavenly city is destined to reign with God for all eternity. The earthly city is begotten from Cain; the heavenly city, from Abel. The earthly city is born of nature, like Ishmael; the heavenly city is born of promise, like Isaac. And the earthly city is divided against itself; the heavenly city enjoys eternal and perfect peace (*City of God*, XIV, 28—XV, 1-5).

This is not to say that the parallels are always clear and consistent. Thus, Augustine sometimes writes of the earthly city as if it had two aspects itself: one good and one evil: "One part of the earthly city has been made into an image of the Heavenly City, by symbolizing something other than itself, namely that other City; and for that reason it is a servant. For it was established not for its own sake but in order to symbolize another City . . ." (XV, 2). The evil part, in turn, is divided against itself as were Remus and Romulus, ". . . for this is how Rome was founded, when Remus, as Roman history witnesses, was slain by his brother Romulus. The difference from the primal crime was that both brothers were citizens of the earthly city" (XV, 5).

An even more pronounced identification of the Kingdom of God and the Church is found in the succeeding centuries in such writings as those of Pope Gregory the Great, who interpreted Luke 9:27 ("I assure you, there are some standing here who will not taste death until they see the reign of God") to apply to the Church, which is opposed to the "power and glory" of the world.

Once the Franks came to power in the West, this ecclesiastical interpretation of the Kingdom of God was fully *politicized*. Charlemagne was the new David who had taken over the reins of royal lordship in the Church, allowing the pope the role of Moses at prayer (see his *Letter to Leo III*), while remaining himself the sovereign who shared in the reign of Christ and of God. This same notion was one of the inspirations of the Crusades and was used to justify the investiture of bishops by kings.

Apocalyptic notions were then added to the political. The kingdom of the Franks along with that of the Romans was regarded as the "third kingdom" mentioned in the seventh chapter of Daniel, following the kingdoms of the Greeks and the Persians. Thus, the world awaited a last ruler to restore the empire to its glory and lay down his crown in Jerusalem, before the coming of the Antichrist. The most direct opposition to this imperial notion of the Kingdom of God was formulated by Pope Boniface VIII's bull, *Unam Sanctam* (1303), in which he declared that the pope alone has supreme authority over the whole world.

Joachim of Fiore (d. 1202) was the principal source of yet another interpretation of the Kingdom in the medieval period. He divided history into three great periods: (1) the age of the Father (the time of the Old Testament when the human community lived under the Law); (2) the age of the Son (the time of the New Testament and for forty-two generations of about thirty years each, or until the year 1260, during which the human community lived under grace); and (3) the age of the Spirit, in which there would be new religious orders leading to the conversion of the world and the establishment of a spiritual church. Some carried Joachim's vision to extremes—e.g., the Spiritual Franciscans, who saw Francis of Assisi as the "angel with the sign of the living God" ushering in the age of the Spirit, and the Fraticelli, who regarded themselves as the new order of spiritual men foretold by Joachim. This view of the Kingdom persisted well into the Middle Ages and would influence some of the Protestant sects at the margin of the Reformation movement—e.g., Bohemian Brethren and the Anabaptists.

Dominican *mysticism*—e.g., Meister Eckhart, Tauler, Suso—saw the Kingdom of God as "God himself with all his riches" in the depths of the soul, but this notion coexisted with the more ecclesiastical and political interpretations put forth by Martin Bucer (d. 1551), Tommaso Campanella (d. 1639), and Thomas More (d. 1535) in his *Utopia* (1516).

Luther's doctrine of the two kingdoms rejected both the sectarian interpretations as well as the grand theocratic understanding of the Kingdom as proposed by some Catholics. God's reign is essentially invisible and spiritual. The law is the affair of the secular powers. The Church is concerned only with the preaching of the Gospel. Salvation is through faith, not works. The two kingdoms "must be sharply distinguished," he wrote ("Secular Authority: To What Extent It Should Be Obeyed," in *Martin Luther: Selections From His Writings*, John Dillenberger, ed., New York: Doubleday Anchor, 1961, p. 371). The one kingdom produces piety; the other brings about external peace and prevents evil deeds. Each needs the other. Without piety, there is only hypocrisy. Without law, however, evil is given free reign. (For an understanding of Protestant thought on this question as it developed in the United States from its beginnings, see H. Richard

Niebuhr, *The Kingdom of God in America*, New York: Harper & Row, 1937.)

By the eighteenth century, and particularly under the impact of the *Enlightenment*, the Kingdom of God was once again perceived not only as an earthly reality but even as the product of human initiative and effort. It comes about through the establishment of human society according to moral principles. Immanuel Kant defined the Kingdom as an "ethical commonwealth" (*Religion Within the Limits of Pure Reason Alone*). Other philosophical interpretations were placed upon it. Hegel, for example, saw it as the final manifestation of the spirit in which it becomes fully conscious of itself. It is the completion and perfection of history. The same evolutionary and historical understanding shaped the thinking of Karl Marx and then, in the twentieth century, of the Marxist philosopher Ernst Bloch (d. 1977) who inspired much of the "theology of hope" movement in Europe in the 1960s. The future now becomes decisive. *Praxis* replaces reflection, or theory. We are called to participate in the struggle to bring the future kingdom into the present, to narrow the gap between justice and injustice, freedom and oppression. But in none of these views is the sovereignty of God the "incalculable and impenetrable irruption of grace in love" (Peter Hünermann, "Reign of God," *The Concise Sacramentum Mundi*, p. 1356). The Kingdom of God becomes equivalently the kingdom of humankind. It was against this Liberal (i.e., anti-transcendental) interpretation that modern biblical scholarship reacted, as we shall see in the next section (on twentieth-century biblical theology).

At the same time, other interpretations of the Kingdom of God from within the churches adhered to a less historical, more *"spiritual "* line. Thus, for Blaise Pascal (d. 1662) the Kingdom was the order of charity which takes us out of ourselves, and the realm where we experience the forgiveness of sins and the friendship of God. With the rise of the Tübingen School in Germany (see chapter 25), the Kingdom of God becomes "the idea of Christianity which contains and produces all others" (e.g., J. S. Drey, *Introduction to the Study of Theology*). J. B. Hirscher took it to be the "basic idea" for Christian moral theology. Entrance is gained by conversion, and the Kingdom itself is the rule of God in every realm of life.

Twentiety-Century Biblical Theology

Futurist Eschatology: The Kingdom as Future

There is a sense in which it can be said that modern New Testament scholarship begins with the debate about the eschatological question. Over against the dominant nineteenth-century Liberal Protestant view that the Kingdom of God is an earthly reality produced by human hands (Albrecht Ritschl, d. 1889), New Testament exegetes like Albert Schweitzer (d. 1965) and Johannes Weiss (d. 1914) argued that the disciples were to pray for the coming of the Kingdom but that neither they nor we could do anything to establish it. Not even Jesus could do that. When the Kingdom comes, God will destroy this old order which is ruled and spoiled by the devil and will create a completely new world (see Johannes Weiss, *Jesus' Proclamation of the Kingdom of God*, Philadelphia: Fortress Press, 1971; originally published in 1892). A more recent expression of this school of thought, known as *futurist (or consequent, consistent, or thorough-going) eschatology*, is offered by Martin Werner. The irruption of the Kingdom, he argues, signified for Jesus the end of the present natural world. The Kingdom, therefore, was in no sense a present reality. It is always in the future, but imminent (*The Formation of Christian Dogma*, Boston: Beacon Press, 1965).

Realized Eschatology: The Kingdom As Past

Selecting a different set of New Testament passages, the British scholar Charles H. Dodd (d. 1973) argued that "in the earliest tradition Jesus was understood to have proclaimed that the Kingdom of God, the hope of many generations, had at last come. It is not merely imminent; it is here. . . . The *eschaton* has moved from the future to the present, from the sphere of expectation into that of realized experience" (*The Parables of the Kingdom*, London: Collins/Fontana, 1963, pp. 40-41; originally published in 1935). For Dodd, however, the challenge of the Kingdom is a challenge for individuals and for the immediate situation, for "Jesus passed directly from the immediate situation to the eternal order lying beyond all history" (p. 154). History moves by crisis, not by evolution. The Church proclaims the Gospel of the Kingdom that each might experience the "hour of decision" that Jesus brought (p. 152). The school of "realized eschatology" assumes, therefore, that "history in the individual life is of the same stuff as history at large; that is, it is significant in so far as it serves to bring men face to face with God in his Kingdom, power and glory." (See also Joachim Jeremias, *The Parables of Jesus*, New York: Charles Scribner's Sons, 1955.)

Existentialist Eschatology: The Kingdom As Present

For Rudolf Bultmann (d. 1976) the Kingdom of God is a new mode of existential existence, for ". . . the question of God and the question of myself are identical" (*Jesus Christ and Mythology*, London: SCM Press, 1958, p. 53). The living God encounters us here and now in the Word, i.e., in the preaching instituted by Jesus Christ. "The idea of the omnipresent and almighty God becomes real in my personal existence only by His Word spoken here and now" (p. 79). The decisive significance of Jesus Christ is that he—in his person, his coming, his passion, and his glorification—is the eschatological event. That event happens here and now in the preaching of the Word regardless of whether this Word is accepted or rejected (p. 81). "It is only in the light of the proclaimed word that what has happened or is happening here or there assumes the character of God's action for the believer" (p. 85). Our relation to the world remains paradoxical. It is our world, but it is really God's. We must live as if it is not ours at all.

This highly existential, present-oriented, and anti-political understanding of the Kingdom is even more explicitly developed in *Jesus and the Word* (London: Collins/Fontana, 1958; originally published in 1934). The Kingdom of God is "no ideal social order" (p. 78). Jesus paid no apparent attention to the social and economic conditions of his time. "*No programme for world-reformation is derived from the will of God*" (p. 79). Instead, every person stands under the judgment of God at this moment. The decision is against the world and for God. Every claim of one's own is to be silenced. "The *real* future stands before man in decision, not the false future over which he already has control, but the future which will give him a character which he does not yet have" (p. 96).

Salvation-History Eschatology: The Kingdom As Past, Present, and Future

Directly opposed to Bultmann's existentialist interpretation is Oscar Cullmann's notion of salvation history. The Kingdom of God has its beginning at creation, reaches its zenith or midpoint in Jesus Christ, and will be brought to completion at the *Parousia*, or Second Coming. We live now "between-the-times," i.e., between the first and second comings of Christ. This is also "church-time." The mission of the Church is to recall what God has already accomplished in Christ, to focus the attention of the world on the events to come, and to make possible, here and now, a meeting with the Lord through the preaching of the Word and the celebration of the sacraments. What finally distinguishes Christian faith, therefore, from other views of reality is the Christian's conviction that history itself is salvific and that it moves with purpose and direction. Everything leads up to, and flows from, the central Christ-event (see *Christ and Time*, Philadelphia: Westminster Press, 1947).

In a later work he acknowledged the bitter dispute with Bultmann evoked by *Christ and Time*. Cullmann insists in his *Salvation in History* (New York: Harper & Row, 1967) that he agrees with Bultmann that the call to decision is essential to the New Testament faith. Where they disagree, he insists, is over Bultmann's exclusion of salvation history as if it were simply opposed to Christian existence as portrayed in the New Testament. Rather, we find both elements there: the call to decision and salvation history. "By our decision in faith we align ourselves with this very special history, salvation history... comprehending past, present, and future..." (p. 21).

Other contemporary biblical scholars who recognize the threefold temporal dimension of the Kingdom include Rudolf

Schnackenburg (*God's Rule and Kingdom*, 1963), Werner G. Küm-mel (*Promise and Fulfillment: The Eschatological Message of Jesus*, London: SCM Press, 1956), and Norman Perrin (*Jesus and the Language of the Kingdom*, Philadelphia: Fortress Press, 1976).

Twentieth-Century Systematic Theology

Catholic Theologians

Karl Rahner: The Kingdom of God and the Church are not one and the same. The Church is the sacrament of the Kingdom in the "eschatological phase of sacred history which began with Christ, the phase which brings about the kingdom of God" ("Church and World," *The Concise Sacramentum Mundi*, p. 239). The Kingdom will not be definitively present until history ends with the Second Coming of Christ and the last judgment. On the other hand, the Kingdom is not something totally in the future. It is already coming to be in the history of the world, wherever obedience to God occurs in grace as the acceptance of God's self-communica-tion. But this does not take place solely in the Church nor solely in the personal inwardness of conscience, but in the concrete fulfill-ment of an earthly task, of active love of others, even of collective love of others.

All of this follows from basic Catholic principles: (1) that grace and justification are to be found also outside the Church; (2) that there is an inseparable unity between material and formal morality, between action and intention; and (3) that there is a fundamental unity between love of God and love of neighbor. This Kingdom is manifested in the "unity, activity, fraternity, etc., of the *world*" (p. 240).

Is the Kingdom the work of God, or the product of human effort? Rahner argues that this question can be answered only dialectically, i.e., by holding in balance two apparently opposed principles: (1) the Kingdom of God will come about at the end of history as an action of God; and (2) human history enters somehow into that endpoint. Thus, human history has ultimate validity, and yet it will undergo radical transformation. These two propositions remain unresolved and so must remain dialectically related in order to keep the future open (God will give the Kingdom when God wills) and to allow the present to keep its basic importance (human effort somehow enters into God's final act). What is permanent in history is the concrete work of love.

Why can it be said that history enters into God's own fullness? "Because the Word of God has himself both made and endured history" ("Christianity and the new earth," *Theology Digest*, 15, Winter 1967, p. 281). Rahner's notion of the Kingdom, therefore, is rooted in the basic Catholic principle of sacramentality, centered in the incarnation.

Edward Schillebeeckx: Schillebeeckx notes that one of the first changes effected by the Second Vatican Council was its abandoning of the earlier tendency to identify the Church too easily with the Kingdom of God. The council also acknowledged the presence of saving grace outside the Church. For Schillebeeckx the Church and the world are on the way to the Kingdom, but are not yet the Kingdom. The powers of the Kingdom, however, are already actively present in the Church and in the world at large. It is, in fact, our common hope in the radically new and final Kingdom that stimulates us never to rest satisfied with what has already been achieved in this world. Historically, we can never say that *this* is the promised future. The Gospel message calls us always to overcome the limitations of the present. It contains a permanent criticism of the present: institutions, structures, mentalities. It urges constant improvement. "Eschatological hope makes the commitment to the temporal order *radical* and by the same token declares any already existing temporal order to be only relative. Thus the Christian's social and political commitment, rooted in his care for mankind, is the hermeneutic of what in Revelation the Kingdom of God's promise implies" (*God the Future of Man*, New York: Sheed & Ward, 1968, p. 161).

For Schillebeeckx, the Kingdom of God is "the divine power itself in its saving activity within our history, but at the same time the final, eschatological state of affairs that brings to an end the evil world, dominated by the forces of calamity and woe, and initiates the new world in which God 'appears to full advantage'; 'your kingdom come' (Matthew 6:10)" (*Jesus: An Experiment in*

Christology, New York: Seabury Press, 1979, p. 141). Thus, present and future are essentially interrelated.

God's Lordship is God's mode of being God. God is shown as a loving and caring God who is mindful of humanity (Titus 3:4). The Kingdom of God is our well-being. To surrender to the Lordship of God is to love the other, to work for the other's well-being. "Man's caring for his fellow-men is the visible form and aspect in which the coming of God's kingdom is manifested; it is the way God's Lordship takes" (p. 153). In its fullness, therefore, Jesus' message of the Kingdom is that we must love one another as God loves us, and he (Jesus) discloses this in and through his own mode of conduct, i.e., his *praxis* of the Kingdom. Jesus brings the message that God says "No" to the continuing course of human suffering, to all forms of hunger and poverty, and that the purpose of life and history is "peace, laughter, total satisfaction: the 'final good' of salvation and happiness. . . . Showing mercy is, despite everything, the deepest purpose that God intends to fulfill in history" (p. 177).

Jesus is the sacrament of God's universal love for us. He is "God translated" for us. Jesus shows us a "most human God" (*Deus humanissimus*). "The cause of God as the cause of man is personified in the very person of Jesus Christ. . . . He is the firstborn and 'the leader' of a new mankind in that he has lived out proleptically in his own experience, the praxis of the kingdom of God and because that praxis has been endorsed by God" (p. 670).

Hans Küng: In the light of modern exegesis, Küng asserts, it is impossible to speak of the Church as the Kingdom of God on earth, nor does the Church build up the Kingdom. The Kingdom is *God's* Kingdom. "Man's part is the way of readiness and openness, obedience and watchfulness, faith and repentance" (*The Church*, New York: Sheed & Ward, 1968, p. 92). The Church is the work of humanity; the Kingdom is the work of God. It is not the Church but the Kingdom which is the goal of creation. To belong to the Church is no guarantee of entrance into the Kingdom. The Church is the anticipatory sign of the Kingdom. The Church moves always toward the Kingdom as its goal. It does not bring the Kingdom; it announces it. God alone brings about the Kingdom; the Church is devoted entirely to its service.

Thus, the Kingdom is not merely God's continuing rule, existing from the moment of creation, but is that which is promised for the future. It is not a religio-political theocracy or democracy, but the immediate, unrestricted rule of God over the world, to be awaited without recourse to violence. It is not for an elite but is the glad tidings of God's infinite goodness and unconditional grace, particularly for the abandoned and the destitute. It is not constructed by human effort but is an act of God. It will, therefore, be a Kingdom of "absolute righteousness, of unsurpassable freedom, of dauntless love, of universal reconciliation, of everlasting peace" (*On Being a Christian*, New York: Doubleday, 1976, p. 215). Just as a false interiorizing of the Kingdom once had to be avoided, so a false secularizing of the Kingdom now is to be avoided. In language close to Bultmann's, Küng insists that our situation is critical. We are "pressed to make a final decision, to accept the offer to commit [ourselves] *to the reality of God*, which is ahead....It is a decision in which everything is at stake: an either-or, for or against God" (p. 225).

Walter Kasper: A similar approach is taken by Walter Kasper. The Kingdom of God is "totally and exclusively God's doing. It cannot be earned by religious or moral effort, imposed by political struggle, or projected in calculation. We cannot plan for it, organize it, make it or build it, we cannot invent or imagine it. It is given (Matthew 21:43, Luke 12:32), 'appointed' (Luke 22:29). We can only inherit it (Matthew 25:34)" (*Jesus the Christ*, New York: Paulist Press, 1976, p. 81). This is not to say that we can do nothing at all in relation to the Kingdom. We are not condemned to Quietism or pure passivity. "What is demanded of us is repentance and faith (Mark 1:15 and parallels)." It means ceasing to rely on one's own capabilities, admitting human powerlessness. It means expecting nothing from oneself and everything from God.

With an explicitly Hegelian flavor, Kasper insists that God's divinity consists in God's self-giving, or God's entering into the other without losing "himself." Indeed, "...he is himself precisely when he enters into that which is other than himself. It is by surrendering himself that he shows his divinity. Concealment is therefore the way in which God's glory is revealed in the world" (p. 83). Jesus' message announces that the "ultimate source and meaning of all reality is now becoming a reality in a new and final form. The final decision about the meaning of reality is now being made. With the entry of the Kingdom of God the world enters into salvation."

Johannes Metz: If Küng and Kasper emphasize the role of God in the coming of the Kingdom, Johannes Metz stresses the role of human effort in the political realm.

Christian theology veered too far in an existentialist, personalist, indeed *privatized* direction under the influence of Rudolf Bultmann, Metz argues. The future dimension was all but lost, and so, too, the critical function of theology. "Modern man" no longer experiences the world as an imposed fate, but rather as raw material which has to be shaped and directed into something greater. Christian faith is guided by hope, a "crucified hope for the world." Such a hope is "an initiative for the passionate innovating and changing of the world toward the Kingdom of God" (*Theology of the World*, New York: Herder & Herder, 1969, p. 93). The Church exists within that world as that part of the world which calls the world in question when it takes itself with ultimate seriousness. "The eschatological City of God is *now* coming into existence, for our hopeful approach *builds* this city. We are workers building this future, and not just interpreters of this future. . . . The Christian is a 'co-worker' in bringing the promised universal era of peace and justice. The orthodoxy of a Christian's faith must constantly *make itself* true in the 'orthopraxy' of his actions orientated toward the final future, because the promised *truth* is a truth which must be *made* (see John 3:21ff.)" (pp. 94-95).

Metz rejects, therefore, an eschatology like Bultmann's which focuses on the "making present" of the Kingdom in the moment of personal decision, and also the eschatology of Weiss, Werner, and others, which makes life in this world a time of waiting until God brings about the Kingdom. Metz's eschatology is the basis of a *political theology*, a theology of the emerging social and political order. Political theology, therefore, is "a positive attempt to formulate the eschatological message under the conditions of our present society" (p. 107). It is theology which attends always to the relation between theory and practice, between understanding the faith and social practice.

Gustavo Gutierrez: A similarly strong emphasis on the social and political dimension of the Kingdom is given in Latin American liberation theology. Gustavo Gutierrez warns against a spiritualizing of the reality of the Kingdom. It is "inevitably historical, temporal, earthly, social, and material" (*A Theology of Liberation*, Maryknoll, N.Y.: Orbis Books, 1973, p. 167). The prophets announced a kingdom of peace, but peace presupposes justice. It presupposes the defense of the rights of the poor, punishment of the oppressors, liberation from oppression. The struggle for justice *is* the struggle for the Kingdom of God (p. 168). On the other hand, the Kingdom of God "must not be confused with the establishment of a just society" (p. 231).

The proclamation of the Kingdom, Gutierrez writes, opens up new horizons and leads us to see unsuspected dimensions and to pursue unexplored paths. Only within a commitment to liberation and in solidarity with the oppressed can we understand the meaning of the Kingdom and the implications of the Gospel message (p. 269). The alleviation of poverty and oppression is not identical with the Kingdom, but poverty and oppression are certainly incompatible with the Kingdom of love and justice (p. 295).

And this was the vision of Jesus as well. Misery and social injustice reveal a "sinful situation," a disintegration of community. By freeing us from sin, Jesus attacks the roots of an unjust social order. "Far from showing no interest in...liberation, Jesus rather placed it on a deeper level, with far reaching consequences" (p. 231). Jesus' announcement of the Kingdom is subversive because it heralds the end of domination of human beings over human beings. In preaching the universal love of the Father, Jesus inevitably preached against all injustice, privilege, oppression, and narrow nationalism (p. 232).

Protestant Theologians

Paul Tillich (d. 1965):   The entire fifth part of Tillich's *Systematic Theology* is devoted to the Kingdom of God and its relation to history. For Tillich, the Kingdom is the answer to the ambiguities of history. It has both an inner-historical and transhistorical side. "As inner-historical, it participates in the dynamics of history; as transhistorical, it answers the questions implied in the ambiguities of the dynamics of history" (*Systematic Theology*, vol. III, Chicago: University of Chicago Press, 1963, p. 357).

The first connotation of the Kingdom symbol is *political*, in that it is a manifestation of the power of God. The second characteristic is *social*, since there is no holiness without justice. The third element is *personal*, in that the Kingdom gives eternal meaning to the individual person. And the fourth characteristic is its *universality*, in that it is the fulfillment of all life and not only of human life.

The appearance of Jesus as the Christ is the historical event in which history becomes aware of itself and of its meaning. This is the central manifestation of the Kingdom (pp. 368-369). The churches represent the Kingdom of God but are not themselves identical with it (pp. 376-377). As for individuals, ". . . one cannot reach the transcendent Kingdom of God without participating in the struggle of the inner-historical Kingdom of God" (p. 392). The Kingdom is already present. We stand now in the face of the eternal. But we do so looking ahead toward the end of history and the end of all that is temporal in the eternal (p. 396).

Jürgen Moltmann: The Kingdom of God is a symbol for the "comprehensive Christian horizon of life" (*The Church in the Power of the Spirit*, New York: Harper & Row, 1977, p. 134). It requires conversion to the God of the future, and it brings liberation from the godless and inhuman relationships of this world. The Kingdom of God, therefore, is the "eschatological fulfillment of the liberating lordship of God in history" (p. 190). It is both the actual rule of God in the world and the universal goal of that divine rule. It is thus at once present and future. As present, it is relevant to our earthly concerns. As future, it cannot be identified with anything in history. It draws us into history and beyond history.

Through his own mission and resurrection Jesus has brought the Kingdom into history. It has become the power of the future which determines the present. We can already live in the light of the "new era" in the circumstances of the "old" one. "Since the eschatological becomes historical in this way, the historical also becomes eschatological" (p. 192). Moltmann calls this "messianic mediation." The Lordship of Christ points beyond itself to the Kingdom of God.

The presence of the Holy Spirit puts the new creation into force. Past, present, and future are brought together: "Just as the messianic era stands under the token of the 'not yet', so it also stands under the sign of 'no longer' and therefore under the sign of 'already'....The dreams of hope lead to the pains of love" (p. 193). The Kingdom of God is the goal of history in the midst of history (p. 196).

The Church in the Power of the Spirit, in effect, broadens the horizon of Moltmann's earlier, and better known, *Theology of Hope* (New York: Harper & Row, 1967, pp. 325-338). Since the Kingdom has not yet come, everything is to be called into question which already identifies itself with the Kingdom. The Church is called to engage in the historic transformation of life into the Kingdom of righteousness, peace, freedom, and humanity. Its mission is shaped by its expectation of the coming Kingdom. To disclose to the world "the horizon of the future of the crucified Christ is the task of the Christian Church" (p. 338).

Wolfhart Pannenberg: Pannenberg defines the Kingdom of God variously as "that perfect society of men which is to be realized in history by God himself," as "the utterly concrete reality of justice and love," and as "the destiny of present society" (*Theology and the Kingdom of God*, Philadelphia: Westminster Press, 1969, pp. 76, 79, and 84). It is the rule, or sovereignty, of God; its principal effect is unity among humankind. That is why Jesus explained the will of God by the commandment of love. But it is not a purely interpersonal love. There is no dualism of religion and society, of love and justice. "Subjective behavior is related always to social institutions.... Obviously, then, the Kingdom of God is pointedly political" (pp. 79-80). Our present world, with its wars, injustices, and brutalities, demonstrates the gap between itself and the Kingdom of God. God's Kingdom has not yet come in all its fullness. No present form of life or society is ultimate. But this situation need not lead to political paralysis. "The future of the Kingdom releases a dynamic in the present that again and again kindles the vision of man and gives meaning to his fervent quest for the political forms of justice and love" (p. 80).

Harvey Cox: Much less emphatic about the *coming* character of the Kingdom and much more insistent on its this-wordly, socio-political dimension is Harvey Cox's *The Secular City* (New York: Macmillan, 1965). Close to the tradition of the Social Gospel Movement, which tended to identify the Kingdom with social and political reform (see Walter Rauschenbusch, *A Theology for the Social Gospel*, New York: Abingdon Press, 1945, pp. 131-145), Cox refers to the Kingdom as "the fullest possible disclosure of the partnerhsip of God and man in history" (p. 112). It is present in history, offering us "an objectively new social situation" and providing us an "occasion within which we are summoned to discard the old and take up something different" (p. 113).

Cox identifies himself thereby with those Protestant sectarians who have worked for the transformation of society: the Anabaptists, Congregationalists, Quakers, and others. "The mainline Reformers," he argues, "never developed a viable theology for social change, one of the most nagging needs of the modern church" (*The Secular City Debate*, Daniel Callahan, ed., New York: Macmillan, 1967, p. 193). Cox agrees, however, that the sectarians sometimes identified the marks of the Kingdom too quickly. Theologians like Reinhold Niebuhr were right in criticizing this tendency. But we may have gone too far in the opposite direction. "In guarding the Kingdom of God from ideological perversion, we rendered it politically irrelevant" (p. 194).

Reinhold Niebuhr (d. 1971): It was Reinhold Niebuhr more than any other Protestant theologian who challenged both the Liberal equation of Kingdom and "secular city" and the progressive view of history upon which the equation was often based. It is not that history is static or that we have no tasks and obligations within it. Niebuhr insists, however, that grace is related to nature partly as fulfillment and partly as negation. "If the contradiction between 'nature' and 'grace' is not recognized, and the continued power of 'nature' in the realm of 'grace' is not conceded, new sins are brought into history by the pretension that sin has been progressively eliminated" (*The Nature and Destiny of Man*, vol. 2, New York; Charles Scribner's Sons, 1943, pp. 245-246).

"Nature" here represents "the historical possibilities of justice," and "grace" represents the "ideal possibility of perfect love....[in] the complete obedience of all wills to the will of God" (p. 246). Thus, the relation between historical justice and the love of the Kingdom of God is dialectical. "Love is both the fulfillment and the negation of all achievements of justice in history. Or expressed from the opposite standpoint, the achievements of justice in history may rise in indeterminate degrees to find their fulfillment in a more perfect love and brotherhood; but each new level of fulfillment also contains elements which stand in contradiction to perfect love." We are bound to bring about justice in indeterminate degrees, but we can never achieve the perfection of justice within history. "Sanctification in the realm of social relations demands recognition of the impossibility of perfect sanctification" (p. 247).

The Kingdom, or sovereignty, of God, therefore, has the same two relations as eternity has to time. "It is on the one hand the authority of the source of life over all life at any moment. It is on the other hand a sovereignty which is finally vindicated in 'the end' " (p. 300, n. 1). History after Christ is an 'interim between the disclosure of its true meaning and the fulfillment of that meaning....Sin is overcome in principle but not in fact. Love must continue to be suffering love rather than triumphant love. The distinction," he argues, "becomes a basic category of interpreting history in all profound versions of the Christian faith..." (p. 49).

The spirit of Niebuhr influenced even such activist Christians as Martin Luther King, Jr., who acknowledged that Niebuhr helped him to "recognize the complexity of man's social involvement and the glaring reality of collective evil" as well as "the illusions of a superficial optimism concerning human nature and the dangers of false idealism" (*Stride Toward Freedom*, New York: Harper & Row, 1958, p. 81).

Anglican Theologians

John A. T. Robinson: The former bishop of Woolwich in South London is best known for his controversial *Honest to God* (1963). In an earlier and must less heralded piece in *The Historic Episcopate in the Fullness of the Church* (Kenneth M. Carey, ed., London: Dacre Press, 1960), Robinson argued that the Kingdom of God is "the controlling category of biblical theology for both Old and New Testaments" (p. 15). The whole constitution of the universe has been transformed through Christ, although the transformation still remains to be acknowledged and fulfilled in obedience. To see all reality, including the Church, always in subordination to the Kingdom is to view everything as situated between the two great moments of Christ's sovereignty over the world: the finished work of Calvary and the Second Coming in glory.

Eschatology, therefore, is not just the teaching about the "last things" but rather the teaching about the relation of all things to the "last things," or about the finality of things. The Christian lives not *at* the end of time, but rather *from* the end and *in* the end. Everything is seen from an eschatological perspective, and every moment is, in turn, an eschatological moment. "What the Christian faith provides is not a blue-print for the future of man....Its assurance rests in the fact that the whole of life is *response*, that the initiative—whether in the Beginning or the End—does not lie with us. It speaks of an evocation, a trust, an endurance, by which, in freedom, men find themselves impelled and drawn on. It points to those whose whole way of life betokens a 'beyond' that will not let them rest..." (*In the End God*, New York: Harper & Row, 1968, p. 139).

John Macquarrie: The Kingdom of God is "the full manifestation of the holiness of Being" (*Principles of Christian Theology*, New York: Charles Scribner's Sons, 1977, 2nd. ed., p. 369). It will issue forth in "a commonwealth of free beings, united in Being and with each other through love...." The Kingdom, although not to be identified with the Church, is already present in history. Macquarrie rejects both the extremes of a Liberalism which exaggerates human effort in the coming of the Kingdom, and of an apocalypticism which makes the Kingdom totally otherworldly. But his concern is directed perhaps more strongly against the former: "It is God who is the author of the kingdom, and it is his grace that is realizing it, albeit with the free cooperation of human beings. And while the eschatological interpretation may seem to become otherworldly in placing the kingdom beyond history, it is only being realistic. It is utopian and foolish to suppose that the kingdom could be realized on earth, though on the other hand it is not foolish to strive toward its increasing realization..." (p. 370). He returns to this point: "The eschatological consummation of the kingdom of God is a mystery to be realized by the movement of Being, not by creaturely striving, even if this makes an indispensable contribution. We delude ourselves if we think that some ideal state of affairs is attainable on earth, or that the main business of Christianity is to establish a super welfare state" (p. 519).

Norman Pittenger: Norman Pittenger is, as we have noted in chapter 14, a theologian of the process school of thought. God works in the world, Pittenger argues against the traditional eschatology, by providing "initial aims" for each occasion or event or occurrence or "entity." God's "power" is persuasion. God is present to history as a "lure" (Whitehead's term), not as a coercive force. For the Christian, Christ is the disclosure of what God is up to in the world. Talk about the "last things" is not talk about something that will happen only in the future, after death; rather, it is talk about us as we now live, in this world and with this world's responsibilities as well as its privileges.

Our purpose in life is to be the personalized instruments of cosmic Love. Everything we are and do has to be understood in light of that purpose. Thus, death reminds us that we are mortal and have only a relatively short time to contribute to humankind. Judgment means that we are what our decisions have made us. They cannot be undone. Heaven is the sheer joy of relationship with God and with one another. Hell is the absence of God. It is always and only a possibility—a possibility of rejecting God in freedom. But God's action surrounds us with love, and we respond in love. "The Lord came from God precisely in order to love, in order to be the humanly visible instrument of the divine charity. Christian theology... is nothing other than the explication and application of what that statement *means*" (*"The Last Things" in a Process Perspective,* London: Epworth Press, 1970, p. 105).

Orthodox Theology

John Meyendorff: The Kingdom of God is not one of the major categories of Orthodox theology (see the index of John

Meyendorff's *Byzantine Theology: Historical Trends and Doctrinal Themes*, New York: Fordham University Press, 1974). Where it is mentioned, it is linked always with the Holy Spirit, which is its "content" (p. 169). The prayer "Thy Kingdom come" is understood as "May Thy Holy Spirit come upon us and cleanse us." The Byzantine liturgical tradition addresses the Holy Spirit as "Heavenly King." The Spirit is the firstfruits of the eschatological transfiguration of creation. If salvation is understood essentially in terms of *participation* in, and *communion* with, the deified humanity of the incarnate Logos, it is the Spirit who makes this possible (p. 171). On the other hand, nowhere except in the *sacraments* can we achieve the "truly liberating divine life. . . . The Kingdom to come is already realized in the sacraments, but each individual Christian is called to grow into it, by exercising his own efforts and by using his own God-given freedom with the cooperation of the Spirit" (p. 176). But those efforts are not of a political or even ethical nature. They are part of the process toward "perfection" and "holiness."

Eschatology, however, qualifies the whole of Orthodox theology (p. 218). Everything is viewed in relation to the end, to our destiny in God. But that future reality is also a present experience, accessible in Christ through the gifts of the Spirit. Orthodox eschatology is a realized eschatology. The movement of humankind towards its goal is a mystical movement, not an historical movement (p. 219). We are moving "from glory to glory," i.e., to the moment when we will be restored to our original stature, which has been corrupted by sin and death. This will be the resurrection of the flesh.

Significantly, the last things (Second Coming, cosmic transfiguration, resurrection, and judgment) "are not subjects of detailed speculation by Byzantine theologians; yet they stand at the very center of Byzantine liturgical experience" (p. 220).

Official Teachings of the Church

Nowhere has the Kingdom of God been defined by the official magisterium, nor has any official position been taken regarding the

precise relationship between the divine and the human, the transcendental and the immanent, the spiritual and the political in the
Kingdom of God. One has to infer a doctrinal position from the
explicit teachings on grace, Original Sin, and Jesus Christ (see
chapters 4, 5, and 13).

Second Vatican Council

The most explicit conciliar declaration on the meaning of the
Kingdom was given by the Second Vatican Council (1965) in its
Pastoral Constitution on the Church in the Modern World. It
describes the Kingdom variously as "the consummation of the
earth and of humanity," "a new dwelling place and a new earth
where justice will abide, and whose blessedness will answer and
surpass all the longings for peace which spring up in the human
heart," a "new age," and as a reality "of truth and life, of holiness
and grace, of justice, love, and peace" (n. 39). That Kingdom is
already growing on this earth, but it is present only in mystery, i.e.,
sacramentally.

What are some of the signs of God's growing rule? The
nurturing on earth of the values of "human dignity, brotherhood
and freedom, and indeed all the good fruits of our nature and
enterprise," which we shall find again at the end, "but freed of
stain, burnished and transfigured."

To what extent is human effort incorporated into, or necessary for, the Kingdom of God? Although the Kingdom will be
given in the end by God, ". . . the expectation of a new earth must
not weaken but rather stimulate our concern for cultivating this
one. For here grows the body of a new human family, a body which
even now is able to give some kind of foreshadowing of the new
age." Accordingly, "Earthly progress must be carefully distinguished from the growth of Christ's kingdom. Nevertheless, to the
extent that the former can contribute to the better ordering of
human society, it is of vital concern to the Kingdom of God."

This same Kingdom was at the center of Jesus' own proclamation, and he revealed it to humankind in his word, his works,
and his presence (*Dogmatic Constitution on the Church*, n. 5).
Although the council describes the Church as the "initial budding

forth" of the Kingdom, the Church nonetheless must strain toward the consummation of the Kingdom at history's end. The whole of human history meanwhile is moving toward the same final goal, which it will reach "in the Holy City, whose light shall be the glory of God, when the nations will walk in his light" (*Declaration on the Relationship of the Church to Non-Christian Religions*, n. 1). Human solidarity and all human activity will attain their final destiny therein (*Pastoral Constitution*, nn. 32, 39). For Christ is both the beginning and the end of all creation (n. 45). And so the "final stage of time has already come upon us (see 1 Corinthians 10:11). The renewal of the world is irrevocably determined and, in some real manner, it is anticipated in the present era..." (*Dogmatic Constitution on the Church*, n. 48).

Pope Paul VI, *Evangelii Nuntiandi*

This Apostolic Exhortation, *On Evangelization in the Modern World* (1975), acknowledges at the outset that the whole mission of Jesus is summed up in his own declaration that he was sent to proclaim the good news of the Kingdom of God (Luke 4:43), and in a particular way to the poor (Luke 4:18; Isaiah 61:1). Jesus' evangelizing activities, however, were not restricted to verbal proclamation. Christ also proclaimed the Kingdom by "innumerable signs...: the sick are cured, water is changed into wine, bread is multiplied, the dead come back to life. And among these signs there is the one to which he attached great importance: the humble and the poor are evangelized..." (n. 12). Evangelization,therefore, consists also of "liberation from everything that oppresses man but...is above all liberation from sin and the Evil One..." (n. 9). However closely linked it is with human liberation, the Kingdom of God is not simply identical with it (n. 35). Some notions of liberation are, in fact, incompatible with the Gospel, and the Kingdom itself will not come about even through proper expressions of liberation, well-being, and human development alone.

This Kingdom, of course, is available to every human being "as grace and mercy," and yet each individual gains entrance "through a total interior renewal which the Gospel calls *meta-noia*; it is radical conversion, a profound change of mind and heart" (n. 10; see also n. 36). The Church itself comes into being as a community gathered in Jesus' name "in order to seek together the Kingdom, build it up and live it" (n. 13). This means that the Church's call to evangelization, i.e., to the proclamation of the good news of the Kingdom of God, is directed to its total mission. It is a proclamation in word, in sacrament, in witness, and in service.

THE LAST THINGS: THE DESTINY OF INDIVIDUALS
The Destiny of Each Individual: Death and Judgment
Death

Old Testament: Because of the ancient Hebrew concept of the human person as an *animated body* rather than as an incarnated spirit, death was perceived as a state in which the spirit had departed from the body. The deceased continued to exist in *Sheol* (the underworld, or the abode of the dead), but completely shorn of their human powers (Psalms 6:6; 30:10; 88:11; 115:17; Isaiah 38:11,18). Ideally, death comes in the fullnes of age to a person of undiminished powers (Genesis 25:8; Job 21:23-24; 29:18-20). Such a one dies easily and quickly and goes immediately down to *Sheol* (Job 21:13). Death is the natural end of the human person (2 Samuel 14:14), but it is the consequence of sin (Genesis 2-3). On occasion, there is an expression of hope that death is not terminal. In Psalm 16:10 the poet rejoices that Yahweh will not abandon him to *Sheol* ("the nether world") nor permit him to "undergo corruption." In Psalm 49:16 the poet is assured that God will redeem him from *Sheol*. Psalm 73:23-28 is even clearer. If Yahweh's promises and loving kindness are everlasting, then there must be some way in which the faithful Israelite will experience them. Only gradually, however, did this subordinate line of thought emerge as a more dominant force in the Israelite theology of death. Thus, there is no trace of a clear belief in the resurrection of the dead before the second century B.C., in Daniel (12:2).

New Testament: The New Testament is explicit and unequivocal about the origin of death: It is the consequence of sin and a punishment for it (Romans 5:12-14). Likewise in 1 Corinthians 15:22, Paul asserts that we all die in Adam, but rise to life in Christ. Indeed, Jesus overcame death by his own death (15:25-26). He has deprived death of its power (2 Timothy 1:10), rendering the devil, the lord of death, impotent (Hebrews 2:14). Death no longer has power over Christ (Romans 6:9), and so he rules over the living and the dead (14:9). The Christian experiences Jesus' victory over death by sharing in his death (6:2-11). To die with Christ is to live with him (6:8). We overcome death by being baptized into Christ (6:4) and by partaking of the Eucharist (John 6:50-51).

On the other hand, death is at once final and unique. There is no question of *reincarnation*: "...those who might wish to cross from here to you cannot do so, nor can anyone cross from your side to us" (Luke 16:26; see also John 9:4; 2 Corinthians 5:10; Galatians 6:10).

Official Teachings of the Church: At first the Church's eschatological vision centered on the Second Coming of Christ and the entrance of the whole Church into the final Kingdom. The individual received much less attention. The Middle Ages brought about a shift from the communal to the individual. Theologians focused on the moment of death as the key point at which individual destiny was to be decided.

Church documents on the subject of death and the afterlife are comparatively few in number. Since they belong for the most part to the Middle Ages, they also reflect an individual rather than a communal or ecclesial perspective. They deal primarily with the beatific vision and the resurrection of the individual body (as we shall see below). Not until the Second Vatican Council is there once again a fuller, more comprehensive statement on the reality of death and its universal significance.

Council of Trent (1546): Adam's sin not only involved a loss of holiness and justice but also brought death with it as a punishment. This punishment was applied not only to Adam but to all of his offspring. The council cites Romans 5:12 (*Decree on Original Sin,* Session V).

Second Vatican Council (1965): "It is in the face of death that the riddle of human existence becomes most acute....All the endeavors of technology, though useful in the extreme, cannot calm his [the individual's] anxiety" (*Pastoral Constitution on the Church in the Modern World*, n. 18). Only faith can overcome this anxiety. We have been "created by God for a blissful purpose beyond the reach of earthly misery." We are all called to an "endless sharing of a divine life beyond all corruption," and this was won for us by the death and resurrection of Christ. "Through Christ and in Christ, the riddles of sorrow and death grow meaningful. Apart from his gospel, they overwhelm us" (n. 22).

Congregation for the Doctrine of the Faith, "Letter on Certain Questions Concerning Eschatology" (May 1979): This document reaffirms the Church's traditional belief in the resurrection of the dead, the resurrection of the whole person, survival of the human self after death, the meaningfulness of prayers for the dead, the Second Coming and general judgment, the assumption of the Blessed Virgin Mary, and heaven, hell, and purgatory. The document also warns, however, against "arbitrary imaginative representations" of life after death and calls such excesses "a major cause of the difficulties that Christian faith often encounters." At the same time, the document encourages continued theological exploration of these issues.

Theological Reflections: All romantic, idealized versions of human life are brought low by the reality of death. More than anything else, death forces us to acknowledge the radical finitude of our existence. But this is not to say that death nullifies everything, rendering all life absurd and meaningless. On the contrary, death projects an ambiguous character. In spite of the certainty of death, we go on living with a deeply rooted conviction that life does make sense, or at least can make sense. Death itself can be an affirmative, even courageous act. An individual's life—not to say a nation's or a world's—can assume extraordinary significance by the manner in which death is faced. A person dies that another might live, as in the case of Maximilian Kolbe (d. 1941), the Polish priest who went to his death at Auschwitz to spare the life of a family man marked out for execution by the Nazis. The circumstances of a person's death, too, can be understood as in some way redeeming the blameworthy actions of his or her life, as in the case of Sydney Carton in Charles Dickens' *A Tale of Two Cities.*

Although theologians such as Karl Rahner and Ladislas Boros and scientists such as Elisabeth Kubler-Ross have attempted in recent years to illuminate the darkness surrounding this perennial mystery of death (see E. Kubler-Ross, *On Death and Dying*, New York: Macmillan, 1969; K. Rahner, *On the Theology of Death*, New York: Herder & Herder, 1961; and L. Boros, *The Mystery of Death*, New York: Herder & Herder, 1965), perhaps no one has substantially improved upon the fundamental insights of the existentialist philosopher Martin Heidegger (d. 1976). Death is the horizon that closes off the future. All human possibilities are seen in the context of death, because it brings into existence a responsibility and a seriousness that it could scarcely have had otherwise. Death, therefore, not only destroys; it brings some degree of unity and coherence and purpose into one's life. We shape and direct our lives with the certainty of future death in mind. We do not have unlimited time at our disposal. We have a certain amount of time, and everything has to be arranged in relation to that "deadline." Moreover, death exposes the superficiality and triviality of much of what we count as important and to which we dedicate so much of our resources and energies. In the face of death, things get put into perspective (see *Being and Time*, New York: Harper & Row, 1962, pp. 279-311).

For the Christian, of course, the death of Jesus is the model and norm of every human death. He accepted death in freedom. He could have escaped but did not. Moreover, only in death was he able to accomplish what he had proclaimed in life. In dying he made possible the release of the Holy Spirit as the firstfruits of the final Kingdom. Only in death did he reveal to others the ultimate seriousness of the claims of God. His whole existence was oriented toward his death, for he knew that a final conflict between the powers of this world and the Word of God was inevitable, and that this conflict would be played out in the conflict between the contemporary religious establishment and himself (see chapter 12). Such a death brought a wholeness (integrity) to his life, and so it can to ours.

Judgment

Old Testament: Judgment is both *defense* and *vindication* of Israel by Yahweh (Isaiah 1:27; 30:18) and also *punishment* (Ezekiel 5:7-15; 7:3-27; 16:38; 11:10; 24:13-14). Yahweh is also judge of the whole world (Psalms 7:8; 9:9-10; 96:13; 110:6; Genesis 18:25; 1 Samuel 2:10). The idea of the judgment of all nations is characteristic of apocalyptic literature (Joel 4:9-12; Daniel 7:9-11).

New Testament: In the Synoptics, judgment is often condemnation of sinners (e.g., Matthew 5:22; 23:33; Luke 12:58). In Paul such judgment is not only in the future (Romans 2:1-3,16; 3:5-6) but also in the past (Romans 5:16,18) and in the present (1 Corinthians 11:29,32). In any event, the judgment of God is unsearchable (Romans 11:33). In John the judgment is always in the present (3:18; 5:24; 12:31; 16:11). Hebrews looks to the resurrection of the dead and eternal judgment (6:2). It will not go well with those who were unfaithful (10:27; 13:4). Those who break the law, according to James, will be judged mercilessly (2:12-13), and so, too, will unfaithful teachers (3:1). On the other hand, we should be careful not to judge others (4:12; see also Matthew 7:1; Luke 6:37). God will judge the living and the dead (1 Peter 4:5), and that process will begin with the Church (4:17). In 2 Peter and Jude the judgment has an apocalyptic tone, comparable to the judgment of Sodom and Gomorrah (2 Peter 2:6,9; 3:7). This is even more explicit in Revelation, where judgment is the downfall of a world power (17:1—19:2). All will be judged in the end (11:18; 10:12-13).

Biblical belief, therefore, is that the judgment of God is final, that it is outside and beyond history, and that it is *the act by which evil is overcome once and for all.* On the other hand, the judgment also occurs even now in our acceptance or rejection of Christ and the Gospel (Matthew 25:31-46). In faith and hope the future judgment and salvation are already a reality (John 5:24; 12:31; 16:8). The Spirit is already given (Philippians 1:19; Romans 8:23), and the resurrection has already taken place (John 5:25;28; 2 Timothy 2:18).

Official Teachings of the Church: The *fact* of the final judgment is attested to throughout the history of the Church: In the *Apostles' Creed* ("... he shall come again to judge the living and the dead");

the *Nicene Creed* (325) ("He ascended to the heavens and shall come again to judge the living and the dead"); the *Nicene-Constantinopolitan Creed* (381) from the Council of Constantinople ("He shall come again in glory to judge the living and the dead..."); the so-called *Athanasian Creed* (end of the fifth century) ("...He shall come to judge the living and the dead"); the *Fourth Lateran Council* (1215), which added the words: "and to render to each one according to his works, to the reprobate as well as to the elect"; the *Second Council of Lyons* (1274), which said essentially the same thing as Lateran IV; the Constitution *Benedictus Deus* (1336) of Pope Benedict XII (d. 1342); and the *Council of Florence* (1439). The *Second Vatican Council* simply presumes this line of teaching (see the *Pastoral Constitution on the Church in the Modern World*, nn. 17 and 45).

Theological Reflections: One must distinguish always between the general judgment and the particular judgment. The *general judgment* applies to the consummation of the whole world and of history itself. It is connected with the Second Coming, or *Parousia*, of Christ. Because is affects all it is called the "general" judgment. Because it is the act which terminates history it is also called the "last" judgment. Everything in the first part of this chapter, on the Kingdom of God, is applicable to this general or last judgement.

The *particular judgment*, which is also the subject of the preceding biblical texts and of the official teachings of the Church, underscores the uniqueness and particularity of every human person before God. We are not simply part of some larger, impersonal collective reality. Just as it is erroneous to exaggerate the destiny of the individual and to forget the cosmic and communal destiny which is the Kingdom of God, so it is wrong to deny the hope that burns in each individual heart that his or her own life has final meaning and purpose. Correspondingly, we are to be judged not simply on the basis of our community's activity but on the basis of our own as well.

If everything were to return to a kind of undifferentiated unity, then creation itself would have been pointless in the first place. What we look forward to in the end is a community of free and responsible persons united in love. But such a community is impossible unless the persons within it are preserved in some kind of individual identity. It is hardly "good news" to hear that we are worth something on this earth while we are still alive but that we are not worth anything thereafter, for eternity.

The Destiny of the Faithful:
Beatific Vision, Purgatory, Resurrection of the Body

Beatific Vision/Heaven/Eternal Life

New Testament: The vision of God after death, known as the *beatific vision*, is rarely referred to in the New Testament and not at all in the Old Testament. The Old Testament's belief in the invisibility of God generally persists into the New Testament (1 John 3:6; 4:12,20; John 1:18: 1 Timothy 1:17; 6:16). The promise of the vision of God, however, is found in Matthew 5:8: "Blest are the single-hearted for they shall see God." Given the background of Jewish thought, it is remarkable that the promise is uttered without any refinement or explanation. The vision of God which is promised to the peacemakers is the fruit of love in 1 Corinthians 13:12. Paul contrasts the vision of God after death with the dim view seen in a mirror. He chooses the expression "face to face," which echoes the traditions of Moses; a veil concealed the glory of God reflected in the face of Moses. Paul insists that the Christian will behold the glory of the Lord without such a veil (2 Corinthians 3:12-18). In 1 John 3:2 we are assured that we shall see God and that the vision will transform us into God's likeness.

Such a vision inaugurates us into a new life, "eternal life." God gives eternal life to those who are faithful (Romans 2:7; 6:23). It comes through faith (1 Timothy 1:16; John 3:15,36; 20:31) and is assured by hope (Titus 1:2; 3:7). It becomes a present reality by Baptism (Romans 6:4). Jesus has the words of eternal life (John 6:68). His followers retain eternal life by loving one another (12:50). Thus, death is never final (6:39,44,54). Those who partake of the Son will have eternal life (1 John 5:11-12). It consists of the knowledge of the one true God and of Jesus, whom God has sent (John 17:3).

Official Teachings of the Church: The principal texts are the Constitution *Benedictus Deus* (1336) of Pope Benedict XII and the Council of Florence's *Decree for the Greeks* (1439). Both insist that the souls of the faithful, provided they are in no need of purification, will immediately see "the divine essence with an intuitive vision and even face to face, without the mediation of any creature by way of object of vision; rather the divine essence immediately manifests itself to them, plainly, clearly and openly, and in this vision they enjoy the divine essence" (*Benedictus Deus*). Such faithful will "see clearly God, one and three, as God is, though some more perfectly than others, according to the diversity of merits" (Council of Florence). It is made possible by the *lumen gloriae* ("light of glory"). The traditional teaching is reaffirmed by Pope Pius XII (d. 1958) in his encyclical *Mystici Corporis* (1943), by Pope Paul VI (d. 1978) in his *Credo of the People of God* (1968), and by the Congregation for the Doctrine of the Faith, "Letter on Certain Questions Concerning Eschatology" (May 1979).

Theological Reflections: The beatific vision is *the full union of the human person with God*. It is that toward which every person strives. It is that which transcends the person on this earth and draws the person beyond himself or herself to become something other than he or she is at present. It is the goal of every human inquiry, search, and gesture toward the other. It is the completion of all that we are as human beings. "Our hearts are restless," Augustine cried out to God, "until they rest in Thee."

We thereby become fully like God. No trace of selfishness remains. We are fully open to the other. We cling to nothing of our own. We pour out our own being as God poured out the divine Being in Christ. This is why the early Church believed that the martyrs went directly to heaven without purification. The martyrs completely transcended selfish being and attained a likeness to Christ, and so to God. Heaven for them is not a reward for being good. Rather, ". . . it is the reward of having been delivered from any seeking for rewards" (John Macquarrie, *Principles of Christian Theology*, p. 366). The only reward for such self-giving love is an increased capacity for it. Heaven, therefore, is neither mythological nor simply the satisfaction of all egocentric human longings. It is the goal of human existence as such.

Purgatory

Biblical Foundations: There is, for all practical purposes, no biblical basis for the doctrine of purgatory. This is not to say that there is no basis at all for the doctrine, but only that there is no clear *biblical* basis for it. On the other hand, there is no contradictory evidence in either Old or New Testaments. The classic text is 2 Maccabees 12:38-46: ". . . for if he were not expecting the fallen to rise again, it would have been useless and foolish to pray for them in death. . . . Thus he made atonement for the dead that they might be freed from this sin" (12:44,46). The New Testament was insistent on the fact that the Kingdom of God had already come in Jesus Christ, and the Christian's attention was drawn to the immediate and imminent consummation and to the decision required of everyone in the face of the Kingdom's drawing near. The real testing of faith and its works is expected in the "fire" of the last judgment, not in the particular judgment (1 Corinthians 3:12-15). It is clear that notions of *Sheol* are still operative (Luke 16:19-31).

History of the Doctrine: In the *patristic period,* Justin and Tertullian shared this Lucan perspective and taught that the dead are waiting "in the grave" for the consummation. Origen argued that everyone will be saved but that there is a particular purification for each individual. The purification occurs, however, at the moment of judgment and not as some intermediate state between the particular judgment and the final passage into the sight of God. The Origenist belief in universal salvation (*apokatastasis*) was condemned by the provincial council of Constantinople in 543, a judgment approved by all the Eastern patriarchs and confirmed by Pope Vigilius (d. 555).

Augustine emphasized that all the just, not only the martyrs, enter immediately into heaven. But gradually the fire of judgment referred to in 1 Corinthians 3:12-15 becomes after Augustine the purgatorial fire and appears as an intermediate realm after death. The very fact of not yet being totally with God constitutes a punishment, according to Pope Gregory the Great.

The Western theology of the *Middle Ages* emphasized the penal and expiatory character of purgatory. The Christian East, however, rejected this highly juridical approach and stressed instead the more mystical nature of purgatory, as a process of maturation and spiritual growth. The Orientals also denied that the beatific vision was available to anyone, including the just, before the general resurrection and the final judgment. The traditional doctrine is enunciated by the Second Council of Lyons (1274), Benedict XII's *Benedictus Deus* (1336), and especially in the Council of Florence's *Decree for the Greeks* (1439), which tried to strike a careful balance between the Western concept of satisfaction and expiation and the Eastern emphasis on purification. Out of consideration for the Orientals, the council deliberately omitted all reference to fire (which the Orientals considered an echo of Origen's notion that all are saved by the one purifying fire) and avoided any language that would lead to a concept of purgatory as a place.

The *Reformation*, however, called into question what, until now, no one had questioned, either in the East or the West—namely, the appropriateness of prayers for the dead. From 1530 onwards, Luther and Melanchton joined Calvin and Zwingli in rejecting this doctrine, consistently with their teaching that salvation is by grace alone. In reply the Council of Trent defined the existence of purgatory, insisted that the souls detained there are helped by acts of intercession of the faithful, and especially by the sacrifice of the Mass. On the other hand, the council explicitly warned against any dwelling upon "the more difficult and subtle questions which do not make for edification and, for the most part, are not conducive to an increase of piety." These should not be included in popular sermons to uneducated people. Likewise, doubtful theological views should not be given wide circulation, and whatever belongs to the realm of "curiosity or superstition" or smacks of "dishonorable gain" should be forbidden as "scandalous and injurious to the faithful" (*Decree on Purgatory*, Session XXV, 1563).

The doctrine is reaffirmed in Pope Paul VI's *Credo of the People of God* (1968) and by the Congregation for the Doctrine of the Faith's "Letter on Certain Questions Concerning Eschatology" (1979) and is assumed by the Second Vatican Council's *Dogmatic Constitution on the Church*, n. 51.

Theological Reflections: Purgatory is best understood as *a process by which we are purged of our residual selfishness so that we can really become one with the God who is totally oriented to others, i.e., the self-giving God.* It is also part of that larger process by which we are called out of nothingness into existence, from existence to selfhood, or responsible human existence, from responsible human existence to Christian existence, and from Christian existence to full and final incorporation into God. The kind of suffering associated with purgatory, therefore, is not suffering inflicted upon us from the outside as a punishment for sin, but *the intrinsic pain that we all feel when we are asked to surrender our ego-centered self so that the God-centered loving self may take its place.* It is part of the process by which we are called to die and rise with Christ.

A Note on Indulgences: From the earliest days the Church imposed penances upon those who had sinned after Baptism (see chapter 22). It was not enough to be sorry for one's sins; that only removed the *guilt* of sin. One also had to pay the *penalty* of sin. Since sin always involves some violation of the Church which is called to be a holy community and the sacrament of Christ's presence in the world, the Church is also involved in the process by which the sinner is reconciled to God. Not only did the Church decide when the penitent was ready to be restored to communion, but the Church also prayed with the penitent as he or she pursued the path of repentance. At times, the Church drew upon its own spiritual treasury of grace and merit to cancel out some (partial indulgence) or all (plenary indulgence) of the punishment still due to an individual's sin.

The first actual indulgences appeared in France in the eleventh century. They were at once a remission of some penance and a remission of the temporal punishment due to sin. Even into the thirteenth century, however, indulgences were regarded as concessions to the imperfect, which more faithful Christians should not claim. (They are not to be confused with redemptions and commutations, which came out of the Germanic period. These applied only to imposed penances and not to punishment due to sin.) At first, some theologians contested the bishop's right to grant indulgences, but as the actual practice became more widespread, theological opposition diminished.

On the other hand, the practice itself changed. Where previously the Church only *prayed for* the remission of temporal punishment due to sin and had excused a canonical penance on that account, now the Church definitively declared that such temporal punishment was canceled on the basis of the Church's control over the treasury of grace and merit. By the middle of the thirteenth century, the granting of indulgences became increasingly divorced from the sacrament of Penance, and more and more an act of the pope. The number of indulgences multiplied, and the need for doing some penitential work declined. Any reasonable cause was now regarded as sufficient grounds for granting an indulgence (Aquinas, *Summa Theologica*, Supplement, q. 25, a. 2).

Plenary indulgences, i.e., the remission of all temporal punishment due to sin, had come into prominence during the Crusades in the eleventh century when the crusaders were promised complete remission of punishment in return for their military service (Pope Urban II, d. 1099). Indulgences for the dead began to be granted from the middle of the fifteenth century. Their connection with almsgiving was established as early as the eleventh century. In the later Middle Ages, however, they became a convenient source of income for the Church and, as such, were multiplied to scandalous proportions. Simony (i.e., buying and selling spiritual goods) was not unknown. Some preached indulgences in a theologically unsound and exaggerated way. The Council of Trent condemned such practices in its *Decree on Indulgences* (1563), but perhaps too late, since those very abuses were among the proximate causes of the Reformation.

The most recent and fullest official exposition of the meaning of indulgences is contained in Pope Paul VI's Apostolic Constitution *Indulgentiarum Doctrina* (1967). The pope linked the doctrine of indulgences with the doctrine of the Communion of Saints. The Church on earth is united with the Church in heaven and in purgatory. The "treasury of the Church" is not "akin to a hoard of material wealth accumulated over the centuries" but is the "infinite and inexhaustible value which the expiation and merits of Christ have in the sight of God . . . ." An indulgence, he declares, is "the remission in the sight of God of the temporal punishment due to sins which have already been blotted out as far as guilt is concerned." They are either plenary or partial, and they can be applied to the dead. Henceforth, however, partial indulgences will be described without reference to numbers of days and years. (The medieval approach had been to specify the precise amount of time subtracted from one's purgatorial "sentence".) It is, of course, always required that an individual be truly contrite, be a member of the Church in good standing, perform the work attached to the indulgence, and at least have the general intention of gaining the indulgence.

The doctrine of indulgences is best understood in the context of the whole mystery of Christian existence. We are all members of the Body of Christ. As such, we are beneficiaries of Christ's saving work on our behalf. Death is not the end of life, nor, therefore, is it the end of our relationships with our loved ones or with our brothers and sisters in the Church. Our obligations of concern and mutual assistance do not lapse with their death. Accordingly, decline of interest in indulgences is inconsistent with Catholic principles if that decline reflects a growing indifference to the Communion of Saints and/or to our abiding spiritual responsibility toward our dead relatives and friends. On the other hand, a calculating, egocentric approach to Christian destiny, where an individual is concerned primarily with the accumulation of spiritual "credits," is so antithetical to sound theological and doctrinal principles that the disappearance of that sort of interest in indulgences can only be welcomed.

Resurrection of the Body

Old Testament: The Hebrew concept of the human person as an animated body made it impossible for any idea of the afterlife to arise which did not involve a restoration of life to the body. This came, as we have already seen, very late in the Old Testament (Daniel 12:2; 2 Maccabees 7:9,11,23; 14:46). Isaiah 26:19 mentions the resurrection of the dead, but it may refer, as Ezekiel 37:1-14 does, to the restoration of Israel. By the time of the New Testament, resurrection was affirmed by the Pharisees but not by the Sadducees (Matthew 22:23; Mark 12:18; Luke 20:27; Acts of the Apostles 23:8).

New Testament: In his discussion with Sadducees (Mark 12:16-27), Jesus refutes their denial of the resurrection by an appeal to the Torah and above all to the power of God. But he also corrects the Pharisees' doctrine that the resurrection meant a return to the conditions of earthly life (12:25). In the Synoptics no mention is made of the resurrection of the sinner, although it might be implied in what is said about God's judgment upon every person at the end. The reward granted in the resurrection of the just (Luke 14:14) reflects a Jewish rather than a Christian approach.

A resurrection to life is mentioned in John 5:28-29 (see also 6:39-40; 11:25-26) in terms very close to Daniel 12:2, and the same conception is contained in 2 Corinthians 5:10 (see also 1 Corinthians 15:19; Philippians 3:21). Hebrews 6:2 counts it among the basic doctrines of Christian faith. The Book of Revelation alone speaks of a double resurrection, the second being the general resurrection of all the dead at the last judgment (20:11-15); the first is reserved to the martyrs who will then rule with Christ for one thousand years (20:4-6).

Most of the references to the resurrection in the New Testament, however, are references not to the resurrection of the body after death but to the Christian's *present* resurrection with Christ by being baptized into his death and rising with him unto new life (e.g., Romans 6:4-11). Other texts look to the *future* (e.g., 2 Corinthians 4:14; Philippians 3:11; John 11:25; 6:39-44,54; 1 Corinthians 15), but they are not explicit about the *bodily* character of this resurrection.

In fact, whenever the New Testament speaks about the resurrection, it speaks of the resurrection of the dead, never of the resurrection of the body, which is not found until Clement of Rome and Justin's *Dialogue* (80,5). Resurrection of the body, in the sense of resurrection of the flesh (*sarx*), would not have been consistent with Paul's distinction between *sarx* and *soma* ("body"). The latter embraces the whole person, whereas the former is something weak, perishable, and even sinful. The body (*sarx*) cannot rise, because "flesh and blood cannot inherit the kingdom of God; no more can corruption inherit incorruption" (1 Corinthians 15:50).

Some Protestant scholars like Oscar Cullmann have interpreted such texts to mean that death does not consist in the soul's being separated from the body and continuing to live on its own in some intermediate state, awaiting the resurrection of the body, but rather that death is the destruction of the whole person. Only at the general resurrection will there be a completely new creation. We live on between death and resurrection in the mind of God alone. Such a position has to reconcile itself with such texts as Philippians 1:21; 2 Corinthians 5:6-8; Luke 23:42-43; and Revelation 6:9; 20:4.

Official Teachings of the Church: The resurrection of the body is attested to in the *Apostles' Creed* ("I believe in. . .the resurrection of the body. . ."); the *Nicene-Constantinopolitan Creed* (381); the so-called *Athanasian Creed* (late fifth century); the Fourth Lateran Council (1215); the Second Council of Lyons (1274); and in the Constitution *Benedictus Deus* of Pope Benedict XII (1336). Usually the belief was simply included with other essential elements of Christian faith. Sometimes, however, the doctrine was deliberately and specifically formulated over against a heretical tendency to deny the radical goodness of the body, as in Lateran IV's rejection of Catharism, Albigensianism, and the Manichaeism upon which they were based. More recently, the belief is reaffirmed by the Second Vatican Council in its *Dogmatic Constitution on the Church* (n. 51) and in its *Pastoral Constitution on the Church in the Modern World* (n. 39), and also by the aforementioned Vatican "Letter on Certain Questions Concerning Eschatology" (1979).

Theological Reflections: We must reassert here what has already been presented in chapter 5—namely, that the human person is not simply an embodied spirit, in the sense that the body is base, inhuman, and without intrinsic worth. "Holiness is wholeness" (Goldbrunner) because the human person is bodily as well as spiritual, or, in biblical terms, is an animated body (*soma*). Our hope is not simply the salvation of our soul but the salvation of our whole being. Our immortality is not something required by philosophical speculation (namely, because the soul is spiritual, it is indestructible) but is grounded on God's promise of eternal life and the conferral of new life in the resurrection of Jesus Christ himself. And not life for part of us, i.e., the soul, but for all that we are, i.e., animated body.

Nor is our resurrection at the end the resurrection only of so many individuals. Our bodiliness also is the natural basis of our solidarity with others and through them with God. We are human insofar as we are oriented toward others. And our orientation toward others is made possible and necessary by our bodiliness. The doctrine of the resurrection of the *body* is a foundation for the doctrine of the Communion of Saints. Thus, life after death is also communal life. And thus, too, the resurrection of the body cannot be achieved until the consummation of history itself.

The Destiny of the Unfaithful: Hell

Old Testament

The word *hell* is not used in the Old Testament. Its counterpart is *Gehenna*, which is an abbreviation of "valley of the son of Hinnon." Gehenna was an actual place on the boundary between the tribes of Judah and Benjamin; it was regarded as unholy because it was the site of a shrine where human sacrifices were offered (2 Kings 23:10; 2 Chronicles 28:3; 33:6; Jeremiah 7:31; 19:2-5; 32:35). It was considered, therefore, to be the place where the dead bodies of those who rebelled against Yahweh would lie (Isaiah 66:24). The term is frequently used in extrabiblical Jewish writings and applies there to a fiery abyss, a place of darkness, chains, etc.

New Testament

Gehenna is mentioned seven times in Matthew, three times in Mark, once in Luke, and once in James. It is a place of unquenchable fire (Mark 9:43; Matthew 5:22; 18:9; James 3:6), a pit into which people are cast (Matthew 5:29-30; 18:9; Mark 9:45,47; Luke 12:5). The wicked are destroyed there (Matthew 10:28). The place is described, although not named, elsewhere (e.g., Matthew 3:10,12; 7:19; Luke 3:9,17). It is the final destination of the wicked (Revelation 19:20; 20:9-15; 21:8). It is a place of weeping and gnashing of teeth (Matthew 8:12; 13:42,50; 22:13; 24:51; 25:30), where the worm does not die (Mark 9:48); it is shrouded in darkness (Matthew 8:12; 22:13; 25:30).

Elsewhere in the New Testament the language is less concrete. Paul speaks of a day of wrath (Romans 2:5) and of death as the wages of sin (6:23). Sinners will have no share in the Kingdom of God (1 Corinthians 6:10; Galatians 5:19-21). The enemies of the cross of Christ are doomed to destruction, and so are all the impious (Philippians 3:19; 2 Thessalonians 1:9). It is a terrible and fearful thing to fall into the hands of the living God (Hebrews 10:26-31).

Official Teachings of the Church

The existence of hell as a condition of eternal punishment for sin is attested to in the *Athanasian Creed* (end of fifth century); the Fourth Lateran Council (1215), which speaks of "perpetual punishment with the devil"; the Second Council of Lyons (1274), which taught that not only those who die in mortal sin but also those who die with Original Sin only "go down immediately to hell, to be punished however with different punishments"—a teaching which differed from an earlier letter of Pope Innocent III to Humbert, the Archbishop of Arles, in 1201, in which the pope made a distinction between those who commit mortal sin and merit the "torture of hell" and those who are not yet baptized and suffer instead the "loss of the beatific vision" (see the discussion of limbo below); and in Benedict XII's Constitution *Benedictus Deus* (1336). Significantly, hell is not mentioned in the Second Vatican Council nor even in Pope Paul VI's otherwise very complete *Credo of the People of God* (1968). There *is* reference to "eternal punishment for the sinner" in the Congregation for the Doctrine of the Faith's "Letter on Certain Questions Concerning Eschatology" (1979).

Theological Reflections

The word *hell* is derived from the German *hel* ("realm of the dead"). The New Testament really assumes rather than affirms its existence when it simply takes over the notions and imagery of later Judaism. What the New Testament says about hell is to be interpreted according to the same principles which govern our interpretation of apocalyptic literature. Apocalypticism is too individualistic, too much oriented to worlds beyond this one, too elitist or Gnostic in its approach to revelation and salvation, and too fascinated with the esoteric and the ominous. Hence what the New Testament says about hell is not to be taken literally, nor is it to be taken as a balanced theological statement of the case.

When Jesus used this imagery, he did so not to describe a particular place but to dramatize the urgency of his proclamation of the Kingdom and the seriousness of our decisions for or against the Kingdom. The stakes are as high as they can be. Our personal integrity and destiny are at issue. To turn our backs on God is to be finally and fully alienated and estranged from God. It is to choose inauthentic existence. It is to reject community with God and with others. It is to opt for isolation and separation.

Neither Jesus, nor the Church after him, ever stated that persons actually go to hell or are there now. He—as does the Church—restricts himself to the *possibility*. *If* somone really and deliberately rejected God, *this* is what he or she would be choosing instead of God: a totally isolated existence. Even in this sense, hell is not the product of divine vindictiveness. Rather, *it is God's yielding to our freedom*. To reject God is to reject life in community. Conversely, it is to choose life in isolation. Hell is absolute isolation. The radical sinner *chooses* that. God does not impose it as a punishment.

Some have argued that if an individual really chooses hell, i.e., a totally isolated existence, that individual is choosing self-annihilation, for one cannot even exist that way. To reject God completely and absolutely is to reject Being itself. It is to opt for non-being, for nothingness. Hell, in this conception, is not a place or a state but simply the condition of non-being.

Jesus' own "descent into hell," to which the Apostles' Creed attests, is the underworld (*Sheol*) rather than the place of fire. By dying Jesus entered the company of those who had died before him and thereby shared with them what he had achieved. The words "he descended into hell," therefore, mean simply that he died and that he remained dead, at least for a short time.

A Note on Demonology: In the *Old Testament*, belief in demons was generally excluded by the severe prohibitions against magic in Hebrew law. This is not to say that Israel knew no superstition at all. There is evidence of it here and there (1 Samuel 28:13; Psalm 106:37; Isaiah 13:21; 34:14). The situation changes, however, in the intertestamental and early New Testament periods. The belief in evil forces that was prevalent in Mesopotamian culture was assimilated almost whole, without change. The apocryphal literature traces the origin of demons to the fallen angels, the sons of God who married the daughters of men (Genesis 6:1-4).

The mention of demons is much rarer in the *New Testament* than in later Judaism. The victims of heathen sacrifices are offered to demons (1 Corinthians 10:20-21). Deceiving spirits are behind false teachings (1 Timothy 4:1). The spirits of demons perform wonders (Revelation 16:14), and the ruins of Babylon are haunted by demons (18:2). The demons are called the angels of Satan, for whom eternal fire is prepared (Matthew 25:41). They are the "principalities" who separate Christians from the love of God (Romans 8:38), but they are disarmed by the crucifixion of Christ (Colossians 2:15).

Demons do not occupy a significant place in the *official teachings of the Church*. The Council of Braga (561), in Portugal, rejected the teachings of Priscillian (d. 385), founder of a Manichaean sect in Spain. The council denied the radical dualism of matter and spirit. All that exists is from God and is under the authority and power of God. Thus, even the devil was created by God and was in the beginning a good angel. The existence of demons is simply presupposed by the provincial council of Constantinople (543) and by the *Decree on Original Sin* of the Council of Trent (1546).

The Church has taught, therefore, that there is evil in the world which transcends the particular evil that human beings do (see chapter 9). But no clear theology of demons emerged until the Middle Ages, when it appeared as part of the discussions of creation. Insofar as a theology of demons has any relevance today, it is more appropriately an element of the theology of sin. Demonology is "an expression of the personal basis of our guilt and mortality which is not within our power to control or reach by any human action in history. It is also an expression of the fact that, as a human situation, evil in the world has a certain depth which is not simply attributable to man and the history which is subject to his autonomous control, but is something that can only be overcome by God's eschatological act in Christ in fulfillment of his promise" (Karl Rahner, "Demonology," *The Concise Sacramentum Mundi*, p. 334).

Beyond that, who really knows, or can know?

The Destiny of the Unbaptized: Limbo

The word *limbo* is derived from the Latin *limbus* ("border"). It is the *state or place*, according to some, *reserved for the dead who deserved neither the beatific vision nor eternal punishment*. The *limbus patrum* ("limbo of the fathers"), containing the pre-Christian just who had to await the opening of heaven by Christ (Luke 16:22; 1 Peter 3:18-22), was distinguished from the *limbus puerorum*, containing unbaptized infants and children, who, therefore, remained in Original Sin without ever incurring any actual sins.

Over against the Pelagians, Augustine (d. 430) had argued that such children were condemned to real, though diminished, pains of hell. Anselm of Canterbury (d. 1109) and the Scholastics after him held to the Augustinian belief that such individuals were forever excluded from eternal happiness, but they allowed them a place of natural happiness, i.e., limbo. The belief was maintained throughout the Middle Ages and into the twentieth century. With the Second Vatican Council and the theological climate it reflected and sanctioned, however, the idea of limbo has seemed less and less tenable in light of the universality of grace from the very beginning of each person's existence (the "supernatural existential").

The Catholic Church continues to endorse, indeed mandate, the practice of immediately baptizing infants in danger of death. There is no indication in the new rites of Baptism, however, that the practice is based on a belief in limbo. Rather, the texts speak of the Church's desire to associate the child with the death and resurrection of Christ, to become a member of Christ's Church, and to share in the glory of the Kingdom of God.

The issue is, therefore, linked with the questions of grace (see chapter 5), of the necessity of the Church for salvation (see chapter 20), and infant Baptism (see chapter 21). Insofar as membership in the Church is not necessary for the salvation of each individual, and insofar as grace is present to each person from the beginning of existence, the Baptism of a dying infant seems unnecessary and perhaps even unwarranted. Insofar as membership in the Church is a call from God without regard for age, talent, or longevity, and insofar as the Church has a wider dimension beyond death in the Communion of Saints, the Baptism of a dying infant may, in fact, be legitimated and perhaps even required. In neither instance, however, is belief in limbo a necessary component of the answer.

THE COMMUNION OF SAINTS

The article on the "communion of saints" was first found in the Apostles' Creed at the end of the fifth century and was used much earlier in the East, through not as a part of the creed. It was understood as our participation in the blessings of salvation and in the fellowship of God's holy people. Although this community of salvation encompassed the whole Church, the term *communion of saints* only gradually came to apply principally to the communion between the heavenly Church and the earthly Church. More recently still, the term has come to apply only to the exchange of graces and blessings between individuals here on earth and the saints in heaven and the souls in purgatory (the Church militant, triumphant, and suffering). Its fundamental biblical and theological meaning, however, remains locked in the noun *communion* (*koinonia*). The Church is, first and foremost, a communion, a fellowship called by the Father, in Christ, through the power of the Spirit (Hebrews 2:14-17; Romans 5:8-10; 8:3,32-35; John 1:14; and especially 2 Corinthians 13:13).

The doctrine is explicitly affirmed in the Second Vatican Council's *Dogmatic Constitution on the Church* (and reaffirmed in Pope Paul VI's *Credo of the People of God*): "For all who belong to Christ, having his Spirit, form one Church and cleave together in him (see Ephesians 4:16). Therefore the union of the pilgrims with the brethren who have gone to sleep in the peace of Christ is not in the least interrupted." Those in heaven, because of their close union with Christ, "establish the whole Church more firmly in holiness, lend nobility to the worship which the Church offers on earth to God, and in many ways contribute to its great upbuilding (see 1 Corinthians 12:12-27)" (n. 49). Such persons intercede for those of us on earth and place their merits at our disposal.

Because of this sense of union linking all Christians, both living and dead, the Church has "from the first ages . . . cultivated with great piety the memory of the dead," through the offering of prayers on their behalf (n. 50). The Church has also always venerated the saints, especially the Blessed Mother, and has sought their aid. "For when we look at the lives of those who have faithfully followed Christ, we are inspired with a new reason for seeking the city which is to come (Hebrews 13:14; 11:10). . . . In the lives of those who shared in our humanity and yet were transformed into especially successful images of Christ (see 2 Corinthians 3:18), God vividly manifests to humankind the divine presence and face. God speaks to us in them, and gives us a sign of the kingdom, to which we are powerfully drawn, surrounded as we are by so many witnesses (see Hebrews 12:1)" (n. 50).

The council's vision is eschatologically wide-ranging. When Christ appears at the end and the glorious resurrection of the dead occurs, ". . . the splendor of God will brighten the heavenly city and the Lamb will be the lamp thereof (see Revelation 21:24)" (n. 51). At that supreme moment, the charity of the whole Church will be manifested in adoration of God and of the Lamb who was slain, and all will proclaim with one voice: "To the One seated on the throne, and to the Lamb, be praise and honor, glory and might, forever and ever!" (Revelation 5:13).

Herein, cosmic eschatology and individual eschatology converge. Our hope in the Kingdom of God for all humankind and for all the world and its history is at once our hope in our own personal entrance into that Kingdom, that we might share with others and with the whole cosmos the fruits of the saving work which the Father has accomplished in Jesus Christ, by the power of the Holy Spirit.

SUMMARY

1. *Christian destiny* is not distinct from human destiny, nor is either distinct from the destiny of the world and of its history: *the Kingdom of God*.

2. *Eschatology* is that area of theology which is directly concerned with the "study of the last thing(s)," i.e., the Kingdom of God (the "last thing") and death, particular judgment, heaven, hell, purgatory, Second Coming of Christ, resurrection of the body, general judgment, and the consummation of all things in the Kingdom (the "last things").

3. The *Kingdom of God* is the redemptive presence of God actualized through the power of God's reconciling Spirit.

4. Since the Kingdom is not only in the *future*, eschatology is concerned also with the *present* and the *past*. The final events are grounded in the redemptive work of Jesus Christ and are anticipated even now in faith, hope, charity, in the sacraments, and in the Church itself, the carrier of the divine glory.

5. Our movement toward the Kingdom is believed not only because it is *promised* but also because it seems to be *demanded* by graced human nature itself. Otherwise, there is no basis at all for our endless quest for truth and love (the meaning of "intentionality"), nor is there any real possibility of ultimate human fulfillment.

6. Through the mediation of humanity, the world itself also has "intentionality," i.e., purpose, direction, conscious freedom. In other words, *the world has a history* and *is* history. The outcome is already decided in Christ, but there are powers at work which impede the movement of history toward the Kingdom of God. These evil forces are focused in the one known as *Satan*. They have decisively been overcome by the passion of Christ.

7. The *Kingdom of God*, the destiny of creation and humanity, was a reality woven into the texture of Israel's faith from the beginning. It referred to the provident and protective kingship of God over the chosen people. It was a kingship that was at once *in* history and *beyond* history, *local* (e.g., in the ark of the covenant) and *universal*, over *Israel* and over *all* people and all *creation*, in the *present* and in the *future*.

8. The *fruit* of the Kingdom is a whole *new moral order* of peace, justice, and mercy. This is the vision of *Deutero-Isaiah* (61:1), which Jesus made his own (Luke 4:18).

9. *Later Judaism* gave the Kingdom a more *nationalistic* orientation, a conception with which Jesus had to contend. But there was also an *apocalyptic* notion (Daniel) which saw the Kingdom as the heavenly Jerusalem and saw paradise as the abode of the elect. The emphasis was

always on God's action, and attention was focused constantly on the signs and portents of the coming Kingdom.

10. Jesus startled his listeners not because he proclaimed the Kingdom of God but because he proclaimed it as *near at hand* (Mark 1:15). He called, therefore, for conversion and repentance and for watchfulness.

11. He emphasized, too, the *mercy of God*: that the Kingdom was for sinners and outcasts, the poor and the despised. Entrance into the Kingdom will be determined by our response to the neighbor in need.

12. Although there were political implications to the proclamation, Jesus excluded a *political* interpretation of the Kingdom. He was not a Zealot, nor did he cooperate with the Zealots. And he discouraged people from calling him the Messiah because of the political and nationalistic overtones of the term.

13. Jesus' preaching of the Kingdom was underscored by his *praxis*: healings, exorcisms, eating with outcasts, etc.

14. Where Jesus proclaimed the Kingdom, the *early Church* proclaimed Jesus as the personification of the Kingdom. We are living between-the-times, i.e., between the first and second comings of Christ (Luke); Christ is destined to rule over all creation, even beyond the Church (Paul); in the meantime we are pilgrims, still on the way to the Kingdom (1 Peter); the final Kingdom is anticipated in the Eucharist (Luke 22:30).

15. *Early patristic theology* (Ignatius of Antioch, Justin, Tertullian, Origen, *et al.*) emphasized the Lordship of Jesus, the imminence of the Kingdom, and its interior, or spiritual, character. *Western theology*, however, increasingly identified the Kingdom with the *Church* (Augustine, Gregory the Great), and Christian political leaders even identified it with the Holy Roman Empire (Charlemagne). This notion would be vigorously rejected by Pope Boniface VIII in 1303. Emphasis on God's action, even to the detriment of human collaboration, was strong in Augustine (the two cities).

16. Coinciding with the Augustinian and Gregorian tendency to equate the Kingdom and the visible, institutional Church was another medieval tendency to identify the Kingdom with a *spiritual* sectarian Church (Joachim of Fiore).

17. Other *medieval notions* of the Kingdom included those of the Dominican *mystics* (Eckhart, Tauler, Suso), who saw the Kingdom as God in the depths of the soul, and of *Luther*, who rejected both the sectarian and the theocratic understandings of the Kingdom, insisting instead on the sharp distinction between the kingdom of humankind and the Kingdom of God.

18. With the *Enlightenment* of the eighteenth century, the Kingdom was once again perceived not only as an earthly reality but as the product of human initiative and effort. It is an ethical commonweal (Kant), the completion of history (Hegel), the classless society (Marx). But other, more spiritual interpretations continued in the Church (Pascal), and the symbol "Kingdom of God" became the central idea of Christianity in the *Tübingen School* in Germany in the nineteenth century.

19. Modern New Testament scholarship begins as a reaction against the more Liberal Protestant views of the Kingdom (Ritschl). The sequence of biblical theologies of the Kingdom follows:

a. *Futurist eschatology* (Schweitzer, Weiss, Werner): The Kingdom is in the *future*; it is God's act alone; when it comes, history as we know it will end; the Kingdom is now imminent.

b. *Realized eschatology* (C. H. Dodd): The Kingdom is already realized in the *past*; the "hour of decision" has to be experienced anew by each individual.

c. *Existentialist eschatology* (Bultmann): The Kingdom is present; we are called to decide for or against God, to choose authentic or inauthentic existence.

d. *Salvation-history eschatology* (Cullmann and Catholic biblical theology generally): The Kingdom is *past, present, and future*; it proceeds in linear fashion through history, from the moment of creation, through the central Christ-event, to the Second Coming of Christ. Between the first and second coming of Christ is the time of the Church.

20. Twentieth-century *Catholic systematic theology* insists that the Church and Kingdom of God are not the same, that the Kingdom is the product of divine initiative and human collaboration alike, and that this follows from the universality of grace, the incarnation, and the fundamental unity of the love of God and the love of neighbor (*Karl Rahner*). A stronger emphasis on the human and prophetic side of the Kingdom is given by *Edward Schillebeeckx* (the Kingdom of God is our "well-being"), and a correspondingly stronger emphasis on divine initiative is given by *Hans Küng*, who worries as much about a false secularizing of the Kingdom as we once worried about a false interiorizing of it. *Walter Kasper* makes a similar point. *Johannes Metz*, on the other hand, stresses, like Schillebeeckx, the role of human effort in the political realm and speaks even of a "political theology" which formulates the eschatological message under the conditions of our present society. Finally, *Gustavo*

Gutierrez and Latin American liberation theology carry the point even further, insisting that the struggle for justice and for liberation *is* the struggle for the Kingdom of God.

21.   *Protestant systematic theology* sees the Kingdom of God as the "answer to the ambiguities of history," at once present and future, cosmic, social, and individual (*Tillich*), the "eschatological fulfillment of the liberating lordship of God in history" (*Moltmann*), "the utterly concrete reality of justice and love" (*Pannenberg*), and the renewed "secular city" *(Cox)*. A more traditional, neo-Reformation warning comes from *Reinhold Niebuhr*, who notes that the relationship between historical justice and the love of the Kingdom of God is a dialectical one, as is the relationship nature and grace. We are bound to realize justice as far as we can, but we can never forget that God alone can bring about the Kingdom in all its fullness beyond history.

22.   *Anglican theology* emphasizes the supremacy of the Kingdom of God as a theological category (*J. A. T. Robinson*), warns at the same time against identifying it with social or political achievements (*Macquarrie*), and insists on its evolutionary character as a processive unfolding of the cosmic Love that is God (*Pittenger*).

23.   *Orthodox theology (Meyendorff)* sees everything in terms of the destiny of humankind and the world, but it speaks more of the Holy Spirit than of the Kingdom of God. In fact, the Spirit is the Kingdom's "content." The Kingdom is realized already in a mystical rather than a social or political way, especially in the sacraments.

24.   The Catholic Church has never officially defined the meaning of the Kingdom of God. One has to infer a doctrinal position from explicit teachings on grace, Original Sin, and Jesus Christ. The *Second Vatican Council's Pastoral Constitution on the Church in the Modern World* speaks of it as "the consummation of the earth and of humanity," signified in the present by the realization of human dignity, brotherhood, and freedom. Pope Paul VI's *Evangelii Nuntiandi* links, but does not completely identify, the Kingdom with "liberation from everything that oppresses man but which is above all liberation from sin and the Evil One." It is the center of the Church's proclamation, as it was of Jesus'.

25.   The *last things* pertain to the destiny of *individuals* as well as the whole of humanity and the world. *The destiny of each individual* includes *death* and *judgment*.

26.   *Death* was perceived in the *Old Testament* as a state in which the spirit had departed from the body to dwell in *Sheol*, the underground or abode of the dead. For the *New Testament* we overcome death by sharing in Christ's victory over it. The *post-biblical Church* at first

emphasized the Second Coming and the destiny of the Church, but in the Middle Ages there was a shift to the death of individuals and to life after death for the individual. Vatican II restored the fuller, more comprehensive view.

27.   Death forces us to confront the *radical finitude* of our existence, but it also gives our lives *shape and direction*. It can be an affirmative act, providing significance to our lives (as in a hero's death). The death of Jesus is our model. Only in death did he reveal the ultimate seriousness of the claims of God's Kingdom.

28.   *Judgment* is both vindication and punishment in the *Old Testament*. For the *New Testament* the judgment of God occurs even now in our acceptance or rejection of Christ and the Gospel and in the giving of the Spirit. But it is also to take place outside and beyond history, and it will be the act by which evil is finally overcome. The *fact* of judgment is consistently taught by the official Church.

29.   We must distinguish between the *general judgment*, as the consummation of the whole world, and the *particular judgment*, as the fulfillment of the individual's personal life.

30.   The *destiny of the faithful* includes the *beatific vision* (heaven, eternal life), *purgatory*, and the *resurrection of the body*.

31.   The *beatific vision* (heaven, eternal life) is not a part of the *Old Testament*, in which God is always invisible, veiled. The *New Testament* speaks of seeing God without a veil, "face to face" (Paul). We are already tasting eternal life in Christ (John). The reality of the beatific vision is affirmed by *Benedictus Deus* of Pope Benedict XII (1336) and the *Council of Florence* (1439).

32.   The beatific vision is the *full union* of the human person with God, and so with one another in God. It is not a reward for being good, but the *fulfillment* of who we are and who we have been called to become.

33.   *Purgatory* is without clear *biblical* foundation. On the other hand, there is no contradictory evidence in the Bible. The classic text is 2 Maccabees 12:38-46. *Origen's* notion of the universal salvation *(apokatastasis)* was condemned by the provincial council of Constantinople (543). *Augustine* insisted that the just enter heaven immediately. Only gradually, by the time of the Middle Ages, did the idea of a penal and expiatory state develop in the West. The *East* did not reject purgatory, only its juridical character. Rather, purgatory is a process of maturation and spiritual growth after death. The Western and Eastern traditions were blended in the Council of Florence's *Decree for the Greeks* (1439). The *Reformers* rejected purgatory on the principle that

grace alone saves. Prayers for the dead are useless. The *Council of Trent* defined its existence and defended prayers for the dead, especially the Mass. But it also warned against superstition and other spiritual excesses.

34.   Purgatory is best understood as a *process* by which we are purged of our residual selfishness so that we can really become one with the God who is totally oriented to others.

35.   *Indulgences* are the remission of punishment still due to sins which, however, have already been forgiven. If the indulgences remit all punishment, they are *plenary*. Otherwise, they are *partial*. At first they were linked with the sacrament of Penance, but gradually, in the Middle Ages, became an act of the pope. They were applied to the dead, beginning in the fifteenth century. In the later Middle Ages they became a convenient source of income. Abuses followed, and so, too, did the Protestant Reformation.

36.   The doctrine of indulgences at best reflects a proper understanding of the *Communion of Saints*. At worst, it reflects a selfish, calculating approach to Christian destiny.

37.   In the *Bible* the *resurrection of the body* is always the resurrection of the whole person *(soma)* and not of the flesh alone *(sarx)*, since the Bible knew no sharp distinction between body and soul. The New Testament speaks rather of the resurrection of the *dead*. Our resurrection has already begun by our Baptism into Christ's death and resurrection (Paul). The official Church taught the resurrection of the body against those who denied the goodness of the body; see especially *Lateran IV, Lyons II,* and *Benedictus Deus* of Pope Benedict XII. It is also an integral part of the traditional *creeds* of the Church.

38.   The doctrine of the resurrection of the body testifies to the importance of our *bodiliness* as the basis of our *solidarity* with one another, and through others with God. Our hope, therefore, is not simply in the salvation of our soul but in the salvation of our whole being.

39.   The *destiny of the unfaithful* is *hell*.

40.   In the *Old Testament* it is called *Gehenna*. In later Judaism it is understood as a fiery abyss, a place of darkness and chains. This carries over in the *New Testament*. When *Jesus* used such imagery, he did so not to describe a place but to dramatize the urgency of his proclamation of the Kingdom and the seriousness of our decision for or against God. *Paul* is less concrete, speaking instead of a day of wrath and death as the wages of sin. Hell is attested to in the Athanasian Creed, Lateran IV, Lyons II, and *Benedictus Deus* of Pope Benedict XII. Significantly, it is not mentioned in Vatican II or Pope Paul VI's *Credo of the People of God*.

41.   The Church has never defined that anyone is actually *in* hell, only that it exists as a *possibility* for those who totally and deliberately reject God. Hell is not a punishment by God, but it is God's yielding to our freedom to reject the Kingdom.

42.   What of the "occupants" of hell, i.e., the *demons*? Demonology was prevalent in Mesopotamian culture, but the *Old Testament* generally rejected it because of Israel's severe prohibitions against magic. Later Judaism, however, tended to assimilate such beliefs. There are some few references to demons in the *New Testament*. Demons do not occupy a significant place in the official teachings of the Church, except where the Church wanted to insist that whatever exists, including evil spirits, exists by the creative act of God and is under the authority of God (Council of Braga, 561).

43.   Demonology is to be linked with our understanding of *Original Sin*. There is evil in the world which is not simply attributable to our free choice, and it can only be overcome by God's final act in Christ.

44.   The *destiny of the unbaptized* is *limbo* (literally, "border").

45.   There is the limbo of the *pre-Christian just*, and the limbo of *unbaptized infants* and young children. The belief was maintained throughout the Middle Ages and into the twentieth century. Although the Catholic Church continues to endorse and even mandate the Baptism of infants who are in danger of death, the idea of limbo seems less tenable in light of the universality of grace from the very beginning of each person's existence.

46.   Cosmic and individual eschatology converge in the doctrine of the *Communion of Saints*. First found in the Apostles' Creed at the end of the fifth century, it meant from the beginning our participation in the blessings of salvation and in the fellowship of God's holy people. In turn, it became identified with the union of earthly and heavenly Churches, and then with the exchange of spiritual benefits between individuals on earth and individuals in heaven and purgatory.

47.   The doctrine is explicitly affirmed and elaborated upon in the *Second Vatican Council's Dogmatic Constitution on the Church*, where it is described as the foundation of our union with one another in Christ, of our veneration of the saints, and of our hope in the final Kingdom. Our communion with one another in Christ will be brought to fulfillment at the Second Coming and the resurrection of the dead.

SUGGESTED READINGS

Bright, John. *The Kingdom of God: The Biblical Concept and Its Meaning for the Church*. Nashville: Abingdon Press, 1953.

Fortman, Edmund J. *Everlasting Life After Death*. New York: Alba House, 1976.

Guardini, Romano. *The Last Things*. New York: Pantheon Books, 1954.

Pannenberg, Wolfhart. *Theology and the Kingdom of God*. Philadelphia: Westminster Press, 1969.

Papin, Joseph, ed. *The Eschaton: A Community of Love*. Villanova, Pa.: Villanova University Press, 1971.

Schnackenburg, Rudolf. *God's Rule and Kingdom*. London: Nelson, 1963.

Simpson, Michael. *The Theology of Death and Eternal Life*. Notre Dame, Ind.: Fides Publishers, 1971.

CONCLUSION

· XXX ·

CATHOLICISM: A SYNTHESIS

CATHOLICISM IN CONTEXT

Catholicism is not a reality that stands by itself. The word *Catholic* is a qualification of *Christian*, and *Christian* is a qualification of *religious*, and *religious* is a qualification of *human*. Thus, the Catholic Church is a community of persons (the *human*) which believes in the reality of God and shapes its life according to that belief (the *religious*). The Church's belief in, and response to, the reality of God is focused in its fundamental attitude toward Jesus Christ. For the Catholic, as for every *Christian*, the old order has passed away and we are a "new creation" in Christ, for God has "reconciled us to himself through Christ" (2 Corinthians 5:17,19).

If Catholicism is to be described, much less defined, it must be described (and defined) according to a method which respects, and takes into account, each of these constitutive relationships: the human, the religious, and the Christian. And that, in fact, is how we have proceeded throughout this book.

Following some introductory probings into the present crisis in which Catholicism finds itself (chapter 1) and some explorations into the meaning and interrelationships of faith, theology, and belief (chapter 2), we moved in *Part I* to the question of *human existence*. To be a Catholic is, before all else, to be human. Catholicism is an understanding and affirmation of human existence before it is a corporate conviction about the pope, or the seven sacraments, or even about Jesus Christ.

But Catholicism is also more than a corporate understanding and affirmation of what it means to be human. To put it another way: Catholicism answers the question of meaning in terms of ultimacy. With Dietrich Bonhoeffer, Catholicism affirms that there is more to life than meets the eye, that there is "a beyond in our midst." With Paul Tillich, Catholicism affirms that there is a ground of all being which is Being itself. With Thomas Aquinas, Catholicism affirms that all reality is rooted in the creative, loving power of that which is most real (*ens realissimum*). Catholicism answers the question of meaning in terms of the reality of God. In a word, Catholicism is a *religious* perspective, and not simply a philosophical or an anthropological one. And so in *Part II* we raised the issues of belief and unbelief, of revelation, of religion and the plurality of religions, and of the triune *God*.

But Catholicism is not some undifferentiated religious view. Indeed, religion *as such* does not exist. There are particular religions. They share a belief in the Transcendent, but they "name" and "interpret" the Transcendent differently, and they shape their response to the Transcendent (worship, moral behavior, institutional expressions) in accord with those names and interpretations. For the Christian, the ultimate dimension of human experience is a triune God: a God who creates and sustains us, a God who draws near to us and identifies with our historical condition, and a God who empowers us to live according to the vocation to which we have been called. More specifically, the God of Christians is the God of Jesus Christ. In *Part III*, therefore, the book developed the thesis that Catholicism is a *Christian* religious perspective, and not a generically religious one.

Christianity itself, however, is not some undifferentiated Christian reality. Christian faith *as such* is an abstraction. It is always a mediated faith, in terms of its origin, its forms of expression, and its exercise. *Part IV* examined the context in which Christian faith is mediated in the community of faith, *the Church*. But the Church is itself composed of churches. The Church universal is a communion of local churches, and the Body of Christ is composed of denominations (for want of a better term). Thus, the noun *Church* is always modified: the Catholic Church, the Methodist Church, the Orthodox Church, the Lutheran Church, and so forth. Moreover, even these modifiers are themselves modified: the Lutheran Church, Missouri Synod; the Lutheran Church in America; the American Lutheran Church, and so forth. The Body of Christ "subsists in" the Catholic Church (Second Vatican Council, *Dogmatic Constitution on the Church*, n. 8), but it is not coextensive with it. There are other churches which have "a right to be honored by the title Christian." Their members are "incorporated into Christ" through Baptism, and they are "properly regarded" as brothers and sisters "in the Lord" by the Catholic Church (*Decree on Ecumenism*, n. 3).

We moved, therefore, in *Part V* to the ecclesial dimension of *Christian existence* and to its *moral* vision and commitments, its *spiritual* resources, and its *hopes* for the future, in light of which its whole understanding of human existence, of God, of Jesus Christ, and of itself is fashioned, refined, and deepened.

THE QUESTION OF CATHOLICISM'S DISTINCTIVENESS

To what extent, however, is the *ecclesial experience* of Jesus Christ *distinctively Catholic*? To what extent are the *moral vision and commitments distinctively Catholic*? To what extent are the *hopes* in the coming Kingdom of God *distinctively Catholic*?

If Catholicism is distinguishable within the Body of Christ from Protestantism, Anglicanism, and Eastern Orthodoxy, it must be on the basis of some belief(s) or characteristic(s) which Catholicism alone possesses. One belief that is obviously distinctive is Catholicism's commitment to the Petrine office, the papacy. At this point in the history of the Church, the Catholic Church alone affirms that the Petrine ministry is an integral institutional element in the Body of Christ, and that without the papal office the Church universal lacks something essential to its wholeness. It is the one issue which still finally divides the Catholic from all other Christian churches and traditions, notwithstanding various other differences regarding liturgy, spirituality, theology, polity, and doctrinal formulations. When all else is stripped away, the official Catholic position on the Petrine ministry and office is different from every other official and/or representative position of every other formal Christian Church. This is not to suggest that it must always be so, however, and therein lies the difficulty in linking Catholic distinctiveness with the papacy alone.

The Lutheran-Roman Catholic consultation in the United States, for example, has achieved a remarkable measure of consensus already on the question of papal primacy (see chapter 23), giving promise of even greater breakthroughs. It is conceivable, in other words, that Catholicism's affirmations about the Petrine ministry will, at some later date, no longer be Catholicism's affirmations alone. They may be shared by Lutherans, Anglicans, the Orthodox, Presbyterians, Methodists, and others. Will all of Christianity at that point be identified simply with Catholicism? Will Lutheranism, Calvinism, Anglicanism, and Orthodox Christianity fade from the scene once and for all? Will there, then, be one theology, one spirituality, one liturgy, one canon law, one vehicle of doctrinal formulation? If so, it would be the first time in the entire history of the Church, not excluding the New Testament period itself (see, for example, Raymond E. Brown's *The Community of the Beloved Disciple*, New York: Paulist Press, 1979; see also chapters 17 and 18 of this book).

A more fruitful, and more theologically and historically naunced, approach to the question of Catholic distinctiveness would seem to lie in the direction of identifying and describing various *characteristics* of Catholicism, each of which (apart from the commitment to the papacy) Catholicism shares with one or another Christian church or tradition. But how can one distinguish Catholicism from other theological, doctrinal, spiritual, liturgical, and institutional expressions of Christianity on the basis of characteristics which Catholicism presumably *shares* with one or another Christian church? It is true: There is no one characteristic, apart from the Petrine doctrine, which sets the Catholic Church apart from *all other* churches. On the other hand, a case can be made that nowhere else except in the Catholic Church are *all* of Catholicism's characteristics present in the precise *configuration* in which they are found within Catholicism.

The point is crucial to the central thesis of this chapter. An example may help to illustrate it. The flag of the United States of America has individual characteristics which it shares with the flags of other nations of the world. (1) It is *tri-colored*. But so, too, are the flags of Australia, Belgium, Botswana, Colombia, the United Kingdom, France, Ireland, Italy, the Federal Republic of

Germany. (2) Its three colors are *red, white, and blue*. But so, too, are the flags of Burma, Cuba, Czechoslovakia, France, the Netherlands, Panama, the United Kingdom, New Zealand, Yugoslavia. (3) It has *stars* in its basic design. But so, too, do the flags of Australia, the People's Republic of China, Honduras, Venezuela.

Despite these common characteristics, no flag in the entire community of nations is identical with the flag of the United States, a reasonably close similarity to the flag of the African nation of Liberia notwithstanding. What is *distinctive* about the United States' flag is not any one of its several *characteristics* but the precise *configuration* of those characteristics. So, too, with the Catholic Church in relation to all of the other churches and traditions within the Body of Christ.

GENERAL CHARACTERISTICS OF CATHOLICISM

As its very name suggests, Catholicism is characterized by a *radical openness to all truth and to every value*. It is *comprehensive* and *all-embracing* toward the totality of Christian experience and tradition, in all the theological, doctrinal, spiritual, liturgical, canonical, institutional, and social richness and diversity of that experience and tradition. Catholicism is not a post-biblical phenomenon. It does not emerge from some historical moment and from particular historical (i.e., national, cultural, political) circumstances which are removed in time from Jesus' proclamation of the Kingdom, his gathering of disciples, and the formation of the Church in the period encompassed by the New Testament. Catholicism does not begin as a distinctive expression of Christian faith in the sixteenth century, nor are its basic lines already fixed by the fourteenth. It is not itself a sect or a schismatic entity, although sectarianism and schism are not unknown to it. Nor is it inextricably linked with the culture of a particular nation or region of the world. Catholicism is, in principle, as Asian as it is European, as Slavic as it is Latin, as Mexican or Nigerian as it is Irish or Polish.

There is no list of "Catholic Fathers" (or Catholic "Mothers," for that matter) which does not include the great theological and spiritual writers of the period *before* as well as after the division of East and West and the divisions within the West. Gregory of Nyssa is as much a Catholic Father as is Augustine or Thomas Aquinas.

Nor are there *schools of theology* which Catholicism excludes, variations in their inherent strengths and weaknesses notwithstanding. Catholicism continues to read Ignatius of Antioch and Clement of Alexandria, Athanasius and Cyril of Jerusalem, Gregory of Nazianzen and Augustine, Anselm of Canterbury and Bernard of Clairvaux, Abelard and Hugh of St. Victor, Thomas Aquinas and Bonaventure, Robert Bellarmine and Johann Adam Möhler, Karl Rahner and Charles Journet, not to mention John and Luke (see chapters 2, 9, 13, 18, and 25).

Nor are there *spiritualities* which Catholicism excludes, their variations again notwithstanding. Catholicism is open to *The Cloud of Unknowing* and the *Introduction to the Devout Life*, to the way of Francis of Assisi and of Bernard of Clairvaux, to Ignatius Loyola and John of the Cross, to Marmion and Merton (see chapter 28).

Nor are there *doctrinal* streams and mighty rivers that Catholicism closes off. Catholics are guided by Nicea as by Vatican I, by Chalcedon as by Lateran IV, by Trent as by Vatican II. They read Gregory the Great as well as Paul VI, Clement of Rome as well as Leo XIII, Pius XII as well as John XXIII.

Catholicism is characterized, therefore, by a *both/and* rather than an *either/or* approach. It is not nature *or* grace, but graced nature; not reason *or* faith, but reason illumined by faith; not law *or* Gospel, but law inspired by the Gospel; not Scripture *or* tradition, but normative tradition within Scripture; not faith *or* works, but faith issuing in works and works as expressions of faith; not authority *or* freedom, but authority in the service of freedom; not the past *versus* the present, but the present in continuity with the past; not stability *or* change, but change in fidelity to stable principle, and principle fashioned and refined in response to change; not unity *or* diversity, but unity in diversity, and diversity which prevents uniformity, the antithesis of unity.

There have been many moments in the history of the Catholic Church when these delicate balances were disrupted, often through events beyond anyone's control and at other times through narrow-mindedness, blindness, stubbornness, and malice. But the Church is at once holy and sinful, not in the sense that sin exists *alongside* grace, but in the sense that even graced existence is ambiguous, fragile, and subject to disintegration. The record is always mixed. The Kingdom of God is neither coextensive with the Church nor totally divorced from the Church (see chapter 20).

One person looks at a glass and sees that it is half empty; another looks at the same glass and declares it half full. One person looks at the story of the Church and sees only the Church's complicity in the feudal system, the Crusades, the pretentious claims of Innocent III and Boniface VIII, its blindness to the gathering storm clouds of the Reformation, its insensitivities to the East, its arid Scholasticism of the post-Reformation period, its handling of the Galileo affair, its declaration of war against modernity in the nineteenth century, its suppressions of theological freedom under Pope Pius X, its diplomatic hesitancies in the face of Nazism.

Another looks at the same Church and notes the extraordinary, and finally inexplicable, manner in which it drew unity out of seeming chaos in the Christological controversies of the fourth and fifth centuries. Still another marvels at how the Church can be the Church of both John and Paul, of Luke and Timothy, of the martyrs and apologists, of Gregory of Nyssa and Augustine of Hippo, of Gregory the Great and Anselm of Canterbury, of Francis of Assisi and Thomas Aquinas, of monasticism as a protest against political and social privilege and later as the carrier of Western civilization, of heroic reformers like Catherine of Siena, of contemporary saints like John XXIII or Dorothy Day (see chapters 18 and 28).

But perhaps more than anything or anyone else, one must marvel at the Church of *Vatican II*: a *pluralistic* Church open to pluralism, a *modern* Church open to modernity, an *ecumenical* Church open to the whole wide world (the literal meaning of *ecumenical*), a *living* Church open to new life and to the change it brings and requires, a *catholic* Church open in principle to all truth and to every value (see chapter 19.)

For Lutheran Church historian Martin Marty, of the University of Chicago, "Catholicism is a family of apostolic churches, rich in regional, national, ethnic diversity; it is a faith that teaches me that because you have a *core* or center, you can make room for a variety of apparently competitive and interactive elements" ("Something Real and Lumpy," *U.S. Catholic*, vol. 44, May 1979, p. 24).

Like the flag of the United States of America, there are colors here that others share; there are patterns here that others display; there are symbols here that others use. But no other church or tradition within the Body of Christ puts them all together in quite this way. It is in their special configuration that the distinctiveness of Catholicism is disclosed and expressed. It is expressed in its systematic theology, in its body of doctrines, in its liturgical life, especially its Eucharist, in its variety of spiritualities, in its religious congregations and lay apostolates, in its social teachings and commitments to justice, peace, and human rights, in its exercise of collegiality, and in its Petrine ministry.

THE PHILOSOPHICAL FOCUS OF CATHOLICISM: CHRISTIAN REALISM

Catholicism is not bound to any one school of theology, although there is something distinctively Catholic in the way the pluralism of theologies is integrated, systematized, and applied within the Catholic tradition. If the Catholic Church is not linked exclusively to a particular theology, much less is it linked to a particular philosophy: existentialist, process, phenomenological, even Thomistic. And yet there is a distinctively Catholic way of integrating the pluralism of philosophies underlying its various theological and doctrinal orientations. For want of a better term, that distinctively Catholic philosophical focus is "Christian realism," as outlined, for example, by Bernard J.F. Lonergan (see his "The Origins of Christian Realism" in *A Second Collection*, William Ryan and Bernard Tyrrell, eds., Philadelphia: Westminster Press, 1974, pp. 239-261).

Lonergan reminds us that infants, in contrast to adults, do not speak. They live, therefore, in a world of immediacy: of sights and sounds, of tastes and smells, of touching and feeling, of pleasure and pain. But as infants learn to speak, they gradually move into a larger world, a world mediated by meaning. That world includes the past and the future as well as the present, the possible and the probable as well as the actual, rights and duties as well as the facts.

The criteria of reality in the infant's world of immediacy are given in immediate experience. They are simply the occurrence of seeing, hearing, tasting, smelling, touching, pleasure and pain. But the criteria of reality in the world mediated by meaning are far more complex. They include immediate experience but also go beyond it.

"For the world mediated by meaning is not just given," Lonergan insists. "Over and above what is given there is the universe that is intended by questions, that is organized by intelligence, that is described by language, that is enriched by tradition. It is an enormous world far beyond the comprehension of the nursery. But it is also an insecure world, for besides fact there is fiction, besides truth there is error, besides science there is myth, besides honesty there is deceit" (p. 241).

Now this insecurity and ambiguity does not really bother too many people. But it does trouble philosophers and those whose sciences, like theology, depend in some significant measure on correct philosophical presuppositions. Philosophical answers to the question of reality differ. First, there is *naive realism*, which insists that knowing is simply a matter of taking a good look; objectivity is a matter of seeing what is there to be seen; reality is whatever is given in immediate experience. The offspring of naive realism is *empiricism*. The empiricist takes naive realism seriously. The only reality that counts is the reality that one can determine by quantitative measurement. Empiricism, in turn, begets its philosophical opposite, *critical idealism* (Kant), in which the categories of understanding of themselves are empty and refer to objects only insofar as the categories are applied to the data of the senses. This is the world of *phenomena*. We cannot know things in themselves, the *noumena*.

"Insofar as Christianity is a reality, it is involved in the problems of realism," Lonergan suggests. First, Christianity itself is mediated by meaning. "It is mediated by meaning in its communicative function inasmuch as it is preached. It is mediated by meaning in its cognitive function inasmuch as it is believed. It is mediated by meaning in its constitutive function inasmuch as it is a way of life that is lived. It is mediated by meaning in its effective function inasmuch as its precepts are put into practice" (p. 244).

But there is ambiguity within the Christian's world, as there is in human life itself. For the Christian world is not *exclusively* a world mediated by meaning. There is also the immediacy of God's grace creating the new creature in Christ by the power of the Holy Spirit. The grace of God is not produced by the preacher, nor is it the result of believing the Gospel, nor does it come as a reward for good works. Grace is present to the individual person, as we have seen (chapter 5), from the very beginning of the person's existence. Grace enters into the definition of what it means to be human.

Thus, the real is not only what I can see and touch, as naive realism suggests. Nor is the real just an idea in the mind, as idealism insists. The real is what I judge to be real. The reality of the world mediated by meaning is known not by experience alone, nor by ideas alone, but by judgments and beliefs.

It is this commitment to *critical* realism that has moved the Catholic Church, first at Nicea (325) and again and again in its official teachings, to deliberate, to issue decrees, to condemn, to explain, to defend, to make distinctions, to use technical terms, to engage in the most acute rational reflection. Indeed, it is this commitment to critical realism that is at the foundation of the medieval effort toward systematization and of our own contemporary systematic enterprises as well.

What does all this mean? It means that the Catholic tradition philosophically rejects both naive realism and idealism as adequate bases for Catholicism's theological vision. One contemporary form of naive realism is *biblicism*. For the biblicist, the meaning of the Word of God is obvious. "Just take a look," the biblicist seems to say. "The requirements of Christian existence are clear. The answers are readily available in the pages of Sacred Scripture." *Moralism* is another contemporary form of naive realism. "Just consult your gut feelings, or use your common sense," the moralist insists. "Of course, violence is against the Gospel of Jesus Christ." Or: "Of course, violence can be justified to counteract oppressive violence." But moralism provides no arguments, no warrants, no reasons. It is assumed that the convictions are self-evidently true and their intrinsic power compelling.

Idealism, on the other hand, makes of Christianity a system of principles and ideas, but without clear or meaningful connection with the pastoral situation or the human condition at large. One need not worry about the effectiveness of preaching and teaching, for example, if one is convinced that the ideas to be preached and taught are plainly, even though not infallibly, true. One need not engage in time-consuming and ultimately diverting moral speculation about what it is one must do in such-and-such a conflict-situation when there is a clear statement of moral principle already "on the books." The contemporary forms of idealism are *dogmatism* and *legalism*. Dogmatism assumes that salvation is linked primarily to "right belief" and that the rightness of beliefs is clear and almost self-evident. Legalism assumes that salvation is linked primarily to "right practice," i.e., of obedience to Church laws. There is never any serious doubt about what the law demands, so specific and so detailed is it.

Critical realism, or what Lonergan calls Christian realism, insists that experience itself is not enough. One can "take a look," but one cannot be sure that what one sees corresponds entirely to what is real. "Appearances can be deceiving," the old saying has it. Christian realism also rejects the notion that clear and distinct ideas (doctrines, dogmas, canonical directives) are equivalent to the real itself. Ideas are never formulated except in relation to other ideas, to events, to one's associates, to the problems and resources at hand, to the historical circumstances, to social, economic, and political conditions, to one's own background, age, sex, nationality, occupation, income level, social status, and the like. Just as Christian realism rejects biblicism and moralism in favor of a critical and systematic approach to reality, so Christian realism rejects dogmatism and legalism in favor of a critical and systematic approach to reality, an approach that goes beyond what seems to be there and that takes historicity into account in the use and interpretation of ideas and principles.

This critical realism carries over into everything the Church does. Thus, the Church's moral vision and its approach to the demands of Christian existence are qualified always by its confidence in the power of grace and by its readiness to expect and understand the weaknesses and failures rooted in Original Sin. And so Catholicism is a moral universe of laws but also of dispensations, of rules but also of exceptions, of respect for authority but also for freedom of conscience, of high ideals but also of minimal requirements, of penalties but also of indulgences, of censures and excommunications but also of absolution and of reconciliation.

THE THEOLOGICAL FOCI OF CATHOLICISM: SACRAMENTALITY, MEDIATION, COMMUNION

No theological principle or focus is more characteristic of Catholicism or more central to its identity than the principle of *sacramentality*. The Catholic vision sees God in and through all things: other people, communities, movements, events, places, objects, the world at large, the whole cosmos. The visible, the tangible, the finite, the historical—all these are actual or potential carriers of the divine presence. Indeed, it is only in and through these material realities that we can even encounter the invisible God. The great sacrament of our encounter with God and of God's encounter with us is Jesus Christ. The Church, in turn, is the sacrament of our encounter with Christ and of Christ's with us, and the sacraments, in turn, are the signs and instruments by which that ecclesial encounter with Christ is expressed, celebrated, and made effective for the glory of God and the salvation of men and women.

A corollary of the principle of sacramentality is the principle of *mediation*. A sacrament not only signifies; it also causes what it signifies. Thus, created realities not only contain, reflect, or embody the presence of God. They make that presence effective for those who avail themselves of these realities. Just as we noted in the previous section that the world is mediated by meaning, so the universe of grace is a mediated reality: mediated principally by Christ, and secondarily by the Church and by other signs and instruments of salvation outside and beyond the Church.

Catholicism rejects naive realism, which hold to the immediacy of the experience of God as the normal or exclusive kind of encounter with the divine presence. Catholicism also rejects idealism, which holds that the encounter with God occurs solely in the inwardness of conscience and the inner recesses of consciousness. Catholicism holds, on the contrary, that the encounter with God is a mediated experience but a *real* experience, rooted in the historical and affirmed as real by the critical and systematic judgment that God is truly present and active here or there, in this event or that, in this person or that, in this object or that.

Finally, Catholicism affirms the principle of *communion*: that our way to God and God's way to us is not only a mediated way but a communal way. And even when the divine-human encounter is most personal and individual, it is still communal in that the encounter is made possible by the mediation of the community. Thus, there is *not* simply an individual personal relationship with God or Jesus Christ that is established and sustained by meditative reflection on Sacred Scripture, for the Bible itself is the Church's book and is the testimony of the Church's original faith. The mystic (even in the narrow sense of the word) relies on language, ideas, concepts, presuppositions when he or she enters into, or reflects upon, an intimate, contemplative relationship with God. We are radically social beings; our use of language is clear evidence of that. There is no relationship with God, however intense, profound, and unique, that dispenses entirely with the communal context of *every* human relationship with God.

And this is why, for Catholicism, the mystery of the Church has so significant a place in theology, doctrine, pastoral practice, moral vision and commitment, and devotion. Catholics have always emphasized the place of the Church as both the *sacrament* of Christ, *mediating* salvation through sacraments, ministries, and other institutional elements and forms, and as the *Communion of Saints*, the preview or foretaste, as it were, of the perfect communion to which the whole of humankind is destined in the final Kingdom of God.

And so it is with the *mystery of the Church* that we come at last to the point at which the distinctively Catholic understanding and practice of Christian faith most clearly emerges. For here we find the convergence of those principles which have always been so characteristic of Catholicism: sacramentality, mediation, and communion—principles grasped and interpreted according to the mode of critical realism rather than of naive realism or idealism.

These principles, at once philosophical and theological, have shaped, and continue to shape, Catholicism's Christology, ecclesiology, sacramentology, canon law, spirituality, Mariology, theological anthropology, moral theology, liturgy, social doctrine, and the whole realm of art and aesthetics. The last item is a particular case in point. In contrast, Protestantism, as a religion of the word, has had a "mixed" record when it comes to the arts. It has been "uneasy about objectification of the divine drama in images which might themselves draw the devotion of the supplicant from the invisible God beyond the gods. It has often and maybe even usually been uneasy about unrestricted bodily attention, and has rather consistently feared the ecstasy of the dance through most of the years of its history" (Martin Marty, *Protestantism*, p. 228; for a broader view of Catholicism's aesthetical impact, see Kenneth Clark's *Civilisation*, pp. 167-192).

Baptist theologian Langdon Gilkey saw many of the same characteristics when he probed the reality of Catholicism in search of its distinctive identity. First, he concluded, there is Catholicism's "sense of reality, importance, and 'weight' of tradition and history in the formation of this people and so of her religious truths, religious experience, and human wisdom."

Secondly, there is, "especially to a Protestant, a remarkable sense of humanity and grace in the communal life of Catholics.... Consequently the love of life, the appreciation of the body and the senses, of joy and celebration, the tolerance of the sinner, these natural, worldly and 'human' virtues are far more clearly and universally embodied in Catholics and in Catholic life than in Protestants and in Protestantism."

Thirdly, there is Catholicism's "continuing experience, unequalled in other forms of Western Christianity, of the presence of God and of grace mediated through symbols to the entire course of ordinary human life." For Gilkey, a symbol points to and communicates the reality of God which lies beyond it. A symbol can be viewed and appropriated "as *relative*, as a 'symbol' and not God, without sacrificing this relation to the *absoluteness* that makes it a vehicle of the sacred." The experience of the symbol can unite "sensual, aesthetic, and intellectual experience more readily than the experiences of proclamation or of an ecstatic spiritual presence." The Catholic principle of symbol or sacramentality, according to Gilkey, "may provide the best entrance into a new synthesis of the Christian tradition with the vitalities as well as the relativities of contemporary existence."

Finally, there has been "throughout Catholic history a drive toward rationality, the insistence that the divine mystery manifest in tradition and sacramental presence be insofar as possible penetrated, defended, and explicated by the most acute rational reflection" (*Catholicism Confronts Modernity: A Protestant View*, pp. 17-18, 20-22).

A CONCLUDING WORD

It is not a question here in this chapter, or indeed in this book, of arguing that the Catholic Church and the Catholic tradition are necessarily superior to all of the other churches and traditions on this point or that, but only that there is within Catholicism a configuration of values which one does not discover elsewhere and which commends Catholicism on its own merits, without regard for competing configurations.

These values include Catholicism's sense of *sacramentality* (God is present everywhere, the invisible in the visible, within us and within the whole created order); its principle of *mediation* (the divine is available to us as a transforming, healing, renewing power through the ordinary things of life: persons, communities, events, places, institutions, natural objects, etc.); its sense of *communion*, or of peoplehood (we are radically social and so, too, is our relationship with God and God's with us); its drive toward *rationality* and its *critical realism* (reality is neither self-evident nor confined to the realm of ideas); its corresponding respect for *history*, for *tradition*, and for *continuity* (we are products of our past as well as shapers of our present and our future); its conviction that we can have as radical a notion of *sin* as we like so long as our understanding and appreciation of *grace* is even more radical; its high regard for *authority* and *order* as well as for *conscience* and *freedom*; indeed its *fundamental openness to all truth and to every value*—in a word, its *catholicity*.

SUMMARY

1. Catholicism is not a reality that stands by itself. The word *Catholic* is a qualification of *Christian*, and *Christian* is a qualification of *religious*, and *religious* is a qualification of *human*.

2. The larger *context* of Catholicism has dictated the structure of this book: the meaning of human existence (Part I), the experience of God as the ground of human existence (Part II), the experience of Jesus Christ as the focal point of our experience of God (Part III), the experience of Church as the sacrament of Christ (Part IV), and the moral vision and hopes evoked by such meanings and experiences (Part V).

3. The Catholic Church alone affirms that the *Petrine ministry*, or papacy, is an integral institutional element in the Body of Christ, and that without the papal office the universal Church lacks something essential to its wholeness. It is the one issue which finally divides the Catholic from all other Christians. But this may not always be so, as the Lutheran-Roman Catholic consultation in the U.S.A. suggests.

4. The *distinctiveness* of Catholicism, therefore, lies not simply in its affirmation of the Petrine office but in the unique *configuration of characteristics* which Catholicism possesses and manifests as a Church and as a tradition within the Body of Christ and Christianity at large.

5. *In general*, Catholicism is characterized by a *radical openness to all truth and to every value*. Catholicism does not emerge from a particular time after the foundational period of the New Testament, nor is it tied to a particular nation or culture. It endorses no one school of theology or spirituality and no single interpretation of doctrine.

6. Catholicism is characterized by a *both/and* rather than an either/or approach to nature and grace, reason and faith, law and Gospel, Scripture and tradition, faith and works, authority and freedom, past and present, stability and change, unity and diversity.

7. The *historical record* of Catholicism is mixed: There are, e.g., the triumphalism and even the decadence of the medieval papacy and the simplicity and sanctity of Francis of Assisi, the condemnatory spirit of Pius IX and the openness of John XXIII.

8. Nowhere is the *catholicity* of the Church more evident, however, than at *Vatican II*: A Church at once *pluralistic* and open to pluralism, *modern* and open to modernity, *ecumenical* and open to the

whole wide world, *alive* and open to new life, and *catholic* and open in principle to all truth and every value.

9. Catholicism is not alone in possessing or manifesting such characteristics, no more than the flag of the United States of America is the only tri-colored flag in the world, or the only one using red, white, and blue, or the only one with stars in its design. But that flag is unique in the configuration of those characteristics. There is no other flag exactly like it. So, too, with Catholicism.

10. *Specifically*, Catholicism's *philosophical focus* is *critical*, or *Christian, realism*. It sees the world as mediated by meaning. Thus, it sees neither a world of immediate experience alone (naive realism, empiricism) nor a world of ideas alone (idealism).

11. Christian realism insists that experience ("taking a look") is not enough, as biblicism and moralism suppose, and that reality is not to be identified simply with clear and distinct ideas (doctrines, dogmas, canonical directives), as dogmatism and legalism suppose. It maintains that "appearances can be deceiving," on the one hand, and that ideas are always historically conditioned, on the other.

12. This critical realism carries over into everything the Church does. In the realm of moral demands, for example, Catholicism is a religion of laws but also of dispensations, of censures but also of absolutions.

13. The *theological foci* of Catholicism include the principles of *sacramentality, mediation,* and *communion*.

14. The principle of *sacramentality* means that God is present and operative in and through the visible, the concrete, the tangible, the finite, the historical: persons, communities, places, events, natural objects, the whole created order. The great sacrament of encounter with God is *Christ*, and the *Church*, in turn, is the sacrament of encounter with Christ, and the *sacraments*, in turn, are the signs and instruments by which that ecclesial encounter with Christ is expressed, celebrated, and made effective for all.

15. The principle of *mediation* is a corollary of the principle of sacramentality. God uses signs and instruments to communicate grace—i.e., to become present to the whole of creation. Catholicism rejects naive realism, which holds to the immediacy of the experience of God as the normal or exclusive kind of encounter with God, and also idealism, which holds that the encounter with God occurs solely in the inwardness of conscience and consciousness.

16. The principle of *communion* means that our way to God and God's way to us is mediated through community: the human community

at large and the Church in particular. Communion is both the way and the goal. The *Communion of Saints* is the preview or foretaste of the perfect communion to which the whole of humankind is destined in the final Kingdom of God.

17. These principles, philosophical and theological alike, have shaped, and continue to shape, the total reality that is Catholicism: e.g., theology, liturgy, spirituality, structures, art.

18. By way of contrast, for example *Protestantism*, a religion mainly of the word, has had a "mixed" record when it comes to the arts, the celebration of the bodily, and bodily expression.

19. *Langdon Gilkey* identifies the following as characteristic of Catholicism: its sense of tradition and history, its sense of peoplehood and community, its sense of symbol and sacrament, and its drive toward rationality and rational reflection.

20. It was not the purpose of this chapter or of this book to establish the superiority of Catholicism but to identify its *distinctiveness* by calling attention to the *configuration of values* which one finds nowhere else in the Body of Christ or in Christianity at large: sacramentality, mediation, communion, rationality, continuity, the triumph of grace over sin, the regard for authority and order as well as conscience and freedom, and its fundamental openness to all truth and to every value. In a word, its *catholicity*.

SUGGESTED READINGS

Clark, Kenneth. *Civilisation*, New York: Harper & Row, 1969.

Delaney, John J., ed. *Why Catholic?* New York: Doubleday, 1979.

Gilkey, Langdon. *Catholicism Confronts Modernity: A Protestant View.* New York: Seabury Press, 1975.

Lossky, Vladimir. *The Mystical Theology of the Eastern Church.* London: Clarke, 1957.

Marty, Martin E. *Protestantism.* New York: Holt, Rinehart and Winston, 1972.

APPENDIX

The Creed of the Council of Constantinople (381) (The council of Constantinople was convened to reaffirm the faith of the council of Nicea, of 325. Though not itself promulgated by the council of Constantinople, this creed soon acquired greater authority than even the Nicene Creed. Since the seventh century it has been known as the *Nicene-Constantinopolitan Creed.)*

We believe in one God,
  the Father, the Almighty,
  maker of heaven and earth,
  of all that is seen and unseen.
We believe in one Lord, Jesus Christ,
  the only Son of God,
  eternally begotten of the Father,
  God from God, Light from Light,
  true God from true God,
  begotten, not made, one in Being with the Father.
  Through him all things were made.
For us men and for our salvation
  he came down from heaven:
by the power of the Holy Spirit
  he was born of the Virgin Mary, and became man.
For our sake he was crucified under Pontius Pilate;
  he suffered, died, and was buried.
  On the third day he rose again
    in fulfillment of the Scriptures;
  he ascended into heaven
    and is seated at the right hand of the Father.
He will come again in glory to judge the living and the
  dead,
  and his kingdom will have no end.
We believe in the Holy Spirit, the Lord, the giver of life,
  who proceeds from the Father and the Son.
  With the Father and the Son he is worshiped and
    glorified.
He has spoken through the Prophets.
We believe in one holy catholic and apostolic Church.
We acknowledge one baptism for the forgiveness of sins.
We look for the resurrection of the dead,
  and the life of the world to come. Amen.

Instruction on the Historical Truth of the Gospels, Pontifical Biblical Commission, April 21, 1964. (Excerpt. Full text in the *Catholic Biblical Quarterly,* vol. 26, July 1964, pp. 305-312.)

1. The Catholic exegete, under the guidance of the Church, must turn to account all the resources for the understanding of the sacred text which have been put at his disposal by previous interpreters, especially the holy Fathers and Doctors of the Church, whose labors it is for him to take up and to carry on. In order to bring out with fullest clarity the enduring truth and authority of the Gospels he must, whilst carefully observing the rules of rational and of Catholic hermeneutics, make skillful use of the new aids to exegesis, especially those which the historical method, taken in its widest sense, has provided; that method, namely, which minutely investigates sources, determining their nature and bearing, and availing itself of the findings of textual criticism, literary criticism, and linguistic studies. The interpreter must be alert to the reminder given him by Pope Pius XII of happy memory when he charged him "to make judicious inquiry as to how far the form of expression or the type of literature adopted by the sacred writer may help towards the true and genuine interpretation, and to remain convinced that this part of his task cannot be neglected without great detriment to Catholic exegesis."[5] In this reminder Pius XII of happy memory is laying down a general rule of hermeneutics, one by whose help the books both of the Old Testament and of the New are to be explained, since the sacred writers when composing them followed the way of thinking and of writing current amongst their contemporaries. In a word, the exegete must make use of every means which will help him to reach a deeper understanding of the character of the gospel testimony, of the religious life of the first churches, and of the significance and force of the apostolic tradition.

In appropriate cases the interpreter is free to seek out what sound elements there are in "the Method of Form-history," and these he can duly make use of to gain a fuller understanding of the Gospels. He must be circumspect in doing so, however, because the method in question is often found alloyed with principles of a philosophical or theological nature which are quite inadmissible, and which not infrequently vitiate both the method itself and the conclusions arrived at regarding literary questions. For certain exponents of this method, led astray by rationalistic prejudices, refuse to admit that there exists a supernatural order, or that a personal God intervenes in the world by revelation properly so called, or that miracles and prophecies are possible and have actually occurred. There are others who have as their starting-point a wrong notion of faith, taking it that faith is indifferent to historical truth, and is indeed incompatible with it. Others practically deny *a priori* the histori-cal value and character of the documents of revelation. Others finally there are who on the one hand underestimate the authority which the Apostles had as witnesses of Christ, and the office and influence which they wielded in the primitive community, whilst on the other hand they overestimate the creative capacity of the community itself. All these aberrations are not only opposed to Catholic doctrine, but are also devoid of any scientific foundation, and are foreign to the genuine principles of the historical method.

2. In order to determine correctly the trustworthiness of what is transmitted in the Gospels, the interpreter must take careful note of the three stages of tradition by which the teaching and the life of Jesus have come down to us.

Christ our Lord attached to Himself certain chosen disciples[6] who had followed Him from the beginning,[7] who had seen His works and had heard His words, and thus were qualified to become witnesses of His life and teaching.[8] Our Lord, when expounding His teaching by word of mouth, observed the methods of reasoning and of exposition which were in common use at the time; in this way He accommodated Himself to the mentality of His hearers, and ensured that His teachings would be deeply impressed on their minds and would be easily retained in memory by His disciples. These latter grasped correctly the idea that the miracles and other events of the life of Jesus were things purposely performed or arranged by Him in such a way that men would thereby be led to believe in Christ and to accept by faith the doctrine of salvation.

The Apostles, bearing testimony to Jesus,[9] proclaimed first and fore-most the death and resurrection of the Lord, faithfully recounting His life and words[10] and, as regards the manner of their preaching, taking into account the circumstances of their hearers.[11] After Jesus had risen from the dead, and when His divinity was clearly perceived,[12] the faith of the disciples, far from blotting out the remembrance of the events that had happened, rather consolidated it, since their faith was based on what Jesus had done and taught.[13] Nor was Jesus transformed into a "mythi-cal" personage, and His teaching distorted, by reason of the worship which the disciples now paid Him, revering Him as Lord and Son of God. Yet it need not be denied that the Apostles, when handing on to their hearers the things which in actual fact the Lord had said and done, did so in the light of that fuller understanding which they enjoyed as a result of being schooled by the glorious things accomplished in Christ,[14] and of being illuminated by the Spirit of Truth.[15] Thus it came about that, just as Jesus Himself after His resurrection had "interpreted to them"[16] both the words of the Old Testament and the words which He Himself had spoken,[17] so now they in their turn interpreted His words and deeds according to the needs of their hearers. "Devoting (themselves) to the ministry of the word,"[18] they made use, as they preached, of such various forms of speech as were adapted to their own purposes and to the mentality of their hearers; for it was "to Greek and barbarian, to learned and simple,"[19] that they had a duty to discharge.[20] These varied ways of speaking which the heralds of Christ made use of in proclaiming Him must be distinguished one from the other and carefully appraised: catecheses, narratives, testimonies, hymns, doxologies, prayers and any other such literary forms as were customarily employed in Sacred Scripture and by people of that time.

The sacred authors, for the benefit of the churches, took this earliest body of instruction, which had been handed on orally at first and then in writing—for many soon set their hands to "drawing up a narrative"[21] of matters concerning the Lord Jesus—and set it down in the four Gospels. In doing this each of them followed a method suitable to the special purpose which he had in view. They selected certain things out of the many which had been handed on; some they synthesized, some they explained with an eye to the situation of the churches, painstakingly using every means of bringing home to their readers the solid truth of the things in which they had been instructed.[22] For, out of the material which they had received, the sacred authors selected especially those items which were adapted to the varied circumstances of the faithful as well as to the end which they themselves wished to attain; these they recounted in a manner consonant with those circumstances and with that end. And since the meaning of a statement depends, amongst other things, on the place which it has in a given sequence, the Evangelists, in handing on the words or the deeds of our Savior, explained them for the advantage of their readers by respectively setting them, one Evangelist in one context, another in another. For this reason the exegete must ask himself what the Evangelist intended by recounting a saying or a fact in a certain way, or by placing it in a certain context. For the truth of the narrative is not affected in the slightest by the fact that the Evangelists report the sayings or the doings of our Lord in a different order,[23] and that they use different words to express what He said, not keeping to the very letter, but nevertheless preserving the sense.[24] For, as St. Augustine says: "Where it is a question only of those matters whose order in the narrative may be indifferently this or that without in any way taking from the truth and authority of the Gospel, it is probable enough that each Evangelist believed he should narrate them in that same order in which God was pleased to suggest them to his recollection. The Holy Spirit distributes His gifts to each one according as He wills;[25] therefore, too, for the sake of those Books which were to be set so high at the very summit of authority, He undoubtedly guided and controlled the minds of the holy writers in their recollection of what they were to write; but as to why, in doing so, He should have permitted them, one to follow this order in his narrative, another to follow that—that is a question whose answer may possibly be found with God's help, if one seeks it out with reverent care."[26]

Unless the exegete, then, pays attention to all those factors which have a bearing on the origin and the composition of the Gospels, and makes due use of the acceptable findings of modern research, he will fail in his duty of ascertaining what the intentions of the sacred writers were, and what it is that they have actually said. The results of recent study have made it clear that the teachings and the life of Jesus were not simply recounted for the mere purpose of being kept in remembrance, but were "preached" in such a way as to furnish the Church with the foundation on which to build up faith and morals. It follows that the interpreter who subjects the testimony of the Evangelists to persevering scrutiny will be in a position to shed further light on the enduring theological value of the Gospels, and to throw into clearest relief the vital importance of the Church's interpretation.

[5] *Divino afflante Spiritu; EB* 560.
[6] Cf. *Mc.* 3,14; *Lc.* 6,13.
[7] Cf. *Lc.* 1,2; *Act.* 1,21-22.
[8] Cf. *Lc.* 24,48; *Jn.* 15,27; *Act.* 1,8; 10,39; 13,31.
[9] Cf. *Lc.* 24, 44-48; *Act.* 2,32; 3,15; 5,30-32.
[10] Cf. *Act.* 10,36-41.
[11] Cf. *Act.* 13,16-41 with *Act.* 17,22-31.
[12] *Act.* 2,36; *Jn.* 20,28.
[13] *Act* 2,22; 10,37-39.
[14] *Jn.* 2,22; 12,16; 11,51-52; cf. 14,26; 16,12-13; 7,39.
[15] Cf. *Jn.* 14,26; 16,13.
[16] *Lc.* 24,27.
[17] Cf. *Lc.* 24,44-45; *Act.* 1,3.
[18] *Act.* 6,4.
[19] *Rom.* 1,14.
[20] *1 Cor.* 9,19-23.
[21] Cf. *Lc.* 1,1.
[22] Cf. *Lc.* 1,4.
[23] Cf. St. John Chrys., *In Mat. Hom.* I,3; *PG* 57,16,17.
[24] Cf. St August., *De consensu Evang.* 2,12,28; *PL* 34, 1090-1091.
[25] *I Cor.* 12,11.
[26] *De consensu Evang.,* 2, 21, 51 s.; *PL* 34,1102.

Declaration in Defense of the Catholic Doctrine on the Church Against Certain Errors of the Present Day (Mysterium Ecclesiae), Congregation for the Doctrine of the Faith, June 24, 1973. (Excerpt. Full text in *Origins: NC Documentary Service,* vol. 3, July 19, 1973, pp. 97,99,100.)

The transmission of divine Revelation by the Church encounters difficulties of various kinds. These arise from the fact that the hidden mysteries of God 'by their nature so far transcend the human intellect that even if they are revealed to us and accepted by faith, they remain concealed by the veil of faith itself and are as it were wrapped in darkness'. Difficulties arise also from the historical condition that affects the expression of Revelation.

With regard to this historical condition, it must first be observed that the meaning of the pronouncements of faith depend partly upon the expressive power of the language used at a certain point in time and in particular circumstances. Moreover, it sometimes happens that some dogmatic truth is first expressed incompletely (but not falsely), and at a later date, when considered in a broader context of faith or human knowledge, it receives a fuller and more perfect expression. In addition, when the Church makes new pronouncements she intends to confirm or clarify what is in some way contained in Sacred Scripture or in previous expressions of Tradition; but at the same time she usually has the intention of solving certain questions or removing certain errors. All these things have to be taken into account in order that these pronouncements may be properly interpreted. Finally, even though the truths which the Church intends to teach through her dogmatic formulas are distinct from the changeable conceptions of a given epoch and can be expressed without them, nevertheless it can sometimes happen that these truths may be enunciated by the Sacred Magisterium in terms that bear traces of such conceptions.

In view of the above, it must be stated that the dogmatic formulas of the Church's Magisterium were from the very beginning suitable for communicating revealed truth, and that as they are they remain for ever suitable for communicating this truth to those who interpret them correctly. It does not however follow that every one of these formulas has always been or will always be so to the same extent. For this reason theologians seek to define exactly the intention of teaching proper to the various formulas, and in carrying out this work they are of considerable assistance to the living Magisterium of the Church, to which they remain subordinated. For this reason also it oftens happens that ancient dogmatic formulas and others closely connected with them remain living and fruitful in the habitual usage of the Church, but with suitable expository and explanatory additions that maintain and clarify their original meaning. In addition, it has sometimes happened that in this habitual usage of the Church certain of these formulas gave way to new expressions which, proposed and approved by the Sacred Magisterium, presented more clearly or more completely the same meaning.

As for the meaning of dogmatic formulas, this remains ever true and constant in the Church, even when it is expressed with greater clarity or [is] more developed. The faithful therefore must shun the opinion, first, that dogmatic formulas (or some category of them) cannot signify truth in a determinate way, but can only offer changeable approximations to it, which to a certain extent distort or alter it; secondly, that these formulas signify the truth only in an indeterminate way, this truth being like a goal that is constantly being sought by means of such approximations. Those who hold such an opinion do not avoid dogmatic relativism and they corrupt the concept of the Church's infallibility relative to the truth to be taught or held in a determinate way.

· · ·

"A Courageous Worldwide Theology," an address by Karl Rahner, S.J., at John Carroll University, Cleveland, Ohio, April 6, 1979, on the occasion of receiving an honorary degree marking his seventy-fifth birthday. (Excerpt. Full text in *National Jesuit News,* vol. 8, June 1979, p. 10.)

It is my preference that both the tribute and my thanks be directed toward the contemporary theology in its entirety—that theology shaped in the last 30 years and recognized somewhat officially by the Second Vatican Council.

Of course, I have in mind an orthodox Catholic theology. That goes without saying. A theology which would not be obedient and docile under the word of God as it is proclaimed in the Church would not be Catholic theology. But I am envisaging a Catholic theology that is courageous and does not shun relative and restricted conflicts with Church authorities. I am thinking of a theology which can no longer be uniform in a neoscholastic approach.

I call that time of uniformity the "Pius epoch," but that era of the Popes who bore the name "Pius" has after all come to an end. I envisage a theology which is in dialogue with its time and lives courageously with it and in it.

This is all the more possible because it is characteristic of this time to be at a critical distance from itself, something *God makes possible.* It is a special grace to this age to be able now to have a critical distance from ourselves given us from the Cross of Christ.

From this more critical distance, I envisage a theology which in the Church at large must be the theology of a worldwide Church. That means a theology which does not only recite its own medieval history, but one that can listen to the wisdom of the East, to the longing for freedom in Latin America, and also to the sound of African drums.

I envisage a systematic theology that is an inner unity and what Trinitarian theologians call *perichoresis* (literally a dancing around together) of fundamental and dogmatic theology. I envisage a theology that enables human beings of our time to have a real grasp on the message of freedom and redemption, a theology that courageously abandons external stanchions of seemingly self-evident truths and things, something which does not stem necessarily from what is Christian, but rather from the changing historical situation structured by its intellectual and social elements.

I envisage a theology that does not only move along the numbers in our familiar friend "Denzinger" interpreting old ecclesiastical pronouncements, but a theology which breaks new ground for *new* pronouncements of the Church.

It would be a theology which takes seriously the hierarchy of truths, a theology which lives by the ecumenical hope that baptized Christians should be able to communicate in that which they all live in their faith. Such a communication should be possible without losing sight of the multiplicity of charisms of life and thought.

I envisage a theology which comprehends itself as an interpretation of the reality which through grace is present in every human being; a reality which is not only given to man by external indoctrination.

It would be a theology through which this reality would find itself, and which would not pride itself upon its clear concepts but would force them to open over and over again into the incomprehensibility of God himself. Such a theology would not secretly seek to understand itself as *the* theoretical underpinning of a life of middle-class ethics supervised by God.

One could continue in this vein for long. But my purpose is not to degrade the old theology, whose grateful children we are and remain. It has been rather to hint from afar that our time calls also us theologians sleeping under the broom tree of orthodoxy like Elijah in old days: *Surge, grandis tibi restat via*—Arise, a long journey lies ahead of you.

GLOSSARY

(The purpose of this glossary is *not* to provide new information or greater precision. Each term has already been explained, and in most cases defined, in the text itself. The reader should consult the Index of Subjects for such references. The glossary is provided instead as a convenience to the reader, as a quick memory-refresher and time-saver.)

ADOPTIONISM General term for views which look upon Jesus Christ as the purely human, "adopted" son of God.

AGNOSTICISM The suspension of belief regarding the reality of God.

ALEXANDRIA, SCHOOL OF Theological and catechetical center in Egypt, from the end of the second century, which emphasized the divinity of Christ. (Principal representatives: Clement, Origen.)

ANATHEMA An official condemnation by the Church of a doctrinal or moral position.

ANNULMENT An official declaration by the Church that a presumed marriage never really existed in the first place—e.g., because the couple was psychologically incapable of making a permanent commitment.

ANTHROPOLOGY, THEOLOGICAL The meaning of human existence in light of God, Christ, redemption, etc.

ANTICHRIST The embodiment of all historical forces hostile to God.

ANTINOMIANISM An attitude which rejects any and every law as the basis of Christian conduct.

ANTIOCH, SCHOOL OF Theological and catechetical center in Syria, from the end of the second century, which emphasized the humanity of Jesus. (Principal representatives: Arius, Theodore of Mopsuestia, John Chrysostom.)

APOCALYPTICISM A comprehensive name for a style of thought and writing associated with the later period of the Old Testament (e.g., Daniel), the period between the two Testaments, and the New Testament itself. Emphasis is on visions, signs, and predictions of future events brought about entirely by divine power, beyond history.

APOKATASTASIS   The belief, associated especially with Origen, that every human being will eventually be saved.

APOLOGETICS.   That part of theology which tries to show the reasonableness of Christian faith.

APOSTLE   A missionary or messenger of the Church in the New Testament period. The term is not coextensive with *the Twelve* (see below).

APOSTOLIC SUCCESSION   In the wider sense, the process by which the whole Church continues, and is faithful to, the word, the witness, and the service of the Apostles. In the stricter sense, the legitimation of the bishops' office and authority by their valid derivation from the Apostles.

ARIANISM   The heresy, condemned by the council of Nicea (325), which made the Son of God the highest of creatures, greater than we but less than God.

ASCETICISM   Exercises undertaken to live the Gospel more faithfully, especially in light of the cross of Christ and the sacrificial nature of his whole life.

ASSUMPTION   Dogma defined in 1950 by Pope Pius XII that the body of the Blessed Virgin Mary was taken directly to heaven after her life on earth had ended.

ATHEISM   The denial of the reality of God.

ATONEMENT   The act of healing the breach between God and humankind opened by sin. Usually associated with the crucifixion of Christ.

AUTHENTICITY OF CHURCH TEACHINGS   A quality of teachings which have authority because they are issued by persons holding a canonically recognized teaching office in the Church.

AUTHENTICITY OF SACRED SCRIPTURE   A quality of the various books of the Bible by which they are recognized to have been produced by the individuals or communities with whom the Church associates these writings.

BAIANISM   Unorthodox sixteenth-century view which held that after Original Sin everything we do is sinful. We have no real freedom of choice.

BAPTISM OF DESIRE   The process by which individuals are said to merit eternal life because of their good will, even though, through no fault of their own, they have not been baptized with water.

BASILEIA   The Greek word for "Kingdom (of God)."

BEATIFIC VISION   Our final union with God in heaven.

BELIEF   Any expression of faith. Not all beliefs are *doctrines* or *dogmas* (see below).

CANON   A list which seves as a "measure" or standard.

CANON LAW   The code of Church laws promulgated in 1918. More generally, any official code, or listing, of Church laws.

CANON OF SCRIPTURE   The official list of inspired books of the Bible, solemnly defined by the Council of Trent (1546).

CANONICAL FORM   The requirement of the Catholic Church that every Catholic be married in the presence of a priest and two witnesses, unless specifically dispensed.

CASUISTRY   An approach to the solution of moral problems which reduces theology to canon law, i.e., to a solver of "cases" ("Is it sinful? If so, how seriously?").

CATECHESIS   The process of "echoing" the Gospel, of introducing young people or adult converts to the main elements of the Christian faith.

CATECHISM   A handbook for catechesis. Usually in question-and-answer form.

CATECHUMEN   One who is undergoing catechesis.

CATECHUMENATE   The formal stage of preparation for entrance into the Church.

CHALCEDON   The city in Asia Minor where in 451 the fourth ecumenical council was held in which it was defined that Jesus Christ is true God and true man, and that his divine and human natures are united in one divine person, without confusion, change, division, or separation.

CHARACTER, MORAL   That which gives orientation, direction, and shape to our lives. The cluster of virtues which make a person what he or she is.

CHARACTER, SACRAMENTAL   The permanent effect of three sacraments: Baptism, Confirmation, and Holy Order. (Hence, these sacraments are never conferred more than once.)

CHARISM   A gift of the Holy Spirit—e.g., wisdom.

CHARISMATIC   One who manifests and is attentive to the gifts of the Holy Spirit.

CHRISTOCENTRISM   Seeing all reality, and therefore all of theology, in light of Jesus Christ.

CHRISTOLOGY   The theological study of Jesus Christ: natures, person, ministry, consciousness, etc. Christology "from above" starts with the Word of God (*Logos*) in heaven and views Jesus as the Word who has come down to earth for our salvation (John and Paul). Christology "from below" starts with the Jesus of history and shows how his earthly life is significant for our salvation (the Synoptics).

CHRISTOMONISM   Seeing all reality, and doing all theology, only in light of Jesus Christ, so that there is no revelation or salvation apart from Christ and apart from explicit faith in him.

CIRCUMINCESSION   The presence, or indwelling, of the three divine Persons in one another. The Son and the Holy Spirit are present in the Father, and the Father in the Son and the Holy Spirit. The Father and the Son are present in the Holy Spirit, and the Holy Spirit in the Father and the Son. And so forth. Known also as *perichoresis.*

CLASSICISM   The philosophical world view which holds that reality (truth) is essentially static, unchanging, and unaffected by history. Such truth can readily be captured in propositions or statements whose meaning is fixed and clear from century to century.

COGNITIVE   Pertaining to knowledge. A theological approach is said to be "cognitive" if it emphasizes knowledge, the intellect, principles rather than emotions, imagination, the will, the subject, the situation, and circumstances.

COLLEGIALITY   The principle that the Church is a community (college) of local churches which together make up the Church universal. In practice, collegiality introduces a mode of decision-making in the Church which emphasizes coresponsibility not only between the pope and the bishops but also among all communities and groups within the Body of Christ.

COMMUNICATIO IDIOMATUM   The "communication of properties" between the divine and human natures of Jesus Christ because both natures are united in one divine Person, without confusion. The properties of both natures can and must be applied to, or predicated of, the one divine person; e.g., "The Word of God was crucified."

COMMUNICATIO IN SACRIS   Literally, "communication in sacred things." It refers to Catholic and non-Catholic Christians sharing in the Eucharist by receiving Holy Communion in one or another's liturgy.

COMMUNION OF SAINTS The whole community of believers in Christ, living and dead. Those on earth are called the *Church Militant*. Those in purgatory are the *Church Suffering*. Those in heaven are the *Church Triumphant*.

CONCILIARISM The medieval movement which viewed an ecumenical council as superior in authority to the pope.

CONCUPISCENCE Natural "desires," impulses, or instincts of the human person which move the person toward something morally good or morally evil even before he or she has begun any moral reflection about it.

CONSCIENCE The experience of ourselves as moral agents, as persons responsible for our actions. Decisions are made in light of who we think we are and are called to become.

CONSERVATISM, BIBLICAL The tendency to take the accounts of Sacred Scripture at face value—e.g., Jesus really understood himself to be the Messiah and the Son of God right from the beginning of his life and ministry.

CONSERVATISM, THEOLOGICAL The tendency to adhere to the literal meaning of the official teachings of the Church and to emphasize their decisive authority in matters under discussion among theologians.

CONSUBSTANTIATION The Reformation view that the bread and wine remain along with the body and blood of Christ after the eucharistic consecration ("This is my body. . . . This is my blood. . . ."). It is distinguished from *transubstantiation* (see below).

CONTEMPLATION Conscious attention to the presence of God in the depths of oneself, in others, and in the world. A form of prayer.

CONTEMPLATIVE Generally, one whose life is governed by the spirit and practice of contemplation. Specifically, a member of a monastic community.

CONVENIENCE, ARGUMENT FROM A method of reaching theological conclusions not on the basis of sources (Bible, doctrines, etc.) but on the basis of the seeming appropriateness of a particular conclusion. The usual form of such an argument is: It is fitting that God should have done so; God had the power to do so; therefore, God must have done so. Especially applicable to *Mariology* (see below).

CONVERSION The fundamental change of heart (*metanoia*) by which a person accepts Jesus as the Christ and orients his or her whole life around Christ and the Kingdom of God which he proclaimed.

COREDEMPTRIX A title sometimes given to the Blessed Virgin Mary to emphasize her cooperative role in the redemption of the human race by Christ.

COUNCIL An official church assembly. It is *ecumenical*, or *general*, if it draws representatives from the "whole wide world." It is *regional* if it draws representatives from various dioceses in a particular region of the world or of a particular nation. It is *local* if it involves only a particular diocese, or local church.

COUNTER-REFORMATION The Catholic response to the Protestant Reformation of the sixteenth century. At the center was the *Council of Trent* and its reform of doctrine, liturgy, and law.

COVENANT The bond, contract, or "testament" between God and Israel in the Old Testament, established with Noah, Abraham, Moses, and David, and between God and the whole human community in the New Testament, established by the blood of Christ.

COVENANTAL Pertaining to the close bond of love and friendship between God and ourselves.

CREED An official profession of faith, usually promulgated by a council of the Church and used in the Church's liturgy.

CRITICISM, FORM A method of biblical study employed to uncover the second layer of tradition in the composition of the Gospels, namely, the oral proclamation of the Apostles and the disciples (catechesis, narratives, hymns, prayers, etc.).

CRITICISM, HISTORICAL A method of biblical study employed to uncover the first layer of tradition in the composition of the Gospels, namely, the original words and deeds of Jesus. It asks, "How can we know the historical Jesus?"

CRITICISM, REDACTION A method of biblical study employed to uncover the third layer of tradition in the composition of the Gospels, namely, the writings themselves. It tries to identify the dominant ideas which governed the final editing of the texts as we have them today.

DECALOGUE The Ten Commandments.

DEISM A view of God which looks upon God as a divine "watch-maker." Once the world has been created, God no longer takes an active part in its course. Rejected by Vatican I (1869).

DEMYTHOLOGIZATION A method of New Testament interpretation originated by Rudolf Bultmann. It seeks to get back to the original message of Jesus by stripping away all irrelevant stories (myths) about Jesus' divine powers and his comings and goings between heaven and earth.

DEONTOLOGICAL Pertaining to a way of doing moral theology which emphasizes duty and obligation (*deontos*) in relation to law.

DEPOSIT OF FAITH The "content" of Christian faith given by Christ and the Apostles and preserved as a treasury by the Church ever since.

DESCENT INTO HELL The item in the Apostles' Creed which refers to the time between the crucifixion and the resurrection when Jesus was "among the dead." It does not refer to hell as a state of eternal punishment for sin, but rather to *Sheol* (see below).

DIACONATE The ministry of, and state of being, a deacon of the Church, i.e., an ordained assistant to the bishop or the *presbyter* (see below).

DIALECTICAL Pertaining to a way of understanding reality by noting and keeping in balance seemingly opposite values—e.g., God is wholly Other, but God is also one with us in Christ; the Bible is the Word of God, but it is also the product of human effort; we are sinners, but we are also graced and redeemed.

DISCERNMENT The process, associated with the virtue of prudence, by which we try to decide what God wills us to do in these particular circumstances and for the future.

DISCIPLE A follower of Christ. One who literally "learns from" Christ. All Apostles were disciples, but not all disciples were *Apostles* (see above).

DISPENSATION An action of the official Church by which an individual or individuals are exempted from an ecclesiastical law, temporarily or permanently.

DOCETIC Pertaining to a theological attitude which tends to deny the reality of the material and the bodily in creation, redemption, and salvation.

DOCETISM A view which held that Christ only "seemed" to have a human body.

DOCTRINE   An official teaching of the Church.

DOCTRINE, DEVELOPMENT OF   The process by which official teachings are revised in accordance with changes in historical circumstances and understanding.

DOGMA   A doctrine which is promulgated with the highest authority and solemnity. Its denial is a *heresy* (see below). Every dogma is a doctrine, but not every doctrine is a dogma.

DOGMATIC THEOLOGY   Systematic reflection on the Christian faith as that faith has been articulated by the official Church.

DONATISM   A North African movement of the fourth century which held that Baptism had to be administered a second time to those who had left the Church and then returned. Opposed strongly by Augustine.

DOUBLE EFFECT, PRINCIPLE OF   The principle which holds that an evil effect can be permitted so long as it is not directly intended, is not the means of achieving a good effect, and is not out of proportion to the good effect.

DUALISM   The general theological view that all reality is composed of, and arises from, two distinct, absolutely independent, antagonistic, and co-equal principles: Good and Evil.

ECCLESIAL   Pertaining to the Church as a mystery, i.e., as the Body of Christ and the Temple of the Holy Spirit, as distinguished from *ecclesiastical*, which pertains to the Church as an institution.

ECCLESIOLOGY   The theological study of the Church.

ECUMENICAL   Pertaining to a theological attitude which is attentive to the experience and critical reflections of other churches and traditions.

ECUMENISM   The movement which seeks to achieve unity of Christians within the Church and ultimately of all humankind throughout the "whole wide world" (the literal meaning of the word).

ENCYCLICAL   A letter written by the pope and "circulated" throughout the whole Church and even the whole world beyond the Church.

ENLIGHTENMENT   The eighteenth-century philosophical movement which exalted freedom of inquiry and freedom in decision-making. A *post-Enlightenment* mentality criticizes the Enlightenment for its "uncritical" celebration of reason and its failure to attend to the imagination and the larger social context of our ideas.

EPHESUS A city in Asia Minor where the third ecumenical council was held in 431. It condemned *Nestorianism* (see below) and held that Mary is truly the Mother of God (*theotokos*).

EPISCOPACY The highest level of the sacrament of Holy Order. Those who are ordained to the episcopacy are called "bishops." The word is derived from *episkopos*, meaning "overseer."

EPISCOPATE The body of bishops.

ESCHATOLOGICAL Pertaining to a theological attitude which sees all reality in light of the coming Kingdom of God.

ESCHATOLOGY Literally, "the study of the last things." That area of theology which focuses on the Kingdom of God, judgment, heaven, hell, purgatory, the resurrection of the body, and the Second Coming of Christ.

EUCHARIST Literally, a "thanksgiving." The common name for the Mass, or Lord's Supper.

EVANGELICAL Pertaining to the Gospel and to a theological approach which emphasizes the preaching of Jesus and the biblical expression of that preaching.

EVANGELIZATION The proclamation of the Gospel.

EX OPERE OPERANTIS "From the work of the worker." A phrase explaining how a *sacramental* (see below) achieves its effect: not only by the prayer of the Church but also, and necessarily, by the faith and disposition of the recipient and minister.

EX OPERE OPERATO "From the work done." A phrase explaining how a sacrament achieves its effect: not because of the faith of the recipient and/or the worthiness of the minister but because of the power of Christ who acts within and through it.

EXCOMMUNICATION The expulsion of an individual from the Church, more particularly from the Eucharist.

EXEGESIS The scientific interpretation of the texts of Sacred Scripture.

EXISTENTIALIST THEOLOGY An approach to theology which emphasizes the value of the individual person, the primacy of conscience, and the importance of freedom and authenticity in decision-making.

EXPIATION See *atonement*.

EXTRA ECCLESIAM NULLA SALUS "Outside the Church no salvation." The belief that unless one is somehow related to the

Church, that person cannot be saved. The meaning of the formula has been disputed. Father Leonard Feeney, S.J., of Boston, was condemned by the Vatican in 1949 for an extreme interpretation of the principle.

EXTREME UNCTION   The former name for the sacrament of the Anointing of the Sick.

FAITH   Personal knowledge of God. Christian faith is personal knowledge of God as disclosed in Jesus Christ.

FAITH DEVELOPMENT   The process by which faith advances progressively through various stages of human growth—e.g., from an adolescent's desire to win approval to a mature adult's commitment to values apart from self-interest.

FATHERS OF THE CHURCH   Writers of Christian antiquity who had a major impact on the doctrinal tradition of the Church. The period of the Fathers is said to have ended by the mid-eighth century.

FIDEISM   The nineteenth-century view that faith has no rational content at all. Conviction is rooted in the heart, not the mind.

FIDES FIDUCIALIS   Luther's notion of faith as "trust." This view was rejected by the Council Trent (1547) because it seemed to deny any objective content to faith.

FILIOQUE   Literally, "and from the Son." This word was added to the Creed of Nicea-Constantinople at the end of the seventh century, contending that the Holy Spirit proceeds from the Father and the Son as from a single principle. It was opposed by the Greek Church, which preferred the term *"per Filium"* to emphasize the primacy of God the Father in the work of salvation.

FLORENCE   An ecumenical council, held in this Italian city in 1439, which not only tried to heal the East-West schism but also defined the seven sacraments.

FUNDAMENTAL OPTION   The radical orientation of one's whole life toward or away from God. Akin to conversion. Our destiny is determined by this fundamental "choice" and not by individual acts, unless those acts are such that our basic relationship with God is fully engaged.

FUNDAMENTAL THEOLOGY   That area of theology which deals with the most basic introductory questions: e.g., revelation, faith, authority, the ways of knowing God, the nature and task of theology itself.

GALLICANISM A form of national *conciliarism* (see above) peculiar to France (Gaul), and implicitly rejected by the First Vatican Council (1869-1870).

GAUDIUM ET SPES Vatican II's *Pastoral Constitution on the Church in the Modern World*.

GNOSTIC Pertaining to a theological attitude which exaggerates the role of knowledge (*gnosis*) in salvation and which insists that such saving knowledge is available to only a select few.

GNOSTICISM The earliest of Christian heresies, first refuted in the Fourth Gospel. Besides stressing the role of saving knowledge, it also denied the goodness of creation and of the material order.

GOSPEL The "good news" proclaimed by Jesus Christ and thereafter by the Apostles and the Church. The Gospel is interpreted and recorded in the four Gospels of Matthew, Mark, Luke, and John.

GRACE The presence of God.

GRACE, ACTUAL The presence of God given as a power to guide particular human actions.

GRACE, CREATED The presence of God in particular persons, manifested in virtues, in gifts of the Holy Spirit, etc.

GRACE, SANCTIFYING The abiding presence of God in the human person.

GRACE, UNCREATED God. The uncreated Word of God in Jesus Christ. The Holy Spirit.

HEILSGESCHICHTE See *salvation history*.

HELLENISM Theological and philosophical movements dictated and shaped by Greek culture, where the emphasis is on the realm of ideas and universal principles rather than on the world of the concrete and the changeable.

HELLENIZATION OF DOGMA The progressive introduction of Greek categories in the formulation and interpretation of the Christian faith. They are often distinguished from biblical categories of faith.

HERESY Literally, a "choice." It is the denial of a *dogma* (see above).

HERMENEUTICS The science of interpretation; the body of principles which governs the interpretation of any statement or text.

HIERARCHICAL Pertaining to a theological mentality which emphasizes the role of ecclesiastical officers in the life and teaching of the Church.

HIERARCHY Literally, "rule by priests." It is the body of ordained ministers in the Church: pope, bishops, priests, and deacons.

HISTORICAL CONSCIOUSNESS A theological and philosophical mentality which is attentive to the impact of history on human thought and action and which, therefore, takes into account the concrete and the changeable. Distinguished from *classicism* (see above).

HISTORICITY That fundamental human condition by which we are set in time and shaped by the movement of history.

HISTORY The movement of the world toward the final Kingdom of God under the impact of God's grace and the shaping influence of human freedom.

HOMOIOUSIOS Literally, "of a *similar* substance." This term was proposed by Eusebius of Caesarea, who thought it was closer to the teaching of Sacred Scripture, namely, that the Son is *like* the Father. It is simply a different emphasis and approach and is not regarded as unorthodox if correctly understood.

HOMOOUSIOS Literally, "of the *same* substance." Used in the teaching of the early Christological councils, especially Nicea (325), to affirm that the Father and the *Logos* (see below) are of the same substance, or nature. Therefore, Jesus is truly divine.

HORIZON A philosophical term meaning the range, or context, of one's view of reality and, therefore, the spectrum of questions one is prepared to ask about human existence, the world, meaning, etc.

HUMANAE VITAE The 1968 encyclical of Pope Paul VI in which he condemned as immoral all artificial means of regulating births.

HUMANIZATION The process by which the world and its history, through heightened consciousness and freedom, become progressively truer to their vocation and closer to their final destiny in the Kingdom of God.

HYLOMORPHISM A medieval Scholastic notion which regarded all reality as composed of matter and form. The notion was applied to the theology of the Eucharist, grace, the human person, and the sacraments in general; e.g., the *matter* of a sacrament is what is used (water in Baptism), the *form* of a sacrament is the words and gestures (pouring the water and saying the baptismal formula); or, the body is the *matter* of the human person, the soul is the *form*.

HYPOSTATIC UNION   The word *hypostasis* refers to the person of the *Logos* (see below). The hypostatic union is the permanent union of divine and human natures in the one divine Person of the Word in Jesus Christ (see *Chalcedon* above).

ICONOCLASM   Literally, "the destroying of images." The negative attitude toward images (*icons*) and their veneration. An iconoclastic controversy raged in the East during the eighth and ninth centuries.

IDEALISM   The philosophical attitude which identifies reality with ideas. It is distinguished from *realism* (see below).

IDOLATRY   The worship of idols. The term applies to any tendency to equate something finite with the infinite (God).

IMMACULATE CONCEPTION   The dogma defined by Pope Pius IX in 1854 which holds that the Blessed Virgin Mary was free from sin from the very first moment of her existence. This is not to be confused with the *virgin birth* (see below).

IMPECCABILITAS   The attribute of Jesus Christ by which he is incapable of sinning.

IMPECCANTIA   The sinlessness of Jesus. Even if Jesus Christ were capable of sinning, in fact he did not sin.

INCARNATION   The process by which the Word of God became flesh. (See also *hypostatic union*.)

INDIFFERENTISM   A theological attitude which holds that one religion is as good, or as bad, as another.

INDISSOLUBILITY   The quality of permanence (literally "unbreakability") which applies to marriage.

INDULGENCE   The partial or full remission of the penalties still due to sins which have already been forgiven.

INERRANCY   The immunity of Sacred Scripture from fundamental error about God and the things of God.

INFALLIBILITY   Literally, "immunity from error." The charism by which the Church is protected from fundamental error in matters of faith and morals. It can be exercised by the pope and by an ecumenical council.

INFRALAPSARIAN Pertaining to the period of history after the "fall" of Adam.

INITIATION, CHRISTIAN The total liturgical and catechetical process of becoming a Christian through Baptism, Confirmation, and Eucharist.

INITIUM FIDEI Literally, the "beginning of faith." The grace of God is necessary for the whole process of faith, from beginning to end. There is no point at which the movement of, and toward, faith is possible without the impulse of divine grace.

INSPIRATION, BIBLICAL The guidance of the Holy Spirit in the writing of Sacred Scripture. More generally, inspiration refers to the guidance of the Holy Spirit over the whole Church.

INTEGRALISM A theological attitude, prevalent especially in France in the nineteenth and twentieth centuries, which insists that everything must become formally and explicitly Christian before it is good. Literally, nothing is "whole" (integral) unless and until it is brought within the orbit of the Church.

INTENTIONALITY A philosophical and theological term which refers to the purposive character of human decision-making and behavior.

INTERCOMMUNION See *communicatio in sacris* (above).

INTERNAL FORUM The realm of conscience and/or of the sacrament of Penance. A decision reached in the "internal forum" is known only to God, the individual, and the confessor or spiritual director.

IURE DIVINO Literally, "by divine law." The term refers to institutions (e.g., sacraments) which are said to exist by the explicit will of God, as articulated by Christ and/or the Church. Hence, they are not subject to abolition or substantial tampering by the Church or other human agents.

JANSENISM A seventeenth- and eighteenth-century movement in Europe, especially France, which stressed moral austerity, the evil of the human body and of human desires, and an elitist notion of salvation (Jesus died for a few).

JANSENISTIC Pertaining to a moral attitude which displays a negative appreciation of the bodily and a fear of the sexual. It passed from France to Ireland and then to the United States of America in the late nineteenth and early twentieth centuries.

JESUS OF HISTORY/CHRIST OF FAITH Refers to the distinction between Jesus as he actually was (and whom we can never fully know on the basis of historical evidence) and Jesus as he was understood and interpreted by the Church after the resurrection (namely, as the Christ).

JOHANNINE Pertaining to the writings of the New Testament attributed to John, the Evangelist and the "beloved disciple," or at least to those influenced by him. These are the Fourth Gospel, the three epistles, and the Book of Revelation. They present a high Christology ("from above") and emphasize the law of love and the work of the Spirit.

JURIDICAL Pertaining to a theological attitude which stresses the importance of law in the formation and exercise of Christian life.

JUSTIFICATION The event by which God, acting in Jesus Christ, makes us holy (just) in the divine sight. The immediate effect of justification is *sanctification* (see below). The ultimate effect is *salvation* (see below). The foundation of justification is the *redemption* (see below).

KENOSIS A biblical term (Philippians 2: 5-11) which refers to the "self-emptying" of Christ. He did not cling to his divinity but became obedient even unto death.

KERYGMA The "message" of the Gospel. That which was originally proclaimed.

KERYGMATIC THEOLOGY A theology which adheres closely to the literal meaning and emphasis of the biblical message (see also *evangelical*).

KINGDOM OF GOD The reign, or rule, of God. It is the presence of God in the heart, in groups, in the world at large, renewing and reconciling all things. It is both a process ("reign of God") and the reality towards which the process is moving ("Kingdom of God").

KOINONIA Community, or fellowship, produced by the Holy Spirit.

LAST THINGS Death, judgment, heaven, hell, purgatory, Second Coming of Christ, resurrection of the body, and the fulfillment of the Kingdom of God.

LAW In the Old Testament: the Ten Commandments, the Torah, and other norms of conduct, founded in the *Covenant* (see above). In the New Testament: the law of the Gospel, fulfilled in the commandment of love of God and love of neighbor.

LAXISM   A moral attitude which tries to find ways of getting around Christian obligations and which always resolves the doubt in favor of exemption, even when good reasons are not present.

LEGALISM   A moral attitude which identifies morality with the literal observance of laws, even if the spirit of the law requires something more or different.

LEX ORANDI, LEX CREDENDI   "The law of praying is the law of believing." Christian belief is expressed in Christian worship. Christian worship is, in turn, a norm of faith.

LIBERALISM, BIBLICAL   The tendency to reduce the content of the Bible to its most natural meaning; e.g., Jesus had no idea that he was the Messiah or the Son of God.

LIBERALISM, THEOLOGICAL   The tendency to place a rational or humanistic interpretation on all dogmas and doctrines so that they are devoid of supernatural content. The word is sometimes used in Catholic circles to describe those who assume a critical attitude toward the teaching authority of the Church or toward traditional doctrines of the faith.

LIBERATION THEOLOGY   A type of theology which emphasizes the motif of liberation in both Old and New Testaments and which reinterprets all doctrines in terms of that motif. Forms of liberation theology include: Latin American, black, and feminist.

LITURGY   The official public worship of the Church, especially the Eucharist and the sacraments.

LOGOS   The Word of God, the Second Person of the Trinity, who became flesh in the *incarnation* (see above).

LUMEN GENTIUM   Vatican II's *Dogmatic Constitution on the Church.*

LUMEN GLORIAE   "The light of glory." That power by which we are enabled to "see God face to face" in heaven. (See also *beatific vision.*)

MACEDONIANISM   A fourth-century heresy which denied the divinity of the Holy Spirit. It was condemned by the Council of Constantinople (381).

MAGISTERIUM   The teaching authority of the Church, which belongs to some by reason of office (pope and bishops) and to others by reason of scholarly competence (theologians). The term also applies to the body of teachers.

MANICHAEISM   A blend of *dualism* and *Gnosticism* (see above for both terms), which began in the mid-third century and did not finally die out until the fourteenth.

MARIOLOGY   The theological study of the Blessed Virgin Mary in terms of her role in the Church and in our redemption.

MARTYR   Literally, a "witness." One who is put to death because of his or her faith in Jesus Christ.

MASS   The Eucharist, or Lord's Supper.

MATER ET MAGISTRA   The 1961 encyclical of Pope John XXIII on social justice.

MEDIATION   The theological principle that God is available to us and acts upon us through secondary causes: persons, places, events, things, nature, history.

MEDIEVAL   Pertaining to the period known as the Middle Ages, the beginning of which some place as early as the seventh century and the end as late as the sixteenth. The high Middle Ages are the twelfth and thirteenth centuries, which are sometimes mistakenly identified with the origins of Catholicism itself.

MERIT   Spiritual "credit" earned with God for having performed some good action.

METANOIA   See *conversion*.

METHOD   A regular and recurrent pattern of operations. A fundamental way of doing theology. Thus, an historical method treats every question from the point of view of its development from its origins to the present time.

MINISTRY   Literally, a "service." Any service publicly designated by the Church to assist in the fulfillment of its mission.

MIRACLE   An unusual event by which God makes a special impact on history. A special manifestation of the presence and power of God.

MISSION OF THE CHURCH   That for which the Church has been "sent"; i.e., its purpose: to proclaim the Gospel in word, in sacrament, in witness, and in service.

MIXED MARRIAGE   A marriage between a Catholic and one who is not a Catholic.

MODALISM   A general theological approach to the Trinity which sees the three Persons as three different modes of the one God's operations (creation, incarnation, and sanctification).

MODERNISM An early-twentieth-century movement in Catholicism condemned by Pope Pius X because it seemed to deny the permanence of dogmas and tended to reduce all doctrines to their rational or humanistic components. (See also *liberalism, theological.*)

MODERNITY A frame of mind induced by technology, and especially by the innovations effected by advances in communications and transportation. The modern mentality is characterized by its stress on the necessity of making choices from among a relatively large number of possibilities and, therefore, of consulting as wide a spectrum of views as possible. (See also *pluralism.*)

MONASTICISM A style of Christian life, begun in the third century as a flight to the desert to avoid persecution and later to protest the newly privileged status of the Church; it emphasizes life-in-community, common prayer, silence, and contemplation.

MONOGENISM The view that the whole human race is descended from a single couple, Adam and Eve. It is distinguished from *polygenism.*

MONOPHYSITISM The teaching, condemned by the Council of Chalcedon (451), that the human nature of Christ was totally absorbed by the divine nature. As an expression of the *Alexandrian School* (see above), it emphasized the divinity of Christ.

MONOTHEISM The belief in one God. It is distinguished from *polytheism.*

MONOTHELITISM The view, rejected by the Third Council of Constantinople (681), that there is only one will in Christ, the divine will. This is also known as *Monenergism.*

MONTANISM A second-century charismatic belief which stressed the imminent end of the world and imposed an austere morality in preparation for the event. Tertullian was its best-known adherent.

MORAL THEOLOGY That branch of theology which attends to the individual and social implications of the Gospel, and which draws normative inferences for the conduct of the Church and its individual members.

MORTAL SIN So fundamental a rejection of the Gospel and/or the will of God that it merits eternal punishment. Thus, the adjective "mortal."

MYSTERIUM ECCLESIAE   The 1973 declaration of the Congregation for the Doctrine of the Faith on infallibility and on the development of doctrine. The document is especially significant because it
acknowledges the historicity of doctrinal and dogmatic statements.

MYSTERY   A reality imbued with the hidden presence of God. The
term is most akin to the word *sacrament*. It also refers to the plan of
God for our salvation, as worked out historically in Christ.

MYSTICISM   A human's experience of God. Christian mysticism is the
experiencing of God in Jesus Christ in light of the Holy Spirit.

NATURAL LAW   The whole order of reality which, by the will of
God, defines us as human persons and contributes to human development. For the Greeks, it was a "given" of reality; for the Romans, it
was something to be discovered and reshaped through common
sense and intelligence.

NATURE   The human condition apart from grace, but with the radical capacity to receive grace. ("Pure" nature, i.e., without the
capacity for grace, does not exist.)

NEO-ORTHODOXY   The early-twentieth-century movement within
Protestantism (especially Karl Barth) which sought to return to the
basic principles of Reformation theology: the primacy of the Word of
God, e.g.

NEOPLATONISM   The final stage of ancient Greek philosophy
which strongly influenced certain Christian thinkers, especially Origen and Augustine. It stressed the reality of God as *Logos*, of finite
beings as participants in the *Logos*, and as always in movement back
to their source in God. Negatively, it tended to underestimate the
goodness of the material order and the importance of the individual
person.

NESTORIANISM   The teaching, condemned by the council of
Ephesus (431), that posited two separate persons in Jesus Christ, the
one human and the other divine. Therefore, Mary was the mother of
the human Jesus only. As an expression of the *Antioch School* of
theology (see above), it emphasized the humanity of Christ.

NICEA   The city in Asia Minor where in 325 the first ecumenical
council was held to condemn *Arianism* (see above).

NOMINALISM   A medieval philosophical view which denied the reality of universal principles. Emphasis was always on the individual
person, situation, or term, and on its uniqueness.

ORDAINED MINISTRY   A *ministry* (see above) conferred by the imposition of hands: diaconate, presbyterate (priesthood), and the episcopate.

ORDINATION   A sacramental act, usually involving a laying on of hands by a bishop, through which an individual is admitted to the diaconate, the presbyterate (priesthood), or the episcopate.

ORIGENISM   A tendency in Eastern theology of the third through fifth centuries which emphasized the necessity and eternity of the world and of souls and which looked upon matter as a consequence of sin.

ORIGINAL JUSTICE   The state in which the first human beings were thought to have existed before Original Sin.

ORIGINAL SIN   The state in which all human beings are now born. It is a situation or condition in which the possibility of sin becomes instead a probability because grace is not at our disposal in the manner and to the degree that God intended.

ORTHODOXY   Literally, "right praise." Consistency with the faith of the Church as embodied in Sacred Scripture, the Fathers, official teachings, and the liturgy.

PACEM IN TERRIS   The 1963 encyclical of Pope John XXIII on social justice and international development.

PARABLE   A story which makes a theological point through the use of metaphors.

PAROUSIA   The Second Coming of Christ at the end of history.

PARTHENOGENESIS   See *virgin birth*.

PASTORAL   Pertaining to the actual life of the Church, especially at the parish and diocesan levels.

PATRISTIC   Pertaining to the *Fathers of the Church* (see above).

PAULINE   Pertaining to the writings of the New Testament attributed to Paul. They are known as Epistles, or letters: Romans, 1 and 2 Corinthians, Galatians, etc.

PAULINE PRIVILEGE   Based on 1 Corinthians 7:10-16, the principle which allows a convert to the Church to remarry if his or her unbaptized spouse does not also become a Christian.

PELAGIAN   Pertaining to a theological attitude which exaggerates the role of human effort in moral life.

PELAGIANISM   A heresy with roots in the fifth century which declared that salvation is possible through human effort alone, without grace.

PENTATEUCH   The first five books of the Old Testament: Genesis, Exodus, Leviticus, Numbers, and Deuteronomy. Also known as the *Torah*, or the *Law* (see above).

PERICHORESIS   See *circumincession*.

PERSON   An existing being with the capacity for consciousness and freedom. In the Trinity, the word "person" is used analogically; i.e., Father, Son, and Holy Spirit are "like" human persons, but there are not three separate Gods, only different relationships within the Godhead and different ways in which the one God acts outside the Godhead itself. (See also *subject*.)

PERSONALISM   A theological and philosophical view which stresses the importance of the individual human being, or person, in reaching moral decisions.

PETRINE MINISTRY, OFFICE   The service rendered the Church by the pope. The papacy. Both ministry and office attend to the universal Church's need for unity in life and mission.

PETRINE PRIVILEGE   Also known as the "Privilege of the Faith." It allows the pope to dissolve a marriage between a Christian and a non-Christian when the Christian wishes to marry another Christian or the non-Christian wishes to become a Catholic and remarry.

PHENOMENOLOGY   A philosophical and theological view which begins with, and emphasizes, observable realities (phenomena) rather than general principles.

PHILOSOPHY   The branch of knowledge concerned with the ultimate meaning of reality, but it does not assume responsibility (as *theology* does) for articulating that meaning in terms of particular religious traditions. Closely related to, and sometimes indistinguishable from, theology itself.

PIETISM   A seventeenth- and eighteenth-century movement within German Lutheranism which stressed the interior life, the experience of conversion, and personal devotion to Jesus.

PIETISTIC   Pertaining to a spiritual or moral attitude which stresses personal devotion at the expense of sound biblical, theological, and doctrinal principles.

PLURALISM   The inevitable variety of human experiences and of expressions. The "discovery" of pluralism is a modern phenomenon

xli

brought about especially by advances in communications and in transportation.

PNEUMA   The Greek word for "spirit." It refers to the spiritual principle in human existence, opposed to the flesh (*sarx*).

PNEUMATOLOGICAL   Pertaining to the Holy Spirit.

POLITICAL THEOLOGY   A type of theology which stresses the relationship between Christian faith and the socio-political order or, more generally, between theory and practice.

POLYTHEISM   Belief in many gods.

POSITIVISM   A philosophical and theological view which not only begins with observable realities, as does the *phenomenological* approach (see *phenomenology* above), but insists that reality consists *only* of the concrete, the visible, and the particular. In theology it leads to reflection on God not in terms of the totality of reality but in terms of the understanding of God as given in certain sources—e.g., the Bible, the teachings of the Church.

POTENTIA OBEDIENTIALIS   The fundamental human capacity for grace.

PRAXIS   Reflective action. Reflection which is the fruit of one's concrete experience and situation. Action which is the expression of such reflection. Not identical, therefore, simply with "practice." A central term in *liberation theology* (see above).

PREDESTINATION   The eternal decree of God regarding the destination, or final goal, of all reality and especially of humankind.

PREDESTINATIONISM   The Calvinist doctrine that God decides, independently of a person's exercise of freedom and manifestation of good will, who will be saved and who will be damned. The latter decree is also known as *antecedent negative reprobation*.

PRESBYTER   A priest of the second "order"—i.e., less than a bishop but more than a deacon. A priest.

PRESBYTERATE   The body of priests.

PRIMACY   The authority which the pope has over the whole Church.

PROBABILISM   The moral principle which holds that one can safely follow a theological opinion if it is proposed by someone having sufficient theological authority and standing. *Equiprobabilism* requires that the more lenient opinion be at least as strong as the stricter opinion. *Probabiliorism* requires that the more lenient opinion be stronger than the stricter opinion.

PROCESS THEOLOGY   A type of theology which emphasizes the movement, dynamism, changeability, and relativity of God, of history, and of all reality. Closely linked on the Catholic side with the writings of Teilhard de Chardin; on the Protestant side, with Alfred North Whitehead.

PROPHECY   Literally, a "speaking on behalf (of God)." More specifically, the proclamation of a word and the doing of a deed on behalf of the Kingdom of God.

PROTOLOGY   The "study of the first things" (creation, Original Justice, Original Sin).

PROVIDENCE   God's abiding guidance of the whole created order toward the final Kingdom.

PURGATORY   The state of purification and/or maturation which one may need to enter after death and before the *beatific vision* (see above).

QUIETISM   A seventeenth-century movement in France which held that we can do nothing at all for our salvation and that the way of Christian spirituality is a way of inwardness, of resignation, and of complete passivity.

RATIONALISM   The philosophical view which holds that nothing can be accepted as true unless it can be proved by reason alone.

RATIONALISTIC   Pertaining to a philosophical and theological approach which exaggerates the powers of human reason to know truth and even God to the point where revelation is denied.

REALISM   A philosophical view which emphasizes the objectivity of things, apart from the person thinking about them. *Naive* realism assumes that things are exactly what they seem to be ("Just take a look"). *Critical* realism insists that all reality is "mediated by meaning"—i.e., the real is what we *judge* to be true, on the basis of our experience.

REAL PRESENCE   The sacramental presence of Christ in the Eucharist.

REDEMPTION   The act by which we are literally "bought back" into the grace of God by the work of Jesus Christ. See also *soteriology.*

REIGN OF GOD   The more active, or dynamic, expression for the Kingdom of God (see above). It is the Kingdom as it is now in process.

xliii

RELIC   An object regarded as worthy of veneration because of its connection with a saint—e.g., a piece of bone.

RELIGION   The external, social, institutionalized expression of our faith in God.

RELIGIOUS   Pertaining to an attitude of seeing all reality in light of the presence and action of God, and of responding to God's presence and action with reverence, gratitude, and appropriate moral behavior.

RELIGIOUS CONGREGATION, ORDER   An organized group of Christians who have taken vows to live in community and to observe the evangelical counsels of poverty, chastity, and obedience.

RELIGIOUS EDUCATION   That field which comes into existence at the point of intersection between theology and education. It is concerned with interpreting and directing human experience in light of the conviction that God is present to that experience, that Jesus Christ is the sacrament of God's presence in the world, and that the Church is the primary place where the presence of God in Christ is acknowledged, celebrated, and lived out.

RES ET SACRAMENTUM   Literally, "the reality and the sign." In sacramental theology, it refers to the lasting effect of a sacrament—e.g., the Real Presence of Christ in the Eucharist.

RES TANTUM   Literally, "the reality alone." In sacramental theology, it refers to the immediate effect of a sacrament, namely, grace.

REVELATION   God's self-disclosure (literally, "unveiling") to humankind through creation, events, persons, and especially Jesus Christ.

REVIVISCENCE   The revival of grace from a *character* sacrament (see above) received in *mortal sin* (see above). If a person receives a character sacrament in the state of mortal sin, the grace of that sacrament is not given. But that grace "revives" and is applied to the individual as soon as contrition blots out the sin.

RIGHT   A power that we have to do things which are necessary for achieving the end or purpose for which we are destined as rational and free persons.

RIGHTEOUSNESS   The state of being just in the sight of God.

SABELLIANISM   A third- and fourth-century heresy which held that God is three only in relation to the world. There is no trinity of Persons *within* the godhead. A form of *Modalism* (see above).

SACRAMENT   In general, any visible sign of God's invisible presence. Specifically, a sign through which the Church manifests its faith and communicates the saving reality (grace) of God which is present in the Church and in the signs themselves. In Catholic doctrine there are Baptism, Confirmation, Eucharist, Penance, Marriage, Holy Order, and the Anointing of the Sick.

SACRAMENTAL   A grace-bearing sign which does not so fully express the nature of the Church and which, according to Catholic doctrine, does not carry the guarantee of grace associated with the seven sacraments—e.g., holy water, the palm branches used on Palm Sunday, a crucifix.

SACRAMENTALITY, PRINCIPLE OF   The fundamentally Catholic notion that all reality is potentially and in fact the bearer of God's presence and the instrument of divine action on our behalf. Closely related to the principle of *mediation* (see above).

SACRAMENTUM TANTUM   Literally, "the sign alone." In sacramental theology, it is a rite or sacred action—e.g., the pouring of the water and the recitation of the formula "I baptize you...."

SALVATION   From the Latin word *salus*, meaning "health." It is the goal and end-product of creation, the incarnation, the redemption, conversion, justification, and sanctification. To be saved is to be fully and permanently united with God and with one another in God.

SALVATION-HISTORY   History perceived as the arena in which God progressively brings humankind toward the Kingdom. Salvation-history begins with creation, ends with the Second Coming of Christ, and has its midpoint in Jesus Christ. Such a view of history is associated with Luke in the New Testament and with Oscar Cullmann in modern theology.

SANCTIFICATION   The state of holiness by reason of the presence of God within oneself. It is not to be confused with *justification* (see above), which is the act or process by which we are made holy, or just, in God's sight.

SANCTIFYING GRACE   See *grace*.

SARX   The Greek word for "flesh." It is the body apart from the spirit, and even opposed to it.

SATAN   Literally, "the evil one." The personification of evil. The one in whom all evil is focused.

xlv

SCHISM   A breach of Church unity which occurs when a whole group or community separates itself from the rest of the Body of Christ. In Catholic theology, this happens when communion with the pope is broken.

SCHOLASTIC   Pertaining to a general approach to the doing of theology which derives its style from the medieval "schools." Such theology is deductive, abstract, doctrinal, and *classicist* (see above).

SCHOLASTICISM   A theological and philosophical movement in the Middle Ages attached to certain "schools" (thus, the term "scholastic") and emphasizing the interpretation of texts, especially of other theologians and philosophers rather than of the Bible and the Fathers of the Church.

SEMI-PELAGIANISM   The heresy, condemned by the Second Council of Orange (527), which held that the beginning of faith (*initium fidei*) is made independently of God's grace but that thereafter the grace of God is necessary for salvation.

SENSUS FIDELIUM   Literally, "the sense of the faithful." It is one of the norms of theological truth, namely, the actual belief of Christians down through the centuries.

SHEOL   The Old Testament name for the "underworld" inhabited by all the dead. Not to be confused with hell, which is a state of eternal alienation from God because of sin.

SIMONY   The buying and selling of spiritual goods.

SIMUL JUSTUS ET PECCATOR   Literally, "at the same time just and sinner." A formula made famous by Martin Luther to make the point that even though we have been declared just by God because of Christ, we are still as corrupt as ever inside. Catholic doctrine insists that *justification* leads to *sanctification* (see above).

SIN   Any deliberate infidelity to the will of God. It can be individual or social. The condition that makes sin possible, not to say probable, is *Original Sin* (see above). Sins which reverse our *fundamental option* (see above) for God, are *mortal sins*. Sins which reflect poorly on our commitment to God but which do not reverse our course toward God are *serious sins*. Less serious sins are *venial sins*. Below those in gravity are *imperfections*.

SOCIAL DOCTRINE   The body of official teachings, developed since Pope Leo XIII in 1891, which identify the implications of the Gospel in matters pertaining to social justice, peace, and human rights.

xlvi

SOCIALIZATION   A process by which nations and humankind in general are becoming increasingly interdependent. Emphasized by Pope John XXIII's social encyclicals, *Mater et Magistra* (1961) and *Pacem in Terris* (1963).

SOLA FIDE   Literally, "by faith alone." The Protestant principle that we are saved by faith alone, not by good works. Catholic doctrine insists that faith must issue in good works and that good works are saving insofar as they are expressions of faith.

SOLA GRATIA   Literally, "by grace alone." The Protestant principle that we are saved by grace alone, i.e., by God's action and not at all by our own. Catholic doctrine insists that God requires our free cooperation although it is God alone who makes that cooperation possible.

SOLA SCRIPTURA   Literally, "by Scripture alone." The Protestant principle that the Word of God is given to us in the Bible alone and not in the official teachings of the Church. Catholic doctrine insists that the Bible itself is the Church's book—i.e., that the authority of the Church has determined which books are inspired and, therefore, *canonical* (see above). Furthermore, all official teachings are subject to the authority of the Word of God as contained in the Bible.

SOMA   The Greek word for "body." But in contradistinction to *sarx* (see above), *soma* stands for the whole person: flesh and spirit together.

SOTERIOLOGY   Literally, "the study of salvation." It is that area of theology which focuses on the passion, death, resurrection, and exaltation of Christ insofar as they bring about our salvation.

SPIRITUAL   Pertaining to an attitude and style which reflect an attentiveness to the presence and action of God within us and in the world around us.

SPIRITUALITY   Our way of being *religious* (see above). *Christian* spirituality is the cultivation of a style of life consistent with the presence of the Spirit of the Risen Christ within us and with our status as members of the Body of Christ.

SUBJECT   The human *person* (see above) insofar as the person is conscious, interrelates with others, and freely determines who and what he or she will become.

SUBJECTIVE   Pertaining to a philosophical and theological attitude which emphasizes the values of individual consciousness and freedom.

SUBORDINATIONISM A second- and third-century heresy which held that the Son and the Holy Spirit are less than the Father because they proceed from the Father. Therefore, the Son and the Spirit are not fully divine.

SUBSIDIARITY A principle in Catholic social doctrine which holds that nothing should be done by a higher agency which can be done as well, or better, by a lower agency.

SUMMA THEOLOGICA The major work of systematic theology done by Thomas Aquinas.

SUPERNATURAL Pertaining to that which exceeds the power and capacity of human nature apart from the grace of God.

"SUPERNATURAL EXISTENTIAL" A term used by Karl Rahner, meaning our radical capacity for God. It is the permanent modification of the human person, in the depths of one's being, by which the person is transformed from within and oriented toward God. It is not grace itself, but God's offer of grace.

SYMBOL A sign which embodies what it signifies. Close to the meaning of *sacrament* (see above). Therefore, it is not an arbitrary sign, but a sign that is intimately connected with what it signifies.

SYNOD An official assembly of the Church at the international, national, regional, provincial, or diocesan level.

SYNOPTICS The first three Gospels, Matthew, Mark, and Luke, so called because when they are read side by side (synoptically), certain parallels in structure and content readily emerge.

SYSTEMATIC THEOLOGY That theology which tries to see the Christian tradition as a whole, by understanding the whole in terms of the interrelationships among all its parts, and each part in terms of its relationships to other parts and to the whole.

TELEOLOGICAL Pertaining to a way of doing moral theology which emphasizes the end (*telos*), or purpose, of human existence.

THEOLOGY The ordered effort to bring our experience of God to the level of intelligent expression. It is "faith seeking understanding" (Anselm).

THEOTOKOS Literally, "the Bearer of God." The title given to Mary at the Council of Ephesus (431), which taught that there is one divine person in Jesus Christ, not two as the Nestorians argued. Therefore, Mary is truly the "Mother of God" and not only the mother of the human Jesus.

THOMISM   An approach to theology derived from Thomas Aquinas. It is based on *critical realism* (see above under *realism*) and follows a strongly *systematic* method (see above). It is not to be confused with *Scholasticism* (see above).

TRADITION   Both the process of "handing on" the faith and that which has been handed on. Tradition (upper-case) includes Scripture, the essential doctrines of the Church, the major writings and teachings of the Fathers, the liturgical life of the Church, and the living and lived faith of the whole Church down through the centuries. Tradition (upper-case) is not to be confused with tradition (lower-case), which includes customs, institutions, practices which are simply usual ways of thinking about, and giving expression to, the Christian faith.

TRADITIONALISM   The nineteenth-century opinion, rejected by Vatican I, that reason can know nothing at all about religious truth because such knowledge comes only through the revelation that has been "handed down" to us. As a modern term, it refers to the attitude of those Catholics who are opposed to the reforms of Vatican II and who wish the Church would return to its traditional pre-Vatican II ways.

TRANSCENDENTAL   Pertaining to that which is above and beyond the ordinary, the concrete, the tangible—i.e., to God.

TRANSCENDENTAL THOMISM   That twentieth-century approach to theology which is rooted in the principle that God is already present to life as a principle that renders all life open to becoming something more than it is already.

TRANSUBSTANTIATION   The official Catholic teaching, given by the Council of Trent, that the substance of the bread and the wine are changed into the substance of Christ's body and blood at the Eucharist, so that nothing of the bread and wine remains except what is accidental—e.g., taste, shape, weight. This teaching is distinguished from *consubstantiation* (see above).

TRENT   The Italian city in which the nineteenth ecumenical council was held from 1545 to 1563, and hence the council itself. This council was the Catholic Church's principal response to the Protestant Reformation. It defined the canon of Sacred Scripture, Original Sin, grace, justification, the seven sacraments, etc. Trent was the primary influence on Catholic life until the pontificate of John XXIII (1958-1963).

TRINITARIAN   Pertaining to a theological emphasis which views all doctrines in light of the creative activity of the Father, the redemptive work of the Son, and the reconciling action of the Holy Spirit.

TRINITY, ECONOMIC   The reality of the Trinity insofar as the triune God is active and manifested in the world and its history: the Father as creator, the Son as redeemer, the Spirit as reconciler. Refers, therefore, to the exterior activity of the Trinity in history.

TRINITY, IMMANENT   The reality of the Trinity insofar as the three Persons are different not in terms of their different work on our behalf but in terms of their different relationships, one to another; e.g., the Father is unbegotten, the Son is begotten. Refers, therefore, to the inner life of the Trinity.

TRITHEISM   Belief in three gods. An exaggeration of the doctrine of the Trinity.

TWELVE, THE   The twelve men directly called by Jesus to carry his message of the Kingdom of God to the world. All of the Twelve were apostles, but not all apostles were among the original Twelve.

TYPE   A person in whom the qualities of a greater or later reality are somehow "typified" or anticipated—e.g., Mary as a "type" of the Church, and Moses as a "type" of Christ.

ULTRAMONTANISM   Literally, "beyond the mountains" (the Alps). It is a form of rigid *traditionalism* (see above) developed in France, distrustful of theological reflection, and excessively loyal to the Holy See "beyond the mountains."

VATICAN   The territory politically operated and controlled by the papacy, and the site of the twentieth (1869-1870) and twenty-first (1962-1965) ecumenical councils. *Vatican I* addressed itself to the questions of reason and faith, on the one hand, and papal primacy and papal infallibility, on the other. *Vatican II* opened the Church to more of its own members, to other Christians, and to the whole world.

VENIAL SIN   A less serious infidelity to the will of God, sufficient to diminish one's Christian character (see *character, moral*) but not to reverse one's fundamental orientation toward God.

VIATICUM   Literally, "on the way with you." The last sacrament, i.e., the final reception of Holy Communion before death.

1

VIRGIN BIRTH   The belief that Jesus became a human being without the cooperation of a human father. This is not to be confused with the *Immaculate Conception* (see above).

VIRGINAL CONCEPTION   The belief that Jesus was conceived in the womb of Mary without the cooperation of a human father.

VIRGINITY OF MARY   The belief that Mary was a virgin throughout her life, including the time when she conceived and brought forth Jesus, her Son.

VIRTUE   The power to realize moral good and to do it joyfully and with perseverance in spite of obstacles. *Theological* virtues are those which have been *infused* by God: faith, hope, and charity. The *moral* virtues—prudence, justice, temperance, and fortitude—are those which have to be *acquired* through cooperation with God's grace and which, in turn, are the linchpins (*cardinal* virtues) of other, lesser virtues.

VOLUNTARISM   A theological and philosophical view which exaggerates the place and function of the human will in the attainment of truth as well as moral good. It is the opposite of *rationalism*.

VULGATE   The name given since the thirteenth century to the Latin translation of the Bible done by St. Jerome.

WORLD   The totality of created reality. Insofar as the world is shaped and directed by human consciousness and human freedom under the grace of God, the world is identical with *history* (see above).

YAHWEH   The Old Testament name for God.

INDEX OF PERSONAL NAMES

INDEX OF SUBJECTS

This index should be used in conjunction with the Table of Contents, Index of Personal Names, and Glossary.

Faith: 23-75, *esp.* 24-5, 31-46; and
reason, 12-13, 38, 40, 41, 43-4,
113, 214, 1174; as knowledge,
25, 35, 37, 38; object of, 25, 34;
and "the faith," 25; and
religious education, 26; and
theology, 26; and Baptism, 33,
34; and repentance, 33; and
justification, 34, 38, 42-3;
content of, 34, 43; and grace,
35, 38, 40-1, 43, 44; and eternal
life, 35; and love, 35, 36, 42, 43,
145, 909, 910; and the Holy
Spirit, 35, 42; and circumcision,
35; and evidence, 36, 38, 39, 40,
42, 44, 188; and hope, 36, 42,
43, 145; and works, 36, 43,
1174; as assent, 37, 38, 41, 42,
44, 967; and salvation, 38, 41,
43, 145; as free gift of God, 38,
41, 45; and freedom, 43, 45; and
science, 93, 96; and philosophy,
113; and belief, 186; and
understanding, 189; and
revelation, 209, 236; and
miracles, 326; and evil, 331; and
temporal activities, 674; and
religious freedom, 678; as
theological virtue, 966-72, 1077;
as trust, 967-8; and doctrine,
967; and *praxis*, 968; and the
Kingdom of God, 968; stages of,
969-72; and the ministry of
Jesus, 918-19; and spirituality,
1080
Faith development, 969-72
False Decretals, 833
Family, 924-6
Fatherhood of God. *See* God
Fathers of the Church, 37
Fatima, 881
"Fear of the Lord," 32
Febronianism, 639
Fetishism, 257
Feudalism, 462, 616-17, 619-21,
641, 1175
Fideism, 43, 216, 217, 233, 291, 641
Fides fiducialis, 42, 967-8
Fides quae creditur, 972
Filioque, 354

"Five ways" of Aquinas, 305
Florence, Council of, 301, 306-7,
354, 355, 780, 1142
Form criticism, 395, 396
Formal norms, 993-4
"Formula of Union," 452-3, 455
Fortitude, 988-90
Forty Hours devotions, 637
Franciscan spirituality, 1074
Franciscanism, 623, 825, 1064
Frankfurt School of social criticism,
111, 500
Fraticelli, 1115
Freedom: 102, 103, 111, 130, 136,
137, 475, 529-30, 912, 940,
954-7; defined, 954; and law, 36;
and grace, 159, 161, 325, 911;
and evil, 331; limitations on,
954-5, 957; and responsibility,
956; and authority, 1174, 1183-4
French Revolution, 641, 806
Frequens, 630
Fruits of the Holy Spirit, 1089
Fundamental option, 955, 957,
958, 959
Fundamentalism, biblical, 39, 398-9
Fundamentalism, dogmatic, 70
Futurist eschatology, 1117

Gallicanism, 311, 639, 641, 833,
839, 840
General judgment, 1103, 1140
Gentiles, mission to, 6, 572, 578,
590, 607, 610-11
German Catechism, 18
Germanization of Christianity,
616-18, 805
Gifts, diversity of, 1090
Glossalalia, 1086-8
Gnosticism, 7-8, 37, 156, 225, 289,
375, 384, 413, 417, 440, 441,
444, 446, 476, 477, 517, 611,
761, 832, 837, 871, 928,
1060, 1086
God: our knowledge of, 24, 25, 26,
27, 32, 35, 129, 130-1, 160, 195,
201, 228, 230, 233, 234, 267,
283, 302, 310; as Supreme
Being, 50; as Father, 51, 290,
333-4, 352-3; and history, 60,

284, 344; and the Holy Spirit,
821; and the Kingdom of God,
1111, 1127
Lourdes, 880, 882
Love: 975-8, 1102; as theological
virtue, 1077; and justice, 1129
Love of God and love of neighbor,
921-2, 927-8, 937, 953, 963, 975,
977, 1072, 1075, 1077, 1078,
1120, 1122, 1133
Lumen gloriae, 1142
Lutheran-Roman Catholic Dialogue,
765-6, 840
Lutheranism, 1172
Lyons, Second Council of, 306-7

Macedonianism, 297
Magic, 1153
Magisterium: 68-72, 660; Aquinas on,
68; credibility of, 1018-19, 1021.
See also Teaching authority
Marian devotions, 637, 889-93
Marian maximalism, 891
Marian minimalism, 889-91
Manichaeism, 135, 225, 303, 383,
611, 790, 929, 1149
Marcionism, 62, 211, 229, 246, 289
Mariology: 865-6; and Christology,
865; and Nestorianism, 872
Marks of the Church, 661, 708
Maronite church, 680
Marriage: 378, 557, 638, 788-98, 847,
924-6; *res et sacramentum* of,
740; purpose of, 788, 789-90,
791; in the Old Testament, 788;
and the Covenant, 788; and the
Kingdom of God, 789; and the
Second Coming, 789; in Paul,
789; in Augustine, 790;
consummation of, 792-3; and
faith, 792, 793; witnesses of,
795; ecumenical consensus on,
797-8
Marriage Encounter, 1079
Martyrdom, 1060
Martyrs, 1142, 1143, 1148
Mary, Blessed Virgin: 513-18, 865-96;
appearances of, 238; as Mother
of God, 445, 450, 456, 615, 872;

in the New Testament, 866-9;
and Eve, 870-1; as Mediatrix,
873, 874, 878; as Co-
Redemptrix, 876; as Mother of
the Church, 882; and
redemption, 894. *See also*
Assumption of Mary,
Immaculate Conception,
Marian..., Virginity of Mary
Marxism, 643
Mass: etymology, 760; daily, 761;
private, 763, 764; Sunday
obligation, 958. *See also*
Eucharist
Masturbation, 1026, 1029
Mater et Magistra, 647, 673, 938,
985, 1045
Material norms, 992-4
Materialism, 217
Matrimony. *See* Marriage
Medellin documents, 707
Mediation, principle of, 731-2, 890,
894-5, 1066, 1180, 1183
Mennonites, 383
Mercy, 990-1, 1122
Merit, 470
Metanoia. See Conversion
"Method of immanence," 190, 219
Metropolitans, 850
Millenarianism, 606
Ministeria Quaedam, 844, 848
Ministry: 592, 842-8; ordained,
807-10; mutual recognition of,
808; etymology, 843; in the New
Testament, 843; and the mission
of the Church, 845; theological
principles of, 845-6; ecumenical
discussion on, 845
Miracles, 325-8
Missionary movement, the, 647, 648
Missions, the, 679
Mixed marriage, 795
Modalism, 291, 298, 360
Modernism: 11, 54-5, 56, 218-19,
294, 399, 644-6; and dogma, 55;
and revelation, 218-19, 234, 236
Modernity, 11, 14, 15, 87, 644, 836,
1175
Modernization, 95, 96
Molinism, 157, 323